LEARNSMART ADVANTAGE WORKS

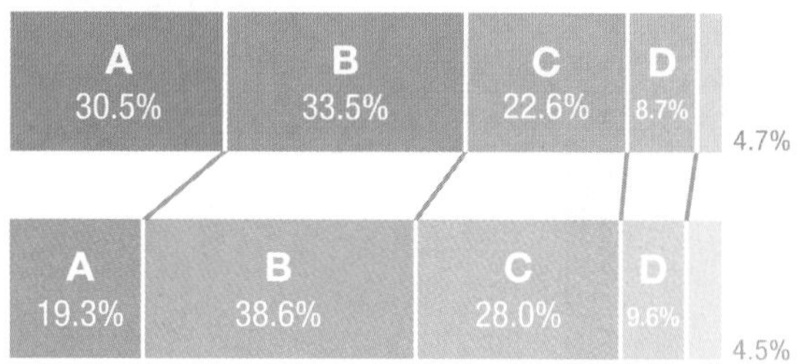

Without LearnSmart

More C students earn B's

*Study: 690 students / 6 institutions

Over 20% more students pass the class with LearnSmart

*A&P Research Study

LEARNSMART Pass Rate - 70%

Without LearnSmart Pass Rate - 57%

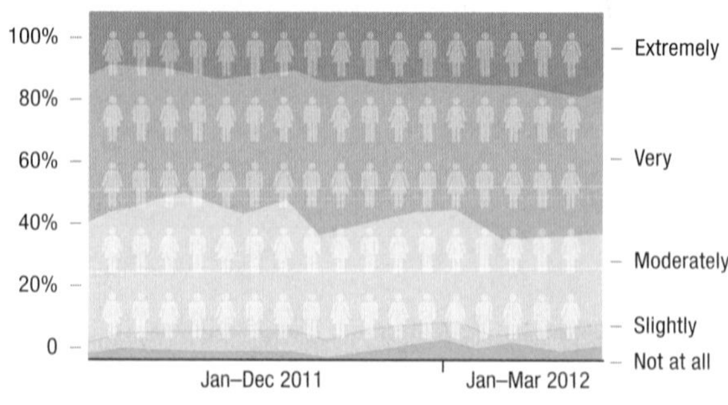

More than 60% of all students agreed LearnSmart was a very or extremely helpful learning tool

*Based on 750,000 student survey responses

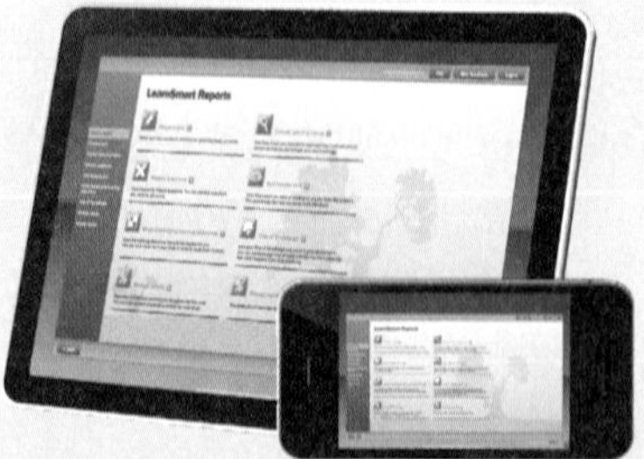

> AVAILABLE ON-THE-GO

http://bit.ly/LS4Apple

http://bit.ly/LS4Droid

How do you rank against your peers?

SMARTBOOK

Standings for all

25855. Jemarkus Parker. 593

25856. Paul Joseph. 593

25857. Professor

25858. Kayla Geddes. 592

25859. Gabriel Ross. 591

Type your answer in the box

________ is a business's concern for the welfare of society.

Do you know the answer?

I KNOW IT | THINK SO | UNSURE | NO IDEA

Let's see how confident you are on the questions.

What you know (green) and what you still need to review (yellow), based on your answers.

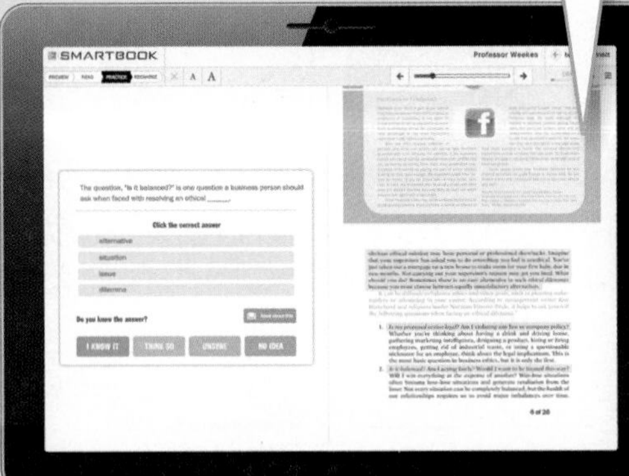

COMPARE AND CHOOSE WHAT'S RIGHT FOR YOU

	BOOK	LEARNSMART	ASSIGNMENTS	
connect	✓	✓	✓	LearnSmart, assignments, and SmartBook—all in one digital product for maximum savings!
connect Looseleaf	✓	✓	✓	Pop the pages into your own binder or carry just the pages you need.
connect Bound Book	✓	✓	✓	The #1 Student Choice!
SMARTBOOK™ Access Code	✓	✓		The first and only book that adapts to you!
LEARNSMART® ADVANTAGE Access Code		✓		The smartest way to get from a B to an A.
CourseSmart eBook	✓			Save some green and some trees!
create™	✓	✓	✓	Check with your instructor about a custom option for your course.

> Buy directly from the source at http://shop.mheducation.com.

Crafting and Executing Strategy

Concepts and Readings

Crafting and Executing Strategy

Concepts and Readings | TWENTIETH EDITION

Arthur A. Thompson
The University of Alabama

Margaret A. Peteraf
Dartmouth College

John E. Gamble
Texas A&M University–Corpus Christi

A. J. Strickland III
The University of Alabama

CRAFTING AND EXECUTING STRATEGY: THE QUEST FOR COMPETITIVE ADVANTAGE, CONCEPTS AND READINGS, TWENTIETH EDITION

Published by McGraw-Hill Education, 2 Penn Plaza, New York, NY 10121.

Some ancillaries, including electronic and print components, may not be available to customers outside the United States.

This book is printed on acid-free paper.

1 2 3 4 5 6 7 8 9 0 DOW/DOW 1 0 9 8 7 6 5

ISBN 978-1-259-29707-6
MHID 1-259-29707-1

Senior Vice President, Products & Markets: *Kurt L. Strand*
Vice President, General Manager, Products & Markets: *Michael Ryan*
Vice President, Content Design & Delivery: *Kimberly Meriwether David*
Managing Director: *Susan Gouijnstook*
Director: *Michael Ablassmeir*
Director, Product Development: *Meghan Campbell*
Product Developer: *Trina Hauger*
Marketing Manager: *Elizabeth Trepkowski*
Director, Content Design & Delivery: *Terri Schiesl*
Program Manager: *Mary Conzachi*
Content Project Managers: *Mary E. Powers, Daryl Bruflodt*
Buyer: *Michael McCormick*
Design: *Srdjan Savanovic*
Content Licensing Specialists: *Keri Johnson*
Cover Image: © *D-BASE/iStock, Getty Images*
Compositor: *Laserwords Private Limited*
Printer: *R. R. Donnelley*

Library of Congress Cataloging-in-Publication Data

Thompson, Arthur A., 1940-
Crafting and executing strategy : the quest for competitive advantage : concepts and readings/ Arthur A. Thompson, Margaret A. Peteraf, John E. Gamble, A. J. Strickland III.—Twentieth edition.
pages cm
ISBN 978-1-259-29707-6 (alk. paper)
1. Strategic planning. 2. Business planning. I. Title.
HD30.28.T525 2015
658.4'012--dc23

2014033214

www.mhhe.com

To our families and especially our spouses:
Hasseline, Paul, and Kitty.

ABOUT THE AUTHORS

Arthur A. Thompson, Jr., earned his B.S. and Ph.D. degrees in economics from The University of Tennessee, spent three years on the economics faculty at Virginia Tech, and served on the faculty of The University of Alabama's College of Commerce and Business Administration for 24 years. In 1974 and again in 1982, Dr. Thompson spent semester-long sabbaticals as a visiting scholar at the Harvard Business School.

His areas of specialization are business strategy, competition and market analysis, and the economics of business enterprises. In addition to publishing over 30 articles in some 25 different professional and trade publications, he has authored or co-authored five textbooks and six computer-based simulation exercises. His textbooks and strategy simulations have been used at well over 1,000 college and university campuses worldwide.

Dr. Thompson spends much of his off-campus time giving presentations, putting on management development programs, working with companies, and helping operate a business simulation enterprise in which he is a major partner.

Dr. Thompson and his wife of 53 years have two daughters, two grandchildren, and a Yorkshire Terrier.

Margaret A. Peteraf is the Leon E. Williams Professor of Management at the Tuck School of Business at Dartmouth College. She is an internationally recognized scholar of strategic management, with a long list of publications in top management journals. She has earned myriad honors and prizes for her contributions, including the 1999 Strategic Management Society Best Paper Award recognizing the deep influence of her work on the field of Strategic Management. Professor Peteraf is a fellow of the Strategic Management Society and the Academy of Management. She served previously as a member of the Board of Governors of both the Society and the Academy of Management and as Chair of the Business Policy and Strategy Division of the Academy. She has also served in various editorial roles and on numerous editorial boards, including the *Strategic Management Journal,* the *Academy of Management Review,* and *Organization Science.* She has taught in Executive Education programs in various programs around the world and has won teaching awards at the MBA and Executive level.

Professor Peteraf earned her Ph.D., M.A., and M.Phil. at Yale University and held previous faculty appointments at Northwestern University's Kellogg Graduate School of Management and at the University of Minnesota's Carlson School of Management.

John E. Gamble is a Professor of Management and Dean of the College of Business at Texas A&M University–Corpus Christi. His teaching and research for nearly 20 years has focused on strategic management at the undergraduate and graduate levels. He has conducted courses in strategic management in Germany since 2001, which have been sponsored by the University of Applied Sciences in Worms.

Dr. Gamble's research has been published in various scholarly journals and he is the author or co-author of more than 75 case studies published in an assortment of strategic management and strategic marketing texts. He has done consulting on industry and market analysis for clients in a diverse mix of industries.

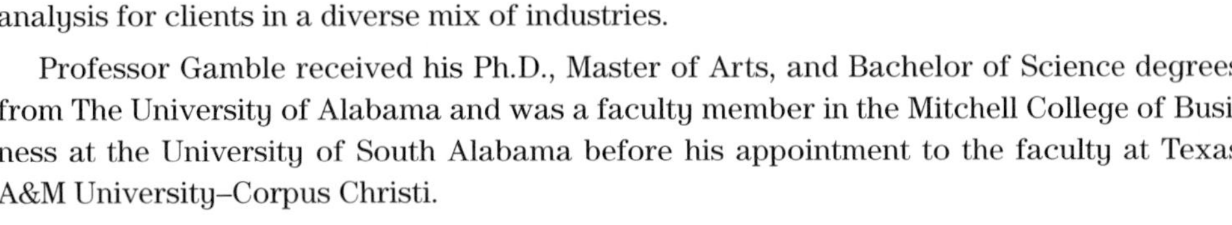

Professor Gamble received his Ph.D., Master of Arts, and Bachelor of Science degrees from The University of Alabama and was a faculty member in the Mitchell College of Business at the University of South Alabama before his appointment to the faculty at Texas A&M University–Corpus Christi.

Dr. A. J. (Lonnie) Strickland is the Thomas R. Miller Professor of Strategic Management at the Culverhouse School of Business at The University of Alabama. He is a native of north Georgia, and attended the University of Georgia, where he received a Bachelor of Science degree in math and physics; Georgia Institute of Technology, where he received a Master of Science in industrial management; and Georgia State University, where he received his Ph.D. in business administration.

Lonnie's experience in consulting and executive development is in the strategic management arena, with a concentration in industry and competitive analysis. He has developed strategic planning systems for numerous firms all over the world. He served as Director of Marketing and Strategy at BellSouth, has taken two companies to the New York Stock Exchange, is one of the founders and directors of American Equity Investment Life Holding (AEL), and serves on numerous boards of directors. He is a very popular speaker in the area of strategic management.

Lonnie and his wife, Kitty, have been married for 48 years. They have two children and two grandchildren. Each summer, Lonnie and his wife live on their private game reserve in South Africa where they enjoy taking their friends on safaris.

PREFACE

By offering the most engaging, clearly articulated, and conceptually sound text on strategic management, *Crafting and Executing Strategy* has been able to maintain its position as the leading textbook in strategic management for 30 years. With this latest edition, we build on this strong foundation, maintaining the attributes of the book that have long made it the most teachable text on the market, while updating the content, sharpening its presentation, and providing enlightening new illustrations and examples.

The distinguishing mark of the 20th edition is its enriched and enlivened presentation of the material in each of the 12 chapters, providing an as up-to-date and engrossing discussion of the core concepts and analytical tools as you will find anywhere. As with each of our new editions, there is an accompanying collection of new, contemporary readings that amplify important topics in managing a company's strategy-making, strategy-executing process and help drive the chapter lessons home.

While this 20th edition retains the 12-chapter structure of the prior edition, every chapter—indeed every paragraph and every line—has been reexamined, refined, and refreshed. New content has been added to keep the material in line with the latest developments in the theory and practice of strategic management. In other areas, coverage has been trimmed to keep the book at a more manageable size. Scores of new examples have been added, along with 15 new Illustration Capsules, to enrich understanding of the content and to provide students with a ringside view of strategy in action. The result is a text that cuts straight to the chase in terms of what students really need to know and gives instructors a leg up on teaching that material effectively. It remains, as always, solidly mainstream and balanced, mirroring *both* the penetrating insight of academic thought and the pragmatism of real-world strategic management.

A standout feature of this text is the tight linkage between the content of the chapters and the selected readings—two or three new readings for each chapter. The lineup of readings that accompany the 20th edition is outstanding in this respect—a truly appealing mix of strategically relevant and practically oriented readings, certain to engage students and sharpen their thinking on how to apply the concepts and tools of strategic analysis. We are confident you will be impressed with how well the readings work as discussion vehicles and the amount of student interest they will spark.

For some years now, growing numbers of strategy instructors at business schools worldwide have been transitioning from a purely text-readings course structure to a more robust and energizing text-readings-simulation course structure. Incorporating a competition-based strategy simulation has the strong appeal of providing class members with *an immediate and engaging opportunity to apply the concepts and analytical tools covered in the chapters and to become personally involved in crafting and executing a strategy for a virtual company that they have been assigned to manage and that competes head-to-head with companies run by other class members.* Two widely used and pedagogically effective online strategy simulations, *The Business Strategy Game* and *GLO-BUS,* are optional companions for this text. Both simulations were created by Arthur Thompson, one of the text authors, and, like the readings, are closely linked to the content of each chapter in the text. The Exercises for Simulation Participants, found at the end of each chapter, provide clear guidance to class members in applying the concepts and analytical tools covered in the chapters to the issues and decisions that they have to wrestle with in managing their simulation company.

To assist instructors in assessing student achievement of program learning objectives, in line with the latest AACSB requirements, the 20th edition includes a set of Assurance of Learning Exercises at the end of each chapter that link to the specific learning objectives appearing at the beginning of each chapter and highlighted throughout the text. An important instructional feature of the 20th edition is its more closely *integrated* linkage of selected chapter-end Assurance of Learning Exercises to the publisher's web-based assignment and assessment platform called Connect™. Your students will be able to use the online Connect™ supplement to (1) complete two of the Assurance of Learning Exercises appearing at the end of each of the 12 chapters, and (2) complete chapter-end quizzes. Many of the Connect™ exercises are automatically graded, thereby enabling you to easily assess the learning that has occurred.

In addition, both of the companion strategy simulations have a built-in Learning Assurance Report that quantifies how well each member of your class performed on nine skills/learning measures *versus tens of thousands of other students worldwide* who completed the simulation in the past 12 months. We believe the chapter-end Assurance of Learning Exercises, the all-new online and automatically graded Connect exercises, and the Learning Assurance Report generated at the conclusion of *The Business Strategy Game* and *GLO-BUS* simulations provide you with easy-to-use, empirical measures of student learning in your course. All can be used in conjunction with other instructor-developed or school-developed scoring rubrics and assessment tools to comprehensively evaluate course or program learning outcomes and measure compliance with AACSB accreditation standards.

Taken together, the various components of the 20th-edition package and the supporting set of instructor resources provide you with enormous course design flexibility and a powerful kit of teaching/learning tools. We've done our very best to ensure that the elements constituting the 20th edition will work well for you in the classroom, help you economize on the time needed to be well prepared for each class, and cause students to conclude that your course is one of the very best they have ever taken—from the standpoint of both enjoyment and learning.

DIFFERENTIATING FEATURES OF THE 20TH EDITION

Six standout features strongly differentiate this text and the accompanying instructional package from others in the field:

1. *Our integrated coverage of the two most popular perspectives on strategic management—positioning theory and resource-based theory—is unsurpassed by any other leading strategy text.* Principles and concepts from both the positioning perspective and the resource-based perspective are prominently and comprehensively integrated into our coverage of crafting both single-business and multibusiness strategies. By highlighting the relationship between a firm's resources and capabilities to the activities it conducts along its value chain, we show explicitly how these two perspectives relate to one another. Moreover, in Chapters 3 through 8 it is emphasized repeatedly that a company's strategy must be matched *not only*

to its external market circumstances *but also* to its internal resources and competitive capabilities.

2. *Our coverage of cooperative strategies and the role that interorganizational activity can play in the pursuit of competitive advantage, is similarly distinguished.* The topics of the value net (newly added), strategic alliances, licensing, joint ventures, and other types of collaborative relationships are featured prominently in a number of chapters and are integrated into other material throughout the text. We show how strategies of this nature can contribute to the success of single-business companies as well as multibusiness enterprises, whether with respect to firms operating in domestic markets or those operating in the international realm.
3. *With a stand-alone chapter devoted to this topic, our coverage of business ethics, corporate social responsibility, and environmental sustainability goes well beyond that offered by any other leading strategy text.* Chapter 9, "Ethics, Corporate Social Responsibility, Environmental Sustainability, and Strategy," fulfills the important functions of (1) alerting students to the role and importance of ethical and socially responsible decision making and (2) addressing the accreditation requirement of the AACSB International that business ethics be visibly and thoroughly embedded in the core curriculum. Moreover, discussions of the roles of values and ethics are integrated into portions of other chapters to further reinforce why and how considerations relating to ethics, values, social responsibility, and sustainability should figure prominently into the managerial task of crafting and executing company strategies.
4. *Long known as a valuable accompaniment to this text, the readings collection in the 20th edition is truly unrivaled* from the standpoints of student appeal, teachability, and suitability for sparking discussions of the application of the concepts in Chapters 1 through 12. The 25 readings included in this edition are the very latest, the best, and the most on target that we could find.
5. *The text is now more tightly linked to the publisher's trailblazing web-based assignment and assessment platform called Connect*™. This will enable professors to gauge class members' prowess in accurately completing (a) selected chapter-end exercises and (b) chapter-end quizzes.
6. *Two cutting-edge and widely used strategy simulations*—The Business Strategy Game *and* GLO-BUS—*are optional companions to the 20th edition.* These give you an unmatched capability to employ a text-readings-simulation model of course delivery.

ORGANIZATION, CONTENT, AND FEATURES OF THE 20TH-EDITION TEXT CHAPTERS

- Chapter 1 serves as a brief, general introduction to the topic of strategy, focusing on the central questions of *"What is strategy?"* and "Why *is it important?"* As such, it serves as the perfect accompaniment for your opening-day lecture on what the course is all about and why it matters. Using the newly added example of Starbucks to drive home the concepts in this chapter, we introduce students to what we mean by "competitive advantage" and the key features of business-level strategy. Describing strategy making as a process, we explain why a company's strategy is partly planned and partly reactive and why a strategy tends to co-evolve with its environment over time. We show that a viable business model must provide both an attractive value proposition for the company's customers and a formula for making profits for the company. New to this chapter is a depiction of how the Value-Price-Cost Framework can be used to frame this discussion. We show how the mark of a winning strategy is its ability to pass three tests: (1) the *fit test* (for internal and external fit), (2) the *competitive advantage test,* and (3) the *performance test.* And we explain why good company performance depends not only upon a sound strategy but upon solid strategy execution as well.

- Chapter 2 presents a more complete overview of the strategic management process, covering topics ranging from the role of vision, mission, and values to what constitutes good corporate governance. It makes a great assignment for the second day of class and provides a smooth transition into the heart of the course. It introduces students to such core concepts as strategic versus financial objectives, the balanced scorecard, strategic intent, and business-level versus corporate-level strategies. It explains why *all managers are on a company's strategy-making, strategy-executing team* and why a company's strategic plan is a collection of strategies devised by different managers at different levels in the organizational hierarchy. The chapter concludes with a section on the role of the board of directors in the strategy-making, strategy-executing process and examines the conditions that led to recent high-profile corporate governance failures.
- The next two chapters introduce students to the two most fundamental perspectives on strategy making: the positioning view, exemplified by Michael Porter's "five forces model of competition"; and the resource-based view. Chapter 3 provides *what has long been the clearest, most straightforward discussion of the five forces framework to be found in any text on strategic management.* It also offers a set of complementary analytical tools for conducting competitive analysis and demonstrates the importance of tailoring strategy to fit the circumstances of a company's industry and competitive environment. What's new in this edition is the inclusion of the value net framework for conducting analysis of how cooperative as well as competitive moves by various parties contribute to the creation and capture of value in an industry.
- Chapter 4 presents the resource-based view of the firm, showing why resource and capability analysis is such a powerful tool for sizing up a company's competitive assets. It offers a simple framework for identifying a company's resources and capabilities and explains how the VRIN framework can be used to determine whether they can provide the company with a sustainable competitive advantage over its competitors. Other topics covered in this chapter include dynamic capabilities, SWOT analysis, value chain analysis, benchmarking, and competitive strength assessments, thus enabling a solid appraisal of a company's relative cost position and customer value proposition vis-à-vis its rivals. *An important feature of this chapter is a table showing how key financial and operating ratios are calculated and how to interpret them.* Students will find this table handy in doing the number crunching needed to evaluate whether a company's strategy is delivering good financial performance.
- Chapter 5 sets forth the basic approaches available for competing and winning in the marketplace in terms of the five generic competitive strategies—low-cost leadership, differentiation, best-cost provider, focused differentiation, and focused low cost. It describes when each of these approaches works best and what pitfalls to avoid. It explains the role of *cost drivers* and *uniqueness drivers* in reducing a company's costs and enhancing its differentiation, respectively.

- Chapter 6 focuses on *other strategic actions* a company can take to complement its competitive approach and maximize the power of its overall strategy. These include a variety of offensive or defensive competitive moves, and their timing, such as blue-ocean strategies and first-mover advantages and disadvantages. It also includes choices concerning the breadth of a company's activities (or its *scope* of operations along an industry's entire value chain), ranging from horizontal mergers and acquisitions, to vertical integration, outsourcing, and strategic alliances. This material serves to segue into the scope issues covered in the next two chapters on international and diversification strategies.
- Chapter 7 takes up the topic of how to compete in international markets. It begins with a discussion of why differing market conditions across countries must necessarily influence a company's strategic choices about how to enter and compete in foreign markets. It presents five major strategic options for expanding a company's geographic scope and competing in foreign markets: export strategies, licensing, franchising, establishing a wholly owned subsidiary via acquisition or "greenfield" venture, and alliance strategies. It includes coverage of topics such as Porter's Diamond of National Competitive Advantage, profit sanctuaries, and the choice between multidomestic, global, and transnational strategies. This chapter explains the impetus for sharing, transferring, or accessing valuable resources and capabilities across national borders in the quest for competitive advantage, connecting the material to that on the resource-based view from Chapter 4. The chapter concludes with a discussion of the unique characteristics of competing in developing-country markets.
- Chapter 8 concerns strategy making in the multibusiness company, introducing the topic of corporate-level strategy with its special focus on diversification. The first portion of this chapter describes when and why diversification makes good strategic sense, the different means of diversifying a company's business lineup, and the pros and cons of related versus unrelated diversification strategies. The second part of the chapter looks at how to evaluate the attractiveness of a diversified company's business lineup, how to decide whether it has a good diversification strategy, and what the strategic options are for improving a diversified company's future performance. The evaluative technique integrates material concerning both industry analysis and the resource-based view, in that it considers the relative attractiveness of the various industries the company has diversified into, the company's competitive strength in each of its lines of business, and the extent to which its different businesses exhibit both *strategic fit* and *resource fit.*
- Although the topic of ethics and values comes up at various points in this textbook, Chapter 9 brings more direct attention to such issues and may be used as a stand-alone assignment in either the early, middle, or late part of a course. It concerns the themes of ethical standards in business, approaches to ensuring consistent ethical standards for companies with international operations, corporate social responsibility, and environmental sustainability. The contents of this chapter are sure to give students some things to ponder, rouse lively discussion, and help to make students more *ethically aware* and conscious of *why all companies should conduct their business in a socially responsible and sustainable manner.*
- The next three chapters (Chapters 10, 11, and 12) comprise a module on strategy execution that is presented in terms of a 10-step framework. Chapter 10 provides an overview of this framework and then explores the first three of these

tasks: (1) staffing the organization with people capable of executing the strategy well, (2) building the organizational capabilities needed for successful strategy execution, and (3) creating an organizational structure supportive of the strategy execution process.

- Chapter 11 discusses five additional managerial actions that advance the cause of good strategy execution: (1) *allocating resources* to enable the strategy execution process, (2) ensuring that *policies and procedures* facilitate rather than impede strategy execution, (3) using *process management tools* and *best practices* to drive continuous improvement in the performance of value chain activities, (4) installing *information and operating systems* that help company personnel carry out their strategic roles, and (5) using *rewards and incentives* to encourage good strategy execution and the achievement of performance targets.
- Chapter 12 completes the framework with a consideration of the roles of corporate culture and leadership in promoting good strategy execution. The recurring theme throughout the final three chapters is that executing strategy involves deciding on the specific actions, behaviors, and conditions needed for a smooth strategy-supportive operation and then following through to get things done and deliver results. The goal here is to ensure that students understand that the strategy-executing phase is a *make-things-happen and make-them-happen-right* kind of managerial exercise—one that is critical for achieving operating excellence and reaching the goal of strong company performance.

In this latest edition, we have put our utmost effort into ensuring that the 12 chapters are consistent with the latest and best thinking of academics and practitioners in the field of strategic management and provide the topical coverage required for both undergraduate and MBA-level strategy courses. The ultimate test of the text, of course, is the positive pedagogical impact it has in the classroom. If this edition sets a more effective stage for your lectures and does a better job of helping you persuade students that the discipline of strategy merits their rapt attention, then it will have fulfilled its purpose.

THE COLLECTION OF READINGS

The 25 readings in this edition are flush with practical examples and valuable lessons for students of the art and science of crafting and executing strategy. There are two or three readings for each chapter—all chosen with three criteria in mind: relevance, readability, and recency of publication. The *relevance* criterion led us to seek out articles that connected clearly to the material in the text chapters and either extended the chapter coverage or expanded on a topic of strategic importance. The *readability* criterion helped us identify articles that were clearly written, engaging, practically oriented, and relatively short. The *recency* criterion limited our selections to those that appeared in the 2012–2014 period, with the exception of one important article from 2011. We endeavored to be highly selective in our choices, deciding that a manageable number of on-target readings was a better fit with the teaching/learning objectives of most senior and MBA courses in strategy than a more sweeping collection of readings. The readings we chose came from recent issues of *Harvard Business Review, MIT Sloan Management Review, McKinsey Quarterly, Business Strategy Review, Business Horizons, Journal of Business Strategy, Ivey Business Journal,* and *Long Range Planning,* among others.

The first reading, by Richard Rumelt, "The Perils of Bad Strategy," makes an excellent accompaniment to the introductory chapter with its focus on the question of "What distinguishes good strategy from bad strategy?" It reminds readers that strategy is as much about what NOT to do as it is about what TO do and explains why having a compelling vision, mission, and set of core values is not enough. The second reading, "The Role of the Chief Strategy Officer," provides an outstanding discussion of the different ways in which an empowered strategist can contribute to the strategy formulation and strategy execution capabilities of a company.

The third reading, "Managing the Strategy Journey," focuses on the process of developing strategies and making strategic decisions, arguing that there are ten big things that top management teams always need to do. The fourth reading, "The Balanced Scorecard in China: Does it Work?" addresses another key topic from Chapter 2. It suggests that there are limitations to the balanced scorecard approach but provides recommendations for how to overcome these and successfully implement this management tool in China.

The next article, "Competing in Network Markets: Can the Winner Take All?" provides a wonderful complement to the value net and five forces frameworks in Chapter 3. It describes the factors that influence success and failure in network markets and concludes with a set of recommendations for increasing the likelihood of success for both entrepreneurs and incumbent firms. "BlackBerry Forgot to Manage the Ecosystem," by Michael Jacobides, draws attention to the importance of viewing the competitive landscape through an ecosystem lens. This short piece derives from a framework that can be seen as a valuable extension of, and complement to, the familiar five-forces framework and the value net.

Reading 7, by David Teece, continues the theme of the need for shaping the ecosytem, but focuses instead on the role of dynamic capabilities, as its title, "Dynamic Capabilities: Routines versus Entrepreneurial Action," suggests. Reading 8, "Meta-SWOT: Introducing a New Strategic Planning Tool," offers an enhancement to another of Chapter 4's most widely employed frameworks. The short piece, titled "Are You Ready for the Digital Value Chain?" completes the readings for Chapter 4, showing how the increasing digitization of the value chain is likely to transform all industry sectors.

The next two readings provide valuable supplements to the material on generic strategies covered in Chapter 5. The first, "Limits to Growing Customer Value: Being Squeezed between the Past and the Future," discusses the importance of value engineering in managing trade-offs and driving growth. The second, "Organizational Ambidexterity," argues that the key to surviving in extreme competitive conditions is striking a balance between competing effectively today and innovating for the future.

The article by Constantinos Markides and Lourdes Sosa makes a perfect accompaniment to Chapter 6. In "Pioneering and First Mover Advantages: The Importance of Business Models," they argue that pioneering has both advantages and disadvantages; which predominates will depend on the business model chosen for both attacking and defending one's position. The next reading, "Adding Value through Offshoring," by Joan Enric Ricart and Pablo Agnese, adds the topic of offshoring to the discussion about outsourcing covered in Chapter 6. They offer insight on modern offshoring practices, showing how companies can not only lower costs through such practices but create value as well.

Reading 14, by Vijay Govindarajan and Chris Trimble, focuses on a topic of concern in the area of international strategies. The authors suggest that traditional approaches for entering emerging markets may not be appropriate for poor countries like India and China, where market needs are so different from those of rich countries that companies are advised to pursue "Reverse Innovation: A Global Growth Strategy That Could Pre-empt Disruption at Home." The next article, "How Emerging Giants Can Take on the World," focuses on the strategies of successful and ambitious companies headquartered in developing countries. The authors argue that the key to their continuing growth and success depends upon their ability to acquire needed capabilities and they propose a four-stage approach.

The next two readings complement and extend the material on corporate strategy presented in Chapter 8. Reading 16, "Why Conglomerates Thrive (Outside the U.S.)," describes the path to success taken by many widely diversified foreign companies. The next reading, "Diversification: Best Practices of the Leading Companies," describes the contrasting case of how successful diversifiers such as GE and McDonald's manage this aspect of their businesses.

Readings 18 and 19 deal with the core material found in Chapter 9. "Pragmatic Business Ethics," as its title suggests, takes on the topic of business ethics. It offers an approach for assessing and resolving ethical dilemmas in the gray areas of business ethics. Gary Hamel's piece, "Leaders as Stewards," urges managers to embrace the responsibility of stewardship and argues that what matters is the bedrock values of companies and their leaders.

The next six readings comprise a set of readings that cover various aspects concerning strategy execution. The first of these, also by Hamel and titled "Attract Top Talent: Become a Passion Multiplier," argues that to attract creative young workers and magnify their passions you need to reinvent your management practices to align with their expectations. The second, titled "Building Superior Capabilities for Strategic Sourcing," describes how firms can create more value by investing in capability-building in the purchasing domain.

Readings 22 and 23 link to the topical material found in Chapter 11. The point of the first of these is well captured by its title: "How Collaboration Technologies Are Improving Process, Workforce, and Business Performance." The second, "The ROI of Employee Recognition," complements the material of the first, showing how well-designed reward and recognition programs can also enhance company performance.

The last two readings were chosen to expand upon and complement the central themes of Chapter 12. As its title suggests, "The Critical Few: Components of a Truly Effective Culture" contends that a few key practices can make all the difference in building a performance-enhancing culture. In "How Strategists Lead," the closing article, corporate strategy expert Cynthia Montgomery reflects upon the unique value that strategic leaders can bring to their companies, thus providing a strong and thoughtful conclusion for a course on strategic management.

THE TWO STRATEGY SIMULATION SUPPLEMENTS: *THE BUSINESS STRATEGY GAME* AND *GLO-BUS*

The Business Strategy Game and *GLO-BUS: Developing Winning Competitive Strategies*—two competition-based strategy simulations that are delivered online and that feature automated processing and grading of performance—are being marketed by the publisher as companion supplements for use with the 20th edition (and other texts in the field).

- *The Business Strategy Game* is the world's most popular strategy simulation, having been used by over 2,500 instructors in courses involving approximately 750,000 students on 1,050+ university campuses in 60 countries.
- *GLO-BUS,* a somewhat simpler strategy simulation introduced in 2004, has been used by more than 1,450+ instructors in courses involving over 180,000 students at 640+ university campuses in 48+ countries.

How the Strategy Simulations Work

In both *The Business Strategy Game (BSG)* and *GLO-BUS,* class members are divided into teams of one to five persons and assigned to run a company that competes head-to-head against companies run by other class members.

- In *BSG,* team members run an athletic footwear company, producing and marketing both branded and private-label footwear.
- In *GLO-BUS,* team members operate a digital camera company that designs, assembles, and markets entry-level digital cameras and upscale, multifeatured cameras.

In both simulations, companies compete in a global market arena, selling their products in four geographic regions—Europe-Africa, North America, Asia-Pacific, and Latin America. Each management team is called upon to craft a strategy for their company and make decisions relating to plant operations, workforce compensation, pricing and marketing, social responsibility/citizenship, and finance.

Company co-managers are held accountable for their decision making. Each company's performance is scored on the basis of earnings per share, return-on-equity investment, stock price, credit rating, and image rating. Rankings of company performance, along with a wealth of industry and company statistics, are available to company co-managers after each decision round to use in making strategy adjustments and operating decisions for the next competitive round. You can be certain that the market environment, strategic issues, and operating challenges that company co-managers must contend with are *very tightly linked* to what your class members will be reading about in the text chapters. The circumstances that co-managers face in running their simulation company embrace the very concepts, analytical tools, and strategy options they encounter in the text chapters (this is something you can quickly confirm by skimming through some of the Exercises for Simulation Participants that appear at the end of each chapter).

We suggest that you schedule 1 or 2 practice rounds and anywhere from 4 to 10 regular (scored) decision rounds (more rounds are better than fewer rounds). Each decision round represents a year of company operations and will entail roughly two hours of time for company co-managers to complete. In traditional 13-week, semester-long courses, there is merit in scheduling one decision round per week. In courses that run 5 to 10 weeks, it is wise to schedule two decision rounds per week for the last several weeks of the term (sample course schedules are provided for courses of varying length and varying numbers of class meetings).

When the instructor-specified deadline for a decision round arrives, the simulation server automatically accesses the saved decision entries of each company, determines the competitiveness and buyer appeal of each company's product offering relative to the other companies being run by students in your class, and then awards sales and market shares to the competing companies, geographic region by geographic region. The unit sales volumes awarded to each company *are totally governed by:*

- How its prices compare against the prices of rival brands.
- How its product quality compares against the quality of rival brands.
- How its product line breadth and selection compare.
- How its advertising effort compares.
- And so on, for a total of 11 competitive factors that determine unit sales and market shares.

The competitiveness and overall buyer appeal of each company's product offering *in comparison to the product offerings of rival companies* is all-decisive—this algorithmic feature is what makes *BSG* and *GLO-BUS* "competition-based" strategy simulations. Once each company's sales and market shares are awarded based on the competitiveness of its respective overall product offering, the various company and industry reports detailing the outcomes of the decision round are then generated. Company co-managers can access the results of the decision round 15 to 20 minutes after the decision deadline.

The Compelling Case for Incorporating Use of a Strategy Simulation

There are *three exceptionally important benefits* associated with using a competition-based simulation in strategy courses taken by seniors and MBA students:

- *A three-pronged text-readings-simulation course model delivers significantly more teaching-learning power than the traditional text-readings model.* Using *both* readings and a strategy simulation to drill students in thinking strategically and applying what they read in the text chapters is a stronger, more effective means of helping them connect theory with practice and develop better business judgment. But what a competition-based strategy simulation does far better is thrust class members squarely into *an active, hands-on managerial role* where they are totally responsible for assessing market conditions, determining how to respond to the actions of competitors, forging a long-term direction and strategy for their company, and making all kinds of operating decisions. Because they are held fully accountable for their decisions and their company's performance, *co-managers are strongly motivated* to dig deeply into company operations, probe for ways to be more cost-efficient and competitive, and ferret out strategic moves and decisions calculated to boost company performance. *Consequently, incorporating both readings assignments and a strategy simulation to develop the skills of class members in thinking strategically and applying the concepts and tools of strategic analysis turns out to be more pedagogically powerful than relying solely on readings assignments—there's stronger retention of the lessons learned and better achievement of course learning objectives.*

  To provide you with quantitative evidence of the learning that occurs with using *The Business Strategy Game* or *GLO-BUS,* there is a built-in Learning Assurance Report showing how well each class member performs on nine skills/learning measures versus tens of thousands of students worldwide who have completed the simulation in the past 12 months.
- *The competitive nature of a strategy simulation arouses positive energy and steps up the whole tempo of the course by a notch or two.* Nothing sparks class excitement quicker or better than the concerted efforts on the part of class members at each decision round to achieve a high industry ranking and avoid the perilous

consequences of being outcompeted by other class members. Students really enjoy taking on the role of a manager, running their own company, crafting strategies, making all kinds of operating decisions, trying to outcompete rival companies, and getting immediate feedback on the resulting company performance. Lots of back-and-forth chatter occurs when the results of the latest simulation round become available and co-managers renew their quest for strategic moves and actions that will strengthen company performance. Co-managers become *emotionally invested* in running their company and figuring out what strategic moves to make to boost their company's performance. Interest levels climb. All this stimulates learning and causes students to see the practical relevance of the subject matter and the benefits of taking your course.

As soon as your students start to say "Wow! Not only is this fun but I am learning a lot," *which they will,* you have won the battle of engaging students in the subject matter and moved the value of taking your course to a much higher plateau in the business school curriculum. This translates into *a livelier, richer learning experience from a student perspective and better instructor-course evaluations.*

- *Use of a fully automated online simulation reduces the time instructors spend on course preparation, course administration, and grading.* Since the simulation exercise involves a 20- to 30-hour workload for student teams (roughly 2 hours per decision round times 10 to 12 rounds, plus optional assignments), simulation adopters often compensate by trimming the number of assigned readings from, say, 10 to 12 to perhaps 4 to 6. Not only does use of a simulation permit assigning fewer readings, but it also permits you to eliminate at least one assignment that entails considerable grading on your part. Grading one less essay exam or other written assignment saves enormous time. With *BSG* and *GLOBUS,* grading is effortless and takes only minutes; once you enter percentage weights for each assignment in your online grade book, a suggested overall grade is calculated for you. You'll be pleasantly surprised—and quite pleased—at how little time it takes to gear up for and administer *The Business Strategy Game* or *GLO-BUS.*

In sum, incorporating use of a strategy simulation turns out to be *a win–win proposition for both students and instructors.* Moreover, a very convincing argument can be made that a competition-based strategy simulation is *the single most effective teaching/learning tool that instructors can employ to teach the discipline of business and competitive strategy, to make learning more enjoyable, and to promote better achievement of course learning objectives.*

A Bird's-Eye View of *The Business Strategy Game*

The setting for *The Business Strategy Game (BSG)* is the global athletic footwear industry (there can be little doubt in today's world that a globally competitive strategy simulation is *vastly superior* to a simulation with a domestic-only setting). Global market demand for footwear grows at the rate of 7 to 9 percent annually for the first five years and 5 to 7 percent annually for the second five years. However, market growth rates vary by geographic region—North America, Latin America, Europe-Africa, and Asia-Pacific.

Companies begin the simulation producing branded and private-label footwear in two plants, one in North America and one in Asia. They have the option to establish production facilities in Latin America and Europe-Africa, either by constructing new plants or by buying previously constructed plants that have been sold by competing companies. Company co-managers exercise control over production costs on the basis of the styling and quality they opt to manufacture, plant location (wages and incentive compensation vary from region to region), the use of best practices and Six Sigma programs to reduce the production of defective footwear and to boost worker productivity, and compensation practices.

All newly produced footwear is shipped in bulk containers to one of four geographic distribution centers. All sales in a geographic region are made from footwear inventories in that region's distribution center. Costs at the four regional distribution centers are a function of inventory storage costs, packing and shipping fees, import tariffs paid on incoming pairs shipped from foreign plants, and exchange rate impacts. At the start of the simulation, import tariffs average $4 per pair in Europe-Africa, $6 per pair in Latin America, and $8 in the Asia-Pacific region. However, the Free Trade Treaty of the Americas allows tariff-free movement of footwear between North America and Latin America. Instructors have the option to alter tariffs as the game progresses.

Companies market their brand of athletic footwear to footwear retailers worldwide and to individuals buying online at the company's website. Each company's sales and market share in the branded footwear segments hinge on its competitiveness on 11 factors: attractive pricing, footwear styling and quality, product line breadth, advertising, use of mail-in rebates, appeal of celebrities endorsing a company's brand, success in convincing footwear retailers to carry its brand, number of weeks it takes to fill retailer orders, effectiveness of a company's online sales effort at its website, and customer loyalty. Sales of private-label footwear hinge solely on being the low-price bidder.

All told, company co-managers make as many as 53 types of decisions each period that cut across production operations (up to 10 decisions per plant, with a maximum of four plants), plant capacity additions/sales/upgrades (up to 6 decisions per plant), worker compensation and training (3 decisions per plant), shipping (up to 8 decisions per plant), pricing and marketing (up to 10 decisions in four geographic regions), bids to sign celebrities (2 decision entries per bid), financing of company operations (up to 8 decisions), and corporate social responsibility and environmental sustainability (up to 6 decisions).

Each time company co-managers make a decision entry, an assortment of on-screen calculations instantly shows the projected effects on unit sales, revenues, market shares, unit costs, profit, earnings per share, ROE, and other operating statistics. The on-screen calculations help team members evaluate the relative merits of one decision entry versus another and put together a promising strategy.

Companies can employ any of the five generic competitive strategy options in selling branded footwear—low-cost leadership, differentiation, best-cost provider, focused low cost, and focused differentiation. They can pursue essentially the same strategy worldwide or craft slightly or very different strategies for the Europe-Africa, Asia-Pacific, Latin America, and North America markets. They can strive for competitive advantage based on more advertising, a wider selection of models, more appealing styling/quality, bigger rebates, and so on.

Any well-conceived, well-executed competitive approach is capable of succeeding, provided it is not overpowered by the strategies of competitors or defeated by the presence of too many copycat strategies that dilute its effectiveness. The challenge for each company's management team is to craft and execute a competitive strategy that produces good performance on five measures: earnings per share, return on equity investment, stock price appreciation, credit rating, and brand image.

All activity for *The Business Strategy Game* takes place at **www.bsg-online.com**.

A Bird's-Eye View of *GLO-BUS*

The industry setting for *GLO-BUS* is the digital camera industry. Global market demand grows at the rate of 8 to 10 percent annually for the first five years and 4 to 6 percent annually for the second five years. Retail sales of digital cameras are seasonal, with about 20 percent of consumer demand coming in each of the first three quarters of each calendar year and 40 percent coming during the big fourth-quarter retailing season.

Companies produce entry-level and upscale, multifeatured cameras of varying designs and quality in a Taiwan assembly facility and ship assembled cameras directly to retailers in North America, Asia-Pacific, Europe-Africa, and Latin America. All cameras are assembled as retail orders come in and are shipped immediately upon completion of the assembly process—companies maintain no finished-goods inventories, and all parts and components are delivered on a just-in-time basis (which eliminates the need to track inventories and simplifies the accounting for plant operations and costs). Company co-managers exercise control over production costs on the basis of the designs and components they specify for their cameras, workforce compensation and training, the length of warranties offered (which affects warranty costs), the amount spent for technical support provided to buyers of the company's cameras, and their management of the assembly process.

Competition in each of the two product market segments (entry-level and multifeatured digital cameras) is based on 10 factors: price, camera performance and quality, number of quarterly sales promotions, length of promotions in weeks, size of the promotional discounts offered, advertising, number of camera models, size of the retail dealer network, warranty period, and amount/caliber of technical support provided to camera buyers. Low-cost leadership, differentiation strategies, best-cost provider strategies, and focus strategies are all viable competitive options. Rival companies can strive to be the clear market leader in either entry-level cameras or upscale multifeatured cameras or both. They can focus on one or two geographic regions or strive for geographic balance. They can pursue essentially the same strategy worldwide or craft slightly or very different strategies for the Europe-Africa, Asia-Pacific, Latin America, and North America markets. Just as with *The Business Strategy Game,* almost any well-conceived, well-executed competitive approach is capable of succeeding, *provided it is not overpowered by the strategies of competitors or defeated by the presence of too many copycat strategies that dilute its effectiveness.*

Company co-managers make 49 types of decisions each period, ranging from R&D, camera components, and camera performance (10 decisions) to production operations and worker compensation (15 decisions) to pricing and marketing (15 decisions) to the financing of company operations (4 decisions) to corporate social responsibility (5 decisions). *Each time participants make a decision entry, an assortment of on-screen calculations instantly shows the projected effects on unit sales, revenues, market shares, unit costs, profit, earnings per share, ROE, and other operating statistics. These on-screen calculations help team members evaluate the relative merits of one decision entry versus another and stitch the separate decisions into a cohesive and promising strategy.* Company performance is judged on five criteria: earnings per share, return on equity investment, stock price, credit rating, and brand image.

All activity for *GLO-BUS* occurs at **www.glo-bus.com**.

Administration and Operating Features of the Two Simulations

The Internet delivery and user-friendly designs of both *BSG* and *GLO-BUS* make them incredibly easy to administer, even for first-time users. And the menus and controls are so similar that you can readily switch between the two simulations or use one in your undergraduate class and the other in a graduate class. If you have not yet used either of the two simulations, you may find the following of particular interest:

- Setting up the simulation for your course is done online and takes about 10 to 15 minutes. Once setup is completed, no other administrative actions are required beyond those of moving participants to a different team (should the need arise) and monitoring the progress of the simulation (to whatever extent desired).
- Participant's Guides are delivered electronically to class members at the website—students can read the guide on their monitors or print out a copy, as they prefer.
- There are 2- to 4-minute Video Tutorials scattered throughout the software (including each decision screen and each page of each report) that provide on-demand guidance to class members who may be uncertain about how to proceed.
- Complementing the Video Tutorials are detailed and clearly written Help sections explaining "all there is to know" about (a) each decision entry and the relevant cause-effect relationships, (b) the information on each page of the Industry Reports, and (c) the numbers presented in the Company Reports. *The Video Tutorials and the Help screens allow company co-managers to figure things out for themselves, thereby curbing the need for students to ask the instructor "how things work."*
- Team members running the same company who are logged in simultaneously on different computers at different locations can click a button to enter Collaboration Mode, enabling them to work collaboratively from the same screen in viewing reports and making decision entries, and click a second button to enter Audio Mode, letting them talk to one another.
    - When in "Collaboration Mode," each team member sees the same screen at the same time as all other team members who are logged in and have joined Collaboration Mode. If one team member chooses to view a particular decision screen, that same screen appears on the monitors for all team members in Collaboration Mode.
    - Each team member controls their own color-coded mouse pointer (with their first-name appearing in a color-coded box linked to their mouse pointer) and can make a decision entry or move the mouse to point to particular on-screen items.
    - A decision entry change made by one team member is seen by all, in real time, and all team members can immediately view the on-screen calculations that result from the new decision entry.
    - If one team member wishes to view a report page and clicks on the menu link to the desired report, that same report page will immediately appear for the other team members engaged in collaboration.
    - Use of Audio Mode capability requires that each team member work from a computer with a built-in microphone (if they want to be heard by their team members) and speakers (so they may hear their teammates) or else have a headset with a microphone that they can plug into their desktop or laptop. A headset is recommended for best results, but most laptops now are equipped

with a built-in microphone and speakers that will support use of our new voice chat feature.

  - Real-time VoIP audio chat capability among team members who have entered both the Audio Mode and the Collaboration Mode is a tremendous boost in functionality that enables team members to go online simultaneously on computers at different locations and conveniently and effectively collaborate in running their simulation company.
  - In addition, instructors have the capability to join the online session of any company and speak with team members, thus circumventing the need for team members to arrange for and attend a meeting in the instructor's office. Using the standard menu for administering a particular industry, instructors can connect with the company desirous of assistance. Instructors who wish not only to talk but also to enter Collaboration (highly recommended because all attendees are then viewing the same screen) have a red-colored mouse pointer linked to a red box labeled Instructor.

  Without a doubt, the Collaboration and Voice-Chat capabilities are hugely valuable for students enrolled in online and distance-learning courses where meeting face-to-face is impractical or time-consuming. Likewise, the instructors of online and distance-learning courses will appreciate having the capability to join the online meetings of particular company teams when their advice or assistance is requested.

- Both simulations are quite suitable for use in distance-learning or online courses (and are currently being used in such courses on numerous campuses).
- Participants and instructors are notified via e-mail when the results are ready (usually about 15 to 20 minutes after the decision round deadline specified by the instructor/game administrator).
- Following each decision round, participants are provided with a complete set of reports—a six-page Industry Report, a one-page Competitive Intelligence report for each geographic region that includes strategic group maps and bulleted lists of competitive strengths and weaknesses, and a set of Company Reports (income statement, balance sheet, cash flow statement, and assorted production, marketing, and cost statistics).
- Two "open-book" multiple-choice tests of 20 questions are built into each simulation. The quizzes, which you can require or not as you see fit, are taken online and automatically graded, with scores reported instantaneously to participants and automatically recorded in the instructor's electronic grade book. Students are automatically provided with three sample questions for each test.
- Both simulations contain a three-year strategic plan option that you can assign. Scores on the plan are automatically recorded in the instructor's online grade book.
- At the end of the simulation, you can have students complete online peer evaluations (again, the scores are automatically recorded in your online grade book).
- Both simulations have a Company Presentation feature that enables each team of company co-managers to easily prepare PowerPoint slides for use in describing their strategy and summarizing their company's performance in a presentation to either the class, the instructor, or an "outside" board of directors.
- *A Learning Assurance Report provides you with hard data concerning how well your students performed vis-à-vis students playing the simulation worldwide over the past 12 months.* The report is based on nine measures of student proficiency,

business know-how, and decision-making skill and can also be used in evaluating the extent to which your school's academic curriculum produces the desired degree of student learning insofar as accreditation standards are concerned.

For more details on either simulation, please consult Section 2 of the Instructor's Manual accompanying this text or register as an instructor at the simulation websites (**www.bsg-online.com** and **www.glo-bus.com**) to access even more comprehensive information. You should also consider signing up for one of the webinars that the simulation authors conduct several times each month (sometimes several times weekly) to demonstrate how the software works, walk you through the various features and menu options, and answer any questions. You have an open invitation to call the senior author of this text at (205) 722-9145 to arrange a personal demonstration or talk about how one of the simulations might work in one of your courses. We think you'll be quite impressed with the cutting-edge capabilities that have been programmed into *The Business Strategy Game* and *GLO-BUS,* the simplicity with which both simulations can be administered, and their exceptionally tight connection to the text chapters, core concepts, and standard analytical tools.

RESOURCES AND SUPPORT MATERIALS FOR THE 20TH EDITION

For Students

Key Points Summaries At the end of each chapter is a synopsis of the core concepts, analytical tools, and other key points discussed in the chapter. These chapter-end synopses, along with the core concept definitions and margin notes scattered throughout each chapter, help students focus on basic strategy principles, digest the messages of each chapter, and prepare for tests.

Two Sets of Chapter-End Exercises Each chapter concludes with two sets of exercises. The *Assurance of Learning Exercises* can be used as the basis for class discussion, oral presentation assignments, and short written reports. The *Exercises for Simulation Participants* are designed expressly for use by adopters who have incorporated use of a simulation and want to go a step further in tightly and explicitly connecting the chapter content to the simulation company their students are running. The questions in both sets of exercises (along with those Illustration Capsules that qualify as "mini-cases") can be used to round out the rest of a 75-minute class period should your lecture on a chapter last for only 50 minutes.

The Connect™ Management Web-Based Assignment and Assessment Platform Beginning with the 18th edition, we began taking advantage of the publisher's innovative Connect™ assignment and assessment platform and created several features that simplify the task of assigning and grading three types of exercises for students:

- There are self-scoring chapter tests consisting of 20 to 25 multiple-choice questions that students can take to measure their grasp of the material presented in each of the 12 chapters.

- There are two author-developed Interactive Application exercises for each of the 12 chapters that drill students in the use and application of the concepts and tools of strategic analysis.

All of the Connect™ exercises are automatically graded (with the exception of those exercise components that entail student entry of short-answer and/or essay answers), thereby simplifying the task of evaluating each class member's performance and monitoring the learning outcomes. The progress-tracking function built into the Connect™ Management system enables you to:

- View scored work immediately and track individual or group performance with assignment and grade reports.
- Access an instant view of student or class performance relative to learning objectives.
- Collect data and generate reports required by many accreditation organizations, such as AACSB.

LearnSmart and SmartBook TM LearnSmart is an adaptive study tool proven to strengthen memory recall, increase class retention, and boost grades. Students are able to study more efficiently because they are made aware of what they know and don't know. Real-time reports quickly identify the concepts that require more attention from individual students—or the entire class. SmartBook is the first and only adaptive reading experience designed to change the way students read and learn. It creates a personalized reading experience by highlighting the most impactful concepts a student needs to learn at that moment in time. As a student engages with SmartBook, the reading experience continuously adapts by highlighting content based on what the student knows and doesn't know. This ensures that the focus is on the content he or she needs to learn, while simultaneously promoting long-term retention of material. Use SmartBook's real-time reports to quickly identify the concepts that require more attention from individual students—or the entire class. The end result? Students are more engaged with course content, can better prioritize their time, and come to class ready to participate.

For Instructors

Instructor Library The Connect Management Instructor Library is your repository for additional resources to improve student engagement in and out of class. You can select and use any asset that enhances your lecture.

Instructor's Manual The accompanying IM contains:

- A section on suggestions for organizing and structuring your course.
- Sample syllabi and course outlines.
- A set of lecture notes on each chapter.
- Answers to the chapter-end Assurance of Learning Exercises.
- A copy of the test bank.
- Discussion questions and suggested answers for the readings.

Test Bank and EZ Test Online There is a test bank containing over 900 multiple-choice questions and short-answer/essay questions. It has been tagged with

AACSB and Bloom's Taxonomy criteria. All of the test bank questions are also accessible within a computerized test bank powered by McGraw-Hill's flexible electronic testing program, EZ Test Online (**www.eztestonline.com**). Using EZ Test Online allows you to create paper and online tests or quizzes. With EZ Test Online, instructors can select questions from multiple McGraw-Hill test banks or author their own and then either print the test for paper distribution or give it online.

PowerPoint Slides To facilitate delivery preparation of your lectures and to serve as chapter outlines, you'll have access to approximately 500 colorful and professional-looking slides displaying core concepts, analytical procedures, key points, and all the figures in the text chapters.

***The Business Strategy Game* and *GLO-BUS* Online Simulations** Using one of the two companion simulations is a powerful and constructive way of emotionally connecting students to the subject matter of the course. We know of no more effective way to arouse the competitive energy of students and prepare them for the challenges of real-world business decision making than to have them match strategic wits with classmates in running a company in head-to-head competition for global market leadership.

ACKNOWLEDGMENTS

A great number of colleagues and students at various universities, business acquaintances, and people at McGraw-Hill provided inspiration, encouragement, and counsel during the course of this project. Like all text authors in the strategy field, we are intellectually indebted to the many academics whose research and writing have blazed new trails and advanced the discipline of strategic management. In addition, we'd like to thank the following reviewers who provided seasoned advice and splendid suggestions over the years for improving the chapters:

Robert B. Baden, Edward Desmarais, Stephen F. Hallam, Joy Karriker, Wendell Seaborne, Joan H. Bailar, David Blair, Jane Boyland, William J. Donoher, Stephen A. Drew, Jo Anne Duffy, Alan Ellstrand, Susan Fox-Wolfgramm, Rebecca M. Guidice, Mark Hoelscher, Sean D. Jasso, Xin Liang, Paul Mallette, Dan Marlin, Raza Mir, Mansour Moussavi, James D. Spina, Monica A. Zimmerman, Dennis R. Balch, Jeffrey R. Bruehl, Edith C. Busija, Donald A. Drost, Randall Harris, Mark Lewis Hoelscher, Phyllis Holland, James W. Kroeger, Sal Kukalis, Brian W. Kulik, Paul Mallette, Anthony U. Martinez, Lee Pickler, Sabine Reddy, Thomas D. Schramko, V. Seshan, Charles Strain, Sabine Turnley, S. Stephen Vitucci, Andrew Ward, Sibin Wu, Lynne Patten, Nancy E. Landrum, Jim Goes, Jon Kalinowski, Rodney M. Walter, Judith D. Powell, Seyda Deligonul, David Flanagan, Esmerlda Garbi, Mohsin Habib, Kim Hester, Jeffrey E. McGee, Diana J. Wong, F. William Brown, Anthony F. Chelte, Gregory G. Dess, Alan B. Eisner, John George, Carle M. Hunt, Theresa Marron-Grodsky, Sarah Marsh, Joshua D. Martin, William L. Moore, Donald Neubaum, George M. Puia, Amit Shah, Lois M. Shelton, Mark Weber, Steve Barndt, J. Michael Geringer, Ming-Fang Li, Richard Stackman, Stephen Tallman, Gerardo R. Ungson, James Boulgarides, Betty Diener, Daniel F. Jennings, David Kuhn, Kathryn Martell, Wilbur Mouton, Bobby Vaught, Tuck Bounds, Lee Burk, Ralph Catalanello, William Crittenden, Vince Luchsinger, Stan

Mendenhall, John Moore, Will Mulvaney, Sandra Richard, Ralph Roberts, Thomas Turk, Gordon Von Stroh, Fred Zimmerman, S. A. Billion, Charles Byles, Gerald L. Geisler, Rose Knotts, Joseph Rosenstein, James B. Thurman, Ivan Able, W. Harvey Hegarty, Roger Evered, Charles B. Saunders, Rhae M. Swisher, Claude I. Shell, R. Thomas Lenz, Michael C. White, Dennis Callahan, R. Duane Ireland, William E. Burr II, C. W. Millard, Richard Mann, Kurt Christensen, Neil W. Jacobs, Louis W. Fry, D. Robley Wood, George J. Gore, and William R. Soukup.

We owe a debt of gratitude to Professors Catherine A. Maritan, Jeffrey A. Martin, Richard S. Shreve, and Anant K. Sundaram for their helpful comments on various chapters. We'd also like to thank the following students of the Tuck School of Business for their assistance with the revisions: Sarah Boole, Kenneth P. Fraser, John L. Gardner, Dennis L. Huggins, Peter Jacobson, Jacob Adam Johnson, Heather Levy, Judith H. Lin, Brian R. McKenzie, Andrew J. Miller, Kiera O'Brien, Sara Paccamonti, Avni V. Patel, Maximilian A. Pinto, Christopher C. Sukenik, Ross M. Templeton, and Nicholas J. Ziemba. And we'd like to acknowledge the help of Dartmouth students Mathieu A. Bertrand, Meghan L. Cooney, Harold W. Greenstone, Campbell Haynes, Alexander P. Judson, Sarah E. Knapp, Amy Li, Roger L. Melick, Alexander C. Olesen, Mahala S. Pagan, Jenna Pfeffer, Jordan M. West, and Sean Zhang, as well as Tuck staff member Mary Biathrow.

As always, we value your recommendations and thoughts about the book. Your comments regarding coverage and contents will be taken to heart, and we always are grateful for the time you take to call our attention to printing errors, deficiencies, and other shortcomings. Please e-mail us at **athompso@cba.ua.edu**, **margaret.a.peteraf@tuck.dartmouth.edu**, **john.gamble@tamucc.edu**, or **astrickl@cba.ua.edu**.

Arthur A. Thompson

Margaret A. Peteraf

John E. Gamble

A. J. Strickland

Crafting and Executing Strategy

Concepts and Readings

GUIDED TOUR

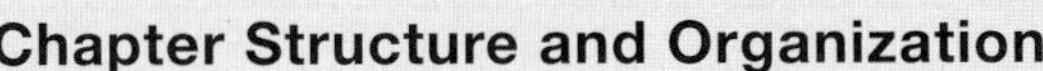

Chapter Structure and Organization

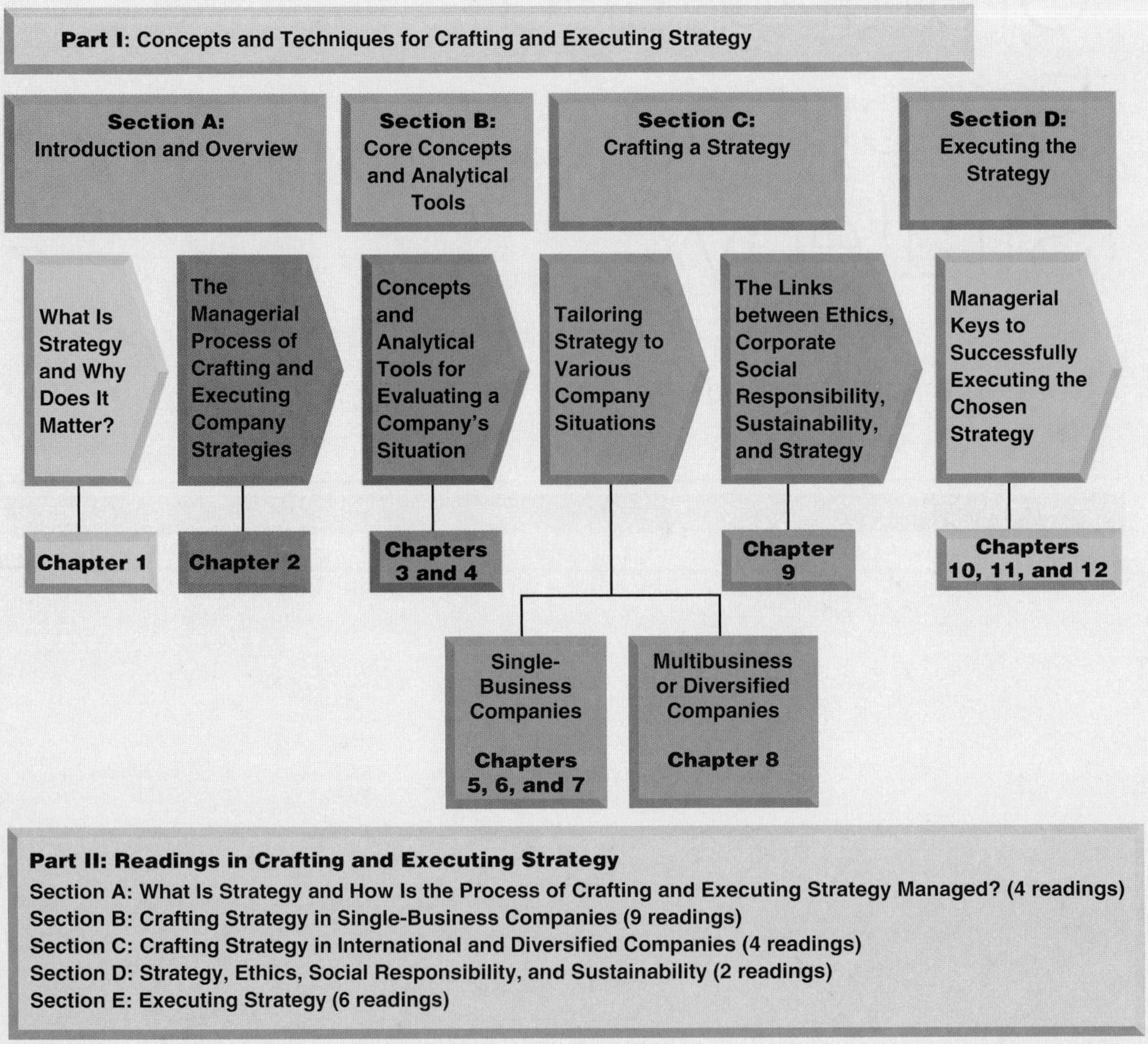

Part I: Concepts and Techniques for Crafting and Executing Strategy

Section A: Introduction and Overview

- What Is Strategy and Why Does It Matter? — **Chapter 1**
- The Managerial Process of Crafting and Executing Company Strategies — **Chapter 2**

Section B: Core Concepts and Analytical Tools

- Concepts and Analytical Tools for Evaluating a Company's Situation — **Chapters 3 and 4**

Section C: Crafting a Strategy

- Tailoring Strategy to Various Company Situations
  - Single-Business Companies — **Chapters 5, 6, and 7**
  - Multibusiness or Diversified Companies — **Chapter 8**
- The Links between Ethics, Corporate Social Responsibility, Sustainability, and Strategy — **Chapter 9**

Section D: Executing the Strategy

- Managerial Keys to Successfully Executing the Chosen Strategy — **Chapters 10, 11, and 12**

Part II: Readings in Crafting and Executing Strategy

Section A: What Is Strategy and How Is the Process of Crafting and Executing Strategy Managed? (4 readings)
Section B: Crafting Strategy in Single-Business Companies (9 readings)
Section C: Crafting Strategy in International and Diversified Companies (4 readings)
Section D: Strategy, Ethics, Social Responsibility, and Sustainability (2 readings)
Section E: Executing Strategy (6 readings)

CHAPTER 1

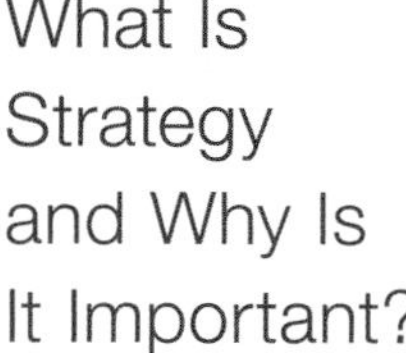

What Is Strategy and Why Is It Important?

Learning Objectives

THIS CHAPTER WILL HELP YOU UNDERSTAND:

LO 1 What we mean by a company's *strategy.*

LO 2 The concept of a *sustainable competitive advantage.*

LO 3 The five most basic strategic approaches for setting a company apart from rivals and winning a sustainable competitive advantage.

LO 4 That a company's strategy tends to evolve because of changing circumstances and ongoing efforts by management to improve the strategy.

LO 5 Why it is important for a company to have a viable business model that outlines the company's customer value proposition and its profit formula.

LO 6 The three tests of a winning strategy.

Learning Objectives are listed at the beginning of each chapter; corresponding numbered indicators in the margins show where learning objectives are covered in the text.

Illustration Capsules appear in boxes throughout each chapter to provide in-depth examples, connect the text presentation to real-world companies, and convincingly demonstrate "strategy in action." Some are appropriate for use as mini-cases.

ILLUSTRATION CAPSULE 9.4

TOMS's Well-Balanced Triple Bottom Line

Having sold over 2 million pairs of shoes worldwide, self-designated "Chief Shoe Giver" Blake Mycoskie founded TOMS on the principle of "One for One." Operating under the belief that "the way you shop can change the world," TOMS donates a pair of shoes to a child in need in over 50 different countries for every pair purchased. Each pair is made with sustainable materials that include organic canvas and recycled materials that minimize TOMS's ecological footprint. TOMS has been recognized with the Award for Corporate Excellence by the Office of the Secretary of State, while *Fortune* magazine has named Mycoskie to its "40 under 40" list.

Mycoskie credits much of TOMS's growth not to success in traditional avenues of advertising but, rather, to the story behind the TOMS shoe as told by TOMS's customers. By focusing on the story behind its product and the importance of sustainable giving, TOMS generates brand awareness through motivated customers who share their feel-good purchases with friends and family. By utilizing user marketing rather than corporate marketing, TOMS successfully pitches a grassroots company-image and bundles a lifestyle with its product.

TOMS's environmental sustainability approach includes offering a line of vegan shoes, which contain no animal by-products, and maintaining its commitment to use earth and animal-friendly materials whenever possible. Its shoeboxes are made with 80 percent recycled waste and are printed with soy ink. Through these production considerations, TOMS caters to an environmentally conscious demographic with few established competitors and with loyal consumers who have helped TOMS experience sustained growth despite the global recession.

From Shoe Giving Trips to employee training on the importance of environmental sustainability, TOMS aspires to offer its employees "more than a 9-to-5" job. This commitment to a worthwhile cause creates not only happier employees but also more autonomous and creative global citizens who work together to inspire change. By attaining *economic* growth through an emphasis on *social* justice and *environmental* sustainability, TOMS has maintained a well-balanced triple bottom line.

Note: Developed with Sean Zhang.

Source: Keynote statements by Blake Mycoskie and other information posted at www.toms.com.

Margin Notes define core concepts and call attention to important ideas and principles.

LO 4

The concepts of corporate social responsibility and environmental sustainability and how companies balance these duties with economic responsibilities to shareholders.

CORE CONCEPT

Corporate social responsibility (CSR) refers to a company's *duty* to operate in an honorable manner, provide good working conditions for employees, encourage workforce diversity, be a good steward of the environment, and actively work to better the quality of life in the local communities where it operates and in society at large.

The idea that businesses have an obligation to foster social betterment, a much-debated topic over the past 50 years, took root in the 19th century when progressive companies in the aftermath of the industrial revolution began to provide workers with housing and other amenities. The notion that corporate executives should balance the interests of all stakeholders—shareholders, employees, customers, suppliers, the communities in which they operate, and society at large—began to blossom in the 1960s. Some years later, a group of chief executives of America's 200 largest corporations, calling themselves the Business Roundtable, came out in strong support of the concept of **corporate social responsibility (CSR):**

> Balancing the shareholder's expectations of maximum return against other priorities is one of the fundamental problems confronting corporate management. The shareholder must receive a good return but the legitimate concerns of other constituencies (customers, employees, communities, suppliers and society at large) also must have the appropriate attention. . . . [Leading managers] believe that by giving enlightened consideration to balancing the legitimate claims of all its constituents, a corporation will best serve the interest of its shareholders.

Today, corporate social responsibility is a concept that resonates in western Europe, the United States, Canada, and such developing nations as Brazil and India.

The Concepts of Corporate Social Responsibility and Good Corporate Citizenship

The essence of socially responsible business behavior is that a company should balance strategic actions to benefit shareholders against the *duty* to be a good corporate citizen. The underlying thesis is that company managers should display a *social conscience* in operating the business and specifically take into account how management decisions and company actions affect the well-being of employees, local communities, the environment, and society at large.[20] Acting in a socially responsible manner thus encompasses more than just participating in community service projects and donating money to charities and other worthy causes. Demonstrating

Figures scattered throughout the chapters provide conceptual and analytical frameworks.

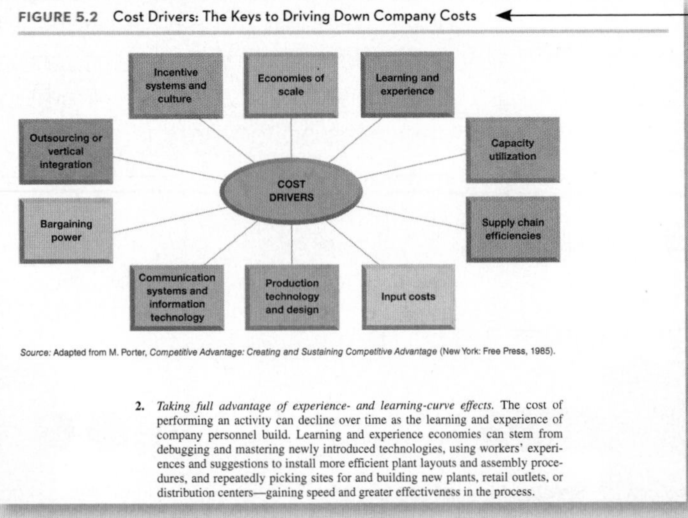

2. *Taking full advantage of experience- and learning-curve effects.* The cost of performing an activity can decline over time as the learning and experience of company personnel build. Learning and experience economies can stem from debugging and mastering newly introduced technologies, using workers' experiences and suggestions to install more efficient plant layouts and assembly procedures, and repeatedly picking sites for and building new plants, retail outlets, or distribution centers—gaining speed and greater effectiveness in the process.

Key Points at the end of each chapter provide a handy summary of essential ideas and things to remember.

KEY POINTS

1. Deciding which of the five generic competitive strategies to employ—overall low cost, broad differentiation, focused low cost, focused differentiation, or best cost—is perhaps the most important strategic commitment a company makes. It tends to drive the remaining strategic actions a company undertakes and sets the whole tone for pursuing a competitive advantage over rivals.
2. In employing a low-cost provider strategy and trying to achieve a low-cost advantage over rivals, a company must do a better job than rivals of cost-effectively managing value chain activities and/or it must find innovative ways to eliminate cost-producing activities. An effective use of cost drivers is key. Low-cost provider strategies work particularly well when price competition is strong and the products of rival sellers are virtually identical, when there are not many ways to differentiate, when buyers are price-sensitive or have the power to bargain down prices, when buyer switching costs are low, and when industry newcomers are likely to use a low introductory price to build market share.
3. Broad differentiation strategies seek to produce a competitive edge by incorporating attributes that set a company's product or service offering apart from rivals in ways that buyers consider valuable and worth paying for. This depends on the appropriate use of value drivers. Successful differentiation allows a firm to (1) command a premium price for its product, (2) increase unit sales (if additional buyers are won over by the differentiating features), and/or (3) gain buyer loyalty to its brand (because some buyers are strongly attracted to the differentiating

EXERCISE FOR SIMULATION PARTICIPANTS

1. Is your company's strategy ethical? Why or why not? Is there anything that your company has done or is now doing that could legitimately be considered "shady" by your competitors? **LO 1**
2. In what ways, if any, is your company exercising corporate social responsibility? What are the elements of your company's CSR strategy? Are there any changes to this strategy that you would suggest? **LO 4**
3. If some shareholders complained that you and your co-managers have been spending too little or too much on corporate social responsibility, what would you tell them? **LO 3, LO 4**
4. Is your company striving to conduct its business in an environmentally sustainable manner? What specific *additional* actions could your company take that would make an even greater contribution to environmental sustainability? **LO 4**
5. In what ways is your company's environmental sustainability strategy in the best long-term interest of shareholders? Does it contribute to your company's competitive advantage or profitability? **LO 4**

Exercises at the end of each chapter, linked to learning objectives, provide a basis for class discussion, oral presentations, and written assignments. Several chapters have exercises that qualify as mini-cases.

ENDNOTES

[1] James E. Post, Anne T. Lawrence, and James Weber, *Business and Society: Corporate Strategy, Public Policy, Ethics*, 10th ed. (New York: McGraw-Hill, 2002).
[2] Mark S. Schwartz, "Universal Moral Values for Corporate Codes of Ethics," *Journal of Business Ethics* 59, no. 1 (June 2005), pp. 27–44.
[3] Mark S. Schwartz, "A Code of Ethics for Corporate Codes of Ethics," *Journal of Business Ethics* 41, no. 1–2 (November–December 2002), pp. 27–43.
[4] T. L. Beauchamp and N. E. Bowie, *Ethical Theory and Business* (Upper Saddle River, NJ: Prentice-Hall, 2001).
[5] www.cnn.com/2013/10/15/world/child-labor-index-2014/ (accessed February 6, 2014).
[6] U.S. Department of Labor, "The Department of Labor's 2012 Findings on the Worst Forms of Child Labor," www.dol.gov/ilab/programs/ocft/PDF/2012OCFTreport.pdf.
[7] W. M. Greenfield, "In the Name of Corporate Social Responsibility," *Business Horizons* 47, no. 1 (January–February 2004), p. 22.
[8] Rajib Sanyal, "Determinants of Bribery in
[12] Thomas Donaldson and Thomas W. Dunfee, "Towards a Unified Conception of Business Ethics: Integrative Social Contracts Theory," *Academy of Management Review* 19, no. 2 (April 1994), pp. 252–284; Andrew Spicer, Thomas W. Dunfee, and Wendy J. Bailey, "Does National Context Matter in Ethical Decision Making? An Empirical Test of Integrative Social Contracts Theory," *Academy of Management Journal* 47, no. 4 (August 2004), p. 610.
[13] Lynn Paine, Rohit Deshpandé, Joshua D. Margolis, and Kim Eric Bettcher, "Up to Code: Does Your Company's Conduct Meet World-Class Standards?" *Harvard Business Review* 83, no. 12 (December 2005), pp. 122–133.
[14] John F. Veiga, Timothy D. Golden, and Kathleen Dechant, "Why Managers Bend Company Rules," *Academy of Management Executive* 18, no. 2 (May 2004).
[15] www.reuters.com/article/2014/02/06/us-sac-martoma-idUSBREA131TL20140206.
[16] Lorin Berlin and Emily Peck, "National Mortgage Settlement: States, Big Banks Reach $25 Billion Deal," *Huff Post Business*, February 9, 2012, www.huffingtonpost.
[20] Timothy M. Devinney, "Is the Socially Responsible Corporation a Myth? The Good, the Bad, and the Ugly of Corporate Social Responsibility," *Academy of Management Perspectives* 23, no. 2 (May 2009), pp. 44–56.
[21] Information posted at www.generalmills.com (accessed March 13, 2013).
[22] Adrian Henriques, "ISO 26000: A New Standard for Human Rights?" *Institute for Human Rights and Business*, March 23, 2010, www.institutehrb.org/blogs/guest/iso_26000_a_new_standard_for_human_rights.html?gclid=CJih7NjN2alCFVs65QodrVOdyQ (accessed July 7, 2010).
[23] Gerald I.J.M. Zetsloot and Marcel N. A. van Marrewijk, "From Quality to Sustainability," *Journal of Business Ethics* 55 (2004), pp. 79–82.
[24] Tilde Herrera, "PG&E Claims Industry First with Supply Chain Footprint Project," *GreenBiz.com*, June 30, 2010, www.greenbiz.com/news/2010/06/30/-pge-claims-industry-first-supply-chain-carbon-footprint-project.
[25] J. G. Speth, *The Bridge at the End of the World: Capitalism, the Environment, and*

The 25 readings in this edition are flush with practical examples and valuable lessons for students of the art and science of crafting and executing strategy. There are two or three readings for each chapter—all chosen with three criteria in mind: relevance, readability, and recency of publication.

READING 09

Are You Ready for the Digital Value Chain?

connect

Rüdiger Stern
Accenture

Matthias Ziegler
Accenture

Music, books, art, maps, the ways we communicate—these and countless other things that used to be primarily physical or analog are now digital as well, and that has changed the ways we live, work, learn and play. But that is just the tip of the iceberg. Today, technology is enabling the digitization of almost everything—even manufacturing. Want your own special protective case for your mobile phone? One device manufacturer has made available digital files that will let consumers design a custom case for their phone, then have the case made on a 3D printer.

In fact, innovative examples of digitization are arising across the entire corporate value chain—not just manufacturing but also new-product development, sourcing, marketing, distribution and service (see chart). Sooner or later, every company will have to deal with the impact of digitization on its business model. Innovative digital solutions can reduce costs and add value at every stage of a product's lifecycle, both within each stage of the value chain and across its entirety. Digitization enables businesses and governments to operate with greater transparency and efficiency, and it boosts consumers' access to everything from innovative products to public services.

Although the focus of media reports is often on specific examples of digitization, it is essential for businesses to see the bigger picture—the truly revolutionary possibilities available by harnessing the synergies of a fully integrated digital value chain. Companies also now need to see data management as a core competence. In the digital age, data is a strategic asset. A company's data must be able to yield the relevant information for improved or new products and services across intelligent, digital networks.

INNOVATIVE APPLICATIONS ACROSS THE DIGITAL VALUE CHAIN

How is digitization altering specific steps in the value chain, and even optimizing the makeup of the chain itself? The marketplace is seeing vibrant innovation in many specific areas; the next step will be to integrate these one-off innovations to help create an end-to-end digital value chain that creates unparalleled business opportunities.

Sourcing and Procurement: eKanban

Kanban is a scheduling system for lean and just-in-time production. For decades, Kanban has been helping companies keep inventories low by ensuring that goods and equipment arrive just before a production run begins. Today, electronic Kanban (eKanban) uses the Internet to route messages to external suppliers, providing real-time visibility into the entire supply chain. These methods can lead to a host of benefits, including lower inventory stock levels, less physical transportation, a reduction in working capital and increased liquidity.

Auto manufacturer BMW implemented an eKanban system together with Lear Corp., a supplier of car seats. Based on BMW's daily demand and supported by an enterprise resource planning

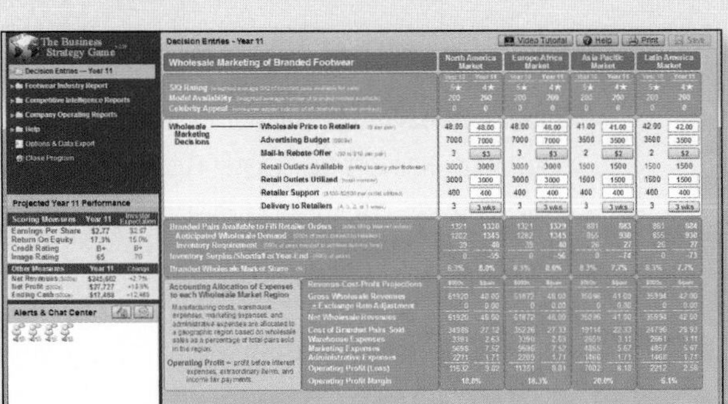

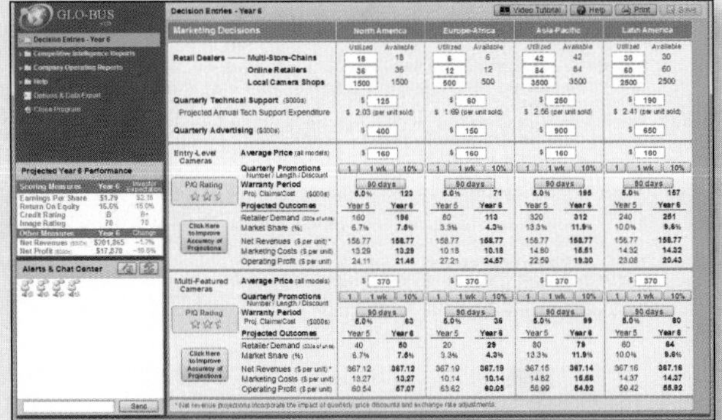

***The Business Strategy Game* or *GLO-BUS* Simulation Exercises** Either one of these text supplements involves teams of students managing companies in a head-to-head contest for global market leadership. Company co-managers have to make decisions relating to product quality, production, workforce compensation and training, pricing and marketing, and financing of company operations. The challenge is to craft and execute a strategy that is powerful enough to deliver good financial performance despite the competitive efforts of rival companies. Each company competes in America, Latin America, Europe-Africa, and Asia-Pacific.

Crafting and Executing Strategy

Concepts and Readings

BRIEF CONTENTS

PART 1 Concepts and Techniques for Crafting and Executing Strategy

PART 2 Readings in Crafting and Executing Strategy

CONTENTS

PART 1

Concepts and Techniques for Crafting and Executing Strategy

CHAPTER 1

What Is Strategy and Why Is It Important?

Learning Objectives

THIS CHAPTER WILL HELP YOU UNDERSTAND:

LO 1 What we mean by a company's *strategy.*

LO 2 The concept of a *sustainable competitive advantage.*

LO 3 The five most basic strategic approaches for setting a company apart from rivals and winning a sustainable competitive advantage.

LO 4 That a company's strategy tends to evolve because of changing circumstances and ongoing efforts by management to improve the strategy.

LO 5 Why it is important for a company to have a viable business model that outlines the company's customer value proposition and its profit formula.

LO 6 The three tests of a winning strategy.

Strategy is about making choices, trade-offs; it's about deliberately choosing to be different.

Michael Porter – *Professor and Consultant*

If your firm's strategy can be applied to any other firm, you don't have a very good one.

David J. Collis and Michael G. Rukstad – *Consultants and Professors*

If you don't have a competitive advantage, don't compete.

Jack Welch – *Former CEO of General Electric*

According to *The Economist,* a leading publication on business, economics, and international affairs, "In business, strategy is king. Leadership and hard work are all very well and luck is mighty useful, but it is strategy that makes or breaks a firm."[1] Luck and circumstance can explain why some companies are blessed with initial, short-lived success. But only a well-crafted, well-executed, constantly evolving strategy can explain why an elite set of companies somehow manages to rise to the top and stay there, year after year, pleasing their customers, shareholders, and other stakeholders alike in the process. Companies such as ExxonMobil, IBM, Southwest Airlines, FedEx, Google, Apple, Coca-Cola, Procter & Gamble, McDonald's, and Berkshire Hathaway come to mind—but long-lived success is not just the province of U.S. companies. Diverse kinds of companies, both large and small, from many different countries have been able to sustain strong performance records, including Russia's Gazprom (in energy), Korea's Samsung (in electronics), Singapore Airlines, Sweden's IKEA (in home furnishings), Mexico's America Movil (in telecommunications), and Japan's Toyota Motor.

In this opening chapter, we define the concept of strategy and describe its many facets. We explain what is meant by a competitive advantage, discuss the relationship between a company's strategy and its business model, and introduce you to the kinds of competitive strategies that can give a company an advantage over rivals in attracting customers and earning above-average profits. We look at what sets a winning strategy apart from others and why the caliber of a company's strategy determines whether the company will enjoy a competitive advantage over other firms. By the end of this chapter, you will have a clear idea of why the tasks of crafting and executing strategy are core management functions and why excellent execution of an excellent strategy is the most reliable recipe for turning a company into a standout performer over the long term.

WHAT DO WE MEAN BY *STRATEGY*?

A company's **strategy** is the set of actions that its managers take to outperform the company's competitors and achieve superior profitability. The objective of a well-crafted strategy is not merely temporary competitive success and profits in the short run, but rather the sort of lasting success that can support growth and secure the

CORE CONCEPT

A company's **strategy** is the set of actions that its managers take to outperform the company's competitors and achieve superior profitability.

company's future over the long term. Achieving this entails making a managerial commitment to a coherent array of well-considered choices about how to compete.[2] These include choices about:

- *How* to attract and please customers.
- *How* to compete against rivals.
- *How* to position the company in the marketplace and capitalize on attractive opportunities to grow the business.
- *How* to respond to changing economic and market conditions.
- *How* to manage each functional piece of the business (R&D, supply chain activities, production, sales and marketing, distribution, finance, and human resources).
- *How* to achieve the company's performance targets.

LO 1

What we mean by a company's *strategy.*

In most industries, companies have considerable freedom in choosing the *hows* of strategy.[3] Thus some companies strive to achieve lower costs than rivals, while others aim for product superiority or more personalized customer service or enhanced quality dimensions that rivals cannot match. Some companies opt for wide product lines, while others concentrate their energies on a narrow product lineup. Some competitors deliberately confine their operations to local or regional markets; others opt to compete nationally, internationally (several countries), or globally (all or most of the major country markets worldwide).

Strategy Is about Competing Differently

Mimicking the strategies of successful industry rivals—with either copycat product offerings or maneuvers to stake out the same market position—rarely works. Rather, every company's strategy needs to have some distinctive element that draws in customers and produces a competitive edge. Strategy, at its essence, is about competing differently—doing what rival firms *don't* do or what rival firms *can't* do.[4] This does not mean that the key elements of a company's strategy have to be 100 percent different, but rather that they must differ in at least *some important respects.* A strategy stands a better chance of succeeding when it is predicated on actions, business approaches, and competitive moves aimed at (1) appealing to buyers in ways that *set a company apart from its rivals* and (2) staking out a market position that is not crowded with strong competitors.

Strategy is about competing differently from rivals—doing what competitors *don't* do or, even better, doing what they *can't* do!

A company's strategy provides direction and guidance, in terms of not only what the company *should* do but also what it *should not* do. Knowing what not to do can be as important as knowing what to do, strategically. At best, making the wrong strategic moves will prove a distraction and a waste of company resources. At worst, it can bring about unintended long-term consequences that put the company's very survival at risk.

Figure 1.1 illustrates the broad types of actions and approaches that often characterize a company's strategy in a particular business or industry. For a more concrete example of the specific actions constituting a firm's strategy, see Illustration Capsule 1.1, describing Starbucks's strategy in the specialty coffee market.

LO 2

The concept of a *sustainable competitive advantage.*

Strategy and the Quest for Competitive Advantage

The heart and soul of any strategy are the actions and moves in the marketplace that managers are taking to gain a competitive advantage over rivals. A company achieves a competitive advantage whenever it has some type of edge over rivals in attracting buyers and coping with competitive forces. There are many routes to competitive advantage, but they all involve either giving buyers what they perceive as superior value

FIGURE 1.1 Identifying a Company's Strategy—What to Look For

compared to the offerings of rival sellers or giving buyers the same value as others at a lower cost to the firm. Superior value can mean a good product at a lower price, a superior product that is worth paying more for, or a best-value offering that represents an attractive combination of price, features, quality, service, and other attributes. Delivering superior value or delivering value more efficiently—whatever form it takes—nearly always requires performing value chain activities differently than rivals do and building competencies and resource capabilities that are not readily matched. In Illustration Capsule 1.1, it's evident that Starbucks has gained a competitive advantage over its rivals in the coffee shop industry through its efforts to create an upscale experience for coffee drinkers by catering to individualized tastes, enhancing the atmosphere and comfort of the shops, and delivering a premium product produced under environmentally sound, Fair Trade practices. By differentiating itself in this manner from other coffee purveyors, Starbucks has been able to charge prices for its coffee that are well above those of its rivals and far exceed the low cost of its inputs. Its expansion policies have allowed the company to make it easy for customers to find a Starbucks shop almost anywhere, further enhancing the brand and cementing customer loyalty. A creative *distinctive* strategy such as that used by Starbucks is a company's most reliable ticket for developing a competitive advantage over its rivals. If a strategy is not distinctive, then there can be no competitive advantage, since no firm would be meeting customer needs better or operating more efficiently than any other.

ILLUSTRATION CAPSULE 1.1

Starbucks's Strategy in the Coffeehouse Market

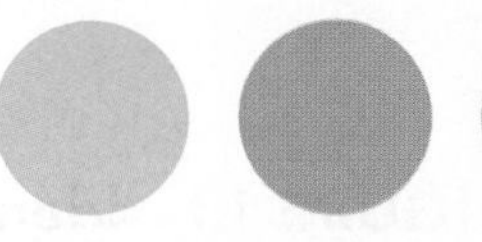

Since its founding in 1985 as a modest nine-store operation in Seattle, Washington, Starbucks had become the premier roaster and retailer of specialty coffees in the world, with over 18,800 store locations as of April 2013. In fiscal 2013, its annual sales were expected to exceed $15 billion—an all-time high for revenues and net earnings. The key elements of Starbucks's strategy in the coffeehouse industry included:

- *Train "baristas" to serve a wide variety of specialty coffee drinks that allow customers to satisfy their individual preferences in a customized way.* Starbucks essentially brought specialty coffees, such as cappuccinos, lattes, and macchiatos, to the mass market in the United States, encouraging customers to personalize their coffee-drinking habits. Requests for such items as an "Iced Grande Hazelnut Macchiato with Soy Milk, and no Hazelnut Drizzle" could be served up quickly with consistent quality.
- *Emphasize store ambience and elevation of the customer experience at Starbucks stores.* Starbucks's management viewed each store as a billboard for the company and as a contributor to building the company's brand and image. The company went to great lengths to make sure the store fixtures, the merchandise displays, the artwork, the music, and the aromas all blended to create an inviting environment that evoked the romance of coffee and signaled the company's passion for coffee. Free Wi-Fi drew those who needed a comfortable place to work while they had their coffee.
- *Purchase and roast only top-quality coffee beans.* The company purchased only the highest-quality arabica beans and carefully roasted coffee to exacting standards of quality and flavor. Starbucks did not use chemicals or artificial flavors when preparing its roasted coffees.
- *Foster commitment to corporate responsibility.* Starbucks was protective of the environment and contributed positively to the communities where Starbucks stores were located. In addition, Starbucks promoted Fair Trade practices and paid above-market prices for coffee beans to provide its growers and suppliers with sufficient funding to sustain their operations and provide for their families.
- *Expand the number of Starbucks stores domestically and internationally.* Starbucks operated stores in high-traffic, high-visibility locations in the United States and abroad. The company's ability to vary store size and format made it possible to locate stores in settings such as downtown and suburban shopping areas, office buildings, and university campuses. The company also focused on making Starbucks a global brand, expanding its reach to more than 60 countries in 2013.
- *Broaden and periodically refresh in-store product offerings.* Noncoffee products by Starbucks included teas, fresh pastries and other food items, candy, juice drinks, music CDs, and coffee mugs and coffee accessories.
- *Fully exploit the growing power of the Starbucks name and brand image with out-of-store sales.* Starbucks's Consumer Packaged Goods division included domestic and international sales of Frappuccino, coffee ice creams, and Starbucks coffees.

Source: Company documents, 10-Ks, and information posted on Starbucks's website.

If a company's competitive edge holds promise for being *sustainable* (as opposed to just temporary), then so much the better for both the strategy and the company's future profitability. What makes a competitive advantage **sustainable** (or durable), as opposed to temporary, are elements of the strategy that give buyers lasting reasons to prefer a company's products or services over those of competitors—*reasons that competitors are unable to nullify or overcome despite their best efforts.* In the case of Starbucks, the company's unparalleled name recognition, its reputation for high-quality specialty coffees served in a comfortable, inviting atmosphere, and the accessibility of the shops make it difficult for competitors to weaken or overcome Starbucks's competitive advantage. Not only has Starbucks's strategy provided the company with a sustainable competitive advantage, but it has made Starbucks one of the most admired companies on the planet.

CORE CONCEPT

A company achieves a **competitive advantage** when it provides buyers with superior value compared to rival sellers or offers the same value at a lower cost to the firm. The advantage is **sustainable** if it persists despite the best efforts of competitors to match or surpass this advantage.

Five of the most frequently used and dependable strategic approaches to setting a company apart from rivals, building strong customer loyalty, and winning a competitive advantage are:

LO 3

The five most basic strategic approaches for setting a company apart from rivals and winning a sustainable competitive advantage.

1. *A low-cost provider strategy*—achieving a cost-based advantage over rivals. Walmart and Southwest Airlines have earned strong market positions because of the low-cost advantages they have achieved over their rivals. Low-cost provider strategies can produce a durable competitive edge when rivals find it hard to match the low-cost leader's approach to driving costs out of the business.
2. *A broad differentiation strategy*—seeking to differentiate the company's product or service from that of rivals in ways that will appeal to a broad spectrum of buyers. Successful adopters of differentiation strategies include Apple (innovative products), Johnson & Johnson in baby products (product reliability), LVMH (luxury and prestige), and BMW (engineering design and performance). One way to sustain this type of competitive advantage is to be sufficiently innovative to thwart the efforts of clever rivals to copy or closely imitate the product offering.
3. *A focused low-cost strategy*—concentrating on a narrow buyer segment (or market niche) and outcompeting rivals by having lower costs and thus being able to serve niche members at a lower price. Private-label manufacturers of food, health and beauty products, and nutritional supplements use their low-cost advantage to offer supermarket buyers lower prices than those demanded by producers of branded products.
4. *A focused differentiation strategy*—concentrating on a narrow buyer segment and outcompeting rivals by offering buyers customized attributes that meet their specialized needs and tastes better than rivals' products. Lululemon, for example, specializes in high-quality yoga clothing and the like, attracting a devoted set of buyers in the process. Jiffy Lube International in quick oil changes, McAfee in virus protection software, and The Weather Channel in cable TV provide some other examples of this strategy.
5. *A best-cost provider strategy*—giving customers more value for the money by satisfying their expectations on key quality features, performance, and/or service attributes while beating their price expectations. This approach is a hybrid strategy that blends elements of low-cost provider and differentiation strategies; the aim is to have lower costs than rivals while simultaneously offering better differentiating attributes. Target is an example of a company that is known for its hip product design (a reputation it built by featuring cheap-chic designers such as Isaac Mizrahi), as well as a more appealing shopping ambience for discount store shoppers. Its dual focus on low costs as well as differentiation shows how a best-cost provider strategy can offer customers great value for the money.

Winning a *sustainable* competitive edge over rivals with any of the preceding five strategies generally hinges as much on building competitively valuable expertise and capabilities that rivals cannot readily match as it does on having a distinctive product offering. Clever rivals can nearly always copy the attributes of a popular product or service, but for rivals to match the experience, know-how, and specialized capabilities that a company has developed and perfected over a long period of time is substantially harder to do and takes much longer. FedEx, for example, has superior capabilities in next-day delivery of small packages, while Google is known for its Internet search capabilities. Apple has demonstrated impressive product innovation capabilities in digital music players, smartphones, and e-readers. Hyundai has become the world's fastest-growing automaker as a result of its advanced manufacturing processes and unparalleled quality control system. Each of these capabilities has proved hard for competitors to imitate or best.

LO 4

A company's strategy tends to evolve because of changing circumstances and ongoing efforts by management to improve the strategy.

Why a Company's Strategy Evolves over Time

The appeal of a strategy that yields a sustainable competitive advantage is that it offers the potential for an enduring edge over rivals. However, managers of every company must be willing and ready to modify the strategy in response to changing market conditions, advancing technology, unexpected moves by competitors, shifting buyer needs, emerging market opportunities, and new ideas for improving the strategy. Most of the time, a company's strategy evolves incrementally as management fine-tunes various pieces of the strategy and adjusts the strategy in response to unfolding events.[5] However, on occasion, major strategy shifts are called for, such as when the strategy is clearly failing or when industry conditions change in dramatic ways. Industry environments characterized by high-velocity change require companies to repeatedly adapt their strategies.[6] For example, companies in industries with rapid-fire advances in technology like medical equipment, electronics, and wireless devices often find it essential to adjust key elements of their strategies several times a year, sometimes even finding it necessary to "reinvent" their approach to providing value to their customers.

Changing circumstances and ongoing management efforts to improve the strategy cause a company's strategy to evolve over time—a condition that makes the task of crafting strategy a *work in progress*, not a one-time event.

Regardless of whether a company's strategy changes gradually or swiftly, the important point is that the task of crafting strategy is not a one-time event but always a work in progress. Adapting to new conditions and constantly evaluating what is working well enough to continue and what needs to be improved are normal parts of the strategy-making process, resulting in an *evolving strategy*.[7]

A Company's Strategy Is Partly Proactive and Partly Reactive

A company's strategy is shaped partly by management analysis and choice and partly by the necessity of adapting and learning by doing.

The evolving nature of a company's strategy means that the typical company strategy is a blend of (1) *proactive*, planned initiatives to improve the company's financial performance and secure a competitive edge and (2) *reactive* responses to unanticipated developments and fresh market conditions. The biggest portion of a company's current strategy flows from previously initiated actions that have proven themselves in the marketplace and newly launched initiatives aimed at edging out rivals and boosting financial performance. This part of management's action plan for running the company is its **deliberate strategy,** consisting of proactive strategy

FIGURE 1.2 A Company's Strategy Is a Blend of Proactive Initiatives and Reactive Adjustments

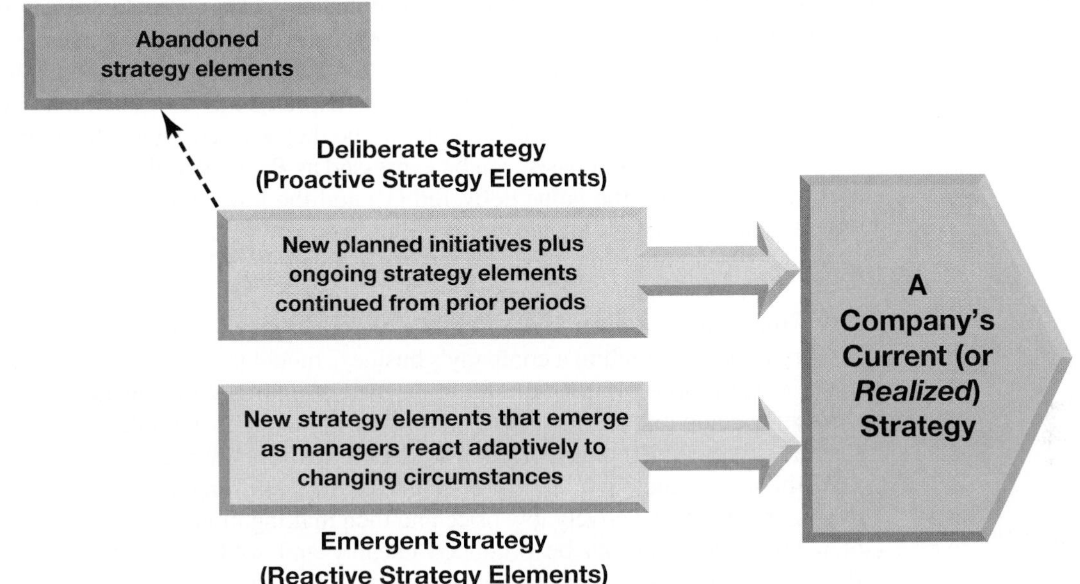

elements that are both planned and realized as planned (while other planned strategy elements may not work out and are abandoned in consequence)—see Figure 1.2.[8]

> **CORE CONCEPT**
>
> A company's **deliberate strategy** consists of *proactive* strategy elements that are planned; its **emergent strategy** consists of *reactive* strategy elements that emerge as changing conditions warrant.

But managers must always be willing to supplement or modify the proactive strategy elements with as-needed reactions to unanticipated conditions. Inevitably, there will be occasions when market and competitive conditions take an unexpected turn that calls for some kind of strategic reaction. Hence, *a portion of a company's strategy is always developed on the fly,* coming as a response to fresh strategic maneuvers on the part of rival firms, unexpected shifts in customer requirements, fast-changing technological developments, newly appearing market opportunities, a changing political or economic climate, or other unanticipated happenings in the surrounding environment. These adaptive strategy adjustments make up the firm's **emergent strategy.** A company's strategy *in toto* (its **realized strategy**) thus tends to be a *combination* of proactive and reactive elements, with certain strategy elements being *abandoned* because they have become obsolete or ineffective. A company's realized strategy can be observed in the pattern of its actions over time, which is a far better indicator than any of its strategic plans on paper or any public pronouncements about its strategy.

A COMPANY'S STRATEGY AND ITS BUSINESS MODEL

At the core of every sound strategy is the company's **business model.** A business model is management's blueprint for delivering a valuable product or service to customers in a manner that will generate revenues sufficient to cover costs and yield an

LO 5

Why it is important for a company to have a viable business model that outlines the company's customer value proposition and its profit formula.

attractive profit.[9] The two elements of a company's business model are (1) its *customer value proposition* and (2) its *profit formula*. The customer value proposition lays out the company's approach to satisfying buyer wants and needs at a price customers will consider a good value. The profit formula describes the company's approach to determining a cost structure that will allow for acceptable profits, given the pricing tied to its customer value proposition. Figure 1.3 illustrates the elements of the business model in terms of what is known as the *Value-Price-Cost Framework*.[10] As the framework indicates, the customer value proposition can be expressed as $V - P$, which is essentially the customers' perception of how much value they are getting for the money. The profit formula, on a per-unit basis, can be expressed as $P - C$. Plainly, from a customer perspective, the greater the value delivered (V) and the lower the price (P), the more attractive is the company's value proposition. On the other hand, the lower the costs (C), given the customer value proposition ($V - P$), the greater the ability of the business model to be a moneymaker. Thus the profit formula reveals how efficiently a company can meet customer wants and needs and deliver on the value proposition. The nitty-gritty issue surrounding a company's business model is whether it can execute its customer value proposition profitably. Just because company managers have crafted a strategy for competing and running the business, this does not automatically mean that the strategy will lead to profitability—it may or it may not.

CORE CONCEPT

A company's **business model** sets forth the logic for how its strategy will create value for customers and at the same time generate revenues sufficient to cover costs and realize a profit.

Gillette's business model in razor blades involves selling a "master product"—the razor—at an attractively low price and then making money on repeat purchases of razor blades that can be produced cheaply and sold at high profit margins. Printer manufacturers like Hewlett-Packard, Canon, and Epson pursue much the same business model as Gillette—selling printers at a low (virtually break-even) price and making large profit margins on the repeat purchases of printer supplies, especially ink cartridges. McDonald's invented the business model for fast food—providing value to customers in the form of economical quick-service meals at clean, convenient locations. Its profit formula involves such elements as standardized cost-efficient store design, stringent specifications for ingredients, operating procedures specified in detail for each unit, and heavy reliance on advertising and in-store promotions to drive volume. Illustration Capsule 1.2 describes three contrasting business models in radio broadcasting.

FIGURE 1.3 The Business Model and the Value-Price-Cost Framework

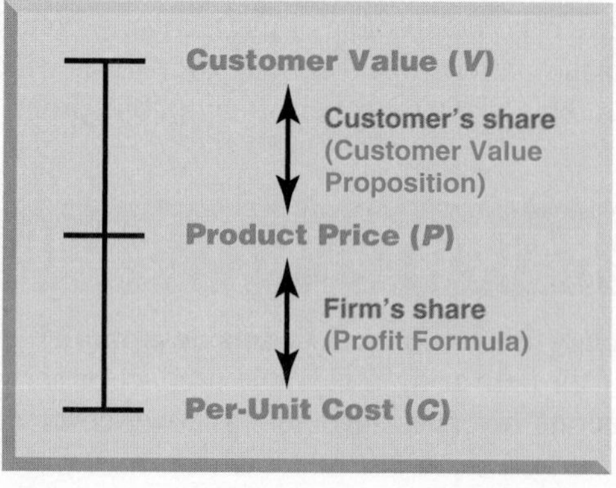

ILLUSTRATION CAPSULE 1.2

Pandora, Sirius XM, and Over-the-Air Broadcast Radio: Three Contrasting Business Models

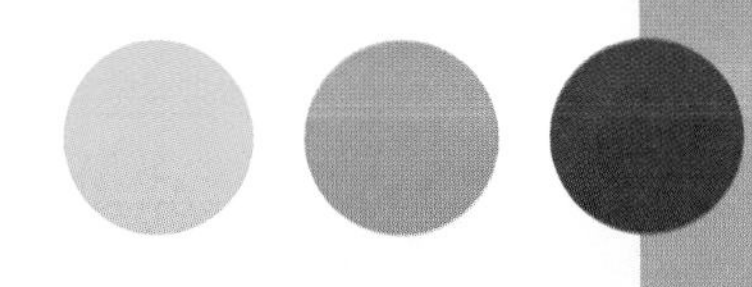

	Pandora	Sirius XM	Over-the-Air Radio Broadcasters
Customer value proposition	• Through free-of-charge Internet radio service, allowed PC, tablet computer, and smartphone users to create up to 100 personalized music and comedy stations. • Utilized algorithms to generate playlists based on users' predicted music preferences. • Offered programming interrupted by brief, occasional ads; eliminated advertising for Pandora One subscribers.	• For a monthly subscription fee, provided Satellite-based music, news, sports, national and regional weather, traffic reports in limited areas, and talk radio programming. • Also offered subscribers streaming Internet channels and the ability to create personalized commercial-free stations for online and mobile listening. • Offered programming interrupted only by brief, occasional ads.	• Provided free-of-charge music, national and local news, local traffic reports, national and local weather, and talk radio programming. • Included frequent programming interruption for ads.
Profit formula	*Revenue generation:* Display, audio, and video ads targeted to different audiences and sold to local and national buyers; subscription revenues generated from an advertising-free option called Pandora One. *Cost structure:* Fixed costs associated with developing software for computers, tablets, and smartphones. Fixed and variable costs related to operating data centers to support streaming network, content royalties, marketing, and support activities.	*Revenue generation:* Monthly subscription fees, sales of satellite radio equipment, and advertising revenues. *Cost structure:* Fixed costs associated with operating a satellite-based music delivery service and streaming Internet service. Fixed and variable costs related to programming and content royalties, marketing, and support activities.	*Revenue generation:* Advertising sales to national and local businesses. *Cost structure:* Fixed costs associated with terrestrial broadcasting operations. Fixed and variable costs related to local news reporting, advertising sales operations, network affiliate fees, programming and content royalties, commercial production activities, and support activities.
	Profit margin: Profitability dependent on generating sufficient advertising revenues and subscription revenues to cover costs and provide attractive profits.	*Profit margin:* Profitability dependent on attracting a sufficiently large number of subscribers to cover costs and provide attractive profits.	*Profit margin:* Profitability dependent on generating sufficient advertising revenues to cover costs and provide attractive profits.

WHAT MAKES A STRATEGY A WINNER?

LO 6

The three tests of a winning strategy.

A **winning strategy** must pass three tests:
1. The Fit Test
2. The Competitive Advantage Test
3. The Performance Test

Three tests can be applied to determine whether a strategy is a *winning strategy:*

1. ***The Fit Test:*** *How well does the strategy fit the company's situation?* To qualify as a winner, a strategy has to be well matched to industry and competitive conditions, a company's best market opportunities, and other pertinent aspects of the business environment in which the company operates. No strategy can work well unless it exhibits good *external fit* and is in sync with prevailing market conditions. At the same time, a winning strategy must be tailored to the company's resources and competitive capabilities and be supported by a complementary set of functional activities (i.e., activities in the realms of supply chain management, operations, sales and marketing, and so on). That is, it must also exhibit *internal fit* and be compatible with a company's ability to execute the strategy in a competent manner. Unless a strategy exhibits good fit with both the external and internal aspects of a company's overall situation, it is likely to be an underperformer and fall short of producing winning results. Winning strategies also exhibit *dynamic fit* in the sense that they evolve over time in a manner that maintains close and effective alignment with the company's situation even as external and internal conditions change.[11]
2. ***The Competitive Advantage Test:*** *Is the strategy helping the company achieve a sustainable competitive advantage?* Strategies that fail to achieve a durable competitive advantage over rivals are unlikely to produce superior performance for more than a brief period of time. Winning strategies enable a company to achieve a competitive advantage over key rivals that is long-lasting. The bigger and more durable the competitive advantage, the more powerful it is.
3. ***The Performance Test:*** *Is the strategy producing good company performance?* The mark of a winning strategy is strong company performance. Two kinds of performance indicators tell the most about the caliber of a company's strategy: (1) competitive strength and market standing and (2) profitability and financial strength. Above-average financial performance or gains in market share, competitive position, or profitability are signs of a winning strategy.

Strategies that come up short on one or more of the preceding tests are plainly less appealing than strategies passing all three tests with flying colors. Managers should use the same questions when evaluating either proposed or existing strategies. New initiatives that don't seem to match the company's internal and external situations should be scrapped before they come to fruition, while existing strategies must be scrutinized on a regular basis to ensure they have good fit, offer a competitive advantage, and are contributing to above-average performance or performance improvements.

WHY CRAFTING AND EXECUTING STRATEGY ARE IMPORTANT TASKS

Crafting and executing strategy are top-priority managerial tasks for two big reasons. First, a clear and reasoned strategy is management's prescription for doing business, its road map to competitive advantage, its game plan for pleasing customers, and its formula for improving performance. High-achieving enterprises are nearly always the product of astute, creative, and proactive strategy making. Companies don't get to the top of the industry rankings or stay there with illogical strategies, copycat strategies, or timid attempts to try to do better. Only a handful of companies can boast of hitting home runs in the marketplace due to lucky breaks or the good fortune of having stumbled into the right market at the right time with the right product. Even if this is the case, success will not be lasting unless the companies subsequently craft a strategy that capitalizes on their luck, builds on what is working, and discards the rest. So there can be little argument that the process of crafting a company's strategy matters—and matters a lot.

Second, even the best of strategies will lead to failure if it is not executed proficiently. The processes of crafting and executing strategies must go hand in hand if a company is to be successful in the long term. The chief executive officer of one successful company put it well when he said:

> In the main, our competitors are acquainted with the same fundamental concepts and techniques and approaches that we follow, and they are as free to pursue them as we are. More often than not, the difference between their level of success and ours lies in the relative thoroughness and self-discipline with which we and they develop and execute our strategies for the future.

Good Strategy + Good Strategy Execution = Good Management

Crafting and executing strategy are thus core management functions. Among all the things managers do, nothing affects a company's ultimate success or failure more fundamentally than how well its management team charts the company's direction, develops competitively effective strategic moves and business approaches, and pursues what needs to be done internally to produce good day-in, day-out strategy execution and operating excellence. Indeed, *good strategy and good strategy execution are the most telling signs of good management.* The rationale for using the twin standards of good strategy making and good strategy execution to determine whether a company is well managed is therefore compelling: *The better conceived a company's strategy and the more competently it is executed, the more likely the company will be a standout performer in the marketplace.* In stark contrast, a company that lacks clear-cut direction, has a flawed strategy, or can't execute its strategy competently is a company whose financial performance is probably suffering, whose business is at long-term risk, and whose management is sorely lacking.

THE ROAD AHEAD

Throughout the chapters to come and in Part 2 of this text, the spotlight is trained on the foremost question in running a business enterprise: *What must managers do, and do well, to make a company a winner in the marketplace?* The answer that emerges is that doing a good job of managing inherently requires good strategic thinking and good management of the strategy-making, strategy-executing process.

> How well a company performs is directly attributable to the caliber of its strategy and the proficiency with which the strategy is executed.

The mission of this book is to provide a solid overview of what every business student and aspiring manager needs to know about crafting and executing strategy. We will explore what good strategic thinking entails, describe the core concepts and tools of strategic analysis, and examine the ins and outs of crafting and executing strategy. The accompanying cases will help build your skills in both diagnosing how well the strategy-making, strategy-executing task is being performed and prescribing actions for how the strategy in question or its execution can be improved. The strategic management course that you are enrolled in may also include a strategy simulation exercise in which you will run a company in head-to-head competition with companies run by your classmates. Your mastery of the strategic management concepts presented in the following chapters will put you in a strong position to craft a winning strategy for your company and figure out how to execute it in a cost-effective and profitable manner. As you progress through the chapters of the text and the activities assigned during the term, we hope to convince you that first-rate capabilities in crafting and executing strategy are essential to good management.

As you tackle the content and accompanying activities of this book, ponder the following observation by the essayist and poet Ralph Waldo Emerson: "Commerce is a game of skill which many people play, but which few play well." If your efforts help you become a savvy player and better equip you to succeed in business, the time and energy you spend here will indeed prove worthwhile.

KEY POINTS

1. A company's strategy is its game plan to attract and please customers, outperform its competitors, and achieve superior profitability.
2. The central thrust of a company's strategy is undertaking moves to build and strengthen the company's long-term competitive position and financial performance by *competing differently* from rivals and gaining a sustainable competitive advantage over them.
3. A company achieves a *competitive advantage* when it provides buyers with superior value compared to rival sellers or offers the same value at a lower cost to the firm. The advantage is *sustainable* if it persists despite the best efforts of competitors to match or surpass this advantage.
4. A company's strategy typically evolves over time, emerging from a blend of (1) proactive deliberate actions on the part of company managers to improve the strategy and (2) reactive emergent responses to unanticipated developments and fresh market conditions.
5. A company's business model sets forth the logic for how its strategy will create value for customers and at the same time generate revenues sufficient to cover costs and realize a profit. Thus, it contains two crucial elements: (1) the *customer value proposition*—a plan for satisfying customer wants and needs at a price customers will consider good value, and (2) the *profit formula*—a plan for a cost structure that will enable the company to deliver the customer value proposition profitably. These elements are illustrated by the Value-Price-Cost Framework.
6. A winning strategy will pass three tests: (1) *Fit* (external, internal, and dynamic consistency), (2) *Competitive Advantage* (durable competitive advantage), and (3) *Performance* (outstanding financial and market performance).
7. Crafting and executing strategy are core management functions. How well a company performs and the degree of market success it enjoys are directly attributable to the caliber of its strategy and the proficiency with which the strategy is executed.

ASSURANCE OF LEARNING EXERCISES

1. Based on your experiences as a coffee consumer, does Starbucks's strategy (as described in Illustration Capsule 1.1) seem to set it apart from rivals? Does the strategy seem to be keyed to a cost-based advantage, differentiating features, serving the unique needs of a niche, or some combination of these? What is there about Starbucks's strategy that can lead to sustainable competitive advantage? connect **LO 1, LO 2, LO 3**
2. Elements of eBay's strategy have evolved in meaningful ways since the company's founding in 1995. After reviewing all of the links at the company's investor relations site, which can be found at **investor.ebayinc.com**, prepare a one- to two-page report that discusses how its strategy has evolved. Your report should also assess how well eBay's strategy passes the three tests of a winning strategy. **LO 4, LO 6**
3. Go to **www.nytco.com/investors** and check whether *The New York Times*' recent financial reports indicate that its business model is working. Does the company's business model remain sound as more consumers go to the Internet to find general information and stay abreast of current events and news stories? Is its revenue stream from advertisements growing or declining? Are its subscription fees and circulation increasing or declining? connect **LO 5**

EXERCISE FOR SIMULATION PARTICIPANTS

Three basic questions must be answered by managers of organizations of all sizes as they begin the process of crafting strategy:

- What is our present situation?
- Where do we want to go from here?
- How are we going to get there?

After you have read the Participant's Guide or Player's Manual for the strategy simulation exercise that you will participate in during this academic term, you and your co-managers should come up with brief one- or two-paragraph answers to these three questions *prior* to entering your first set of decisions. While your answer to the first of the three questions can be developed from your reading of the manual, the second and third questions will require a collaborative discussion among the members of your company's management team about how you intend to manage the company you have been assigned to run.

1. *What is our company's current situation?* A substantive answer to this question should cover the following issues: connect **LO 1, LO 2, LO 3**
   - Is your company in a good, average, or weak competitive position vis-à-vis rival companies?
   - Does your company appear to be in a sound financial condition?
   - Does it appear to have a competitive advantage, and is it likely to be sustainable?
   - What problems does your company have that need to be addressed?

connect

LO 4, LO 6

2. *Where do we want to take the company during the time we are in charge?* A complete answer to this question should say something about each of the following:
   - What goals or aspirations do you have for your company?
   - What do you want the company to be known for?
   - What market share would you like your company to have after the first five decision rounds?
   - By what amount or percentage would you like to increase total profits of the company by the end of the final decision round?
   - What kinds of performance outcomes will signal that you and your co-managers are managing the company in a successful manner?

connect

LO 4, LO 5

3. *How are we going to get there?* Your answer should cover these issues:
   - Which of the basic strategic and competitive approaches discussed in this chapter do you think makes the most sense to pursue?
   - What kind of competitive advantage over rivals will you try to achieve?
   - How would you describe the company's business model?
   - What kind of actions will support these objectives?

ENDNOTES

[1] B. R, "Strategy," *The Economist,* October 19, 2012, www.economist.com/blogs/schumpeter/2012/10/z-business-quotations-1 (accessed January 4, 2014).

[2] Jan Rivkin, "An Alternative Approach to Making Strategic Choices," Harvard Business School case 9-702-433, 2001.

[3] Michael E. Porter, "What Is Strategy?" *Harvard Business Review* 74, no. 6 (November–December 1996), pp. 65–67.

[4] Ibid.

[5] Eric T. Anderson and Duncan Simester, "A Step-by-Step Guide to Smart Business Experiments," *Harvard Business Review* 89, no. 3 (March 2011).

[6] Shona L. Brown and Kathleen M. Eisenhardt, *Competing on the Edge: Strategy as Structured Chaos* (Boston, MA: Harvard Business School Press, 1998).

[7] Cynthia A. Montgomery, "Putting Leadership Back into Strategy," *Harvard Business Review* 86, no. 1 (January 2008).

[8] Henry Mintzberg and J. A. Waters, "Of Strategies, Deliberate and Emergent," *Strategic Management Journal* 6 (1985); Costas Markides, "Strategy as Balance: From 'Either-Or' to 'And,'" *Business Strategy Review* 12, no. 3 (September 2001).

[9] Mark W. Johnson, Clayton M. Christensen, and Henning Kagermann, "Reinventing Your Business Model," *Harvard Business Review* 86, no. 12 (December 2008); Joan Magretta, "Why Business Models Matter," *Harvard Business Review* 80, no. 5 (May 2002).

[10] A. Brandenburger and H. Stuart, "Value-Based Strategy," *Journal of Economics and Management Strategy* 5 (1996), pp. 5–24; D. Hoopes, T. Madsen, and G. Walker, "Guest Editors' Introduction to the Special Issue: Why Is There a Resource-Based View? Toward a Theory of Competitive Heterogeneity," *Strategic Management Journal* 24 (2003), pp. 889–992; and M. Peteraf and J. Barney, "Unravelling the Resource-Based Tangle," *Managerial and Decision Economics* 24 (2003), pp. 309–323.

[11] Rivkin, "An Alternative Approach to Making Strategic Choices."

CHAPTER 2

Charting a Company's Direction

Its Vision, Mission, Objectives, and Strategy

Learning Objectives

THIS CHAPTER WILL HELP YOU UNDERSTAND:

LO 1 Why it is critical for company managers to have a clear strategic vision of where a company needs to head and why.

LO 2 The importance of setting both strategic and financial objectives.

LO 3 Why the strategic initiatives taken at various organizational levels must be tightly coordinated to achieve companywide performance targets.

LO 4 What a company must do to achieve operating excellence and to execute its strategy proficiently.

LO 5 The role and responsibility of a company's board of directors in overseeing the strategic management process.

Vision without action is merely a dream. . . .Vision with action can change the world.

Joel A. Barker – *Consultant and Author*

A good goal is like a strenuous exercise—it makes you stretch.

Mary Kay Ash – *Founder of Mary Kay Cosmetics*

To succeed in your mission, you must have single-minded devotion to your goal.

Abdul Kalam – *Former President of India*

If crafting and executing strategy are critically important managerial tasks, then it is essential to know exactly what is involved in developing a strategy and executing it proficiently. Is any analysis required? What goes into charting a company's strategic course and long-term direction? Does a company need a strategic plan? What are the various components of the strategy-making, strategy-executing process and to what extent are company personnel—aside from senior management—involved in the process?

This chapter presents an overview of the ins and outs of crafting and executing company strategies. Special attention is given to management's direction-setting responsibilities—charting a strategic course, setting performance targets, and choosing a strategy capable of producing the desired outcomes. We also explain why strategy making is a task for a company's entire management team and discuss which kinds of strategic decisions tend to be made at which levels of management. The chapter concludes with a look at the roles and responsibilities of a company's board of directors and how good corporate governance protects shareholder interests and promotes good management.

WHAT DOES THE STRATEGY-MAKING, STRATEGY-EXECUTING PROCESS ENTAIL?

The process of crafting and executing a company's strategy is an ongoing, continuous process consisting of five interrelated stages:

1. *Developing a strategic vision* that charts the company's long-term direction, a *mission statement* that describes the company's purpose, and a set of *core values* to guide the pursuit of the vision and mission.
2. *Setting objectives* for measuring the company's performance and tracking its progress in moving in the intended long-term direction.
3. *Crafting a strategy* for advancing the company along the path management has charted and achieving its performance objectives.
4. *Executing the chosen strategy* efficiently and effectively.

FIGURE 2.1 The Strategy-Making, Strategy-Executing Process

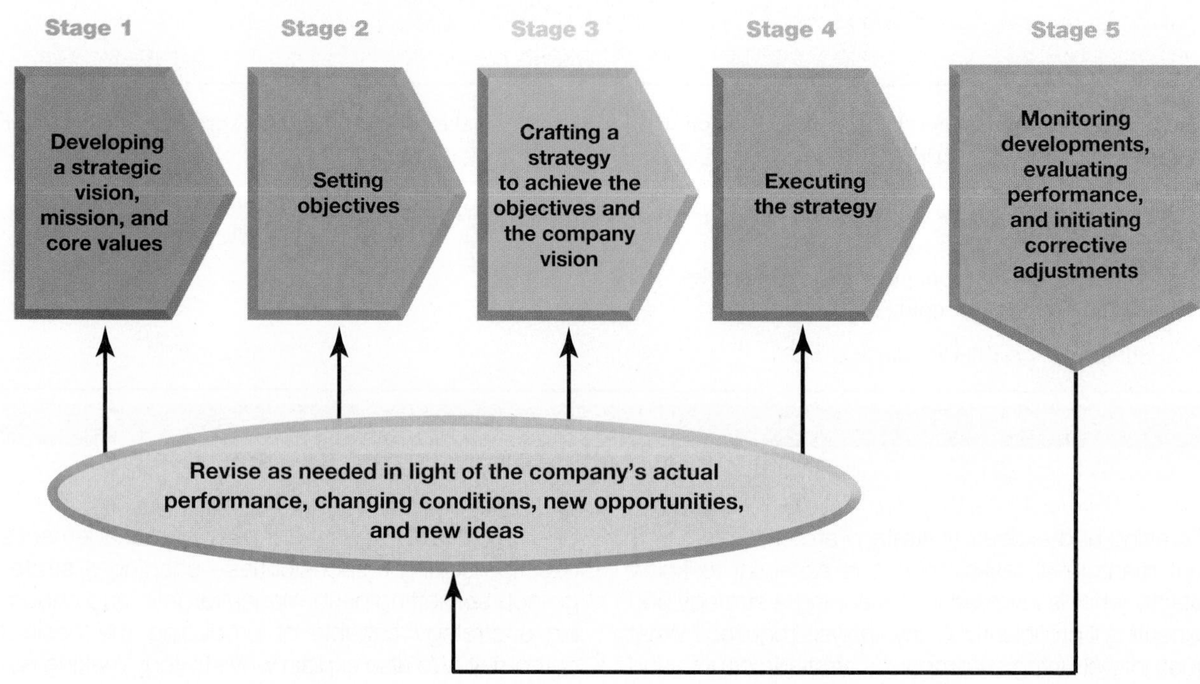

5. *Monitoring developments, evaluating performance, and initiating corrective adjustments* in the company's vision and mission statement, objectives, strategy, or approach to strategy execution in light of actual experience, changing conditions, new ideas, and new opportunities.

A company's **strategic plan** lays out its future direction, performance targets, and strategy.

Figure 2.1 displays this five-stage process, which we examine next in some detail. The first three stages of the strategic management process involve making a strategic plan. A **strategic plan** maps out where a company is headed, establishes strategic and financial targets, and outlines the competitive moves and approaches to be used in achieving the desired business results.[1]

STAGE 1: DEVELOPING A STRATEGIC VISION, MISSION STATEMENT, AND SET OF CORE VALUES

LO 1

Why it is critical for company managers to have a clear strategic vision of where a company needs to head and why.

Very early in the strategy-making process, a company's senior managers must wrestle with the issue of what directional path the company should take. Can the company's prospects be improved by changing its product offerings, or the markets in which it participates, or the customers it aims to serve? Deciding to commit the company to one path versus another pushes managers to draw some carefully reasoned conclusions about whether the company's present strategic course offers attractive opportunities for growth and profitability or whether changes of one kind or another in the company's strategy and long-term direction are needed.

Developing a Strategic Vision

Top management's views and conclusions about the company's long-term direction and what product-market-customer business mix seems optimal for the road ahead constitute a **strategic vision** for the company. A strategic vision delineates management's aspirations for the business, providing a panoramic view of "where we are going" and a convincing rationale for why this makes good business sense for the company. A strategic vision thus points an organization in a particular direction, charts a strategic path for it to follow, builds commitment to the future course of action, and molds organizational identity. A clearly articulated strategic vision communicates management's aspirations to stakeholders (customers, employees, stockholders, suppliers, etc.) and helps steer the energies of company personnel in a common direction. For instance, Henry Ford's vision of a car in every garage had power because it captured the imagination of others, aided internal efforts to mobilize the Ford Motor Company's resources, and served as a reference point for gauging the merits of the company's strategic actions.

CORE CONCEPT

A **strategic vision** describes "where we are going"—management's aspirations for the company and the course and direction charted to achieve them.

Well-conceived visions are *distinctive* and *specific* to a particular organization; they avoid generic, feel-good statements like "We will become a global leader and the first choice of customers in every market we serve."[2] Likewise, a strategic vision proclaiming management's quest "to be the market leader" or "to be the most innovative" or "to be recognized as the best company in the industry" offers scant guidance about a company's direction or the kind of company that management is striving to build.

A surprising number of the vision statements found on company websites and in annual reports are vague and unrevealing, saying very little about the company's future direction. Some could apply to almost any company in any industry. Many read like a public relations statement—high-sounding words that someone came up with because it is fashionable for companies to have an official vision statement.[3] But the real purpose of a vision statement is to serve as a management tool for giving the organization a sense of direction.

For a strategic vision to function as a valuable management tool, it must convey what top executives want the business to look like and provide managers at all organizational levels with a reference point in making strategic decisions and preparing the company for the future. It must say something definitive about how the company's leaders intend to position the company beyond where it is today. Table 2.1 provides some dos and don'ts in composing an effectively worded vision statement. Illustration Capsule 2.1 provides a critique of the strategic visions of several prominent companies.

An effectively communicated vision is a valuable management tool for enlisting the commitment of company personnel to actions that move the company in the intended direction.

Communicating the Strategic Vision

A strategic vision has little value to the organization unless it's effectively communicated down the line to lower-level managers and employees. A vision cannot provide direction for middle managers or inspire and energize employees unless everyone in the company is familiar with it and can observe management's commitment to the vision. It is particularly important for executives to provide a compelling rationale for a dramatically *new* strategic vision and company direction. When company personnel don't understand or accept the need for redirecting organizational efforts, they are prone to resist change. Hence, explaining the basis for the new direction, addressing employee concerns head-on, calming fears, lifting spirits, and providing updates and progress reports as events unfold all become part of the task in mobilizing support for the vision and winning commitment to needed actions.

Winning the support of organization members for the vision nearly always means putting "where we are going and why" in writing, distributing the statement

TABLE 2.1 Wording a Vision Statement—the Dos and Don'ts

The Dos	The Don'ts
Be graphic. Paint a clear picture of where the company is headed and the market position(s) the company is striving to stake out.	**Don't be vague or incomplete.** Never skimp on specifics about where the company is headed or how the company intends to prepare for the future.
Be forward-looking and directional. Describe the strategic course that will help the company prepare for the future.	**Don't dwell on the present.** A vision is not about what a company once did or does now; it's about "where we are going."
Keep it focused. Focus on providing managers with guidance in making decisions and allocating resources.	**Don't use overly broad language.** Avoid all-inclusive language that gives the company license to pursue any opportunity.
Have some wiggle room. Language that allows some flexibility allows the directional course to be adjusted as market, customer, and technology circumstances change.	**Don't state the vision in bland or uninspiring terms.** The best vision statements have the power to motivate company personnel and inspire shareholder confidence about the company's future.
Be sure the journey is feasible. The path and direction should be within the realm of what the company can accomplish; over time, a company should be able to demonstrate measurable progress in achieving the vision.	**Don't be generic.** A vision statement that could apply to companies in any of several industries (or to any of several companies in the same industry) is not specific enough to provide any guidance.
Indicate why the directional path makes good business sense. The directional path should be in the long-term interests of stakeholders (especially shareholders, employees, and suppliers).	**Don't rely on superlatives.** Visions that claim the company's strategic course is the "best" or "most successful" usually lack specifics about the path the company is taking to get there.
Make it memorable. To give the organization a sense of direction and purpose, the vision needs to be easily communicated. Ideally, it should be reducible to a few choice lines or a memorable slogan.	**Don't run on and on.** A vision statement that is not short and to the point will tend to lose its audience.

Sources: John P. Kotter, *Leading Change* (Boston: Harvard Business School Press, 1996); Hugh Davidson, *The Committed Enterprise* (Oxford: Butterworth Heinemann, 2002); and Michel Robert, *Strategy Pure and Simple II* (New York: McGraw-Hill, 1992).

organizationwide, and having top executives personally explain the vision and its rationale to as many people as feasible. Ideally, executives should present their vision for the company in a manner that reaches out and grabs people. An engaging and convincing strategic vision has enormous motivational value—for the same reason that a stonemason is more inspired by the opportunity to build a great cathedral for the ages than a house. Thus, executive ability to paint a convincing and inspiring picture of a company's journey to a future destination is an important element of effective strategic leadership.

Expressing the Essence of the Vision in a Slogan The task of effectively conveying the vision to company personnel is assisted when management can capture the vision of where to head in a catchy or easily remembered slogan. A number of organizations have summed up their vision in a brief phrase. Nike's slogan is "to bring

ILLUSTRATION CAPSULE 2.1

Examples of Strategic Visions—How Well Do They Measure Up?

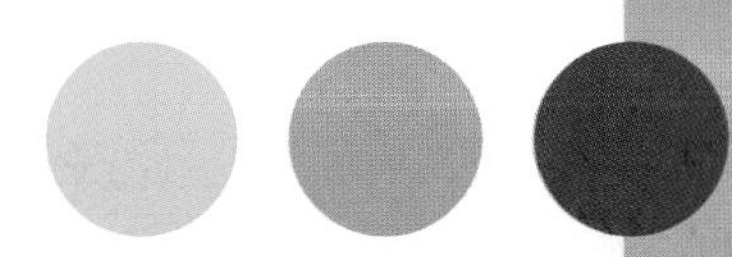

Vision Statement	Effective Elements	Shortcomings
Coca-Cola Our vision serves as the framework for our Roadmap and guides every aspect of our business by describing what we need to accomplish in order to continue achieving sustainable, quality growth. • People: Be a great place to work where people are inspired to be the best they can be. • Portfolio: Bring to the world a portfolio of quality beverage brands that anticipate and satisfy people's desires and needs. • Partners: Nurture a winning network of customers and suppliers; together we create mutual, enduring value. • Planet: Be a responsible citizen that makes a difference by helping build and support sustainable communities. • Profit: Maximize long-term return to shareowners while being mindful of our overall responsibilities. • Productivity: Be a highly effective, lean, and fast-moving organization.	• Graphic • Focused • Flexible • Makes good business sense	• Long • Not forward-looking
Procter & Gamble We will provide branded products and services of superior quality and value that improve the lives of the world's consumers, now and for generations to come. As a result, consumers will reward us with leadership sales, profit and value creation, allowing our people, our shareholders and the communities in which we live and work to prosper.	• Forward-looking • Flexible • Feasible • Makes good business sense	• Not graphic • Not focused • Not memorable
Heinz We define a compelling, sustainable future and create the path to achieve it.	• Forward-looking • Flexible	• Not graphic • Not focused • Confusing • Not memorable • Not necessarily feasible

Note: Developed with Jenna P. Pfeffer.

Source: Company documents and websites (accessed February 12, 2012).

innovation and inspiration to every athlete in the world." The Mayo Clinic's vision is to provide "the best care to every patient every day," while Greenpeace's aspires "to halt environmental abuse and promote environmental solutions." Even Scotland Yard has a catchy vision, which is "to make London the safest major city in the world." Creating a short slogan to illuminate an organization's direction and purpose and using it repeatedly as a reminder of "where we are headed and why" helps rally organization members to hurdle whatever obstacles lie in the company's path and maintain their focus.

Why a Sound, Well-Communicated Strategic Vision Matters

A well-thought-out, forcefully communicated strategic vision pays off in several respects: (1) It crystallizes senior executives' own views about the firm's long-term direction; (2) it reduces the risk of rudderless decision making; (3) it is a tool for winning the support of organization members to help make the vision a reality; (4) it provides a beacon for lower-level managers in setting departmental objectives and crafting departmental strategies that are in sync with the company's overall strategy; and (5) it helps an organization prepare for the future. When top executives are able to demonstrate significant progress in achieving these five benefits, the first step in organizational direction setting has been successfully completed.

The distinction between a strategic vision and a mission statement is fairly clear-cut: A **strategic vision** portrays a company's aspirations for its *future* ("where we are going"), whereas a company's **mission** describes the scope and purpose of its *present* business ("who we are, what we do, and why we are here").

Developing a Company Mission Statement

The defining characteristic of a strategic vision is what it says about the company's *future strategic course*—"the direction we are headed and the shape of our business in the future." It is aspirational. In contrast, a **mission statement** describes the enterprise's *present business and purpose*—"who we are, what we do, and why we are here." It is purely descriptive. Ideally, a company mission statement (1) identifies the company's products and/or services, (2) specifies the buyer needs that the company seeks to satisfy and the customer groups or markets that it serves, and (3) gives the company its own identity. The mission statements that one finds in company annual reports or posted on company websites are typically quite brief; some do a better job than others of conveying what the enterprise is all about.

Consider, for example, the mission statement of Trader Joe's (a specialty grocery chain):

> The mission of Trader Joe's is to give our customers the best food and beverage values that they can find anywhere and to provide them with the information required for informed buying decisions. We provide these with a dedication to the highest quality of customer satisfaction delivered with a sense of warmth, friendliness, fun, individual pride, and company spirit.

Note that Trader Joe's mission statement does a good job of conveying "who we are, what we do, and why we are here" but it provides no sense of "where we are headed."

An example of a well-stated mission statement with ample specifics about what the organization does is that of the Occupational Safety and Health Administration (OSHA): "to assure the safety and health of America's workers by setting and enforcing standards; providing training, outreach, and education; establishing partnerships; and encouraging continual improvement in workplace safety and health." YouTube's mission statement, while short, still captures the essence of what the company is about: "to provide fast and easy video access and the ability to share videos frequently." An example of a not-so-revealing mission statement is that of Microsoft. "To help people and businesses throughout the world realize their full potential" says nothing about its products or business makeup and could apply to many companies in many different industries. A person unfamiliar with Microsoft could not discern from its mission statement that it is a globally known provider of PC software and a leading maker of video game consoles (the popular Xbox 360). Coca-Cola, which markets nearly 400 beverage brands in over 200 countries, also has an uninformative mission statement: "to refresh the world; to inspire moments of optimism and happiness; to create value and make a difference." The usefulness of a mission statement that cannot convey the essence of a company's business activities and purpose is unclear.

To be well worded, a company mission statement must employ language specific enough to distinguish its business makeup and purpose from those of other enterprises and give the company its own identity.

Occasionally, companies couch their mission in terms of making a profit. This, too, is flawed. Profit is more correctly an *objective* and a *result* of what a company does. Moreover, earning a profit is the obvious intent of every commercial enterprise. Such companies as Volkswagen, Wegmans, Edward Jones, The Boston Consulting Group, DreamWorks Animation, and Intuit are each striving to earn a profit for shareholders; but plainly the fundamentals of their businesses are substantially different when it comes to "who we are and what we do." It is management's answer to "make a profit doing what and for whom?" that reveals the substance of a company's true mission and business purpose.

Linking the Vision and Mission with Company Values

Many companies have developed a set of values to guide the actions and behavior of company personnel in conducting the company's business and pursuing its strategic vision and mission. By **values** (or **core values,** as they are often called), we mean certain designated beliefs, traits, and behavioral norms that management has determined should guide the pursuit of its vision and mission. Values relate to such things as fair treatment, honor and integrity, ethical behavior, innovativeness, teamwork, a passion for top-notch quality or superior customer service, social responsibility, and community citizenship.

CORE CONCEPT

A company's **values** are the beliefs, traits, and behavioral norms that company personnel are expected to display in conducting the company's business and pursuing its strategic vision and mission.

Most companies have articulated four to eight core values that company personnel are expected to display and that are supposed to be mirrored in how the company conducts its business. At Kodak, the core values are respect for the dignity of the individual, uncompromising integrity, unquestioned trust, constant credibility, continual improvement and personal renewal, and open celebration of individual and team achievements. At Foster Wheeler, a global engineering and construction firm, the five core values are integrity, accountability, high performance, valuing people, and teamwork. In its quest to be the world's leading home-improvement retailer, Home Depot embraces eight values—entrepreneurial spirit, excellent customer service, giving back to the community, respect for all people, doing the right thing, taking care of people, building strong relationships, and creating shareholder value.

Do companies practice what they preach when it comes to their professed values? Sometimes no, sometimes yes—it runs the gamut. At one extreme are companies with window-dressing values; the values are given lip service by top executives but have little discernible impact on either how company personnel behave or how the company operates. Such companies have value statements because they are in vogue and make the company look good. At the other extreme are companies whose executives are committed to grounding company operations on sound values and principled ways of doing business. Executives at these companies deliberately seek to ingrain the designated core values into the corporate culture—the core values thus become an integral part of the company's DNA and what makes the company tick. At such values-driven companies, executives "walk the talk" and company personnel are held accountable for embodying the stated values in their behavior.

At companies where the stated values are real rather than cosmetic, managers connect values to the pursuit of the strategic vision and mission in one of two ways. In companies with values that are deeply entrenched in the corporate culture, senior managers are careful to craft a vision, mission, strategy, and set of operating practices that match established values; moreover, they repeatedly emphasize how the value-based behavioral norms contribute to the company's business success. If the company changes to a different vision or strategy, executives take care to explain how and why the core values continue to be relevant. Few companies with sincere commitment to established core values ever undertake strategic moves that conflict with ingrained values. In new

ILLUSTRATION CAPSULE 2.2 Patagonia, Inc.: A Values-Driven Company

PATAGONIA'S MISSION STATEMENT

Build the best product, cause no unnecessary harm, use business to inspire and implement solutions to the environmental crisis.

PATAGONIA'S CORE VALUES

Quality: Pursuit of ever-greater quality in everything we do.

Integrity: Relationships built on integrity and respect.

Environmentalism: Serve as a catalyst for personal and corporate action.

Not Bound by Convention: Our success—and much of the fun—lies in developing innovative ways to do things.

Patagonia, Inc., is an American outdoor clothing and gear company that clearly "walks the talk" with respect to its mission and values. While its mission is relatively vague about the types of products Patagonia offers, it clearly states the foundational "how" and "why" of the company. The four core values individually reinforce the mission in distinct ways, charting a defined path for employees to follow. At the same time, each value is reliant on the others for maximum effect. The values' combined impact on internal operations and public perception has made Patagonia a strong leader in the outdoor gear world.

While many companies espouse the pursuit of **quality** as part of their strategy, at Patagonia quality must come through honorable practices or not at all. Routinely, the company opts for more expensive materials and labor to maintain internal consistency with the mission. Patagonia learned early on that it could not make good products in bad factories, so it holds its manufacturers accountable through a variety of auditing partnerships and alliances. In this way, the company maintains relationships built on **integrity** and respect. In addition to keeping faith with those who make its products, Patagonia relentlessly pursues integrity in sourcing production inputs. Central to its **environmental** mission and core values, it targets for use sustainable and recyclable materials, ethically procured. Demonstrating leadership in environmentalism, Patagonia established foundations to support ecological causes, even **defying convention** by giving 1 percent of profits to conservation causes. These are but a few examples of the ways in which Patagonia's core values fortify each other and support the mission.

For Patagonia, quality would not be possible without integrity, unflinching environmentalism, and the company's unconventional approach. Since its founding in 1973 by rock climber Yvon Chouinard, Patagonia has remained remarkably consistent to the spirit of these values. This has endeared the company to legions of loyal customers while leading other businesses in protecting the environment. More than an apparel and gear company, Patagonia inspires everyone it touches to do their best for the planet and each other, in line with its mission and core values.

Note: Developed with Nicholas J. Ziemba.

Sources: Patagonia, Inc., "Corporate Social Responsibility," *The Footprint Chronicles,* 2007, and "Becoming a Responsible Company," www.patagonia.com/us/patagonia.go?assetid=2329 (accessed February 28, 2014).

---

companies, top management has to consider what values and business conduct should characterize the company and then draft a value statement that is circulated among managers and employees for discussion and possible modification. A final value statement that incorporates the desired behaviors and that connects to the vision and mission is then officially adopted. Some companies combine their vision, mission, and values into a single statement or document, circulate it to all organization members, and in many instances post the vision, mission, and value statement on the company's website. Illustration Capsule 2.2 describes how core values underlie the company's mission at Patagonia, Inc., a widely known and quite successful outdoor clothing and gear company.

STAGE 2: SETTING OBJECTIVES

LO 2

The importance of setting both strategic and financial objectives.

CORE CONCEPT

Objectives are an organization's performance targets—the specific results management wants to achieve.

The managerial purpose of setting **objectives** is to convert the vision and mission into specific performance targets. Objectives reflect management's aspirations for company performance in light of the industry's prevailing economic and competitive conditions and the company's internal capabilities. Well-stated objectives must be *specific, quantifiable* or *measurable,* and *challenging* and must contain a *deadline for achievement.* As Bill Hewlett, cofounder of Hewlett-Packard, shrewdly observed, "You cannot manage what you cannot measure. . . . And what gets measured gets done."[4] Concrete, measurable objectives are managerially valuable for three reasons: (1) They focus organizational attention and align actions throughout the organization, (2) they serve as *yardsticks* for tracking a company's performance and progress, and (3) they motivate employees to expend greater effort and perform at a high level.

The Imperative of Setting Stretch Objectives

CORE CONCEPT

Stretch objectives set performance targets high enough to *stretch* an organization to perform at its full potential and deliver the best possible results.

The experiences of countless companies teach that one of the best ways to promote outstanding company performance is for managers to deliberately set performance targets high enough to *stretch an organization to perform at its full potential and deliver the best possible results.* Challenging company personnel to go all out and deliver "stretch" gains in performance pushes an enterprise to be more inventive, to exhibit more urgency in improving both its financial performance and its business position, and to be more intentional and focused in its actions. Stretch objectives spur exceptional performance and help build a firewall against contentment with modest gains in organizational performance.

Manning Selvage & Lee (MS&L), a U.S. public relations firm, used ambitious stretch objectives to triple its revenues in three years. A company exhibits *strategic intent* when it relentlessly pursues an ambitious strategic objective, concentrating the full force of its resources and competitive actions on achieving that objective. MS&L's strategic intent was to become one of the leading global PR firms, which it achieved with the help of its stretch objectives. Honda's long-standing strategic intent of producing an ultra-light jet was finally realized in 2012 when the five-passenger plane dubbed the "Honda Civic of the sky" went into production. Google has the strategic intent of developing drones for the delivery of online orders through Amazon and has been making good progress toward meeting that stretch goal.

CORE CONCEPT

A company exhibits **strategic intent** when it relentlessly pursues an ambitious strategic objective, concentrating the full force of its resources and competitive actions on achieving that objective.

What Kinds of Objectives to Set

Two distinct types of performance targets are required: those relating to financial performance and those relating to strategic performance. **Financial objectives** communicate management's goals for financial performance. **Strategic objectives** are goals concerning a company's marketing standing and competitive position. A company's set of financial and strategic objectives should include both near-term and longer-term performance targets. Short-term (quarterly or annual) objectives focus attention on delivering performance improvements in the current period and satisfy shareholder expectations for near-term progress. Longer-term targets (three to five years off) force managers to consider what to do *now* to put the company in position to perform better later. Long-term objectives are critical for achieving optimal long-term performance

CORE CONCEPT

Financial objectives relate to the financial performance targets management has established for the organization to achieve.

Strategic objectives relate to target outcomes that indicate a company is strengthening its market standing, competitive position, and future business prospects.

and stand as a barrier to a nearsighted management philosophy and an undue focus on short-term results. When trade-offs have to be made between achieving long-term objectives and achieving short-term objectives, long-term objectives should take precedence (unless the achievement of one or more short-term performance targets has unique importance). Examples of commonly used financial and strategic objectives are listed in Table 2.2.

The Need for a Balanced Approach to Objective Setting

The importance of setting and attaining financial objectives is obvious. Without adequate profitability and financial strength, a company's long-term health and ultimate survival are jeopardized. Furthermore, subpar earnings and a weak balance sheet alarm shareholders and creditors and put the jobs of senior executives at risk. However, good financial performance, by itself, is not enough. Of equal or greater importance is a company's strategic performance—outcomes that indicate whether a company's market position and competitiveness are deteriorating, holding steady, or improving. *A stronger market standing and greater competitive vitality—especially when accompanied by competitive advantage—is what enables a company to improve its financial performance.*

Moreover, a company's financial performance measures are really *lagging indicators* that reflect the results of past decisions and organizational activities.[5] But a company's past or current financial performance is not a reliable indicator of its future prospects—poor financial performers often turn things around and do better, while good financial performers can fall upon hard times. The best and most reliable *leading indicators* of a company's future financial performance and business prospects are strategic outcomes that indicate whether the company's competitiveness and market position are stronger or weaker. The accomplishment of strategic objectives signals that the company is well positioned to sustain or improve its performance. For instance, if a

TABLE 2.2 Common Financial and Strategic Objectives

Financial Objectives	Strategic Objectives
• An *x* percent increase in annual revenues • Annual increases in after-tax profits *of x* percent • Annual increases in earnings per share of *x* percent • Annual dividend increases of *x* percent • Profit margins of *x* percent • An *x* percent return on capital employed (ROCE) or return on shareholders' equity (ROE) investment • Increased shareholder value in the form of an upward-trending stock price • Bond and credit ratings of *x* • Internal cash flows of *x* dollars to fund new capital investment	• Winning an *x* percent market share • Achieving lower overall costs than rivals • Overtaking key competitors on product performance, quality, or customer service • Deriving *x* percent of revenues from the sale of new products introduced within the past five years • Having broader or deeper technological capabilities than rivals • Having a wider product line than rivals • Having a better-known or more powerful brand name than rivals • Having stronger national or global sales and distribution capabilities than rivals • Consistently getting new or improved products to market ahead of rivals

ILLUSTRATION CAPSULE 2.3 Examples of Company Objectives

WALGREENS

Increase revenues from $72 billion in 2012 to more than $130 billion in 2016; increase operating income from $3.5 billion in 2012 to $8.5 billion to $9.0 billion by 2016; increase operating cash flow from $4.4 billion in 2012 to approximately $8 billion in 2016; generate $1 billion in cost savings from combined pharmacy and general merchandise purchasing synergies by 2016.

PEPSICO

Accelerate top-line growth; build and expand our better-for-you snacks and beverages and nutrition businesses; improve our water use efficiency by 20 percent per unit of production by 2015; reduce packaging weight by 350 million pounds; improve our electricity use efficiency by 20 percent per unit of production by 2015; maintain appropriate financial flexibility with ready access to global capital and credit markets at favorable interest rates.

YUM! BRANDS (KFC, PIZZA HUT, TACO BELL, WINGSTREET)

Increase operating profit derived from operations in emerging markets from 48 percent in 2010 to 57 percent in 2015; increase number of KFC units in Africa from 655 in 2010 to 2,100 in 2020; increase KFC revenues in Africa from $865 million in 2010 to $1.94 billion in 2014; increase number of KFC units in India from 101 in 2010 to 1,250 in 2020; increase number of KFC units in Vietnam from 87 in 2010 to 500 in 2020; increase number of KFC units in Russia from 150 in 2010 to 500 in 2020; open 100 new Taco Bell units in international markets in 2015; increase annual cash flows from operations from $1.5 billion in 2010 to $2.1 billion in 2015.

Source: Information posted on company websites.

company is achieving ambitious strategic objectives such that its competitive strength and market position are on the rise, then there's reason to expect that its *future* financial performance will be better than its current or past performance. If a company is losing ground to competitors and its market position is slipping—outcomes that reflect weak strategic performance (and, very likely, failure to achieve its strategic objectives)—then its ability to maintain its present profitability is highly suspect.

Consequently, it is important to use a performance measurement system that strikes a *balance* between financial objectives and strategic objectives.[6] The most widely used framework of this sort is known as the **Balanced Scorecard.**[7] This is a method for linking financial performance objectives to specific strategic objectives that derive from a company's business model. It provides a company's employees with clear guidelines about how their jobs are linked to the overall objectives of the organization, so they can contribute most productively and collaboratively to the achievement of these goals. In 2010, nearly 50 percent of global companies used a balanced-scorecard approach to measuring strategic and financial performance.[8] Organizations that have adopted the balanced-scorecard approach include 7-Eleven, Allianz Italy, Wells Fargo, Ford Motor, Verizon, SAS Institute, ExxonMobil, Caterpillar, Pfizer, and DuPont.[9] Illustration Capsule 2.3 provides selected strategic and financial objectives of three prominent companies.

CORE CONCEPT

The **Balanced Scorecard** is a widely used method for combining the use of both strategic and financial objectives, tracking their achievement, and giving management a more complete and balanced view of how well an organization is performing.

Setting Objectives for Every Organizational Level

Objective setting should not stop with top management's establishing of companywide performance targets. Company objectives need to be broken down into performance targets for each of the organization's separate businesses, product lines, functional departments, and individual work units. Employees within various functional areas and operating levels will be guided much better by specific objectives relating directly to their departmental activities than broad organizational-level goals. Objective setting is thus a *top-down process* that must extend to the lowest organizational levels. This means that each organizational unit must take care to set performance targets that support—rather than conflict with or negate—the achievement of companywide strategic and financial objectives.

The ideal situation is a team effort in which each organizational unit strives to produce results that contribute to the achievement of the company's performance targets and strategic vision. Such consistency signals that organizational units know their strategic role and are on board in helping the company move down the chosen strategic path and produce the desired results.

STAGE 3: CRAFTING A STRATEGY

LO 3

Why the strategic initiatives taken at various organizational levels must be tightly coordinated to achieve companywide performance targets.

As indicated in Chapter 1, the task of stitching a strategy together entails addressing a series of "hows": *how* to attract and please customers, *how* to compete against rivals, *how* to position the company in the marketplace, *how* to respond to changing market conditions, *how* to capitalize on attractive opportunities to grow the business, and *how* to achieve strategic and financial objectives. Astute entrepreneurship is called for in choosing among the various strategic alternatives and in proactively searching for opportunities to do new things or to do existing things in new or better ways.[10] The faster a company's business environment is changing, the more critical it becomes for its managers to be good entrepreneurs in diagnosing the direction and force of the changes under way and in responding with timely adjustments in strategy. Strategy makers have to pay attention to early warnings of future change and be willing to experiment with dare-to-be-different ways to establish a market position in that future. When obstacles appear unexpectedly in a company's path, it is up to management to adapt rapidly and innovatively. *Masterful strategies come from doing things differently from competitors where it counts—out-innovating them, being more efficient, being more imaginative, adapting faster—rather than running with the herd.* Good strategy making is therefore inseparable from good business entrepreneurship. One cannot exist without the other.

Strategy Making Involves Managers at All Organizational Levels

A company's senior executives obviously have lead strategy-making roles and responsibilities. The chief executive officer (CEO), as captain of the ship, carries the mantles of chief direction setter, chief objective setter, chief strategy maker, and chief strategy implementer for the total enterprise. Ultimate responsibility for *leading* the strategy-making, strategy-executing process rests with the CEO. And the CEO is always fully accountable for the results the strategy produces, whether good or bad. In some enterprises, the CEO or owner functions as chief architect of the strategy, personally deciding what the key elements of the company's strategy will be, although he or she may seek the advice of key subordinates and board members. A CEO-centered approach to strategy development is characteristic of small owner-managed companies and some large corporations that were founded by the present CEO or that have a CEO with strong strategic leadership skills. Steve Jobs at Apple, Reed Hastings at Netflix, Meg Whitman at eBay and now at Hewlett-Packard, Warren Buffet at Berkshire Hathaway, and Howard Schultz at Starbucks are prominent examples of corporate CEOs who have wielded a heavy hand in shaping their company's strategy.

In most corporations, however, strategy is the product of more than just the CEO's handiwork. Typically, other senior executives—business unit heads, the chief financial officer, and vice presidents for production, marketing, and other functional departments have influential strategy-making roles and help fashion the chief strategy components. Normally, a company's chief financial officer is in charge of devising and implementing an appropriate financial strategy; the production vice president takes the lead in developing the company's production strategy; the marketing vice president orchestrates sales and marketing strategy; a brand manager is in charge of the strategy for a particular brand in the company's product lineup; and so on. Moreover, the strategy-making efforts of top managers are complemented by advice and counsel from the company's board of directors; normally, all major strategic decisions are submitted to the board of directors for review, discussion, and official approval.

But strategy making is by no means solely a *top* management function, the exclusive province of owner-entrepreneurs, CEOs, high-ranking executives, and board members. The more a company's operations cut across different products, industries, and geographic areas, the more that headquarters executives have little option but to delegate considerable strategy-making authority to down-the-line managers in charge of particular subsidiaries, divisions, product lines, geographic sales offices, distribution centers, and plants. On-the-scene managers who oversee specific operating units can be reliably counted on to have more detailed command of the strategic issues and choices for the particular operating unit under their supervision—knowing the prevailing market and competitive conditions, customer requirements and expectations, and all the other relevant aspects affecting the several strategic options available. Managers with day-to-day familiarity of, and authority over, a specific operating unit thus have a big edge over headquarters executives in making wise strategic choices for their operating unit. The result is that, in most of today's companies, crafting and executing strategy is a *collaborative team effort* in which *every company manager plays a strategy-making role*—ranging from minor to major—for the area he or she heads.

In most companies, crafting and executing strategy is a *collaborative team effort* in which every manager has a role for the area he or she heads; it is rarely something that only high-level managers do.

Take, for example, a company like General Electric, a global corporation with more than $220 billion in revenues, more than 300,000 employees, operations in some 160 countries, and businesses that include jet engines, lighting, power generation, electric transmission and distribution equipment, housewares and appliances, medical equipment, media and entertainment, locomotives, security devices, water purification, and financial services. While top-level headquarters executives may well be personally involved in shaping GE's *overall* strategy and fashioning *important* strategic moves, they simply cannot know enough about the situation in every GE organizational unit to direct every strategic move made in GE's worldwide organization. Rather, it takes involvement on the part of GE's whole management team—top executives, business group heads, the heads of specific business units and product categories, and key managers in plants, sales offices, and distribution centers—to craft the thousands of strategic initiatives that end up composing the whole of GE's strategy.

A Company's Strategy-Making Hierarchy

In diversified companies like GE, where multiple and sometimes strikingly different businesses have to be managed, crafting a full-fledged strategy involves four distinct types of strategic actions and initiatives. Each of these involves different facets of the company's overall strategy and calls for the participation of different types of managers, as shown in Figure 2.2.

> **CORE CONCEPT**
>
> **Corporate strategy** establishes an overall game plan for managing a *set of businesses* in a diversified, multibusiness company.
> **Business strategy** is primarily concerned with strengthening the company's market position and building competitive advantage in a *single-business company* or in a *single business unit* of a diversified multibusiness corporation.

As shown in Figure 2.2, **corporate strategy** is orchestrated by the CEO and other senior executives and establishes an overall strategy for managing a *set of businesses* in a diversified, multibusiness company. Corporate strategy concerns how to improve the combined performance of the set of businesses the company has diversified into by capturing cross-business synergies and turning them into competitive advantage. It addresses the questions of what businesses to hold or divest, which new markets to enter, and how to best enter new markets (by acquisition, creation of a strategic alliance, or through internal development, for example). Corporate strategy and business diversification are the subjects of Chapter 8, in which they are discussed in detail.

Business strategy is concerned with strengthening the market position, building competitive advantage, and improving the performance of a single line of business unit. Business strategy is primarily the responsibility of business unit heads, although corporate-level executives may well exert strong influence; in diversified companies it is not unusual for corporate officers to insist that business-level objectives and strategy conform to corporate-level objectives and strategy themes. The business head has at least two other strategy-related roles: (1) seeing that lower-level strategies are well conceived, consistent, and adequately matched to the overall business strategy, and (2) keeping corporate-level officers (and sometimes the board of directors) informed of emerging strategic issues.

> **CORE CONCEPT**
>
> **Business strategy** is strategy at the *single-business level,* concerning how to improve performance or gain a competitive advantage in a particular line of business.

Functional-area strategies concern the approaches employed in managing particular functions within a business—like research and development (R&D), production, procurement of inputs, sales and marketing, distribution, customer service, and finance. A company's marketing strategy, for example, represents the managerial game plan for running the sales and marketing part of the business. A company's product development strategy represents the game plan for keeping the company's product lineup in tune with what buyers are looking for.

Functional strategies flesh out the details of a company's business strategy. Lead responsibility for functional strategies within a business is normally delegated to the heads of the respective functions, with the general manager of the business having final approval. Since the different functional-level strategies must be compatible with the overall business strategy and with one another to have beneficial impact, the general business manager may at times exert stronger influence on the content of the functional strategies.

Operating strategies concern the relatively narrow approaches for managing key operating units (e.g., plants, distribution centers, purchasing centers) and specific operating activities with strategic significance (e.g., quality control, materials purchasing, brand management, Internet sales). A plant manager needs a strategy for accomplishing the plant's objectives, carrying out the plant's part of the company's overall manufacturing game plan, and dealing with any strategy-related problems that exist at the plant. A company's advertising manager needs a strategy for getting maximum audience exposure and sales impact from the ad budget. Operating strategies, while of limited scope, add further detail and completeness to functional strategies and to

FIGURE 2.2 A Company's Strategy-Making Hierarchy

Orchestrated by the CEO and other senior executives.

Corporate Strategy (for the set of businesses as a whole)
- How to gain advantage from managing a set of businesses

Two-Way Influence

Orchestrated by the senior executives of each line of business, often with advice from the heads of functional areas within the business and other key people.

Business Strategy (one for each business the company has diversified into)
- How to gain and sustain a competitive advantage for a single line of business

In the case of a single-business company, these two levels of the strategy-making hierarchy merge into one level—*Business Strategy*—that is orchestrated by the company's CEO and other top executives.

Two-Way Influence

Orchestrated by the heads of major functional activities within a particular business, often in collaboration with other key people.

Functional Area Strategies (within each business)
- How to manage a particular activity within a business in ways that support the business strategy

Two-Way Influence

Orchestrated by brand managers, plant managers, and the heads of other strategically important activities, such as distribution, purchasing, and website operations, often with input from other key people.

Operating Strategies (within each functional area)
- How to manage activities of strategic significance within each functional area, adding detail and completeness

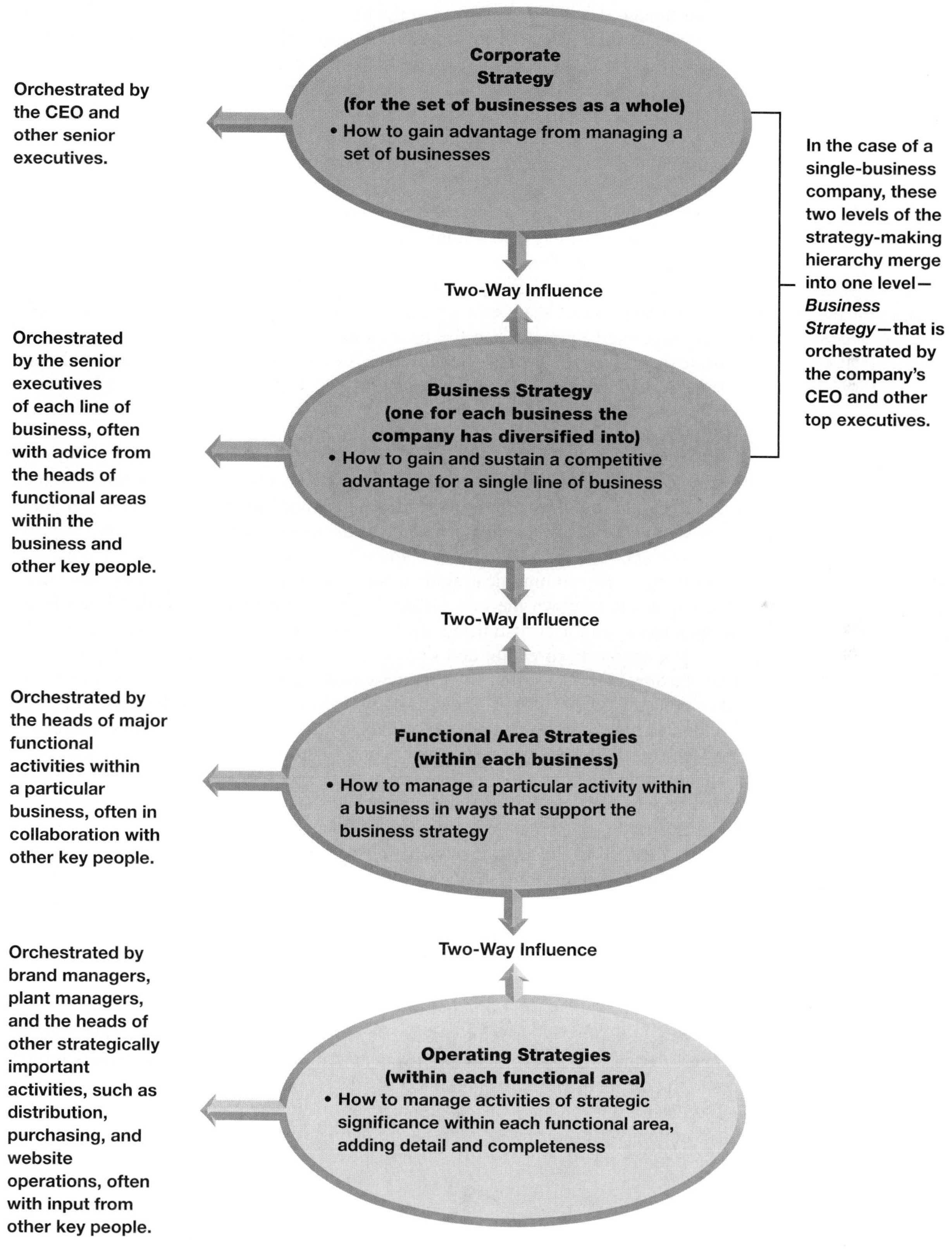

the overall business strategy. Lead responsibility for operating strategies is usually delegated to frontline managers, subject to the review and approval of higher-ranking managers.

Even though operating strategy is at the bottom of the strategy-making hierarchy, its importance should not be downplayed. A major plant that fails in its strategy to achieve production volume, unit cost, and quality targets can damage the company's reputation for quality products and undercut the achievement of company sales and profit objectives. Frontline managers are thus an important part of an organization's strategy-making team. One cannot reliably judge the strategic importance of a given action simply by the strategy level or location within the managerial hierarchy where it is initiated.

In single-business companies, the uppermost level of the strategy-making hierarchy is the business strategy, so a single-business company has three levels of strategy: business strategy, functional-area strategies, and operating strategies. Proprietorships, partnerships, and owner-managed enterprises may have only one or two strategy-making levels since their strategy-making process requires only a few key people. The larger and more diverse the operations of an enterprise, the more points of strategic initiative it has and the more levels of management that have a significant strategy-making role.

A company's strategy is at full power only when its many pieces are united.

Uniting the Strategy-Making Hierarchy

Ideally, the pieces of a company's strategy up and down the strategy hierarchy should be cohesive and mutually reinforcing, fitting together like a jigsaw puzzle. *Anything less than a unified collection of strategies weakens the overall strategy and is likely to impair company performance.*[11] It is the responsibility of top executives to achieve this unity by clearly communicating the company's vision, objectives, and major strategy components to down-the-line managers and key personnel. Midlevel and frontline managers cannot craft unified strategic moves without first understanding the company's long-term direction and knowing the major components of the corporate and/or business strategies that their strategy-making efforts are supposed to support and enhance. Thus, as a general rule, strategy making must start at the top of the organization and then proceed downward from the corporate level to the business level and then from the business level to the associated functional and operating levels. Once strategies up and down the hierarchy have been created, lower-level strategies must be scrutinized for consistency with and support of higher-level strategies. Any strategy conflicts must be addressed and resolved, either by modifying the lower-level strategies with conflicting elements or by adapting the higher-level strategy to accommodate what may be more appealing strategy ideas and initiatives bubbling up from below.

A Strategic Vision + Mission + Objectives + Strategy = A Strategic Plan

CORE CONCEPT

A company's **strategic plan** lays out its future direction, business purpose, performance targets, and strategy.

Developing a strategic vision and mission, setting objectives, and crafting a strategy are basic direction-setting tasks. They map out where a company is headed, its purpose, the targeted strategic and financial outcomes, the basic business model, and the competitive moves and internal action approaches to be used in achieving the desired business results. Together, these elements constitute a **strategic plan** for coping with industry conditions, outcompeting rivals, meeting objectives, and making progress toward aspirational goals.[12] Typically, a strategic plan includes a commitment to allocate resources to the plan and specifies a time period for achieving goals (usually three to five years).

In companies that do regular strategy reviews and develop explicit strategic plans, the strategic plan usually ends up as a written document that is circulated to most managers. Near-term performance targets are the part of the strategic plan most often communicated to employees more generally and spelled out explicitly. A number of companies summarize key elements of their strategic plans in the company's annual report to shareholders, in postings on their websites, or in statements provided to the business media; others, perhaps for reasons of competitive sensitivity, make only vague, general statements about their strategic plans.[13] In small, privately owned companies, it is rare for strategic plans to exist in written form. Small-company strategic plans tend to reside in the thinking and directives of owner-executives; aspects of the plan are revealed in conversations with company personnel about where to head, what to accomplish, and how to proceed.

STAGE 4: EXECUTING THE STRATEGY

LO 4

What a company must do to achieve operating excellence and to execute its strategy proficiently.

Managing the implementation of a strategy is easily the most demanding and time-consuming part of the strategy management process. Converting strategic plans into actions and results tests a manager's ability to direct organizational change, motivate employees, build and strengthen competitive capabilities, create and nurture a strategy-supportive work climate, and meet or beat performance targets. Initiatives to put the strategy in place and execute it proficiently must be launched and managed on many organizational fronts.

Management's action agenda for executing the chosen strategy emerges from assessing what the company will have to do to achieve the targeted financial and strategic performance. Each company manager has to think through the answer to the question "What needs to be done in my area to execute my piece of the strategic plan, and what actions should I take to get the process under way?" How much internal change is needed depends on how much of the strategy is new, how far internal practices and competencies deviate from what the strategy requires, and how well the present work culture supports good strategy execution. Depending on the amount of internal change involved, full implementation and proficient execution of the company strategy (or important new pieces thereof) can take several months to several years.

In most situations, managing the strategy execution process includes the following principal aspects:

- Creating a strategy-supporting structure.
- Staffing the organization to obtain needed skills and expertise.
- Developing and strengthening strategy-supporting resources and capabilities.
- Allocating ample resources to the activities critical to strategic success.
- Ensuring that policies and procedures facilitate effective strategy execution.
- Organizing the work effort along the lines of best practice.
- Installing information and operating systems that enable company personnel to perform essential activities.
- Motivating people and tying rewards directly to the achievement of performance objectives.
- Creating a company culture conducive to successful strategy execution.
- Exerting the internal leadership needed to propel implementation forward.

Good strategy execution requires diligent pursuit of operating excellence. It is a job for a company's whole management team. Success hinges on the skills and cooperation of operating managers who can push for needed changes in their organizational units and consistently deliver good results. Management's handling of the strategy implementation process can be considered successful if things go smoothly enough that the company meets or beats its strategic and financial performance targets and shows good progress in achieving management's strategic vision.

STAGE 5: EVALUATING PERFORMANCE AND INITIATING CORRECTIVE ADJUSTMENTS

The fifth component of the strategy management process—monitoring new external developments, evaluating the company's progress, and making corrective adjustments—is the trigger point for deciding whether to continue or change the company's vision and mission, objectives, strategy, and/or strategy execution methods.[14] As long as the company's strategy continues to pass the three tests of a winning strategy discussed in Chapter 1 (good fit, competitive advantage, strong performance), company executives may decide to stay the course. Simply fine-tuning the strategic plan and continuing with efforts to improve strategy execution are sufficient.

But whenever a company encounters disruptive changes in its environment, questions need to be raised about the appropriateness of its direction and strategy. If a company experiences a downturn in its market position or persistent shortfalls in performance, then company managers are obligated to ferret out the causes—do they relate to poor strategy, poor strategy execution, or both?—and take timely corrective action. A company's direction, objectives, and strategy have to be revisited anytime external or internal conditions warrant.

A company's vision, mission, objectives, strategy, and approach to strategy execution are never final; managing strategy is an ongoing process.

Likewise, managers are obligated to assess which of the company's operating methods and approaches to strategy execution merit continuation and which need improvement. Proficient strategy execution is always the product of much organizational learning. It is achieved unevenly—coming quickly in some areas and proving troublesome in others. Consequently, top-notch strategy execution entails vigilantly searching for ways to improve and then making corrective adjustments whenever and wherever it is useful to do so.

CORPORATE GOVERNANCE: THE ROLE OF THE BOARD OF DIRECTORS IN THE STRATEGY-CRAFTING, STRATEGY-EXECUTING PROCESS

LO 5

The role and responsibility of a company's board of directors in overseeing the strategic management process.

Although senior managers have the *lead responsibility* for crafting and executing a company's strategy, it is the duty of a company's board of directors to exercise strong oversight and see that management performs the various tasks involved in each of the five stages of the strategy-making, strategy-executing process in a manner that best serves the interests of shareholders and other stakeholders.[15] A company's board of directors has four important obligations to fulfill:

1. *Oversee the company's financial accounting and financial reporting practices.* While top executives, particularly the company's CEO and CFO (chief financial

officer), are primarily responsible for seeing that the company's financial statements fairly and accurately report the results of the company's operations, board members have a *legal obligation* to warrant the accuracy of the company's financial reports and protect shareholders. It is their job to ensure that generally accepted accounting principles (GAAP) are used properly in preparing the company's financial statements and that proper financial controls are in place to prevent fraud and misuse of funds. Virtually all boards of directors have an audit committee, always composed entirely of *outside directors* (*inside directors* hold management positions in the company and either directly or indirectly report to the CEO). The members of the audit committee have the lead responsibility for overseeing the decisions of the company's financial officers and consulting with both internal and external auditors to ensure accurate financial reporting and adequate financial controls.

2. *Critically appraise the company's direction, strategy, and business approaches.* Board members are also expected to guide management in choosing a strategic direction and to make independent judgments about the validity and wisdom of management's proposed strategic actions. This aspect of their duties takes on heightened importance when the company's strategy is failing or is plagued with faulty execution, and certainly when there is a precipitous collapse in profitability. But under more normal circumstances, many boards have found that meeting agendas become consumed by compliance matters with little time left to discuss matters of strategic importance. The board of directors and management at Philips Electronics hold annual two- to three-day retreats devoted exclusively to evaluating the company's long-term direction and various strategic proposals. The company's exit from the semiconductor business and its increased focus on medical technology and home health care resulted from management-board discussions during such retreats.[16]

3. *Evaluate the caliber of senior executives' strategic leadership skills.* The board is always responsible for determining whether the current CEO is doing a good job of strategic leadership (as a basis for awarding salary increases and bonuses and deciding on retention or removal).[17] Boards must also exercise due diligence in evaluating the strategic leadership skills of other senior executives in line to succeed the CEO. When the incumbent CEO steps down or leaves for a position elsewhere, the board must elect a successor, either going with an insider or deciding that an outsider is needed to perhaps radically change the company's strategic course. Often, the outside directors on a board visit company facilities and talk with company personnel personally to evaluate whether the strategy is on track, how well the strategy is being executed, and how well issues and problems are being addressed by various managers. For example, independent board members at GE visit operating executives at each major business unit once a year to assess the company's talent pool and stay abreast of emerging strategic and operating issues affecting the company's divisions. Home Depot board members visit a store once per quarter to determine the health of the company's operations.[18]

4. *Institute a compensation plan for top executives that rewards them for actions and results that serve shareholder interests.* A basic principle of corporate governance is that the owners of a corporation (the shareholders) delegate operating authority and managerial control to top management in return for compensation. In their role as *agents* of shareholders, top executives have a clear and

unequivocal duty to make decisions and operate the company in accord with shareholder interests. (This does not mean disregarding the interests of other stakeholders—employees, suppliers, the communities in which the company operates, and society at large.) Most boards of directors have a compensation committee, composed entirely of directors from *outside* the company, to develop a salary and incentive compensation plan that rewards senior executives for boosting the company's *long-term* performance on behalf of shareholders. The compensation committee's recommendations are presented to the full board for approval. But during the past 10 to 15 years, many boards of directors have done a poor job of ensuring that executive salary increases, bonuses, and stock option awards are tied tightly to performance measures that are truly in the long-term interests of shareholders. Rather, compensation packages at many companies have increasingly rewarded executives for short-term performance improvements—most notably, for achieving quarterly and annual earnings targets and boosting the stock price by specified percentages. This has had the perverse effect of causing company managers to become preoccupied with actions to improve a company's near-term performance, often motivating them to take unwise business risks to boost short-term earnings by amounts sufficient to qualify for multimillion-dollar compensation packages (that many see as obscenely large). The focus on short-term performance has proved damaging to long-term company performance and shareholder interests—witness the huge loss of shareholder wealth that occurred at many financial institutions in 2008–2009 because of executive risk taking in subprime loans, credit default swaps, and collateralized mortgage securities. As a consequence, the need to overhaul and reform executive compensation has become a hot topic in both public circles and corporate boardrooms. Illustration Capsule 2.4 discusses how weak governance at the mortgage companies Fannie Mae and Freddie Mac allowed opportunistic senior managers to secure exorbitant bonuses while making decisions that imperiled the futures of the companies they managed.

Effective corporate governance requires the board of directors to oversee the company's strategic direction, evaluate its senior executives, handle executive compensation, and oversee financial reporting practices.

Every corporation should have a strong independent board of directors that (1) is well informed about the company's performance, (2) guides and judges the CEO and other top executives, (3) has the courage to curb management actions the board believes are inappropriate or unduly risky, (4) certifies to shareholders that the CEO is doing what the board expects, (5) provides insight and advice to management, and (6) is intensely involved in debating the pros and cons of key decisions and actions.[19] Boards of directors that lack the backbone to challenge a strong-willed or "imperial" CEO or that rubber-stamp almost anything the CEO recommends without probing inquiry and debate abdicate their fiduciary duty to represent and protect shareholder interests.

ILLUSTRATION CAPSULE 2.4

Corporate Governance Failures at Fannie Mae and Freddie Mac

Excessive executive compensation in the financial services industry ranks high among examples of failed corporate governance. Corporate governance at the government-sponsored mortgage giants Fannie Mae and Freddie Mac was particularly weak. The politically appointed boards at both enterprises failed to understand the risks of the subprime loan strategies being employed, did not adequately monitor the decisions of the CEO, did not exercise effective oversight of the accounting principles being employed (which led to inflated earnings), and approved executive compensation systems that allowed management to manipulate earnings to receive lucrative performance bonuses. The audit and compensation committees at Fannie Mae were particularly ineffective in protecting shareholder interests, with the audit committee allowing the company's financial officers to audit reports prepared under their direction and used to determine performance bonuses. Fannie Mae's audit committee also was aware of management's use of questionable accounting practices that reduced losses and recorded one-time gains to achieve financial targets linked to bonuses. In addition, the audit committee failed to investigate formal charges of accounting improprieties filed by a manager in the Office of the Controller.

Fannie Mae's compensation committee was equally ineffective. The committee allowed the company's CEO, Franklin Raines, to select the consultant employed to design the mortgage firm's executive compensation plan and agreed to a tiered bonus plan that would permit Raines and other senior managers to receive maximum bonuses without great difficulty. The compensation plan allowed Raines to earn performance-based bonuses of $52 million and a total compensation of $90 million between 1999 and 2004. Raines was forced to resign in December 2004 when the Office of Federal Housing Enterprise Oversight found that Fannie Mae executives had fraudulently inflated earnings to receive bonuses linked to financial performance. Securities and Exchange Commission investigators also found evidence of improper accounting at Fannie Mae and required the company to restate its earnings between 2002 and 2004 by $6.3 billion.

Poor governance at Freddie Mac allowed its CEO and senior management to manipulate financial data to receive performance-based compensation as well. Freddie Mac CEO Richard Syron received 2007 compensation of $19.8 million while the mortgage company's share price declined from a high of $70 in 2005 to $25 at year-end 2007. During Syron's tenure as CEO, the company became embroiled in a multibillion-dollar accounting scandal, and Syron personally disregarded internal reports dating to 2004 that cautioned of an impending financial crisis at the company. Forewarnings within Freddie Mac and by federal regulators and outside industry observers proved to be correct, with loan underwriting policies at Freddie Mac and Fannie Mae leading to combined losses at the two firms in 2008 of more than $100 billion. The price of Freddie Mac's shares had fallen to below $1 by the time of Syron's resignation in September 2008.

Both organizations were placed into a conservatorship under the direction of the U.S. government in September 2008 and were provided bailout funds of more than $180 billion by mid-2012. At that point, the U.S. Treasury amended the organizations' bailout terms to require that all profits be transferred to the government while downsizing the firms. By early 2014, the bailout had finally been fully repaid.

Sources: Chris Isidore, "Mortgage Bailout Now Profitable for Taxpayers," *CNNMoney,* February 21, 2014; Alan Zibel and Nick Timiraos "Fannie, Freddie Bailout Receives Revamp," *The Wall Street Journal Online,* August 17, 2012; Eric Dash, "Fannie Mae to Restate Results by $6.3 Billion because of Accounting," *The New York Times Online,* December 7, 2006; Annys Shin, "Fannie Mae Sets Executive Salaries," *The Washington Post,* February 9, 2006, p. D4; and Scott DeCarlo, Eric Weiss, Mark Jickling, and James R. Cristie, *Fannie Mae and Freddie Mac: Scandal in U.S. Housing* (Nova, 2006), pp. 266–286.

KEY POINTS

The strategic management process consists of five interrelated and integrated stages:

1. *Developing a strategic vision* of the company's future, a *mission statement* that defines the company's current purpose, and a set of *core values* to guide the pursuit of the vision and mission. This stage of strategy making provides direction for the company, motivates and inspires company personnel, aligns and guides actions throughout the organization, and communicates to stakeholders management's aspirations for the company's future.
2. *Setting objectives* to convert the vision and mission into performance targets that can be used as yardsticks for measuring the company's performance. Objectives need to spell out *how much* of *what kind* of performance *by when.* Two broad types of objectives are required: *financial objectives* and *strategic objectives.* A *balanced-scorecard* approach for measuring company performance entails setting both *financial objectives and strategic objectives.*
3. *Crafting a strategy* to achieve the objectives and move the company along the strategic course that management has charted. Masterful strategies come from doing things differently from competitors where it counts—out-innovating them, being more efficient, being more imaginative, adapting faster—rather than running with the herd. In large diversified companies, the strategy-making hierarchy consists of four levels, each of which involves a corresponding level of management: corporate strategy (multibusiness strategy), business strategy (strategy for individual businesses that compete in a single industry), functional-area strategies within each business (e.g., marketing, R&D, logistics), and operating strategies (for key operating units, such as manufacturing plants). Thus, strategy making is an inclusive collaborative activity involving not only senior company executives but also the heads of major business divisions, functional-area managers, and operating managers on the frontlines.
4. *Executing the chosen strategy* and converting the strategic plan into action. Management's agenda for executing the chosen strategy emerges from assessing what the company will have to do to achieve the targeted financial and strategic performance. Management's handling of the strategy implementation process can be considered successful if things go smoothly enough that the company meets or beats its strategic and financial performance targets and shows good progress in achieving management's strategic vision.
5. *Monitoring developments, evaluating performance, and initiating corrective adjustments* in light of actual experience, changing conditions, new ideas, and new opportunities. This stage of the strategy management process is the trigger point for deciding whether to continue or change the company's vision and mission, objectives, strategy, and/or strategy execution methods.

The sum of a company's strategic vision, mission, objectives, and strategy constitutes a *strategic plan* for coping with industry conditions, outcompeting rivals, meeting objectives, and making progress toward aspirational goals. *Stretch objectives* spur exceptional performance and help build a firewall against contentment with modest gains in organizational performance. A company exhibits *strategic intent* when it relentlessly pursues an ambitious strategic objective, concentrating the full force of its resources and competitive actions on achieving that objective.

Boards of directors have a duty to shareholders to play a vigilant role in overseeing management's handling of a company's strategy-making, strategy-executing process. This entails four important obligations: (1) Ensure that the company issues accurate financial reports and has adequate financial controls, (2) critically appraise the company's direction, strategy, and strategy execution, (3) evaluate the caliber of senior executives' strategic leadership skills, and (4) institute a compensation plan for top executives that rewards them for actions and results that serve shareholder interests.

ASSURANCE OF LEARNING EXERCISES

connect
LO 1

1. Using the information in Table 2.1, critique the adequacy and merit of the following vision statements, listing effective elements and shortcomings. Rank the vision statements from best to worst once you complete your evaluation.

Vision Statement	Effective Elements	Shortcomings
Amazon Our vision is to be earth's most customer centric company; to build a place where people can come to find and discover anything they might want to buy online.		
BASF We are "The Chemical Company" successfully operating in all major markets. • Our customers view BASF as their partner of choice. • Our innovative products, intelligent solutions and services make us the most competent worldwide supplier in the chemical industry. • We generate a high return on assets. • We strive for sustainable development. • We welcome change as an opportunity. • We, the employees of BASF, together ensure our success.		
MasterCard • A world beyond cash.		
Hilton Hotels Corporation Our vision is to be the first choice of the world's travelers. Hilton intends to build on the rich heritage and strength of our brands by: • Consistently delighting our customers • Investing in our team members • Delivering innovative products and services • Continuously improving performance • Increasing shareholder value • Creating a culture of pride • Strengthening the loyalty of our constituents		

Source: Company websites and annual reports.

LO 2 2. Go to the company websites for ExxonMobil (ir.exxonmobil.com), Pfizer (www.pfizer.com/investors), and Intel (www.intc.com) to find some examples of strategic and financial objectives. Make a list of four objectives for each company, and indicate which of these are strategic and which are financial.

LO 3 3. American Airlines' Chapter 11 reorganization plan filed in 2012 involved the company reducing operating expenses by $2 billion while increasing revenues by $1 billion. The company's strategy to increase revenues included expanding the number of international flights and destinations and increasing daily departures for its five largest markets by 20 percent. The company also intended to upgrade its fleet by spending $2 billion to purchase new aircraft and refurbish the first-class cabins for planes not replaced. A final component of the restructuring plan included a merger with US Airways to create a global airline with more than 56,700 daily flights to 336 destinations in 56 countries. The merger was expected to produce cost savings from synergies of more than $1 billion and result in a stronger airline capable of paying creditors and rewarding employees and shareholders. Explain why the strategic initiatives at various organizational levels and functions require tight coordination to achieve the results desired by American Airlines.

LO 4 4. Go to the investor relations website for Walmart (investors.walmartstores.com) and review past presentations Walmart has made during various investor conferences by clicking on the Events option in the navigation bar. Prepare a one- to two-page report that outlines what Walmart has said to investors about its approach to strategy execution. Specifically, what has management discussed concerning staffing, resource allocation, policies and procedures, information and operating systems, continuous improvement, rewards and incentives, corporate culture, and internal leadership at the company?

connect LO 5 5. Based on the information provided in Illustration Capsule 2.4, explain how corporate governance at Freddie Mac failed the enterprise's shareholders and other stakeholders. Which important obligations to shareholders were fulfilled by Fannie Mae's board of directors? What is your assessment of how well Fannie Mae's compensation committee handled executive compensation at the government-sponsored mortgage giant?

EXERCISE FOR SIMULATION PARTICIPANTS

LO 1 1. Meet with your co-managers and prepare a strategic vision statement for your company. It should be at least one sentence long and no longer than a brief paragraph. When you are finished, check to see if your vision statement meets the conditions for an effectively worded strategic vision set forth in Table 2.1. If not, then revise it accordingly. What would be a good slogan that captures the essence of your strategic vision and that could be used to help communicate the vision to company personnel, shareholders, and other stakeholders?

LO 2 2. What are your company's financial objectives? What are your company's strategic objectives?

LO 3 3. What are the three to four key elements of your company's strategy?

ENDNOTES

[1] Gordon Shaw, Robert Brown, and Philip Bromiley, "Strategic Stories: How 3M Is Rewriting Business Planning," *Harvard Business Review* 76, no. 3 (May–June 1998); David J. Collis and Michael G. Rukstad, "Can You Say What Your Strategy Is?" *Harvard Business Review* 86, no. 4 (April 2008).

[2] Hugh Davidson, *The Committed Enterprise: How to Make Vision and Values Work* (Oxford: Butterworth Heinemann, 2002); W. Chan Kim and Renée Mauborgne, "Charting Your Company's Future," *Harvard Business Review* 80, no. 6 (June 2002), pp. 77–83; James C. Collins and Jerry I. Porras, "Building Your Company's Vision," *Harvard Business Review* 74, no. 5 (September–October 1996), pp. 65–77; Jim Collins and Jerry Porras, *Built to Last: Successful Habits of Visionary Companies* (New York: HarperCollins, 1994); Michel Robert, *Strategy Pure and Simple II: How Winning Companies Dominate Their Competitors* (New York: McGraw-Hill, 1998).

[3] Davidson, *The Committed Enterprise,* pp. 20 and 54.

[4] As quoted in Charles H. House and Raymond L. Price, "The Return Map: Tracking Product Teams," *Harvard Business Review* 60, no. 1 (January–February 1991), p. 93.

[5] Robert S. Kaplan and David P. Norton, *The Strategy-Focused Organization* (Boston: Harvard Business School Press, 2001); Robert S. Kaplan and David P. Norton, *The Balanced Scorecard: Translating Strategy into Action* (Boston: Harvard Business School Press, 1996).

[6] Ibid.; Kevin B. Hendricks, Larry Menor, and Christine Wiedman, "The Balanced Scorecard: To Adopt or Not to Adopt," *Ivey Business Journal* 69, no. 2 (November–December 2004), pp. 1–7; Sandy Richardson, "The Key Elements of Balanced Scorecard Success," *Ivey Business Journal* 69, no. 2 (November–December 2004), pp. 7–9.

[7] Kaplan and Norton, *The Balanced Scorecard.*

[8] Information posted on the website of Bain and Company, www.bain.com (accessed May 27, 2011).

[9] Information posted on the website of the Balanced Scorecard Institute, balancedscorecard.org (accessed May 27, 2011).

[10] Henry Mintzberg, Bruce Ahlstrand, and Joseph Lampel, *Strategy Safari: A Guided Tour through the Wilds of Strategic Management* (New York: Free Press, 1998); Bruce Barringer and Allen C. Bluedorn, "The Relationship between Corporate Entrepreneurship and Strategic Management," *Strategic Management Journal* 20 (1999), pp. 421–444; Jeffrey G. Covin and Morgan P. Miles, "Corporate Entrepreneurship and the Pursuit of Competitive Advantage," *Entrepreneurship: Theory and Practice* 23, no. 3 (Spring 1999), pp. 47–63; David A. Garvin and Lynne C. Levesque, "Meeting the Challenge of Corporate Entrepreneurship," *Harvard Business Review* 84, no. 10 (October 2006), pp. 102–112.

[11] Joseph L. Bower and Clark G. Gilbert, "How Managers' Everyday Decisions Create or Destroy Your Company's Strategy," *Harvard Business Review* 85, no. 2 (February 2007), pp. 72–79.

[12] Gordon Shaw, Robert Brown, and Philip Bromiley, "Strategic Stories: How 3M Is Rewriting Business Planning," *Harvard Business Review* 76, no. 3 (May–June 1998), pp. 41–50.

[13] David J. Collis and Michael G. Rukstad, "Can You Say What Your Strategy Is?" *Harvard Business Review* 86, no. 4 (April 2008), pp. 82–90.

[14] Cynthia A. Montgomery, "Putting Leadership Back into Strategy," *Harvard Business Review* 86, no. 1 (January 2008), pp. 54–60.

[15] Jay W. Lorsch and Robert C. Clark, "Leading from the Boardroom," *Harvard Business Review* 86, no. 4 (April 2008), pp. 105–111.

[16] Ibid.

[17] Stephen P. Kaufman, "Evaluating the CEO," *Harvard Business Review* 86, no. 10 (October 2008), pp. 53–57.

[18] Ibid.

[19] David A. Nadler, "Building Better Boards," *Harvard Business Review* 82, no. 5 (May 2004), pp. 102–105; Cynthia A. Montgomery and Rhonda Kaufman, "The Board's Missing Link," *Harvard Business Review* 81, no. 3 (March 2003), pp. 86–93; John Carver, "What Continues to Be Wrong with Corporate Governance and How to Fix It," *Ivey Business Journal* 68, no. 1 (September–October 2003), pp. 1–5. See also Gordon Donaldson, "A New Tool for Boards: The Strategic Audit," *Harvard Business Review* 73, no. 4 (July–August 1995), pp. 99–107.

CHAPTER 3

Evaluating a Company's External Environment

Learning Objectives

THIS CHAPTER WILL HELP YOU UNDERSTAND:

LO 1 How to recognize the factors in a company's broad macro-environment that may have strategic significance.

LO 2 How to use analytic tools to diagnose the competitive conditions in a company's industry.

LO 3 How to map the market positions of key groups of industry rivals.

LO 4 How to use multiple frameworks to determine whether an industry's outlook presents a company with sufficiently attractive opportunities for growth and profitability.

Without competitors, there would be no need for strategy.

Kenichi Ohmae – *Consultant and Author*

It is nice to have valid competition; it pushes you to do better.

Gianni Versace – *Entrepreneur and Founder of Gianni Versace S.p.A.*

In essence, the job of a strategist is to understand and cope with competition.

Michael Porter – *Harvard Business School Professor and Cofounder of Monitor Consulting*

In order to chart a company's strategic course wisely, managers must first develop a deep understanding of the company's present situation. Two facets of a company's situation are especially pertinent: (1) its external environment—most notably, the competitive conditions of the industry in which the company operates; and (2) its internal environment—particularly the company's resources and organizational capabilities.

Insightful diagnosis of a company's external and internal environments is a prerequisite for managers to succeed in crafting a strategy that is an excellent *fit* with the company's situation—the first test of a winning strategy. As depicted in Figure 3.1, strategic thinking begins with an appraisal of the company's external and internal environments (as a basis for deciding on a long-term direction and developing a strategic vision), moves toward an evaluation of the most promising alternative strategies and business models, and culminates in choosing a specific strategy.

This chapter presents the concepts and analytic tools for zeroing in on those aspects of a company's external environment that should be considered in making strategic choices. Attention centers on the broad environmental context, the specific market arena in which a company operates, the drivers of change, the positions and likely actions of rival companies, and the factors that determine competitive success. In Chapter 4, we explore the methods of evaluating a company's internal circumstances and competitive capabilities.

THE STRATEGICALLY RELEVANT FACTORS IN THE COMPANY'S MACRO-ENVIRONMENT

LO 1

How to recognize the factors in a company's broad macro-environment that may have strategic significance.

Every company operates in a broad **"macro-environment"** that comprises six principal components: political factors, economic conditions in the firm's general environment (local, country, regional, worldwide), sociocultural forces, technological factors, environmental factors (concerning the natural environment), and legal/regulatory conditions. Each of these components has the potential to affect the firm's more immediate industry and competitive environment, although some are likely to have a more important effect than others (see Figure 3.2). An analysis of the impact of these factors is often referred to as **PESTEL analysis,** an acronym that serves as a reminder of the six components

FIGURE 3.1 From Thinking Strategically about the Company's Situation to Choosing a Strategy

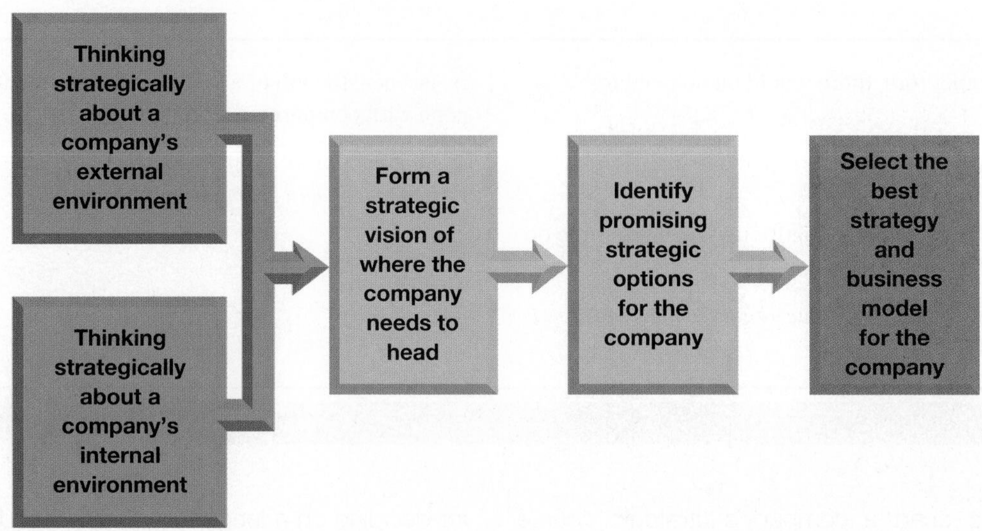

involved (political, economic, sociocultural, technological, environmental, legal/regulatory).

CORE CONCEPT

The **macro-environment** encompasses the broad environmental context in which a company's industry is situated.

CORE CONCEPT

PESTEL analysis can be used to assess the strategic relevance of the six principal components of the macro-environment: **P**olitical, **E**conomic, **S**ocial, **T**echnological, **E**nvironmental, and **L**egal/Regulatory forces.

Since macro-economic factors affect different industries in different ways and to different degrees, it is important for managers to determine which of these represent the most *strategically relevant factors* outside the firm's industry boundaries. By *strategically relevant,* we mean important enough to have a bearing on the decisions the company ultimately makes about its long-term direction, objectives, strategy, and business model. The impact of the outer-ring factors depicted in Figure 3.2 on a company's choice of strategy can range from big to small. But even if those factors change slowly or are likely to have a low impact on the company's business situation, they still merit a watchful eye.

For example, the strategic opportunities of cigarette producers to grow their businesses are greatly reduced by antismoking ordinances, the decisions of governments to impose higher cigarette taxes, and the growing cultural stigma attached to smoking. Motor vehicle companies must adapt their strategies to customer concerns about high gasoline prices and to environmental concerns about carbon emissions. Companies in the food processing, restaurant, sports, and fitness industries have to pay special attention to changes in lifestyles, eating habits, leisure-time preferences, and attitudes toward nutrition and fitness in fashioning their strategies. Table 3.1 provides a brief description of the components of the macro-environment and some examples of the industries or business situations that they might affect.

As company managers scan the external environment, they must be alert for potentially important outer-ring developments, assess their impact and influence, and adapt the company's direction and strategy as needed. However, the factors in a company's environment having the *biggest* strategy-shaping impact typically pertain to the company's immediate industry and competitive environment. Consequently, it is on a company's industry and competitive environment that we concentrate the bulk of our attention in this chapter.

FIGURE 3.2 The Components of a Company's Macro-Environment

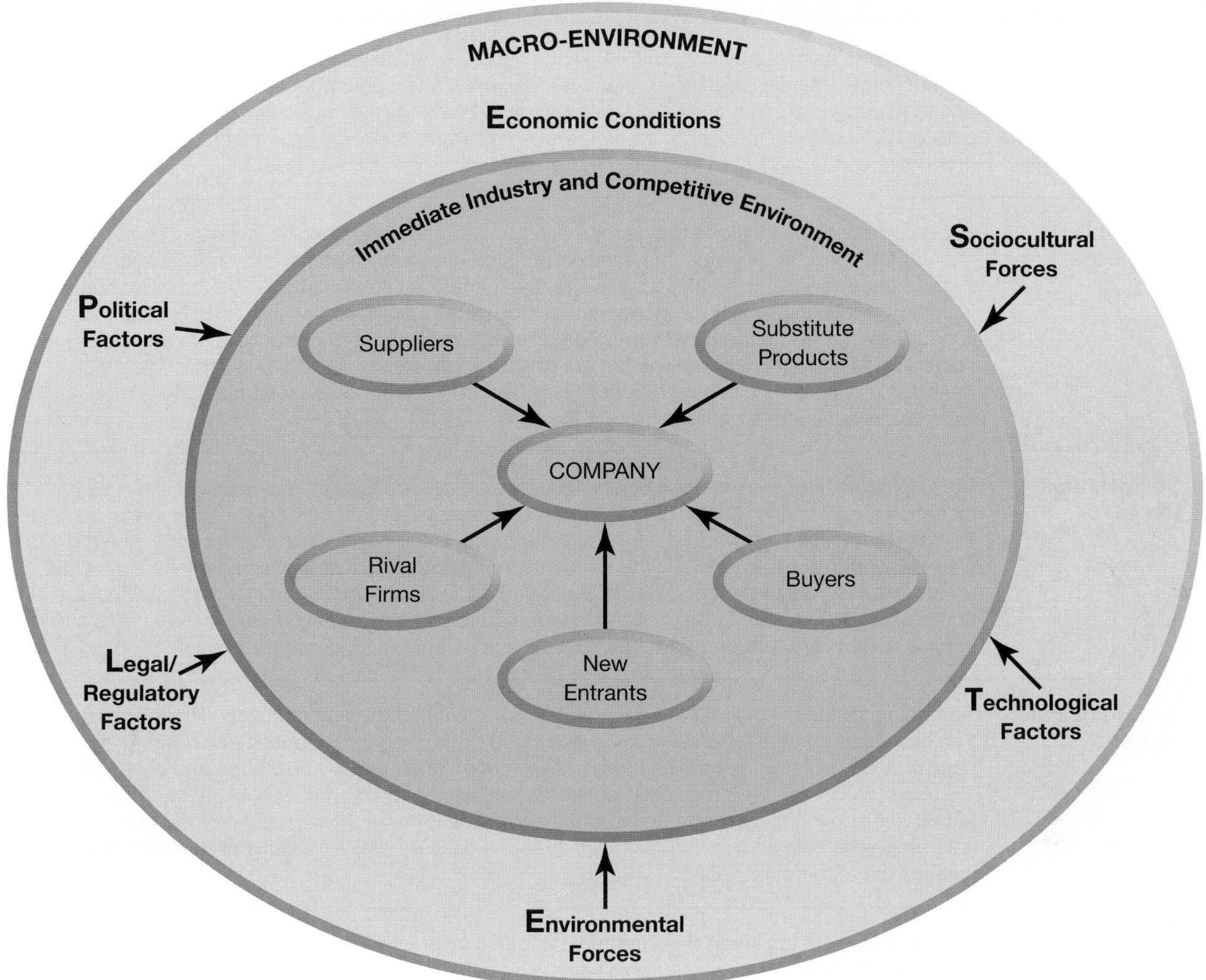

ASSESSING THE COMPANY'S INDUSTRY AND COMPETITIVE ENVIRONMENT

Thinking strategically about a company's industry and competitive environment entails using some well-validated concepts and analytic tools. These include the five forces framework, the value net, driving forces, strategic groups, competitor analysis, and key success factors. Proper use of these analytic tools can provide managers with the understanding needed to craft a strategy that fits the company's situation within their industry environment. The remainder of this chapter is devoted to describing how managers can use these tools to inform and improve their strategic choices.

LO 2

How to use analytic tools to diagnose the competitive conditions in a company's industry.

TABLE 3.1 The Six Components of the Macro-Environment

Component	Description
Political factors	These factors include political policies, including the extent to which a government intervenes in the economy. They include such matters as tax policy, fiscal policy, tariffs, the political climate, and the strength of institutions such as the federal banking system. Some political policies affect certain types of industries more than others. An example is energy policy, which affects energy producers and heavy users of energy more than other types of businesses.
Economic conditions	Economic conditions include the general economic climate and specific factors such as interest rates, exchange rates, the inflation rate, the unemployment rate, the rate of economic growth, trade deficits or surpluses, savings rates, and per-capita domestic product. Economic factors also include conditions in the markets for stocks and bonds, which can affect consumer confidence and discretionary income. Some industries, such as construction, are particularly vulnerable to economic downturns but are positively affected by factors such as low interest rates. Others, such as discount retailing, may benefit when general economic conditions weaken, as consumers become more price-conscious.
Sociocultural forces	Sociocultural forces include the societal values, attitudes, cultural influences, and lifestyles that impact demand for particular goods and services, as well as demographic factors such as the population size, growth rate, and age distribution. Sociocultural forces vary by locale and change over time. An example is the trend toward healthier lifestyles, which can shift spending toward exercise equipment and health clubs and away from alcohol and snack foods. Population demographics can have large implications for industries such as health care, where costs and service needs vary with demographic factors such as age and income distribution.
Technological factors	Technological factors include the pace of technological change and technical developments that have the potential for wide-ranging effects on society, such as genetic engineering and nanotechnology. They include institutions involved in creating new knowledge and controlling the use of technology, such as R&D consortia, university-sponsored technology incubators, patent and copyright laws, and government control over the Internet. Technological change can encourage the birth of new industries, such as the delivery drone industry, and disrupt others, such as the recording industry.
Environmental forces	These include ecological and environmental forces such as weather, climate, climate change, and associated factors like water shortages. These factors can directly impact industries such as insurance, farming, energy production, and tourism. They may have an indirect but substantial effect on other industries such as transportation and utilities.
Legal and regulatory factors	These factors include the regulations and laws with which companies must comply, such as consumer laws, labor laws, antitrust laws, and occupational health and safety regulation. Some factors, such as banking deregulation, are industry-specific. Others, such as minimum wage legislation, affect certain types of industries (low-wage, labor-intensive industries) more than others.

THE FIVE FORCES FRAMEWORK

The character and strength of the competitive forces operating in an industry are never the same from one industry to another. The most powerful and widely used tool for diagnosing the principal competitive pressures in a market is the *five forces framework*.[1] This framework, depicted in Figure 3.3, holds that competitive pressures on

FIGURE 3.3 The Five Forces Model of Competition: A Key Analytic Tool

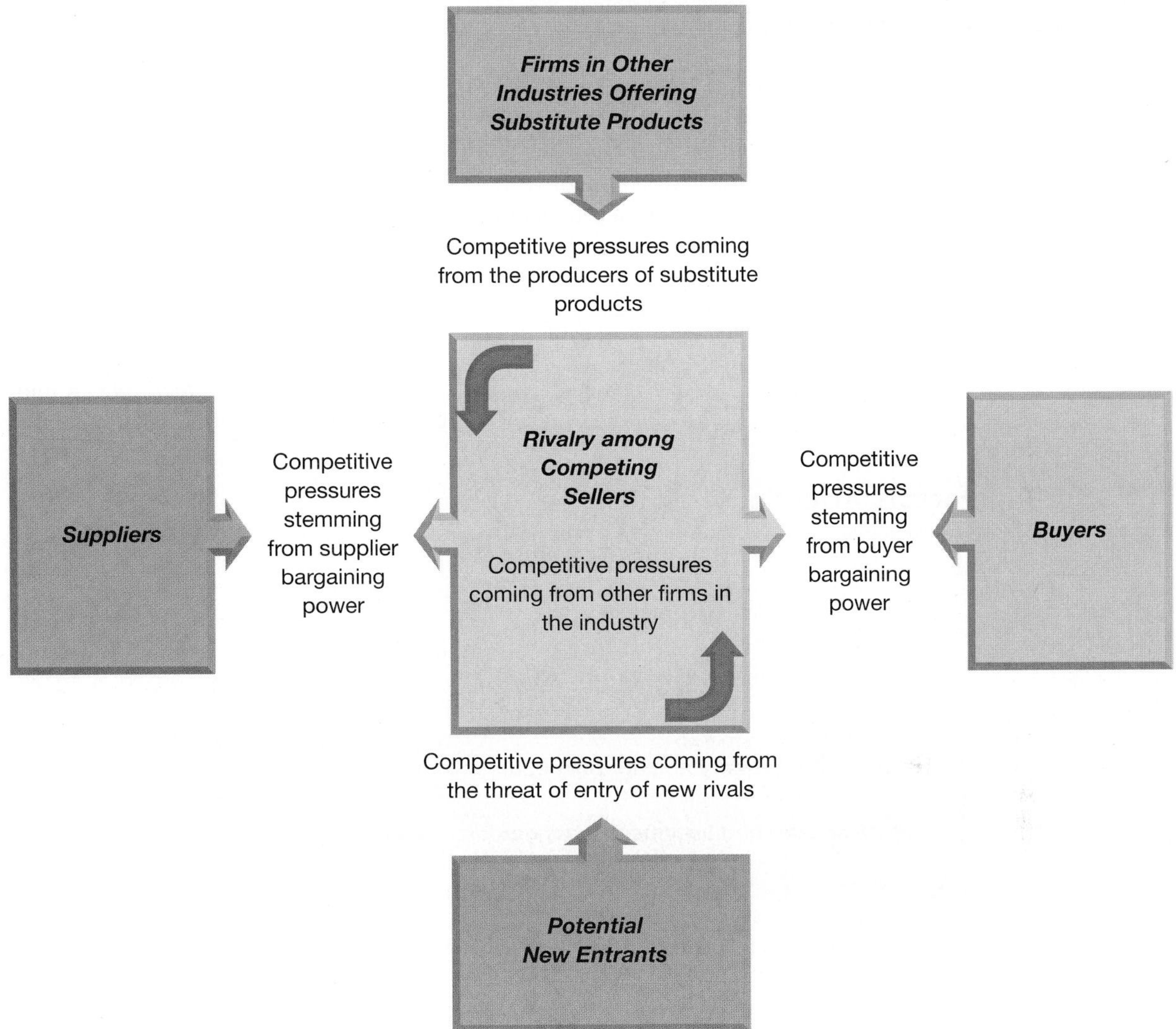

Sources: Adapted from M. E. Porter, "How Competitive Forces Shape Strategy," *Harvard Business Review* 57, no. 2 (1979), pp. 137–145; and M. E. Porter, "The Five Competitive Forces That Shape Strategy," *Harvard Business Review* 86, no. 1 (2008), pp. 80–86.

companies within an industry come from five sources. These include (1) competition from *rival sellers,* (2) competition from *potential new entrants* to the industry, (3) competition from producers of *substitute products,* (4) *supplier* bargaining power, and (5) *customer* bargaining power.

Using the five forces model to determine the nature and strength of competitive pressures in a given industry involves three steps:

- *Step 1:* For each of the five forces, identify the different parties involved, along with the specific factors that bring about competitive pressures.

- *Step 2:* Evaluate how strong the pressures stemming from each of the five forces are (strong, moderate, or weak).
- *Step 3:* Determine whether the five forces, overall, are supportive of high industry profitability.

Competitive Pressures Created by the Rivalry among Competing Sellers

The strongest of the five competitive forces is often the rivalry for buyer patronage among competing sellers of a product or service. The intensity of rivalry among competing sellers within an industry depends on a number of identifiable factors. Figure 3.4 summarizes these factors, identifying those that intensify or weaken rivalry among direct competitors in an industry. A brief explanation of why these factors affect the degree of rivalry is in order:

- *Rivalry increases when buyer demand is growing slowly or declining.* Rapidly expanding buyer demand produces enough new business for all industry members

FIGURE 3.4 Factors Affecting the Strength of Rivalry

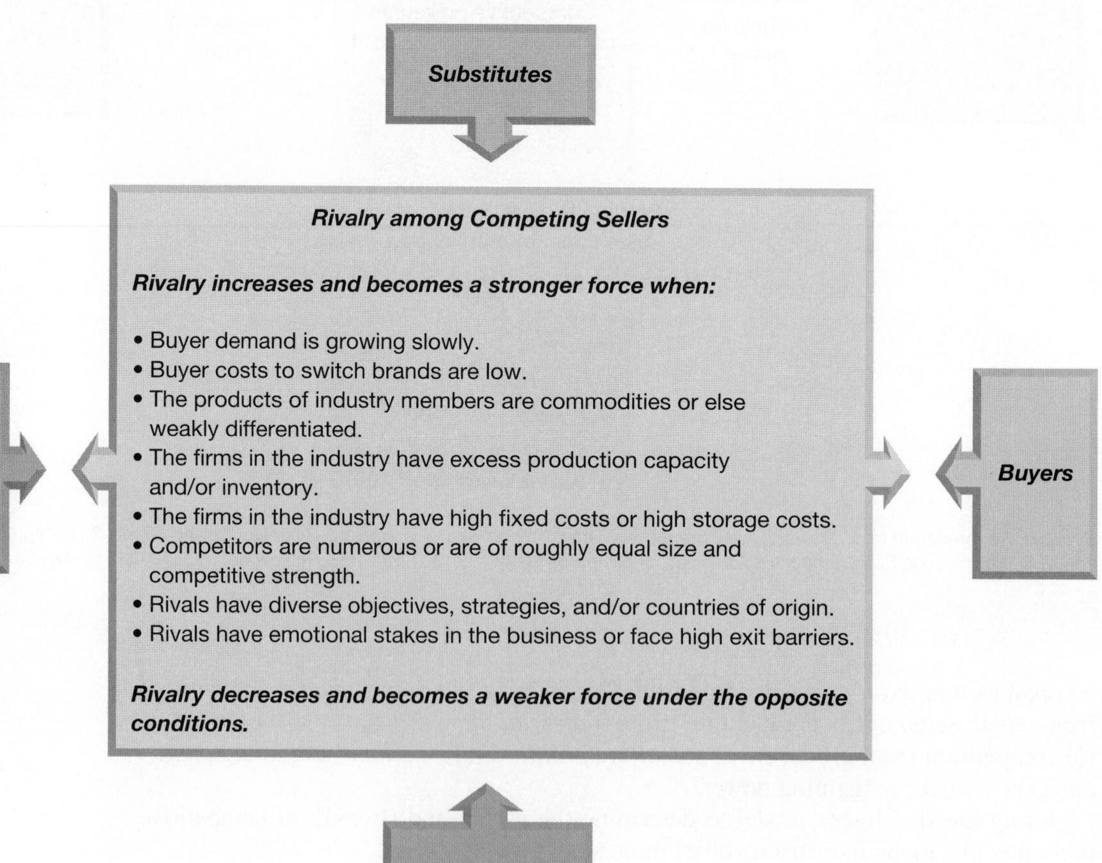

to grow without having to draw customers away from rival enterprises. But in markets where buyer demand is slow-growing or shrinking, companies desperate to gain more business typically employ price discounts, sales promotions, and other tactics to increase their sales volumes at the expense of rivals, sometimes to the point of igniting a fierce battle for market share.

- *Rivalry increases as it becomes less costly for buyers to switch brands.* The less costly it is for buyers to switch their purchases from one seller to another, the easier it is for sellers to steal customers away from rivals. When the cost of switching brands is higher, buyers are less prone to brand switching and sellers have protection from rivalrous moves. Switching costs include not only monetary costs but also the time, inconvenience, and psychological costs involved in switching brands. For example, retailers may not switch to the brands of rival manufacturers because they are hesitant to sever long-standing supplier relationships or incur any technical support costs or retraining expenses in making the switchover.
- *Rivalry increases as the products of rival sellers become less strongly differentiated.* When rivals' offerings are identical or weakly differentiated, buyers have less reason to be brand-loyal—a condition that makes it easier for rivals to convince buyers to switch to their offerings. Moreover, when the products of different sellers are virtually identical, shoppers will choose on the basis of price, which can result in fierce price competition among sellers. On the other hand, strongly differentiated product offerings among rivals breed high brand loyalty on the part of buyers who view the attributes of certain brands as more appealing or better suited to their needs.
- *Rivalry is more intense when there is excess supply or unused production capacity, especially if the industry's product has high fixed costs or high storage costs.* Whenever a market has excess supply (overproduction relative to demand), rivalry intensifies as sellers cut prices in a desperate effort to cope with the unsold inventory. A similar effect occurs when a product is perishable or seasonal, since firms often engage in aggressive price cutting to ensure that everything is sold. Likewise, whenever fixed costs account for a large fraction of total cost so that unit costs are significantly lower at full capacity, firms come under significant pressure to cut prices whenever they are operating below full capacity. Unused capacity imposes a significant cost-increasing penalty because there are fewer units over which to spread fixed costs. The pressure of high fixed or high storage costs can push rival firms into price concessions, special discounts, rebates, and other volume-boosting competitive tactics.
- *Rivalry intensifies as the number of competitors increases and they become more equal in size and capability.* When there are many competitors in a market, companies eager to increase their meager market share often engage in price-cutting activities to drive sales, leading to intense rivalry. When there are only a few competitors, companies are more wary of how their rivals may react to their attempts to take market share away from them. Fear of retaliation and a descent into a damaging price war leads to restrained competitive moves. Moreover, when rivals are of comparable size and competitive strength, they can usually compete on a fairly equal footing—an evenly matched contest tends to be fiercer than a contest in which one or more industry members have commanding market shares and substantially greater resources than their much smaller rivals.
- *Rivalry becomes more intense as the diversity of competitors increases in terms of long-term directions, objectives, strategies, and countries of origin.* A diverse

group of sellers often contains one or more mavericks willing to try novel or rule-breaking market approaches, thus generating a more volatile and less predictable competitive environment. Globally competitive markets are often more rivalrous, especially when aggressors have lower costs and are intent on gaining a strong foothold in new country markets.

- *Rivalry is stronger when high exit barriers keep unprofitable firms from leaving the industry.* In industries where the assets cannot easily be sold or transferred to other uses, where workers are entitled to job protection, or where owners are committed to remaining in business for personal reasons, failing firms tend to hold on longer than they might otherwise—even when they are bleeding red ink. Deep price discounting of this sort can destabilize an otherwise attractive industry.

Evaluating the strength of rivalry in an industry is a matter of determining whether the factors stated here, taken as a whole, indicate that the rivalry is relatively strong, moderate, or weak. When rivalry is *strong,* the battle for market share is generally so vigorous that the profit margins of most industry members are squeezed to bare-bones levels. When rivalry is *moderate,* a more normal state, the maneuvering among industry members, while lively and healthy, still allows most industry members to earn acceptable profits. When rivalry is *weak,* most companies in the industry are relatively well satisfied with their sales growth and market shares and rarely undertake offensives to steal customers away from one another. Weak rivalry means that there is no downward pressure on industry profitability due to this particular competitive force.

The Choice of Competitive Weapons

Competitive battles among rival sellers can assume many forms that extend well beyond lively price competition. For example, competitors may resort to such marketing tactics as special sales promotions, heavy advertising, rebates, or low-interest-rate financing to drum up additional sales. Rivals may race one another to differentiate their products by offering better performance features or higher quality or improved customer service or a wider product selection. They may also compete through the rapid introduction of next-generation products, the frequent introduction of new or improved products, and efforts to build stronger dealer networks, establish positions in foreign markets, or otherwise expand distribution capabilities and market presence. Table 3.2 provides a sampling of the types of competitive weapons available to rivals, along with their primary effects with respect to price (P), cost (C), and value (V)—the elements of an effective business model and the value-price-cost framework, as discussed in Chapter 1.

Competitive Pressures Associated with the Threat of New Entrants

New entrants into an industry threaten the position of rival firms since they usually compete fiercely for market share and add to the production capacity and number of rivals in the process. But even the *threat* of new entry increases the competitive pressures in an industry. This is because incumbent firms typically lower prices and increase defensive actions in an attempt to deter new entry when the threat of entry is high. Just how serious the threat of entry is in a particular market depends on two classes of factors: the *expected reaction of incumbent firms to new entry* and what are known as *barriers to entry.* The threat of entry is low when incumbent firms are

TABLE 3.2 Common "Weapons" for Competing with Rivals

Types of Competitive Weapons	Primary Effects
Discounting prices, holding clearance sales	Lowers price (*P*), increases total sales volume and market share, lowers profits if price cuts are not offset by large increases in sales volume
Offering coupons, advertising items on sale	Increases sales volume and total revenues, lowers price (*P*), increases unit costs (*C*), may lower profit margins per unit sold (*P* – *C*)
Advertising product or service characteristics, using ads to enhance a company's image	Boosts buyer demand, increases product differentiation and perceived value (*V*), increases total sales volume and market share, but may increase unit costs (*C*) and lower profit margins per unit sold
Innovating to improve product performance and quality	Increases product differentiation and value (*V*), boosts buyer demand, boosts total sales volume, likely to increase unit costs (*C*)
Introducing new or improved features, increasing the number of styles to provide greater product selection	Increases product differentiation and value (*V*), strengthens buyer demand, boosts total sales volume and market share, likely to increase unit costs (*C*)
Increasing customization of product or service	Increases product differentiation and value (*V*), increases buyer switching costs, boosts total sales volume, often increases unit costs (*C*)
Building a bigger, better dealer network	Broadens access to buyers, boosts total sales volume and market share, may increase unit costs (*C*)
Improving warranties, offering low-interest financing	Increases product differentiation and value (*V*), increases unit costs (*C*), increases buyer switching costs, boosts total sales volume and market share

likely to retaliate against new entrants with sharp price discounting and other moves designed to make entry unprofitable and when entry barriers are high. Entry barriers are high under the following conditions:[2]

- *Industry incumbents enjoy large cost advantages over potential entrants.* Existing industry members frequently have costs that are hard for a newcomer to replicate. The cost advantages of industry incumbents can stem from (1) scale economies in production, distribution, advertising, or other activities, (2) the learning-based cost savings that accrue from experience in performing certain activities such as manufacturing or new product development or inventory management, (3) cost-savings accruing from patents or proprietary technology, (4) exclusive partnerships with the best and cheapest suppliers of raw materials and components, (5) favorable locations, and (6) low fixed costs (because incumbents have older facilities that have been mostly depreciated). The bigger the cost advantages of industry incumbents, the riskier it becomes for outsiders to attempt entry (since they will have to accept thinner profit margins or even losses until the cost disadvantages can be overcome).
- *Customers have strong brand preferences and high degrees of loyalty to seller.* The stronger buyers' attachment to established brands, the harder it is for a newcomer

to break into the marketplace. In such cases, a new entrant must have the financial resources to spend enough on advertising and sales promotion to overcome customer loyalties and build its own clientele. Establishing brand recognition and building customer loyalty can be a slow and costly process. In addition, if it is difficult or costly for a customer to switch to a new brand, a new entrant may have to offer a discounted price or otherwise persuade buyers that its brand is worth the switching costs. Such barriers discourage new entry because they act to boost financial requirements and lower expected profit margins for new entrants.

- *Patents and other forms of intellectual property protection are in place.* In a number of industries, entry is prevented due to the existence of intellectual property protection laws that remain in place for a given number of years. Often, companies have a "wall of patents" in place to prevent other companies from entering with a "me too" strategy that replicates a key piece of technology.
- *There are strong "network effects" in customer demand.* In industries where buyers are more attracted to a product when there are many other users of the product, there are said to be "network effects," since demand is higher the larger the network of users. Video game systems are an example, since users prefer to have the same systems as their friends so that they can play together on systems they all know and can share games. When incumbents have a large existing base of users, new entrants with otherwise comparable products face a serious disadvantage in attracting buyers.
- *Capital requirements are high.* The larger the total dollar investment needed to enter the market successfully, the more limited the pool of potential entrants. The most obvious capital requirements for new entrants relate to manufacturing facilities and equipment, introductory advertising and sales promotion campaigns, working capital to finance inventories and customer credit, and sufficient cash to cover startup costs.
- *There are difficulties in building a network of distributors/dealers or in securing adequate space on retailers' shelves.* A potential entrant can face numerous distribution-channel challenges. Wholesale distributors may be reluctant to take on a product that lacks buyer recognition. Retailers must be recruited and convinced to give a new brand ample display space and an adequate trial period. When existing sellers have strong, well-functioning distributor–dealer networks, a newcomer has an uphill struggle in squeezing its way into existing distribution channels. Potential entrants sometimes have to "buy" their way into wholesale or retail channels by cutting their prices to provide dealers and distributors with higher markups and profit margins or by giving them big advertising and promotional allowances. As a consequence, a potential entrant's own profits may be squeezed unless and until its product gains enough consumer acceptance that distributors and retailers are anxious to carry it.
- *There are restrictive regulatory policies.* Regulated industries like cable TV, telecommunications, electric and gas utilities, radio and television broadcasting, liquor retailing, and railroads entail government-controlled entry. Government agencies can also limit or even bar entry by requiring licenses and permits, such as the medallion required to drive a taxicab in New York City. Government-mandated safety regulations and environmental pollution standards also create entry barriers because they raise entry costs.
- *There are restrictive trade policies.* In international markets, host governments commonly limit foreign entry and must approve all foreign investment

applications. National governments commonly use tariffs and trade restrictions (antidumping rules, local content requirements, quotas, etc.) to raise entry barriers for foreign firms and protect domestic producers from outside competition.

Whether an industry's entry barriers ought to be considered high or low depends on the resources and capabilities possessed by the pool of potential entrants.

Figure 3.5 summarizes the factors that cause the overall competitive pressure from potential entrants to be strong or weak. An analysis of these factors can help managers determine whether the threat of entry into their industry is high or low, *in general*. But certain kinds of companies—those with sizable financial resources, proven competitive capabilities, and a respected brand name—may be able to hurdle an industry's entry barriers even when they are high.[3] For example, when Honda opted to enter the U.S. lawn-mower market in competition against Toro, Snapper, Craftsman,

FIGURE 3.5 Factors Affecting the Threat of Entry

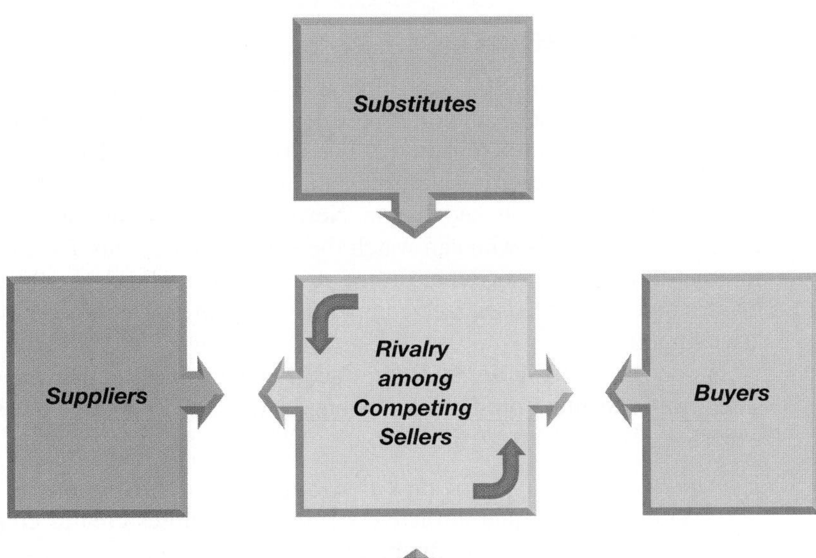

Competitive Pressures from Potential Entrants

Threat of entry is a stronger force when incumbents are unlikely to make retaliatory moves against new entrants and entry barriers are low. Entry barriers are high (and threat of entry is low) when:

- Incumbents have large cost advantages over potential entrants due to:
  - High economies of scale
  - Significant experience-based cost advantages or learning curve effects
  - Other cost advantages (e.g., favorable access to inputs, technology, location, or low fixed costs)
- Customers have strong brand preferences and/or loyalty to incumbent sellers.
- Patents and other forms of intellectual property protection are in place.
- There are strong network effects.
- Capital requirements are high.
- There is limited new access to distribution channels and shelf space.
- Government policies are restrictive.
- There are restrictive trade policies.

High entry barriers and weak entry threats today do not always translate into high entry barriers and weak entry threats tomorrow.

John Deere, and others, it was easily able to hurdle entry barriers that would have been formidable to other newcomers because it had long-standing expertise in gasoline engines and a reputation for quality and durability in automobiles that gave it instant credibility with homeowners. As a result, Honda had to spend relatively little on inducing dealers to handle the Honda lawn-mower line or attracting customers.

It is also important to recognize that the threat of entry changes as the industry's prospects grow brighter or dimmer and as entry barriers rise or fall. For example, key patents that have prevented new entry in the market for functional 3-D printers expired in February 2014, opening the way for new competition in this industry. Use of the Internet for shopping has made it much easier for e-tailers to enter into competition against some of the best-known retail chains. On the other hand, new strategic actions by incumbent firms to increase advertising, strengthen distributor–dealer relations, step up R&D, or improve product quality can erect higher roadblocks to entry.

Competitive Pressures from the Sellers of Substitute Products

Companies in one industry are vulnerable to competitive pressure from the actions of companies in a closely adjoining industry whenever buyers view the products of the two industries as good substitutes. For instance, the producers of sugar experience competitive pressures from the sales and marketing efforts of the makers of Equal, Splenda, Sweet 'N Low, and Truvia. Newspapers are struggling to maintain their relevance to subscribers who can watch the news on numerous TV channels and use the Internet to read blogs or other online news sources. Similarly, the producers of eyeglasses and contact lenses face competitive pressures from doctors who do corrective laser surgery.

As depicted in Figure 3.6, three factors determine whether the competitive pressures from substitute products are strong or weak. Competitive pressures are stronger when:

1. *Good substitutes are readily available and attractively priced.* The presence of readily available and attractively priced substitutes creates competitive pressure by placing a ceiling on the prices industry members can charge without risking sales erosion. This price ceiling, at the same time, puts a lid on the profits that industry members can earn unless they find ways to cut costs.
2. *Buyers view the substitutes as comparable or better in terms of quality, performance, and other relevant attributes.* The availability of substitutes inevitably invites customers to compare performance, features, ease of use, and other attributes as well as price. The users of paper cartons constantly weigh the price-performance trade-offs with plastic containers and metal cans, for example.
3. *The costs that buyers incur in switching to the substitutes are low.* Low switching costs make it easier for the sellers of attractive substitutes to lure buyers to their offerings; high switching costs deter buyers from purchasing substitute products.

Before assessing the competitive pressures coming from substitutes, company managers must identify the substitutes, which is less easy than it sounds since it involves (1) determining where the industry boundaries lie and (2) figuring out which other products or services can address the same basic customer needs as those produced by industry members. Deciding on the industry boundaries is necessary for

FIGURE 3.6 Factors Affecting Competition from Substitute Products

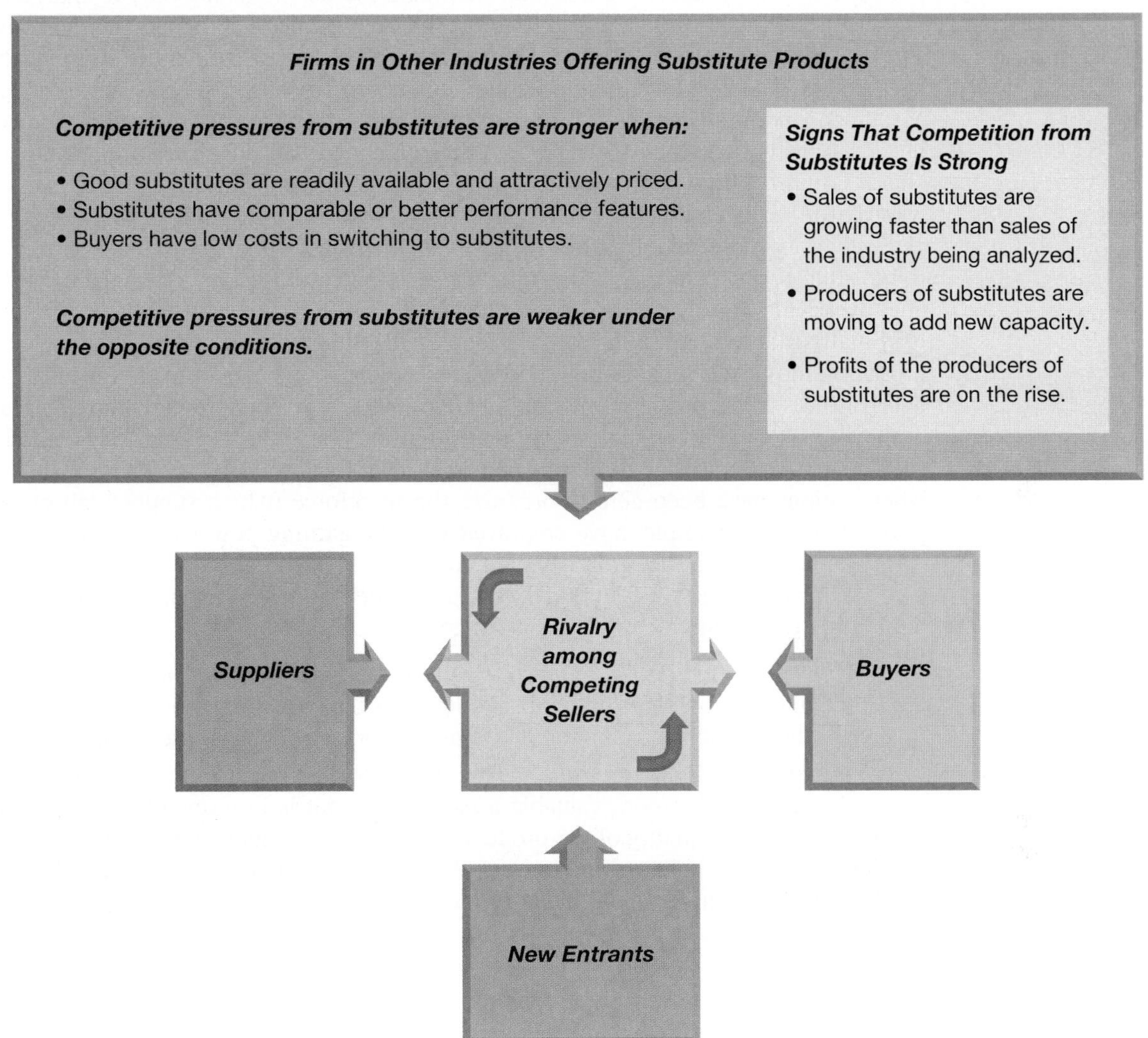

determining which firms are direct rivals and which produce substitutes. This is a matter of perspective—there are no hard-and-fast rules, other than to say that other brands of the same basic product constitute rival products and not substitutes.

Competitive Pressures Stemming from Supplier Bargaining Power

Whether the suppliers of industry members represent a weak or strong competitive force depends on the degree to which suppliers have sufficient *bargaining power* to influence the terms and conditions of supply in their favor. Suppliers with strong bargaining power can erode industry profitability by charging industry members higher prices, passing costs on to them, and limiting their opportunities to find better deals. For instance, Microsoft and Intel, both of which supply PC makers with essential components, have been known to use their dominant market status not only to charge PC makers premium prices but also to leverage their power over PC makers in other ways. The bargaining power of these two companies over their customers is so great that both companies have faced antitrust charges on numerous occasions. Prior to a legal agreement ending the practice, Microsoft pressured PC makers to load only Microsoft products on the PCs they shipped. Intel has defended itself against similar antitrust charges, but in filling orders for newly introduced Intel chips, it continues to give top priority to PC makers that use the biggest percentages of Intel chips in their PC models. Being on Intel's list of preferred customers helps a PC maker get an early allocation of Intel's latest chips and thus allows the PC maker to get new models to market ahead of rivals.

Small-scale retailers often must contend with the power of manufacturers whose products enjoy well-known brand names, since consumers expect to find these products on the shelves of the retail stores where they shop. This provides the manufacturer with a degree of pricing power and often the ability to push hard for favorable shelf displays. Supplier bargaining power is also a competitive factor in industries where unions have been able to organize the workforce (which supplies labor). Air pilot unions, for example, have employed their bargaining power to increase pilots' wages and benefits in the air transport industry.

As shown in Figure 3.7, a variety of factors determine the strength of suppliers' bargaining power. Supplier power is stronger when:

- *Demand for suppliers' products is high and the products are in short supply.* A surge in the demand for particular items shifts the bargaining power to the suppliers of those products; suppliers of items in short supply have pricing power.
- *Suppliers provide differentiated inputs that enhance the performance of the industry's product.* The more valuable a particular input is in terms of enhancing the performance or quality of the products of industry members, the more bargaining leverage suppliers have. In contrast, the suppliers of commodities are in a weak bargaining position, since industry members have no reason other than price to prefer one supplier over another.
- *It is difficult or costly for industry members to switch their purchases from one supplier to another.* Low switching costs limit supplier bargaining power by enabling industry members to change suppliers if any one supplier attempts to raise prices by more than the costs of switching. Thus, the higher the switching costs of industry members, the stronger the bargaining power of their suppliers.
- *The supplier industry is dominated by a few large companies and it is more concentrated than the industry it sells to.* Suppliers with sizable market shares and strong demand for the items they supply generally have sufficient bargaining power to charge high prices and deny requests from industry members for lower prices or other concessions.
- *Industry members are incapable of integrating backward to self-manufacture items they have been buying from suppliers.* As a rule, suppliers are safe from the threat of self-manufacture by their customers until the volume of parts a customer needs becomes large enough for the customer to justify backward integration into self-manufacture of the component. When industry members can threaten credibly to self-manufacture suppliers' goods, their bargaining power over suppliers increases proportionately.

FIGURE 3.7 Factors Affecting the Bargaining Power of Suppliers

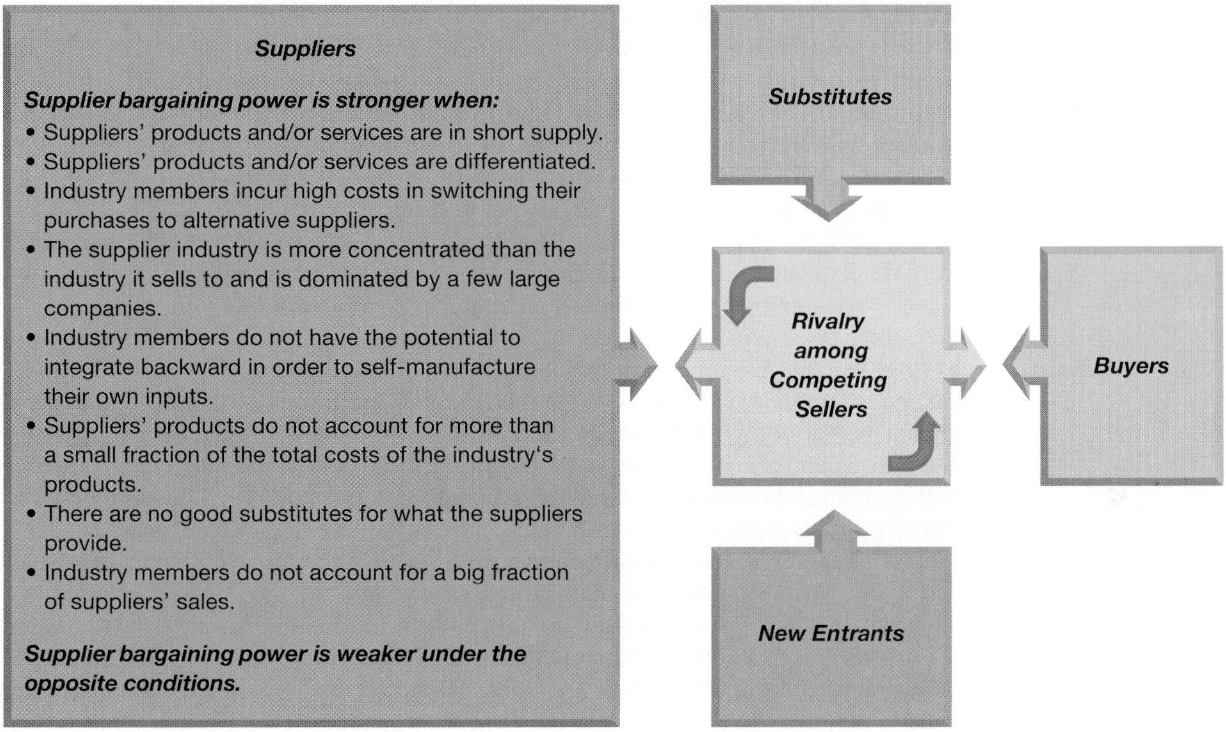

- *Suppliers provide an item that accounts for no more than a small fraction of the costs of the industry's product.* The more that the cost of a particular part or component affects the final product's cost, the more that industry members will be sensitive to the actions of suppliers to raise or lower their prices. When an input accounts for only a small proportion of total input costs, buyers will be less sensitive to price increases. Thus, suppliers' power increases when the inputs they provide do *not* make up a large proportion of the cost of the final product
- *Good substitutes are not available for the suppliers' products.* The lack of readily available substitute inputs increases the bargaining power of suppliers by increasing the dependence of industry members on the suppliers.
- *Industry members are not major customers of suppliers.* As a rule, suppliers have less bargaining leverage when their sales to members of the industry constitute a big percentage of their total sales. In such cases, the well-being of suppliers is closely tied to the well-being of their major customers, and their dependence upon them increases. The bargaining power of suppliers is stronger, then, when they are *not* bargaining with major customers.

In identifying the degree of supplier power in an industry, it is important to recognize that different types of suppliers are likely to have different amounts of bargaining power. Thus, the first step is for managers to identify the different types of suppliers, paying particular attention to those that provide the industry with important inputs. The next step is to assess the bargaining power of each type of supplier separately.

Competitive Pressures Stemming from Buyer Bargaining Power and Price Sensitivity

Whether buyers are able to exert strong competitive pressures on industry members depends on (1) the degree to which buyers have bargaining power and (2) the extent to which buyers are price-sensitive. Buyers with strong bargaining power can limit industry profitability by demanding price concessions, better payment terms, or additional features and services that increase industry members' costs. Buyer price sensitivity limits the profit potential of industry members by restricting the ability of sellers to raise prices without losing revenue due to lost sales.

The leverage that buyers have in negotiating favorable terms of sale can range from weak to strong. Individual consumers, for example, rarely have much bargaining power in negotiating price concessions or other favorable terms with sellers. However, their price sensitivity varies by individual and by the type of product they are buying (whether it's a necessity or a discretionary purchase, for example). Business buyers, in contrast, can have considerable bargaining power. Retailers tend to have greater bargaining power over industry sellers if they have influence over the purchase decisions of the end user or if they are critical in providing sellers with access to the end user. For example, large retail chains like Walmart, Best Buy, Staples, and Home Depot typically have considerable negotiating leverage in purchasing products from manufacturers because of manufacturers' need for access to their broad base of customers. Major supermarket chains like Kroger, Safeway, and Publix have sufficient bargaining power to demand promotional allowances and lump-sum payments (called *slotting fees*) from food products manufacturers in return for stocking certain brands or putting them in the best shelf locations. Motor vehicle manufacturers have strong bargaining power in negotiating to buy original-equipment tires from tire makers not only because they buy in large quantities but also because consumers are more likely to buy replacement tires that match the tire brand on their vehicle at the time of its purchase.

Figure 3.8 summarizes the factors determining the strength of buyer power in an industry. Note that the first five factors are the mirror image of those determining the bargaining power of suppliers, as described next.

Buyer bargaining power is stronger when:

- *Buyer demand is weak in relation to industry supply.* Weak or declining demand and the resulting excess supply create a "buyers' market," in which bargain-hunting buyers are able to press for better deals and special treatment.
- *Industry goods are standardized or differentiation is weak.* In such circumstances, buyers make their selections on the basis of price, which increases price competition among vendors.
- *Buyers' costs of switching to competing brands or substitutes are relatively low.* Switching costs put a cap on how much industry producers can raise prices or reduce quality before they will lose the buyer's business.
- *Buyers are large and few in number relative to the number of sellers.* The larger the buyers, the more important their business is to the seller and the more sellers will be willing to grant concessions.
- *Buyers pose a credible threat of integrating backward into the business of sellers.* Companies like Anheuser-Busch, Coors, and Heinz have partially integrated backward into metal-can manufacturing to gain bargaining power in obtaining the balance of their can requirements from otherwise powerful metal-can manufacturers.

FIGURE 3.8 Factors Affecting the Bargaining Power of Buyers

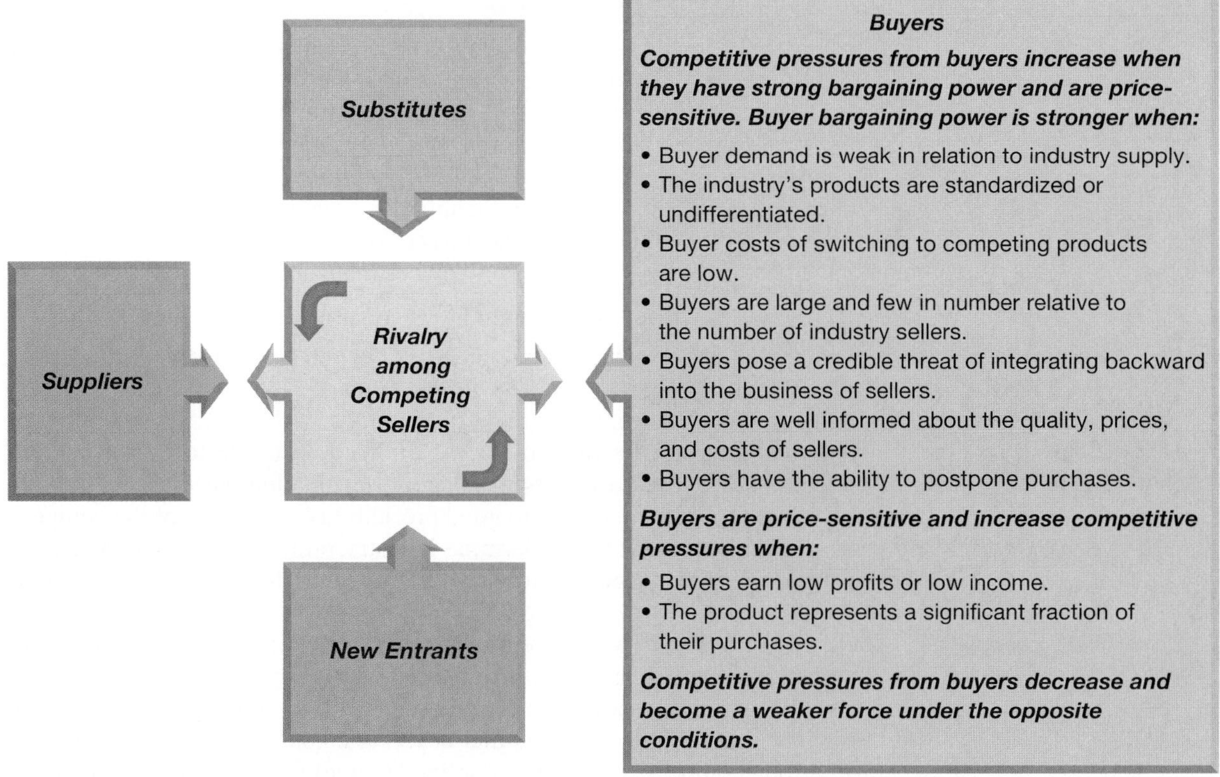

- *Buyers are well informed about sellers' products, prices, and costs.* The more information buyers have, the better bargaining position they are in. The mushrooming availability of product information on the Internet (and its ready access on smartphones) is giving added bargaining power to consumers, since they can use this to find or negotiate better deals.
- *Buyers have discretion to delay their purchases or perhaps even not make a purchase at all.* Consumers often have the option to delay purchases of durable goods, such as major appliances, or discretionary goods, such as hot tubs and home entertainment centers, if they are not happy with the prices offered. Business customers may also be able to defer their purchases of certain items, such as plant equipment or maintenance services. This puts pressure on sellers to provide concessions to buyers so that the sellers can keep their sales numbers from dropping off.

The following factors increase buyer price sensitivity and result in greater competitive pressures on the industry as a result:

- *Buyer price sensitivity increases when buyers are earning low profits or have low income.* Price is a critical factor in the purchase decisions of low-income consumers and companies that are barely scraping by. In such cases, their high price sensitivity limits the ability of sellers to charge high prices.

- *Buyers are more price-sensitive if the product represents a large fraction of their total purchases.* When a purchase eats up a large portion of a buyer's budget or represents a significant part of his or her cost structure, the buyer cares more about price than might otherwise be the case.

The starting point for the analysis of buyers as a competitive force is to identify the different types of buyers along the value chain—then proceed to analyzing the bargaining power and price sensitivity of each type separately. It is important to recognize that *not all buyers of an industry's product have equal degrees of bargaining power with sellers, and some may be less sensitive than others to price, quality, or service differences.* For example, apparel manufacturers confront significant bargaining power when selling to big retailers like Target, Macy's, or L.L.Bean, but they can command much better prices selling to small owner-managed apparel boutiques.

Is the Collective Strength of the Five Competitive Forces Conducive to Good Profitability?

Assessing whether each of the five competitive forces gives rise to strong, moderate, or weak competitive pressures sets the stage for evaluating whether, overall, the strength of the five forces is conducive to good profitability. Are some of the competitive forces sufficiently powerful to undermine industry profitability? Can companies in this industry reasonably expect to earn decent profits in light of the prevailing competitive forces?

The most extreme case of a "competitively unattractive" industry occurs when all five forces are producing strong competitive pressures: Rivalry among sellers is vigorous, low entry barriers allow new rivals to gain a market foothold, competition from substitutes is intense, and both suppliers and buyers are able to exercise considerable leverage. Strong competitive pressures coming from all five directions drive industry profitability to unacceptably low levels, frequently producing losses for many industry members and forcing some out of business. But an industry can be competitively unattractive without all five competitive forces being strong. In fact, *intense competitive pressures from just one of the five forces may suffice to destroy the conditions for good profitability and prompt some companies to exit the business.*

CORE CONCEPT

The strongest of the five forces determines the extent of the downward pressure on an industry's profitability.

As a rule, *the strongest competitive forces determine the extent of the competitive pressure on industry profitability.* Thus, in evaluating the strength of the five forces overall and their effect on industry profitability, managers should look to the strongest forces. Having more than one strong force will not worsen the effect on industry profitability, but it does mean that the industry has multiple competitive challenges with which to cope. In that sense, an industry with three to five strong forces is even more "unattractive" as a place to compete. Especially intense competitive conditions seem to be the norm in tire manufacturing, apparel, and commercial airlines, three industries where profit margins have historically been thin.

In contrast, when the overall impact of the five competitive forces is moderate to weak, an industry is "attractive" in the sense that the *average* industry member can reasonably expect to earn good profits and a nice return on investment. The ideal competitive environment for earning superior profits is one in which both suppliers and customers are in weak bargaining positions, there are no good substitutes, high barriers block further entry, and rivalry among present sellers is muted. Weak competition is the best of all possible worlds for also-ran companies because even they can usually eke out a decent profit—if a company can't make a decent profit when competition is weak, then its business outlook is indeed grim.

Matching Company Strategy to Competitive Conditions

A company's strategy is increasingly effective the more it provides some insulation from competitive pressures, shifts the competitive battle in the company's favor, and positions the firm to take advantage of attractive growth opportunities.

Working through the five forces model step by step not only aids strategy makers in assessing whether the intensity of competition allows good profitability but also promotes sound strategic thinking about how to better match company strategy to the specific competitive character of the marketplace. Effectively matching a company's business strategy to prevailing competitive conditions has two aspects:

1. Pursuing avenues that shield the firm from as many of the different competitive pressures as possible.
2. Initiating actions calculated to shift the competitive forces in the company's favor by altering the underlying factors driving the five forces.

But making headway on these two fronts first requires identifying competitive pressures, gauging the relative strength of each of the five competitive forces, and gaining a deep enough understanding of the state of competition in the industry to know which strategy buttons to push.

COMPLEMENTORS AND THE VALUE NET

Not all interactions among industry participants are necessarily competitive in nature. Some have the potential to be cooperative, as the value net framework demonstrates. Like the five forces framework, the value net includes an analysis of buyers, suppliers, and substitutors (see Figure 3.9). But it differs from the five forces framework in several important ways.

First, the analysis focuses on the interactions of industry participants with a particular company. Thus it places that firm in the center of the framework, as Figure 3.9 shows. Second, the category of "competitors" is defined to include not only the focal firm's direct competitors or industry rivals but also the sellers of substitute products and potential entrants. Third, the value net framework introduces a new category of industry participant that is not found in the five forces framework—that of "complementors." **Complementors** are the producers of complementary products, which are products that enhance the value of the focal firm's products when they are used together. Some examples include snorkels and swim fins or shoes and shoelaces.

CORE CONCEPT

Complementors are the producers of complementary products, which are products that enhance the value of the focal firm's products when they are used together.

The inclusion of complementors draws particular attention to the fact that success in the marketplace need not come at the expense of other industry participants. Interactions among industry participants may be cooperative in nature rather than competitive. In the case of complementors, an increase in sales for them is likely to increase the sales of the focal firm as well. But the value net framework also encourages managers to consider other forms of cooperative interactions and realize that value is created jointly by all industry participants. For example, a company's success in the marketplace depends on establishing a reliable supply chain for its inputs, which implies the need for cooperative relations with its suppliers. Often a firm works hand in hand with its suppliers to ensure a smoother, more efficient operation for both parties. Newell-Rubbermaid, for example, works cooperatively as a supplier to companies such as Kmart and Kohl's. Even direct rivals may work cooperatively if they participate in industry trade associations or engage in joint lobbying efforts. Value net analysis can help managers discover the potential to improve their position through cooperative as well as competitive interactions.

FIGURE 3.9 The Value Net

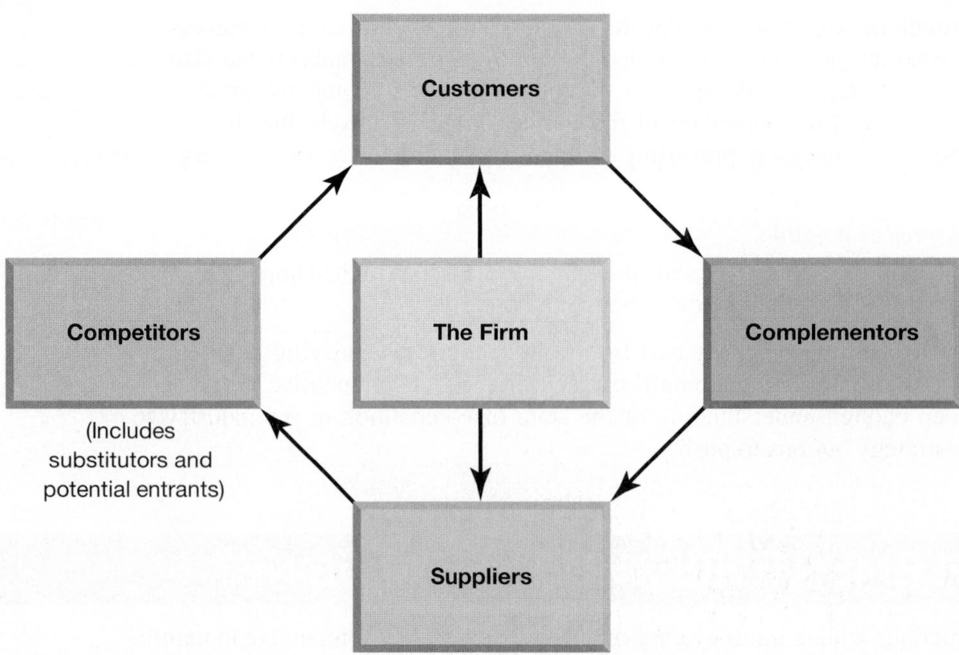

INDUSTRY DYNAMICS AND THE FORCES DRIVING CHANGE

While it is critical to understand the nature and intensity of competitive and cooperative forces in an industry, it is equally critical to understand that the intensity of these forces is fluid and subject to change. All industries are affected by new developments and ongoing trends that alter industry conditions, some more speedily than others. Any strategies devised by management will therefore play out in a dynamic industry environment, so it's imperative that managers consider the factors driving industry change and how they might affect the industry environment. Moreover, with early notice, managers may be able to influence the direction or scope of environmental change and improve the outlook.

CORE CONCEPT

Driving forces are the major underlying causes of change in industry and competitive conditions.

Industry and competitive conditions change because forces are enticing or pressuring certain industry participants (competitors, customers, suppliers, complementors) to alter their actions in important ways. The most powerful of the change agents are called **driving forces** because they have the biggest influences in reshaping the industry landscape and altering competitive conditions. Some driving forces originate in the outer ring of the company's macro-environment (see Figure 3.2), but most originate in the company's more immediate industry and competitive environment.

Driving-forces analysis has three steps: (1) identifying what the driving forces are, (2) assessing whether the drivers of change are, on the whole, acting to make the industry more or less attractive, and (3) determining what strategy changes are needed to prepare for the impact of the driving forces. All three steps merit further discussion.

Identifying the Forces Driving Industry Change

Many developments can affect an industry powerfully enough to qualify as driving forces. Some drivers of change are unique and specific to a particular industry situation, but most drivers of industry and competitive change fall into one of the following categories:

- *Changes in an industry's long-term growth rate.* Shifts in industry growth up or down have the potential to affect the balance between industry supply and buyer demand, entry and exit, and the character and strength of competition. Whether demand is growing or declining is one of the key factors influencing the intensity of rivalry in an industry, as explained earlier. But the strength of this effect will depend on how changes in the industry growth rate affect entry and exit in the industry. If entry barriers are low, then growth in demand will attract new entrants, increasing the number of industry rivals and changing the competitive landscape.
- *Increasing globalization.* Globalization can be precipitated by such factors as the blossoming of consumer demand in developing countries, the availability of lower-cost foreign inputs, and the reduction of trade barriers, as has occurred recently in many parts of Latin America and Asia. The forces of globalization are sometimes such a strong driver that companies find it highly advantageous, if not necessary, to spread their operating reach into more and more country markets.
- *Emerging new Internet capabilities and applications.* The Internet of the future will feature faster speeds, dazzling applications, and over a billion connected gadgets performing an array of functions, thus driving a host of industry and competitive changes. But Internet-related impacts vary from industry to industry. The challenges are to assess precisely how emerging Internet developments are altering a particular industry's landscape and to factor these impacts into the strategy-making equation.
- *Shifts in buyer demographics.* Shifts in buyer demographics and the ways products are used can greatly alter industry and competitive conditions. Longer life expectancies and growing percentages of relatively well-to-do retirees, for example, are driving demand growth in such industries as health care, prescription drugs, recreational living, and vacation travel.
- *Technological change and manufacturing process innovation.* Advances in technology can cause disruptive change in an industry by introducing substitutes or can alter the industry landscape by opening up whole new industry frontiers. For instance, advances in battery technology are beginning to change how motor vehicles are powered.
- *Product innovation.* An ongoing stream of product innovations tends to alter the pattern of competition in an industry by attracting more first-time buyers, rejuvenating industry growth, and/or increasing product differentiation, with concomitant effects on rivalry, entry threat, and buyer power. Product innovation has been a key driving force in industries such as smartphones, video games, and prescription drugs.
- *Entry or exit of major firms.* Entry by a major firm thus often produces a new ball game, not only with new key players but also with new rules for competing. Similarly, exit of a major firm changes the competitive structure by reducing the number of market leaders and increasing the dominance of the leaders who remain.

- *Diffusion of technical know-how across companies and countries.* As knowledge about how to perform a particular activity or execute a particular manufacturing technology spreads, products tend to become more commodity-like. Knowledge diffusion can occur through scientific journals, trade publications, onsite plant tours, word of mouth among suppliers and customers, employee migration, and Internet sources.
- *Changes in cost and efficiency.* Widening or shrinking differences in the costs among key competitors tend to dramatically alter the state of competition. Declining costs of producing PCs have enabled price cuts and spurred PC sales (especially lower-priced models) by making them more affordable to lower-income households worldwide.
- *Reductions in uncertainty and business risk.* Many companies are hesitant to enter industries with uncertain futures or high levels of business risk because it is unclear how much time and money it will take to overcome various technological hurdles and achieve acceptable production costs (as is the case in the infant solar power industry). Over time, however, diminishing risk levels and uncertainty tend to stimulate new entry and capital investments on the part of growth-minded companies seeking new opportunities, thus dramatically altering industry and competitive conditions.
- *Regulatory influences and government policy changes.* Government regulatory actions can often mandate significant changes in industry practices and strategic approaches—as has recently occurred in the world's banking industry. New rules and regulations pertaining to government-sponsored health insurance programs are driving changes in the health care industry. In international markets, host governments can drive competitive changes by opening their domestic markets to foreign participation or closing them to protect domestic companies.
- *Changing societal concerns, attitudes, and lifestyles.* Emerging social issues as well as changing attitudes and lifestyles can be powerful instigators of industry change. Mounting consumer concerns about the use of chemical additives and the nutritional content of food products are driving changes in the restaurant and food industries. Shifting societal concerns, attitudes, and lifestyles alter the pattern of competition, favoring those players that respond with products targeted to the new trends and conditions.

The most important part of driving-forces analysis is to determine whether the collective impact of the driving forces will increase or decrease market demand, make competition more or less intense, and lead to higher or lower industry profitability.

While many forces of change may be at work in a given industry, *no more than three or four* are likely to be true driving forces powerful enough to qualify as the *major determinants* of why and how the industry is changing. Thus, company strategists must resist the temptation to label every change they see as a driving force. Table 3.3 lists the most common driving forces

Assessing the Impact of the Forces Driving Industry Change

The real payoff of driving-forces analysis is to help managers understand what strategy changes are needed to prepare for the impacts of the driving forces.

The second step in driving-forces analysis is to determine whether the prevailing change drivers, on the whole, are acting to make the industry environment more or less attractive. Getting a handle on the collective impact of the driving forces requires looking at the likely effects of each factor separately, since the driving forces may not all be pushing change in the same direction. For example, one driving force may be acting to spur demand for the industry's product while another is working to curtail demand. Whether the net effect on industry demand is up or down hinges on which driver of change is the more powerful.

TABLE 3.3 The Most Common Drivers of Industry Change

- Changes in the long-term industry growth rate
- Increasing globalization
- Emerging new Internet capabilities and applications
- Shifts in buyer demographics
- Technological change and manufacturing process innovation
- Product and marketing innovation
- Entry or exit of major firms
- Diffusion of technical know-how across companies and countries
- Changes in cost and efficiency
- Reductions in uncertainty and business risk
- Regulatory influences and government policy changes
- Changing societal concerns, attitudes, and lifestyles

Adjusting the Strategy to Prepare for the Impacts of Driving Forces

The third step in the strategic analysis of industry dynamics—where the real payoff for strategy making comes—is for managers to draw some conclusions about *what strategy adjustments will be needed to deal with the impacts of the driving forces.* But taking the "right" kinds of actions to prepare for the industry and competitive changes being wrought by the driving forces first requires accurate diagnosis of the forces driving industry change and the impacts these forces will have on both the industry environment and the company's business. To the extent that managers are unclear about the drivers of industry change and their impacts, or if their views are off-base, the chances of making astute and timely strategy adjustments are slim. So driving-forces analysis is not something to take lightly; it has practical value and is basic to the task of thinking strategically about where the industry is headed and how to prepare for the changes ahead.

LO 3

How to map the market positions of key groups of industry rivals.

STRATEGIC GROUP ANALYSIS

Within an industry, companies commonly sell in different price/quality ranges, appeal to different types of buyers, have different geographic coverage, and so on. Some are more attractively positioned than others. Understanding which companies are strongly positioned and which are weakly positioned is an integral part of analyzing an industry's competitive structure. The best technique for revealing the market positions of industry competitors is **strategic group mapping.**

CORE CONCEPT

Strategic group mapping is a technique for displaying the different market or competitive positions that rival firms occupy in the industry.

Using Strategic Group Maps to Assess the Market Positions of Key Competitors

A **strategic group** consists of those industry members with similar competitive approaches and positions in the market. Companies in the same strategic group can resemble one another in a variety of ways. For example, they may have comparable product-line breadth, emphasize the same distribution channels, depend on identical technological approaches, or offer buyers essentially the same product attributes or similar services and technical assistance.[4] Evaluating strategy options entails examining what strategic groups exist, identifying the companies within each group, and determining if a competitive "white space" exists where industry competitors are able to create and capture altogether new demand. As part of this process, the number of strategic groups in an industry and their respective market positions can be displayed on a strategic group map.

The procedure for constructing a *strategic group map* is straightforward:

CORE CONCEPT

A **strategic group** is a cluster of industry rivals that have similar competitive approaches and market positions.

- Identify the competitive characteristics that delineate strategic approaches used in the industry. Typical variables used in creating strategic group maps are price/quality range (high, medium, low), geographic coverage (local, regional, national, global), product-line breadth (wide, narrow), degree of service offered (no frills, limited, full), use of distribution channels (retail, wholesale, Internet, multiple), degree of vertical integration (none, partial, full), and degree of diversification into other industries (none, some, considerable).
- Plot the firms on a two-variable map using pairs of these variables.
- Assign firms occupying about the same map location to the same strategic group.
- Draw circles around each strategic group, making the circles proportional to the size of the group's share of total industry sales revenues.

This produces a two-dimensional diagram like the one for the U.S. beer industry in Illustration Capsule 3.1.

Several guidelines need to be observed in creating strategic group maps. First, the two variables selected as axes for the map should *not* be highly correlated; if they are, the circles on the map will fall along a diagonal and reveal nothing more about the relative positions of competitors than would be revealed by comparing the rivals on just one of the variables. For instance, if companies with broad product lines use multiple distribution channels while companies with narrow lines use a single distribution channel, then looking at the differences in distribution-channel approaches adds no new information about positioning.

Second, the variables chosen as axes for the map should reflect important differences among rival approaches—when rivals differ on both variables, the locations of the rivals will be scattered, thus showing how they are positioned differently. Third, the variables used as axes don't have to be either quantitative or continuous; rather, they can be discrete variables, defined in terms of distinct classes and combinations. Fourth, drawing the sizes of the circles on the map proportional to the combined sales of the firms in each strategic group allows the map to reflect the relative sizes of each strategic group. Fifth, if more than two good variables can be used as axes for the map, then it is wise to draw several maps to give different exposures to the competitive positioning relationships present in the industry's structure—there is not necessarily one best map for portraying how competing firms are positioned.

ILLUSTRATION CAPSULE 3.1

Comparative Market Positions of Producers in the U.S. Beer Industry: A Strategic Group Map Example

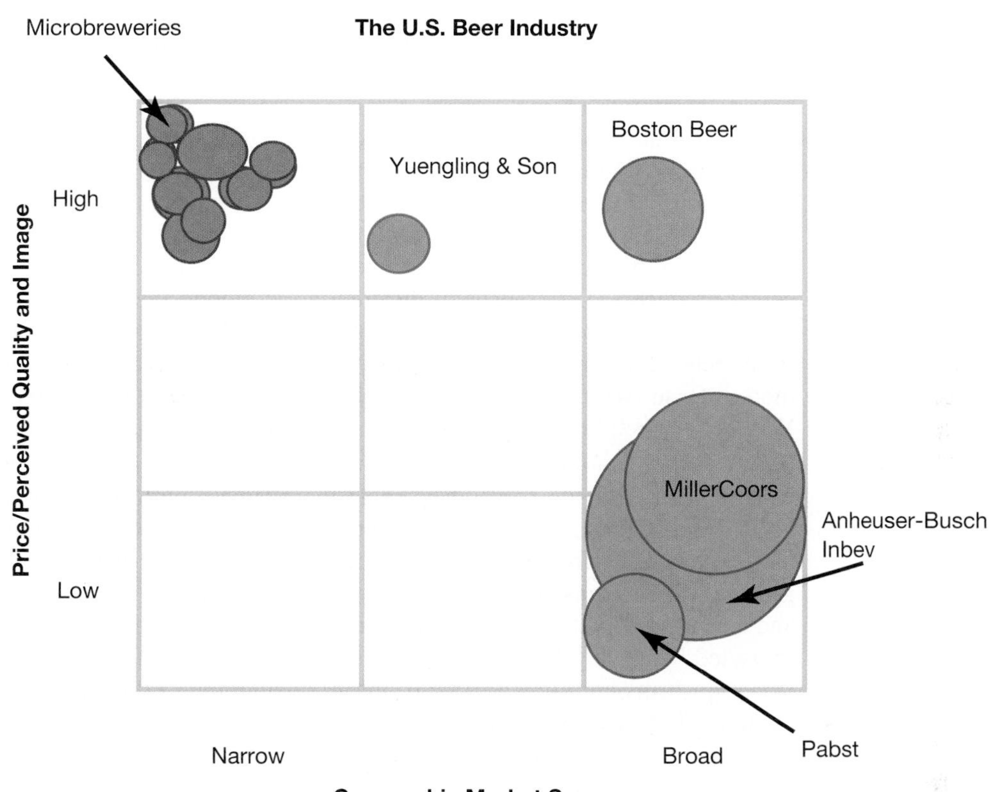

Note: Circles are drawn roughly proportional to the sizes of the chains, based on revenues.

The Value of Strategic Group Maps

Strategic group maps are revealing in several respects. The most important has to do with identifying which industry members are close rivals and which are distant rivals. Firms in the same strategic group are the closest rivals; the next closest rivals are in the immediately adjacent groups. Often, firms in strategic groups that are far apart on the map hardly compete at all. For instance, Walmart's clientele, merchandise selection, and pricing points are much too different to justify calling Walmart a close competitor of Neiman Marcus or Saks Fifth Avenue. For the same reason, the beers produced by Yuengling & Son are really not in competition with the beers produced by Pabst.

Strategic group maps reveal which companies are close competitors and which are distant competitors.

The second thing to be gleaned from strategic group mapping is that *not all positions on the map are equally attractive*.[5] Two reasons account for why some positions can be more attractive than others:

1. *Prevailing competitive pressures from the industry's five forces may cause the profit potential of different strategic groups to vary.* The profit prospects of firms in different strategic groups can vary from good to poor because of differing degrees of competitive rivalry within strategic groups, differing pressures from potential entrants to each group, differing degrees of exposure to competition from substitute products outside the industry, and differing degrees of supplier or customer bargaining power from group to group. For instance, in the ready-to-eat cereal industry, there are significantly higher entry barriers (capital requirements, brand loyalty, etc.) for the strategic group comprising the large branded-cereal makers than for the group of generic-cereal makers or the group of small natural-cereal producers. Differences in differentiation among the branded rivals versus the generic cereal makers make rivalry stronger within the generic strategic group. In the retail chain industry, the competitive battle between Walmart and Target is more intense (with consequently smaller profit margins) than the rivalry among Versace, Chanel, Fendi, and other high-end fashion retailers.
2. *Industry driving forces may favor some strategic groups and hurt others.* Likewise, industry driving forces can boost the business outlook for some strategic groups and adversely impact the business prospects of others. In the news industry, for example, Internet news services and cable news networks are gaining ground at the expense of newspapers and networks due to changes in technology and changing social lifestyles. Firms in strategic groups that are being adversely impacted by driving forces may try to shift to a more favorably situated position. If certain firms are known to be trying to change their competitive positions on the map, then attaching arrows to the circles showing the targeted direction helps clarify the picture of competitive maneuvering among rivals.

Some strategic groups are more favorably positioned than others because they confront weaker competitive forces and/or because they are more favorably impacted by industry driving forces.

Thus, part of strategic group map analysis always entails drawing conclusions about where on the map is the "best" place to be and why. Which companies/strategic groups are destined to prosper because of their positions? Which companies/strategic groups seem destined to struggle? What accounts for why some parts of the map are better than others?

COMPETITOR ANALYSIS

Unless a company pays attention to the strategies and situations of competitors and has some inkling of what moves they will be making, it ends up flying blind into competitive battle. As in sports, scouting the opposition is an essential part of game plan development. Having good information about the strategic direction and likely moves of key competitors allows a company to prepare defensive countermoves, to craft its own strategic moves with some confidence about what market maneuvers to expect from rivals in response, and to exploit any openings that arise from competitors' missteps. The question is where to look for such information, since rivals rarely reveal their strategic intentions openly. If information is not directly available, what are the best indicators?

Studying competitors' past behavior and preferences provides a valuable assist in anticipating what moves rivals are likely to make next and outmaneuvering them in the marketplace.

Michael Porter's **Framework for Competitor Analysis** points to four indicators of a rival's likely strategic moves and countermoves. These include a rival's *current* *strategy, objectives, resources and capabilities,* and *assumptions* about itself and the industry, as shown in Figure 3.10. A strategic profile of a rival that provides good clues to its behavioral proclivities can be constructed by characterizing the rival along these four dimensions.

Current Strategy To succeed in predicting a competitor's next moves, company strategists need to have a good understanding of each rival's current strategy, as an indicator of its pattern of behavior and best strategic options. Questions to consider include: How is the competitor positioned in the market? What is the basis for its competitive advantage (if any)? What kinds of investments is it making (as an indicator of its growth trajectory)?

Objectives An appraisal of a rival's objectives should include not only its financial performance objectives but strategic ones as well (such as those concerning market share). What is even more important is to consider the extent to which the rival is meeting these objectives and whether it is under pressure to improve. Rivals with good financial performance are likely to continue their present strategy with only minor fine-tuning. Poorly performing rivals are virtually certain to make fresh strategic moves.

Resources and Capabilities A rival's strategic moves and countermoves are both enabled and constrained by the set of resources and capabilities the rival has at hand. Thus a rival's resources and capabilities (and efforts to acquire new resources and capabilities) serve as a strong signal of future strategic actions (and reactions to your company's moves). Assessing a rival's resources and capabilities involves sizing up not only its strengths in this respect but its weaknesses as well.

FIGURE 3.10 A Framework for Competitor Analysis

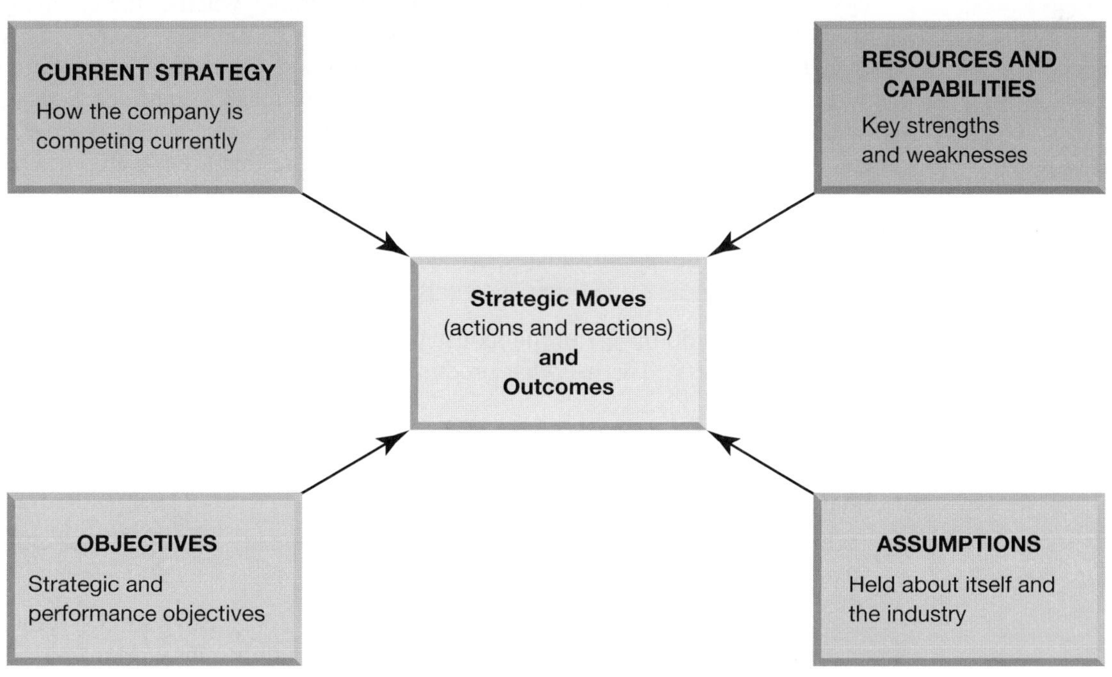

Assumptions How a rival's top managers think about their strategic situation can have a big impact on how the rival behaves. Banks that believe they are "too big to fail," for example, may take on more risk than is financially prudent. Assessing a rival's assumptions entails considering its assumptions about itself as well as about the industry it participates in.

Information regarding these four analytic components can often be gleaned from company press releases, information posted on the company's website (especially the presentations management has recently made to securities analysts), and such public documents as annual reports and 10-K filings. Many companies also have a competitive intelligence unit that sifts through the available information to construct up-to-date strategic profiles of rivals. Doing the necessary detective work can be time-consuming, but scouting competitors well enough to anticipate their next moves allows managers to prepare effective countermoves (perhaps even beat a rival to the punch) and to take rivals' probable actions into account in crafting their own best course of action.

KEY SUCCESS FACTORS

CORE CONCEPT

Key success factors are the strategy elements, product and service attributes, operational approaches, resources, and competitive capabilities that are essential to surviving and thriving in the industry.

An industry's **key success factors (KSFs)** are those competitive factors that most affect industry members' ability to survive and prosper in the marketplace: the particular strategy elements, product attributes, operational approaches, resources, and competitive capabilities that spell the difference between being a strong competitor and a weak competitor—and between profit and loss. KSFs by their very nature are so important to competitive success that *all firms* in the industry must pay close attention to them or risk becoming an industry laggard or failure. To indicate the significance of KSFs another way, how well the elements of a company's strategy measure up against an industry's KSFs determines whether the company can meet the basic criteria for surviving and thriving in the industry. Identifying KSFs, in light of the prevailing and anticipated industry and competitive conditions, is therefore always a top priority in analytic and strategy-making considerations. Company strategists need to understand the industry landscape well enough to separate the factors most important to competitive success from those that are less important.

Key success factors vary from industry to industry, and even from time to time within the same industry, as drivers of change and competitive conditions change. But regardless of the circumstances, an industry's key success factors can always be deduced by asking the same three questions:

1. On what basis do buyers of the industry's product choose between the competing brands of sellers? That is, what product attributes and service characteristics are crucial?
2. Given the nature of competitive rivalry prevailing in the marketplace, what resources and competitive capabilities must a company have to be competitively successful?
3. What shortcomings are almost certain to put a company at a significant competitive disadvantage?

Only rarely are there more than five key factors for competitive success. And even among these, two or three usually outrank the others in importance. Managers should therefore bear in mind the purpose of identifying key success factors—to determine which factors are most important to competitive success—and resist the temptation to label a factor that has only minor importance as a KSF.

In the beer industry, for example, although there are many types of buyers (wholesale, retail, end consumer), it is most important to understand the preferences and buying behavior of the beer drinkers. Their purchase decisions are driven by price, taste, convenient access, and marketing. Thus the KSFs include a *strong network of wholesale distributors* (to get the company's brand stocked and favorably displayed in retail outlets, bars, restaurants, and stadiums, where beer is sold) and *clever advertising* (to induce beer drinkers to buy the company's brand and thereby pull beer sales through the established wholesale and retail channels). Because there is a potential for strong buyer power on the part of large distributors and retail chains, competitive success depends on some mechanism to offset that power, of which advertising (to create demand pull) is one. Thus the KSFs also include *superior product differentiation* (as in microbrews) or *superior firm size and branding capabilities* (as in national brands). The KSFs also include *full utilization of brewing capacity* (to keep manufacturing costs low and offset the high advertising, branding, and product differentiation costs).

Correctly diagnosing an industry's KSFs raises a company's chances of crafting a sound strategy. The key success factors of an industry point to those things that every firm in the industry needs to attend to in order to retain customers and weather the competition. If the company's strategy cannot deliver on the key success factors of its industry, it is unlikely to earn enough profits to remain a viable business.

THE INDUSTRY OUTLOOK FOR PROFITABILITY

LO 4

How to use multiple frameworks to determine whether an industry's outlook presents a company with sufficiently attractive opportunities for growth and profitability.

Each of the frameworks presented in this chapter—PESTEL, five forces analysis, driving forces, strategy groups, competitor analysis, and key success factors—provides a useful perspective on an industry's outlook for future profitability. Putting them all together provides an even richer and more nuanced picture. Thus, the final step in evaluating the industry and competitive environment is to use the results of each of the analyses performed to determine whether the industry presents the company with strong prospects for competitive success and attractive profits. The important factors on which to base a conclusion include:

- How the company is being impacted by the state of the macro-environment.
- Whether strong competitive forces are squeezing industry profitability to subpar levels.
- Whether the presence of complementors and the possibility of cooperative actions improve the company's prospects.
- Whether industry profitability will be favorably or unfavorably affected by the prevailing driving forces.
- Whether the company occupies a stronger market position than rivals.
- Whether this is likely to change in the course of competitive interactions.
- How well the company's strategy delivers on the industry key success factors.

As a general proposition, *the anticipated industry environment is fundamentally attractive if it presents a company with good opportunity for above-average*

The degree to which an industry is attractive or unattractive is not the same for all industry participants and all potential entrants.

profitability; the industry outlook is fundamentally unattractive if a company's profit prospects are unappealingly low.

However, it is a mistake to think of a particular industry as being equally attractive or unattractive to all industry participants and all potential entrants.[6] Attractiveness is relative, not absolute, and conclusions one way or the other have to be drawn from the perspective of a particular company. For instance, a favorably positioned competitor may see ample opportunity to capitalize on the vulnerabilities of weaker rivals even though industry conditions are otherwise somewhat dismal. At the same time, industries attractive to insiders may be unattractive to outsiders because of the difficulty of challenging current market leaders or because they have more attractive opportunities elsewhere.

When a company decides an industry is fundamentally attractive and presents good opportunities, a strong case can be made that it should invest aggressively to capture the opportunities it sees and to improve its long-term competitive position in the business. When a strong competitor concludes an industry is becoming less attractive, it may elect to simply protect its present position, investing cautiously—if at all—and looking for opportunities in other industries. A competitively weak company in an unattractive industry may see its best option as finding a buyer, perhaps a rival, to acquire its business.

KEY POINTS

Thinking strategically about a company's external situation involves probing for answers to the following questions:

1. *What are the strategically relevant factors in the macro-environment, and how do they impact an industry and its members?* Industries differ significantly as to how they are affected by conditions in the broad macro-environment. Using PESTEL analysis to identify which of these factors is strategically relevant is the first step to understanding how a company is situated in its external environment.
2. *What kinds of competitive forces are industry members facing, and how strong is each force?* The strength of competition is a composite of five forces: (1) rivalry within the industry, (2) the threat of new entry into the market, (3) inroads being made by the sellers of substitutes, (4) supplier bargaining power, and (5) buyer bargaining power. All five must be examined force by force, and their collective strength evaluated. One strong force, however, can be sufficient to keep average industry profitability low. Working through the five forces model aids strategy makers in assessing how to insulate the company from the strongest forces, identify attractive arenas for expansion, or alter the competitive conditions so that they offer more favorable prospects for profitability.
3. *What cooperative forces are present in the industry, and how can a company harness them to its advantage?* Interactions among industry participants are not only competitive in nature but cooperative as well. This is particularly the case when complements to the products or services of an industry are important. The value net framework assists managers in sizing up the impact of cooperative as well as competitive interactions on their firm.

4. *What factors are driving changes in the industry, and what impact will they have on competitive intensity and industry profitability?* Industry and competitive conditions change because certain forces are acting to create incentives or pressures for change. The first step is to identify the three or four most important drivers of change affecting the industry being analyzed (out of a much longer list of potential drivers). Once an industry's change drivers have been identified, the analytic task becomes one of determining whether they are acting, individually and collectively, to make the industry environment more or less attractive.
5. *What market positions do industry rivals occupy—who is strongly positioned and who is not?* Strategic group mapping is a valuable tool for understanding the similarities, differences, strengths, and weaknesses inherent in the market positions of rival companies. Rivals in the same or nearby strategic groups are close competitors, whereas companies in distant strategic groups usually pose little or no immediate threat. The lesson of strategic group mapping is that some positions on the map are more favorable than others. The profit potential of different strategic groups may not be the same because industry driving forces and competitive forces likely have varying effects on the industry's distinct strategic groups.
6. *What strategic moves are rivals likely to make next?* Anticipating the actions of rivals can help a company prepare effective countermoves. Using the Framework for Competitor Analysis is helpful in this regard.
7. *What are the key factors for competitive success?* An industry's key success factors (KSFs) are the particular strategy elements, product attributes, operational approaches, resources, and competitive capabilities that all industry members must have in order to survive and prosper in the industry. For any industry, they can be deduced by answering three basic questions: (1) On what basis do buyers of the industry's product choose between the competing brands of sellers, (2) what resources and competitive capabilities must a company have to be competitively successful, and (3) what shortcomings are almost certain to put a company at a significant competitive disadvantage?
8. *Is the industry outlook conducive to good profitability?* The last step in industry analysis is summing up the results from applying each of the frameworks employed in answering questions 1 to 6: PESTEL, five forces analysis, driving forces, strategic group mapping, competitor analysis, and key success factors. Applying multiple lenses to the question of what the industry outlook looks like offers a more robust and nuanced answer. If the answers from each framework, seen as a whole, reveal that a company's profit prospects in that industry are above-average, then the industry environment is basically attractive *for that company.* What may look like an attractive environment for one company may appear to be unattractive from the perspective of a different company.

Clear, insightful diagnosis of a company's external situation is an essential first step in crafting strategies that are well matched to industry and competitive conditions. To do cutting-edge strategic thinking about the external environment, managers must know what questions to pose and what analytic tools to use in answering these questions. This is why this chapter has concentrated on suggesting the right questions to ask, explaining concepts and analytic approaches, and indicating the kinds of things to look for.

ASSURANCE OF LEARNING EXERCISES

connect
LO 2

1. Prepare a brief analysis of the coffee industry using the information provided on the industry trade association websites. Based upon the information provided on these websites, draw a five forces diagram for the coffee industry and briefly discuss the nature and strength of each of the five competitive forces.

connect
LO 3

2. Based on the strategic group map in Illustration Capsule 3.1, which producers are Yuengling & Son's closest competitors? Between which two strategic groups is competition the strongest? Why do you think no beer producers are positioned in the lower left corner of the map? Which company/strategic group faces the weakest competition from the members of other strategic groups?

LO 1, LO 4

3. The National Restaurant Association publishes an annual industry fact book that can be found at **www.restaurant.org**. Based on information in the latest report, does it appear that macro-environmental factors and the economic characteristics of the industry will present industry participants with attractive opportunities for growth and profitability? Explain.

EXERCISE FOR SIMULATION PARTICIPANTS

LO 1, LO 2, LO 3, LO 4

1. Which of the factors listed in Table 3.1 might have the most strategic relevance for your industry?
2. Which of the five competitive forces is creating the strongest competitive pressures for your company?
3. What are the "weapons of competition" that rival companies in your industry can use to gain sales and market share? See Table 3.2 to help you identify the various competitive factors.
4. What are the factors affecting the intensity of rivalry in the industry in which your company is competing? Use Figure 3.4 and the accompanying discussion to help you in pinpointing the specific factors most affecting competitive intensity. Would you characterize the rivalry and jockeying for better market position, increased sales, and market share among the companies in your industry as fierce, very strong, strong, moderate, or relatively weak? Why?
5. Are there any driving forces in the industry in which your company is competing? If so, what impact will these driving forces have? Will they cause competition to be more or less intense? Will they act to boost or squeeze profit margins? List at least two actions your company should consider taking in order to combat any negative impacts of the driving forces.
6. Draw a strategic group map showing the market positions of the companies in your industry. Which companies do you believe are in the most attractive position on the map? Which companies are the most weakly positioned? Which companies

do you believe are likely to try to move to a different position on the strategic group map?

7. What do you see as the key factors for being a successful competitor in your industry? List at least three.
8. Does your overall assessment of the industry suggest that industry rivals have sufficiently attractive opportunities for growth and profitability? Explain.

ENDNOTES

[1] Michael E. Porter, *Competitive Strategy* (New York: Free Press, 1980); Michael E. Porter, "The Five Competitive Forces That Shape Strategy," *Harvard Business Review* 86, no. 1 (January 2008), pp. 78–93.

[2] J. S. Bain, *Barriers to New Competition* (Cambridge, MA: Harvard University Press, 1956); F. M. Scherer, *Industrial Market Structure and Economic Performance* (Chicago: Rand McNally, 1971).

[3] C. A. Montgomery and S. Hariharan, "Diversified Expansion by Large Established Firms," *Journal of Economic Behavior & Organization* 15, no. 1 (January 1991).

[4] Mary Ellen Gordon and George R. Milne, "Selecting the Dimensions That Define Strategic Groups: A Novel Market-Driven Approach," *Journal of Managerial Issues* 11, no. 2 (Summer 1999), pp. 213–233.

[5] Avi Fiegenbaum and Howard Thomas, "Strategic Groups as Reference Groups: Theory, Modeling and Empirical Examination of Industry and Competitive Strategy," *Strategic Management Journal* 16 (1995), pp. 461–476; S. Ade Olusoga, Michael P. Mokwa, and Charles H. Noble, "Strategic Groups, Mobility Barriers, and Competitive Advantage," *Journal of Business Research* 33 (1995), pp. 153–164.

[6] B. Wernerfelt and C. Montgomery, "What Is an Attractive Industry?" *Management Science* 32, no. 10 (October 1986), pp. 1223–1230.

CHAPTER 4

Evaluating a Company's Resources, Capabilities, and Competitiveness

Learning Objectives

THIS CHAPTER WILL HELP YOU UNDERSTAND:

LO 1 How to take stock of how well a company's strategy is working.

LO 2 Why a company's resources and capabilities are centrally important in giving the company a competitive edge over rivals.

LO 3 How to assess the company's strengths and weaknesses in light of market opportunities and external threats.

LO 4 How a company's value chain activities can affect the company's cost structure and customer value proposition.

LO 5 How a comprehensive evaluation of a company's competitive situation can assist managers in making critical decisions about their next strategic moves.

A new strategy nearly always involves acquiring new resources and capabilities.

Laurence Capron and Will Mitchell – *INSEAD and University of Toronto Professors and Consultants*

Only firms who are able to continually build new strategic assets faster and cheaper than their competitors will earn superior returns over the long term.

C. C. Markides and P. J. Williamson – *London Business School Professors and Consultants*

The greatest achievement of the human spirit is to live up to one's opportunities and make the most of one's resources.

Luc de Clapiers – *Writer and Moralist*

Chapter 3 described how to use the tools of industry and competitor analysis to assess a company's external environment and lay the groundwork for matching a company's strategy to its external situation. This chapter discusses techniques for evaluating a company's internal situation, including its collection of resources and capabilities and the activities it performs along its value chain. Internal analysis enables managers to determine whether their strategy is likely to give the company a significant competitive edge over rival firms. Combined with external analysis, it facilitates an understanding of how to reposition a firm to take advantage of new opportunities and to cope with emerging competitive threats. The analytic spotlight will be trained on six questions:

1. How well is the company's present strategy working?
2. What are the company's most important resources and capabilities, and will they give the company a lasting competitive advantage over rival companies?
3. What are the company's strengths and weaknesses in relation to the market opportunities and external threats?
4. How do a company's value chain activities impact its cost structure and customer value proposition?
5. Is the company competitively stronger or weaker than key rivals?
6. What strategic issues and problems merit front-burner managerial attention?

In probing for answers to these questions, five analytic tools—resource and capability analysis, SWOT analysis, value chain analysis, benchmarking, and competitive strength assessment—will be used. All five are valuable techniques for revealing a company's competitiveness and for helping company managers match their strategy to the company's own particular circumstances.

QUESTION 1: HOW WELL IS THE COMPANY'S PRESENT STRATEGY WORKING?

In evaluating how well a company's present strategy is working, the best way to start is with a clear view of what the strategy entails. Figure 4.1 shows the key components of a single-business company's strategy. The first thing to examine is the company's

LO 1

How to take stock of how well a company's strategy is working.

competitive approach. What moves has the company made recently to attract customers and improve its market position—for instance, has it cut prices, improved the design of its product, added new features, stepped up advertising, entered a new geographic market, or merged with a competitor? Is it striving for a competitive advantage based on low costs or a better product offering? Is it concentrating on serving a broad spectrum of customers or a narrow market niche? The company's functional strategies in R&D, production, marketing, finance, human resources, information technology, and so on further characterize company strategy, as do any efforts to establish alliances with other enterprises.

The three best indicators of how well a company's strategy is working are (1) whether the company is achieving its stated financial and strategic objectives, (2) whether its financial performance is above the industry average, and (3) whether it is gaining customers and increasing its market share. Persistent shortfalls in meeting company performance targets and weak marketplace performance relative to rivals are reliable warning signs that the company has a weak strategy, suffers from poor strategy execution, or both. Specific indicators of how well a company's strategy is working include:

- Trends in the company's sales and earnings growth.
- Trends in the company's stock price.
- The company's overall financial strength.

FIGURE 4.1 Identifying the Components of a Single-Business Company's Strategy

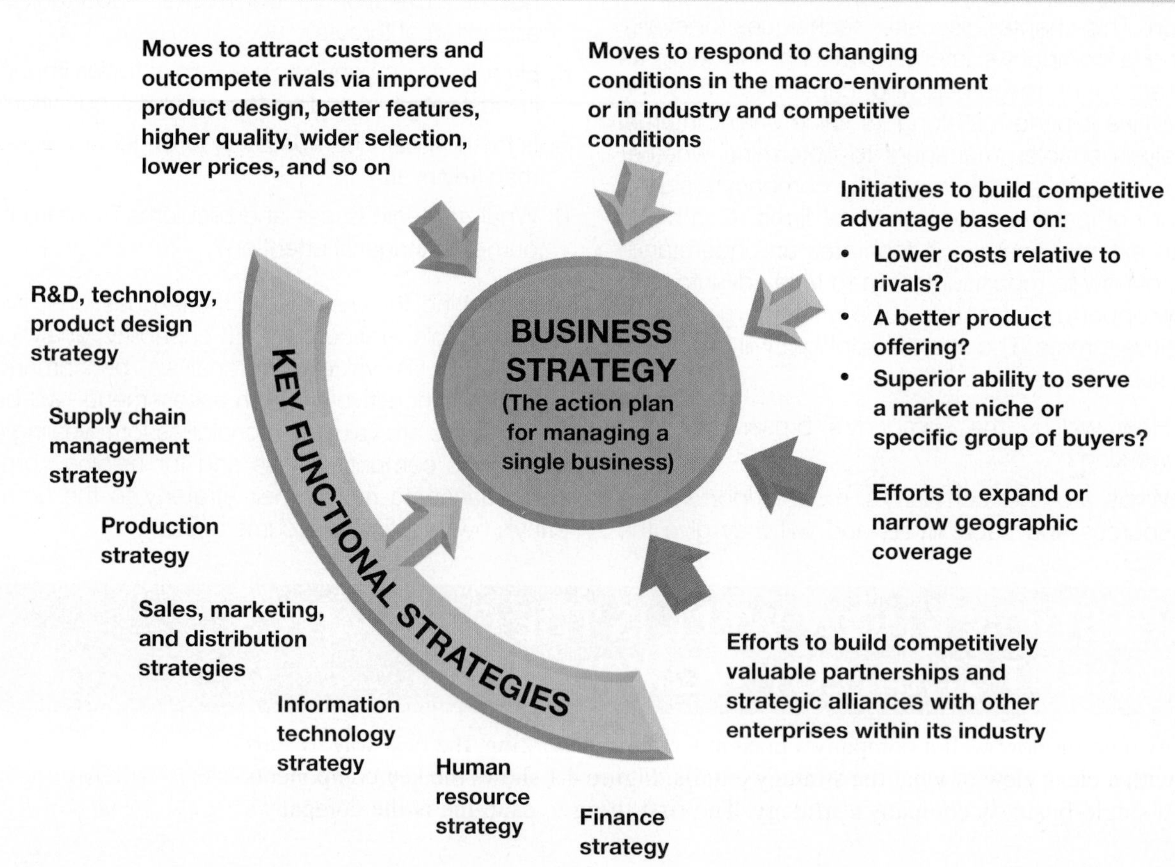

- The company's customer retention rate.
- The rate at which new customers are acquired.
- Evidence of improvement in internal processes such as defect rate, order fulfillment, delivery times, days of inventory, and employee productivity.

The stronger a company's current overall performance, the more likely it has a well-conceived, well-executed strategy. The weaker a company's financial performance and market standing, the more its current strategy must be questioned and the more likely the need for radical changes. Table 4.1 provides a compilation of the financial ratios most commonly used to evaluate a company's financial performance and balance sheet strength.

Sluggish financial performance and second-rate market accomplishments almost always signal weak strategy, weak execution, or both.

TABLE 4.1 Key Financial Ratios: How to Calculate Them and What They Mean

Ratio	How Calculated	What It Shows
Profitability ratios		
1. Gross profit margin	$\frac{\text{Sales revenues} - \text{Cost of goods sold}}{\text{Sales revenues}}$	Shows the percentage of revenues available to cover operating expenses and yield a profit.
2. Operating profit margin (or return on sales)	$\frac{\text{Sales revenues} - \text{Operating expenses}}{\text{Sales revenues}}$ *or* $\frac{\text{Operating income}}{\text{Sales revenues}}$	Shows the profitability of current operations without regard to interest charges and income taxes. Earnings before interest and taxes is known as *EBIT* in financial and business accounting.
3. Net profit margin (or net return on sales)	$\frac{\text{Profits after taxes}}{\text{Sales revenues}}$	Shows after-tax profits per dollar of sales.
4. Total return on assets	$\frac{\text{Profits after taxes} + \text{Interest}}{\text{Total assets}}$	A measure of the return on total investment in the enterprise. Interest is added to after-tax profits to form the numerator, since total assets are financed by creditors as well as by stockholders.
5. Net return on total assets (ROA)	$\frac{\text{Profits after taxes}}{\text{Total assets}}$	A measure of the return earned by stockholders on the firm's total assets.
6. Return on stockholders' equity (ROE)	$\frac{\text{Profits after taxes}}{\text{Total stockholders' equity}}$	The return stockholders are earning on their capital investment in the enterprise. A return in the 12%–15% range is average.
7. Return on invested capital (ROIC)—sometimes referred to as return on capital employed (ROCE)	$\frac{\text{Profits after taxes}}{\text{Long-term debt} + \text{Total stockholders' equity}}$	A measure of the return that shareholders are earning on the monetary capital invested in the enterprise. A higher return reflects greater bottom-line effectiveness in the use of long-term capital.
Liquidity ratios		
1. Current ratio	$\frac{\text{Current assets}}{\text{Current liabilities}}$	Shows a firm's ability to pay current liabilities using assets that can be converted to cash in the near term. Ratio should be higher than 1.0.

(continued)

TABLE 4.1 *(continued)*

Ratio	How Calculated	What It Shows
2. Working capital	Current assets − Current liabilities	The cash available for a firm's day-to-day operations. Larger amounts mean the company has more internal funds to (1) pay its current liabilities on a timely basis and (2) finance inventory expansion, additional accounts receivable, and a larger base of operations without resorting to borrowing or raising more equity capital.
Leverage ratios		
1. Total debt-to-assets ratio	$\frac{\text{Total debt}}{\text{Total assets}}$	Measures the extent to which borrowed funds (both short-term loans and long-term debt) have been used to finance the firm's operations. A low ratio is better—a high fraction indicates overuse of debt and greater risk of bankruptcy.
2. Long-term debt-to-capital ratio	$\frac{\text{Long-term debt}}{\text{Long-term debt} + \text{Total stockholders' equity}}$	A measure of creditworthiness and balance sheet strength. It indicates the percentage of capital investment that has been financed by both long-term lenders and stockholders. A ratio below 0.25 is preferable since the lower the ratio, the greater the capacity to borrow additional funds. Debt-to-capital ratios above 0.50 indicate an excessive reliance on long-term borrowing, lower creditworthiness, and weak balance sheet strength.
3. Debt-to-equity ratio	$\frac{\text{Total debt}}{\text{Total stockholders' equity}}$	Shows the balance between debt (funds borrowed both short term and long term) and the amount that stockholders have invested in the enterprise. The further the ratio is below 1.0, the greater the firm's ability to borrow additional funds. Ratios above 1.0 put creditors at greater risk, signal weaker balance sheet strength, and often result in lower credit ratings.
4. Long-term debt-to-equity ratio	$\frac{\text{Long-term debt}}{\text{Total stockholders' equity}}$	Shows the balance between long-term debt and stockholders' equity in the firm's *long-term* capital structure. Low ratios indicate a greater capacity to borrow additional funds if needed.
5. Times-interest-earned (or coverage) ratio	$\frac{\text{Operating income}}{\text{Interest expenses}}$	Measures the ability to pay annual interest charges. Lenders usually insist on a minimum ratio of 2.0, but ratios above 3.0 signal progressively better creditworthiness.
Activity ratios		
1. Days of inventory	$\frac{\text{Inventory}}{\text{Cost of goods sold} \div 365}$	Measures inventory management efficiency. Fewer days of inventory are better.
2. Inventory turnover	$\frac{\text{Cost of goods sold}}{\text{Inventory}}$	Measures the number of inventory turns per year. Higher is better.
3. Average collection period	$\frac{\text{Accounts receivable}}{\text{Total sales} \div 365}$ *or* $\frac{\text{Accounts receivable}}{\text{Average daily sales}}$	Indicates the average length of time the firm must wait after making a sale to receive cash payment. A shorter collection time is better.

(continued)

TABLE 4.1 *(concluded)*

Ratio	How Calculated	What It Shows
Other important measures of financial performance		
1. Dividend yield on common stock	$\frac{\text{Annual dividends per share}}{\text{Current market price per share}}$	A measure of the return that shareholders receive in the form of dividends. A "typical" dividend yield is 2%–3%. The dividend yield for fast-growth companies is often below 1%; the dividend yield for slow-growth companies can run 4%–5%.
2. Price-to-earnings (P/E) ratio	$\frac{\text{Current market price per share}}{\text{Earnings per share}}$	P/E ratios above 20 indicate strong investor confidence in a firm's outlook and earnings growth; firms whose future earnings are at risk or likely to grow slowly typically have ratios below 12.
3. Dividend payout ratio	$\frac{\text{Annual dividends per share}}{\text{Earnings per share}}$	Indicates the percentage of after-tax profits paid out as dividends.
4. Internal cash flow	After-tax profits + Depreciation	A rough estimate of the cash a company's business is generating after payment of operating expenses, interest, and taxes. Such amounts can be used for dividend payments or funding capital expenditures.
5. Free cash flow	After-tax profits + Depreciation − Capital expenditures − Dividends	A rough estimate of the cash a company's business is generating after payment of operating expenses, interest, taxes, dividends, and desirable reinvestments in the business. The larger a company's free cash flow, the greater its ability to internally fund new strategic initiatives, repay debt, make new acquisitions, repurchase shares of stock, or increase dividend payments.

QUESTION 2: WHAT ARE THE COMPANY'S MOST IMPORTANT RESOURCES AND CAPABILITIES, AND WILL THEY GIVE THE COMPANY A LASTING COMPETITIVE ADVANTAGE OVER RIVAL COMPANIES?

An essential element of deciding whether a company's overall situation is fundamentally healthy or unhealthy entails examining the attractiveness of its resources and capabilities. A company's resources and capabilities are its **competitive assets** and determine whether its competitive power in the marketplace will be impressively strong or disappointingly weak. Companies with second-rate competitive assets nearly always are relegated to a trailing position in the industry.

CORE CONCEPT

A company's resources and capabilities represent its **competitive assets** and are determinants of its competitiveness and ability to succeed in the marketplace.

Resource and capability analysis provides managers with a powerful tool for sizing up the company's competitive assets and determining whether they can provide the foundation necessary for competitive success in the marketplace. This is a two-step process. The first step is to identify the company's resources and

Resource and capability analysis is a powerful tool for sizing up a company's competitive assets and determining whether the assets can support a sustainable competitive advantage over market rivals.

capabilities. The second step is to examine them more closely to ascertain which are the most competitively important and whether they can support a sustainable competitive advantage over rival firms.[1] This second step involves applying the *four tests of a resource's competitive power.*

Identifying the Company's Resources and Capabilities

LO 2

Why a company's resources and capabilities are centrally important in giving the company a competitive edge over rivals.

A firm's resources and capabilities are the fundamental building blocks of its competitive strategy. In crafting strategy, it is essential for managers to know how to take stock of the company's full complement of resources and capabilities. But before they can do so, managers and strategists need a more precise definition of these terms.

In brief, a **resource** is a productive input or competitive asset that is owned or controlled by the firm. Firms have many different types of resources at their disposal that vary not only in kind but in quality as well. Some are of a higher quality than others, and some are more competitively valuable, having greater potential to give a firm a competitive advantage over its rivals. For example, a company's brand is a resource, as is an R&D team—yet some brands such as Coca-Cola and Kleenex are well known, with enduring value, while others have little more name recognition than generic products. In similar fashion, some R&D teams are far more innovative and productive than others due to the outstanding talents of the individual team members, the team's composition, its experience, and its chemistry.

CORE CONCEPT

A **resource** is a competitive asset that is owned or controlled by a company; a **capability** or **competence** is the capacity of a firm to perform some internal activity competently. Capabilities are developed and enabled through the deployment of a company's resources.

A **capability** is the capacity of a firm to perform some internal activity competently. Like resources, capabilities vary in form, quality, and competitive importance, with some being more competitively valuable than others. Apple's product innovation capabilities are widely recognized as being far superior to those of its competitors; Nordstrom is known for its superior incentive management capabilities; PepsiCo is admired for its marketing and brand management capabilities. *Organizational capabilities are developed and enabled through the deployment of a company's resources.*[2]

Types of Company Resources

A useful way to identify a company's resources is to look for them within categories, as shown in Table 4.2. Broadly speaking, resources can be divided into two main categories: **tangible** and **intangible** resources. Although *human resources* make up one of the most important parts of a company's resource base, we include them in the intangible category to emphasize the role played by the skills, talents, and knowledge of a company's human resources.

Tangible resources are the most easily identified, since tangible resources are those that can be *touched* or *quantified* readily. Obviously, they include various types of *physical resources* such as manufacturing facilities and mineral resources, but they also include a company's *financial resources, technological resources,* and *organizational resources* such as the company's communication and control systems. Note that technological resources are included among tangible resources, *by convention,* even though some types, such as copyrights and trade secrets, might be more logically categorized as intangible.

Intangible resources are harder to discern, but they are often among the most important of a firm's competitive assets. They include various sorts of *human assets and intellectual capital,* as well as a company's *brands, image, and reputational assets.* While intangible resources have no material existence on their own, they are often embodied in something material. Thus, the skills and knowledge resources of a firm

TABLE 4.2 Types of Company Resources

Tangible resources
• *Physical resources:* land and real estate; manufacturing plants, equipment, and/or distribution facilities; the locations of stores, plants, or distribution centers, including the overall pattern of their physical locations; ownership of or access rights to natural resources (such as mineral deposits)
• *Financial resources:* cash and cash equivalents; marketable securities; other financial assets such as a company's credit rating and borrowing capacity
• *Technological assets:* patents, copyrights, production technology, innovation technologies, technological processes
• *Organizational resources:* IT and communication systems (satellites, servers, workstations, etc.); other planning, coordination, and control systems; the company's organizational design and reporting structure
Intangible resources
• *Human assets and intellectual capital:* the education, experience, knowledge, and talent of the workforce, cumulative learning, and tacit knowledge of employees; collective learning embedded in the organization, the intellectual capital and know-how of specialized teams and work groups; the knowledge of key personnel concerning important business functions; managerial talent and leadership skill; the creativity and innovativeness of certain personnel
• *Brands, company image, and reputational assets:* brand names, trademarks, product or company image, buyer loyalty and goodwill; company reputation for quality, service, and reliability; reputation with suppliers and partners for fair dealing
• *Relationships:* alliances, joint ventures, or partnerships that provide access to technologies, specialized know-how, or geographic markets; networks of dealers or distributors; the trust established with various partners
• *Company culture and incentive system:* the norms of behavior, business principles, and ingrained beliefs within the company; the attachment of personnel to the company's ideals; the compensation system and the motivation level of company personnel

are embodied in its managers and employees; a company's brand name is embodied in the company logo or product labels. Other important kinds of intangible resources include a company's *relationships* with suppliers, buyers, or partners of various sorts, and the *company's culture and incentive system.* A more detailed listing of the various types of tangible and intangible resources is provided in Table 4.2.

Listing a company's resources category by category can prevent managers from inadvertently overlooking some company resources that might be competitively important. At times, it can be difficult to decide exactly how to categorize certain types of resources. For example, resources such as a work group's specialized expertise in developing innovative products can be considered to be technological assets or human assets or intellectual capital and knowledge assets; the work ethic and drive of a company's workforce could be included under the company's human assets or its culture and incentive system. In this regard, it is important to remember that *it is not exactly how a resource is categorized that matters but, rather, that all of the company's different types of resources are included in the inventory.* The real purpose of using categories in identifying a company's resources is *to ensure that none of a company's resources go unnoticed when sizing up the company's competitive assets.*

Identifying Capabilities Organizational capabilities are more complex entities than resources; indeed, they are built up through the use of resources and draw on some combination of the firm's resources as they are exercised. Virtually all organizational capabilities are *knowledge-based, residing in people and in a company's intellectual capital, or in organizational processes and systems, which embody tacit knowledge.* For example, Procter & Gamble's brand management capabilities draw on the knowledge of the company's brand managers, the expertise of its marketing department, and the company's relationships with retailers, since brand building is a cooperative activity requiring retailer support. The video game design capabilities for which Electronic Arts is known derive from the creative talents and technological expertise of its highly talented game developers, the company's culture of creativity, and a compensation system that generously rewards talented developers for creating best-selling video games.

Because of their complexity, capabilities are harder to categorize than resources and more challenging to search for as a result. There are, however, two approaches that can make the process of uncovering and identifying a firm's capabilities more systematic. The first method takes the completed listing of a firm's resources as its starting point. Since capabilities are built from resources and utilize resources as they are exercised, a firm's resources can provide a strong set of clues about the types of capabilities the firm is likely to have accumulated. This approach simply involves looking over the firm's resources and considering whether (and to what extent) the firm has built up any related capabilities. So, for example, a fleet of trucks, the latest RFID tracking technology, and a set of large automated distribution centers may be indicative of sophisticated capabilities in logistics and distribution. R&D teams composed of top scientists with expertise in genomics may suggest organizational capabilities in developing new gene therapies or in biotechnology more generally.

The second method of identifying a firm's capabilities takes a functional approach. Many capabilities relate to fairly specific functions; these draw on a limited set of resources and typically involve a single department or organizational unit. Capabilities in injection molding or continuous casting or metal stamping are manufacturing-related; capabilities in direct selling, promotional pricing, or database marketing all connect to the sales and marketing functions; capabilities in basic research, strategic innovation, or new product development link to a company's R&D function. This approach requires managers to survey the various functions a firm performs to find the different capabilities associated with each function.

A problem with this second method is that many of the most important capabilities of firms are inherently *cross-functional.* Cross-functional capabilities draw on a number of different kinds of resources and are multidimensional in nature—they spring from the effective collaboration among people with different types of expertise working in different organizational units. An example is Nike's cross-functional design process, spanning R&D activities, marketing research efforts, styling expertise, and manufacturing. Cross-functional capabilities and other complex capabilities involving numerous linked and closely integrated competitive assets are sometimes referred to as **resource bundles.**

> **CORE CONCEPT**
>
> A **resource bundle** is a linked and closely integrated set of competitive assets centered around one or more cross-functional capabilities.

It is important not to miss identifying a company's resource bundles, since they can be the most competitively important of a firm's competitive assets. Resource bundles can sometimes pass the four tests of a resource's competitive power (described below) even when the individual components of the resource bundle cannot. For example, although Callaway Golf Company's engineering capabilities and market research capabilities are matched relatively well by rivals Cobra Golf and Ping Golf, the company's bundling of resources used in its product development process (including cross-functional development systems, technological capabilities, knowledge of consumer preferences, and a collaborative organizational culture) gives it a competitive advantage that has allowed it to remain the largest seller of golf equipment for more than a decade.

Assessing the Competitive Power of a Company's Resources and Capabilities

To assess their competitive power, one must go beyond merely identifying a company's resources and capabilities to probe their *caliber.*[3] Thus, the second step in resource and capability analysis is designed to ascertain which of a company's resources and capabilities are competitively superior and to what extent they can support a company's quest for a sustainable competitive advantage over market rivals. When a company has competitive assets that are central to its strategy and superior to those of rival firms, they can support a competitive advantage, as defined in Chapter 1. If this advantage proves durable *despite the best efforts of competitors to overcome it,* then the company is said to have a ***sustainable* competitive advantage.** While it may be difficult for a company to achieve a sustainable competitive advantage, it is an important strategic objective because it imparts a potential for attractive and long-lived profitability.

The Four Tests of a Resource's Competitive Power The competitive power of a resource or capability is measured by how many of four specific tests it can pass.[4] These tests are referred to as the **VRIN tests for sustainable competitive advantage**—*VRIN* is a shorthand reminder standing for *Valuable, Rare, Inimitable,* and *Nonsubstitutable.* The first two tests determine whether a resource or capability can support a competitive advantage. The last two determine whether the competitive advantage can be sustained.

> **CORE CONCEPT**
>
> The **VRIN tests for sustainable competitive advantage** ask whether a resource is Valuable, Rare, Inimitable, and Nonsubstitutable.

1. *Is the resource or capability competitively **Valuable?*** To be competitively valuable, a resource or capability must be directly relevant to the company's strategy, making the company a more effective competitor. Unless the resource or capability contributes to the effectiveness of the company's strategy, it cannot pass this first test. An indicator of its effectiveness is whether the resource enables the company to strengthen its business model by improving its customer value proposition and/or profit formula (see Chapter 1). Companies have to guard against contending that something they do well is necessarily competitively valuable. Apple's operating system for its personal computers by some accounts is superior to Microsoft's Windows 8, but Apple has failed in converting its resources devoted to operating system design into anything more than moderate competitive success in the global PC market.
2. *Is the resource or capability **Rare**—is it something rivals lack?* Resources and capabilities that are common among firms and widely available cannot be a source of competitive advantage. All makers of branded cereals have valuable marketing capabilities and brands, since the key success factors in the ready-to-eat cereal industry demand this. They are not rare. However, the brand strength of Oreo cookies is uncommon and has provided Kraft Foods with greater market share as well as the opportunity to benefit from brand extensions such as Double Stuf Oreos and Mini Oreos. A resource or capability is considered rare if it is held by only a small number of firms in an industry or specific competitive domain. Thus, while general management capabilities are not rare in an absolute sense, they are relatively rare in some of the less developed regions of the world and in some business domains.

3. *Is the resource or capability* ***Inimitable****—is it hard to copy?* The more difficult and more costly it is for competitors to imitate a company's resource or capability, the more likely that it can also provide a *sustainable* competitive advantage. Resources and capabilities tend to be difficult to copy when they are unique (a fantastic real estate location, patent-protected technology, an unusually talented and motivated labor force), when they must be built over time in ways that are difficult to imitate (a well-known brand name, mastery of a complex process technology, years of cumulative experience and learning), and when they entail financial outlays or large-scale operations that few industry members can undertake (a global network of dealers and distributors). Imitation is also difficult for resources and capabilities that reflect a high level of *social complexity* (company culture, interpersonal relationships among the managers or R&D teams, trust-based relations with customers or suppliers) and *causal ambiguity*, a term that signifies the hard-to-disentangle nature of the complex resources, such as a web of intricate processes enabling new drug discovery. Hard-to-copy resources and capabilities are important competitive assets, contributing to the longevity of a company's market position and offering the potential for sustained profitability.

CORE CONCEPT

Social complexity and **causal ambiguity** are two factors that inhibit the ability of rivals to imitate a firm's most valuable resources and capabilities. Causal ambiguity makes it very hard to figure out how a complex resource contributes to competitive advantage and therefore exactly what to imitate.

4. *Is the resource or capability* ***Nonsubstitutable****—is it invulnerable to the threat of substitution from different types of resources and capabilities?* Even resources that are competitively valuable, rare, and costly to imitate may lose much of their ability to offer competitive advantage if rivals possess equivalent substitute resources. For example, manufacturers relying on automation to gain a cost-based advantage in production activities may find their technology-based advantage nullified by rivals' use of low-wage offshore manufacturing. Resources can contribute to a sustainable competitive advantage only when resource substitutes aren't on the horizon.

The vast majority of companies are not well endowed with standout resources or capabilities, capable of passing all four tests with high marks. Most firms have a mixed bag of resources—one or two quite valuable, some good, many satisfactory to mediocre. Resources and capabilities that are valuable pass the first of the four tests. As key contributors to the effectiveness of the strategy, they are relevant to the firm's competitiveness but are no guarantee of competitive advantage. They may offer no more than competitive parity with competing firms.

Passing both of the first two tests requires more—it requires resources and capabilities that are not only valuable but also rare. This is a much higher hurdle that can be cleared only by resources and capabilities that are *competitively superior.* Resources and capabilities that are competitively superior are the company's true strategic assets. They provide the company with a competitive advantage over its competitors, if only in the short run.

To pass the last two tests, a resource must be able to maintain its competitive superiority in the face of competition. It must be resistant to imitative attempts and efforts by competitors to find equally valuable substitute resources. Assessing the availability of substitutes is the most difficult of all the tests since substitutes are harder to recognize, but the key is to look for resources or capabilities held by other firms or being developed that *can serve the same function* as the company's core resources and capabilities.[5]

Very few firms have resources and capabilities that can pass all four tests, but those that do enjoy a sustainable competitive advantage with far greater profit potential. Walmart is a notable example, with capabilities in logistics and supply chain management that have surpassed those of its competitors for over 40 years. Lincoln Electric Company, less well known but no less notable in its achievements, has been the world leader in welding products for over 100 years as a result of its unique piecework incentive system for compensating production workers and the unsurpassed worker productivity and product quality that this system has fostered.

A Company's Resources and Capabilities Must Be Managed Dynamically Even companies like Walmart and Lincoln Electric cannot afford to rest on their laurels. Rivals that are initially unable to replicate a key resource may develop better and better substitutes over time. Resources and capabilities can depreciate like other assets if they are managed with benign neglect. Disruptive changes in technology, customer preferences, distribution channels, or other competitive factors can also destroy the value of key strategic assets, turning resources and capabilities "from diamonds to rust."[6]

A company requires a dynamically evolving portfolio of resources and capabilities to sustain its competitiveness and help drive improvements in its performance.

Resources and capabilities must be continually strengthened and nurtured to sustain their competitive power and, at times, may need to be broadened and deepened to allow the company to position itself to pursue emerging market opportunities.[7] Organizational resources and capabilities that grow stale can impair competitiveness unless they are refreshed, modified, or even phased out and replaced in response to ongoing market changes and shifts in company strategy. Management's challenge in managing the firm's resources and capabilities dynamically has two elements: (1) attending to the ongoing modification of existing competitive assets, and (2) casting a watchful eye for opportunities to develop totally new kinds of capabilities.

The Role of Dynamic Capabilities Companies that know the importance of recalibrating and upgrading their most valuable resources and capabilities ensure that these activities are done on a continual basis. By incorporating these activities into their routine managerial functions, they gain the experience necessary to be able to do them consistently well. At that point, their ability to freshen and renew their competitive assets becomes a capability in itself—a **dynamic capability.** A dynamic capability is the ability to modify, deepen, or augment the company's existing resources and capabilities.[8] This includes the capacity to improve existing resources and capabilities incrementally, in the way that Toyota aggressively upgrades the company's capabilities in fuel-efficient hybrid engine technology and constantly fine-tunes its famed Toyota production system. A dynamic capability also includes the capacity to add new resources and capabilities to the company's competitive asset portfolio. An example is Pfizer's acquisition capabilities, which have enabled it to replace degraded resources such as expiring patents with newly acquired capabilities in biotechnology.

CORE CONCEPT

A **dynamic capability** is an ongoing capacity of a company to modify its existing resources and capabilities or create new ones.

QUESTION 3: WHAT ARE THE COMPANY'S STRENGTHS AND WEAKNESSES IN RELATION TO THE MARKET OPPORTUNITIES AND EXTERNAL THREATS?

LO 3

How to assess the company's strengths and weaknesses in light of market opportunities and external threats.

In evaluating a company's overall situation, a key question is whether the company is in a position to pursue attractive market opportunities and defend against external threats to its future well-being. The simplest and most easily applied tool for conducting this examination is widely known as *SWOT analysis,* so named because it zeros in on a company's internal **S**trengths and **W**eaknesses, market **O**pportunities, and external **T**hreats. A first-rate SWOT analysis provides the basis for crafting a strategy that capitalizes on the company's strengths, overcomes its weaknesses, aims squarely at

SWOT analysis is a simple but powerful tool for sizing up a company's strengths and weaknesses, its market opportunities, and the external threats to its future well-being.

capturing the company's best opportunities, and defends against competitive and macro-environmental threats.

Identifying a Company's Internal Strengths

A **strength** is something a company is good at doing or an attribute that enhances its competitiveness in the marketplace. A company's strengths depend on the quality of its resources and capabilities. Resource and capability analysis provides a way for managers to assess the quality objectively. While resources and capabilities that pass the VRIN tests of sustainable competitive advantage are among the company's greatest strengths, other types can be counted among the company's strengths as well. A capability that is not potent enough to produce a sustainable advantage over rivals may yet enable a series of temporary advantages if used as a basis for entry into a new market or market segment. A resource bundle that fails to match those of top-tier competitors may still allow a company to compete successfully against the second tier.

Basing a company's strategy on its most competitively valuable strengths gives the company its best chance for market success.

Assessing a Company's Competencies—What Activities Does It Perform Well? One way to appraise the degree of a company's strengths has to do with the company's skill level in performing key pieces of its business—such as supply chain management, R&D, production, distribution, sales and marketing, and customer service. A company's skill or proficiency in performing different facets of its operations can range from the extreme of having minimal ability to perform an activity (perhaps having just struggled to do it the first time) to the other extreme of being able to perform the activity better than any other company in the industry.

CORE CONCEPT

A **competence** is an activity that a company has learned to perform with proficiency—a capability, in other words.

When a company's proficiency rises from that of mere ability to perform an activity to the point of being able to perform it consistently well and at acceptable cost, it is said to have a **competence**—a true *capability,* in other words. A **core competence** is a proficiently performed internal activity that is *central* to a company's strategy and competitiveness. A core competence is a more competitively valuable strength than a competence because of the activity's key role in the company's strategy and the contribution it makes to the company's market success and profitability. Often, core competencies can be leveraged to create new markets or new product demand, as the engine behind a company's growth. 3M Corporation has a core competence in product innovation—its record of introducing new products goes back several decades and new product introduction is central to 3M's strategy of growing its business.

CORE CONCEPT

A **core competence** is an activity that a company performs proficiently and that is also central to its strategy and competitive success.

A **distinctive competence** is a competitively valuable activity that a company *performs better than its rivals.* A distinctive competence thus signifies greater proficiency than a core competence. Because a distinctive competence represents a level of proficiency that rivals do not have, it qualifies as a *competitively superior strength* with competitive advantage potential. This is particularly true when the distinctive competence enables a company to deliver standout value to customers (in the form of lower prices, better product performance, or superior service). For instance, Walt Disney has a distinctive competence in feature film animation.

CORE CONCEPT

A **distinctive competence** is a competitively important activity that a company performs better than its rivals—it thus represents a *competitively superior internal strength.*

The conceptual differences between a competence, a core competence, and a distinctive competence draw attention to the fact that a company's strengths and competitive assets are not all equal.[9] All competencies have some value. But mere ability to perform an activity well does not necessarily give a company competitive clout. Some competencies merely enable market survival because most rivals also have them—indeed, not having a competence that rivals have can result in competitive *disadvantage.* An apparel manufacturer cannot survive without the capability to produce its apparel items very cost-efficiently, given the intensely price-competitive nature of the apparel industry. A maker of cell phones cannot survive without good product design and product innovation capabilities.

Identifying Company Weaknesses and Competitive Deficiencies

A **weakness,** or *competitive deficiency,* is something a company lacks or does poorly (in comparison to others) or a condition that puts it at a disadvantage in the marketplace. A company's internal weaknesses can relate to (1) inferior or unproven skills, expertise, or intellectual capital in competitively important areas of the business; (2) deficiencies in competitively important physical, organizational, or intangible assets; or (3) missing or competitively inferior capabilities in key areas. *Company weaknesses are thus internal shortcomings that constitute competitive liabilities.* Nearly all companies have competitive liabilities of one kind or another. Whether a company's internal weaknesses make it competitively vulnerable depends on how much they matter in the marketplace and whether they are offset by the company's strengths.

CORE CONCEPT

A company's **strengths** represent its competitive assets; its **weaknesses** are shortcomings that constitute competitive liabilities.

Table 4.3 lists many of the things to consider in compiling a company's strengths and weaknesses. Sizing up a company's complement of strengths and deficiencies is akin to constructing a *strategic balance sheet,* where strengths represent *competitive assets* and weaknesses represent *competitive liabilities.* Obviously, the ideal condition is for the company's competitive assets to outweigh its competitive liabilities by an ample margin—a 50-50 balance is definitely not the desired condition!

Identifying a Company's Market Opportunities

Market opportunity is a big factor in shaping a company's strategy. Indeed, managers can't properly tailor strategy to the company's situation without first identifying its market opportunities and appraising the growth and profit potential each one holds. Depending on the prevailing circumstances, a company's opportunities can be plentiful or scarce, fleeting or lasting, and can range from wildly attractive to marginally interesting to unsuitable. Table 4.3 displays a sampling of potential market opportunities.

Newly emerging and fast-changing markets sometimes present stunningly big or "golden" opportunities, but it is typically hard for managers at one company to peer into "the fog of the future" and spot them far ahead of managers at other companies.[10] But as the fog begins to clear, golden opportunities are nearly always seized rapidly—and the companies that seize them are usually those that have been actively waiting, staying alert with diligent market reconnaissance, and preparing themselves to capitalize on shifting market conditions by patiently assembling an arsenal of resources to enable aggressive action when the time comes. In mature markets, unusually attractive market opportunities emerge sporadically, often after long periods of relative calm—but future market conditions may be more predictable, making emerging opportunities easier for industry members to detect.

A company is well advised to pass on a particular market opportunity unless it has or can acquire the resources and capabilities needed to capture it.

In evaluating a company's market opportunities and ranking their attractiveness, managers have to guard against viewing every *industry* opportunity as a *company* opportunity. Rarely does a company have the resource depth to pursue all available market opportunities simultaneously without spreading itself too thin. Some

TABLE 4.3 What to Look for in Identifying a Company's Strengths, Weaknesses, Opportunities, and Threats

Potential Strengths and Competitive Assets	Potential Weaknesses and Competitive Deficiencies
• Competencies that are well matched to industry key success factors • Ample financial resources to grow the business • Strong brand-name image and/or company reputation • Economies of scale and/or learning- and experience-curve advantages over rivals • Other cost advantages over rivals • Attractive customer base • Proprietary technology, superior technological skills, important patents • Strong bargaining power over suppliers or buyers • Resources and capabilities that are valuable and rare • Resources and capabilities that are hard to copy and for which there are no good substitutes • Superior product quality • Wide geographic coverage and/or strong global distribution capability • Alliances and/or joint ventures that provide access to valuable technology, competencies, and/or attractive geographic markets	• No clear strategic vision • No well-developed or proven core competencies • No distinctive competencies or competitively superior resources • Lack of attention to customer needs • A product or service with features and attributes that are inferior to those of rivals • Weak balance sheet, short on financial resources to grow the firm, too much debt • Higher overall unit costs relative to those of key competitors • Too narrow a product line relative to rivals • Weak brand image or reputation • Weaker dealer network than key rivals and/or lack of adequate distribution capability • Lack of management depth • A plague of internal operating problems or obsolete facilities • Too much underutilized plant capacity • Resources that are readily copied or for which there are good substitutes
Potential Market Opportunities	**Potential External Threats to a Company's Future Profitability**
• Sharply rising buyer demand for the industry's product • Serving additional customer groups or market segments • Expanding into new geographic markets • Expanding the company's product line to meet a broader range of customer needs • Utilizing existing company skills or technological know-how to enter new product lines or new businesses • Falling trade barriers in attractive foreign markets • Acquiring rival firms or companies with attractive technological expertise or capabilities • Entering into alliances or joint ventures to expand the firm's market coverage or boost its competitive capability	• Increasing intensity of competition among industry rivals—may squeeze profit margins • Slowdowns in market growth • Likely entry of potent new competitors • Growing bargaining power of customers or suppliers • A shift in buyer needs and tastes away from the industry's product • Adverse demographic changes that threaten to curtail demand for the industry's product • Adverse economic conditions that threaten critical suppliers or distributors • Changes in technology—particularly disruptive technology that can undermine the company's distinctive competencies • Restrictive foreign trade policies • Costly new regulatory requirements • Tight credit conditions • Rising prices on energy or other key inputs

companies have resources and capabilities better-suited for pursuing some opportunities, and a few companies may be hopelessly outclassed in competing for any of an industry's attractive opportunities. *The market opportunities most relevant to a company are those that match up well with the company's competitive assets, offer the best prospects for growth and profitability, and present the most potential for competitive advantage.*

Identifying the Threats to a Company's Future Profitability

Often, certain factors in a company's external environment pose *threats* to its profitability and competitive well-being. Threats can stem from such factors as the emergence of cheaper or better technologies, the entry of lower-cost foreign competitors into a company's market stronghold, new regulations that are more burdensome to a company than to its competitors, unfavorable demographic shifts, and political upheaval in a foreign country where the company has facilities. Table 4.3 shows a representative list of potential threats.

External threats may pose no more than a moderate degree of adversity (all companies confront some threatening elements in the course of doing business), or they may be imposing enough to make a company's situation look tenuous. On rare occasions, market shocks can give birth to a *sudden-death* threat that throws a company into an immediate crisis and a battle to survive. Many of the world's major financial institutions were plunged into unprecedented crisis in 2008–2009 by the aftereffects of high-risk mortgage lending, inflated credit ratings on subprime mortgage securities, the collapse of housing prices, and a market flooded with mortgage-related investments (collateralized debt obligations) whose values suddenly evaporated. It is management's job to identify the threats to the company's future prospects and to evaluate what strategic actions can be taken to neutralize or lessen their impact.

Simply making lists of a company's strengths, weaknesses, opportunities, and threats is not enough; the payoff from SWOT analysis comes from the conclusions about a company's situation and the implications for strategy improvement that flow from the four lists.

What Do the SWOT Listings Reveal?

SWOT analysis involves more than making four lists. The two most important parts of SWOT analysis are *drawing conclusions* from the SWOT listings about the company's overall situation and *translating these conclusions into strategic actions* to better match the company's strategy to its internal strengths and market opportunities, to correct important weaknesses, and to defend against external threats. Figure 4.2 shows the steps involved in gleaning insights from SWOT analysis.

The final piece of SWOT analysis is to translate the diagnosis of the company's situation into actions for improving the company's strategy and business prospects. *A company's internal strengths should always serve as the basis of its strategy—placing heavy reliance on a company's best competitive assets is the soundest route to attracting customers and competing successfully against rivals.*[11] As a rule, strategies that place heavy demands on areas where the company is weakest or has unproven competencies should be avoided. Plainly, managers must look toward correcting competitive weaknesses that make the company vulnerable, hold down profitability, or disqualify it from pursuing an attractive opportunity. Furthermore, a company's strategy should be aimed squarely at capturing attractive market opportunities that are suited to the company's collection of capabilities. How much attention to devote to defending against external threats to the company's future performance hinges on how vulnerable the company is, whether defensive moves can be taken to lessen their impact, and whether the costs of undertaking such moves represent the best use of company resources.

FIGURE 4.2 The Steps Involved in SWOT Analysis: Identify the Four Components of SWOT, Draw Conclusions, Translate Implications into Strategic Actions

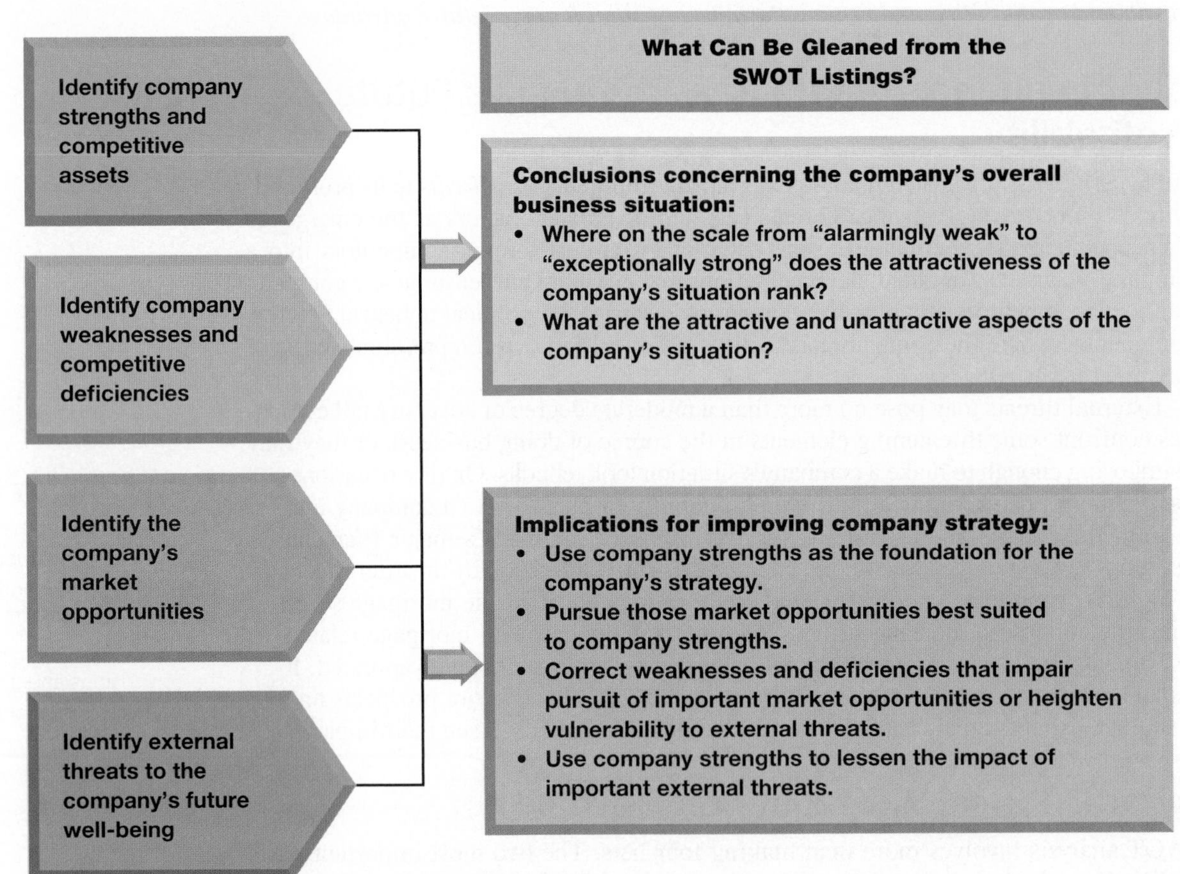

QUESTION 4: HOW DO A COMPANY'S VALUE CHAIN ACTIVITIES IMPACT ITS COST STRUCTURE AND CUSTOMER VALUE PROPOSITION?

LO 4

How a company's value chain activities can affect the company's cost structure and customer value proposition.

Company managers are often stunned when a competitor cuts its prices to "unbelievably low" levels or when a new market entrant introduces a great new product at a surprisingly low price. While less common, new entrants can also storm the market with a product that ratchets the quality level up so high that customers will abandon competing sellers even if they have to pay more for the new product. This is what seems to be happening with Apple's iPad in the market for e-readers and tablet PCs.

Regardless of where on the quality spectrum a company competes, it must remain competitive in terms of its customer value proposition in order to stay in the game.

Tiffany's value proposition, for example, remains attractive to customers who want customer service, the assurance of quality, and a high-status brand despite the availability of cut-rate diamond jewelry online. Target's customer value proposition has withstood the Walmart low-price juggernaut by attention to product design, image, and attractive store layouts in addition to efficiency.

The higher a company's costs are above those of close rivals, the more competitively vulnerable the company becomes.

The value provided to the customer depends on how well a customer's needs are met for the price paid. How well customer needs are met depends on the perceived quality of a product or service as well as on other, more tangible attributes. The greater the amount of customer value that the company can offer profitably compared to its rivals, the less vulnerable it will be to competitive attack. For managers, the key is to keep close track of how *cost effectively* the company can deliver value to customers relative to its competitors. If it can deliver the same amount of value with lower expenditures (or more value at the same cost), it will maintain a competitive edge.

The greater the amount of customer value that a company can offer profitably relative to close rivals, the less competitively vulnerable the company becomes.

Two analytic tools are particularly useful in determining whether a company's costs and customer value proposition are competitive: value chain analysis and benchmarking.

The Concept of a Company Value Chain

Every company's business consists of a collection of activities undertaken in the course of producing, marketing, delivering, and supporting its product or service. All the various activities that a company performs internally combine to form a **value chain**—so called because the underlying intent of a company's activities is ultimately to *create value for buyers.*

CORE CONCEPT

A company's **value chain** identifies the primary activities and related support activities that create customer value.

As shown in Figure 4.3, a company's value chain consists of two broad categories of activities: the *primary activities* foremost in creating value for customers and the requisite *support activities* that facilitate and enhance the performance of the primary activities.[12] The exact natures of the primary and secondary activities that make up a company's value chain vary according to the specifics of a company's business; hence, the listing of the primary and support activities in Figure 4.3 is illustrative rather than definitive. For example, the primary activities at a hotel operator like Starwood Hotels and Resorts mainly consist of site selection and construction, reservations, and hotel operations (check-in and check-out, maintenance and housekeeping, dining and room service, and conventions and meetings); principal support activities that drive costs and impact customer value include hiring and training hotel staff and handling general administration. Supply chain management is a crucial activity for Nissan and Amazon.com but is not a value chain component of Facebook or Twitter. Sales and marketing are dominant activities at Procter & Gamble and Sony but have only minor roles at CBS and Bain Capital.

With its focus on value-creating activities, the value chain is an ideal tool for examining the workings of a company's customer value proposition and business model. It permits a deep look at the company's cost structure and ability to offer low prices. It reveals the emphasis that a company places on activities that enhance differentiation and support higher prices, such as service and marketing. It also includes a profit margin component, since profits are necessary to compensate the company's owners and investors, who bear risks and provide capital. Tracking the profit margin along with the value-creating activities is critical because unless an enterprise succeeds in delivering customer value profitably (with a sufficient return on invested capital), it can't survive for long. Attention to a company's profit formula

FIGURE 4.3 A Representative Company Value Chain

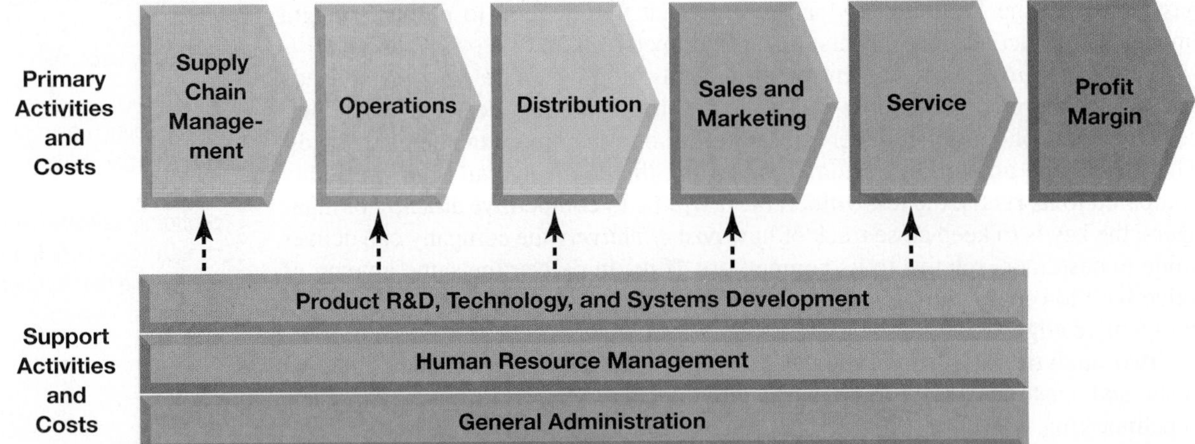

PRIMARY ACTIVITIES

- **Supply Chain Management**—Activities, costs, and assets associated with purchasing fuel, energy, raw materials, parts and components, merchandise, and consumable items from vendors; receiving, storing, and disseminating inputs from suppliers; inspection; and inventory management.
- **Operations**—Activities, costs, and assets associated with converting inputs into final product form (production, assembly, packaging, equipment maintenance, facilities, operations, quality assurance, environmental protection).
- **Distribution**—Activities, costs, and assets dealing with physically distributing the product to buyers (finished goods warehousing, order processing, order picking and packing, shipping, delivery vehicle operations, establishing and maintaining a network of dealers and distributors).
- **Sales and Marketing**—Activities, costs, and assets related to sales force efforts, advertising and promotion, market research and planning, and dealer/distributor support.
- **Service**—Activities, costs, and assets associated with providing assistance to buyers, such as installation, spare parts delivery, maintenance and repair, technical assistance, buyer inquiries, and complaints.

SUPPORT ACTIVITIES

- **Product R&D, Technology, and Systems Development**—Activities, costs, and assets relating to product R&D, process R&D, process design improvement, equipment design, computer software development, telecommunications systems, computer-assisted design and engineering, database capabilities, and development of computerized support systems.
- **Human Resource Management**—Activities, costs, and assets associated with the recruitment, hiring, training, development, and compensation of all types of personnel; labor relations activities; and development of knowledge-based skills and core competencies.
- **General Administration**—Activities, costs, and assets relating to general management, accounting and finance, legal and regulatory affairs, safety and security, management information systems, forming strategic alliances and collaborating with strategic partners, and other “overhead” functions.

Source: Based on the discussion in Michael E. Porter, *Competitive Advantage* (New York: Free Press, 1985), pp. 37–43.

ILLUSTRATION CAPSULE 4.1

American Giant: Using the Value Chain to Compare Costs of Producing a Hoodie in the U.S. and Asia

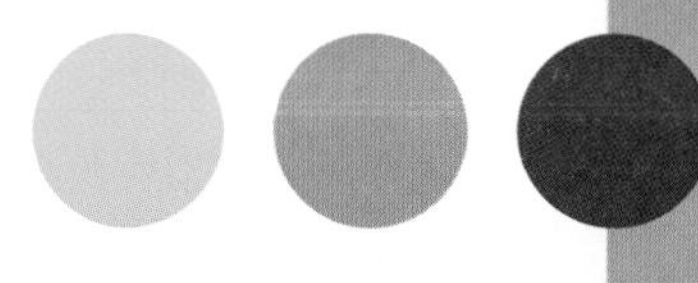

American Giant Clothing Company claims to make the world's best hooded sweatshirt, and it makes them in American plants, despite the higher cost of U.S production, as shown below. Why is this a good choice for the company? Because costs are not the only thing that matters. American Giant's proximity to its factories allows for better communication and control, better quality monitoring, and faster production cycles. This in turn has led to a much higher-quality product—so much higher that the company is selling far more hoodies than it could if it produced lower-cost, lower-quality products overseas. Demand has soared for its hoodies, and American Giant's reputation has soared along with it, giving the company a strong competitive advantage in the hoodie market.

American Giant's Value Chain Activities and Costs in Producing and Selling a Hoodie Sweatshirt: U.S. versus Asian production

	U.S.	Asia
1. Fabric (Highly automated plants make the spinning, knitting, and dyeing of cotton cheaper for American Giant's U.S. suppliers.)	$17.40	$18.40
2. Trim and hardware	3.20	2.30
3. Labor (Without highly automated sweatshirt manufacture, U.S. labor costs would be even higher.)	17.00	5.50
4. Duty	0.00	3.50
5. Shipping (Shipping from overseas is more expensive and takes longer.)	0.50	1.70
6. Total company costs	$38.10	$31.40
7. Wholesale markup over company costs (company operating profit)	41.90	48.60
8. Retail price (American Giant sells online to keep the price lower by avoiding middlemen and their markups.)	$80.00	$80.00

Source: Stephanie Clifford, "U.S. Textile Plants Return, with Floors Largely Empty of People," *The New York Times,* Business Day, September 19, 2013, www.nytimes.com/2013/09/20/business/us-textile-factories-return.html?emc=eta1&_r=0 (accessed February 14, 2014).

in addition to its customer value proposition is the essence of a sound business model, as described in Chapter 1.

Illustration Capsule 4.1 shows representative costs for various activities performed by American Giant, a maker of high-quality sweatshirts, in producing at either U.S. or Asian plants.

Comparing the Value Chains of Rival Companies Value chain analysis facilitates a comparison of how rivals, activity by activity, deliver value to customers. Even rivals in the same industry may differ significantly in terms of the activities they perform. For instance, the "operations" component of the value chain for a manufacturer that makes all of its own parts and components and assembles them into a finished product differs from the "operations" of a rival producer that buys the needed parts and components from outside suppliers and performs only assembly operations. How each activity is performed may affect a company's relative cost position as well as its capacity for differentiation. Thus, even a simple comparison of how the activities of rivals' value chains differ can reveal competitive differences.

A Company's Primary and Secondary Activities Identify the Major Components of Its Internal Cost Structure The combined costs of all the various primary and support activities constituting a company's value chain define its internal cost structure. Further, the cost of each activity contributes to whether the company's overall cost position relative to rivals is favorable or unfavorable. Key purposes of value chain analysis and benchmarking are to develop the data for comparing a company's costs activity by activity against the costs of key rivals and to learn which internal activities are a source of cost advantage or disadvantage.

A company's cost competitiveness depends not only on the costs of internally performed activities (its own value chain) but also on costs in the value chains of its suppliers and distribution-channel allies.

Evaluating a company's cost competitiveness involves using what accountants call *activity-based costing* to determine the costs of performing each value chain activity.[13] The degree to which a company's total costs should be broken down into costs for specific activities depends on how valuable it is to know the costs of specific activities versus broadly defined activities. At the very least, cost estimates are needed for each broad category of primary and support activities, but cost estimates for more specific activities within each broad category may be needed if a company discovers that it has a cost disadvantage vis-à-vis rivals and wants to pin down the exact source or activity causing the cost disadvantage. However, a company's own *internal costs* may be insufficient to assess whether its product offering and customer value proposition are competitive with those of rivals. Cost and price differences among competing companies can have their origins in activities suppliers perform or through distribution allies involved in getting the product to the final customer or end user, in which case the company's entire *value chain system* becomes relevant.

The Value Chain System

A company's value chain is embedded in a larger system of activities that includes the suppliers' value chains and the value chains of whatever wholesale distributors and retailers it uses in getting its product or service to end users. This *value chain system* has implications that extend far beyond the company's costs. It can affect attributes like product quality that enhance differentiation and have importance for the company's customer value proposition, as well as its profitability.[14] Suppliers' value chains are relevant because suppliers perform activities and incur costs in creating and delivering the purchased inputs utilized in a company's own value-creating activities. The costs, performance features, and quality of these inputs influence a company's own costs and product differentiation capabilities. Anything a company can do to help its suppliers drive down the costs of their value chain activities or improve the quality and performance of the items being supplied can enhance its own competitiveness—a powerful reason for working collaboratively with suppliers in managing supply chain activities.[15]

Similarly, the value chains of a company's distribution-channel partners are relevant because (1) the costs and margins of a company's distributors and retail dealers are part of the price the ultimate consumer pays and (2) the activities that distribution allies perform affect sales volumes and customer satisfaction. For these reasons, companies normally work closely with their distribution allies (who are their direct customers) to perform value chain activities in mutually beneficial ways. For instance, motor vehicle manufacturers have a competitive interest in working closely with their automobile dealers to promote higher sales volumes and better customer satisfaction with dealers' repair and maintenance services. Producers of kitchen cabinets are heavily dependent on the sales and promotional activities of their distributors and building supply retailers and on whether distributors and retailers operate cost-effectively enough to be able to sell at prices that lead to attractive sales volumes.

As a consequence, *accurately assessing a company's competitiveness entails scrutinizing the nature and costs of value chain activities throughout the entire value chain system for delivering its products or services to end-use customers.* A typical value chain system that incorporates the value chains of suppliers and forward-channel allies (if any) is shown in Figure 4.4. As was the case with company value chains, the specific activities constituting value chain systems vary significantly from industry to industry. The primary value chain system activities in the pulp and paper industry (timber farming, logging, pulp mills, and papermaking) differ from the primary value chain system activities in the home appliance industry (parts and components manufacture, assembly, wholesale distribution, retail sales) and yet again from the computer software industry (programming, disk loading, marketing, distribution).

Benchmarking: A Tool for Assessing Whether the Costs and Effectiveness of a Company's Value Chain Activities Are in Line

CORE CONCEPT

Benchmarking is a potent tool for improving a company's own internal activities that is based on learning how other companies perform them and borrowing their "best practices."

Benchmarking entails comparing how different companies (and *different types* of companies) perform various value chain activities—how materials are purchased, how inventories are managed, how products are assembled, how fast the company can get new products to market, how customer orders are filled and shipped—and then making cross-company comparisons of the costs and effectiveness of these

FIGURE 4.4 A Representative Value Chain System

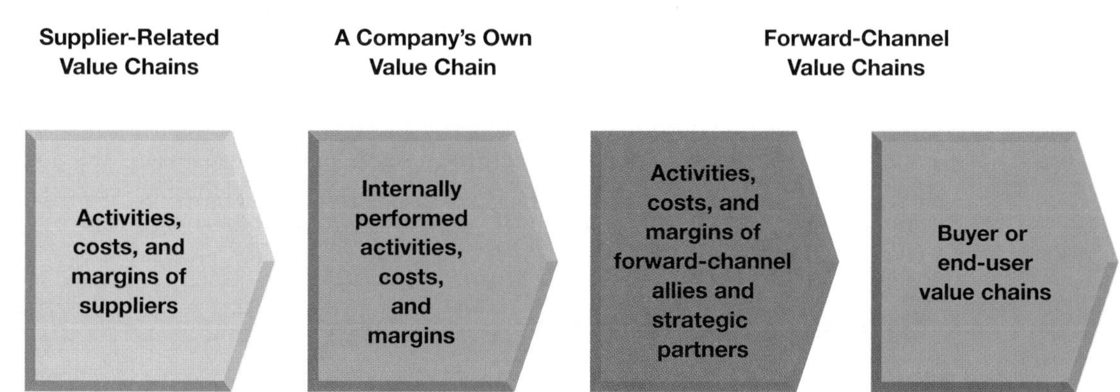

Source: Based in part on the single-industry value chain displayed in Michael E. Porter, *Competitive Advantage* (New York: Free Press, 1985), p. 35.

activities.[16] The objectives of benchmarking are to identify the best practices in performing an activity and to emulate those best practices.

CORE CONCEPT

A **best practice** is a method of performing an activity that consistently delivers superior results compared to other approaches.

A **best practice** is a method of performing an activity or business process that consistently delivers superior results compared to other approaches.[17] To qualify as a legitimate best practice, the method must have been employed by at least one enterprise and shown to be *unusually effective* in lowering costs, improving quality or performance, shortening time requirements, enhancing safety, or achieving some other highly positive operating outcome. Best practices thus identify a path to operating excellence with respect to value chain activities.

Xerox led the way in the use of benchmarking to become more cost-competitive, quickly deciding not to restrict its benchmarking efforts to its office equipment rivals but to extend them to *any company regarded as "world class"* in performing *any activity* relevant to Xerox's business. Other companies quickly picked up on Xerox's approach. Toyota managers got their idea for just-in-time inventory deliveries by studying how U.S. supermarkets replenished their shelves. Southwest Airlines reduced the turnaround time of its aircraft at each scheduled stop by studying pit crews on the auto racing circuit. More than 80 percent of Fortune 500 companies reportedly use benchmarking for comparing themselves against rivals on cost and other competitively important measures.

The tough part of benchmarking is not whether to do it but, rather, how to gain access to information about other companies' practices and costs. Sometimes benchmarking can be accomplished by collecting information from published reports, trade groups, and industry research firms or by talking to knowledgeable industry analysts, customers, and suppliers. Sometimes field trips to the facilities of competing or noncompeting companies can be arranged to observe how things are done, compare practices and processes, and perhaps exchange data on productivity and other cost components. However, such companies, even if they agree to host facilities tours and answer questions, are unlikely to share competitively sensitive cost information. Furthermore, comparing two companies' costs may not involve comparing apples to apples if the two companies employ different cost accounting principles to calculate the costs of particular activities.

Benchmarking the costs of company activities against those of rivals provides hard evidence of whether a company is cost-competitive.

However, a third and fairly reliable source of benchmarking information has emerged. The explosive interest in benchmarking costs and identifying best practices has prompted consulting organizations (e.g., Accenture, A. T. Kearney, Benchnet—The Benchmarking Exchange, and Best Practices, LLC) and several associations (e.g., the Qualserve Benchmarking Clearinghouse, and the Strategic Planning Institute's Council on Benchmarking) to gather benchmarking data, distribute information about best practices, and provide comparative cost data without identifying the names of particular companies. Having an independent group gather the information and report it in a manner that disguises the names of individual companies protects competitively sensitive data and lessens the potential for unethical behavior on the part of company personnel in gathering their own data about competitors. Illustration Capsule 4.2 describes benchmarking practices in the cement industry.

Strategic Options for Remedying a Cost or Value Disadvantage

The results of value chain analysis and benchmarking may disclose cost or value disadvantages relative to key rivals. Such information is vital in crafting strategic actions

ILLUSTRATION CAPSULE 4.2

Delivered-Cost Benchmarking in the Cement Industry

Cement is a dry powder that creates concrete when mixed with water and sand. People interact with concrete every day. It is often the building material of choice for sidewalks, curbs, basements, bridges, and municipal pipes. Cement is manufactured at billion-dollar continuous-process plants by mining limestone, crushing it, scorching it in a kiln, and then milling it again.

About 24 companies (CEMEX, Holcim, and Lafarge are some of the biggest) manufacture cement at 90 U.S. plants with the capacity to produce 110 million tons per year. Plants serve tens of markets distributed across multiple states. Companies regularly benchmark "delivered costs" to understand whether their plants are cost leaders or laggards.

Delivered-cost benchmarking studies typically subdivide manufacturing and logistics costs into five parts: fixed-bin, variable-bin, freight-to-terminal, terminal operating, and freight-to-customer costs. These cost components are estimated using different sources.

Fixed- and variable-bin costs represent the cost of making a ton of cement and moving it to the plant's storage silos. They are the hardest to estimate. Fortunately, the cement industry association PCA publishes key data for every plant that features plant location, age, capacity, technology, and fuel. Companies combine the industry data, satellite imagery revealing quarry characteristics, and news reports with the company's proprietary plant-level financial data to develop their estimates of competitors' costs. The basic assumption is that plants of similar size utilizing similar technologies and raw-material inputs will have similar cost performance.

Logistics costs (including freight-to-terminal, terminal operating, and freight-to-customer costs) are much easier to accurately estimate. Cement companies use common carriers to move their product by barge, train, and truck transit modes. Freight pricing is competitive on a per-mile basis by mode, meaning that the company's per-ton-mile barge cost applies to the competition. By combining the per-ton-mile cost with origin-destination distances, freight costs are easily calculated. Terminal operating costs, the costs of operating barge or rail terminals that store cement and transfer it to trucks for local delivery, represent the smallest fraction of total supply chain cost and typically vary little within mode type. For example, most barge terminals cost $10 per ton to run, whereas rail terminals are less expensive and cost $5 per ton.

By combining all five estimated cost elements, the company benchmarks its estimated relative cost position by market. Using this data, strategists can identify which of the company's plants are most exposed to volume fluctuations, which are in greatest need of investment or closure, which markets the company should enter or exit, and which competitors are the most likely candidates for product or asset swaps.

Note: Developed with Peter Jacobson.

Source: www.cement.org (accessed January 25, 2014).

to eliminate any such disadvantages and improve profitability. Information of this nature can also help a company to find new avenues for enhancing its competitiveness through lower costs or a more attractive customer value proposition. There are three main areas in a company's total value chain system where company managers can try to improve its efficiency and effectiveness in delivering customer value: (1) a company's own internal activities, (2) suppliers' part of the value chain system, and (3) the forward-channel portion of the value chain system.

Improving Internally Performed Value Chain Activities

Managers can pursue any of several strategic approaches to reduce the costs of internally performed value chain activities and improve a company's cost competitiveness. They can *implement best practices* throughout the company, particularly for high-cost activities. They can *redesign the product and/or some of its components* to eliminate high-cost components or facilitate speedier and more economical manufacture or assembly. They can *relocate high-cost activities* (such as manufacturing) to geographic areas where they can be performed more cheaply or *outsource activities* to lower-cost vendors or contractors.

To improve the effectiveness of the company's customer value proposition and enhance differentiation, managers can take several approaches. They can *adopt best practices for quality, marketing, and customer service.* They can *reallocate resources to activities that address buyers' most important purchase criteria,* which will have the biggest impact on the value delivered to the customer. They can *adopt new technologies that spur innovation, improve design, and enhance creativity.* Additional approaches to managing value chain activities to lower costs and/or enhance customer value are discussed in Chapter 5.

Improving Supplier-Related Value Chain Activities Supplier-related cost disadvantages can be attacked by pressuring suppliers for lower prices, switching to lower-priced substitute inputs, and collaborating closely with suppliers to identify mutual cost-saving opportunities.[18] For example, just-in-time deliveries from suppliers can lower a company's inventory and internal logistics costs and may also allow suppliers to economize on their warehousing, shipping, and production scheduling costs—a win-win outcome for both. In a few instances, companies may find that it is cheaper to integrate backward into the business of high-cost suppliers and make the item in-house instead of buying it from outsiders.

Similarly, a company can enhance its customer value proposition through its supplier relationships. Some approaches include selecting and retaining suppliers that meet higher-quality standards, providing quality-based incentives to suppliers, and integrating suppliers into the design process. Fewer defects in parts from suppliers not only improve quality throughout the value chain system but can lower costs as well since less waste and disruption occur in the production processes.

Improving Value Chain Activities of Distribution Partners Any of three means can be used to achieve better cost competitiveness in the forward portion of the industry value chain:

1. Pressure distributors, dealers, and other forward-channel allies to reduce their costs and markups.
2. Collaborate with them to identify win-win opportunities to reduce costs—for example, a chocolate manufacturer learned that by shipping its bulk chocolate in liquid form in tank cars instead of as 10-pound molded bars, it could not only save its candy bar manufacturing customers the costs associated with unpacking and melting but also eliminate its own costs of molding bars and packing them.
3. Change to a more economical distribution strategy, including switching to cheaper distribution channels (selling direct via the Internet) or integrating forward into company-owned retail outlets.

The means to enhancing differentiation through activities at the forward end of the value chain system include (1) engaging in cooperative advertising and promotions with forward allies (dealers, distributors, retailers, etc.), (2) creating exclusive arrangements with downstream sellers or utilizing other mechanisms that increase their incentives to enhance delivered customer value, and (3) creating and enforcing standards for downstream activities and assisting in training channel partners in business practices. Harley-Davidson, for example, enhances the shopping experience and perceptions of buyers by selling through retailers that sell Harley-Davidson motorcycles exclusively and meet Harley-Davidson standards.

Translating Proficient Performance of Value Chain Activities into Competitive Advantage

A company that does a *first-rate job* of managing its value chain activities *relative to competitors* stands a good chance of profiting from its competitive advantage. A company's value-creating activities can offer a competitive advantage in one of two ways (or both):

1. They can contribute to greater efficiency and lower costs relative to competitors.
2. They can provide a basis for differentiation, so customers are willing to pay relatively more for the company's goods and services.

Achieving a cost-based competitive advantage requires determined management efforts to be cost-efficient in performing value chain activities. Such efforts have to be ongoing and persistent, and they have to involve each and every value chain activity. The goal must be continuous cost reduction, not a one-time or on-again–off-again effort. Companies like Dollar General, Nucor Steel, Irish airline Ryanair, Greyhound Lines, and French discount retailer Carrefour have been highly successful in managing their value chains in a low-cost manner.

Ongoing and persistent efforts are also required for a competitive advantage based on differentiation. Superior reputations and brands are built up slowly over time, through continuous investment and activities that deliver consistent, reinforcing messages. Differentiation based on quality requires vigilant management of activities for quality assurance throughout the value chain. While the basis for differentiation (e.g., status, design, innovation, customer service, reliability, image) may vary widely among companies pursuing a differentiation advantage, companies that succeed do so on the basis of a commitment to coordinated value chain activities aimed purposefully at this objective. Examples include Grey Goose Vodka (status), IKEA (design), FedEx (reliability), 3M (innovation), and Nordstrom (customer service).

How Value Chain Activities Relate to Resources and Capabilities There is a close relationship between the value-creating activities that a company performs and its resources and capabilities. An organizational capability or competence implies a *capacity* for action; in contrast, a value-creating activity *initiates* the action. With respect to resources and capabilities, activities are "where the rubber hits the road." When companies engage in a value-creating activity, they do so by drawing on specific company resources and capabilities that underlie and enable the activity. For example, brand-building activities depend on human resources, such as experienced brand managers (including their knowledge and expertise in this arena), as well as organizational capabilities in advertising and marketing. Cost-cutting activities may derive from organizational capabilities in inventory management, for example, and resources such as inventory tracking systems.

Because of this correspondence between activities and supporting resources and capabilities, value chain analysis can complement resource and capability analysis as another tool for assessing a company's competitive advantage. Resources and capabilities that are *both valuable and rare* provide a company with *what it takes* for competitive advantage. For a company with competitive assets of this sort, the potential is there. When these assets are deployed in the form of a value-creating activity, that potential is realized due to their competitive superiority. Resource analysis is one tool for identifying competitively superior resources and capabilities. But their value and the competitive superiority of that value can be assessed objectively only *after* they are deployed. Value chain analysis and benchmarking provide the type of data needed to make that objective assessment.

Performing value chain activities with capabilities that permit the company to either outmatch rivals on differentiation or beat them on costs will give the company a competitive advantage.

There is also a dynamic relationship between a company's activities and its resources and capabilities. Value-creating activities are more than just the embodiment of a resource's or capability's potential. They also contribute to the formation and development of capabilities. The road to competitive advantage begins with management efforts to build organizational expertise in performing certain competitively important value chain activities. With consistent practice and continuous investment of company resources, these activities rise to the level of a reliable organizational capability or a competence. To the extent that top management makes the growing capability a cornerstone of the company's strategy, this capability becomes a core competence for the company. Later, with further organizational learning and gains in proficiency, the core competence may evolve into a distinctive competence, giving the company superiority over rivals in performing an important value chain activity. Such superiority, if it gives the company significant competitive clout in the marketplace, can produce an attractive competitive edge over rivals. Whether the resulting competitive advantage is on the cost side or on the differentiation side (or both) will depend on the company's choice of which types of competence-building activities to engage in over this time period.

QUESTION 5: IS THE COMPANY COMPETITIVELY STRONGER OR WEAKER THAN KEY RIVALS?

LO 5

How a comprehensive evaluation of a company's competitive situation can assist managers in making critical decisions about their next strategic moves.

Using resource analysis, value chain analysis, and benchmarking to determine a company's competitiveness on value and cost is necessary but not sufficient. A more comprehensive assessment needs to be made of the company's *overall* competitive strength. The answers to two questions are of particular interest: First, how does the company rank relative to competitors on each of the important factors that determine market success? Second, all things considered, does the company have a *net* competitive advantage or disadvantage versus major competitors?

An easy-to-use method for answering these two questions involves developing quantitative strength ratings for the company and its key competitors on each industry key success factor and each competitively pivotal resource, capability, and value chain activity. Much of the information needed for doing a competitive strength assessment comes from previous analyses. Industry and competitive analyses reveal the key success factors and competitive forces that separate industry winners from losers. Benchmarking data and scouting key competitors provide a basis for judging rivals' competitive strength on such factors as cost, key product attributes, customer service, image and reputation, financial strength, technological skills, distribution capability, and other factors. Resource and capability analysis reveals which of these are competitively important, given the external situation, and whether the company's competitive advantages are sustainable. SWOT analysis provides a more comprehensive and forward-looking picture of the company's overall situation.

Step 1 in doing a competitive strength assessment is to make a list of the industry's key success factors and other telling measures of competitive strength or weakness (6 to 10 measures usually suffice). Step 2 is to assign weights to each of the measures of competitive strength based on their perceived importance. (The sum of the weights for each measure must add up to 1.) Step 3 is to calculate weighted strength ratings by scoring each competitor on each strength measure (using a 1-to-10 rating scale, where 1 is very weak and 10 is very strong) and multiplying the assigned rating by the assigned weight. Step 4 is to sum the weighted strength ratings on each factor to get an overall measure of competitive strength for each company being rated. Step 5 is to use the overall strength ratings to draw conclusions about the size and extent of the company's net competitive advantage or disadvantage and to take specific note of areas of strength and weakness.

Table 4.4 provides an example of competitive strength assessment in which a hypothetical company (ABC Company) competes against two rivals. In the example, relative cost is the most telling measure of competitive strength, and the other strength measures are of lesser importance. The company with the highest rating on a given measure has an implied competitive edge on that measure, with the size of its edge reflected in the difference between its weighted rating and rivals' weighted ratings. For instance, Rival 1's 3.00 weighted strength rating on relative cost signals a considerable cost advantage over ABC Company (with a 1.50 weighted score on relative cost) and an even bigger cost advantage over Rival 2 (with a weighted score of 0.30). The measure-by-measure ratings reveal the competitive areas in which a company is strongest and weakest, and against whom.

The overall competitive strength scores indicate how all the different strength measures add up—whether the company is at a net overall competitive advantage or disadvantage against each rival. The higher a company's *overall weighted strength rating,* the stronger its *overall competitiveness* versus rivals. The bigger the difference between a company's overall weighted rating and the scores of *lower-rated* rivals, the greater is its implied *net competitive advantage.* Thus, Rival 1's overall weighted score of 7.70 indicates a greater net competitive advantage over Rival 2 (with a score of 2.10) than over ABC Company (with a score of 5.95). Conversely, the bigger the difference between a company's overall rating and the scores of *higher-rated* rivals, the greater its implied *net competitive disadvantage.* Rival 2's score of 2.10 gives it a smaller net competitive disadvantage against ABC Company (with an overall score of 5.95) than against Rival 1 (with an overall score of 7.70).

High-weighted competitive strength ratings signal a strong competitive position and possession of competitive advantage; low ratings signal a weak position and competitive disadvantage.

Strategic Implications of Competitive Strength Assessments

In addition to showing how competitively strong or weak a company is relative to rivals, the strength ratings provide guidelines for designing wise offensive and

TABLE 4.4 A Representative Weighted Competitive Strength Assessment

		Competitive Strength Assessment (rating scale: 1 = very weak, 10 = very strong)					
		ABC Co.		Rival 1		Rival 2	
Key Success Factor/Strength Measure	Importance Weight	Strength Rating	Weighted Score	Strength Rating	Weighted Score	Strength Rating	Weighted Score
Quality/product performance	0.10	8	0.80	5	0.50	1	0.10
Reputation/image	0.10	8	0.80	7	0.70	1	0.10
Manufacturing capability	0.10	2	0.20	10	1.00	5	0.50
Technological skills	0.05	10	0.50	1	0.05	3	0.15
Dealer network/ distribution capability	0.05	9	0.45	4	0.20	5	0.25
New product innovation capability	0.05	9	0.45	4	0.20	5	0.25
Financial resources	0.10	5	0.50	10	1.00	3	0.30
Relative cost position	0.30	5	1.50	10	3.00	1	0.30
Customer service capabilities	0.15	5	0.75	7	1.05	1	0.15
Sum of importance weights	**1.00**						
Overall weighted competitive strength rating			**5.95**		**7.70**		**2.10**

defensive strategies. For example, if ABC Company wants to go on the offensive to win additional sales and market share, such an offensive probably needs to be aimed directly at winning customers away from Rival 2 (which has a lower overall strength score) rather than Rival 1 (which has a higher overall strength score). Moreover, while ABC has high ratings for technological skills (a 10 rating), dealer network/distribution capability (a 9 rating), new product innovation capability (a 9 rating), quality/product performance (an 8 rating), and reputation/image (an 8 rating), these strength measures have low importance weights—meaning that ABC has strengths in areas that don't translate into much competitive clout in the marketplace. Even so, it outclasses Rival 2 in all five areas, plus it enjoys substantially lower costs than Rival 2 (ABC has a 5 rating on relative cost position versus a 1 rating for Rival 2)—and relative cost position carries the highest importance weight of all the strength measures. ABC also has greater competitive strength than Rival 3 regarding customer service capabilities (which carries the second-highest importance weight). Hence, because ABC's strengths are in the very areas where Rival 2 is weak, ABC is in a good position to attack Rival 2. Indeed, ABC may well be able to persuade a number of Rival 2's customers to switch their purchases over to its product.

A company's competitive strength scores pinpoint its strengths and weaknesses against rivals and point directly to the kinds of offensive and defensive actions it can use to exploit its competitive strengths and reduce its competitive vulnerabilities.

But ABC should be cautious about cutting price aggressively to win customers away from Rival 2, because Rival 1 could interpret that as an attack by ABC to win away Rival 1's customers as well. And Rival 1 is in far and away the best position to compete on the basis of low price, given its high rating on relative cost in an industry where low costs are competitively important (relative cost carries an importance weight of 0.30). Rival 1's strong relative cost position vis-à-vis both ABC and Rival 2 arms it with the ability to use its lower-cost advantage to thwart any price cutting on ABC's part. Clearly ABC is vulnerable to any retaliatory price cuts by Rival 1—Rival 1 can easily defeat both ABC and Rival 2 in a price-based battle for sales and market share. If ABC wants to defend against its vulnerability to potential price cutting by Rival 1, then it needs to aim a portion of its strategy at lowering its costs.

The point here is that a competitively astute company should utilize the strength scores in deciding what strategic moves to make. When a company has important competitive strengths in areas where one or more rivals are weak, it makes sense to consider offensive moves to exploit rivals' competitive weaknesses. When a company has important competitive weaknesses in areas where one or more rivals are strong, it makes sense to consider defensive moves to curtail its vulnerability.

QUESTION 6: WHAT STRATEGIC ISSUES AND PROBLEMS MERIT FRONT-BURNER MANAGERIAL ATTENTION?

The final and most important analytic step is to zero in on exactly what strategic issues company managers need to address—and resolve—for the company to be more financially and competitively successful in the years ahead. This step involves drawing on the results of both industry analysis and the evaluations of the company's internal situation. The task here is to get a clear fix on exactly what strategic and competitive challenges confront the company, which of the company's competitive shortcomings need fixing, and what specific problems merit company managers' front-burner attention. *Pinpointing the precise things that management needs to worry about sets the agenda for deciding what actions to take next to improve the company's performance and business outlook.*

Compiling a "worry list" of problems creates an agenda of strategic issues that merit prompt managerial attention.

The "worry list" of issues and problems that have to be wrestled with can include such things as *how* to stave off market challenges from new foreign competitors, *how* to combat the price discounting of rivals, *how* to reduce the company's high costs, *how* to sustain the company's present rate of growth in light of slowing buyer demand, *whether* to correct the company's competitive deficiencies by acquiring a rival company with the missing strengths, *whether* to expand into foreign markets, *whether* to reposition the company and move to a different strategic group, *what to do* about growing buyer interest in substitute products, and *what to do* to combat the aging demographics of the company's customer base. The worry list

A good strategy must contain ways to deal with all the strategic issues and obstacles that stand in the way of the company's financial and competitive success in the years ahead.

thus always centers on such concerns as "how to . . . ," "what to do about . . . ," and "whether to . . ."—the purpose of the worry list is to identify the specific issues and problems that management needs to address, not to figure out what specific actions to take. Deciding what to do—which strategic actions to take and which strategic moves to make—comes later (when it is time to craft the strategy and choose among the various strategic alternatives).

If the items on the worry list are relatively minor—which suggests that the company's strategy is mostly on track and reasonably well matched to the company's overall situation—company managers seldom need to go much beyond fine-tuning the present strategy. If, however, the problems confronting the company are serious and indicate the present strategy is not well suited for the road ahead, the task of crafting a better strategy needs to be at the top of management's action agenda.

KEY POINTS

There are six key questions to consider in evaluating a company's ability to compete successfully against market rivals:

1. *How well is the present strategy working?* This involves evaluating the strategy in terms of the company's financial performance and market standing. The stronger a company's current overall performance, the less likely the need for radical strategy changes. The weaker a company's performance and/or the faster the changes in its external situation (which can be gleaned from PESTEL and industry analysis), the more its current strategy must be questioned.
2. *Do the company's resources and capabilities have sufficient competitive power to give it a sustainable advantage over competitors?* The answer to this question comes from conducting the four tests of a resource's competitive power—the VRIN tests. If a company has resources and capabilities that are competitively *valuable* and *rare,* the firm will have a competitive advantage over market rivals. If its resources and capabilities are also hard to copy *(inimitable),* with no good substitutes *(nonsubstitutable),* then the firm may be able to sustain this advantage even in the face of active efforts by rivals to overcome it.
3. *Is the company able to seize market opportunities and overcome external threats to its future well-being?* The answer to this question comes from performing a SWOT analysis. The two most important parts of SWOT analysis are (1) drawing conclusions about what strengths, weaknesses, opportunities, and threats tell about the company's overall situation and (2) acting on the conclusions to better match the company's strategy to its internal strengths and market opportunities, to correct the important internal weaknesses, and to defend against external threats. A company's strengths and competitive assets are strategically relevant because they are the most logical and appealing building blocks for strategy; internal weaknesses are important because they may represent vulnerabilities that need correction. External opportunities and threats come into play because a good strategy necessarily aims at capturing a company's most attractive opportunities and at defending against threats to its well-being.
4. *Are the company's cost structure and value proposition competitive?* One telling sign of whether a company's situation is strong or precarious is whether its costs

are competitive with those of industry rivals. Another sign is how the company compares with rivals in terms of differentiation—how effectively it delivers on its customer value proposition. Value chain analysis and benchmarking are essential tools in determining whether the company is performing particular functions and activities well, whether its costs are in line with those of competitors, whether it is differentiating in ways that really enhance customer value, and whether particular internal activities and business processes need improvement. They complement resource and capability analysis by providing data at the level of individual activities that provides more objective evidence of whether individual resources and capabilities, or bundles of resources and linked activity sets, are competitively superior.

5. *On an overall basis, is the company competitively stronger or weaker than key rivals?* The key appraisals here involve how the company matches up against key rivals on industry key success factors and other chief determinants of competitive success and whether and why the company has a *net* competitive advantage or disadvantage. Quantitative competitive strength assessments, using the method presented in Table 4.4, indicate where a company is competitively strong and weak and provide insight into the company's ability to defend or enhance its market position. As a rule, a company's competitive strategy should be built around its competitive strengths and should aim at shoring up areas where it is competitively vulnerable. When a company has important competitive strengths in areas where one or more rivals are weak, it makes sense to consider offensive moves to exploit rivals' competitive weaknesses. When a company has important competitive weaknesses in areas where one or more rivals are strong, it makes sense to consider defensive moves to curtail its vulnerability.
6. *What strategic issues and problems merit front-burner managerial attention?* This analytic step zeros in on the strategic issues and problems that stand in the way of the company's success. It involves using the results of industry analysis as well as resource and value chain analysis of the company's competitive situation to identify a "worry list" of issues to be resolved for the company to be financially and competitively successful in the years ahead. Actually deciding on a strategy and what specific actions to take is what comes after the list of strategic issues and problems that merit front-burner management attention is developed.

Like good industry analysis, solid analysis of the company's competitive situation vis-à-vis its key rivals is a valuable precondition for good strategy making.

ASSURANCE OF LEARNING EXERCISES

1. Using the financial ratios provided in Table 4.1 and the financial statement information presented on pp. 110–112 for Costco Wholesale Corporation, calculate the following ratios for Costco for both 2012 and 2013: connect LO 1
   - **a.** Gross profit margin
   - **b.** Operating profit margin
   - **c.** Net profit margin
   - **d.** Times-interest-earned (or coverage) ratio

e. Return on stockholders' equity
f. Return on assets
g. Debt-to-equity ratio
h. Days of inventory
i. Inventory turnover ratio
j. Average collection period

Based on these ratios, did Costco's financial performance improve, weaken, or remain about the same from 2012 to 2013?

Consolidated Statements of Income for Costco Wholesale Corporation, 2012–2013 (in millions, except per share data)

	2013	2012
Revenue		
Net sales	$102,870	$97,062
Membership fees	2,286	2,075
Total revenue	105,156	99,137
Operating Expenses		
Merchandise costs	$ 91,948	$86,823
Selling, general, and administrative	10,104	9,518
Preopening expenses	51	37
Operating income	3,053	2,759
Other income (expense)		
Interest expense	(99)	(95)
Interest income and other, net	97	103
Income before income taxes	3,051	2,767
Provision for income taxes	990	1,000
Net income including noncontrolling interests	2,061	1,767
Net income attributable to noncontrolling interests	(22)	(58)
Net income attributable to Costco	$ 2,039	$ 1,709
Net income per common share attributable to Costco:		
Basic	$ 4.68	$ 3.94
Diluted	$ 4.63	$ 3.89
Shares used in calculation (000's)		
Basic	435,741	433,620
Diluted	440,512	439,373

Consolidated Balance Sheets for Costco Wholesale Corporation, 2012–2013 (in millions, except per share data)

	September 1, 2013	September 2, 2012
Assets		
Current Assets		
Cash and cash equivalents	$ 4,644	$ 3,528
Short-term investments	1,480	1,326
Receivables, net	1,201	1,026
Merchandise inventories	7,894	7,096
Deferred income taxes and other current assets	621	550
Total current assets	$15,840	$13,526
Property and Equipment		
Land	$ 4,409	$ 4,032
Buildings and improvements	11,556	10,879
Equipment and fixtures	4,472	4,261
Construction in progress	585	374
	21,022	19,546
Less accumulated depreciation and amortization	(7,141)	(6,585)
Net property and equipment	13,881	12,961
Other assets	562	653
Total assets	$30,283	$ 27,140
Liabilities and Equity		
Current Liabilities		
Accounts payable	$ 7,872	$ 7,303
Accrued salaries and benefits	2,037	1,832
Accrued member rewards	710	661
Accrued sales and other taxes	382	397
Deferred membership fees	1,167	1,101
Other current liabilities	1,089	966
Total current liabilities	13,257	12,260
Long-term debt, excluding current portion	4,998	1,381
Deferred income taxes and other liabilities	1,016	981

(continued)

Total liabilities	$19,271	$14,622
Commitments and Contingencies		
Equity		
Preferred stock $.005 par value; 100,000,000 shares authorized; no shares issued and outstanding	0	0
Common stock $.005 par value; 900,000,000 shares authorized; 436,839,000 and 432,350,000 shares issued and outstanding	2	2
Additional paid-in capital	$ 4,670	$ 4,369
Accumulated other comprehensive (loss) income	(122)	156
Retained earnings	6,283	7,834
Total Costco stockholders' equity	10,833	12,361
Noncontrolling interests	179	157
Total equity	11,012	12,518
Total Liabilities and Equity	$30,283	$27,140

Source: Costco Wholesale Corporation 2013 10-K.

LO 2, LO 3 2. Panera Bread operates more than 1,600 bakery-cafés in more than 44 states and Canada. How many of the four tests of the competitive power of a resource does the store network pass? Using your general knowledge of this industry, perform a SWOT analysis. Explain your answers.

connect

LO 4 3. Review the information in Illustration Capsule 4.1 concerning American Giant's average costs of producing and selling a hoodie sweatshirt, and compare this with the representative value chain depicted in Figure 4.3. Then answer the following questions:

   a. Which of the company's costs correspond to the primary value chain activities depicted in Figure 4.3?

   b. Which of the company's costs correspond to the support activities described in Figure 4.3?

   c. How would its various costs and activities differ if the company chose to produce its hoodies in Asia?

   d. What value chain activities might be important in securing or maintaining American Giant's competitive advantage? Explain your answer.

LO 5 4. Using the methodology illustrated in Table 4.3 and your knowledge as an automobile owner, prepare a competitive strength assessment for General Motors and its rivals Ford, Chrysler, Toyota, and Honda. Each of the five automobile manufacturers should be evaluated on the key success factors and strength measures of cost competitiveness, product-line breadth, product quality and reliability, financial resources and profitability, and customer service. What does your competitive strength assessment disclose about the overall competitiveness of each automobile manufacturer? What factors account most for Toyota's competitive success? Does Toyota have competitive weaknesses that were disclosed by your analysis? Explain.

EXERCISE FOR SIMULATION PARTICIPANTS

1. Using the formulas in Table 4.1 and the data in your company's latest financial statements, calculate the following measures of financial performance for your company: **LO 1**
    a. Operating profit margin
    b. Total return on total assets
    c. Current ratio
    d. Working capital
    e. Long-term debt-to-capital ratio
    f. Price-to-earnings ratio
2. On the basis of your company's latest financial statements and all the other available data regarding your company's performance that appear in the industry report, list the three measures of financial performance on which your company did best and the three measures on which your company's financial performance was worst. **LO 1**
3. What hard evidence can you cite that indicates your company's strategy is working fairly well (or perhaps not working so well, if your company's performance is lagging that of rival companies)? **LO 1**
4. What internal strengths and weaknesses does your company have? What external market opportunities for growth and increased profitability exist for your company? What external threats to your company's future well-being and profitability do you and your co-managers see? What does the preceding SWOT analysis indicate about your company's present situation and future prospects—where on the scale from "exceptionally strong" to "alarmingly weak" does the attractiveness of your company's situation rank? **LO 2, LO 3**
5. Does your company have any core competencies? If so, what are they? **LO 2, LO 3**
6. What are the key elements of your company's value chain? Refer to Figure 4.3 in developing your answer. **LO 4**
7. Using the methodology presented in Table 4.4, do a weighted competitive strength assessment for your company and two other companies that you and your co-managers consider to be very close competitors. **LO 5**

ENDNOTES

[1] Birger Wernerfelt, "A Resource-Based View of the Firm," *Strategic Management Journal* 5, no. 5 (September–October 1984), pp. 171–180; Jay Barney, "Firm Resources and Sustained Competitive Advantage," *Journal of Management* 17, no. 1 (1991), pp. 99–120.

[2] R. Amit and P. Schoemaker, "Strategic Assets and Organizational Rent," *Strategic Management Journal* 14 (1993).

[3] Jay B. Barney, "Looking Inside for Competitive Advantage," *Academy of Management Executive* 9, no. 4 (November 1995), pp. 49–61; Christopher A. Bartlett and Sumantra Ghoshal, "Building Competitive Advantage through People," *MIT Sloan Management Review* 43, no. 2 (Winter 2002), pp. 34–41; Danny Miller, Russell Eisenstat, and Nathaniel Foote, "Strategy from the Inside Out: Building Capability-Creating Organizations," *California Management Review* 44, no. 3 (Spring 2002), pp. 37–54.

[4] M. Peteraf and J. Barney, "Unraveling the Resource-Based Tangle," *Managerial and Decision Economics* 24, no. 4 (June–July 2003), pp. 309–323.

[5] Margaret A. Peteraf and Mark E. Bergen, "Scanning Dynamic Competitive Landscapes: A Market-Based and Resource-Based Framework," *Strategic Management Journal* 24 (2003), pp. 1027–1042.

[6] C. Montgomery, "Of Diamonds and Rust: A New Look at Resources," in C. Montgomery (ed.), *Resource-Based and Evolutionary Theories of the Firm* (Boston: Kluwer Academic, 1995), pp. 251–268.

[7] Constance E. Helfat and Margaret A. Peteraf, "The Dynamic Resource-Based View: Capability Lifecycles," *Strategic Management Journal* 24, no. 10 (2003).

[8] D. Teece, G. Pisano, and A. Shuen, "Dynamic Capabilities and Strategic Management," *Strategic Management Journal* 18, no. 7 (1997),

pp. 509–533; K. Eisenhardt and J. Martin, "Dynamic Capabilities: What Are They?" *Strategic Management Journal* 21, no. 10–11 (2000), pp. 1105–1121; M. Zollo and S. Winter, "Deliberate Learning and the Evolution of Dynamic Capabilities," *Organization Science* 13 (2002), pp. 339–351; C. Helfat et al., *Dynamic Capabilities: Understanding Strategic Change in Organizations* (Malden, MA: Blackwell, 2007).

[9] David W. Birchall and George Tovstiga, "The Strategic Potential of a Firm's Knowledge Portfolio," *Journal of General Management* 25, no. 1 (Autumn 1999), pp. 1–16; Nick Bontis, Nicola C. Dragonetti, Kristine Jacobsen, and Goran Roos, "The Knowledge Toolbox: A Review of the Tools Available to Measure and Manage Intangible Resources," *European Management Journal* 17, no. 4 (August 1999), pp. 391–401; David Teece, "Capturing Value from Knowledge Assets: The New Economy, Markets for Know-How, and Intangible Assets," *California Management Review* 40, no. 3 (Spring 1998), pp. 55–79.

[10] Donald Sull, "Strategy as Active Waiting," *Harvard Business Review* 83, no. 9 (September 2005), pp. 121–126.

[11] M. Peteraf, "The Cornerstones of Competitive Advantage: A Resource-Based View," *Strategic Management Journal,* March 1993, pp. 179–191.

[12] Michael Porter in his 1985 best seller, *Competitive Advantage* (New York: Free Press).

[13] John K. Shank and Vijay Govindarajan, *Strategic Cost Management* (New York: Free Press, 1993), especially chaps. 2–6, 10, and 11; Robin Cooper and Robert S. Kaplan, "Measure Costs Right: Make the Right Decisions," *Harvard Business Review* 66, no. 5 (September–October, 1988), pp. 96–103; Joseph A. Ness and Thomas G. Cucuzza, "Tapping the Full Potential of ABC," *Harvard Business Review* 73, no. 4 (July–August 1995), pp. 130–138.

[14] Porter, *Competitive Advantage,* p. 34.

[15] Hau L. Lee, "The Triple-A Supply Chain," *Harvard Business Review* 82, no. 10 (October 2004), pp. 102–112.

[16] Gregory H. Watson, *Strategic Benchmarking: How to Rate Your Company's Performance against the World's Best* (New York: Wiley, 1993); Robert C. Camp, *Benchmarking: The Search for Industry Best Practices That Lead to Superior Performance* (Milwaukee: ASQC Quality Press, 1989); Dawn Iacobucci and Christie Nordhielm, "Creative Benchmarking," *Harvard Business Review* 78 no. 6 (November–December 2000), pp. 24–25.

[17] **www.businessdictionary.com/definition/best-practice.html** (accessed December 2, 2009).

[18] Reuben E. Stone, "Leading a Supply Chain Turnaround," *Harvard Business Review* 82, no. 10 (October 2004), pp. 114–121.

CHAPTER 5

The Five Generic Competitive Strategies

Learning Objectives

THIS CHAPTER WILL HELP YOU UNDERSTAND:

LO 1 What distinguishes each of the five generic strategies and why some of these strategies work better in certain kinds of competitive conditions than in others.

LO 2 The major avenues for achieving a competitive advantage based on lower costs.

LO 3 The major avenues to a competitive advantage based on differentiating a company's product or service offering from the offerings of rivals.

LO 4 The attributes of a best-cost provider strategy—a hybrid of low-cost provider and differentiation strategies.

> A strategy delineates a territory in which a company seeks to be unique.
>
> Michael E. Porter – *Professor and Cofounder of Monitor Consulting*

> I'm spending my time trying to understand our competitive position and how we're serving customers.
>
> Lou Gerstner – *Former CEO Credited with IBM's Turnaround*

> I learnt the hard way about positioning in business, about catering to the right segments.
>
> Shaffi Mather –*Social Entrepreneur*

A company can employ any of several basic approaches to competing successfully and gaining a competitive advantage over rivals, but they all involve *delivering more value* to the customer than rivals or *delivering value more efficiently* than rivals (or both). More value for the customer can mean a good product at a lower price, a superior product worth paying more for, or a best-value offering that represents an attractive combination of price, features, service, and other appealing attributes. Greater efficiency means delivering a given level of value to customers at a lower cost to the company. But whatever approach to delivering value the company takes, it nearly always requires performing value chain activities differently than rivals and building competitively valuable resources and capabilities that rivals cannot readily match or trump.

This chapter describes the five *generic competitive strategy options.* Which of the five to employ is a company's foremost choice in crafting an overall strategy and beginning its quest for competitive advantage.

TYPES OF GENERIC COMPETITIVE STRATEGIES

LO1

What distinguishes each of the five generic strategies and why some of these strategies work better in certain kinds of competitive conditions than in others.

A company's competitive strategy *deals exclusively with the specifics of management's game plan for competing successfully*—its specific efforts to position itself in the marketplace, please customers, ward off competitive threats, and achieve a particular kind of competitive advantage. The chances are remote that any two companies—even companies in the same industry—will employ competitive strategies that are exactly alike in every detail. However, when one strips away the details to get at the real substance, the two biggest factors that distinguish one competitive strategy from another boil down to (1) whether a company's market target is broad or narrow and (2) whether the company is pursuing a competitive advantage linked to lower costs or differentiation. These two factors give rise to five competitive strategy options, as shown in Figure 5.1 and listed next.[1]

1. *A low-cost provider strategy*—striving to achieve lower overall costs than rivals on comparable products that attract a broad spectrum of buyers, usually by underpricing rivals.

FIGURE 5.1 The Five Generic Competitive Strategies

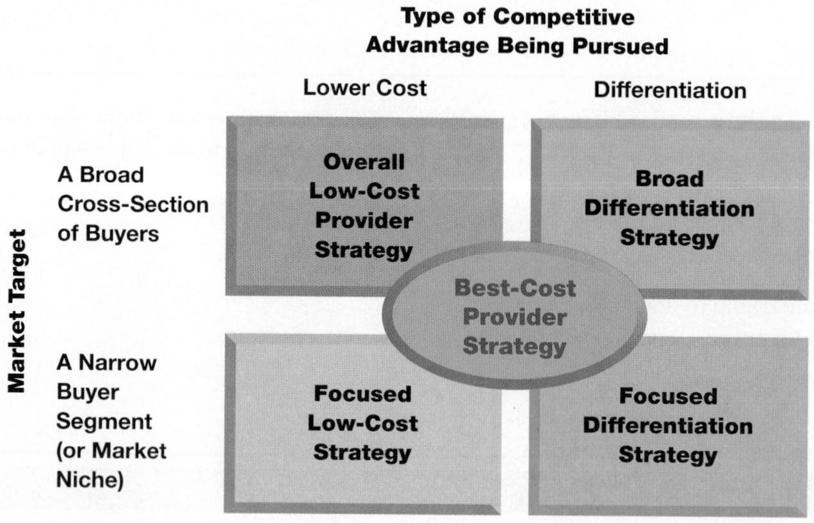

Source: This is an expanded version of a three-strategy classification discussed in Michael E. Porter, *Competitive Strategy* (New York: Free Press, 1980).

2. *A broad differentiation strategy*—seeking to differentiate the company's product offering from rivals' products by offering superior attributes that will appeal to a broad spectrum of buyers.
3. *A focused low-cost strategy*—concentrating on a narrow buyer segment (or market niche) and outcompeting rivals on costs, thus being able to serve niche members at a lower price.
4. *A focused differentiation strategy*—concentrating on a narrow buyer segment (or market niche) and outcompeting rivals by offering niche members customized attributes that meet their tastes and requirements better than rivals' products.
5. *A best-cost provider strategy*—giving customers *more value for their money* by satisfying buyers' expectations on key quality, features, performance, and/or service attributes while beating their price expectations. This option is a *hybrid* strategy that blends elements of low-cost provider and differentiation strategies; the aim is to have the lowest (best) costs and prices among sellers offering products with comparable differentiating attributes.

The remainder of this chapter explores the ins and outs of these five generic competitive strategies and how they differ.

LOW-COST PROVIDER STRATEGIES

Striving to be the industry's overall low-cost provider is a powerful competitive approach in markets with many price-sensitive buyers. A company achieves **low-cost leadership** when it becomes the industry's lowest-cost provider rather than just being one of perhaps several competitors with comparatively low costs. Successful low-cost providers boast lower costs than rivals—but not necessarily the absolutely lowest possible cost. In striving for a cost advantage over rivals, company managers must incorporate features and services that buyers consider essential. A product offering that is too frills-free can be viewed by consumers as offering little value regardless of its pricing.

A company has two options for translating a low-cost advantage over rivals into attractive profit performance. Option 1 is to use the lower-cost edge to underprice competitors and attract price-sensitive buyers in great enough numbers to increase total profits. Option 2 is to maintain the present price, be content with the present market share, and use the lower-cost edge to earn a higher profit margin on each unit sold, thereby raising the firm's total profits and overall return on investment.

While many companies are inclined to exploit a low-cost advantage by using option 1 (attacking rivals with lower prices), this strategy can backfire if rivals respond with their own retaliatory price cuts (in order to protect their customer base). A rush to cut prices can often trigger a price war that lowers the profits of all price discounters. The bigger the risk that rivals will respond with matching price cuts, the more appealing it becomes to employ the second option for using a low-cost advantage to achieve higher profitability.

LO 2

The major avenues for achieving a competitive advantage based on lower costs.

CORE CONCEPT

A **low-cost provider's** basis for competitive advantage is lower overall costs than competitors. Successful **low-cost leaders,** who have the lowest industry costs, are exceptionally good at finding ways to drive costs out of their businesses and still provide a product or service that buyers find acceptable.

The Two Major Avenues for Achieving a Cost Advantage

To achieve a low-cost edge over rivals, a firm's cumulative costs across its overall value chain must be lower than competitors' cumulative costs. There are two major avenues for accomplishing this:[2]

A low-cost advantage over rivals can translate into better profitability than rivals attain.

1. Perform value chain activities more cost-effectively than rivals.
2. Revamp the firm's overall value chain to eliminate or bypass some cost-producing activities.

CORE CONCEPT

A **cost driver** is a factor that has a strong influence on a company's costs.

Cost-Efficient Management of Value Chain Activities

For a company to do a more cost-efficient job of managing its value chain than rivals, managers must diligently search out cost-saving opportunities in every part of the value chain. No activity can escape cost-saving scrutiny, and all company personnel must be expected to use their talents and ingenuity to come up with innovative and effective ways to keep costs down. Particular attention must be paid to a set of factors known as **cost drivers** that have a strong effect on a company's costs and can be used as levers to lower costs. Figure 5.2 shows the most important cost drivers. Cost-cutting approaches that demonstrate an effective use of the cost drivers include:

1. *Capturing all available economies of scale.* Economies of scale stem from an ability to lower unit costs by increasing the scale of operation. Often a large plant or distribution center is more economical to operate than a small one. In global industries, selling a mostly standard product worldwide tends to lower unit costs as opposed to making separate products for each country market, an approach in which costs are typically higher due to an inability to reach the most economic scale of production for each country. There are economies of scale in advertising as well. For example, Anheuser-Busch could afford to pay the $4 million cost of a 30-second Super Bowl ad in 2014 because the cost could be spread out over the hundreds of millions of units of Budweiser that the company sells.

FIGURE 5.2 Cost Drivers: The Keys to Driving Down Company Costs

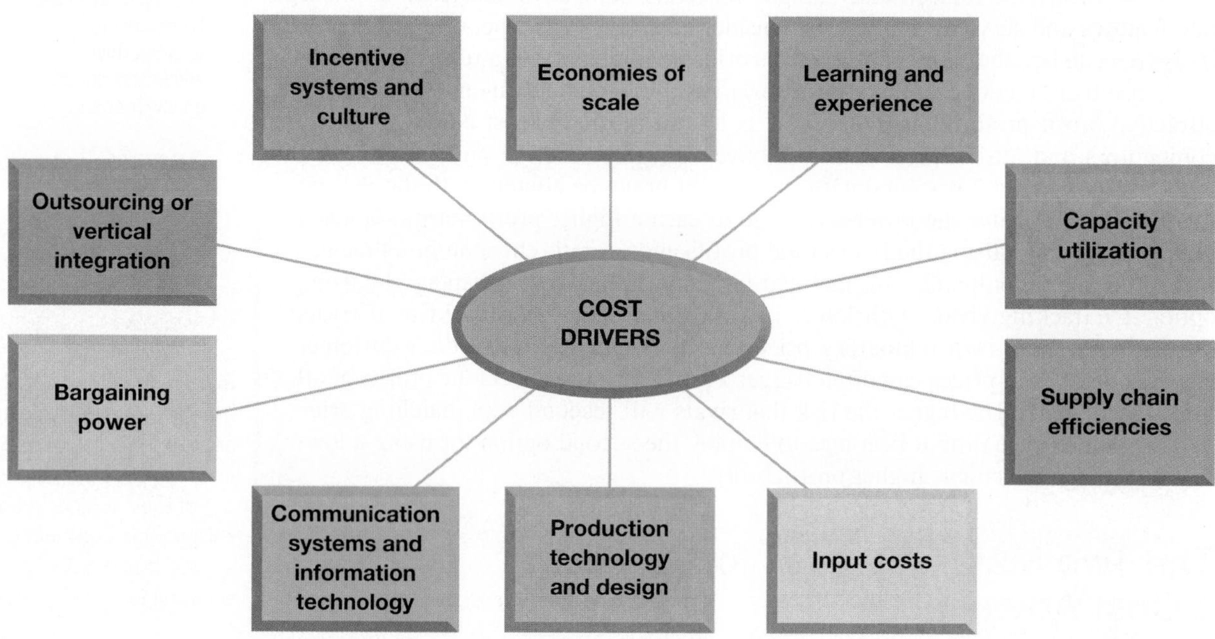

Source: Adapted from M. Porter, *Competitive Advantage: Creating and Sustaining Competitive Advantage* (New York: Free Press, 1985).

2. *Taking full advantage of experience- and learning-curve effects.* The cost of performing an activity can decline over time as the learning and experience of company personnel build. Learning and experience economies can stem from debugging and mastering newly introduced technologies, using workers' experiences and suggestions to install more efficient plant layouts and assembly procedures, and repeatedly picking sites for and building new plants, retail outlets, or distribution centers—gaining speed and greater effectiveness in the process.
3. *Operating facilities at full capacity.* Whether a company is able to operate at or near full capacity has a big impact on unit costs when its value chain contains activities associated with substantial fixed costs. Higher rates of capacity utilization allow depreciation and other fixed costs to be spread over a larger unit volume, thereby lowering fixed costs per unit. The more capital-intensive the business and the higher the fixed costs as a percentage of total costs, the greater the unit-cost penalty for operating at less than full capacity.
4. *Improving supply chain efficiency.* Partnering with suppliers to streamline the ordering and purchasing process, to reduce inventory carrying costs via just-in-time inventory practices, to economize on shipping and materials handling, and to ferret out other cost-saving opportunities is a much-used approach to cost reduction. A company with a distinctive competence in cost-efficient supply chain management, such as BASF (the world's leading chemical company), can sometimes achieve a sizable cost advantage over less adept rivals.
5. *Substituting lower-cost inputs wherever there is little or no sacrifice in product quality or performance.* If the costs of certain raw materials and parts are "too

high," a company can switch to using lower-cost items or maybe even design the high-cost components out of the product altogether.

6. *Using the company's bargaining power vis-à-vis suppliers or others in the value chain system to gain concessions.* Home Depot, for example, has sufficient bargaining clout with suppliers to win price discounts on large-volume purchases.
7. *Using online systems and sophisticated software to achieve operating efficiencies.* For example, sharing data and production schedules with suppliers, coupled with the use of enterprise resource planning (ERP) and manufacturing execution system (MES) software, can reduce parts inventories, trim production times, and lower labor requirements.
8. *Improving process design and employing advanced production technology.* Often production costs can be cut by (1) using design for manufacture (DFM) procedures and computer-assisted design (CAD) techniques that enable more integrated and efficient production methods, (2) investing in highly automated robotic production technology, and (3) shifting to a mass-customization production process. Dell's highly automated PC assembly plant in Austin, Texas, is a prime example of the use of advanced product and process technologies. Many companies are ardent users of total quality management (TQM) systems, business process reengineering, six sigma methodology, and other business process management techniques that aim at boosting efficiency and reducing costs.
9. *Being alert to the cost advantages of outsourcing or vertical integration.* Outsourcing the performance of certain value chain activities can be more economical than performing them in-house if outside specialists, by virtue of their expertise and volume, can perform the activities at lower cost. On the other hand, there can be times when integrating into the activities of either suppliers or distribution-channel allies can lower costs through greater production efficiencies, reduced transaction costs, or a better bargaining position.
10. *Motivating employees through incentives and company culture.* A company's incentive system can encourage not only greater worker productivity but also cost-saving innovations that come from worker suggestions. The culture of a company can also spur worker pride in productivity and continuous improvement. Companies that are well known for their cost-reducing incentive systems and culture include Nucor Steel, which characterizes itself as a company of "20,000 teammates," Southwest Airlines, and Walmart.

Revamping the Value Chain System to Lower Costs Dramatic cost advantages can often emerge from redesigning the company's value chain system in ways that eliminate costly work steps and entirely bypass certain cost-producing value chain activities. Such value chain revamping can include:

- *Selling direct to consumers and bypassing the activities and costs of distributors and dealers.* To circumvent the need for distributors and dealers, a company can (1) create its own direct sales force (which adds the costs of maintaining and supporting a sales force but which may well be cheaper than using independent distributors and dealers to access buyers) and/or (2) conduct sales operations at the company's website (incurring costs for website operations and shipping may be a substantially cheaper way to make sales than going through distributor–dealer channels). Costs in the wholesale and retail portions of the value chain frequently represent 35 to 50 percent of the final price consumers pay, so establishing a direct sales force or selling online may offer big cost savings.

- *Streamlining operations by eliminating low-value-added or unnecessary work steps and activities.* At Walmart, some items supplied by manufacturers are delivered directly to retail stores rather than being routed through Walmart's distribution centers and delivered by Walmart trucks. In other instances, Walmart unloads incoming shipments from manufacturers' trucks arriving at its distribution centers and loads them directly onto outgoing Walmart trucks headed to particular stores without ever moving the goods into the distribution center. Many supermarket chains have greatly reduced in-store meat butchering and cutting activities by shifting to meats that are cut and packaged at the meatpacking plant and then delivered to their stores in ready-to-sell form.
- *Reducing materials handling and shipping costs by having suppliers locate their plants or warehouses close to the company's own facilities.* Having suppliers locate their plants or warehouses close to a company's own plant facilitates just-in-time deliveries of parts and components to the exact workstation where they will be used in assembling the company's product. This not only lowers incoming shipping costs but also curbs or eliminates the company's need to build and operate storerooms for incoming parts and components and to have plant personnel move the inventories to the workstations as needed for assembly.

Illustration Capsule 5.1 describes how Walmart has managed its value chain in the retail grocery portion of its business to achieve a dramatic cost advantage over rival supermarket chains and become the world's biggest grocery retailer.

Examples of Companies That Revamped Their Value Chains to Reduce Costs Nucor Corporation, the most profitable steel producer in the United States and one of the largest steel producers worldwide, drastically revamped the value chain process for manufacturing steel products by using relatively inexpensive electric arc furnaces and continuous casting processes. Using electric arc furnaces to melt recycled scrap steel eliminated many of the steps used by traditional steel mills that made their steel products from iron ore, coke, limestone, and other ingredients using costly coke ovens, basic oxygen blast furnaces, ingot casters, and multiple types of finishing facilities—plus Nucor's value chain system required far fewer employees. As a consequence, Nucor produces steel with a far lower capital investment, a far smaller workforce, and far lower operating costs than traditional steel mills. Nucor's strategy to replace the traditional steelmaking value chain with its simpler, quicker value chain approach has made it one of the world's lowest-cost producers of steel, allowing it to take a huge amount of market share away from traditional steel companies and earn attractive profits. (Nucor reported a profit in 180 out of 184 quarters during 1966–2012—a remarkable feat in a mature and cyclical industry notorious for roller-coaster bottom-line performance.)

Southwest Airlines has achieved considerable cost savings by reconfiguring the traditional value chain of commercial airlines, thereby permitting it to offer travelers dramatically lower fares. Its mastery of fast turnarounds at the gates (about 25 minutes versus 45 minutes for rivals) allows its planes to fly more hours per day. This translates into being able to schedule more flights per day with fewer aircraft, allowing Southwest to generate more revenue per plane on average than rivals. Southwest does not offer assigned seating, baggage transfer to connecting airlines, or first-class seating and service, thereby eliminating all the cost-producing activities associated with these features. The company's fast and user-friendly online reservation system facilitates e-ticketing and reduces staffing requirements at telephone reservation

Success in achieving a low-cost edge over rivals comes from outmanaging rivals in finding ways to perform value chain activities faster, more accurately, and more cost-effectively.

ILLUSTRATION CAPSULE 5.1

How Walmart Managed Its Value Chain to Achieve a Huge Low-Cost Advantage over Rival Supermarket Chains

Walmart has achieved a very substantial cost and pricing advantage over rival supermarket chains both by revamping portions of the grocery retailing value chain and by outmanaging its rivals in efficiently performing various value chain activities. Its cost advantage stems from a series of initiatives and practices:

- Instituting extensive information sharing with vendors via online systems that relay sales at its checkout counters directly to suppliers of the items, thereby providing suppliers with real-time information on customer demand and preferences (creating an estimated 6 percent cost advantage). It is standard practice at Walmart to collaborate extensively with vendors on all aspects of the purchasing and store delivery process to squeeze out mutually beneficial cost savings. Procter & Gamble, Walmart's biggest supplier, went so far as to integrate its enterprise resource planning (ERP) system with Walmart's.
- Pursuing global procurement of some items and centralizing most purchasing activities so as to leverage the company's buying power (creating an estimated 2.5 percent cost advantage).
- Investing in state-of-the-art automation at its distribution centers; operating a truck fleet that makes 24-hour-a-day deliveries to Walmart stores while minimizing the mileage that trucks travel empty, thereby reducing costs and environmental impact; and putting other assorted cost-saving practices into place at its headquarters, distribution centers, and stores (resulting in an estimated 4 percent cost advantage).
- Striving to optimize the product mix and achieve greater sales turnover (resulting in about a 2 percent cost advantage).
- Installing security systems and store operating procedures that lower shrinkage rates (producing a cost advantage of about 0.5 percent).

- Negotiating preferred real estate rental and leasing rates with real estate developers and owners of its store sites (yielding a cost advantage of 2 percent).
- Managing and compensating its workforce in a manner that produces lower labor costs (yielding an estimated 5 percent cost advantage).

Together, these value chain initiatives give Walmart an approximately 22 percent cost advantage over Kroger, Safeway, and other leading supermarket chains. With such a sizable cost advantage, Walmart has been able to underprice its rivals and rapidly become the world's leading supermarket retailer.

In order to maintain its cost advantages, which are very much tied to scale and growth, Walmart has adapted to more broadly reach a changing and growing customer base. Walmart stores range from giant, 24-hour Supercenters to Neighborhood Markets and Express stores that better fit the needs of customers in urban or fast-moving locales, and in the same way the company has tailored its international expansion by country. With further innovation in online and fresh delivery sales, Walmart is well poised to continue its growth and low-cost leadership.

Sources: Information at www.walmart.com; Marco Iansiti and Roy Levien, "Strategy as Ecology," *Harvard Business Review* 82, no. 3 (March 2004), p. 70; and Clare O'Connor, "Wal-Mart vs. Amazon: World's Biggest E-Commerce Battle Could Boil Down to Vegetables," *Forbes* Online, March 2014.

centers and airport counters. Its use of automated check-in equipment reduces staffing requirements for terminal check-in. The company's carefully designed point-to-point route system minimizes connections, delays, and total trip time for passengers, allowing about 75 percent of Southwest passengers to fly nonstop to their destinations and at the same time reducing Southwest's costs for flight operations.

The Keys to Being a Successful Low-Cost Provider

While low-cost providers are champions of frugality, they seldom hesitate to spend aggressively on resources and capabilities *that promise to drive costs out of the business.* Indeed, having competitive assets of this type and ensuring that they remain competitively superior is essential for achieving competitive advantage as a low-cost provider. Walmart has been an early adopter of state-of-the-art technology throughout its operations, as Illustration Capsule 5.1 suggests; *however, Walmart carefully estimates the cost savings of new technologies before it rushes to invest in them.* By continuously investing in complex, cost-saving technologies that are hard for rivals to match, Walmart has sustained its low-cost advantage for over 30 years.

Other companies noted for their successful use of low-cost provider strategies include Vizio in big-screen TVs, Briggs & Stratton in small gasoline engines, Bic in ballpoint pens, Stride Rite in footwear, Poulan in chain saws, and General Electric and Whirlpool in major home appliances.

When a Low-Cost Provider Strategy Works Best

A low-cost provider strategy becomes increasingly appealing and competitively powerful when:

1. *Price competition among rival sellers is vigorous.* Low-cost providers are in the best position to compete offensively on the basis of price, to gain market share at the expense of rivals, to win the business of price-sensitive buyers, to remain profitable despite strong price competition, and to survive price wars.
2. *The products of rival sellers are essentially identical and readily available from many eager sellers.* Look-alike products and/or overabundant product supply set the stage for lively price competition; in such markets, it is the less efficient, higher-cost companies whose profits get squeezed the most.
3. *It is difficult to achieve product differentiation in ways that have value to buyers.* When the differences between product attributes or brands do not matter much to buyers, buyers are nearly always sensitive to price differences, and industry-leading companies tend to be those with the lowest-priced brands.
4. *Most buyers use the product in the same ways.* With common user requirements, a standardized product can satisfy buyers' needs, in which case low price, not features or quality, becomes the dominant factor in causing buyers to choose one seller's product over another's.
5. *Buyers incur low costs in switching their purchases from one seller to another.* Low switching costs give buyers the flexibility to shift purchases to lower-priced sellers having equally good products or to attractively priced substitute products. A low-cost leader is well positioned to use low price to induce potential customers to switch to its brand.

Pitfalls to Avoid in Pursuing a Low-Cost Provider Strategy

Perhaps the biggest mistake a low-cost provider can make is getting carried away with overly aggressive price cutting. *Higher unit sales and market shares do not automatically translate into higher profits.* A lower price improves profitability only if the lower price increases unit sales enough to offset the loss in revenues due to a lower margin on each unit sold.

A second pitfall is *relying on an approach to reduce costs that can be easily copied by rivals.* If rivals find it relatively easy or inexpensive to imitate the leader's low-cost methods, then the leader's advantage will be too short-lived to yield a valuable edge in the marketplace.

A third pitfall is *becoming too fixated on cost reduction.* Low costs cannot be pursued so zealously that a firm's offering ends up being too feature-poor to generate buyer appeal. Furthermore, a company driving hard to push down its costs has to guard against ignoring declining buyer sensitivity to price, increased buyer interest in added features or service, or new developments that alter how buyers use the product. Otherwise, it risks losing market ground if buyers start opting for more upscale or feature-rich products.

Even if these mistakes are avoided, a low-cost provider strategy still entails risk. An innovative rival may discover an even lower-cost value chain approach. Important cost-saving technological breakthroughs may suddenly emerge. And if a low-cost provider has heavy investments in its present means of operating, then it can prove costly to quickly shift to the new value chain approach or a new technology.

A low-cost provider is in the best position to win the business of price-sensitive buyers, set the floor on market price, and still earn a profit.

Reducing price does not lead to higher total profits unless the added gains in unit sales are large enough to offset the loss in revenues due to lower margins per unit sold.

A low-cost provider's product offering must always contain enough attributes to be attractive to prospective buyers—low price, by itself, is not always appealing to buyers.

BROAD DIFFERENTIATION STRATEGIES

Differentiation strategies are attractive whenever buyers' needs and preferences are too diverse to be fully satisfied by a standardized product offering. Successful product differentiation requires careful study to determine what attributes buyers find appealing, valuable, and worth paying for.[3] Then the company must incorporate these desirable features into its product or service to clearly set itself apart from rivals lacking attributes. A differentiation strategy calls for a customer value proposition that is *unique.* The strategy achieves its aim when an attractively large number of buyers find the customer value proposition appealing and become strongly attached to a company's differentiated attributes.

Successful differentiation allows a firm to do one or more of the following:

- Command a premium price for its product.
- Increase unit sales (because additional buyers are won over by the differentiating features).
- Gain buyer loyalty to its brand (because some buyers are strongly attracted to the differentiating features and bond with the company and its products).

Differentiation enhances profitability whenever a company's product can command a sufficiently higher price or produce sufficiently bigger unit sales *to more than cover the added costs of achieving the differentiation.* Company differentiation strategies fail when buyers don't value the brand's uniqueness sufficiently and/or when a company's approach to differentiation is easily matched by its rivals.

LO 3

The major avenues to a competitive advantage based on differentiating a company's product or service offering from the offerings of rivals.

CORE CONCEPT

The essence of a **broad differentiation strategy** is to offer unique product attributes that a wide range of buyers find appealing and worth paying for.

Companies can pursue differentiation from many angles: a unique taste (Red Bull, Listerine); multiple features (Microsoft Office, Apple iPad); wide selection and one-stop shopping (Home Depot, Amazon.com); superior service (Ritz-Carlton, Nordstrom); spare parts availability (Caterpillar in machines); engineering design and performance (Mercedes, BMW); luxury and prestige (Rolex, Gucci); product reliability (Whirlpool and Bosch in large home appliances); quality manufacture (Michelin in tires); technological leadership (3M Corporation in bonding and coating products); a full range of services (Charles Schwab in stock brokerage); and wide product selection (Campbell's soups).

Managing the Value Chain to Create the Differentiating Attributes

Differentiation is not something hatched in marketing and advertising departments, nor is it limited to the catchalls of quality and service. Differentiation opportunities can exist in activities all along an industry's value chain. The most systematic approach that managers can take, however, involves focusing on the **value drivers,** a set of factors—analogous to cost drivers—that are particularly effective in creating differentiation. Figure 5.3 contains a list of important value drivers. Ways that managers can enhance differentiation based on value drivers include the following:

CORE CONCEPT

A **value driver** is a factor that can have a strong differentiating effect.

1. *Create product features and performance attributes that appeal to a wide range of buyers.* This applies to the physical as well as functional attributes of a product, including features such as added user safety or enhanced environmental protection. Styling and appearance are big differentiating factors in the apparel and motor vehicle industries. Size and weight matter in binoculars and smartphones. Most companies employing broad differentiation strategies make a point of incorporating innovative and novel features in their product or service offering, especially those that improve performance.
2. *Improve customer service or add extra services.* Better customer services, in areas such as delivery, returns, and repair, can be as important in creating differentiation as superior product features. Examples include superior technical assistance to buyers, higher-quality maintenance services, more and better product information provided to customers, more and better training materials for end users, better credit terms, quicker order processing, and greater customer convenience.
3. *Invest in production-related R&D activities.* Engaging in production R&D may permit custom-order manufacture at an efficient cost, provide wider product variety and selection through product "versioning," or improve product quality. Many manufacturers have developed flexible manufacturing systems that allow different models and product versions to be made on the same assembly line. Being able to provide buyers with made-to-order products can be a potent differentiating capability.
4. *Strive for innovation and technological advances.* Successful innovation is the route to more frequent first-on-the-market victories and is a powerful differentiator. If the innovation proves hard to replicate, through patent protection or other means, it can provide a company with a first mover advantage that is sustainable.
5. *Pursue continuous quality improvement.* Quality control processes reduce product defects, prevent premature product failure, extend product life, make it economical to offer longer warranty coverage, improve economy of use, result in

FIGURE 5.3 Value Drivers: The Keys to Creating a Differentiation Advantage

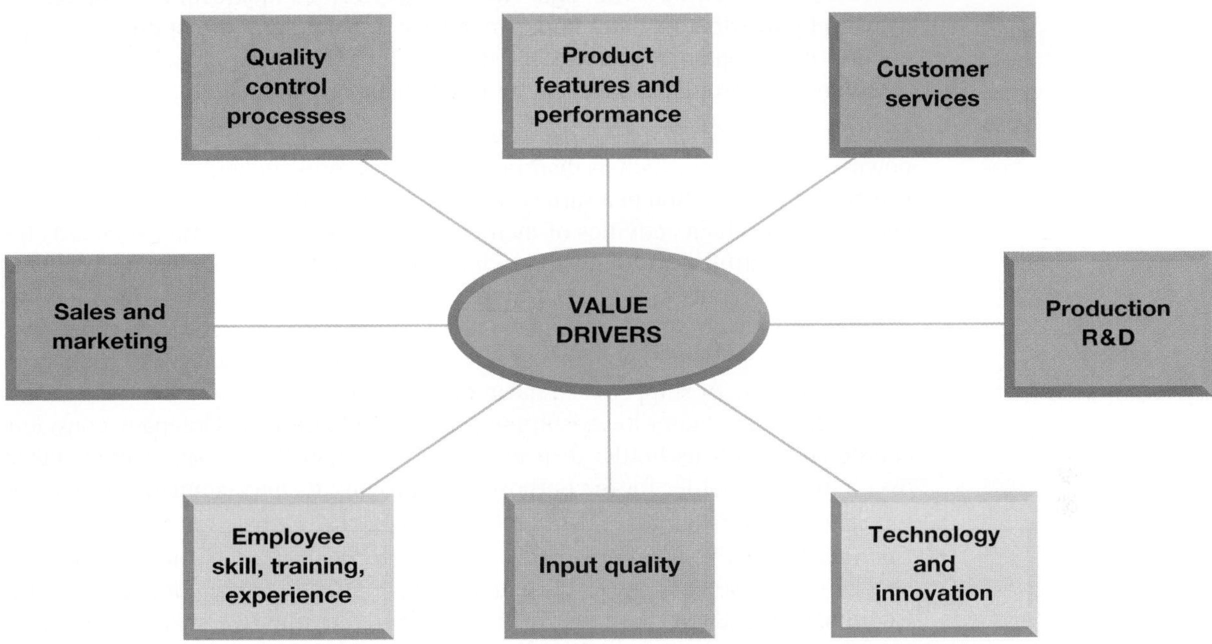

Source: Adapted from M. Porter, *Competitive Advantage: Creating and Sustaining Competitive Advantage* (New York: Free Press, 1985).

more end-user convenience, or enhance product appearance. Companies whose quality management systems meet certification standards, such as the ISO 9001 standards, can enhance their reputation for quality with customers.

6. *Increase marketing and brand-building activities.* Marketing and advertising can have a tremendous effect on the value perceived by buyers and therefore their willingness to pay more for the company's offerings. They can create differentiation even when little tangible differentiation exists otherwise. For example, blind taste tests show that even the most loyal Pepsi or Coke drinkers have trouble telling one cola drink from another.[4] Brands create customer loyalty, which increases the perceived "cost" of switching to another product.
7. *Seek out high-quality inputs.* Input quality can ultimately spill over to affect the performance or quality of the company's end product. Starbucks, for example, gets high ratings on its coffees partly because it has very strict specifications on the coffee beans purchased from suppliers.
8. *Emphasize human resource management activities that improve the skills, expertise, and knowledge of company personnel.* A company with high-caliber intellectual capital often has the capacity to generate the kinds of ideas that drive product innovation, technological advances, better product design and product performance, improved production techniques, and higher product quality. Well-designed incentive compensation systems can often unleash the efforts of talented personnel to develop and implement new and effective differentiating attributes.

Revamping the Value Chain System to Increase Differentiation

Just as pursuing a cost advantage can involve the entire value chain system, the same is true for a differentiation advantage. Activities performed upstream by suppliers or downstream by distributors and retailers can have a meaningful effect on customers' perceptions of a company's offerings and its value proposition. Approaches to enhancing differentiation through changes in the value chain system include:

- *Coordinating with channel allies to enhance customer value.* Coordinating with downstream partners such as distributors, dealers, brokers, and retailers can contribute to differentiation in a variety of ways. Methods that companies use to influence the value chain activities of their channel allies include setting standards for downstream partners to follow, providing them with templates to standardize the selling environment or practices, training channel personnel, or cosponsoring promotions and advertising campaigns. Coordinating with retailers is important for enhancing the buying experience and building a company's image. Coordinating with distributors or shippers can mean quicker delivery to customers, more accurate order filling, and/or lower shipping costs. The Coca-Cola Company considers coordination with its bottler-distributors so important that it has at times taken over a troubled bottler for the purpose of improving its management and upgrading its plant and equipment before releasing it again.[5]
- *Coordinating with suppliers to better address customer needs.* Collaborating with suppliers can also be a powerful route to a more effective differentiation strategy. Coordinating and collaborating with suppliers can improve many dimensions affecting product features and quality. This is particularly true for companies that engage only in assembly operations, such as Dell in PCs and Ducati in motorcycles. Close coordination with suppliers can also enhance differentiation by speeding up new product development cycles or speeding delivery to end customers. Strong relationships with suppliers can also mean that the company's supply requirements are prioritized when industry supply is insufficient to meet overall demand.

Delivering Superior Value via a Broad Differentiation Strategy

Differentiation strategies depend on meeting customer needs in unique ways or creating new needs through activities such as innovation or persuasive advertising. The objective is to offer customers something that rivals can't—at least in terms of the level of satisfaction. There are four basic routes to achieving this aim.

The first route is to incorporate product attributes and user features that *lower the buyer's overall costs* of using the company's product. This is the least obvious and most overlooked route to a differentiation advantage. It is a differentiating factor since it can help business buyers be more competitive in their markets and more profitable. Producers of materials and components often win orders for their products by reducing a buyer's raw-material waste (providing cut-to-size components), reducing a buyer's inventory requirements (providing just-in-time deliveries), using online systems to reduce a buyer's procurement and order processing costs, and providing free technical support. This route to differentiation can also appeal to individual consumers who are looking to economize on their overall costs of consumption. Making a company's product more economical for a buyer to use can be done by incorporating energy-efficient features (energy-saving appliances and lightbulbs help cut buyers' utility bills; fuel-efficient vehicles cut buyer costs for gasoline) and/or by increasing maintenance intervals and product reliability so as to lower buyer costs for maintenance and repairs.

A second route is to incorporate *tangible* features that increase customer satisfaction with the product, such as product specifications, functions, and styling. This can be accomplished by including attributes that add functionality, enhance the design, save time for the user, are more reliable, or make the product cleaner, safer, quieter, simpler to use, more portable, more convenient, or longer-lasting than rival brands. Smartphone manufacturers are in a race to introduce next-generation devices capable of being used for more purposes and having simpler menu functionality.

A third route to a differentiation-based competitive advantage is to incorporate *intangible* features that enhance buyer satisfaction in noneconomic ways. Toyota's Prius appeals to environmentally conscious motorists not only because these drivers want to help reduce global carbon dioxide emissions but also because they identify with the image conveyed. Bentley, Ralph Lauren, Louis Vuitton, Burberry, Cartier, and Coach have differentiation-based competitive advantages linked to buyer desires for status, image, prestige, upscale fashion, superior craftsmanship, and the finer things in life. Intangibles that contribute to differentiation can extend beyond product attributes to the reputation of the company and to customer relations or trust.

Differentiation can be based on *tangible* or *intangible* attributes.

The fourth route is to *signal the value* of the company's product offering to buyers. Typical signals of value include a high price (in instances where high price implies high quality and performance), more appealing or fancier packaging than competing products, ad content that emphasizes a product's standout attributes, the quality of brochures and sales presentations, and the luxuriousness and ambience of a seller's facilities (important for high-end retailers and for offices or other facilities frequented by customers). They make potential buyers aware of the professionalism, appearance, and personalities of the seller's employees and/or make potential buyers realize that a company has prestigious customers. Signaling value is particularly important (1) when the nature of differentiation is based on intangible features and is therefore subjective or hard to quantify, (2) when buyers are making a first-time purchase and are unsure what their experience with the product will be, (3) when repurchase is infrequent, and (4) when buyers are unsophisticated.

Regardless of the approach taken, achieving a successful differentiation strategy requires, first, that the company have capabilities in areas such as customer service, marketing, brand management, and technology that can create and support differentiation. That is, the resources, competencies, and value chain activities of the company must be well matched to the requirements of the strategy. For the strategy to result in competitive advantage, the company's competencies must also be sufficiently unique in delivering value to buyers that they help set its product offering apart from those of rivals. They must be competitively superior. There are numerous examples of companies that have differentiated themselves on the basis of distinctive capabilities. When a major news event occurs, many people turn to Fox News and CNN because they have the capability to devote more airtime to breaking news stories and get reporters on the scene very quickly. Avon and Mary Kay Cosmetics have differentiated themselves from other cosmetics and personal care companies by assembling a sales force numbering in the hundreds of thousands that gives them a direct sales capability—their sales associates personally demonstrate products to interested buyers, take their orders on the spot, and deliver the items to buyers' homes.

The most successful approaches to differentiation are those that are difficult for rivals to duplicate. Indeed, this is the route to a sustainable differentiation advantage. While resourceful competitors can, in time, clone almost any tangible product

Easy-to-copy differentiating features cannot produce sustainable competitive advantage.

attribute, socially complex intangible attributes, such as company reputation, long-standing relationships with buyers, and image are much harder to imitate. Differentiation that creates switching costs that lock in buyers also provides a route to sustainable advantage. For example, if a buyer makes a substantial investment in learning to use one type of system, that buyer is less likely to switch to a competitor's system. (This has kept many users from switching away from Microsoft Office products, despite the fact that there are other applications with superior features.) As a rule, differentiation yields a longer-lasting and more profitable competitive edge when it is based on a well-established brand image, patent-protected product innovation, complex technical superiority, a reputation for superior product quality and reliability, relationship-based customer service, and unique competitive capabilities.

When a Differentiation Strategy Works Best

Differentiation strategies tend to work best in market circumstances where:

- *Buyer needs and uses of the product are diverse.* Diverse buyer preferences allow industry rivals to set themselves apart with product attributes that appeal to particular buyers. For instance, the diversity of consumer preferences for menu selection, ambience, pricing, and customer service gives restaurants exceptionally wide latitude in creating a differentiated product offering. Other industries with diverse buyer needs include magazine publishing, automobile manufacturing, footwear, and kitchen appliances.
- *There are many ways to differentiate the product or service that have value to buyers.* Industries in which competitors have opportunities to add features to products and services are well suited to differentiation strategies. For example, hotel chains can differentiate on such features as location, size of room, range of guest services, in-hotel dining, and the quality and luxuriousness of bedding and furnishings. Similarly, cosmetics producers are able to differentiate based upon prestige and image, formulations that fight the signs of aging, UV light protection, exclusivity of retail locations, the inclusion of antioxidants and natural ingredients, or prohibitions against animal testing. Basic commodities, such as chemicals, mineral deposits, and agricultural products, provide few opportunities for differentiation.
- *Few rival firms are following a similar differentiation approach.* The best differentiation approaches involve trying to appeal to buyers on the basis of attributes that rivals are not emphasizing. A differentiator encounters less head-to-head rivalry when it goes its own separate way in creating value and does not try to outdifferentiate rivals on the very same attributes. When many rivals base their differentiation efforts on the same attributes, the most likely result is weak brand differentiation and "strategy overcrowding"—competitors end up chasing much the same buyers with much the same product offerings.
- *Technological change is fast-paced and competition revolves around rapidly evolving product features.* Rapid product innovation and frequent introductions of next-version products heighten buyer interest and provide space for companies to pursue distinct differentiating paths. In video game hardware and video games, golf equipment, mobile phones, and automobile navigation systems, competitors are locked into an ongoing battle to set themselves apart by introducing the best next-generation products. Companies that fail to come up with new and improved products and distinctive performance features quickly lose out in the marketplace.

Any differentiating feature that works well is a magnet for imitators.

Pitfalls to Avoid in Pursuing a Differentiation Strategy

Differentiation strategies can fail for any of several reasons. *A differentiation strategy keyed to product or service attributes that are easily and quickly copied is always suspect.* Rapid imitation means that no rival achieves differentiation, since whenever one firm introduces some value-creating aspect that strikes the fancy of buyers, fast-following copycats quickly reestablish parity. This is why a firm must seek out sources of value creation that are time-consuming or burdensome for rivals to match if it hopes to use differentiation to win a sustainable competitive edge.

Differentiation strategies can also falter when buyers see little value in the unique attributes of a company's product. Thus, even if a company succeeds in setting its product apart from those of rivals, its strategy can result in disappointing sales and profits if the product does not deliver adequate value to buyers. Any time many potential buyers look at a company's differentiated product offering with indifference, the company's differentiation strategy is in deep trouble.

The third big pitfall is overspending on efforts to differentiate the company's product offering, thus eroding profitability. Company efforts to achieve differentiation nearly always raise costs—often substantially, since marketing and R&D are expensive undertakings. The key to profitable differentiation is either to keep the unit cost of achieving differentiation below the price premium that the differentiating attributes can command (thus increasing the profit margin per unit sold) or to offset thinner profit margins per unit by selling enough additional units to increase total profits. If a company goes overboard in pursuing costly differentiation, it could be saddled with unacceptably low profits or even losses.

Other common mistakes in crafting a differentiation strategy include:

- *Offering only trivial improvements in quality, service, or performance features vis-à-vis rivals' products.* Trivial differences between rivals' product offerings may not be visible or important to buyers. If a company wants to generate the fiercely loyal customer following needed to earn superior profits and open up a differentiation-based competitive advantage over rivals, then its strategy must result in *strong rather than weak product differentiation.* In markets where differentiators do no better than achieve weak product differentiation, customer loyalty is weak, the costs of brand switching are low, and no one company has enough of a market edge to command a price premium over rival brands.
- *Over-differentiating so that product quality, features, or service levels exceed the needs of most buyers.* A dazzling array of features and options not only drives up product price but also runs the risk that many buyers will conclude that a less deluxe and lower-priced brand is a better value since they have little occasion to use the deluxe attributes.
- *Charging too high a price premium.* While buyers may be intrigued by a product's deluxe features, they may nonetheless see it as being overpriced relative to the value delivered by the differentiating attributes. A company must guard against turning off would-be buyers with what is perceived as "price gouging." Normally, the bigger the price premium for the differentiating extras, the harder it is to keep buyers from switching to competitors' lower-priced offerings.

Over-differentiating and overcharging are fatal differentiation strategy mistakes.

A low-cost provider strategy can defeat a differentiation strategy when buyers are satisfied with a basic product and don't think "extra" attributes are worth a higher price.

FOCUSED (OR MARKET NICHE) STRATEGIES

What sets focused strategies apart from low-cost provider and broad differentiation strategies is concentrated attention on a narrow piece of the total market. The target segment, or niche, can be in the form of a geographic segment (such as New England), or a customer segment (such as urban hipsters), or a product segment (such as a class of models or some version of the overall product type). Community Coffee, the largest family-owned specialty coffee retailer in the United States, has a geographic focus on the state of Louisiana and communities across the Gulf of Mexico. Community holds only a small share of the national coffee market but has recorded sales in excess of $100 million and has won a strong following in the 20-state region where its coffee is distributed. Examples of firms that concentrate on a well-defined market niche keyed to a particular product or buyer segment include Zipcar (car rental in urban areas), Comedy Central (cable TV), Blue Nile (online jewelry), Tesla Motors (electric cars), and CGA, Inc. (a specialist in providing insurance to cover the cost of lucrative hole-in-one prizes at golf tournaments). Microbreweries, local bakeries, bed-and-breakfast inns, and retail boutiques have also scaled their operations to serve narrow or local customer segments.

A Focused Low-Cost Strategy

A focused strategy based on low cost aims at securing a competitive advantage by serving buyers in the target market niche at a lower cost and lower price than those of rival competitors. This strategy has considerable attraction when a firm can lower costs significantly by limiting its customer base to a well-defined buyer segment. The avenues to achieving a cost advantage over rivals also serving the target market niche are the same as those for low-cost leadership—use the cost drivers to keep the costs of value chain activities to a bare minimum and search for innovative ways to bypass nonessential activities. The only real difference between a low-cost provider strategy and a focused low-cost strategy is the size of the buyer group to which a company is appealing—the former involves a product offering that appeals broadly to almost all buyer groups and market segments, whereas the latter aims at just meeting the needs of buyers in a narrow market segment.

Focused low-cost strategies are fairly common. Producers of private-label goods are able to achieve low costs in product development, marketing, distribution, and advertising by concentrating on making generic items imitative of name-brand merchandise and selling directly to retail chains wanting a low-priced store brand. The Perrigo Company has become a leading manufacturer of over-the-counter health care products, with 2013 sales of more than $3.5 billion, by focusing on producing private-label brands for retailers such as Walmart, CVS, Walgreens, Rite-Aid, and Safeway. Budget motel chains, like Motel 6, Sleep Inn, and Super 8, cater to price-conscious travelers who just want to pay for a clean, no-frills place to spend the night. Illustration Capsule 5.2 describes how Aravind's focus on lowering the costs of cataract removal allowed it to address the needs of the "bottom of the pyramid" in India's population, where blindness due to cataracts is an endemic problem.

A Focused Differentiation Strategy

Focused differentiation strategies involve offering superior products or services designed to appeal to the unique preferences and needs of a narrow, well-defined group of buyers. Successful use of a focused differentiation strategy depends on (1) the existence of a buyer segment that is looking for special product attributes or seller capabilities and (2) a firm's ability to stand apart from rivals competing in the same target market niche.

ILLUSTRATION CAPSULE 5.2 Aravind Eye Care System's Focused Low-Cost Strategy

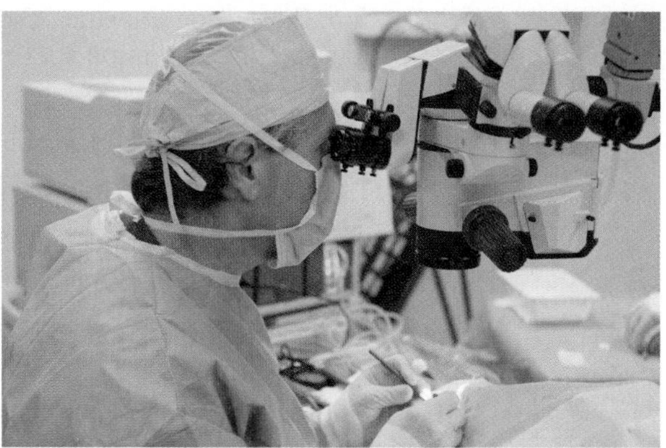

Cataracts, the largest cause of preventable blindness, can be treated with a quick surgical procedure that restores sight; however, poverty and limited access to care prevent millions worldwide from obtaining surgery. The Aravind Eye Care System has found a way to address this problem, with a *focused low-cost strategy* that has made cataract surgery not only affordable for more people in India but free for the very poorest. On the basis of this strategy, Aravind has achieved world renown and become the largest provider of eye care in the world.

High volume and high efficiency are at the cornerstone of Aravind's strategy. The Aravind network, with its nine eye hospitals in India, has become one of the most productive systems in the world, conducting about 350,000 surgeries a year in addition to seeing over 2.8 million outpatients each year. Using the unique model of screening eye camps all over the country, Aravind reaches a broader cross-section of the market for surgical treatment. Additionally, Aravind attains very high staff productivity, with each surgeon performing more than 2,500 surgeries annually compared to 125 for a comparable American surgeon.

What enabled this level of productivity (with no loss in quality of care) was the development of a standardized system of surgical treatment, capitalizing on the fact that cataract removal was already a fairly routine process. Aravind streamlined as much of the process as possible, reducing discretionary elements to a minimum, and tracking outcomes to ensure continuous process improvement. At Aravind's hospitals, there is no wasted time between surgeries, as different teams of support staff prepare patients for surgery and bring them to the operating theater so that surgeons simply need to turn from one table to another to perform surgery on the next prepared patient. Aravind also drove costs down through the creation of its own manufacturing division, Aurolab, to produce intraocular lenses, suture needles, pharmaceuticals, and surgical blades in India.

Aravind's low costs allow it to keep its prices for cataract surgery very low, at 500 rupees ($10) per patient compared to an average cost of $1,500 for surgery in the United States. Nevertheless, the system provides surgical outcomes and quality comparable to clinics in the United States. As a result of its unique fee system and effective management, Aravind is also able to provide free eye care to 60 percent of its patients from the revenue generated from the paying patients.

Note: Developed with Avni V. Patel.

Sources: G. Natchiar, A. L. Robin, R. Thulasiraj, et al., "Attacking the Backlog of India's Curable Blind; The Aravind Eye Hospital Model," *Archives of Ophthalmology* 112 (1994), pp. 987–993; D. F. Chang, "Tackling the Greatest Challenge in Cataract Surgery," *British Journal of Ophthalmology* 89 (2005), pp. 1073–1077; "Driving Down the Cost of High Quality Care," *McKinsey Health International,* December 2011; and S. Kandavel, "Aravind Eye Care to Set Up Next Hospital in Chennai," *The Economic Times* Online, December 25, 2012.

Companies like L. A. Burdick's (gourmet chocolates), Rolls-Royce, and Four Seasons Hotels and Resorts employ successful differentiation-based focused strategies targeted at upscale buyers wanting products and services with world-class attributes. Indeed, most markets contain a buyer segment willing to pay a big price premium for the very finest items available, thus opening the strategic window for some competitors to pursue differentiation-based focused strategies aimed at the very top of the market pyramid. Another successful focused differentiator is "fashion food retailer" Trader Joe's, a 418-store, 39-state chain that is a combination gourmet deli and food warehouse. Customers shop Trader Joe's as much for entertainment as for conventional grocery items—the store stocks out-of-the-ordinary culinary treats like raspberry salsa, salmon burgers, and jasmine fried rice, as well as the standard goods normally found in supermarkets. What sets Trader Joe's apart is not just its unique combination of food novelties and competitively priced grocery items but also its capability to turn an otherwise mundane grocery excursion into a whimsical treasure hunt that is just plain fun. Illustration Capsule 5.3 describes how Popchips has been gaining attention with a focused differentiation strategy.

When a Focused Low-Cost or Focused Differentiation Strategy Is Attractive

A focused strategy aimed at securing a competitive edge based on either low costs or differentiation becomes increasingly attractive as more of the following conditions are met:

- The target market niche is big enough to be profitable and offers good growth potential.
- Industry leaders have chosen not to compete in the niche—in which case focusers can avoid battling head to head against the industry's biggest and strongest competitors.
- It is costly or difficult for multisegment competitors to meet the specialized needs of niche buyers and at the same time satisfy the expectations of their mainstream customers.
- The industry has many different niches and segments, thereby allowing a focuser to pick the niche best suited to its resources and capabilities. Also, with more niches there is more room for focusers to avoid competing for the same customers.
- Few if any rivals are attempting to specialize in the same target segment—a condition that reduces the risk of segment overcrowding.

The advantages of focusing a company's entire competitive effort on a single market niche are considerable, especially for smaller and medium-sized companies that may lack the breadth and depth of resources to tackle going after a broader customer base with a more complex set of needs. YouTube has become a household name by concentrating on short video clips posted online. Papa John's and Domino's Pizza have created impressive businesses by focusing on the home delivery segment.

The Risks of a Focused Low-Cost or Focused Differentiation Strategy

Focusing carries several risks. One is the chance that competitors will find effective ways to match the focused firm's capabilities in serving the target niche—perhaps by coming up with products or brands specifically designed to appeal to buyers in the target niche or by developing expertise and capabilities that offset the focuser's strengths. In the lodging business, large chains like Marriott have launched multibrand strategies that allow them to compete effectively in several lodging segments simultaneously. Marriott has flagship JW Marriott and Ritz-Carlton hotels with deluxe accommodations for business travelers and resort vacationers. Its Courtyard by Marriott and SpringHill Suites brands cater to business travelers looking for moderately priced lodging, while Marriott Residence Inns and TownePlace Suites are designed as a "home away from home" for travelers staying five or more nights, and Fairfield Inn & Suites is intended to appeal to travelers looking for quality lodging at an "affordable" price. Multibrand strategies are attractive to large companies like Marriott precisely because they enable a company to enter a market niche and siphon business away from companies that employ a focused strategy.

ILLUSTRATION CAPSULE 5.3

Popchips' Focused Differentiation Strategy

Potato chips are big business: Americans consume $7 billion worth annually. But the industry is a hard one to break into since it's a mature, slow-growth industry, dominated by a few large competitors. Frito-Lay alone (maker of Lays and Ruffles) has a commanding 60 percent market share. These characteristics are enough to dissuade most potential entrants, but not Popchips, a small potato chip startup. Despite difficult odds, Popchips has made impressive inroads into the industry over the last seven years, with the help of a *focused differentiation strategy*.

Popchips was founded in 2007 by Keith Belling, a serial entrepreneur, and Pat Turpin, a former Costco snack executive. Their idea was simple: Take advantage of high-income purchasers' growing desire for tasty, low-fat snacks. Using an innovative cooking method, they found a way to halve the fat content in potato chips while preserving flavor. Popchips has a differentiated product. But its real point of differentiation is its brand and distribution strategy. Most potato chips have mass distribution and a broad buyer base. Belling and Turpin decided from the outset to narrow their distribution and narrow their targeted buyers. They hoped that focusing on a market niche would allow their product to stand out from the bags of Lays and cans of Pringles in aisles all over America. Popchips' target: upper-income, health-conscious urban and suburban consumers.

To that end, the firm has signed distribution deals with Whole Foods, Target, and, reflecting Turpin's roots, Costco. Popchips' marketing emphasizes social marketing and word-of-mouth recommendations. The company sends out samples to key tastemakers who tweet, blog, or recommend the product in traditional media. Ashton Kutcher, MTV's former *Punk'd* host, was so impressed with the chips that he volunteered to promote them. As with *Punk'd*, Popchips' advertising is similarly irreverent, with taglines like "love. without the handles."

Popchips' differentiation strategy is succeeding. Since 2009, the company's sales have accounted for

nearly all potato chip sales growth at natural supermarket stores, like Whole Foods, giving it a 15 percent market share in this niche distribution channel. The company's 2012 sales were $93 million, nearly doubling since 2010. That's particularly impressive given that the industry growth rate has been a paltry 4 percent. In 2013, *Forbes* put Popchips at number 5 on its list of America's Most Promising Companies.

Note: Developed with Dennis L. Huggins.

Sources: Molly Maier, "Chips, Pretzels and Corn Snacks—US—January 2012," *Mintel,* January 2012, www.oxygen.mintel.com (accessed February 1, 2012); Lindsay Blakely and Caitlin Elsaesser, "One Snacker at a Time: How Popchips Grew without Losing Its Character," *CBS News,* January 2011, www.cbsnews.com (accessed February 1, 2012); Laura Petrecca, "Popchips CEO Keith Belling Is 'Poptimist' on Healthy Snacks," *USA Today,* March 2010, www.usatoday.com (accessed February 13, 2012); www.forbes.com (accessed March 28, 2013); and Popchips' website.

A second risk of employing a focused strategy is the potential for the preferences and needs of niche members to shift over time toward the product attributes desired by the majority of buyers. An erosion of the differences across buyer segments lowers entry barriers into a focuser's market niche and provides an open invitation for rivals in adjacent segments to begin competing for the focuser's customers. A third risk is that the segment may become so attractive that it is soon inundated with competitors, intensifying rivalry and splintering segment profits. And there is always the risk for segment growth to slow to such a small rate that a focuser's prospects for future sales and profit gains become unacceptably dim.

BEST-COST PROVIDER STRATEGIES

As Figure 5.1 indicates, **best-cost provider strategies** stake out a middle ground between pursuing a low-cost advantage and a differentiation advantage and between appealing to the broad market as a whole and a narrow market niche. This permits companies to aim squarely at the sometimes great mass of value-conscious buyers looking for a better product or service at an economical price. Value-conscious buyers frequently shy away from both cheap low-end products and expensive high-end products, but they are quite willing to pay a "fair" price for extra features and functionality they find appealing and useful. The essence of a best-cost provider strategy is giving customers *more value for the money* by satisfying buyer desires for appealing features and charging a lower price for these attributes compared to rivals with similar-caliber product offerings.[6] From a competitive-positioning standpoint, best-cost strategies are thus a *hybrid,* balancing a strategic emphasis on low cost against a strategic emphasis on differentiation (desirable features delivered at a relatively low price).

CORE CONCEPT

Best-cost provider strategies are a *hybrid* of low-cost provider and differentiation strategies that aim at providing more desirable attributes (quality, features, performance, service) while beating rivals on price.

To profitably employ a best-cost provider strategy, a company *must have the capability to incorporate upscale attributes into its product offering at a lower cost than rivals.* When a company can incorporate more appealing features, good to excellent product performance or quality, or more satisfying customer service into its product offering *at a lower cost than rivals,* then it enjoys "best-cost" status—it is the low-cost provider of a product or service with *upscale attributes.* A best-cost provider can use its low-cost advantage to underprice rivals whose products or services have similarly upscale attributes and it still earns attractive profits.

Being a best-cost provider is different from being a low-cost provider because the additional attractive attributes entail additional costs (which a low-cost provider can avoid by offering buyers a basic product with few frills). Moreover, the two strategies aim at a distinguishably different market target. *The target market for a best-cost provider is value-conscious buyers*—buyers who are looking for appealing extras and functionality at a comparatively low price. Value-hunting buyers (as distinct from *price-conscious buyers* looking for a basic product at a bargain-basement price) often constitute a very sizable part of the overall market for a product or service.

LO 4

The attributes of a best-cost provider strategy—a hybrid of low-cost provider and differentiation strategies.

When a Best-Cost Provider Strategy Works Best

A best-cost provider strategy works best in markets where product differentiation is the norm and an attractively large number of value-conscious buyers can be induced to purchase midrange products rather than cheap, basic products or expensive, top-of-the-line products. A best-cost provider needs to position itself *near the middle of the market*

ILLUSTRATION CAPSULE 5.4 American Giant's Best-Cost Provider Strategy

Bayard Winthrop, founder and owner of American Giant, set out to make a hoodie like the soft, ultra-thick Navy sweatshirts his dad used to wear in the 1950s. But he also had two other aims: He wanted it to have a more updated look with a tailored fit, and he wanted it produced cost-effectively so that it could be sold at a great price. To accomplish these aims, he designed the sweatshirt with the help of a former industrial engineer from Apple and an internationally renowned pattern maker, rethinking every aspect of sweatshirt design and production along the way. The result was a hoodie differentiated from others on the basis of extreme attention to fabric, fit, construction, and durability. The hoodie is made from heavy-duty cotton that is run through a machine that carefully picks loops of thread out of the fabric to create a thick, combed, ring-spun fleece fabric that feels three times thicker than most sweatshirts. A small amount of spandex paneling along the shoulders and sides creates the fitted look and maintains the shape, keeping the sweatshirt from looking slouchy or sloppy. It has double stitching with strong thread on critical seams to avoid deterioration and boost durability. The zippers and draw cord are customized to match the sweatshirt's color—an uncommon practice in the business.

American Giant sources yarn from Parkdale, South Carolina, and turns it into cloth at the nearby Carolina Cotton Works. This reduces transport costs, creates a more dependable, durable product that American Giant can easily quality-check, and shortens product turnaround to about a month, lowering inventory costs. This process also enables the company to use a genuine "Made in the U.S.A" label, a perceived quality driver.

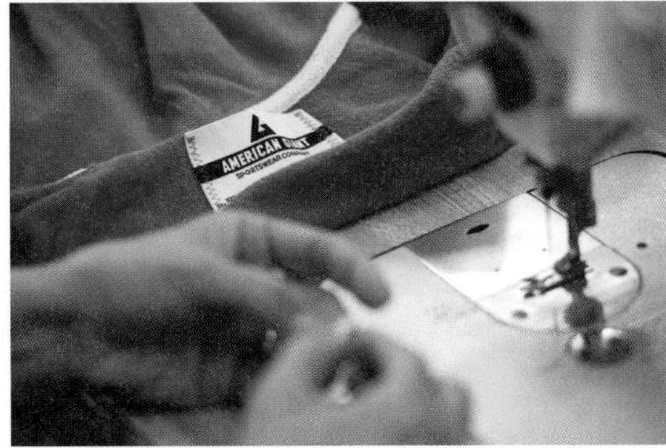

American Giant disrupts the traditional, expensive distribution models by having no stores or resellers. Instead, it sells directly to customers from its website, with free two-day shipping and returns. Much of the company's growth comes from word of mouth and a strong public relations effort that promotes the brand in magazines, newspapers, and key business-oriented television programs. American Giant has a robust refer-a-friend program that offers a discount to friends of, and a credit to, current owners. Articles in popular media proclaiming its product "the greatest hoodie ever made" have made demand for its sweatshirts skyrocket.

At $79 for the original men's hoodie, American Giant is not cheap but offers customers value in terms of both price and quality. The price is higher than what one would pay at The Gap or American Apparel and comparable to Levi's, J.Crew, or Banana Republic. But its quality is more on par with high-priced designer brands, while its price is far more affordable.

Note: Developed with Sarah Boole.

Sources: www.nytimes.com/2013/09/20/business/us-textile-factories-return.html?emc=eta1&_r=0; www.american-giant.com; www.slate.com/articles/technology/technology/2012/12/american_giant_hoodie_this_is_the_greatest_sweatshirt_known_to_man.html; www.businessinsider.com/this-hoodie-is-so-insanely-popular-you-have-to-wait-months-to-get-it-2013-12.

with either a medium-quality product at a below-average price or a high-quality product at an average or slightly higher price. Best-cost provider strategies also work well in recessionary times, when masses of buyers become value-conscious and are attracted to economically priced products and services with more appealing attributes. But unless a company has the resources, know-how, and capabilities to incorporate upscale product or service attributes at a lower cost than rivals, adopting a best-cost strategy is ill-advised. Illustration Capsule 5.4 describes how American Giant has applied the principles of the best-cost provider strategy in producing and marketing its hoodie sweatshirts.

The Risk of a Best-Cost Provider Strategy

A company's biggest vulnerability in employing a best-cost provider strategy is getting squeezed between the strategies of firms using low-cost and high-end differentiation strategies. Low-cost providers may be able to siphon customers away with the appeal of a lower price (despite less appealing product attributes). High-end differentiators may be able to steal customers away with the appeal of better product attributes (even though their products carry a higher price tag). Thus, to be successful, a best-cost provider must achieve significantly lower costs in providing upscale features so that it can outcompete high-end differentiators on the basis of a *significantly* lower price. Likewise, it must offer buyers *significantly* better product attributes to justify a price above what low-cost leaders are charging. In other words, it must offer buyers a more attractive customer value proposition.

THE CONTRASTING FEATURES OF THE FIVE GENERIC COMPETITIVE STRATEGIES: A SUMMARY

A company's competitive strategy should be well matched to its internal situation and predicated on leveraging its collection of competitively valuable resources and capabilities.

Deciding which generic competitive strategy should serve as the framework on which to hang the rest of the company's strategy is not a trivial matter. Each of the five generic competitive strategies *positions* the company differently in its market and competitive environment. Each establishes a *central theme* for how the company will endeavor to outcompete rivals. Each creates some boundaries or guidelines for maneuvering as market circumstances unfold and as ideas for improving the strategy are debated. Each entails differences in terms of product line, production emphasis, marketing emphasis, and means of maintaining the strategy, as shown in Table 5.1.

Thus a choice of which generic strategy to employ spills over to affect many aspects of how the business will be operated and the manner in which value chain activities must be managed. Deciding which generic strategy to employ is perhaps the most important strategic commitment a company makes—it tends to drive the rest of the strategic actions a company decides to undertake.

Successful Competitive Strategies Are Resource-Based

For a company's competitive strategy to succeed in delivering good performance and gain a competitive edge over rivals, it has to be well matched to a company's internal situation and underpinned by an appropriate set of resources, know-how, and competitive capabilities. To succeed in employing a low-cost provider strategy, a company must have the resources and capabilities to keep its costs below those of its competitors. This means having the expertise to cost-effectively manage value chain activities better than rivals, leveraging the cost drivers effectively, and/or having the innovative capability to bypass certain value chain activities being performed by rivals. To succeed in a differentiation strategy, a company must have the resources and capabilities to leverage value drivers effectively and incorporate attributes into its product offering that a broad range of buyers will find appealing. Successful focused strategies (both low cost and differentiation) require the capability to do an outstanding job of

TABLE 5.1 Distinguishing Features of the Five Generic Competitive Strategies

	Low-Cost Provider	Broad Differentiation	Focused Low-Cost Provider	Focused Differentiation	Best-Cost Provider
Strategic target	• A broad cross-section of the market.	• A broad cross-section of the market.	• A narrow market niche where buyer needs and preferences are distinctively different.	• A narrow market niche where buyer needs and preferences are distinctively different.	• Value-conscious buyers. • A middle-market range.
Basis of competitive strategy	• Lower overall costs than competitors.	• Ability to offer buyers something attractively different from competitors' offerings.	• Lower overall cost than rivals in serving niche members.	• Attributes that appeal specifically to niche members.	• Ability to offer better goods at attractive prices.
Product line	• A good basic product with few frills (acceptable quality and limited selection).	• Many product variations, wide selection; emphasis on differentiating features.	• Features and attributes tailored to the tastes and requirements of niche members.	• Features and attributes tailored to the tastes and requirements of niche members.	• Items with appealing attributes and assorted features; better quality, not best.
Production emphasis	• A continuous search for cost reduction without sacrificing acceptable quality and essential features.	• Build in whatever differentiating features buyers are willing to pay for; strive for product superiority.	• A continuous search for cost reduction for products that meet basic needs of niche members.	• Small-scale production or custom-made products that match the tastes and requirements of niche members.	• Build in appealing features and better quality at lower cost than rivals.
Marketing emphasis	• Low prices, good value. • Try to make a virtue out of product features that lead to low cost.	• Tout differentiating features. • Charge a premium price to cover the extra costs of differentiating features.	• Communicate attractive features of a budget-priced product offering that fits niche buyers' expectations.	• Communicate how product offering does the best job of meeting niche buyers' expectations.	• Emphasize delivery of *best value for the money.*
Keys to maintaining the strategy	• Economical prices, good value. • Strive to manage costs down, year after year, in every area of the business.	• Stress constant innovation to stay ahead of imitative competitors. • Concentrate on a few key differentiating features.	• Stay committed to serving the niche at the lowest overall cost; don't blur the firm's image by entering other market segments or adding other products to widen market appeal.	• Stay committed to serving the niche better than rivals; don't blur the firm's image by entering other market segments or adding other products to widen market appeal.	• Unique expertise in simultaneously managing costs down while incorporating upscale features and attributes.
Resources and capabilities required	• Capabilities for driving costs out of the value chain system. • *Examples:* large-scale automated plants, an efficiency-oriented culture, bargaining power.	• Capabilities concerning quality, design, intangibles, and innovation. • *Examples:* marketing capabilities, R&D teams, technology.	• Capabilities to lower costs on niche goods. • *Examples:* lower input costs for the specific product desired by the niche, batch production capabilities.	• Capabilities to meet the highly specific needs of niche members. • *Examples:* custom production, close customer relations.	• Capabilities to simultaneously deliver lower cost and higher-quality/ differentiated features. • *Examples:* TQM practices, mass customization.

satisfying the needs and expectations of niche buyers. Success in employing a best-cost strategy requires the resources and capabilities to incorporate upscale product or service attributes at a lower cost than rivals. *For all types of generic strategies, success in sustaining the competitive edge depends on having resources and capabilities that rivals have trouble duplicating and for which there are no good substitutes.*

KEY POINTS

1. Deciding which of the five generic competitive strategies to employ—overall low cost, broad differentiation, focused low cost, focused differentiation, or best cost—is perhaps the most important strategic commitment a company makes. It tends to drive the remaining strategic actions a company undertakes and sets the whole tone for pursuing a competitive advantage over rivals.
2. In employing a low-cost provider strategy and trying to achieve a low-cost advantage over rivals, a company must do a better job than rivals of cost-effectively managing value chain activities and/or it must find innovative ways to eliminate cost-producing activities. An effective use of cost drivers is key. Low-cost provider strategies work particularly well when price competition is strong and the products of rival sellers are virtually identical, when there are not many ways to differentiate, when buyers are price-sensitive or have the power to bargain down prices, when buyer switching costs are low, and when industry newcomers are likely to use a low introductory price to build market share.
3. Broad differentiation strategies seek to produce a competitive edge by incorporating attributes that set a company's product or service offering apart from rivals in ways that buyers consider valuable and worth paying for. This depends on the appropriate use of value drivers. Successful differentiation allows a firm to (1) command a premium price for its product, (2) increase unit sales (if additional buyers are won over by the differentiating features), and/or (3) gain buyer loyalty to its brand (because some buyers are strongly attracted to the differentiating features and bond with the company and its products). Differentiation strategies work best when buyers have diverse product preferences, when few other rivals are pursuing a similar differentiation approach, and when technological change is fast-paced and competition centers on rapidly evolving product features. A differentiation strategy is doomed when competitors are able to quickly copy the appealing product attributes, when a company's differentiation efforts fail to interest many buyers, and when a company overspends on efforts to differentiate its product offering or tries to overcharge for its differentiating extras.
4. A focused strategy delivers competitive advantage either by achieving lower costs than rivals in serving buyers constituting the target market niche or by developing a specialized ability to offer niche buyers an appealingly differentiated offering that meets their needs better than rival brands do. A focused strategy based on either low cost or differentiation becomes increasingly attractive when the target market niche is big enough to be profitable and offers good growth potential, when it is costly or difficult for multisegment competitors to meet the specialized

needs of the target market niche and at the same time satisfy their mainstream customers' expectations, when there are one or more niches that present a good match for a focuser's resources and capabilities, and when few other rivals are attempting to specialize in the same target segment.

5. Best-cost strategies create competitive advantage by giving buyers *more value for the money*—delivering superior quality, features, performance, and/or service attributes while also beating customer expectations on price. To profitably employ a best-cost provider strategy, a company *must have the capability to incorporate attractive or upscale attributes at a lower cost than rivals.* A best-cost provider strategy works best in markets with large numbers of value-conscious buyers desirous of purchasing better products and services for less money.
6. In all cases, competitive advantage depends on having competitively superior resources and capabilities that are a good fit for the chosen generic strategy. A sustainable advantage depends on maintaining that competitive superiority with resources, capabilities, and value chain activities that rivals have trouble matching and for which there are no good substitutes.

ASSURANCE OF LEARNING EXERCISES

1. Best Buy is the largest consumer electronics retailer in the United States, with 2013 sales of almost $50 billion. The company competes aggressively on price with such rivals as Costco, Sam's Club, Walmart, and Target, but it is also known by consumers for its first-rate customer service. Best Buy customers have commented that the retailer's sales staff is exceptionally knowledgeable about the company's products and can direct them to the exact location of difficult-to-find items. Best Buy customers also appreciate that demonstration models of PC monitors, digital media players, and other electronics are fully powered and ready for in-store use. Best Buy's Geek Squad tech support and installation services are additional customer service features that are valued by many customers. **LO 1, LO 2, LO 3, LO 4**

   How would you characterize Best Buy's competitive strategy? Should it be classified as a low-cost provider strategy? A differentiation strategy? A best-cost strategy? Explain your answer.
2. Illustration Capsule 5.1 discusses Walmart's low-cost position in the supermarket industry. Based on information provided in the capsule, explain how Walmart has built its low-cost advantage in the industry and why a low-cost provider strategy is well suited to the industry. **connect** **LO 2**
3. Stihl is the world's leading manufacturer and marketer of chain saws, with annual sales exceeding $3.7 billion. With innovations dating to its 1929 invention of the gasoline-powered chain saw, the company holds over 1,000 patents related to chain saws and outdoor power tools. The company's chain saws, leaf blowers, and hedge trimmers sell at price points well above competing brands and are sold only by its network of over 40,000 independent dealers in more than 160 countries. **LO 1, LO 2, LO 3, LO 4**

How would you characterize Stihl's competitive strategy? Should it be classified as a low-cost provider strategy? A differentiation strategy? A best-cost strategy? Also, has the company chosen to focus on a narrow piece of the market, or does it appear to pursue a broad market approach? Explain your answer.

connect
LO 3

4. Explore BMW's website at **www.bmwgroup.com** and see if you can identify at least three ways in which the company seeks to differentiate itself from rival automakers. Is there reason to believe that BMW's differentiation strategy has been successful in producing a competitive advantage? Why or why not?

EXERCISE FOR SIMULATION PARTICIPANTS

LO 1, LO 2, LO 3, LO 4

1. Which one of the five generic competitive strategies best characterizes your company's strategic approach to competing successfully?
2. Which rival companies appear to be employing a low-cost provider strategy?
3. Which rival companies appear to be employing a broad differentiation strategy?
4. Which rival companies appear to be employing a best-cost provider strategy?
5. Which rival companies appear to be employing some type of focused strategy?
6. What is your company's action plan to achieve a sustainable competitive advantage over rival companies? List at least three (preferably more than three) specific kinds of decision entries on specific decision screens that your company has made or intends to make to win this kind of competitive edge over rivals.

ENDNOTES

[1] Michael E. Porter, *Competitive Strategy: Techniques for Analyzing Industries and Competitors* (New York: Free Press, 1980), chap. 2; Michael E. Porter, "What Is Strategy?" *Harvard Business Review* 74, no. 6 (November–December 1996).
[2] M. Porter, *Competitive Advantage: Creating and Sustaining Superior Performance* (New York: Free Press, 1985).
[3] Richard L. Priem, "A Consumer Perspective on Value Creation," *Academy of Management Review* 32, no. 1 (2007), pp. 219–235.
[4] **jrscience.wcp.muohio.edu/nsfall01/FinalArticles/Final-IsitWorthitBrandsan.html**
[5] D. Yoffie, "Cola Wars Continue: Coke and Pepsi in 2006," Harvard Business School case 9-706-447.
[6] Peter J. Williamson and Ming Zeng, "Value-for-Money Strategies for Recessionary Times," *Harvard Business Review* 87, no. 3 (March 2009), pp. 66–74.

CHAPTER 6

Strengthening a Company's Competitive Position

Strategic Moves, Timing, and Scope of Operations

Learning Objectives

THIS CHAPTER WILL HELP YOU UNDERSTAND:

LO 1 Whether and when to pursue offensive or defensive strategic moves to improve a company's market position.

LO 2 When being a first mover or a fast follower or a late mover is most advantageous.

LO 3 The strategic benefits and risks of expanding a company's horizontal scope through mergers and acquisitions.

LO 4 The advantages and disadvantages of extending the company's scope of operations via vertical integration.

LO 5 The conditions that favor farming out certain value chain activities to outside parties.

LO 6 When and how strategic alliances can substitute for horizontal mergers and acquisitions or vertical integration and how they can facilitate outsourcing.

The objective is to enlarge the scope of your advantage which can only happen at someone else's expense.

Bruce Henderson – *Founder and Former CEO of the Boston Consulting Group*

Think of your priorities not in terms of what activities you do, but when you do them. Timing is everything.

Dan Millman – *Author and Lecturer*

In the virtual economy, collaboration is a new competitive imperative.

Michael Dell – *Founder and CEO of Dell Inc.*

Once a company has settled on which of the five generic competitive strategies to employ, attention turns to what *other strategic actions* it can take to complement its competitive approach and maximize the power of its overall strategy. The first set of decisions concerns whether to undertake offensive or defensive competitive moves, and the timing of such moves. The second set concerns the breadth of a company's activities (or its *scope* of operations along an industry's entire value chain). All in all, the following measures to strengthen a company's competitive position must be considered:

- Whether to go on the offensive and initiate aggressive strategic moves to improve the company's market position.
- Whether to employ defensive strategies to protect the company's market position.
- When to undertake strategic moves—whether advantage or disadvantage lies in being a first mover, a fast follower, or a late mover.
- Whether to bolster the company's market position by merging with or acquiring another company in the same industry.
- Whether to integrate backward or forward into more stages of the industry value chain system.
- Which value chain activities, if any, should be outsourced.
- Whether to enter into strategic alliances or partnership arrangements with other enterprises.

This chapter presents the pros and cons of each of these strategy-enhancing measures.

LAUNCHING STRATEGIC OFFENSIVES TO IMPROVE A COMPANY'S MARKET POSITION

No matter which of the five generic competitive strategies a firm employs, there are times when a company should *go on the offensive* to improve its market position and performance. **Strategic offensives** are called for when a company spots opportunities to gain profitable market share at its rivals' expense or when a company has no choice but to try to whittle away at a strong rival's competitive advantage. Companies like Samsung, Amazon, Facebook, and Google play hardball, aggressively pursuing competitive advantage and trying to reap the benefits a competitive

LO 1

Whether and when to pursue offensive or defensive strategic moves to improve a company's market position.

Sometimes a company's best strategic option is to seize the initiative, go on the attack, and launch a strategic offensive to improve its market position.

edge offers—a leading market share, excellent profit margins, and rapid growth.[1] The best offensives tend to incorporate several principles: (1) focusing relentlessly on building competitive advantage and then striving to convert it into a sustainable advantage, (2) applying resources where rivals are least able to defend themselves, (3) employing the element of surprise as opposed to doing what rivals expect and are prepared for, and (4) displaying a capacity for swift and decisive actions to overwhelm rivals.[2]

Choosing the Basis for Competitive Attack

As a rule, challenging rivals on competitive grounds where they are strong is an uphill struggle.[3] Offensive initiatives that exploit competitor weaknesses stand a better chance of succeeding than do those that challenge competitor strengths, especially if the weaknesses represent important vulnerabilities and weak rivals can be caught by surprise with no ready defense.

Strategic offensives should exploit the power of a company's strongest competitive assets—its most valuable resources and capabilities such as a better-known brand name, a more efficient production or distribution system, greater technological capability, or a superior reputation for quality. But a consideration of the company's strengths should not be made without also considering the rival's strengths and weaknesses. A strategic offensive should be based on those areas of strength where the company has its greatest competitive advantage over the targeted rivals. If a company has especially good customer service capabilities, it can make special sales pitches to the customers of those rivals that provide subpar customer service. Likewise, it may be beneficial to pay special attention to buyer segments that a rival is neglecting or is weakly equipped to serve.

The best offensives use a company's most powerful resources and capabilities to attack rivals in the areas where they are weakest.

Ignoring the need to tie a strategic offensive to a company's competitive strengths and what it does best is like going to war with a popgun—the prospects for success are dim. For instance, it is foolish for a company with relatively high costs to employ a price-cutting offensive. Likewise, it is ill advised to pursue a product innovation offensive without having proven expertise in R&D and new product development.

The principal offensive strategy options include the following:

1. *Offering an equally good or better product at a lower price.* Lower prices can produce market share gains if competitors don't respond with price cuts of their own and if the challenger convinces buyers that its product is just as good or better. However, such a strategy increases total profits only if the gains in additional unit sales are enough to offset the impact of lower prices and thinner margins per unit sold. Price-cutting offensives should be initiated only by companies that have *first achieved a cost advantage.*[4] British airline EasyJet used this strategy successfully against rivals such as British Air, Alitalia, and Air France by first cutting costs to the bone and then targeting leisure passengers who care more about low price than in-flight amenities and service.[5]
2. *Leapfrogging competitors by being first to market with next-generation products.* In technology-based industries, the opportune time to overtake an entrenched competitor is when there is a shift to the next generation of the technology. Microsoft got its next-generation Xbox 360 to market a full 12 months ahead of Sony's PlayStation 3 and Nintendo's Wii, helping it build a sizable market share and develop a reputation for cutting-edge innovation in the video game industry. Sony was careful to avoid a repeat, releasing its PlayStation 4 in November 2013 just as Microsoft released its Xbox One.

3. *Pursuing continuous product innovation to draw sales and market share away from less innovative rivals.* Ongoing introductions of new and improved products can put rivals under tremendous competitive pressure, especially when rivals' new product development capabilities are weak. But such offensives can be sustained only if a company can keep its pipeline full and maintain buyer enthusiasm for its new and better product offerings.
4. *Pursuing disruptive product innovations to create new markets.* While this strategy can be riskier and more costly than a strategy of continuous innovation, it can be a game changer if successful. Disruptive innovation involves perfecting new products with a few trial users and then quickly rolling them out to the whole market in an attempt to get the vast majority of buyers to embrace an altogether new and better value proposition quickly. Examples include online universities, Facebook, Tumblr, Twitter, Priceline.com, CampusBookRentals, Square (mobile credit card processing), and Amazon's Kindle.
5. *Adopting and improving on the good ideas of other companies (rivals or otherwise).* The idea of warehouse-type home improvement centers did not originate with Home Depot cofounders Arthur Blank and Bernie Marcus; they got the "big-box" concept from their former employer, Handy Dan Home Improvement. But they were quick to improve on Handy Dan's business model and take Home Depot to the next plateau in terms of product-line breadth and customer service. Offensive-minded companies are often quick to adopt any good idea (not nailed down by a patent or other legal protection) and build upon it to create competitive advantage for themselves.
6. *Using hit-and-run or guerrilla warfare tactics to grab market share from complacent or distracted rivals.* Options for "guerrilla offensives" include occasionally lowballing on price (to win a big order or steal a key account from a rival), surprising rivals with sporadic but intense bursts of promotional activity (offering a discounted trial offer to draw customers away from rival brands), or undertaking special campaigns to attract the customers of rivals plagued with a strike or problems in meeting buyer demand.[6] Guerrilla offensives are particularly well suited to small challengers that have neither the resources nor the market visibility to mount a full-fledged attack on industry leaders.
7. *Launching a preemptive strike to secure an industry's limited resources or capture a rare opportunity.*[7] What makes a move preemptive is its one-of-a-kind nature—whoever strikes first stands to acquire competitive assets that rivals can't readily match. Examples of preemptive moves include (1) securing the best distributors in a particular geographic region or country, (2) obtaining the most favorable site at a new interchange or intersection, in a new shopping mall, and so on, (3) tying up the most reliable, high-quality suppliers via exclusive partnerships, long-term contracts, or acquisition, and (4) moving swiftly to acquire the assets of distressed rivals at bargain prices. To be successful, a preemptive move doesn't have to totally block rivals from following; it merely needs to give a firm a prime position that is not easily circumvented.

How long it takes for an offensive to yield good results varies with the competitive circumstances.[8] It can be short if buyers respond immediately (as can occur with a dramatic cost-based price cut, an imaginative ad campaign, or a disruptive innovation). Securing a competitive edge can take much longer if winning consumer acceptance of an innovative product will take some time or if the firm may need several years to debug a new technology or put a new production capacity in place. But how long it takes for an offensive move to improve a company's market standing (and whether it can do so) also depends on whether market rivals recognize the threat and begin a counterresponse. And whether rivals will respond depends on whether they are capable of making an effective response and if they believe that a counterattack is worth the expense and the distraction.[9]

Choosing Which Rivals to Attack

Offensive-minded firms need to analyze which of their rivals to challenge as well as how to mount the challenge. The following are the best targets for offensive attacks:[10]

- *Market leaders that are vulnerable.* Offensive attacks make good sense when a company that leads in terms of market share is not a true leader in terms of serving the market well. Signs of leader vulnerability include unhappy buyers, an inferior product line, aging technology or outdated plants and equipment, a preoccupation with diversification into other industries, and financial problems. Caution is well advised in challenging strong market leaders—there's a significant risk of squandering valuable resources in a futile effort or precipitating a fierce and profitless industrywide battle for market share.
- *Runner-up firms with weaknesses in areas where the challenger is strong.* Runner-up firms are an especially attractive target when a challenger's resources and capabilities are well suited to exploiting their weaknesses.
- *Struggling enterprises that are on the verge of going under.* Challenging a hard-pressed rival in ways that further sap its financial strength and competitive position can weaken its resolve and hasten its exit from the market. In this type of situation, it makes sense to attack the rival in the market segments where it makes the most profits, since this will threaten its survival the most.
- *Small local and regional firms with limited capabilities.* Because small firms typically have limited expertise and resources, a challenger with broader and/or deeper capabilities is well positioned to raid their biggest and best customers—particularly those that are growing rapidly, have increasingly sophisticated requirements, and may already be thinking about switching to a supplier with a more full-service capability.

Blue-Ocean Strategy—A Special Kind of Offensive

CORE CONCEPT

A **blue-ocean strategy** offers growth in revenues and profits by discovering or inventing new industry segments that create altogether new demand.

A **blue-ocean strategy** seeks to gain a dramatic and durable competitive advantage by abandoning efforts to beat out competitors in existing markets and, instead, *inventing a new market segment that renders existing competitors irrelevant and allows a company to create and capture altogether new demand.*[11] This strategy views the business universe as consisting of two distinct types of market space. One is where industry boundaries are well defined, the competitive rules of the game are understood, and companies try to outperform rivals by capturing a bigger share of existing demand. In such markets, intense competition constrains a company's prospects for rapid growth and superior profitability since rivals move quickly to either imitate or counter the successes of competitors. The second type of market space is a "blue ocean," where the industry does not really exist yet, is untainted by competition, and offers wide-open opportunity for profitable and rapid growth if a company can create new demand with a new type of product offering.

A terrific example of such blue-ocean market space is the online auction industry that eBay created and now dominates. Other companies that have created blue-ocean market spaces include NetJets in fractional jet ownership, Drybar in hair blowouts, Tune Hotels in limited service "backpacker" hotels, and Cirque du Soleil in live entertainment. Cirque du Soleil "reinvented the circus" by pulling in a whole new group of customers—adults and corporate clients—who not only were noncustomers of traditional circuses (like Ringling Brothers) but also were willing to pay several times more than the price of a conventional circus ticket to have a "sophisticated entertainment experience" featuring stunning visuals and star-quality acrobatic acts. Zipcar Inc. is presently using a blue-ocean strategy to compete against entrenched rivals in the rental-car industry. It rents cars by the hour or day (rather than by the week) to members who pay a yearly fee for access to cars parked in designated spaces located conveniently throughout large cities. By allowing drivers under 25 years of age to rent cars and by targeting city dwellers who need to supplement their use of public transportation with short-term car rentals, Zipcar entered uncharted waters in the rental-car industry, growing rapidly in the process.

Good defensive strategies can help protect a competitive advantage but rarely are the basis for creating one.

Blue-ocean strategies provide a company with a great opportunity in the short run. But they don't guarantee a company's long-term success, which depends more on whether a company can protect the market position it opened up and sustain its early advantage. See Illustration Capsule 6.1 for an example of a company that opened up new competitive space in online luxury retailing only to see its blue-ocean waters ultimately turn red.

DEFENSIVE STRATEGIES—PROTECTING MARKET POSITION AND COMPETITIVE ADVANTAGE

In a competitive market, all firms are subject to offensive challenges from rivals. The purposes of defensive strategies are to lower the risk of being attacked, weaken the impact of any attack that occurs, and induce challengers to aim their efforts at other rivals. While defensive strategies usually don't enhance a firm's competitive advantage, they can definitely help fortify the firm's competitive position, protect its most valuable resources and capabilities from imitation, and defend whatever competitive advantage it might have. Defensive strategies can take either of two forms: actions to block challengers or actions to signal the likelihood of strong retaliation.

Blocking the Avenues Open to Challengers

The most frequently employed approach to defending a company's present position involves actions that restrict a challenger's options for initiating a competitive attack. There are any number of obstacles that can be put in the path of would-be challengers. A defender can introduce new features, add new models, or broaden its product line to close off gaps and vacant niches to opportunity-seeking challengers. It can thwart rivals' efforts to attack with a lower price by maintaining its own lineup of economy-priced options. It can discourage buyers from trying competitors' brands by lengthening warranties, making early announcements about impending new products or price changes, offering free training and support services, or providing coupons and sample giveaways to buyers most prone to experiment. It can induce potential buyers to reconsider switching. It can challenge the quality or safety of rivals' products.

ILLUSTRATION CAPSULE 6.1

Gilt Groupe's Blue-Ocean Strategy in the U.S. Flash-Sale Industry

Luxury-fashion flash sales exploded onto the U.S. e-commerce scene when Gilt Groupe launched its business in 2007. Flash sales offer limited quantities of high-end designer brands at steep discounts to site members over a very narrow timeframe: The opportunity to snap up an incredible bargain is over in a "flash." The concept of online, time-limited, designer-brand sale events, available to members only, had been invented six years earlier by the French company Vente Privée. But since Vente Privée operated in Europe, the U.S. market represented a wide-open blue ocean of uncontested opportunity. Gilt Groupe's only rival was Ideeli, another U.S. startup that had launched in the same year.

Gilt Groupe thrived and grew rapidly in the calm waters of the early days of the U.S. industry. Its tremendous growth stemmed from its recognition of an underserved segment of the population—the web-savvy, value-conscious fashionista—and also from fortuitous timing. The Great Recession hit the United States in December 2007, causing a sharp decline in consumer buying and leaving designers with unforeseen quantities of luxury items they could not sell. The fledgling flash-sale industry was the perfect channel to offload some of the excess inventory since it still maintained the cachet of exclusivity, with members-only sales and limited-time availability.

Gilt's revenue grew exponentially from $25 million in 2008 to upward of $550 million by 2012. But the company's success prompted an influx of fast followers into the luxury flash-sale industry, including HauteLook, RueLaLa, Lot18, and Vente-Privee.com, which entered the market at around the same time as Gilt. The new rivals not only competed for online customers, who could switch costlessly from site to site (since memberships were free), but also competed for unsold designer inventory. As the U.S. economy came out of the recession, much less of this type of inventory was available. Larger players had also begun to enter the flash-sale market in the United States, with Nordstrom's acquisition of HauteLook, eBay's purchase of RueLaLa, and Amazon.com's 2011 acquisition of MyHabit.com. In late 2011, Vente Privée announced the launch of its U.S. online site, a joint venture with American Express.

As the competitive waters have begun to roil and turn increasingly red, Gilt Groupe has been looking for new ways to compete, expanding into a variety of online luxury product and service niches and venturing overseas. While the company is not yet profitable in traditional terms, under new management at Gilt Groupe, internal measures of operating profits have become positive and the company is more serious than ever about an IPO in 2014 or 2015. Some of Gilt's competitors have successfully gone public in recent years, showing that there may still be plenty of room to survive and prosper in a more crowded competitive space. But only time will tell.

Note: Developed with Judith H. Lin.

Sources: Matthew Carroll, "The Rise of Gilt Groupe," *Forbes.com,* January 2012; Mark Brohan, "The Top 500 Guide," *Internet Retailer,* June 2011; Colleen Debaise, "Launching Gilt Groupe, a Fashionable Enterprise," *The Wall Street Journal,* October 2010, www.wsj.com (accessed February 26, 2012); about.americanexpress.com/news/pr/2011/vente_usa.aspx (accessed March 3, 2012); and J. Del Ray, "Gilt Groupe Eyes Late 2014 IPO—For Real, This Time," *AllThingsD* Online, November 21, 2013 (accessed March 29, 2014).

Finally, a defender can grant volume discounts or better financing terms to dealers and distributors to discourage them from experimenting with other suppliers, or it can convince them to handle its product line *exclusively* and force competitors to use other distribution outlets.

There are many ways to throw obstacles in the path of would-be challengers.

Signaling Challengers That Retaliation Is Likely

The goal of signaling challengers that strong retaliation is likely in the event of an attack is either to dissuade challengers from attacking at all or to divert them to less threatening options. Either goal can be achieved by letting challengers know the battle will cost more than it is worth. Signals to would-be challengers can be given by:

- Publicly announcing management's commitment to maintaining the firm's present market share.
- Publicly committing the company to a policy of matching competitors' terms or prices.
- Maintaining a war chest of cash and marketable securities.
- Making an occasional strong counterresponse to the moves of weak competitors to enhance the firm's image as a tough defender.

To be an effective defensive strategy, signaling needs to be accompanied by a *credible commitment* to follow through.

To be an effective defensive strategy, however, signaling needs to be accompanied by a *credible commitment* to follow through.

TIMING A COMPANY'S OFFENSIVE AND DEFENSIVE STRATEGIC MOVES

When to make a strategic move is often as crucial as *what* move to make. Timing is especially important when **first-mover advantages** or **disadvantages** exist. Under certain conditions, being first to initiate a strategic move can have a high payoff in the form of a competitive advantage that later movers can't dislodge. Moving first is no guarantee of success, however, since first movers also face some significant disadvantages. Indeed, there are circumstances in which it is more advantageous to be a fast follower or even a late mover. Because the timing of strategic moves can be consequential, it is important for company strategists to be aware of the nature of first-mover advantages and disadvantages and the conditions favoring each type of move.[12]

CORE CONCEPT

Because of **first-mover advantages** and **disadvantages,** competitive advantage can spring from *when* a move is made as well as from *what* move is made.

The Potential for First-Mover Advantages

Market pioneers and other types of first movers typically bear greater risks and greater development costs than firms that move later. If the market responds well to its initial move, the pioneer will benefit from a monopoly position (by virtue of being first to market) that enables it to recover its investment costs and make an attractive profit. If the firm's pioneering move gives it a competitive advantage that can be sustained even after other firms enter the market space, its first-mover advantage will be greater still. The extent of this type of advantage, however, will depend on whether and how fast follower firms can piggyback on the pioneer's success and either imitate or improve on its move.

LO 2

When being a first mover or a fast follower or a late mover is most advantageous.

There are five such conditions in which first-mover advantages are most likely to arise:

1. *When pioneering helps build a firm's reputation and creates strong brand loyalty.* Customer loyalty to an early mover's brand can create a tie that binds, limiting the success of later entrants' attempts to poach from the early mover's customer base and steal market share.
2. *When a first mover's customers will thereafter face significant switching costs.* Switching costs can protect first movers when consumers make large investments in learning how to use a specific company's product or in purchasing complementary products that are also brand-specific. Switching costs can also arise from loyalty programs or long-term contracts that give customers incentives to remain with an initial provider.
3. *When property rights protections thwart rapid imitation of the initial move.* In certain types of industries, property rights protections in the form of patents, copyrights, and trademarks prevent the ready imitation of an early mover's initial moves. First-mover advantages in pharmaceuticals, for example, are heavily dependent on patent protections, and patent races in this industry are common. In other industries, however, patents provide limited protection and can frequently be circumvented. Property rights protections also vary among nations, since they are dependent on a country's legal institutions and enforcement mechanisms.
4. *When an early lead enables the first mover to move down the learning curve ahead of rivals.* When there is a steep learning curve and when learning can be kept *proprietary,* a first mover can benefit from volume-based cost advantages that grow ever larger as its experience accumulates and its scale of operations increases. This type of first-mover advantage is self-reinforcing and, as such, can preserve a first mover's competitive advantage over long periods of time. Honda's advantage in small multiuse motorcycles has been attributed to such an effect.
5. *When a first mover can set the technical standard for the industry.* In many technology-based industries, the market will converge around a single technical standard. By establishing the industry standard, a first mover can gain a powerful advantage that, like experience-based advantages, builds over time. The lure of such an advantage, however, can result in standard wars among early movers, as each strives to set the industry standard. The key to winning such wars is to enter early on the basis of strong fast-cycle product development capabilities, gain the support of key customers and suppliers, employ penetration pricing, and make allies of the producers of complementary products.

Illustration Capsule 6.2 describes how Amazon.com achieved a first-mover advantage in online retailing.

The Potential for Late-Mover Advantages or First-Mover Disadvantages

In some instances there are advantages *to being an adept follower* rather than a first mover. Late-mover advantages (or *first-mover disadvantages*) arise in four instances:

- When the costs of pioneering are high relative to the benefits accrued and imitative followers can achieve similar benefits with far lower costs. This is often the case when second movers can learn from a pioneer's experience and avoid making the same costly mistakes as the pioneer.

ILLUSTRATION CAPSULE 6.2

Amazon.com's First-Mover Advantage in Online Retailing

Amazon.com's path to becoming the world's largest online retailer began in 1994 when Jeff Bezos, a Manhattan hedge fund analyst at the time, noticed that the number of Internet users was increasing by 2,300 percent annually. Bezos saw the tremendous growth as an opportunity to sell products online that would be demanded by a large number of Internet users and could be easily shipped. Bezos launched the online bookseller Amazon.com in 1995. The startup's revenues soared to $148 million in 1997, $610 million in 1998, and $1.6 billion in 1999. Bezos's business plan—hatched while on a cross-country trip with his wife in 1994—made him *Time* magazine's Person of the Year in 1999.

The volume-based and reputational benefits of Amazon.com's early entry into online retailing had delivered a first-mover advantage, but between 2000 and 2013 Bezos undertook a series of additional strategic initiatives to solidify the company's number-one ranking in the industry. Bezos undertook a massive building program in the late-1990s that added five new warehouses and fulfillment centers at a total cost of $300 million. The additional warehouse capacity was added years before it was needed, but Bezos wanted to move preemptively against potential rivals and ensure that, as demand continued to grow, the company could continue to offer its customers the best selection, the lowest prices, and the cheapest and most convenient delivery. The company also expanded its product line to include sporting goods, tools, toys, grocery items, electronics, and digital music downloads, giving it another means of maintaining its experience and scale-based advantages. Amazon.com's 2013 revenues of $74.5 billion not only made it the world's leading Internet retailer but made it larger than its 12 biggest competitors combined. As a result, Jeff Bezos's shares in Amazon.com made him the 12th wealthiest person in the United States, with an estimated net worth of $27.2 billion.

Moving down the learning curve in Internet retailing was not an entirely straightforward process for Amazon.com. Bezos commented in a *Fortune* article profiling the company, "We were investors in every bankrupt, 1999-vintage e-commerce startup. Pets.com, living.com, kozmo.com. We invested in a lot of high-profile flameouts." He went on to specify that although the ventures were a "waste of money," they "didn't take us off our own mission." Bezos also suggested that gaining advantage as a first mover is "taking a million tiny steps—and learning quickly from your missteps."

Sources: Mark Brohan, "The Top 500 Guide," *Internet Retailer,* June 2009, www.internetretailer.com (accessed June 17, 2009); Josh Quittner, "How Jeff Bezos Rules the Retail Space," *Fortune,* May 5, 2008, pp. 126–134; S. Banjo and P. Ziobro, "After Decades of Toil, Web Sales Remain Small for Many Retailers," *The Wall Street Journal* Online, August 27, 2013 (accessed March 2014); Company Snapshot, *Bloomberg Businessweek* Online (accessed March 28, 2014); Forbes.com; and company website.

- When an innovator's products are somewhat primitive and do not live up to buyer expectations, thus allowing a follower with better-performing products to win disenchanted buyers away from the leader.
- When rapid market evolution (due to fast-paced changes in either technology or buyer needs) gives second movers the opening to leapfrog a first mover's products with more attractive next-version products.
- When market uncertainties make it difficult to ascertain what will eventually succeed, allowing late movers to wait until these needs are clarified.
- When customer loyalty to the pioneer is low and a first mover's skills, know-how, and actions are easily copied or even surpassed

To Be a First Mover or Not

In weighing the pros and cons of being a first mover versus a fast follower versus a late mover, it matters whether the race to market leadership in a particular industry is a marathon or a sprint. In marathons, a slow mover is not unduly penalized—first-mover advantages can be fleeting, and there's ample time for fast followers and sometimes even late movers to catch up.[13] Thus the speed at which the pioneering innovation is likely to catch on matters considerably as companies struggle with whether to pursue an emerging market opportunity aggressively (as a first mover) or cautiously (as a late mover). For instance, it took 5.5 years for worldwide mobile phone use to grow from 10 million to 100 million, and it took close to 10 years for the number of at-home broadband subscribers to grow to 100 million worldwide. The lesson here is that there is a market penetration curve for every emerging opportunity. Typically, the curve has an inflection point at which all the pieces of the business model fall into place, buyer demand explodes, and the market takes off. The inflection point can come early on a fast-rising curve (like the use of e-mail) or farther up on a slow-rising curve (like the use of broadband). Any company that seeks competitive advantage by being a first mover thus needs to ask some hard questions:

- Does market takeoff depend on the development of complementary products or services that currently are not available?
- Is new infrastructure required before buyer demand can surge?
- Will buyers need to learn new skills or adopt new behaviors?
- Will buyers encounter high switching costs in moving to the newly introduced product or service?
- Are there influential competitors in a position to delay or derail the efforts of a first mover?

When the answers to any of these questions are yes, then a company must be careful not to pour too many resources into getting ahead of the market opportunity—the race is likely going to be closer to a 10-year marathon than a 2-year sprint.[14] On the other hand, if the market is a winner-take-all type of market, where powerful first-mover advantages insulate early entrants from competition and prevent later movers from making any headway, then it may be best to move quickly despite the risks.

STRENGTHENING A COMPANY'S MARKET POSITION VIA ITS SCOPE OF OPERATIONS

CORE CONCEPT

The **scope of the firm** refers to the range of activities that the firm performs internally, the breadth of its product and service offerings, the extent of its geographic market presence, and its mix of businesses.

Apart from considerations of competitive moves and their timing, there is another set of managerial decisions that can affect the strength of a company's market position. These decisions concern the scope of a company's operations—the breadth of its activities and the extent of its market reach. Decisions regarding the **scope of the firm** focus on which activities a firm will perform internally and which it will not.

Consider, for example, Ralph Lauren Corporation. In contrast to Rare Essentials, a boutique clothing store that sells apparel at a single retail store, Ralph Lauren designs, markets, and distributes fashionable apparel and other merchandise to more than 10,000 major department stores and specialty retailers throughout the world. In addition, it operates nearly 400 Ralph Lauren retail stores, more than

200 factory stores, and 7 e-commerce sites. Scope decisions also concern which segments of the market to serve—decisions that can include geographic market segments as well as product and service segments. Almost 40 percent of Ralph Lauren's sales are made outside the United States, and its product line includes apparel, fragrances, home furnishings, eyewear, watches and jewelry, and handbags and other leather goods. The company has also expanded its brand lineup through the acquisitions of Chaps menswear and casual retailer Club Monaco.

Decisions such as these, in essence, determine where the boundaries of a firm lie and the degree to which the operations within those boundaries cohere. They also have much to do with the direction and extent of a business's growth. In this chapter, we introduce the topic of company scope and discuss different types of scope decisions in relation to a company's business-level strategy. In the next two chapters, we develop two additional dimensions of a firm's scope. Chapter 7 focuses on international expansion—a matter of extending the company's geographic scope into foreign markets. Chapter 8 takes up the topic of corporate strategy, which concerns diversifying into a mix of different businesses. *Scope issues are at the very heart of corporate-level strategy.*

Several dimensions of firm scope have relevance for business-level strategy in terms of their capacity to strengthen a company's position in a given market. These include the firm's **horizontal scope,** which is the range of product and service segments that the firm serves within its product or service market. Mergers and acquisitions involving other market participants provide a means for a company to expand its horizontal scope. Expanding the firm's vertical scope by means of vertical integration can also affect the success of its market strategy. **Vertical scope** is the extent to which the firm engages in the various activities that make up the industry's entire value chain system, from initial activities such as raw-material production all the way to retailing and after-sale service activities. *Outsourcing decisions* concern another dimension of scope since they involve narrowing the firm's boundaries with respect to its participation in value chain activities. We discuss the pros and cons of each of these options in the sections that follow. Since *strategic alliances and partnerships* provide an alternative to vertical integration and acquisition strategies and are sometimes used to facilitate outsourcing, we conclude this chapter with a discussion of the benefits and challenges associated with *cooperative arrangements* of this nature.

CORE CONCEPT

Horizontal scope is the range of product and service segments that a firm serves within its focal market.

CORE CONCEPT

Vertical scope is the extent to which a firm's internal activities encompass the range of activities that make up an industry's entire value chain system, from raw-material production to final sales and service activities.

HORIZONTAL MERGER AND ACQUISITION STRATEGIES

LO 3

The strategic benefits and risks of expanding a company's horizontal scope through mergers and acquisitions.

Mergers and acquisitions are much-used strategic options to strengthen a company's market position. A *merger* is the combining of two or more companies into a single corporate entity, with the newly created company often taking on a new name. An *acquisition* is a combination in which one company, the acquirer, purchases and absorbs the operations of another, the acquired. The difference between a merger and an acquisition relates more to the details of ownership, management control, and financial arrangements than to strategy and competitive advantage. The resources and competitive capabilities of the newly created enterprise end up much the same whether the combination is the result of an acquisition or a merger.

Horizontal mergers and acquisitions, which involve combining the operations of firms *within the same product or service market,* provide an effective means for firms to rapidly increase the scale and horizontal scope of their core business. For example, the merger of AMR Corporation (parent of American Airlines) with US Airways has increased the airlines' scale of operations and extended their reach geographically to create the world's largest airline.

Merger and acquisition strategies typically set sights on achieving any of five objectives:[15]

1. *Creating a more cost-efficient operation out of the combined companies.* When a company acquires another company in the same industry, there's usually enough overlap in operations that less efficient plants can be closed or distribution and sales activities partly combined and downsized. Likewise, it is usually feasible to squeeze out cost savings in administrative activities, again by combining and downsizing such administrative activities as finance and accounting, information technology, human resources, and so on. The combined companies may also be able to reduce supply chain costs because of greater bargaining power over common suppliers and closer collaboration with supply chain partners. By helping to consolidate the industry and remove excess capacity, such combinations can also reduce industry rivalry and improve industry profitability.
2. *Expanding a company's geographic coverage.* One of the best and quickest ways to expand a company's geographic coverage is to acquire rivals with operations in the desired locations. Since a company's size increases with its geographic scope, another benefit is increased bargaining power with the company's suppliers or buyers. Greater geographic coverage can also contribute to product differentiation by enhancing a company's name recognition and brand awareness. Banks like JPMorgan Chase, Wells Fargo, and Bank of America have used acquisition strategies to establish a market presence and gain name recognition in an ever-growing number of states and localities. Food products companies like Nestlé, Kraft, Unilever, and Procter & Gamble have made acquisitions an integral part of their strategies to expand internationally.
3. *Extending the company's business into new product categories.* Many times a company has gaps in its product line that need to be filled in order to offer customers a more effective product bundle or the benefits of one-stop shopping. For example, customers might prefer to acquire a suite of software applications from a single vendor that can offer more integrated solutions to the company's problems. Acquisition can be a quicker and more potent way to broaden a company's product line than going through the exercise of introducing a company's own new product to fill the gap. Coca-Cola has increased the effectiveness of the product bundle it provides to retailers by acquiring beverage makers Minute Maid, Odwalla, Hi-C, and Glacéau Vitaminwater.
4. *Gaining quick access to new technologies or other resources and capabilities.* Making acquisitions to bolster a company's technological know-how or to expand its skills and capabilities allows a company to bypass a time-consuming and expensive internal effort to build desirable new resources and capabilities. From 2000 through May 2013, Cisco Systems purchased 106 companies to give it more technological reach and product breadth, thereby enhancing its standing as the world's largest provider of hardware, software, and services for creating and operating Internet networks.
5. *Leading the convergence of industries whose boundaries are being blurred by changing technologies and new market opportunities.* In fast-cycle industries or industries whose boundaries are changing, companies can use acquisition strategies to hedge their bets about the direction that an industry will take, to increase

their capacity to meet changing demands, and to respond flexibly to changing buyer needs and technological demands. News Corporation has prepared for the convergence of media services with the purchase of satellite TV companies to complement its media holdings in TV broadcasting (the Fox network and TV stations in various countries), cable TV (Fox News, Fox Sports, and FX), filmed entertainment (Twentieth Century Fox and Fox studios), newspapers, magazines, and book publishing.

Horizontal mergers and acquisitions can strengthen a firm's competitiveness in five ways: (1) by improving the efficiency of its operations, (2) by heightening its product differentiation, (3) by reducing market rivalry, (4) by increasing the company's bargaining power over suppliers and buyers, and (5) by enhancing its flexibility and dynamic capabilities.

Illustration Capsule 6.3 describes how Bristol-Myers Squibb developed its "string-of-pearls" horizontal acquisition strategy to fill in its pharmaceutical product development gaps.

Why Mergers and Acquisitions Sometimes Fail to Produce Anticipated Results

Despite many successes, mergers and acquisitions do not always produce the hoped-for outcomes.[16] Cost savings may prove smaller than expected. Gains in competitive capabilities may take substantially longer to realize or, worse, may never materialize at all. Efforts to mesh the corporate cultures can stall due to formidable resistance from organization members. Key employees at the acquired company can quickly become disenchanted and leave; the morale of company personnel who remain can drop to disturbingly low levels because they disagree with newly instituted changes. Differences in management styles and operating procedures can prove hard to resolve. In addition, the managers appointed to oversee the integration of a newly acquired company can make mistakes in deciding which activities to leave alone and which activities to meld into their own operations and systems.

A number of mergers and acquisitions have been notably unsuccessful. The 2008 merger of Arby's and Wendy's is a prime example. After only three years, Wendy's decided to sell Arby's due to the roast beef sandwich chain's continued poor profit performance. The jury is still out on whether Microsoft's 2011 acquisition of Skype for $8.5 billion, the United-Continental airlines merger, and Google's $12.5 billion acquisition of cell phone manufacturer Motorola Mobility will prove to be moneymakers or money losers.

VERTICAL INTEGRATION STRATEGIES

LO 4

The advantages and disadvantages of extending the company's scope of operations via vertical integration.

Expanding the firm's vertical scope by means of a vertical integration strategy provides another possible way to strengthen the company's position in its core market. A **vertically integrated firm** is one that participates in multiple stages of an industry's value chain system. Thus, if a manufacturer invests in facilities to produce component parts that it had formerly purchased from suppliers, or if it opens its own chain of retail stores to bypass its former distributors, it is engaging in vertical integration. A good example of a vertically integrated firm is Maple Leaf Foods, a major Canadian producer of fresh and processed meats whose best-selling brands include Maple Leaf

ILLUSTRATION CAPSULE 6.3

Bristol-Myers Squibb's "String-of-Pearls" Horizontal Acquisition Strategy

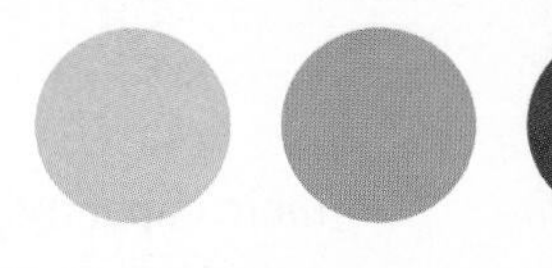

Back in 2007, the pharmaceutical company Bristol-Myers Squibb had a problem: Its top-selling drugs, Plavix and Abilify, would go off patent by 2012 and its drug pipeline was nearly empty. Together these drugs (the first for heart attacks, the second for depression) accounted for nearly half of the company's sales. Not surprisingly, the company's stock price had stagnated and was underperforming that of its peers.

Developing new drugs is difficult: New drugs must be identified, tested in increasingly sophisticated trials, and approved by the Food and Drug Administration. On average, this process takes 13 years and costs $2 billion. The success rate is low: Only one drug in eight manages to pass through clinical testing. In 2007, Bristol-Myers Squibb had only six new drugs at the clinical testing stage.

At the time, many drug companies were diversifying into new markets like over-the-counter drugs to better manage drug development risk. Bristol-Myers Squibb's management pursued a different strategy: product diversification through horizontal acquisitions. Bristol-Myers Squibb targeted small companies in new treatment areas, with the objective of reducing new product development risk by betting on preidentified drugs. The small companies it targeted, with one or two drugs in development, needed cash; Bristol-Myers Squibb needed new drugs. The firm's management called this its "string-of-pearls" strategy.

To implement its approach and obtain the cash it needed, Bristol-Myers Squibb sold its stake in Mead Johnson, a nutritional supplement manufacturer. Then it went on a shopping spree. Starting in 2007, the company spent over $8 billion on 18 transactions, including 12 horizontal acquisitions. In the process, the company acquired many promising new drug candidates for common diseases such as cancer, cardiovascular disease, rheumatoid arthritis, and hepatitis C.

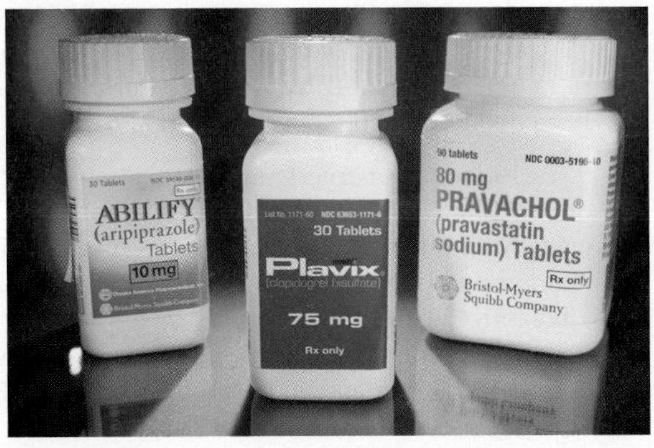

By early 2012, the company's string-of-pearls acquisitions were estimated to have added over $4 billion of new revenue to the company's coffers. Despite management changes over the subsequent year leading to the loss of two of the visionaries of the "string-of-pearls" concept, the new R&D chief remained committed to continuing the strategy. Analysts reported that Bristol-Myers Squibb had one of the best pipelines among drug makers. Investors agreed: The company's stock price has climbed consistently since 2007, outperforming its competitors and experiencing annual growth of over 20 percent in early 2013.

Note: Developed with Dennis L. Huggins.

Sources: D. Armstrong and M. Tirrell, "Bristol's Buy of Inhibitex for Hepatitis Drug Won't Be Last," *Bloomberg Businessweek,* January 2012, www.bloomberg.com (accessed January 30, 2012); S. M. Paul et al., "How to Improve R&D Productivity: The Pharmaceutical Industry's Grand Challenge," *Nature Reviews,* March 2010, pp. 203–214; Bristol-Myers Squibb 2007 and 2011 annual reports; and D. Armstrong, "Bristol-Myers New R&D Chief Plans to Keep Focus on Cancer," *Bloomberg* Online, April 8, 2013.

and Schneiders. Maple Leaf Foods participates in hog and poultry production, with company-owned hog and poultry farms; it has its own meat-processing and rendering facilities; it packages its products and distributes them from company-owned distribution centers; and it conducts marketing, sales, and customer service activities for its wholesale and retail buyers but does not otherwise participate in the final stage of the meat-processing vertical chain—the retailing stage.

CORE CONCEPT

A **vertically integrated firm** is one that performs value chain activities along more than one stage of an industry's value chain system.

A vertical integration strategy can expand the firm's range of activities *backward* into sources of supply and/or *forward* toward end users. When Tiffany & Co., a manufacturer and retailer of fine jewelry, began sourcing, cutting, and polishing its own diamonds, it integrated backward along the diamond supply chain. Mining giant De Beers Group and Canadian miner Aber Diamond integrated forward when they entered the diamond retailing business.

A firm can pursue vertical integration by starting its own operations in other stages of the vertical activity chain or by acquiring a company already performing the activities it wants to bring in-house. Vertical integration strategies can aim at *full integration* (participating in all stages of the vertical chain) or *partial integration* (building positions in selected stages of the vertical chain). Firms can also engage in *tapered integration* strategies, which involve a mix of in-house and outsourced activity in any given stage of the vertical chain. Oil companies, for instance, supply their refineries with oil from their own wells as well as with oil that they purchase from other producers—they engage in tapered backward integration. Boston Beer Company, the maker of Samuel Adams, engages in tapered forward integration, since it operates brew-pubs but sells the majority of its products through third-party distributors.

The Advantages of a Vertical Integration Strategy

Under the right conditions, a vertical integration strategy can add materially to a company's technological capabilities, strengthen the firm's competitive position, and boost its profitability.[17] But it is important to keep in mind that vertical integration has no real payoff strategy-wise or profit-wise unless the extra investment can be justified by compensating improvements in company costs, differentiation, or competitive strength.

Integrating Backward to Achieve Greater Competitiveness It is harder than one might think to generate cost savings or improve profitability by integrating backward into activities such as the manufacture of parts and components (which could otherwise be purchased from suppliers with specialized expertise in making the parts and components). For **backward integration** to be a cost-saving and profitable strategy, a company must be able to (1) achieve the same scale economies as outside suppliers and (2) match or beat suppliers' production efficiency with no drop-off in quality. Neither outcome is easily achieved. To begin with, a company's in-house requirements are often too small to reach the optimum size for low-cost operation. For instance, if it takes a minimum production volume of 1 million units to achieve scale economies and a company's in-house requirements are just 250,000 units, then it falls far short of being able to match the costs of outside suppliers (which may readily find buyers for 1 million or more units). Furthermore, matching the production efficiency of suppliers is fraught with problems when suppliers have considerable production experience, when the technology they employ has elements that are hard to master, and/or when substantial R&D expertise is required to develop next-version components or keep pace with advancing technology in components production.

CORE CONCEPT

Backward integration involves entry into activities previously performed by suppliers or other enterprises positioned along earlier stages of the industry value chain system; **forward integration** involves entry into value chain system activities closer to the end user.

That said, occasions still arise when a company can improve its cost position and competitiveness by performing a broader range of industry value chain activities in-house rather than having such activities performed by outside suppliers. When there are few suppliers and when the item being supplied is a major component, vertical integration can lower costs by limiting supplier power. Vertical integration can also lower costs by facilitating the coordination of production flows and avoiding bottleneck problems. Furthermore, when a company has proprietary know-how that it wants to keep from rivals, then in-house performance of value-adding activities related to this know-how is beneficial even if such activities could otherwise be performed by outsiders.

Apple decided to integrate backward into producing its own chips for iPhones, chiefly because chips are a major cost component, suppliers have bargaining power, and in-house production would help coordinate design tasks and protect Apple's proprietary iPhone technology. International Paper Company backward integrates into pulp mills that it sets up near its paper mills and reaps the benefits of coordinated production flows, energy savings, and transportation economies. It does this, in part, because outside suppliers are generally unwilling to make a site-specific investment for a buyer.

Backward vertical integration can produce a differentiation-based competitive advantage when performing activities internally contributes to a better-quality product or service offering, improves the caliber of customer service, or in other ways enhances the performance of the final product. On occasion, integrating into more stages along the industry value chain system can add to a company's differentiation capabilities by allowing it to strengthen its core competencies, better master key skills or strategy-critical technologies, or add features that deliver greater customer value. Spanish clothing maker Inditex has backward integrated into fabric making, as well as garment design and manufacture, for its successful Zara brand. By tightly controlling the process and postponing dyeing until later stages, Zara can respond quickly to changes in fashion trends and supply its customers with the hottest items. NewsCorp backward integrated into film studios (Twentieth Century Fox) and TV program production to ensure access to high-quality content for its TV stations (and to limit supplier power).

Integrating Forward to Enhance Competitiveness Like backward integration, **forward integration** can lower costs by increasing efficiency and bargaining power. In addition, it can allow manufacturers to gain better access to end users, improve market visibility, and include the end user's purchasing experience as a differentiating feature. For example, Harley's company-owned retail stores are essentially little museums, filled with iconography, that provide an environment conducive to selling not only motorcycles and gear but also memorabilia, clothing, and other items featuring the brand. Insurance companies and brokerages like Allstate and Edward Jones have the ability to make consumers' interactions with local agents and office personnel a differentiating feature by focusing on building relationships.

In many industries, independent sales agents, wholesalers, and retailers handle competing brands of the same product and have no allegiance to any one company's brand—they tend to push whatever offers the biggest profits. To avoid dependence on distributors and dealers with divided loyalties, Goodyear has integrated forward into company-owned and franchised retail tire stores. Consumer-goods companies like Under Armour, Pepperidge Farm, Bath & Body Works, Nike, and Ann Taylor's have integrated forward into retailing and operate their own branded stores in factory outlet malls, enabling them to move overstocked items, slow-selling items, and seconds.

Some producers have opted to integrate forward by selling directly to customers at the company's website. Bypassing regular wholesale and retail channels in favor of direct sales and Internet retailing can have appeal if it reinforces the brand and enhances consumer satisfaction or if it lowers distribution costs, produces a relative cost advantage over certain rivals, and results in lower selling prices to end users. In addition, sellers are compelled to include the Internet as a retail channel when a sufficiently large number of buyers in an industry prefer to make purchases online. However, a company that is vigorously pursuing online sales to consumers at the same time that it is also heavily promoting sales to consumers through its network of wholesalers and retailers is *competing directly against its distribution allies*. Such actions constitute *channel conflict* and create a tricky route to negotiate. A company that is actively trying to expand online sales to consumers is signaling a weak strategic commitment to its dealers *and* a willingness to cannibalize dealers' sales and growth potential. The likely result is angry dealers and loss of dealer goodwill. Quite possibly, a company may stand to lose more sales by offending its dealers than it gains from its own online sales effort. Consequently, in industries where the strong support and goodwill of dealer networks is essential, companies may conclude that it is important to avoid channel conflict and that *their websites should be designed to partner with dealers rather than compete against them.*

The Disadvantages of a Vertical Integration Strategy

Vertical integration has some substantial drawbacks beyond the potential for channel conflict.[18] The most serious drawbacks to vertical integration include the following concerns:

- Vertical integration raises a firm's capital investment in the industry, thereby *increasing business risk.*
- Vertically integrated companies are often *slow to embrace technological advances* or more efficient production methods when they are saddled with older technology or facilities. A company that obtains parts and components from outside suppliers can always shop the market for the newest, best, and cheapest parts, whereas a vertically integrated firm with older plants and technology may choose to continue making suboptimal parts rather than face the high costs of premature abandonment.
- Vertical integration can result in *less flexibility in accommodating shifting buyer preferences.* It is one thing to design out a component made by a supplier and another to design out a component being made in-house (which can mean laying off employees and writing off the associated investment in equipment and facilities). Integrating forward or backward locks a firm into relying on its own in-house activities and sources of supply.
- Vertical integration *may not enable a company to realize economies of scale* if its production levels are below the minimum efficient scale. Small companies in particular are likely to suffer a cost disadvantage by producing in-house.
- Vertical integration poses all kinds of *capacity-matching problems.* In motor vehicle manufacturing, for example, the most efficient scale of operation for making axles is different from the most economic volume for radiators, and different yet again for both engines and transmissions. Consequently, integrating across several production stages in ways that achieve the lowest feasible costs can be a monumental challenge.
- Integration forward or backward often *calls for developing new types of resources and capabilities.* Parts and components manufacturing, assembly operations, wholesale distribution and retailing, and direct sales via the Internet represent different kinds of businesses, operating in different types of industries, with different key success factors. Many manufacturers learn the hard way that company-owned wholesale and retail networks require skills that they lack, fit poorly with what they do best, and detract from their overall profit performance. Similarly, a company that tries to produce many components in-house is likely to find itself very hard-pressed to keep up with technological advances and cutting-edge production practices for each component used in making its product.

Weighing the Pros and Cons of Vertical Integration

All in all, therefore, a strategy of vertical integration can have both strengths and weaknesses. The tip of the scales depends on (1) whether vertical integration can enhance the performance of strategy-critical activities in ways that lower cost, build expertise, protect proprietary know-how, or increase differentiation, (2) what impact vertical integration will have on investment costs, flexibility, and response times, (3) what administrative costs will be incurred by coordinating operations across more vertical chain activities, and (4) how difficult it will be for the company to acquire the set of skills and capabilities needed to operate in another stage of the vertical chain. *Vertical integration strategies have merit according to which capabilities and value-adding activities truly need to be performed in-house and which can be performed better or cheaper by outsiders.* Absent solid benefits, integrating forward or backward is not likely to be an attractive strategy option.

Kaiser Permanente, the largest managed care organization in the United States, has made vertical integration a central part of its strategy, as described in Illustration Capsule 6.4.

OUTSOURCING STRATEGIES: NARROWING THE SCOPE OF OPERATIONS

LO 5

The conditions that favor farming out certain value chain activities to outside parties.

CORE CONCEPT

Outsourcing involves contracting out certain value chain activities that are normally performed in-house to outside vendors.

In contrast to vertical integration strategies, outsourcing strategies narrow the scope of a business's operations, in terms of what activities are performed internally. **Outsourcing** involves contracting out certain value chain activities that are normally performed in-house to outside vendors.[19] Many PC makers, for example, have shifted from assembling units in-house to outsourcing the entire assembly process to manufacturing specialists, which can operate more efficiently due to their greater scale, experience, and bargaining power over components makers. Nike has outsourced most of its manufacturing-related value chain activities, so it can concentrate on marketing and managing its brand.

Outsourcing certain value chain activities makes strategic sense whenever:

- *An activity can be performed better or more cheaply by outside specialists.* A company should generally *not* perform any value chain activity internally that can be performed more efficiently or effectively by outsiders—the chief exception occurs when a particular activity is strategically crucial and internal control over that activity is deemed essential. Dolce & Gabbana, for example, contracts out the production of sunglasses under its label to Luxottica—the world's best sunglass manufacturing company, known for its Oakley and Ray-Ban brands.
- *The activity is not crucial to the firm's ability to achieve sustainable competitive advantage.* Outsourcing of support activities such as maintenance services, data processing, data storage, fringe-benefit management, and website operations has become commonplace. Colgate-Palmolive, for instance, has been able to reduce its information technology operational costs by more than 10 percent per year through an outsourcing agreement with IBM.
- *The outsourcing improves organizational flexibility and speeds time to market.* Outsourcing gives a company the flexibility to switch suppliers in the event that its present supplier falls behind competing suppliers. Moreover, seeking out new suppliers with the needed capabilities already in place is frequently quicker, easier,

ILLUSTRATION CAPSULE 6.4

Kaiser Permanente's Vertical Integration Strategy

Kaiser Permanente's unique business model features a vertical integration strategy that enables it to deliver higher-quality care to patients at a lower cost. Kaiser Permanente is the largest vertically integrated health care delivery system in the United States, with $53.1 billion in revenues and $2.7 billion in net income in 2013. It functions as a health insurance company with over 9 million members and a provider of health care services with 37 hospitals, 618 medical offices, and more than 17,000 physicians. As a result of its vertical integration, Kaiser Permanente is better able to efficiently match demand for services by health plan members to capacity of its delivery infrastructure, including physicians and hospitals. Moreover, its prepaid financial model helps to incentivize the appropriate delivery of health care services.

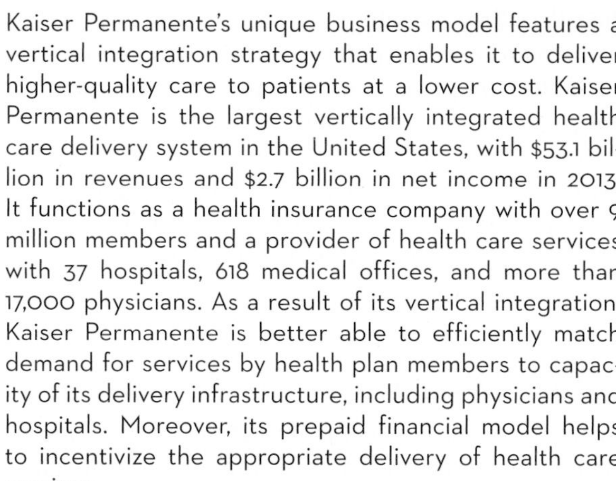

Unlike Kaiser Permanente, the majority of physicians and hospitals in the United States provide care on a fee-for-service revenue model or per-procedure basis. Consequently, most physicians and hospitals earn higher revenues by providing more services, which limits investments in preventive care. In contrast, Kaiser Permanente providers are incentivized to focus on health promotion, disease prevention, and chronic disease management. Kaiser Permanente pays primary care physicians more than local averages to attract top talent, and surgeons are salaried rather than paid by procedure to encourage the optimal level of care. Physicians from multiple specialties work collaboratively to coordinate care and treat the overall health of patients rather than individual health issues.

One result of this strategy is enhanced efficiency, enabling Kaiser Permanente to provide health insurance that is, on average, 10 percent cheaper than that of its competitors. Further, the care provided is of higher quality based on national standards of care. For the sixth year in a row, Kaiser Permanente health plans received the highest overall quality-of-care rating of any health plan in California, which accounts for 7 million of its 9 million members. Kaiser Permanente is also consistently praised for member satisfaction. Four of Kaiser's health plan regions, accounting for 90 percent of its membership, were ranked highest in member satisfaction by J.D. Power and Associates. The success of Kaiser Permanente's vertical integration strategy is the primary reason why many health care organizations are seeking to replicate its model as they transition from a fee-for-service revenue model to an accountable care model.

Note: Developed with Christopher C. Sukenik.

Sources: "Kaiser Foundation Hospitals and Health Plan Report Fiscal Year 2013 and Fourth Quarter Financial Results," *PRNewswire,* February 14, 2014, www.prnewswire.com; Kaiser Permanente website and 2012 annual report; and J. O'Donnell, "Kaiser Permanente CEO on Saving Lives, Money," *USA Today,* October 23, 2012.

less risky, and cheaper than hurriedly retooling internal operations to replace obsolete capabilities or trying to install and master new technologies.

- *It reduces the company's risk exposure to changing technology and buyer preferences.* When a company outsources certain parts, components, and services, its suppliers must bear the burden of incorporating state-of-the-art technologies and/or undertaking redesigns and upgrades to accommodate a company's plans to introduce next-generation products. If what a supplier provides falls out of favor with buyers, or is rendered unnecessary by technological change, it is the supplier's business that suffers rather than the company's.

- *It allows a company to concentrate on its core business, leverage its key resources, and do even better what it already does best.* A company is better able to enhance its own capabilities when it concentrates its full resources and energies on performing only those activities. United Colors of Benetton and Sisley, for example, outsource the production of handbags and other leather goods while devoting their energies to the clothing lines for which they are known. Apple outsources production of its iPod, iPhone, and iPad models to Chinese contract manufacturer Foxconn and concentrates in-house on design, marketing, and innovation.

The Risk of Outsourcing Value Chain Activities

The biggest danger of outsourcing is that a company will farm out the wrong types of activities and thereby hollow out its own capabilities.[20] For example, in recent years, companies anxious to reduce operating costs have opted to outsource such strategically important activities as product development, engineering design, and sophisticated manufacturing tasks—the very capabilities that underpin a company's ability to lead sustained product innovation. While these companies have apparently been able to lower their operating costs by outsourcing these functions to outsiders, *their ability to lead the development of innovative new products is weakened because so many of the cutting-edge ideas and technologies for next-generation products come from outsiders.*

A company must guard against outsourcing activities that hollow out the resources and capabilities that it needs to be a master of its own destiny.

Another risk of outsourcing comes from the lack of direct control. It may be difficult to monitor, control, and coordinate the activities of outside parties via contracts and arm's-length transactions alone. Unanticipated problems may arise that cause delays or cost overruns and become hard to resolve amicably. Moreover, contract-based outsourcing can be problematic because outside parties lack incentives to make investments specific to the needs of the outsourcing company's internal value chain.

Companies like Cisco Systems are alert to these dangers. Cisco guards against loss of control and protects its manufacturing expertise by designing the production methods that its contract manufacturers must use. Cisco keeps the source code for its designs proprietary, thereby controlling the initiation of all improvements and safeguarding its innovations from imitation. Further, Cisco uses the Internet to monitor the factory operations of contract manufacturers around the clock so that it knows immediately when problems arise and can decide whether to get involved.

STRATEGIC ALLIANCES AND PARTNERSHIPS

Strategic alliances and cooperative partnerships provide one way to gain some of the benefits offered by vertical integration, outsourcing, and horizontal mergers and acquisitions while minimizing the associated problems. Companies frequently engage in cooperative strategies as an alternative to vertical integration or horizontal mergers and acquisitions. Increasingly, companies are also employing strategic alliances and partnerships to extend their scope of operations via international expansion and diversification strategies, as we describe in Chapters 7 and 8. Strategic alliances and cooperative arrangements are now a common means of narrowing a company's scope of operations as well, serving as a useful way to manage outsourcing (in lieu of traditional, purely price-oriented contracts).

LO 6

When and how strategic alliances can substitute for horizontal mergers and acquisitions or vertical integration and how they can facilitate outsourcing.

For example, oil and gas companies engage in considerable vertical integration—but Shell Oil Company and Pemex (Mexico's state-owned petroleum company) have found that joint ownership of their Deer Park Refinery in Texas lowers their investment costs and risks in comparison to going it alone. The colossal failure of the Daimler-Chrysler merger formed an expensive lesson for Daimler AG about what can go wrong with horizontal mergers and acquisitions; its 2010 strategic alliance with Renault-Nissan is allowing the two companies to achieve jointly the global scale required for cost competitiveness in cars and trucks while avoiding the type of problems that so plagued Daimler-Chrysler. In 2013, Ford Motor Company joined Daimler and Renault-Nissan in an effort to develop affordable, mass-market hydrogen fuel cell vehicles by 2017.

Many companies employ strategic alliances to manage the problems that might otherwise occur with outsourcing—Cisco's system of alliances guards against loss of control, protects its proprietary manufacturing expertise, and enables the company to monitor closely the assembly operations of its partners while devoting its energy to designing new generations of the switches, routers, and other Internet-related equipment for which it is known.

A **strategic alliance** is a formal agreement between two or more separate companies in which they agree to work collaboratively toward some strategically relevant objective. Typically, they involve shared financial responsibility, joint contribution of resources and capabilities, shared risk, shared control, and mutual dependence. They may be characterized by cooperative marketing, sales, or distribution; joint production; design collaboration; or projects to jointly develop new technologies or products. They can vary in terms of their duration and the extent of the collaboration; some are intended as long-term arrangements, involving an extensive set of cooperative activities, while others are designed to accomplish more limited, short-term objectives.

CORE CONCEPT

A **strategic alliance** is a formal agreement between two or more separate companies in which they agree to work cooperatively toward some common objective.

Collaborative arrangements may entail a contractual agreement, but they commonly stop short of formal ownership ties between the partners (although sometimes an alliance member will secure minority ownership of another member). A special type of strategic alliance involving ownership ties is the **joint venture.** A joint venture entails forming a *new corporate entity that is jointly owned* by two or more companies that agree to share in the revenues, expenses, and control of the newly formed entity. Since joint ventures involve setting up a mutually owned business, they tend to be more durable but also riskier than other arrangements. In other types of strategic alliances, the collaboration between the partners involves a much less rigid structure in which the partners retain their independence from one another. If a strategic alliance is not working out, a partner can choose to simply walk away or reduce its commitment to collaborating at any time.

CORE CONCEPT

A **joint venture** is a partnership involving the establishment of an independent corporate entity that the partners own and control jointly, sharing in its revenues and expenses.

An alliance becomes "strategic," as opposed to just a convenient business arrangement, when it serves any of the following purposes:[21]

1. It facilitates achievement of an important business objective (like lowering costs or delivering more value to customers in the form of better quality, added features, and greater durability).
2. It helps build, strengthen, or sustain a core competence or competitive advantage.

3. It helps remedy an important resource deficiency or competitive weakness.
4. It helps defend against a competitive threat, or mitigates a significant risk to a company's business.
5. It increases bargaining power over suppliers or buyers.
6. It helps open up important new market opportunities.
7. It speeds the development of new technologies and/or product innovations.

Strategic cooperation is a much-favored approach in industries where new technological developments are occurring at a furious pace along many different paths and where advances in one technology spill over to affect others (often blurring industry boundaries). Whenever industries are experiencing high-velocity technological advances in many areas simultaneously, firms find it virtually essential to have cooperative relationships with other enterprises to stay on the leading edge of technology, even in their own area of specialization. In industries like these, alliances are all about fast cycles of learning, gaining quick access to the latest round of technological know-how, and developing dynamic capabilities. In bringing together firms with different skills and knowledge bases, alliances open up learning opportunities that help partner firms better leverage their own resources and capabilities.[22]

It took a $3.2 billion joint venture involving the likes of Sprint-Nextel, Clearwire, Intel, Time Warner Cable, Google, Comcast, and Bright House Networks to roll out next-generation 4G wireless services based on Sprint's and Clearwire's WiMax mobile networks. WiMax was an advanced Wi-Fi technology that allowed people to browse the Internet at speeds as great as 10 times faster than other cellular Wi-Fi technologies. The venture was a necessity for Sprint-Nextel and Clearwire since they lacked the financial resources to handle the rollout on their own. The appeal of the partnership for Time Warner, Comcast, and Bright House was the ability to bundle the sale of wireless services to their cable customers, while Intel had the chip sets for WiMax and hoped that WiMax would become the dominant wireless Internet format. Google's interest in the alliance was its desire to strengthen its lead in desktop searches on wireless devices.

Companies that have formed a host of alliances need to manage their alliances like a portfolio.

Clear Channel Communications has entered into a series of partnerships to provide a multiplatform launchpad for artists like Taylor Swift, Phoenix, and Sara Bareilles. In 2010, Clear Channel partnered with MySpace, Hulu, and the artist management company 19 Entertainment for *If I Can Dream,* an original reality series in which unsigned musicians and actors share a "real world"–style house in Los Angeles and document their attempts at stardom. Clear Channel helped promote the show by conducting exclusive radio interviews and performances with the talent, which in turn helped the show become a top-30 weekly program on Hulu.[23]

The best alliances are highly selective, focusing on particular value chain activities and on obtaining a specific competitive benefit. They enable a firm to build on its strengths and to learn.

Because of the varied benefits of strategic alliances, many large corporations have become involved in 30 to 50 alliances, and a number have formed hundreds of alliances. Genentech, a leader in biotechnology and human genetics, has formed R&D alliances with over 30 companies to boost its prospects for developing new cures for various diseases and ailments. Companies that have formed a host of alliances need to manage their alliances like a portfolio—terminating those that no longer serve a useful purpose or that have produced meager results, forming promising new alliances, and restructuring existing alliances to correct performance problems and/or redirect the collaborative effort.

Capturing the Benefits of Strategic Alliances

The extent to which companies benefit from entering into alliances and partnerships seems to be a function of six factors:[24]

1. *Picking a good partner.* A good partner must bring complementary strengths to the relationship. To the extent that alliance members have nonoverlapping strengths, there is greater potential for synergy and less potential for coordination problems and conflict. In addition, a good partner needs to share the company's vision about the overall purpose of the alliance and to have specific goals that either match or complement those of the company. Strong partnerships also depend on good chemistry among key personnel and compatible views about how the alliance should be structured and managed.
2. *Being sensitive to cultural differences.* Cultural differences among companies can make it difficult for their personnel to work together effectively. Cultural differences can be problematic among companies from the same country, but when the partners have different national origins, the problems are often magnified. Unless there is respect among all the parties for cultural differences, including those stemming from different local cultures and local business practices, productive working relationships are unlikely to emerge.
3. *Recognizing that the alliance must benefit both sides.* Information must be shared as well as gained, and the relationship must remain forthright and trustful. If either partner plays games with information or tries to take advantage of the other, the resulting friction can quickly erode the value of further collaboration. Open, trustworthy behavior on both sides is essential for fruitful collaboration.
4. *Ensuring that both parties live up to their commitments.* Both parties have to deliver on their commitments for the alliance to produce the intended benefits. The division of work has to be perceived as fairly apportioned, and the caliber of the benefits received on both sides has to be perceived as adequate.
5. *Structuring the decision-making process so that actions can be taken swiftly when needed.* In many instances, the fast pace of technological and competitive changes dictates an equally fast decision-making process. If the parties get bogged down in discussions or in gaining internal approval from higher-ups, the alliance can turn into an anchor of delay and inaction.
6. *Managing the learning process and then adjusting the alliance agreement over time to fit new circumstances.* One of the keys to long-lasting success is adapting the nature and structure of the alliance to be responsive to shifting market conditions, emerging technologies, and changing customer requirements. Wise allies are quick to recognize the merit of an evolving collaborative arrangement, where adjustments are made to accommodate changing conditions and to overcome whatever problems arise in establishing an effective working relationship.

Most alliances that aim at sharing technology or providing market access turn out to be temporary, lasting only a few years. This is not necessarily an indicator of failure, however. Strategic alliances can be terminated after a few years simply because they have fulfilled their purpose; indeed, many alliances are intended to be of limited duration, set up to accomplish specific short-term objectives. Longer-lasting collaborative arrangements, however, may provide even greater strategic benefits. Alliances are more likely to be long-lasting when (1) they involve collaboration with partners that do not compete directly, such as suppliers or distribution allies, (2) a trusting relationship has been established, and (3) both parties conclude that continued collaboration is in their mutual interest, perhaps because new opportunities for learning are emerging.

The Drawbacks of Strategic Alliances and Partnerships

While strategic alliances provide a way of obtaining the benefits of vertical integration, mergers and acquisitions, and outsourcing, they also suffer from some of the same drawbacks. Anticipated gains may fail to materialize due to an overly optimistic view of the synergies or a poor fit in terms of the combination of resources and capabilities. When outsourcing is conducted via alliances, there is no less risk of becoming dependent on other companies for essential expertise and capabilities—indeed, this may be the Achilles' heel of such alliances. Moreover, there are additional pitfalls to collaborative arrangements. The greatest danger is that a partner will gain access to a company's proprietary knowledge base, technologies, or trade secrets, enabling the partner to match the company's core strengths and costing the company its hard-won competitive advantage. This risk is greatest when the alliance is among industry rivals or when the alliance is for the purpose of collaborative R&D, since this type of partnership requires an extensive exchange of closely held information.

The question for managers is when to engage in a strategic alliance and when to choose an alternative means of meeting their objectives. The answer to this question depends on the relative advantages of each method and the circumstances under which each type of organizational arrangement is favored.

The principal advantages of strategic alliances over vertical integration or horizontal mergers and acquisitions are threefold:

1. They lower investment costs and risks for each partner by facilitating resource pooling and risk sharing. This can be particularly important when investment needs and uncertainty are high, such as when a dominant technology standard has not yet emerged.
2. They are more flexible organizational forms and allow for a more adaptive response to changing conditions. Flexibility is essential when environmental conditions or technologies are changing rapidly. Moreover, strategic alliances under such circumstances may enable the development of each partner's dynamic capabilities.
3. They are more rapidly deployed—a critical factor when speed is of the essence. Speed is of the essence when there is a winner-take-all type of competitive situation, such as the race for a dominant technological design or a race down a steep experience curve, where there is a large first-mover advantage.

The key advantages of using strategic alliances rather than arm's-length transactions to manage outsourcing are (1) the increased ability to exercise control over the partners' activities and (2) a greater willingness for the partners to make relationship-specific investments. Arm's-length transactions discourage such investments since they imply less commitment and do not build trust.

On the other hand, there are circumstances when other organizational mechanisms are preferable to alliances and partnering. Mergers and acquisitions are especially suited for situations in which strategic alliances or partnerships do not go far enough in providing a company with access to needed resources and capabilities. Ownership ties are more permanent than partnership ties, allowing the operations of the merger or acquisition participants to be tightly integrated and creating more in-house control and autonomy. Other organizational mechanisms are also preferable to alliances when there is limited property rights protection for valuable know-how and when companies fear being taken advantage of by opportunistic partners.

While it is important for managers to understand when strategic alliances and partnerships are most likely (and least likely) to prove useful, it is also important to know how to manage them.

How to Make Strategic Alliances Work

A surprisingly large number of alliances never live up to expectations. Even though the number of strategic alliances increases by about 25 percent annually, about 60 to 70 percent of alliances continue to fail each year.[25] The success of an alliance depends on how well the partners work together, their capacity to respond and adapt to changing internal and external conditions, and their willingness to renegotiate the bargain if circumstances so warrant. A successful alliance requires real in-the-trenches collaboration, not merely an arm's-length exchange of ideas. Unless partners place a high value on the contribution each brings to the alliance and the cooperative arrangement results in valuable win-win outcomes, it is doomed to fail.

While the track record for strategic alliances is poor on average, many companies have learned how to manage strategic alliances successfully and routinely defy this average. Samsung Group, which includes Samsung Electronics, successfully manages an ecosystem of over 1,300 partnerships that enable productive activities from global procurement to local marketing to collaborative R&D. Companies that have greater success in managing their strategic alliances and partnerships often credit the following factors:

- *They create a system for managing their alliances.* Companies need to manage their alliances in a systematic fashion, just as they manage other functions. This means setting up a process for managing the different aspects of alliance management from partner selection to alliance termination procedures. To ensure that the system is followed on a routine basis by all company managers, many companies create a set of explicit procedures, process templates, manuals, or the like.
- *They build relationships with their partners and establish trust.* Establishing strong interpersonal relationships is a critical factor in making strategic alliances work since such relationships facilitate opening up channels of communication, coordinating activity, aligning interests, and building trust.
- *They protect themselves from the threat of opportunism by setting up safeguards.* There are a number of means for preventing a company from being taken advantage of by an untrustworthy partner or unwittingly losing control over key assets. Contractual safeguards, including noncompete clauses, can provide other forms of protection.
- *They make commitments to their partners and see that their partners do the same.* When partners make credible commitments to a joint enterprise, they have stronger incentives for making it work and are less likely to "free-ride" on the efforts of other partners. Because of this, equity-based alliances tend to be more successful than nonequity alliances.[26]
- *They make learning a routine part of the management process.* There are always opportunities for learning from a partner, but organizational learning does not take place automatically. Whatever learning occurs cannot add to a company's knowledge base unless the learning is incorporated systematically into the company's routines and practices.

Finally, managers should realize that alliance management is an organizational capability, much like any other. It develops over time, out of effort, experience, and learning. For this reason, it is wise to begin slowly, with simple alliances designed to meet limited, short-term objectives. Short-term partnerships that are successful often become the basis for much more extensive collaborative arrangements. Even when strategic alliances are set up with the hope that they will become long-term engagements, they have a better chance of succeeding if they are phased in so that the partners can learn how they can work together most fruitfully.

KEY POINTS

1. Once a company has settled on which of the five generic competitive strategies to employ, attention turns to how strategic choices regarding (1) competitive actions, (2) timing of those actions, and (3) scope of operations can complement its competitive approach and maximize the power of its overall strategy.
2. Strategic offensives should, as a general rule, be grounded in a company's strategic assets and employ a company's strengths to attack rivals in the competitive areas where they are weakest.
3. Companies have a number of offensive strategy options for improving their market positions: using a cost-based advantage to attack competitors on the basis of price or value, leapfrogging competitors with next-generation technologies, pursuing continuous product innovation, adopting and improving the best ideas of others, using hit-and-run tactics to steal sales away from unsuspecting rivals, and launching preemptive strikes. A blue-ocean type of offensive strategy seeks to gain a dramatic new competitive advantage by inventing a new industry or distinctive market segment that renders existing competitors largely irrelevant and allows a company to create and capture altogether new demand.
4. The purposes of defensive strategies are to lower the risk of being attacked, weaken the impact of any attack that occurs, and influence challengers to aim their efforts at other rivals. Defensive strategies to protect a company's position usually take one of two forms: (1) actions to block challengers or (2) actions to signal the likelihood of strong retaliation.
5. The timing of strategic moves also has relevance in the quest for competitive advantage. Company managers are obligated to carefully consider the advantages or disadvantages that attach to being a first mover versus a fast follower versus a late mover.
6. Decisions concerning the scope of a company's operations—which activities a firm will perform internally and which it will not—can also affect the strength of a company's market position. The *scope of the firm* refers to the range of its activities, the breadth of its product and service offerings, the extent of its geographic market presence, and its mix of businesses. Companies can expand their scope horizontally (more broadly within their focal market) or vertically (up or down the industry value chain system that starts with raw-material production and ends with sales and service to the end consumer). Horizontal mergers and acquisitions (combinations of market rivals) provide a means for a company to expand its horizontal scope. Vertical integration expands a firm's vertical scope.

7. Horizontal mergers and acquisitions typically have any of five objectives: lowering costs, expanding geographic coverage, adding product categories, gaining new technologies or other resources and capabilities, and preparing for the convergence of industries. They can strengthen a firm's competitiveness in five ways: (1) by improving the efficiency of its operations, (2) by heightening its product differentiation, (3) by reducing market rivalry, (4) by increasing the company's bargaining power over suppliers and buyers, and (5) by enhancing its flexibility and dynamic capabilities.
8. Vertical integration, forward or backward, makes most strategic sense if it strengthens a company's position via either cost reduction or creation of a differentiation-based advantage. Otherwise, the drawbacks of vertical integration (increased investment, greater business risk, increased vulnerability to technological changes, less flexibility in making product changes, and the potential for channel conflict) are likely to outweigh any advantages.
9. Outsourcing involves contracting out pieces of the value chain formerly performed in-house to outside vendors, thereby narrowing the scope of the firm. Outsourcing can enhance a company's competitiveness whenever (1) an activity can be performed better or more cheaply by outside specialists; (2) the activity is not crucial to the firm's ability to achieve sustainable competitive advantage; (3) the outsourcing improves organizational flexibility, speeds decision making, and cuts cycle time; (4) it reduces the company's risk exposure; and (5) it permits a company to concentrate on its core business and focus on what it does best.
10. Strategic alliances and cooperative partnerships provide one way to gain some of the benefits offered by vertical integration, outsourcing, and horizontal mergers and acquisitions while minimizing the associated problems. They serve as an alternative to vertical integration and mergers and acquisitions; they serve as a supplement to outsourcing, allowing more control relative to outsourcing via arm's-length transactions.
11. Companies that manage their alliances well generally (1) create a system for managing their alliances, (2) build relationships with their partners and establish trust, (3) protect themselves from the threat of opportunism by setting up safeguards, (4) make commitments to their partners and see that their partners do the same, and (5) make learning a routine part of the management process.

ASSURANCE OF LEARNING EXERCISES

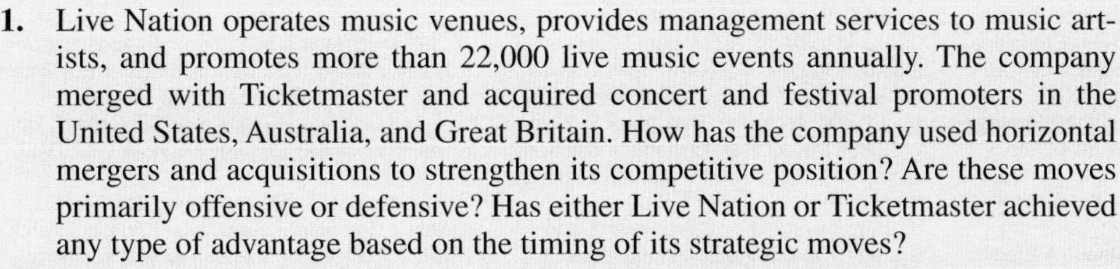

1. Live Nation operates music venues, provides management services to music artists, and promotes more than 22,000 live music events annually. The company merged with Ticketmaster and acquired concert and festival promoters in the United States, Australia, and Great Britain. How has the company used horizontal mergers and acquisitions to strengthen its competitive position? Are these moves primarily offensive or defensive? Has either Live Nation or Ticketmaster achieved any type of advantage based on the timing of its strategic moves?

connect

LO 1, LO 2, LO 3

connect 2. Kaiser Permanente, a standout among managed health care systems, has become a model of how to deliver good health care cost-effectively. Illustration Capsule 6.4 describes how Kaiser Permanente has made vertical integration a central part of its strategy. What value chain segments has Kaiser Permanente chosen to enter and perform internally? How has vertical integration aided the organization in building competitive advantage? Has vertical integration strengthened its market position? Explain why or why not.

LO 4

LO 5 3. Perform an Internet search to identify at least two companies in different industries that have entered into outsourcing agreements with firms with specialized services. In addition, describe what value chain activities the companies have chosen to outsource. Do any of these outsourcing agreements seem likely to threaten any of the companies' competitive capabilities?

LO 6 4. Using your university library's subscription to LexisNexis, EBSCO, or a similar database, find two examples of how companies have relied on strategic alliances or joint ventures to substitute for horizontal or vertical integration.

EXERCISE FOR SIMULATION PARTICIPANTS

LO 1, LO 2 1. Has your company relied more on offensive or defensive strategies to achieve your rank in the industry? What options for being a first mover does your company have? Do any of these first-mover options hold competitive advantage potential?

LO 3 2. Does your company have the option to merge with or acquire other companies? If so, which rival companies would you like to acquire or merge with?

LO 4 3. Is your company vertically integrated? Explain.

LO 5, LO 6 4. Is your company able to engage in outsourcing? If so, what do you see as the pros and cons of outsourcing? Are strategic alliances involved? Explain.

ENDNOTES

[1] George Stalk, Jr., and Rob Lachenauer, "Hardball: Five Killer Strategies for Trouncing the Competition," *Harvard Business Review* 82, no. 4 (April 2004); Richard D'Aveni, "The Empire Strikes Back: Counterrevolutionary Strategies for Industry Leaders," *Harvard Business Review* 80, no. 11 (November 2002); David J. Bryce and Jeffrey H. Dyer, "Strategies to Crack Well-Guarded Markets," *Harvard Business Review* 85, no. 5 (May 2007).

[2] George Stalk, "Playing Hardball: Why Strategy Still Matters," *Ivey Business Journal* 69, no.2 (November–December 2004), pp. 1–2; W. J. Ferrier, K. G. Smith, and C. M. Grimm, "The Role of Competitive Action in Market Share Erosion and Industry Dethronement: A Study of Industry Leaders and Challengers," *Academy of Management Journal* 42, no. 4 (August 1999), pp. 372–388.

[3] David B. Yoffie and Mary Kwak, "Mastering Balance: How to Meet and Beat a Stronger Opponent," *California Management Review* 44, no. 2 (Winter 2002), pp. 8–24.

[4] Ian C. MacMillan, Alexander B. van Putten, and Rita Gunther McGrath, "Global Gamesmanship," *Harvard Business Review* 81, no. 5 (May 2003); Ashkay R. Rao, Mark E. Bergen, and Scott Davis, "How to Fight a Price War," *Harvard Business Review* 78, no. 2 (March–April 2000).

[5] D. B. Yoffie and M. A. Cusumano, "Judo Strategy— the Competitive Dynamics of Internet Time," *Harvard Business Review* 77, no. 1 (January–February 1999), pp. 70–81.

[6] Ming-Jer Chen and Donald C. Hambrick, "Speed, Stealth, and Selective Attack: How Small Firms Differ from Large Firms in Competitive Behavior," *Academy of Management Journal* 38, no. 2 (April 1995), pp. 453–482; William E. Rothschild, "Surprise and the Competitive Advantage," *Journal of Business Strategy* 4, no. 3 (Winter 1984), pp. 10–18.

[7] Ian MacMillan, "Preemptive Strategies," *Journal of Business Strategy* 14, no. 2 (Fall 1983), pp. 16–26.

[8] Ian C. MacMillan, "How Long Can You Sustain a Competitive Advantage?" in Liam Fahey (ed.), *The Strategic Planning Management*

Reader (Englewood Cliffs, NJ: Prentice Hall, 1989), pp. 23–24.

[9] Kevin P. Coyne and John Horn, "Predicting Your Competitor's Reactions," *Harvard Business Review* 87, no. 4 (April 2009), pp. 90–97.

[10] Philip Kotler, *Marketing Management,* 5th ed. (Englewood Cliffs, NJ: Prentice Hall, 1984).

[11] W. Chan Kim and Renée Mauborgne, "Blue Ocean Strategy," *Harvard Business Review* 82, no. 10 (October 2004), pp. 76–84.

[12] Jeffrey G. Covin, Dennis P. Slevin, and Michael B. Heeley, "Pioneers and Followers: Competitive Tactics, Environment, and Growth," *Journal of Business Venturing* 15, no. 2 (March 1999), pp. 175–210; Christopher A. Bartlett and Sumantra Ghoshal, "Going Global: Lessons from Late-Movers," *Harvard Business Review* 78, no. 2 (March–April 2000), pp. 132–145.

[13] Costas Markides and Paul A. Geroski, "Racing to Be 2nd: Conquering the Industries of the Future," *Business Strategy Review* 15, no. 4 (Winter 2004), pp. 25–31.

[14] Fernando Suarez and Gianvito Lanzolla, "The Half-Truth of First-Mover Advantage," *Harvard Business Review* 83, no. 4 (April 2005), pp. 121–127.

[15] Joseph L. Bower, "Not All M&As Are Alike—and That Matters," *Harvard Business Review* 79, no. 3 (March 2001); O. Chatain and P. Zemsky, "The Horizontal Scope of the Firm: Organizational Tradeoffs vs. Buyer-Supplier Relationships," *Management Science* 53, no. 4 (April 2007), pp. 550–565.

[16] Jeffrey H. Dyer, Prashant Kale, and Harbir Singh, "When to Ally and When to Acquire," *Harvard Business Review* 82, no. 4 (July–August 2004), pp. 109–110.

[17] John Stuckey and David White, "When and When Not to Vertically Integrate," *Sloan Management Review* (Spring 1993), pp. 71–83.

[18] Thomas Osegowitsch and Anoop Madhok, "Vertical Integration Is Dead, or Is It?" *Business Horizons* 46, no. 2 (March–April 2003), pp. 25–35.

[19] Ronan McIvor, "What Is the Right Outsourcing Strategy for Your Process?" *European Management Journal* 26, no. 1 (February 2008), pp. 24–34.

[20] Gary P. Pisano and Willy C. Shih, "Restoring American Competitiveness," *Harvard Business Review* 87, no. 7–8 (July–August 2009), pp. 114–125; Jérôme Barthélemy, "The Seven Deadly Sins of Outsourcing," *Academy of Management Executive* 17, no. 2 (May 2003), pp. 87–100.

[21] Jason Wakeam, "The Five Factors of a Strategic Alliance," *Ivey Business Journal* 68, no. 3 (May–June 2003), pp. 1–4.

[22] A. Inkpen, "Learning, Knowledge Acquisition, and Strategic Alliances," *European Management Journal* 16, no. 2 (April 1998), pp. 223–229.

[23] *Advertising Age,* May 24, 2010, p. 14.

[24] Patricia Anslinger and Justin Jenk, "Creating Successful Alliances," *Journal of Business Strategy* 25, no. 2 (2004), pp. 18–23; Rosabeth Moss Kanter, "Collaborative Advantage: The Art of the Alliance," *Harvard Business Review* 72, no. 4 (July–August 1994), pp. 96–108; Gary Hamel, Yves L. Doz, and C. K. Prahalad, "Collaborate with Your Competitors—and Win," *Harvard Business Review* 67, no. 1 (January–February 1989), pp. 133–139.

[25] Jonathan Hughes and Jeff Weiss, "Simple Rules for Making Alliances Work," *Harvard Business Review* 85, no. 11 (November 2007), pp. 122–131.

[26] Y. G. Pan and D. K. Tse, "The Hierarchical Model of Market Entry Modes," *Journal of International Business Studies* 31, no. 4 (2000), pp. 535–554.

CHAPTER 7

Strategies for Competing in International Markets

Learning Objectives

THIS CHAPTER WILL HELP YOU UNDERSTAND:

LO 1 The primary reasons companies choose to compete in international markets.

LO 2 How and why differing market conditions across countries influence a company's strategy choices in international markets.

LO 3 The five major strategic options for entering foreign markets.

LO 4 The three main strategic approaches for competing internationally.

LO 5 How companies are able to use international operations to improve overall competitiveness.

LO 6 The unique characteristics of competing in developing-country markets.

Profit is the most global aspect of a business, and it is cross-functional.

Carlos Ghosn – *Chairman and CEO of Both Renault and Nissan*

Globalization has changed us into a company that searches the world, not just to sell or to source, but to find intellectual capital—the world's best talents and greatest ideas.

Jack Welch – *Former Chairman and CEO of GE*

The response to the Starbucks brand has been phenomenal in our international markets.

Howard Schultz – *Chairman and CEO of Starbucks*

Any company that aspires to industry leadership in the 21st century must think in terms of global, not domestic, market leadership. The world economy is globalizing at an accelerating pace as ambitious, growth-minded companies race to build stronger competitive positions in the markets of more and more countries, as countries previously closed to foreign companies open up their markets, and as information technology shrinks the importance of geographic distance. The forces of globalization are changing the competitive landscape in many industries, offering companies attractive new opportunities and at the same time introducing new competitive threats. Companies in industries where these forces are greatest are therefore under considerable pressure to come up with a strategy for competing successfully in international markets.

This chapter focuses on strategy options for expanding beyond domestic boundaries and competing in the markets of either a few or a great many countries. In the process of exploring these options, we introduce such concepts as multidomestic, transnational, and global strategies; the Porter diamond of national competitive advantage; and profit sanctuaries. The chapter also includes sections on cross-country differences in cultural, demographic, and market conditions; strategy options for entering foreign markets; the importance of locating value chain operations in the most advantageous countries; and the special circumstances of competing in developing markets such as those in China, India, Brazil, Russia, and eastern Europe.

WHY COMPANIES DECIDE TO ENTER FOREIGN MARKETS

A company may opt to expand outside its domestic market for any of five major reasons:

LO 1

The primary reasons companies choose to compete in international markets.

1. *To gain access to new customers.* Expanding into foreign markets offers potential for increased revenues, profits, and long-term growth; it becomes an especially attractive option when a company encounters dwindling growth opportunities in

its home market. Companies often expand internationally to extend the life cycle of their products, as Honda has done with its classic 50-cc motorcycle, the Honda cub (which is still selling well in developing markets, more than 50 years after it was first introduced in Japan). A larger target market also offers companies the opportunity to earn a return on large investments more rapidly. This can be particularly important in R&D-intensive industries, where development is fast-paced or competitors imitate innovations rapidly.

2. *To achieve lower costs through economies of scale, experience, and increased purchasing power.* Many companies are driven to sell in more than one country because domestic sales volume alone is not large enough to capture fully economies of scale in product development, manufacturing, or marketing. Similarly, firms expand internationally to increase the rate at which they accumulate experience and move down the learning curve. International expansion can also lower a company's input costs through greater pooled purchasing power. The relatively small size of country markets in Europe and limited domestic volume explains why companies like Michelin, BMW, and Nestlé long ago began selling their products all across Europe and then moved into markets in North America and Latin America.
3. *To gain access to low-cost inputs of production.* Companies in industries based on natural resources (e.g., oil and gas, minerals, rubber, and lumber) often find it necessary to operate in the international arena since raw-material supplies are located in different parts of the world and can be accessed more cost-effectively at the source. Other companies enter foreign markets to access low-cost human resources; this is particularly true of industries in which labor costs make up a high proportion of total production costs.
4. *To further exploit its core competencies.* A company may be able to extend a market-leading position in its domestic market into a position of regional or global market leadership by leveraging its core competencies further. Walmart is capitalizing on its considerable expertise in discount retailing to expand into the United Kingdom, Japan, China, and Latin America. Walmart executives believe the company has tremendous growth opportunities in China. Companies can often leverage their resources internationally by replicating a successful business model, using it as a basic blueprint for international operations, as Starbucks and McDonald's have done.[1]
5. *To gain access to resources and capabilities located in foreign markets.* An increasingly important motive for entering foreign markets is to acquire resources and capabilities that may be unavailable in a company's home market. Companies often make acquisitions abroad or enter into cross-border alliances to gain access to capabilities that complement their own or to learn from their partners.[2] In other cases, companies choose to establish operations in other countries to utilize local distribution networks, gain local managerial or marketing expertise, or acquire technical knowledge.

In addition, companies that are the suppliers of other companies often expand internationally when their major customers do so, to meet their customers' needs abroad and retain their position as a key supply chain partner. Automotive parts suppliers, for example, have followed automobile manufacturers abroad, and retail-goods suppliers, such as Newell-Rubbermaid, have followed their discount retailer customers, such as Walmart, into foreign markets.

WHY COMPETING ACROSS NATIONAL BORDERS MAKES STRATEGY MAKING MORE COMPLEX

Crafting a strategy to compete in one or more countries of the world is inherently more complex for five reasons. First, different countries have different home-country advantages in different industries; competing effectively requires an understanding of these differences. Second, there are location-based advantages to conducting particular value chain activities in different parts of the world. Third, different political and economic conditions make the general business climate more favorable in some countries than in others. Fourth, companies face risk due to adverse shifts in currency exchange rates when operating in foreign markets. And fifth, differences in buyer tastes and preferences present a challenge for companies concerning customizing versus standardizing their products and services.

LO 2

How and why differing market conditions across countries influence a company's strategy choices in international markets.

Home-Country Industry Advantages and the Diamond Model

Certain countries are known for their strengths in particular industries. For example, Chile has competitive strengths in industries such as copper, fruit, fish products, paper and pulp, chemicals, and wine. Japan is known for competitive strength in consumer electronics, automobiles, semiconductors, steel products, and specialty steel. Where industries are more likely to develop competitive strength depends on a set of factors that describe the nature of each country's business environment and vary from country to country. Because strong industries are made up of strong firms, the strategies of firms that expand internationally are usually grounded in one or more of these factors. The four major factors are summarized in a framework developed by Michael Porter and known as the *Diamond of National Competitive Advantage* (see Figure 7.1).[3]

Demand Conditions The demand conditions in an industry's home market include the relative size of the market, its growth potential, and the nature of domestic buyers' needs and wants. Differing population sizes, income levels, and other demographic factors give rise to considerable differences in market size and growth rates from country to country. Industry sectors that are larger and more important in their home market tend to attract more resources and grow faster than others. For example, owing to widely differing population demographics and income levels, there is a far bigger market for luxury automobiles in the United States and Germany than in Argentina, India, Mexico, and China. At the same time, in developing markets like India, China, Brazil, and Malaysia, market growth potential is far higher than it is in the more mature economies of Britain, Denmark, Canada, and Japan. The potential for market growth in automobiles is explosive in China, where 2013 sales of new vehicles amounted to 18 million, surpassing U.S. sales of 15.6 million and making China the world's largest market for the fourth year in a row.[4] Demanding domestic buyers for an industry's products spur greater innovativeness and improvements in quality. Such conditions foster the development of stronger industries, with firms that are capable of translating a home-market advantage into a competitive advantage in the international arena.

FIGURE 7.1 The Diamond of National Competitive Advantage

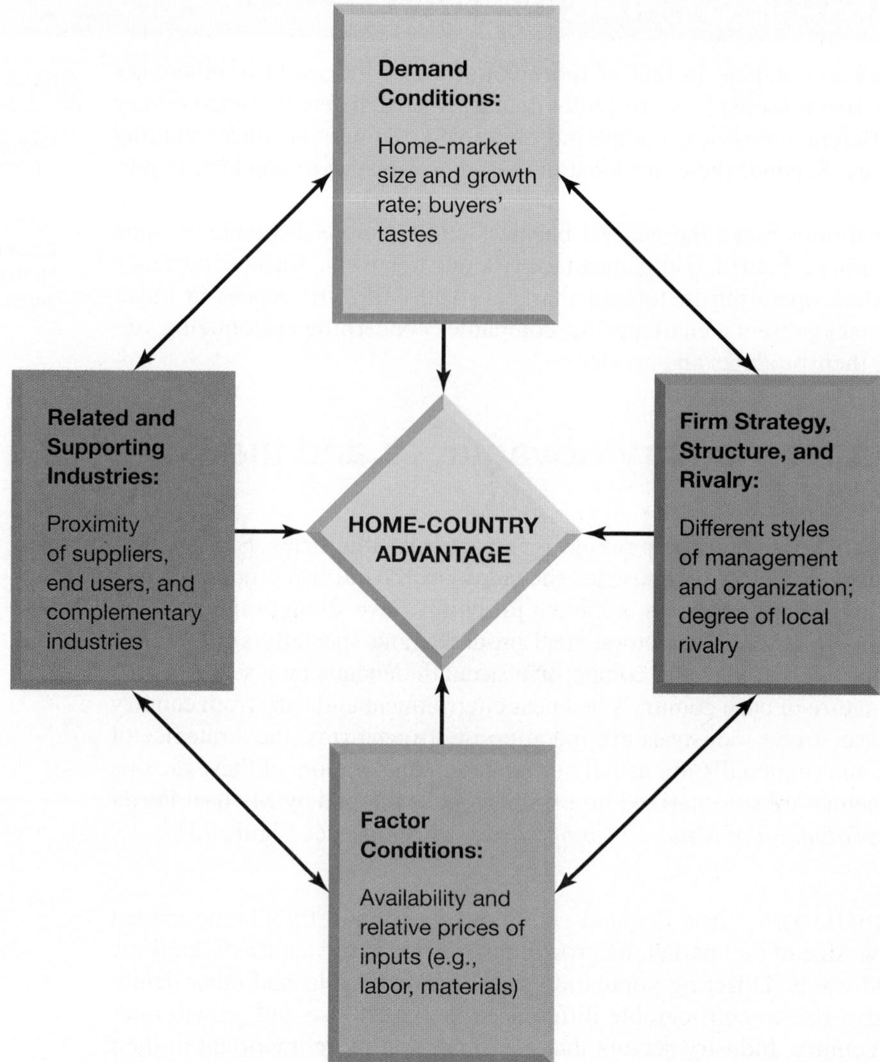

Source: Adapted from M. Porter, "The Competitive Advantage of Nations," *Harvard Business Review,* March–April 1990, pp. 73–93.

Factor Conditions Factor conditions describe the availability, quality, and cost of raw materials and other inputs (called *factors of production*) that firms in an industry require for producing their products and services. The relevant factors of production vary from industry to industry but can include different types of labor, technical or managerial knowledge, land, financial capital, and natural resources. Elements of a country's infrastructure may be included as well, such as its transportation, communication, and banking systems. For instance, in India there are efficient, well-developed national channels for distributing groceries, personal care items, and other packaged products to the country's 3 million retailers, whereas in China distribution is primarily local and there is a limited national network for distributing most products. Competitively strong industries and firms develop where relevant factor conditions are favorable.

Related and Supporting Industries Robust industries often develop in locales where there is a cluster of related industries, including others within the same value chain system (e.g., suppliers of components and equipment, distributors) and the makers of complementary products or those that are technologically related. The sports car makers Ferrari and Maserati, for example, are located in an area of Italy known as the "engine technological district," which includes other firms involved in racing, such as Ducati Motorcycles, along with hundreds of small suppliers. The advantage to firms that develop as part of a related-industry cluster comes from the close collaboration with key suppliers and the greater knowledge sharing throughout the cluster, resulting in greater efficiency and innovativeness.

Firm Strategy, Structure, and Rivalry Different country environments foster the development of different styles of management, organization, and strategy. For example, strategic alliances are a more common strategy for firms from Asian or Latin American countries, which emphasize trust and cooperation in their organizations, than for firms from North America, where individualism is more influential. In addition, countries vary in terms of the competitive rivalry of their industries. Fierce rivalry in home markets tends to hone domestic firms' competitive capabilities and ready them for competing internationally.

For an industry in a particular country to become competitively strong, all four factors must be favorable for that industry. When they are, the industry is likely to contain firms that are capable of competing successfully in the international arena. Thus the diamond framework can be used to reveal the answers to several questions that are important for competing on an international basis. First, it can help predict *where foreign entrants into an industry are most likely to come from.* This can help managers prepare to cope with new foreign competitors, since the framework also reveals something about the basis of the new rivals' strengths. Second, it can reveal the countries in which foreign rivals are likely to be weakest and thus can help managers decide *which foreign markets to enter first.* And third, because it focuses on the attributes of a country's business environment that allow firms to flourish, it reveals something about the advantages of conducting particular business activities in that country. Thus the diamond framework is an aid to deciding *where to locate different value chain activities most beneficially*—a topic that we address next.

Opportunities for Location-Based Advantages

Increasingly, companies are locating different value chain activities in different parts of the world to exploit location-based advantages that vary from country to country. This is particularly evident with respect to the location of manufacturing activities. Differences in wage rates, worker productivity, energy costs, and the like, create sizable variations in manufacturing costs from country to country. By locating its plants in certain countries, firms in some industries can reap major manufacturing cost advantages because of lower input costs (especially labor), relaxed government regulations, the proximity of suppliers and technologically related industries, or unique natural resources. In such cases, the low-cost countries become principal production sites, with most of the output being exported to markets in other parts of the world. Companies that build production facilities in low-cost countries (or that source their products from contract manufacturers in these countries) gain a competitive advantage over rivals with plants in countries where costs are higher. The competitive role of low manufacturing costs is most evident in low-wage countries like China, India,

Pakistan, Cambodia, Vietnam, Mexico, Brazil, Guatemala, the Philippines, and several countries in Africa and eastern Europe that have become production havens for manufactured goods with high labor content (especially textiles and apparel). Hourly compensation for manufacturing workers in 2012 averaged about $1.46 in India, $1.74 in China, $2.10 in the Philippines, $6.36 in Mexico, $8.95 in Hungary, $9.46 in Taiwan, $11.20 in Brazil, $12.10 in Portugal, $20.72 in South Korea, $24.77 in New Zealand, $35.71 in Japan, $35.34 in the United States, $35.67 in Canada, $45.79 in Germany, and $63.36 in Norway.[5] Not surprisingly, China has emerged as the manufacturing capital of the world—virtually all of the world's major manufacturing companies now have facilities in China.

For other types of value chain activities, input quality or availability are more important considerations. Tiffany entered the mining industry in Canada to access diamonds that could be certified as "conflict free" and not associated with either the funding of African wars or unethical mining conditions. Many U.S. companies locate call centers in countries such as India and Ireland, where English is spoken and the workforce is well educated. Other companies locate R&D activities in countries where there are prestigious research institutions and well-trained scientists and engineers. Likewise, concerns about short delivery times and low shipping costs make some countries better locations than others for establishing distribution centers.

The Impact of Government Policies and Economic Conditions in Host Countries

Cross-country variations in government policies and economic conditions affect both the opportunities available to a foreign entrant and the risks of operating within the host country. The governments of some countries are anxious to attract foreign investments, and thus they go all out to create a business climate that outsiders will view as favorable. Governments anxious to spur economic growth, create more jobs, and raise living standards for their citizens usually enact policies aimed at stimulating business innovation and capital investment; Ireland is a good example. They may provide such incentives as reduced taxes, low-cost loans, site location and site development assistance, and government-sponsored training for workers to encourage companies to construct production and distribution facilities. When new business-related issues or developments arise, "pro-business" governments make a practice of seeking advice and counsel from business leaders. When tougher business-related regulations are deemed appropriate, they endeavor to make the transition to more costly and stringent regulations somewhat business-friendly rather than adversarial.

On the other hand, governments sometimes enact policies that, from a business perspective, make locating facilities within a country's borders less attractive. For example, the nature of a company's operations may make it particularly costly to achieve compliance with a country's environmental regulations. Some governments provide subsidies and low-interest loans to domestic companies to enable them to better compete against foreign companies. To discourage foreign imports, governments may enact deliberately burdensome procedures and requirements regarding customs inspection for foreign goods and may impose tariffs or quotas on imports. Additionally, they may specify that a certain percentage of the parts and components used in manufacturing a product be obtained from local suppliers, require prior approval of capital spending projects, limit withdrawal of funds from the country, and require partial ownership of foreign company operations by local companies or investors. There are times when a government may place restrictions on exports to ensure adequate local supplies and regulate the prices of imported and locally produced goods. Such government actions make a country's business climate less attractive and in some cases may be sufficiently onerous as to discourage a company from locating facilities in that country or even selling its products there.

A country's business climate is also a function of the political and economic risks associated with operating within its borders. **Political risks** have to do with the instability of weak governments, growing possibilities that a country's citizenry will revolt against dictatorial government leaders, the likelihood of new onerous legislation or regulations on foreign-owned businesses, and the potential for future elections to produce corrupt or tyrannical government leaders. In industries that a government deems critical to the national welfare, there is sometimes a risk that the government will nationalize the industry and expropriate the assets of foreign companies. In 2012, for example, Argentina nationalized the country's top oil producer, YPF, which was owned by Spanish oil major Repsol. Other political risks include the loss of investments due to war or political unrest, regulatory changes that create operating uncertainties, security risks due to terrorism, and corruption. **Economic risks** have to do with the stability of a country's economy and monetary system—whether inflation rates might skyrocket or whether uncontrolled deficit spending on the part of government or risky bank lending practices could lead to a breakdown of the country's monetary system and prolonged economic distress. In some countries, the threat of piracy and lack of protection for intellectual property are also sources of economic risk. Another is fluctuations in the value of different currencies—a factor that we discuss in more detail next.

CORE CONCEPT

Political risks stem from instability or weakness in national governments and hostility to foreign business. **Economic risks** stem from the stability of a country's monetary system, economic and regulatory policies, and the lack of property rights protections.

The Risks of Adverse Exchange Rate Shifts

When companies produce and market their products and services in many different countries, they are subject to the impacts of sometimes favorable and sometimes unfavorable changes in currency exchange rates. The rates of exchange between different currencies can vary by as much as 20 to 40 percent annually, with the changes occurring sometimes gradually and sometimes swiftly. *Sizable shifts in exchange rates pose significant risks for two reasons:*

1. They are hard to predict because of the variety of factors involved and the uncertainties surrounding when and by how much these factors will change.
2. They shuffle the cards of which countries represent the low-cost manufacturing locations and which rivals have the upper hand in the marketplace.

To illustrate the economic risks associated with fluctuating exchange rates, consider the case of a U.S. company that has located manufacturing facilities in Brazil (where the currency is *reals*—pronounced "ray-alls") and that exports most of the Brazilian-made goods to markets in the European Union (where the currency is euros). To keep the numbers simple, assume that the exchange rate is 4 Brazilian reals for 1 euro and that the product being made in Brazil has a manufacturing cost of 4 Brazilian reals (or 1 euro). Now suppose that the exchange rate shifts from 4 reals per euro to 5 reals per euro (meaning that the real has declined in value and that the euro is stronger). Making the product in Brazil is now more cost-competitive because a Brazilian good costing 4 reals to produce has fallen to only 0.8 euro at the new exchange rate (4 reals divided by 5 reals per euro = 0.8 euro). This clearly puts the producer of the

Brazilian-made good *in a better position to compete* against the European makers of the same good. On the other hand, should the value of the Brazilian real grow stronger in relation to the euro—resulting in an exchange rate of 3 reals to 1 euro—the same Brazilian-made good formerly costing 4 reals (or 1 euro) to produce now has a cost of 1.33 euros (4 reals divided by 3 reals per euro = 1.33 euros), putting the producer of the Brazilian-made good in a weaker competitive position vis-à-vis the European producers. Clearly, the attraction of manufacturing a good in Brazil and selling it in Europe is far greater when the euro is strong (an exchange rate of 1 euro for 5 Brazilian reals) than when the euro is weak and exchanges for only 3 Brazilian reals.

But there is one more piece to the story. When the exchange rate changes from 4 reals per euro to 5 reals per euro, not only is the cost competitiveness of the Brazilian manufacturer stronger relative to European manufacturers of the same item but the Brazilian-made good that formerly cost 1 euro and now costs only 0.8 euro can also be sold to consumers in the European Union for a lower euro price than before. In other words, the combination of a stronger euro and a weaker real acts to *lower the price of Brazilian-made goods* in all the countries that are members of the European Union, which is likely to *spur sales of the Brazilian-made good in Europe and boost Brazilian exports to Europe.* Conversely, should the exchange rate shift from 4 reals per euro to 3 reals per euro—which makes the Brazilian manufacturer less cost-competitive with European manufacturers of the same item—the Brazilian-made good that formerly cost 1 euro and now costs 1.33 euros will sell for a higher price in euros than before, thus weakening the demand of European consumers for Brazilian-made goods and acting to reduce Brazilian exports to Europe. Thus Brazilian exporters are likely to experience (1) rising demand for their goods in Europe whenever the Brazilian real grows weaker relative to the euro and (2) falling demand for their goods in Europe whenever the real grows stronger relative to the euro. Consequently, from the standpoint of a company with Brazilian manufacturing plants, *a weaker Brazilian real is a favorable exchange rate shift* and *a stronger Brazilian real is an unfavorable exchange rate shift.*

It follows from the previous discussion that shifting exchange rates have a big impact on the ability of domestic manufacturers to compete with foreign rivals. For example, U.S.-based manufacturers locked in a fierce competitive battle with low-cost foreign imports benefit from a *weaker* U.S. dollar. There are several reasons why this is so:

- Declines in the value of the U.S. dollar against foreign currencies raise the U.S. dollar costs of goods manufactured by foreign rivals at plants located in the countries whose currencies have grown stronger relative to the U.S. dollar. A *weaker* dollar acts to reduce or eliminate whatever cost advantage foreign manufacturers may have had over U.S. manufacturers (and helps protect the manufacturing jobs of U.S. workers).
- A *weaker* dollar makes foreign-made goods more expensive in dollar terms to U.S. consumers—this curtails U.S. buyer demand for foreign-made goods, stimulates greater demand on the part of U.S. consumers for U.S.-made goods, and reduces U.S. imports of foreign-made goods.
- A *weaker* U.S. dollar enables the U.S.-made goods to be sold at lower prices to consumers in countries whose currencies have grown stronger relative to the U.S. dollar—such lower prices boost foreign buyer demand for the now relatively cheaper U.S.-made goods, thereby stimulating exports of U.S.-made goods to foreign countries and creating more jobs in U.S.-based manufacturing plants.

- A *weaker* dollar has the effect of increasing the dollar value of profits a company earns in foreign-country markets where the local currency is stronger relative to the dollar. For example, if a U.S.-based manufacturer earns a profit of €10 million on its sales in Europe, those €10 million convert to a larger number of dollars when the dollar grows weaker against the euro.

A weaker U.S. dollar is therefore an economically favorable exchange rate shift for manufacturing plants based in the United States. A decline in the value of the U.S. dollar strengthens the cost competitiveness of U.S.-based manufacturing plants and boosts buyer demand for U.S.-made goods. When the value of the U.S. dollar is expected to remain weak for some time to come, foreign companies have an incentive to build manufacturing facilities in the United States to make goods for U.S. consumers rather than export the same goods to the United States from foreign plants where production costs in dollar terms have been driven up by the decline in the value of the dollar. Conversely, a *stronger* U.S. dollar is an *unfavorable exchange rate shift* for U.S.-based manufacturing plants because it makes such plants less cost-competitive with foreign plants and weakens foreign demand for U.S.-made goods. A strong dollar also weakens the incentive of foreign companies to locate manufacturing facilities in the United States to make goods for U.S. consumers. The same reasoning applies to companies that have plants in countries in the European Union where euros are the local currency. A weak euro versus other currencies enhances the cost competitiveness of companies manufacturing goods in Europe vis-à-vis foreign rivals with plants in countries whose currencies have grown stronger relative to the euro; a strong euro versus other currencies weakens the cost competitiveness of companies with plants in the European Union.

Fluctuating exchange rates pose significant economic risks to a company's competitiveness in foreign markets. Exporters are disadvantaged when the currency of the country where goods are being manufactured grows stronger relative to the currency of the importing country.

Domestic companies facing competitive pressure from lower-cost imports benefit when their government's currency grows *weaker* in relation to the currencies of the countries where the lower-cost imports are being made.

Cross-Country Differences in Demographic, Cultural, and Market Conditions

Buyer tastes for a particular product or service sometimes differ substantially from country to country. In France, consumers prefer top-loading washing machines, while in most other European countries consumers prefer front-loading machines. People in Hong Kong prefer compact appliances, but in Taiwan large appliances are more popular. Ice cream flavors like eel, shark fin, and dried shrimp appeal to Japanese customers, whereas fruit-based flavors have more appeal in the United States and in Europe. Sometimes, product designs suitable in one country are inappropriate in another because of differing local standards—for example, in the United States electrical devices run on 110-volt electric systems, but in some European countries the standard is a 240-volt electric system, necessitating the use of different electrical designs and components. Cultural influences can also affect consumer demand for a product. For instance, in South Korea, many parents are reluctant to purchase PCs even when they can afford them because of concerns that their children will be distracted from their schoolwork by surfing the Web, playing PC-based video games, and becoming Internet "addicts."[6]

Consequently, companies operating in an international marketplace have to wrestle with *whether and how much to customize their offerings in each country market to match local buyers' tastes and preferences or whether to pursue a strategy of offering a mostly standardized product worldwide.* While making products that are closely matched to local tastes makes them more appealing to local buyers, customizing a company's products country by country may raise production and distribution costs due to the greater variety of designs and components, shorter production runs, and the complications of added inventory handling and distribution logistics. Greater standardization of a global company's product offering, on the other hand, can lead to scale economies and learning-curve effects, thus contributing to the achievement of a low-cost advantage. *The tension between the market pressures to localize a company's product offerings country by country and the competitive pressures to lower costs is one of the big strategic issues that participants in foreign markets have to resolve.*

STRATEGIC OPTIONS FOR ENTERING INTERNATIONAL MARKETS

LO 3

The five major strategic options for entering foreign markets.

Once a company decides to expand beyond its domestic borders, it must consider the question of how to enter foreign markets. There are five primary strategic options for doing so:

1. Maintain a home-country production base and *export* goods to foreign markets.
2. *License* foreign firms to produce and distribute the company's products abroad.
3. Employ a *franchising* strategy in foreign markets.
4. Establish a *subsidiary* in a foreign market via acquisition or internal development.
5. Rely on *strategic alliances* or joint ventures with foreign companies.

Which option to employ depends on a variety of factors, including the nature of the firm's strategic objectives, the firm's position in terms of whether it has the full range of resources and capabilities needed to operate abroad, country-specific factors such as trade barriers, and the transaction costs involved (the costs of contracting with a partner and monitoring its compliance with the terms of the contract, for example). The options vary considerably regarding the level of investment required and the associated risks—but higher levels of investment and risk generally provide the firm with the benefits of greater ownership and control.

Export Strategies

Using domestic plants as a production base for exporting goods to foreign markets is an excellent initial strategy for pursuing international sales. It is a conservative way to test the international waters. The amount of capital needed to begin exporting is often minimal; existing production capacity may well be sufficient to make goods for export. With an export-based entry strategy, a manufacturer can limit its involvement in foreign markets by contracting with foreign wholesalers experienced in importing to handle the entire distribution and marketing function in their countries or regions of the world. If it is more advantageous to maintain control over these functions, however, a manufacturer can establish its own distribution and sales organizations in some or all of the target foreign markets. Either way, a home-based production and export strategy helps the firm minimize its direct investments in foreign countries. Such strategies are commonly favored by Chinese, Korean, and Italian companies—products are designed and manufactured at home and then distributed through local channels in the importing countries. The primary functions performed abroad relate chiefly to establishing a network of distributors and perhaps conducting sales promotion and brand-awareness activities.

Whether an export strategy can be pursued successfully over the long run depends on the relative cost competitiveness of the home-country production base. In some industries, firms gain additional scale economies and learning-curve benefits from centralizing production in plants whose output capability exceeds demand in any one country market; exporting enables a firm to capture such economies. However, an export strategy is vulnerable when (1) manufacturing costs in the home country are substantially higher than in foreign countries where rivals have plants, (2) the costs of shipping the product to distant foreign markets are relatively high, (3) adverse shifts occur in currency exchange rates, and (4) importing countries impose tariffs or erect other trade barriers. Unless an exporter can keep its production and shipping costs competitive with rivals' costs, secure adequate local distribution and marketing support of its products, and hedge against unfavorable changes in currency exchange rates, its success will be limited.

Licensing Strategies

Licensing as an entry strategy makes sense when a firm with valuable technical know-how, an appealing brand, or a unique patented product has neither the internal organizational capability nor the resources to enter foreign markets. Licensing also has the advantage of avoiding the risks of committing resources to country markets that are unfamiliar, politically volatile, economically unstable, or otherwise risky. By licensing the technology, trademark, or production rights to foreign-based firms, the firm can generate income from royalties while shifting the costs and risks of entering foreign markets to the licensee. The big disadvantage of licensing is the risk of providing valuable technological know-how to foreign companies and thereby losing some degree of control over its use; monitoring licensees and safeguarding the company's proprietary know-how can prove quite difficult in some circumstances. But if the royalty potential is considerable and the companies to which the licenses are being granted are trustworthy and reputable, then licensing can be a very attractive option. Many software and pharmaceutical companies use licensing strategies to compete in foreign markets.

Franchising Strategies

While licensing works well for manufacturers and owners of proprietary technology, franchising is often better suited to the international expansion efforts of service and retailing enterprises. McDonald's, Yum! Brands (the parent of Pizza Hut, KFC, Taco Bell, and WingStreet), the UPS Store, Roto-Rooter, 7-Eleven, and Hilton Hotels have all used franchising to build a presence in foreign markets. Franchising has many of the same advantages as licensing. The franchisee bears most of the costs and risks of establishing foreign locations; a franchisor has to expend only the resources to recruit, train, support, and monitor franchisees. The problem a franchisor faces is maintaining quality control; foreign franchisees do not always exhibit strong commitment to consistency and standardization, especially when the local culture does not stress the same kinds of quality concerns. A question that can arise is whether to allow foreign franchisees to make modifications in the franchisor's product offering so as to better satisfy the tastes and expectations of local buyers. Should McDonald's give franchisees in each nation some leeway in what products they put on their menus? Should the franchised KFC units in China be permitted to substitute spices that appeal to Chinese consumers? Or should the same menu offerings be rigorously and unvaryingly required of all franchisees worldwide?

Foreign Subsidiary Strategies

CORE CONCEPT

A **greenfield venture** is a subsidiary business that is established by setting up the entire operation from the ground up.

While exporting, licensing, and franchising rely upon the resources and capabilities of allies to deliver goods or services to buyers in international markets, companies pursuing international expansion may elect to take responsibility for the performance of all essential value chain activities. Companies that prefer direct control over all aspects of operating in a foreign market can establish a wholly owned subsidiary, either by acquiring a foreign company or by establishing operations from the ground up via internal development. A subsidiary business that is established by setting up the entire operation from the ground up is called a **greenfield venture.**

Acquisition is the quicker of the two options, and it may be the least risky and most cost-efficient means of hurdling such entry barriers as gaining access to local distribution channels, building supplier relationships, and establishing working relationships with government officials and other key constituencies. Buying an ongoing operation allows the acquirer to move directly to the task of transferring resources and personnel to the newly acquired business, redirecting and integrating the activities of the acquired business into its own operation, putting its own strategy into place, and accelerating efforts to build a strong market position.

One thing an acquisition-minded firm must consider is whether to pay a premium price for a successful local company or to buy a struggling competitor at a bargain price. If the buying firm has little knowledge of the local market but ample capital, it is often better off purchasing a capable, strongly positioned firm. However, when the acquirer sees promising ways to transform a weak firm into a strong one and has the resources and managerial know-how to do so, a struggling company can be the better long-term investment.

Entering a new foreign country via a greenfield venture makes sense when a company already operates in a number of countries, has experience in establishing new subsidiaries and overseeing their operations, and has a sufficiently large pool of resources and capabilities to rapidly equip a new subsidiary with the personnel and competencies it needs to compete successfully and profitably. Four other conditions make a greenfield venture strategy appealing:

- When creating an internal startup is cheaper than making an acquisition.
- When adding new production capacity will not adversely impact the supply–demand balance in the local market.
- When a startup subsidiary has the ability to gain good distribution access (perhaps because of the company's recognized brand name).
- When a startup subsidiary will have the size, cost structure, and capabilities to compete head-to-head against local rivals.

Greenfield ventures in foreign markets can also pose problems, just as other entry strategies do. They represent a costly capital investment, subject to a high level of risk. They require numerous other company resources as well, diverting them from other uses. They do not work well in countries without strong, well-functioning markets and institutions that protect the rights of foreign investors and provide other legal protections. Moreover, an important disadvantage of greenfield ventures relative to other means of international expansion is that they are the slowest entry route—particularly if the objective is to achieve a sizable market share. On the other hand, successful greenfield ventures may offer higher returns to compensate for their high risk and slower path.

Collaborative strategies involving alliances or joint ventures with foreign partners are a popular way for companies to edge their way into the markets of foreign countries.

Alliance and Joint Venture Strategies

Strategic alliances, joint ventures, and other cooperative agreements with foreign companies are a widely used means of entering foreign markets.[7] A company can benefit immensely from a foreign partner's familiarity with local government regulations, its knowledge of the buying habits and product preferences of consumers, its distribution-channel relationships, and so on.[8] Both Japanese and American companies are actively forming alliances with European companies to better compete in the 28-nation European Union and to capitalize on the opening of eastern European markets. Many U.S. and European companies are allying with Asian companies in their efforts to enter markets in China, India, Thailand, Indonesia, and other Asian countries.

Cross-border alliances enable a growth-minded company to widen its geographic coverage and strengthen its competitiveness in foreign markets; at the same time, they offer flexibility and allow a company to retain some degree of autonomy and operating control.

Another reason for cross-border alliances is to capture economies of scale in production and/or marketing. By joining forces in producing components, assembling models, and marketing their products, companies can realize cost savings not achievable with their own small volumes. A third reason to employ a collaborative strategy is to share distribution facilities and dealer networks, thus mutually strengthening each partner's access to buyers. A fourth benefit of a collaborative strategy is the learning and added expertise that comes from performing joint research, sharing technological know-how, studying one another's manufacturing methods, and understanding how to tailor sales and marketing approaches to fit local cultures and traditions. A fifth benefit is that cross-border allies can direct their competitive energies more toward mutual rivals and less toward one another; teaming up may help them close the gap on leading companies. And, finally, alliances can be a particularly useful way for companies across the world to gain agreement on important technical standards—they have been used to arrive at standards for assorted PC devices, Internet-related technologies, high-definition televisions, and mobile phones.

Cross-border alliances are an attractive means of gaining the aforementioned types of benefits (as compared to merging with or acquiring foreign-based companies) because they allow a company to preserve its independence (which is not the case with a merger) and avoid using scarce financial resources to fund acquisitions. Furthermore, an alliance offers the flexibility to readily disengage once its purpose has been served or if the benefits prove elusive, whereas mergers and acquisitions are more permanent arrangements.[9]

Illustration Capsule 7.1 shows how California-based Solazyme, a maker of biofuels and other green products, has used cross-border strategic alliances to fuel its growth.

The Risks of Strategic Alliances with Foreign Partners Alliances and joint ventures with foreign partners have their pitfalls, however. Sometimes a local partner's knowledge and expertise turns out to be less valuable than expected (because its knowledge is rendered obsolete by fast-changing market conditions or because its operating practices are archaic). Cross-border allies typically must overcome language and cultural barriers and figure out how to deal with diverse (or conflicting) operating practices. The transaction costs of working out a mutually agreeable

ILLUSTRATION CAPSULE 7.1

Solazyme's Cross-Border Alliances with Unilever, Sephora, Qantas, and Roquette

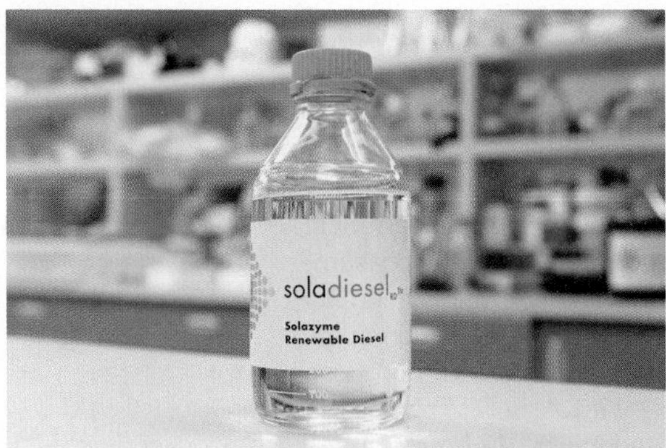

Solazyme, a California-based company that produces oils for nutritional, cosmetic, and biofuel products from algae, was named "America's Fastest-Growing Manufacturing Company" by *Inc. Magazine* in 2011. The company has fueled its rapid growth through a variety of cross-border strategic alliances with much larger partners. These partnerships not only have facilitated Solazyme's entry into new markets but have also created value through resource sharing and risk spreading.

Its partnership with Unilever, a giant British-Dutch consumer-goods company, initially focused on collaborative R&D. Projects were aimed at meeting the growing demand for completely renewable, natural, and sustainable personal care products through the use of algal oils. By further developing Solazyme's technology platform, the partnership has taken off; with the ability to produce Solazyme's oils and other biomaterials efficiently and at large scale, Unilever is now taking the next step of marketing and selling those products as part of its ambitious goal to use only sustainable agricultural raw materials by 2020.

Solazyme has entered into a variety of marketing and distribution agreements with French cosmetics company Sephora (now part of LVMH). In March 2011, Solazyme launched its luxury skin care brand, Algenist, with Sephora's help. Sephora has also agreed to distribute Solazyme's antiaging skin care line, making it available in Sephora stores and at Sephora.com.

In 2011, Solazyme also signed a contract with Australian airline Qantas to supply, test, and refine Solazyme's jet fuel product, SolaJet. Solazyme stands to gain valuable input on how to design and distribute its product while receiving media attention and the marketing advantage of a well-known customer. Likewise, Qantas hopes to better understand how it will achieve its sustainability goals while building its reputation as a sustainability leader in the airline industry.

However, not every partnership ends successfully, regardless of the strength of the initial motivations and relationship. Because its algae require sugar to produce oil, Solazyme developed an interest in securing a stable supply of this feedstock. For this purpose, Solazyme created a 50-50 joint venture with French starch processor Roquette to develop, produce, and market food products globally. By working with Roquette, Solazyme hoped to lower its exposure to sugar price fluctuations, trading the use of its innovative technological resources in return for Roquette's manufacturing infrastructure and expertise. But in 2013, the joint venture dissolved—both parties felt that after the exchange of ideas, technologies, and goals, they would be better off going it alone on the algal food product frontier.

Note: Developed with John L. Gardner and Harold W. Greenstone.

Sources: Company website; gigaom.com/, www.businessgreen.com/, www.reuters.com/, and www.foodnavigator-usa.com/ (all accessed March 4, 2012); S. Daniels, "Solazyme & Roquette to Each Go It Alone on Microalgae-Sourced Ingredients," www.foodnavigator-usa.com (accessed April 1, 2014); and D. Cardwell, "Unilever to Buy Oil Derived from Algae from Solazyme," *The New York Times* Online, September 25, 2013 (accessed April 1, 2014).

arrangement and monitoring partner compliance with the terms of the arrangement can be high. The communication, trust building, and coordination costs are not trivial in terms of management time.[10] Often, partners soon discover they have conflicting objectives and strategies, deep differences of opinion about how to proceed, or important differences in corporate values and ethical standards. Tensions build up, working relationships cool, and the hoped-for benefits never materialize.[11] It is not unusual for there to be little personal chemistry among some of the key people on whom the success or failure of the alliance depends—the rapport such personnel need to work well together may never emerge. And even if allies are able to develop productive personal relationships, they can still have trouble reaching mutually agreeable ways to deal with key issues or launching new initiatives fast enough to stay abreast of rapid advances in technology or shifting market conditions.

One worrisome problem with alliances or joint ventures is that a firm may risk losing some of its competitive advantage if an alliance partner is given full access to its proprietary technological expertise or other competitively valuable capabilities. There is a natural tendency for allies to struggle to collaborate effectively in competitively sensitive areas, thus spawning suspicions on both sides about forthright exchanges of information and expertise. It requires many meetings of many people working in good faith over a period of time to iron out what is to be shared, what is to remain proprietary, and how the cooperative arrangements will work.

Even if the alliance proves to be a win-win proposition for both parties, there is the danger of becoming overly dependent on foreign partners for essential expertise and competitive capabilities. Companies aiming for global market leadership need to develop their own resource capabilities in order to be masters of their destiny. Frequently, experienced international companies operating in 50 or more countries across the world find less need for entering into cross-border alliances than do companies in the early stages of globalizing their operations.[12] Companies with global operations make it a point to develop senior managers who understand how "the system" works in different countries, plus they can avail themselves of local managerial talent and know-how by simply hiring experienced local managers and thereby detouring the hazards of collaborative alliances with local companies. One of the lessons about cross-border partnerships is that they are more effective in helping a company establish a beachhead of new opportunity in world markets than they are in enabling a company to achieve and sustain global market leadership.

INTERNATIONAL STRATEGY: THE THREE MAIN APPROACHES

LO 4

The three main strategic approaches for competing internationally.

Broadly speaking, a firm's **international strategy** is simply its strategy for competing in two or more countries simultaneously. Typically, a company will start to compete internationally by entering one or perhaps a select few foreign markets—selling its products or services in countries where there is a ready market for them. But as it expands further internationally, it will have to confront head-on two conflicting pressures: the demand for responsiveness to local needs versus the prospect of efficiency gains from offering a standardized product globally. Deciding upon the degree to vary its competitive approach to fit the specific market conditions and buyer preferences in each host country is perhaps the foremost strategic issue that must be addressed when a company is operating in two or more foreign markets.[13] Figure 7.2 shows a company's three options for resolving this issue: choosing a *multidomestic, global,* or *transnational* strategy.

CORE CONCEPT

An **international strategy** is a strategy for competing in two or more countries simultaneously.

FIGURE 7.2 Three Approaches for Competing Internationally

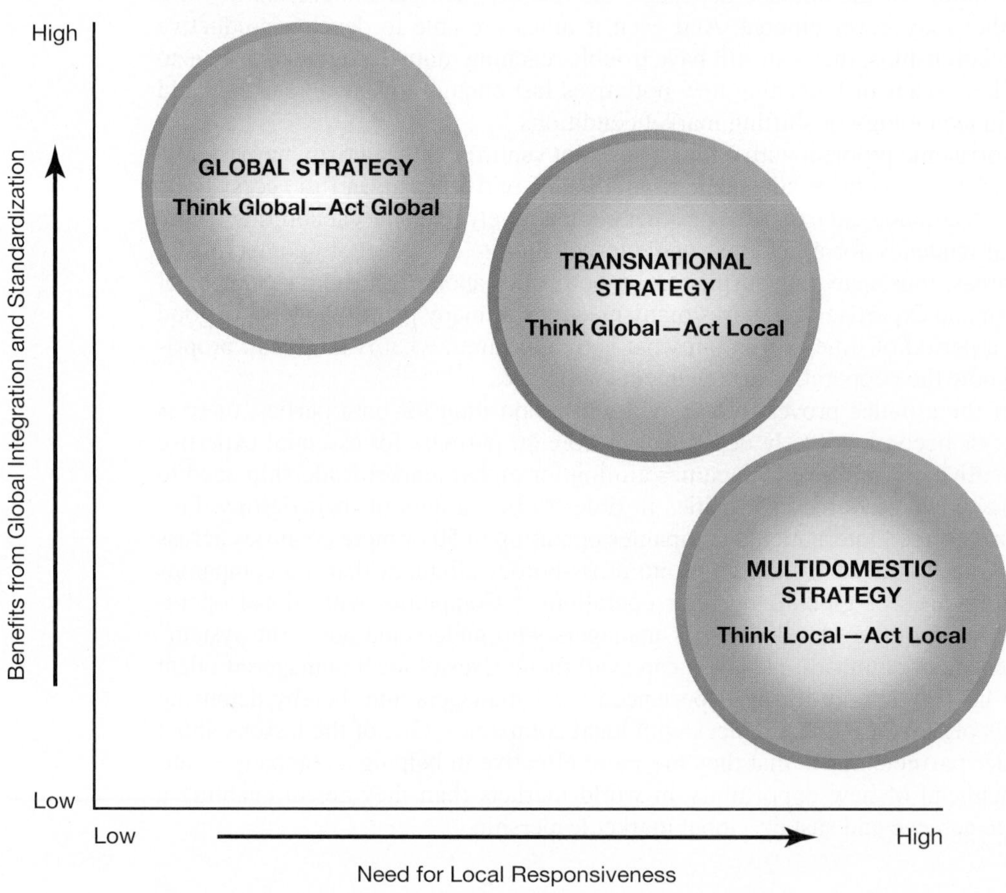

Multidomestic Strategies—A "Think-Local, Act-Local" Approach

> **CORE CONCEPT**
>
> A **multidomestic strategy** is one in which a company varies its product offering and competitive approach from country to country in an effort to be responsive to differing buyer preferences and market conditions. It is a **think-local, act-local** type of international strategy, facilitated by decision making decentralized to the local level.

A **multidomestic strategy** is one in which a company varies its product offering and competitive approach from country to country in an effort to meet differing buyer needs and to address divergent local-market conditions. It involves having plants produce different product versions for different local markets and adapting marketing and distribution to fit local customs, cultures, regulations, and market requirements. Castrol, a specialist in oil lubricants, produces over 3,000 different formulas of lubricants to meet the requirements of different climates, vehicle types and uses, and equipment applications that characterize different country markets. In the food products industry, it is common for companies to vary the ingredients in their products and sell the localized versions under local brand names to cater to country-specific tastes and eating preferences. Motor vehicle manufacturers routinely produce smaller, more fuel-efficient vehicles for European markets, where roads are narrower and gasoline prices are two to three times higher than in the North American market (where many consumers prefer larger vehicles). The models they manufacture for the Asian market are different yet again—and local managers tailor the sales and marketing of these vehicles to local cultures, buyer tastes, and competitive conditions.

In essence, a multidomestic strategy represents a **think-local, act-local** approach to international strategy. A think-local, act-local approach to strategy making is most appropriate when the need for local responsiveness is high due to significant cross-country differences in demographic, cultural, and market conditions and when the potential for efficiency gains from standardization is limited, as depicted in Figure 7.2. A think-local, act-local approach is possible only when decision making is decentralized, giving local managers considerable latitude for crafting and executing strategies for the country markets they are responsible for. Giving local managers decision-making authority allows them to address specific market needs and respond swiftly to local changes in demand. It also enables them to focus their competitive efforts, stake out attractive market positions vis-à-vis local competitors, react to rivals' moves in a timely fashion, and target new opportunities as they emerge.[14]

Despite their obvious benefits, think-local, act-local strategies have three big drawbacks:

1. They hinder transfer of a company's capabilities, knowledge, and other resources across country boundaries, since the company's efforts are not integrated or coordinated across country boundaries. This can make the company less innovative overall.
2. They raise production and distribution costs due to the greater variety of designs and components, shorter production runs for each product version, and complications of added inventory handling and distribution logistics.
3. They are not conducive to building a single, worldwide competitive advantage. When a company's competitive approach and product offering vary from country to country, the nature and size of any resulting competitive edge also tends to vary. At the most, multidomestic strategies are capable of producing a group of local competitive advantages of varying types and degrees of strength.

Global Strategies—A "Think-Global, Act-Global" Approach

A **global strategy** contrasts sharply with a multidomestic strategy in that it takes a standardized, globally integrated approach to producing, packaging, selling, and delivering the company's products and services worldwide. Companies employing a global strategy sell the same products under the same brand names everywhere, utilize much the same distribution channels in all countries, and compete on the basis of the same capabilities and marketing approaches worldwide. Although the company's strategy or product offering may be adapted in minor ways to accommodate specific situations in a few host countries, the company's fundamental competitive approach (low cost, differentiation, best cost, or focused) remains very much intact worldwide and local managers stick close to the global strategy.

A **think-global, act-global** approach prompts company managers to integrate and coordinate the company's strategic moves worldwide and to expand into most, if not all, nations where there is significant buyer demand. It puts considerable strategic emphasis on building a *global* brand name and aggressively pursuing opportunities to transfer ideas, new products, and capabilities from one country to another. Global strategies are characterized by relatively centralized value chain activities, such as production and distribution. While there may be more than one manufacturing plant and distribution center to minimize transportation costs, for example, they tend to be few in number. Achieving the efficiency potential of a global strategy requires that resources and best practices be shared, value chain

CORE CONCEPT

A **global strategy** is one in which a company employs the same basic competitive approach in all countries where it operates, sells standardized products globally, strives to build global brands, and coordinates its actions worldwide with strong headquarters control. It represents a **think-global, act-global** approach.

activities be integrated, and capabilities be transferred from one location to another as they are developed. These objectives are best facilitated through centralized decision making and strong headquarters control.

Because a global strategy cannot accommodate varying local needs, it is an appropriate strategic choice when there are pronounced efficiency benefits from standardization and when buyer needs are relatively homogeneous across countries and regions. A globally standardized and integrated approach is especially beneficial when high volumes significantly lower costs due to economies of scale or added experience (moving the company further down a learning curve). It can also be advantageous if it allows the firm to replicate a successful business model on a global basis efficiently or engage in higher levels of R&D by spreading the fixed costs and risks over a higher-volume output. It is a fitting response to industry conditions marked by global competition.

Ford's global design strategy is a move toward a think-global, act-global strategy, involving the development and production of standardized models with country-specific modifications limited to what is required to meet local country emission and safety standards. The 2010 Ford Fiesta and 2011 Ford Focus were the company's first global design models to be marketed in Europe, North America, Asia, and Australia. Whenever country-to-country differences are small enough to be accommodated within the framework of a global strategy, a global strategy is preferable because a company can more readily unify its operations and focus on establishing a brand image and reputation that are uniform from country to country. Moreover, with a global strategy a company is better able to focus its full resources on securing a sustainable low-cost or differentiation-based competitive advantage over both domestic rivals and global rivals.

There are, however, several drawbacks to global strategies: (1) They do not enable firms to address local needs as precisely as locally based rivals can, (2) they are less responsive to changes in local market conditions, in the form of either new opportunities or competitive threats, (3) they raise transportation costs and may involve higher tariffs, and (4) they involve higher coordination costs due to the more complex task of managing a globally integrated enterprise.

Transnational Strategies—A "Think-Global, Act-Local" Approach

CORE CONCEPT

A **transnational strategy** is a **think-global, act-local** approach that incorporates elements of both multidomestic and global strategies.

A **transnational strategy** (sometimes called *glocalization*) incorporates elements of both a globalized and a localized approach to strategy making. This type of middle-ground strategy is called for when there are relatively high needs for local responsiveness as well as appreciable benefits to be realized from standardization, as Figure 7.2 suggests. A transnational strategy encourages a company to **think global, act local** to balance these competing objectives.

Often, companies implement a transnational strategy with mass-customization techniques that enable them to address local preferences in an efficient, semistandardized manner. McDonald's, KFC, and Starbucks have discovered ways to customize their menu offerings in various countries without compromising costs, product quality, and operating effectiveness. Unilever is responsive to local market needs regarding its consumer products, while realizing global economies of scale in certain functions. Otis Elevator found that a transnational strategy delivers better results than a global strategy when it is competing in countries like China, where local needs are highly differentiated. By switching from its customary single-brand approach to a multibrand strategy aimed at serving different segments of the market, Otis was able to double its market share in China and increased its revenues sixfold over a nine-year period.[15]

As a rule, most companies that operate internationally endeavor to employ as global a strategy as customer needs and market conditions permit. Electronic Arts (EA) has two major design studios—one in Vancouver, British Columbia, and one in Los Angeles—and smaller design studios in San Francisco, Orlando, London, and Tokyo. This dispersion of design studios helps EA to design games that are specific to different cultures—for example, the London studio took the lead in designing the popular FIFA Soccer game to suit European tastes and to replicate the stadiums, signage, and team rosters; the U.S. studio took the lead in designing games involving NFL football, NBA basketball, and NASCAR racing.

A transnational strategy is far more conducive than other strategies to transferring and leveraging subsidiary skills and capabilities. But, like other approaches to competing internationally, transnational strategies also have significant drawbacks:

1. They are the most difficult of all international strategies to implement due to the added complexity of varying the elements of the strategy to situational conditions.
2. They place large demands on the organization due to the need to pursue conflicting objectives simultaneously.
3. Implementing the strategy is likely to be a costly and time-consuming enterprise, with an uncertain outcome.

Illustration Capsule 7.2 explains how Four Seasons Hotels has been able to compete successfully on the basis of a transnational strategy.

Table 7.1 provides a summary of the pluses and minuses of the three approaches to competing internationally.

TABLE 7.1 Advantages and Disadvantages of Multidomestic, Global, and Transnational Strategies

	Advantages	Disadvantages
Multidomestic (think local, act local)	• Can meet the specific needs of each market more precisely • Can respond more swiftly to localized changes in demand • Can target reactions to the moves of local rivals • Can respond more quickly to local opportunities and threats	• Hinders resource and capability sharing or cross-market transfers • Has higher production and distribution costs • Is not conducive to a worldwide competitive advantage
Global (think global, act global)	• Has lower costs due to scale and scope economies • Can lead to greater efficiencies due to the ability to transfer best practices across markets • Increases innovation from knowledge sharing and capability transfer • Offers the benefit of a global brand and reputation	• Cannot address local needs precisely • Is less responsive to changes in local market conditions • Involves higher transportation costs and tariffs • Has higher coordination and integration costs
Transnational (think global, act local)	• Offers the benefits of both local responsiveness and global integration • Enables the transfer and sharing of resources and capabilities across borders • Provides the benefits of flexible coordination	• Is more complex and harder to implement • Entails conflicting goals, which may be difficult to reconcile and require trade-offs • Involves more costly and time-consuming implementation

ILLUSTRATION CAPSULE 7.2 Four Seasons Hotels: Local Character, Global Service

Four Seasons Hotels is a Toronto, Canada–based manager of luxury hotel properties. With 92 properties located in many of the world's most popular tourist destinations and business centers, Four Seasons commands a following of many of the world's most discerning travelers. In contrast to its key competitor, Ritz-Carlton, which strives to create one uniform experience globally, Four Seasons Hotels has gained market share by deftly combining local architectural and cultural experiences with globally consistent luxury service.

When moving into a new market, Four Seasons always seeks out a local capital partner. The understanding of local custom and business relationships this financier brings is critical to the process of developing a new Four Seasons hotel. Four Seasons also insists on hiring a local architect and design consultant for each property, as opposed to using architects or designers it's worked with in other locations. While this can be a challenge, particularly in emerging markets, Four Seasons has found it is worth it in the long run to have a truly local team.

The specific layout and programming of each hotel is also unique. For instance, when Four Seasons opened its hotel in Mumbai, India, it prioritized space for large banquet halls to target the Indian wedding market. In India, weddings often draw guests numbering in the thousands. When moving into the Middle East, Four Seasons designed its hotels with separate prayer rooms for men and women. In Bali, where destination weddings are common, the hotel employs a "weather shaman" who, for some guests, provides reassurance that the weather will cooperate for their special day. In all cases, the objective is to provide a truly local experience.

When staffing its hotels, Four Seasons seeks to strike a fine balance between employing locals who have an innate understanding of the local culture alongside expatriate staff or "culture carriers" who understand the DNA of Four Seasons. It also uses global systems to track customer preferences and employs globally consistent service standards. Four Seasons claims that its guests experience the same high level of service globally but that no two experiences are the same.

While it is much more expensive and time-consuming to design unique architectural and programming experiences, doing so is a strategic trade-off Four Seasons has made to achieve the local experience demanded by its high-level clientele. Likewise, it has recognized that maintaining globally consistent operation processes and service standards is important too. Four Seasons has struck the right balance between thinking globally and acting locally—the marker of a truly transnational strategy. As a result, the company has been rewarded with an international reputation for superior service and a leading market share in the luxury hospitality segment.

Note: Developed with Brian R. McKenzie.

Sources: Four Seasons annual report and corporate website; and interview with Scott Woroch, Executive Vice President of Development, Four Seasons Hotels, February 22, 2014.

INTERNATIONAL OPERATIONS AND THE QUEST FOR COMPETITIVE ADVANTAGE

There are three important ways in which a firm can gain competitive advantage (or offset domestic disadvantages) by expanding outside its domestic market. First, it can use location to lower costs or achieve greater product differentiation. Second, it can transfer competitively valuable resources and capabilities from one country to another or share them across international borders to extend its competitive advantages. And third, it can benefit from cross-border coordination opportunities that are not open to domestic-only competitors.

Using Location to Build Competitive Advantage

LO 5

How companies are able to use international operations to improve overall competitiveness.

To use location to build competitive advantage, a company must consider two issues: (1) whether to concentrate each activity it performs in a few select countries or to disperse performance of the activity to many nations, and (2) in which countries to locate particular activities.

Companies that compete internationally can pursue competitive advantage in world markets by locating their value chain activities in whatever nations prove most advantageous.

When to Concentrate Activities in a Few Locations It is advantageous for a company to concentrate its activities in a limited number of locations when:

- *The costs of manufacturing or other activities are significantly lower in some geographic locations than in others.* For example, much of the world's athletic footwear is manufactured in Asia (Vietnam, China, and Korea) because of low labor costs; much of the production of circuit boards for PCs is located in Taiwan because of both low costs and the high-caliber technical skills of the Taiwanese labor force.
- *Significant scale economies exist in production or distribution.* The presence of significant economies of scale in components production or final assembly means that a company can gain major cost savings from operating a few super-efficient plants as opposed to a host of small plants scattered across the world. Makers of digital cameras and LED TVs located in Japan, South Korea, and Taiwan have used their scale economies to establish a low-cost advantage in this way. Achieving low-cost provider status often requires a company to have the largest worldwide manufacturing share (as distinct from brand share or market share), with production centralized in one or a few giant plants. Some companies even use such plants to manufacture units sold under the brand names of rivals to further boost production-related scale economies. Likewise, a company may be able to reduce its distribution costs by establishing large-scale distribution centers to serve major geographic regions of the world market (e.g., North America, Latin America, Europe and the Middle East, and the Asia-Pacific region).
- *Sizable learning and experience benefits are associated with performing an activity.* In some industries, learning-curve effects can allow a manufacturer to lower unit costs, boost quality, or master a new technology *more quickly* by concentrating production in a few locations. The key to riding down the learning curve is to concentrate production in a few locations to increase the cumulative volume at a plant (and thus the experience of the plant's workforce) as rapidly as possible.
- *Certain locations have superior resources, allow better coordination of related activities, or offer other valuable advantages.* Companies often locate a research unit or a sophisticated production facility in a particular country to take advantage of its pool of technically trained personnel. Samsung became a leader in memory chip technology by establishing a major R&D facility in Silicon Valley and transferring the know-how it gained back to its operations in South Korea. Where just-in-time inventory practices yield big cost savings and/or where an assembly firm has long-term partnering arrangements with its key suppliers, parts manufacturing plants may be clustered around final-assembly plants. A customer service center or sales office may be opened in a particular country to help cultivate strong relationships with pivotal customers located nearby.

When to Disperse Activities across Many Locations In some instances, dispersing activities across locations is more advantageous than concentrating them. Buyer-related activities—such as distribution, marketing, and after-sale service—usually must take place close to buyers. This means physically locating the capability to perform such activities in every country or region where a firm has major customers. For example, firms that make mining and oil-drilling equipment maintain operations in many locations around the world to support customers' needs for speedy equipment repair and technical assistance. Large public accounting firms have offices in numerous countries to serve the foreign operations of their international corporate clients. Dispersing activities to many locations is also competitively important when high transportation costs, diseconomies of large size, and trade barriers make it too expensive to operate from a central location. Many companies distribute their products from multiple locations to shorten delivery times to customers. In addition, dispersing activities helps hedge against the risks of fluctuating exchange rates, supply interruptions (due to strikes, natural disasters, or transportation delays), and adverse political developments. Such risks are usually greater when activities are concentrated in a single location.

Even though global firms have strong reason to disperse buyer-related activities to many international locations, such activities as materials procurement, parts manufacture, finished-goods assembly, technology research, and new product development can frequently be decoupled from buyer locations and performed wherever advantage lies. Components can be made in Mexico; technology research done in Frankfurt; new products developed and tested in Phoenix; and assembly plants located in Spain, Brazil, Taiwan, or South Carolina, for example. Capital can be raised wherever it is available on the best terms.

Sharing and Transferring Resources and Capabilities across Borders to Build Competitive Advantage

When a company has competitively valuable resources and capabilities, it may be able to leverage them further by expanding internationally. If its resources retain their value in foreign contexts, then entering new foreign markets can extend the company's resource-based competitive advantage over a broader domain. For example, companies like Hermes, Prada, and Gucci have utilized their powerful brand names to extend their differentiation-based competitive advantages into markets far beyond their home-country origins. In each of these cases, the luxury brand name represents a valuable competitive asset that can readily be *shared* by all of the company's international stores, enabling them to attract buyers and gain a higher degree of market penetration over a wider geographic area than would otherwise be possible.

Another way for a company to extend its competitive advantage internationally is to *transfer* technological know-how or other important resources and capabilities from its operations in one country to its operations in other countries. For instance, if a company discovers ways to assemble a product faster and more cost-effectively at one plant, then that know-how can be transferred to its assembly plants in other countries. Whirlpool, the leading global manufacturer of home appliances, with 65 manufacturing and technology research centers around the world, uses an online global information technology platform to quickly and effectively transfer key product innovations and improved production techniques both across national borders and across various appliance brands. Walmart is expanding its international operations with a strategy that involves transferring its considerable resource capabilities in distribution and discount retailing to its retail units in 26 foreign countries.

Cross-border sharing or transferring resources and capabilities provides a cost-effective way for a company to leverage its core competencies more fully and extend its competitive advantages into a wider array of geographic markets. The cost of sharing or transferring already developed resources and capabilities across country borders is low in comparison to the time and considerable expense it takes to create them. Moreover, deploying them abroad spreads the fixed development costs over a greater volume of unit sales, thus contributing to low unit costs and a potential cost-based competitive advantage in recently entered geographic markets. Even if the shared or transferred resources or capabilities have to be adapted to local-market conditions, this can usually be done at low additional cost.

Consider the case of Walt Disney's theme parks as an example. The success of the theme parks in the United States derives in part from core resources such as the Disney brand name and characters like Mickey Mouse that have universal appeal and worldwide recognition. These resources can be freely shared with new theme parks as Disney expands internationally. Disney can also replicate its theme parks in new countries cost-effectively since it has already borne the costs of developing its core resources, park attractions, basic park design, and operating capabilities. The cost of replicating its theme parks abroad should be relatively low, even if the parks need to be adapted to a variety of local country conditions. By expanding internationally, Disney is able to enhance its competitive advantage over local theme park rivals. It does so by leveraging the differentiation advantage conferred by resources such as the Disney name and the park attractions. And by moving into new foreign markets, it augments its competitive advantage worldwide through the efficiency gains that come from cross-border resource sharing and low-cost capability transfer and business model replication.

Sharing and transferring resources and capabilities across country borders may also contribute to the development of broader or deeper competencies and capabilities—helping a company achieve *dominating depth* in some competitively valuable area. For example, the reputation for quality that Honda established worldwide began in motorcycles but enabled the company to command a position in both automobiles and outdoor power equipment in multiple-country markets. A one-country customer base is often too small to support the resource buildup needed to achieve such depth; this is particularly true in a developing or protected market, where competitively powerful resources are not required. By deploying capabilities across a larger international domain, a company can gain the experience needed to upgrade them to a higher performance standard. And by facing a more challenging set of international competitors, a company may be spurred to develop a stronger set of competitive capabilities. Moreover, by entering international markets, firms may be able to augment their capability set by learning from international rivals, cooperative partners, or acquisition targets.

However, cross-border resource sharing and transfers of capabilities are not guaranteed recipes for competitive success. For example, whether a resource or capability can confer a competitive advantage abroad depends on the conditions of rivalry in each particular market. If the rivals in a foreign-country market have superior resources and capabilities, then an entering firm may find itself at a competitive disadvantage even if it has a resource-based advantage domestically and can transfer the resources at low cost. In addition, since lifestyles and buying habits differ internationally, resources and capabilities that are valuable in one country may not have value in another. Sometimes a popular or well-regarded brand in one country turns out to have little competitive clout against local brands in other countries.

For example, Netherlands-based Royal Philips Electronics, with 2012 sales of about €25 billion in more than 60 countries, is a leading seller of electric shavers, lighting products, small appliances, televisions, DVD players, and health care products. It has proven competitive capabilities in a number of businesses and countries and has been consistently profitable on a global basis. But the company's Philips and Magnavox brand names and the resources it has invested in its North American organization have proved inadequate in changing its image as a provider of low-end TVs and DVD players, recruiting retailers that can effectively merchandise its Magnavox and Philips products, and exciting consumers with the quality and features of its products. It has lost money in North America every year since 1988.

Benefiting from Cross-Border Coordination

Companies that compete on an international basis have another source of competitive advantage relative to their purely domestic rivals: They are able to benefit from coordinating activities across different countries' domains.[16] For example, an international manufacturer can shift production from a plant in one country to a plant in another to take advantage of exchange rate fluctuations, to cope with components shortages, or to profit from changing wage rates or energy costs. Production schedules can be coordinated worldwide; shipments can be diverted from one distribution center to another if sales rise unexpectedly in one place and fall in another. By coordinating their activities, international companies may also be able to enhance their leverage with host-country governments or respond adaptively to changes in tariffs and quotas. Efficiencies can also be achieved by shifting workloads from where they are unusually heavy to locations where personnel are underutilized.

CROSS-BORDER STRATEGIC MOVES

While international competitors can employ any of the offensive and defensive moves discussed in Chapter 6, there are two types of strategic moves that are particularly suited for companies competing internationally. Both involve the use of "profit sanctuaries."

Profit sanctuaries are country markets (or geographic regions) in which a company derives substantial profits because of a strong or protected market position. In most cases, a company's biggest and most strategically crucial profit sanctuary is its home market, but international and global companies may also enjoy profit sanctuary status in other nations where they have a strong position based on some type of competitive advantage. Companies that compete globally are likely to have more profit sanctuaries than companies that compete in just a few country markets; a domestic-only competitor, of course, can have only one profit sanctuary. Nike, which markets its products in 190 countries, has two major profit sanctuaries: North America and Greater China (where it earned $2.5 billion and $809 million respectively in operating profits in 2013).

Using Profit Sanctuaries to Wage a Strategic Offensive

Profit sanctuaries are valuable competitive assets, providing the financial strength to support strategic offensives in selected country markets and fuel a company's race for world-market leadership. The added financial capability afforded by multiple profit sanctuaries gives an international competitor the financial strength to wage a market offensive against a domestic competitor whose only profit sanctuary is its home market. The international company has the flexibility of lowballing its prices or launching high-cost marketing campaigns in the domestic company's home market and grabbing market share at the domestic company's expense. Razor-thin margins or even losses in these markets can be subsidized with the healthy profits earned in its profit sanctuaries—a practice called **cross-market subsidization.** The international company can adjust the depth of its price cutting to move in and capture market share quickly, or it can shave prices slightly to make gradual market inroads (perhaps over a decade or more) so as not to threaten domestic firms precipitously and trigger protectionist government actions. If the domestic company retaliates with matching price cuts or increased marketing expenses, it thereby exposes its entire revenue stream and profit base to erosion; its profits can be squeezed substantially and its competitive strength sapped, even if it is the domestic market leader.

CORE CONCEPT

Cross-market subsidization—supporting competitive offensives in one market with resources and profits diverted from operations in another market—can be a powerful competitive weapon.

When taken to the extreme, cut-rate pricing attacks by international competitors may draw charges of unfair "dumping." A company is said to be *dumping* when it sells its goods in foreign markets at prices that are (1) well below the prices at which it normally sells them in its home market or (2) well below its full costs per unit. Almost all governments can be expected to retaliate against perceived dumping practices by imposing special tariffs on goods being imported from the countries of the guilty companies. Indeed, as the trade among nations has mushroomed over the past 10 years, most governments have joined the World Trade Organization (WTO), which promotes fair trade practices among nations and actively polices dumping. Companies deemed guilty of dumping frequently come under pressure from their own government to cease and desist, especially if the tariffs adversely affect innocent companies based in the same country or if the advent of special tariffs raises the specter of an international trade war.

Using Profit Sanctuaries to Defend against International Rivals

Cross-border tactics involving profit sanctuaries can also be used as a means of defending against the strategic moves of rivals with multiple profit sanctuaries of their own. If a company finds itself under competitive attack by an international rival in one country market, one way to respond is to conduct a counterattack against the rival in one of its key markets in a different country—preferably where the rival is least protected and has the most to lose. This is a possible option when rivals compete against one another in much the same markets around the world.

For companies with at least one profit sanctuary, having a presence in a rival's key markets can be enough to deter the rival from making aggressive attacks. The reason for this is that the combination of market presence in the rival's key markets and a profit sanctuary elsewhere can send a signal to the rival that the company could quickly ramp up production (funded by the profit sanctuary) to mount a competitive counterattack if the rival attacks one of the company's key markets.

When international rivals compete against one another in multiple-country markets, this type of deterrence effect can restrain them from taking aggressive action against one another, due to the fear of a retaliatory response that might escalate the battle into a cross-border competitive war. **Mutual restraint** of this sort tends to stabilize the competitive position of multimarket rivals against one another. And while it may prevent each firm from making any

CORE CONCEPT

When the same companies compete against one another in multiple geographic markets, the threat of cross-border counterattacks may be enough to deter aggressive competitive moves and encourage **mutual restraint** among international rivals.

major market share gains at the expense of its rival, it also protects against costly competitive battles that would be likely to erode the profitability of both companies without any compensating gain.

STRATEGIES FOR COMPETING IN THE MARKETS OF DEVELOPING COUNTRIES

LO 6

The unique characteristics of competing in developing-country markets.

Companies racing for global leadership have to consider competing in developing-economy markets like China, India, Brazil, Indonesia, Thailand, and Russia—countries where the business risks are considerable but where the opportunities for growth are huge, especially as their economies develop and living standards climb toward levels in the industrialized world.[17] In today's world, a company that aspires to international market leadership (or to sustained rapid growth) cannot ignore the market opportunities or the base of technical and managerial talent such countries offer. For example, in 2013 China was the world's second-largest economy (behind the United States), based on purchasing power and its population of 1.3 billion people. Due to the rapid growth of a wealthy class, it may soon become the world's largest consumer of luxury products. China is already the world's largest consumer of many commodities. Thus, no company that aspires to global market leadership can afford to ignore the strategic importance of establishing competitive market positions in the so-called BRIC countries (Brazil, Russia, India, and China), as well as in other parts of the Asia-Pacific region, Latin America, and eastern Europe.

Tailoring products to fit market conditions in developing countries, however, often involves more than making minor product changes and becoming more familiar with local cultures. McDonald's has had to offer vegetable burgers in parts of Asia and to rethink its prices, which are often high by local standards and affordable only by the well-to-do. Kellogg has struggled to introduce its cereals successfully because consumers in many less developed countries do not eat cereal for breakfast. Single-serving packages of detergents, shampoos, pickles, cough syrup, and cooking oils are very popular in India because they allow buyers to conserve cash by purchasing only what they need immediately. Thus, many companies find that trying to employ a strategy akin to that used in the markets of developed countries is hazardous.[18] Experimenting with some, perhaps many, local twists is usually necessary to find a strategy combination that works.

Strategy Options for Competing in Developing-Country Markets

There are several options for tailoring a company's strategy to fit the sometimes unusual or challenging circumstances presented in developing-country markets:

- *Prepare to compete on the basis of low price.* Consumers in developing markets are often highly focused on price, which can give low-cost local competitors the edge unless a company can find ways to attract buyers with bargain prices as well as better products. For example, in order to enter the market for laundry detergents in India, Unilever had to develop a low-cost detergent (named Wheel), construct new low-cost production facilities, package the detergent in single-use amounts so that it could be sold at a very low unit price, distribute the product to local merchants by handcarts, and craft an economical marketing campaign that included painted signs on buildings and demonstrations near stores. The new brand quickly captured $100 million in sales and was the top detergent brand in India based on 2011 dollar sales. Unilever later replicated the strategy in India with low-priced packets of shampoos and deodorants and in South America with a detergent brand-named Ala.

- *Modify aspects of the company's business model to accommodate the unique local circumstances of developing countries.* For instance, when Dell entered China, it discovered that individuals and businesses were not accustomed to placing orders through the Internet. To adapt, Dell modified its direct sales model to rely more heavily on phone and fax orders while waiting for a greater acceptance of online ordering. Further, because numerous Chinese government departments and state-owned enterprises insisted that hardware vendors make their bids through distributors and systems integrators (as opposed to dealing directly with Dell salespeople as did large enterprises in other countries), Dell opted to use third parties in marketing its products to this buyer segment. But Dell was careful not to abandon the parts of its business model that gave it a competitive edge over rivals.
- *Try to change the local market to better match the way the company does business elsewhere.* An international company often has enough market clout to drive major changes in the way a local country market operates. When Japan's Suzuki entered India, it triggered a quality revolution among Indian auto parts manufacturers. Local component suppliers teamed up with Suzuki's vendors in Japan and worked with Japanese experts to produce higher-quality products. Over the next two decades, Indian companies became proficient in making top-notch components for vehicles, won more prizes for quality than companies in any country other than Japan, and broke into the global market as suppliers to many automakers in Asia and other parts of the world. Mahindra and Mahindra, one of India's premier automobile manufacturers, has been recognized by a number of organizations for its product quality. Among its most noteworthy awards was its number-one ranking by J.D. Power Asia Pacific for new-vehicle overall quality.
- *Stay away from developing markets where it is impractical or uneconomical to modify the company's business model to accommodate local circumstances.* Home Depot's CFO, Carol Tomé, argues that there are few developing countries where Home Depot can operate successfully.[19] The company expanded successfully into Mexico, but it has avoided entry into other developing countries because its value proposition of good quality, low prices, and attentive customer service relies on (1) good highways and logistical systems to minimize store inventory costs, (2) employee stock ownership to help motivate store personnel to provide good customer service, and (3) high labor costs for housing construction and home repairs that encourage homeowners to engage in do-it-yourself projects. Relying on these factors in North American markets has worked spectacularly for Home Depot, but the company found that it could not count on these factors in China, from which it withdrew in 2012.

Profitability in developing markets rarely comes quickly or easily—new entrants have to adapt their business models to local conditions, which may not always be possible.

Company experiences in entering developing markets like Argentina, Vietnam, Malaysia, and Brazil indicate that profitability seldom comes quickly or easily. Building a market for the company's products can often turn into a long-term process that involves reeducation of consumers, sizable investments in advertising to alter tastes and buying habits, and upgrades of the local infrastructure (transportation systems, distribution channels, etc.). In such cases, a company must be patient, work within the system to improve the infrastructure, and lay the foundation for generating sizable revenues and profits once conditions are ripe for market takeoff.

DEFENDING AGAINST GLOBAL GIANTS: STRATEGIES FOR LOCAL COMPANIES IN DEVELOPING COUNTRIES

If opportunity-seeking, resource-rich international companies are looking to enter developing-country markets, what strategy options can local companies use to survive? As it turns out, the prospects for local companies facing global giants are by no means grim. Studies of local companies in developing markets have disclosed five strategies that have proved themselves in defending against globally competitive companies.[20]

1. *Develop business models that exploit shortcomings in local distribution networks or infrastructure.* In many instances, the extensive collection of resources possessed by the global giants is of little help in building a presence in developing markets. The lack of well-established local wholesaler and distributor networks, telecommunication systems, consumer banking, or media necessary for advertising makes it difficult for large internationals to migrate business models proved in developed markets to emerging markets. Emerging markets sometimes favor local companies whose managers are familiar with the local language and culture and are skilled in selecting large numbers of conscientious employees to carry out labor-intensive tasks. Shanda, a Chinese producer of massively multiplayer online role-playing games (MMORPG), overcame China's lack of an established credit card network by selling prepaid access cards through local merchants. The company's focus on online games also protects it from shortcomings in China's software piracy laws. An India-based electronics company carved out a market niche for itself by developing an all-in-one business machine, designed especially for India's millions of small shopkeepers, that tolerates the country's frequent power outages.
2. *Utilize keen understanding of local customer needs and preferences to create customized products or services.* When developing-country markets are largely made up of customers with strong local needs, a good strategy option is to concentrate on customers who prefer a local touch and to accept the loss of the customers attracted to global brands.[21] A local company may be able to astutely exploit its local orientation—its familiarity with local preferences, its expertise in traditional products, its long-standing customer relationships. A small Middle Eastern cell phone manufacturer competes successfully against industry giants Samsung, Apple, Nokia, and Motorola by selling a model designed especially for Muslims—it is loaded with the Koran, alerts people at prayer times, and is equipped with a compass that points them toward Mecca. Shenzhen-based Tencent has become the leader in instant messaging in China through its unique understanding of Chinese behavior and culture.
3. *Take advantage of aspects of the local workforce with which large international companies may be unfamiliar.* Local companies that lack the technological capabilities of foreign entrants may be able to rely on their better understanding of the local labor force to offset any disadvantage. Focus Media is China's largest outdoor advertising firm and has relied on low-cost labor to update its 130,000 LCD displays and billboards in 90 cities in a low-tech manner, while

international companies operating in China use electronically networked screens that allow messages to be changed remotely. Focus uses an army of employees who ride to each display by bicycle to change advertisements with programming contained on a USB flash drive or DVD. Indian information technology firms such as Infosys Technologies and Satyam Computer Services have been able to keep their personnel costs lower than those of international competitors EDS and Accenture because of their familiarity with local labor markets. While the large internationals have focused recruiting efforts in urban centers like Bangalore and Delhi, driving up engineering and computer science salaries in such cities, local companies have shifted recruiting efforts to second-tier cities that are unfamiliar to foreign firms.

4. *Use acquisition and rapid-growth strategies to better defend against expansion-minded internationals.* With the growth potential of developing markets such as China, Indonesia, and Brazil obvious to the world, local companies must attempt to develop scale and upgrade their competitive capabilities as quickly as possible to defend against the stronger international's arsenal of resources. Most successful companies in developing markets have pursued mergers and acquisitions at a rapid-fire pace to build first a nationwide and then an international presence. Hindalco, India's largest aluminum producer, has followed just such a path to achieve its ambitions for global dominance. By acquiring companies in India first, it gained enough experience and confidence to eventually acquire much larger foreign companies with world-class capabilities.[22] When China began to liberalize its foreign trade policies, Lenovo (the Chinese PC maker) realized that its long-held position of market dominance in China could not withstand the onslaught of new international entrants such as Dell and HP. Its acquisition of IBM's PC business allowed Lenovo to gain rapid access to IBM's globally recognized PC brand, its R&D capability, and its existing distribution in developed countries. This has allowed Lenovo not only to hold its own against the incursion of global giants into its home market but to expand into new markets around the world.[23]

5. *Transfer company expertise to cross-border markets and initiate actions to contend on an international level.* When a company from a developing country has resources and capabilities suitable for competing in other country markets, launching initiatives to transfer its expertise to foreign markets becomes a viable strategic option. Televisa, Mexico's largest media company, used its expertise in Spanish culture and linguistics to become the world's most prolific producer of Spanish-language soap operas. By continuing to upgrade its capabilities and learn from its experience in foreign markets, a company can sometimes transform itself into one capable of competing on a worldwide basis, as an emerging global giant. Sundaram Fasteners of India began its foray into foreign markets as a supplier of radiator caps to GM—an opportunity it pursued when GM first decided to outsource the production of this part. As a participant in GM's supplier network, the company learned about emerging technical standards, built its capabilities, and became one of the first Indian companies to achieve QS 9000 quality certification. With the expertise it gained and its recognition for meeting quality standards, Sundaram was then able to pursue opportunities to supply automotive parts in Japan and Europe.

Illustration Capsule 7.3 discusses how a travel agency in China used a combination of these strategies to become that country's largest travel consolidator and online travel agent.

ILLUSTRATION CAPSULE 7.3

How Ctrip Successfully Defended against International Rivals to Become China's Largest Online Travel Agency

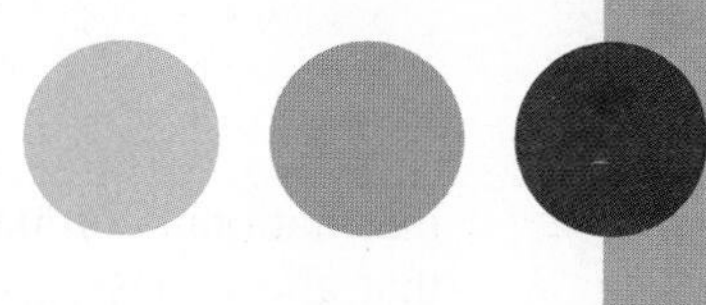

Ctrip has utilized a business model tailored to the Chinese travel market, its access to low-cost labor, and its unique understanding of customer preferences and buying habits to build scale rapidly and defeat foreign rivals such as Expedia and Travelocity in becoming the largest travel agency in China. The company was founded in 1999 with a focus on business travelers, since corporate travel accounts for the majority of China's travel bookings. The company initially placed little emphasis on online transactions, since at the time there was no national ticketing system in China, most hotels did not belong to a national or international chain, and most consumers preferred paper tickets to electronic tickets. To overcome this infrastructure shortcoming and enter the online market, the company established its own central database of 5,600 hotels located throughout China and flight information for all major airlines operating in China. Ctrip set up a call center of 3,000 representatives that could use its proprietary database to provide travel information for up to 100,000 customers per day. Because most of its transactions were not done over the Internet at the start, the company hired couriers in all major cities in China to ride by bicycle or scooter to collect payments and deliver tickets to Ctrip's corporate customers. Ctrip also initiated a loyalty program that provided gifts and incentives to the administrative personnel who arranged travel for business executives, who were more likely to use online services. By 2011, Ctrip.com held 60 percent of China's online travel market, having grown 40 percent every year since 1999, leading to a market cap coming close to those of some major U.S. online travel agencies.

However, the phenomenal growth of the Chinese market for such travel agency services (expected to more than double by 2016), along with changing technological ability and preferences, has led to a new type of competition: online, and more pivotally, mobile travel booking. Dominance in the mobile space has driven a competitor, Qunar, to experience a huge surge in growth. While this competition has been a negative in a traditional financial sense for Ctrip, analysts believe that new technology will ultimately end up benefiting the entire industry. Additionally, Qunar's entry has provided the two companies the opportunity to utilize another important local strategy to grow and remain competitive against global firms—a partnership, which Ctrip and Qunar undertook in 2013, combining their unique advantages to cross-sell travel products. The relative and absolute success of Ctrip and its competitor-partner Qunar will be seen in the coming years, but to date we have already observed the effects of an effective local-market strategy.

Note: Developed with Harold W. Greenstone.

Sources: Arindam K. Bhattacharya and David C. Michael, "How Local Companies Keep Multinationals at Bay," *Harvard Business Review* 86, no. 3 (March 2008), pp. 85–95; B. Perez, "Ctrip Likely to Gain More Business from Stronger Qunar Platform," *South China Morning Press* Online, October 2, 2013 (accessed April 3, 2014); B. Cao, "Qunar Jumps on Mobile User Growth as Ctrip Tumbles," *Bloomberg* Online, January 5, 2014 (accessed April 3, 2014); www.thatsmags.com/shanghai/article/detail/480/a-journey-with-ctrip; and money.cnn.com/quote/quote.html?symb=EXPE (accessed March 28, 2012).

KEY POINTS

1. Competing in international markets allows a company to (1) gain access to new customers, (2) achieve lower costs through greater economies of scale, learning, and increased purchasing power, (3) gain access to low-cost inputs of production, (4) further exploit its core competencies, and (5) gain access to resources and capabilities located outside the company's domestic market.
2. Strategy making is more complex for five reasons: (1) Different countries have *home-country advantages* in different industries; (2) there are location-based advantages to performing different value chain activities in different parts of the world; (3) varying political and economic risks make the business climate of some countries more favorable than others; (4) companies face the risk of adverse shifts in exchange rates when operating in foreign countries; and (5) differences in buyer tastes and preferences present a conundrum concerning the trade-off between customizing and standardizing products and services.
3. The strategies of firms that expand internationally are usually grounded in home-country advantages concerning demand conditions, factor conditions, related and supporting industries, and firm strategy, structure, and rivalry, as described by the Diamond of National Competitive Advantage framework.
4. There are five strategic options for entering foreign markets. These include maintaining a home-country production base and *exporting* goods to foreign markets, *licensing* foreign firms to produce and distribute the company's products abroad, employing a *franchising* strategy, establishing a foreign *subsidiary via an acquisition or greenfield venture,* and using *strategic alliances or other collaborative partnerships.*
5. A company must choose among three alternative approaches for competing internationally: (1) a *multidomestic strategy*—a *think-local, act-local* approach to crafting international strategy; (2) a *global strategy*—a *think-global, act-global* approach; and (3) a combination *think-global, act-local* approach, known as a *transnational strategy.* A multidomestic strategy (think local, act local) is appropriate for companies that must vary their product offerings and competitive approaches from country to country in order to accommodate different buyer preferences and market conditions. The global strategy (think global, act global) works best when there are substantial cost benefits to be gained from taking a standardized, globally integrated approach and there is little need for local responsiveness. A transnational strategy (think global, act local) is called for when there is a high need for local responsiveness as well as substantial benefits from taking a globally integrated approach. In this approach, a company strives to employ the same basic competitive strategy in all markets but still customizes its product offering and some aspect of its operations to fit local market circumstances.
6. There are three general ways in which a firm can gain competitive advantage (or offset domestic disadvantages) in international markets. One way involves locating various value chain activities among nations in a manner that lowers costs or achieves greater product differentiation. A second way draws on an international competitor's ability to extend its competitive advantage by cost-effectively sharing, replicating, or transferring its most valuable resources and capabilities across borders. A third looks for benefits from cross-border coordination that are unavailable to domestic-only competitors.
7. Two types of strategic moves are particularly suited for companies competing internationally. Both involve the use of profit sanctuaries—country markets where a company derives substantial profits because of its strong or protected market position. Profit sanctuaries are useful in waging strategic offenses in international markets through *cross-subsidization*—a practice of supporting competitive offensives in

one market with resources and profits diverted from operations in another market (the profit sanctuary). They may be used defensively to encourage *mutual restraint* among competitors when there is international *multimarket competition* by signaling that each company has the financial capability for mounting a strong counterattack if threatened. For companies with at least one profit sanctuary, having a presence in a rival's key markets can be enough to deter the rival from making aggressive attacks.

8. Companies racing for global leadership have to consider competing in developing markets like the BRIC countries—Brazil, Russia, India, and China—countries where the business risks are considerable but the opportunities for growth are huge. To succeed in these markets, companies often have to (1) compete on the basis of low price, (2) modify aspects of the company's business model to accommodate local circumstances, and/or (3) try to change the local market to better match the way the company does business elsewhere. Profitability is unlikely to come quickly or easily in developing markets, typically because of the investments needed to alter buying habits and tastes, the increased political and economic risk, and/or the need for infrastructure upgrades. And there may be times when a company should simply stay away from certain developing markets until conditions for entry are better suited to its business model and strategy.

9. Local companies in developing-country markets can seek to compete against large international companies by (1) developing business models that exploit shortcomings in local distribution networks or infrastructure, (2) utilizing a superior understanding of local customer needs and preferences or local relationships, (3) taking advantage of competitively important qualities of the local workforce with which large international companies may be unfamiliar, (4) using acquisition strategies and rapid-growth strategies to better defend against expansion-minded international companies, or (5) transferring company expertise to cross-border markets and initiating actions to compete on an international level.

ASSURANCE OF LEARNING EXERCISES

LO 1, LO 3

1. Chile's largest producer of wine, Concha y Toro, chooses to compete in Europe, North America, the Caribbean, and Asia using an export strategy. Go to the Investor Relations section of the company's website (**www.conchaytoro.com/the-company/investor-relations/**) to review the company's press releases, annual reports, and presentations. Why does it seem that the company has avoided developing vineyards and wineries in wine-growing regions outside South America? What reasons does Concha y Toro likely have to pursue exporting rather than stick to a domestic-only sales and distribution strategy?

connect

LO 1, LO 3

2. Collaborative agreements with foreign companies in the form of strategic alliances or joint ventures are widely used as a means of entering foreign markets. They are also used as a means of acquiring resources and capabilities by learning from foreign partners. And they are used to put together powerful combinations of complementary resources and capabilities by accessing the complementary resources and capabilities of a foreign partner. Illustration Capsule 7.1 provides examples of four cross-border strategic alliances that Solazyme has participated in. What were each of these partnerships (with Unilever, Sephora, Qantas, and Roquette) designed to achieve, and why would they make sense for a company like Solazyme? (Analyze each partnership separately based on the information provided in the capsule.)

3. Assume you are in charge of developing the strategy for an international company selling products in some 50 different countries around the world. One of the issues you face is whether to employ a multidomestic strategy, a global strategy, or a transnational strategy. connect LO 2, LO 4
   a. If your company's product is mobile phones, which of these strategies do you think it would make better strategic sense to employ? Why?
   b. If your company's product is dry soup mixes and canned soups, would a multidomestic strategy seem to be more advisable than a global strategy or a transnational strategy? Why?
   c. If your company's product is large home appliances such as washing machines, ranges, ovens, and refrigerators, would it seem to make more sense to pursue a multidomestic strategy, a global strategy, or a transnational strategy? Why?
4. Your company is an American-based footwear producer. Over the past few years, while demand for your products has been increasing, costs have been rising steadily and your production capabilities are limited. What options might you have to decrease costs and increase production to meet rising demand? LO 5
5. Assume you are the CEO of an online retailer looking to expand your services into developing-country markets. Much of the success of your business model depends on the ability to ship items quickly and without delays as well as provide unrivaled customer service. What concerns might you have entering a developing-country market given your business model? What would be the necessary conditions for your business to succeed? LO 2, LO 6

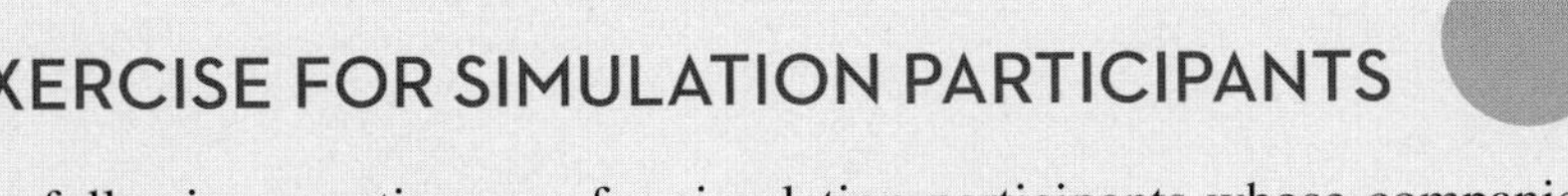

EXERCISE FOR SIMULATION PARTICIPANTS

The following questions are for simulation participants whose companies operate in an international market arena. If your company competes only in a single country, then skip the questions in this section.

1. To what extent, if any, have you and your co-managers adapted your company's strategy to take shifting exchange rates into account? In other words, have you undertaken any actions to try to minimize the impact of adverse shifts in exchange rates? LO 2
2. To what extent, if any, have you and your co-managers adapted your company's strategy to take geographic differences in import tariffs or import duties into account? LO 2
3. Which one of the following best describes the strategic approach your company is taking in trying to compete successfully on an international basis? LO 4
   - Multidomestic or think-local, act-local approach.
   - Global or think-global, act-global approach.
   - Transnational or think-global, act-local approach.

Explain your answer and indicate two or three chief elements of your company's strategy for competing in two or more different geographic regions.

ENDNOTES

[1] Sidney G. Winter and Gabriel Szulanski, "Getting It Right the Second Time," *Harvard Business Review* 80, no. 1 (January 2002), pp. 62–69.
[2] P. Dussauge, B. Garrette, and W. Mitchell, "Learning from Competing Partners: Outcomes and Durations of Scale and Link Alliances in Europe, North America and Asia," *Strategic Management Journal* 21, no. 2 (February 2000), pp. 99–126; K. W. Glaister and P. J. Buckley, "Strategic Motives for International Alliance Formation," *Journal of Management Studies* 33, no. 3 (May 1996), pp. 301–332.
[3] M. Porter, "The Competitive Advantage of Nations," *Harvard Business Review,* March–April 1990, pp. 73–93.
[4] Tom Mitchell and Avantika Chilkoti, "China Car Sales Accelerate Away from US and Brazil in 2013," *Financial Times,* January 9, 2014, www.ft.com/cms/s/0/8c649078-78f8-11e3-b381-00144feabdc0.html#axzz2rpEqjkZO.
[5] U.S. Department of Labor, Bureau of Labor Statistics, "International Comparisons of Hourly Compensation Costs in Manufacturing 2012," August 9, 2013. (The numbers for India and China are estimates.)
[6] Sangwon Yoon, "South Korea Targets Internet Addicts; 2 Million Hooked," *Valley News,* April 25, 2010, p. C2.
[7] Joel Bleeke and David Ernst, "The Way to Win in Cross-Border Alliances," *Harvard Business Review* 69, no. 6 (November–December 1991), pp. 127–133; Gary Hamel, Yves L. Doz, and C. K. Prahalad, "Collaborate with Your Competitors—and Win," *Harvard Business Review* 67, no. 1 (January–February 1989), pp. 134–135.
[8] K. W. Glaister and P. J. Buckley, "Strategic Motives for International Alliance Formation," *Journal of Management Studies* 33, no. 3 (May 1996), pp. 301–332.
[9] Jeffrey H. Dyer, Prashant Kale, and Harbir Singh, "When to Ally and When to Acquire," *Harvard Business Review* 82, no. 7–8 (July–August 2004).
[10] Yves Doz and Gary Hamel, Alliance Advantage: *The Art of Creating Value through Partnering* (Harvard Business School Press, 1998); Rosabeth Moss Kanter, "Collaborative Advantage: The Art of the Alliance," *Harvard Business Review* 72, no. 4 (July–August 1994), pp. 96–108.
[11] Jeremy Main, "Making Global Alliances Work," *Fortune,* December 19, 1990, p. 125.
[12] C. K. Prahalad and Kenneth Lieberthal, "The End of Corporate Imperialism," *Harvard Business Review* 81, no. 8 (August 2003), pp. 109–117.
[13] Pankaj Ghemawat, "Managing Differences: The Central Challenge of Global Strategy," *Harvard Business Review* 85, no. 3 (March 2007).
[14] C. A. Bartlett and S. Ghoshal, *Managing across Borders: The Transnational Solution,* 2nd ed. (Boston: Harvard Business School Press, 1998).
[15] Lynn S. Paine, "The China Rules," *Harvard Business Review* 88, no. 6 (June 2010), pp. 103–108.
[16] C. K. Prahalad and Yves L. Doz, *The Multinational Mission: Balancing Local Demands and Global Vision* (New York: Free Press, 1987).
[17] David J. Arnold and John A. Quelch, "New Strategies in Emerging Markets," *Sloan Management Review* 40, no. 1 (Fall 1998), pp. 7–20.
[18] Tarun Khanna, Krishna G. Palepu, and Jayant Sinha, "Strategies That Fit Emerging Markets," *Harvard Business Review* 83, no. 6 (June 2005), p. 63; Arindam K. Bhattacharya and David C. Michael, "How Local Companies Keep Multinationals at Bay," *Harvard Business Review* 86, no. 3 (March 2008), pp. 94–95.
[19] www.ajc.com/news/business/home-depot-eschews-large-scale-international-expan/nSQBh/ (accessed February 2, 2014).
[20] Tarun Khanna and Krishna G. Palepu, "Emerging Giants: Building World-Class Companies in Developing Countries," *Harvard Business Review* 84, no. 10 (October 2006), pp. 60–69.
[21] Niroj Dawar and Tony Frost, "Competing with Giants: Survival Strategies for Local Companies in Emerging Markets," *Harvard Business Review* 77, no. 1 (January–February 1999), p. 122; Guitz Ger, "Localizing in the Global Village: Local Firms Competing in Global Markets," *California Management Review* 41, no. 4 (Summer 1999), pp. 64–84.
[22] N. Kumar, "How Emerging Giants Are Rewriting the Rules of M&A," *Harvard Business Review,* May 2009, pp. 115–121.
[23] H. Rui and G. Yip, "Foreign Acquisitions by Chinese Firms: A Strategic Intent Perspective," *Journal of World Business* 43 (2008), pp. 213–226.

CHAPTER 8

Corporate Strategy

Diversification and the Multibusiness Company

Learning Objectives

THIS CHAPTER WILL HELP YOU UNDERSTAND:

LO 1 When and how business diversification can enhance shareholder value.

LO 2 How related diversification strategies can produce cross-business strategic fit capable of delivering competitive advantage.

LO 3 The merits and risks of unrelated diversification strategies.

LO 4 The analytic tools for evaluating a company's diversification strategy.

LO 5 What four main corporate strategy options a diversified company can employ for solidifying its strategy and improving company performance.

The desire for reinvention seems to arise most often when companies hear the siren call of synergy and start to expand beyond their core businesses.

James Surowiecki – *Writer on Business and Finance for* The New Yorker

Diversification and globalization are the keys to the future.

Fujio Mitarai – *Legendary Chairman and CEO of Canon, Inc.*

How many senior executives discuss the crucial distinction between competitive strategy at the level of a business and competitive strategy at the level of an entire company?

C. K. Prahalad and Gary Hamel – *Professors, Authors, and Consultants*

In this chapter, we move up one level in the strategy-making hierarchy, from strategy making in a single-business enterprise to strategy making in a diversified enterprise. Because a diversified company is a collection of individual businesses, the strategy-making task is more complicated. In a one-business company, managers have to come up with a plan for competing successfully in only a single industry environment—the result is what Chapter 2 labeled as *business strategy* (or *business-level strategy*). But in a diversified company, the strategy-making challenge involves assessing multiple industry environments and developing a *set of business strategies,* one for each industry arena in which the diversified company operates. And top executives at a diversified company must still go one step further and devise a companywide (or *corporate*) strategy for improving the performance of the company's overall business lineup and for making a rational whole out of its diversified collection of individual businesses.

In the first portion of this chapter, we describe what crafting a diversification strategy entails, when and why diversification makes good strategic sense, the various approaches to diversifying a company's business lineup, and the pros and cons of related versus unrelated diversification strategies. The second part of the chapter looks at how to evaluate the attractiveness of a diversified company's business lineup, how to decide whether it has a good diversification strategy, and the strategic options for improving a diversified company's future performance.

WHAT DOES CRAFTING A DIVERSIFICATION STRATEGY ENTAIL?

The task of crafting a diversified company's overall *corporate strategy* falls squarely in the lap of top-level executives and involves four distinct facets:

1. *Picking new industries to enter and deciding on the means of entry.* The decision to pursue business diversification requires that management decide which new industries to enter and whether to enter by starting a new business from the ground

up, acquiring a company already in the target industry, or forming a joint venture or strategic alliance with another company.

2. *Pursuing opportunities to leverage cross-business value chain relationships, where there is strategic fit, into competitive advantage.* The task here is to determine whether there are opportunities to strengthen a diversified company's businesses by such means as transferring competitively valuable resources and capabilities from one business to another, combining the related value chain activities of different businesses to achieve lower costs, sharing the use of a powerful and well-respected brand name across multiple businesses, and encouraging knowledge sharing and collaborative activity among the businesses.
3. *Establishing investment priorities and steering corporate resources into the most attractive business units.* Typically, this translates into pursuing rapid-growth strategies in the company's most promising businesses, initiating profit improvement or turnaround strategies in weak-performing businesses that have potential, and divesting businesses that are no longer attractive or that don't fit into management's long-range plans.
4. *Initiating actions to boost the combined performance of the corporation's collection of businesses.* Strategic options for improving the corporation's overall performance include (1) sticking closely with the existing business lineup and pursuing opportunities presented by these businesses, (2) broadening the scope of diversification by entering additional industries, (3) retrenching to a narrower scope of diversification by divesting poorly performing businesses, and (4) broadly restructuring the entire company by divesting some businesses and acquiring others so as to put a whole new face on the company's business lineup.

The demanding and time-consuming nature of these four tasks explains why corporate executives generally refrain from becoming immersed in the details of crafting and executing business-level strategies. Rather, the normal procedure is to delegate lead responsibility for business strategy to the heads of each business, giving them the latitude to develop strategies suited to the particular industry environment in which their business operates and holding them accountable for producing good financial and strategic results.

WHEN TO CONSIDER DIVERSIFYING

As long as a company has plentiful opportunities for profitable growth in its present industry, there is no urgency to pursue diversification. But growth opportunities are often limited in mature industries and declining markets. In addition, changing industry conditions—new technologies, inroads being made by substitute products, fast-shifting buyer preferences, or intensifying competition—can undermine a company's ability to deliver ongoing gains in revenues and profits. Consider, for example, what the growing use of debit cards and online bill payment has done to the check-printing business and what mobile phone companies and marketers of Voice over Internet Protocol (VoIP) have done to the revenues of long-distance providers such as AT&T, British Telecommunications, and NTT in Japan. Thus, diversifying into new industries always merits strong consideration whenever a single-business company encounters diminishing market opportunities and stagnating sales in its principal business.

The decision to diversify presents wide-ranging possibilities. A company can diversify into closely related businesses or into totally unrelated businesses. It can diversify its present revenue and earnings base to a small or major extent. It can move into one or two large new businesses or a greater number of small ones. It can achieve diversification by acquiring an existing company, starting up a new business from scratch, or forming a joint venture with one or more companies to enter new businesses. In every case, however, the decision to diversify must start with a strong economic justification for doing so.

BUILDING SHAREHOLDER VALUE: THE ULTIMATE JUSTIFICATION FOR DIVERSIFYING

Diversification must do more for a company than simply spread its business risk across various industries. In principle, diversification cannot be considered a success unless it results in *added long-term economic value for shareholders*—value that shareholders cannot capture on their own by purchasing stock in companies in different industries or investing in mutual funds so as to spread their investments across several industries.

LO 1

When and how business diversification can enhance shareholder value.

Business diversification stands little chance of building shareholder value without passing the following three **Tests of Corporate Advantage.**[1]

1. *The industry attractiveness test.* The industry to be entered through diversification must be structurally attractive (in terms of the five forces), have resource requirements that match those of the parent company, and offer good prospects for growth, profitability, and return on investment.
2. *The cost of entry test.* The cost of entering the target industry must not be so high as to exceed the potential for good profitability. A catch-22 can prevail here, however. The more attractive an industry's prospects are for growth and good long-term profitability, the more expensive it can be to enter. Entry barriers for startup companies are likely to be high in attractive industries—if barriers were low, a rush of new entrants would soon erode the potential for high profitability. And buying a well-positioned company in an appealing industry often entails a high acquisition cost that makes passing the cost of entry test less likely. Since the owners of a successful and growing company usually demand a price that reflects their business's profit prospects, it's easy for such an acquisition to fail the cost of entry test.
3. *The better-off test.* Diversifying into a new business must offer potential for the company's existing businesses and the new business to perform better together under a single corporate umbrella than they would perform operating as independent, stand-alone businesses—an effect known as **synergy.** For example, let's say that company A diversifies by purchasing company B in another industry. If A and B's consolidated profits in the years to come prove no greater than what each could have earned on its own, then A's diversification won't provide its shareholders with any added value. Company A's shareholders could have achieved the same 1 + 1 = 2 result by merely purchasing stock in company B. Diversification does not result in added long-term value for shareholders unless it produces a 1 + 1 = 3 effect, whereby the businesses *perform better together as part of the same firm than they could have performed as independent companies.*

CORE CONCEPT

To add shareholder value, a move to diversify into a new business must pass the three **Tests of Corporate Advantage:**

1. The Industry Attractiveness Test
2. The Cost of Entry Test
3. The Better-off Test

CORE CONCEPT

Creating added value for shareholders via diversification requires building a multibusiness company in which the whole is greater than the sum of its parts—such 1 + 1 = 3 effects are called **synergy.**

Diversification moves must satisfy all three tests to grow shareholder value over the long term. Diversification moves that can pass only one or two tests are suspect.

APPROACHES TO DIVERSIFYING THE BUSINESS LINEUP

The means of entering new businesses can take any of three forms: acquisition, internal startup, or joint ventures with other companies.

Diversifying by Acquisition of an Existing Business

Acquisition is a popular means of diversifying into another industry. Not only is it quicker than trying to launch a new operation, but it also offers an effective way to hurdle such entry barriers as acquiring technological know-how, establishing supplier relationships, achieving scale economies, building brand awareness, and securing adequate distribution. Acquisitions are also commonly employed to access resources and capabilities that are complementary to those of the acquiring firm and that cannot be developed readily internally. Buying an ongoing operation allows the acquirer to move directly to the task of building a strong market position in the target industry, rather than getting bogged down in trying to develop the knowledge, experience, scale of operation, and market reputation necessary for a startup entrant to become an effective competitor.

CORE CONCEPT

An **acquisition premium**, or control premium, is the amount by which the price offered exceeds the preacquisition market value of the target company.

However, acquiring an existing business can prove quite expensive. The costs of acquiring another business include not only the acquisition price but also the costs of performing the due diligence to ascertain the worth of the other company, the costs of negotiating the purchase transaction, and the costs of integrating the business into the diversified company's portfolio. If the company to be acquired is a successful company, the acquisition price will include a hefty *premium* over the preacquisition value of the company for the right to control the company. For example, the $28 billion that Berkshire Hathaway and 3G Capital agreed to pay for H. J. Heinz Company in 2014 included a 30 percent premium over its one-year average share price.[2] Premiums are paid in order to convince the shareholders and managers of the target company that it is in their financial interests to approve the deal. The average premium paid by U.S. companies was 19 percent in 2013, but it was more often in the 20 to 25 percent range over the last 10 years.[3]

While acquisitions offer an enticing means for entering a new business, many fail to deliver on their promise.[4] Realizing the potential gains from an acquisition requires a successful integration of the acquired company into the culture, systems, and structure of the acquiring firm. This can be a costly and time-consuming operation. Acquisitions can also fail to deliver long-term shareholder value if the acquirer overestimates the potential gains and pays a premium in excess of the realized gains. High integration costs and excessive price premiums are two reasons that an acquisition might fail the cost of entry test. Firms with significant experience in making acquisitions are better able to avoid these types of problems.[5]

Entering a New Line of Business through Internal Development

Achieving diversification through *internal development* involves starting a new business subsidiary from scratch. Internal development has become an increasingly important way for companies to diversify and is often referred to as **corporate venturing** or *new venture development.* Although building a new business from the ground up is generally a time-consuming and uncertain process, it avoids the pitfalls associated with entry via acquisition and may allow the firm to realize greater profits in the end. It may offer a viable means of entering a new or emerging industry where there are no good acquisition candidates.

Entering a new business via internal development, however, poses some significant hurdles. An internal new venture not only has to overcome industry entry barriers but also must invest in new production capacity, develop sources of supply, hire and train employees, build channels of distribution, grow a customer base, and so on, unless the new business is quite similar to the company's existing business. The risks associated with internal startups can be substantial, and the likelihood of failure is often high. Moreover, the culture, structures, and organizational systems of some companies may impede innovation and make it difficult for corporate entrepreneurship to flourish.

Generally, internal development of a new business has appeal only when (1) the parent company already has in-house most of the resources and capabilities it needs to piece together a new business and compete effectively; (2) there is ample time to launch the business; (3) the internal cost of entry is lower than the cost of entry via acquisition; (4) adding new production capacity will not adversely impact the supply–demand balance in the industry; and (5) incumbent firms are likely to be slow or ineffective in responding to a new entrant's efforts to crack the market.

CORE CONCEPT

Corporate venturing (or *new venture development*) is the process of developing new businesses as an outgrowth of a company's established business operations. It is also referred to as *corporate entrepreneurship* or *intrapreneurship* since it requires entrepreneurial-like qualities within a larger enterprise.

Using Joint Ventures to Achieve Diversification

Entering a new business via a joint venture can be useful in at least three types of situations.[6] First, a joint venture is a good vehicle for pursuing an opportunity that is too complex, uneconomical, or risky for one company to pursue alone. Second, joint ventures make sense when the opportunities in a new industry require a broader range of competencies and know-how than a company can marshal on its own. Many of the opportunities in satellite-based telecommunications, biotechnology, and network-based systems that blend hardware, software, and services call for the coordinated development of complementary innovations and the tackling of an intricate web of financial, technical, political, and regulatory factors simultaneously. In such cases, pooling the resources and competencies of two or more companies is a wiser and less risky way to proceed. Third, companies sometimes use joint ventures to diversify into a new industry when the diversification move entails having operations in a foreign country. However, as discussed in Chapters 6 and 7, partnering with another company has significant drawbacks due to the potential for conflicting objectives, disagreements over how to best operate the venture, culture clashes, and so on. Joint ventures are generally the least durable of the entry options, usually lasting only until the partners decide to go their own ways.

Choosing a Mode of Entry

The choice of how best to enter a new business—whether through internal development, acquisition, or joint venture—depends on the answers to four important questions:

- Does the company have all of the resources and capabilities it requires to enter the business through internal development, or is it lacking some critical resources?
- Are there entry barriers to overcome?
- Is speed an important factor in the firm's chances for successful entry?
- Which is the least costly mode of entry, given the company's objectives?

The Question of Critical Resources and Capabilities If a firm has all the resources it needs to start up a new business or will be able to easily purchase or lease any missing resources, it may choose to enter the business via internal development. However, if missing critical resources cannot be easily purchased or leased, a firm wishing to enter a new business must obtain these missing resources through either acquisition or joint venture. Bank of America acquired Merrill Lynch to obtain critical investment banking resources and capabilities that it lacked. The acquisition of these additional capabilities complemented Bank of America's strengths in corporate banking and opened up new business opportunities for the company. Firms often acquire other companies as a way to enter foreign markets where they lack local marketing knowledge, distribution capabilities, and relationships with local suppliers or customers. McDonald's acquisition of Burghy, Italy's only national hamburger chain, offers an example.[7] If there are no good acquisition opportunities or if the firm wants to avoid the high cost of acquiring and integrating another firm, it may choose to enter via joint venture. This type of entry mode has the added advantage of spreading the risk of entering a new business, an advantage that is particularly attractive when uncertainty is high. De Beers's joint venture with the luxury goods company LVMH provided De Beers not only with the complementary marketing capabilities it needed to enter the diamond retailing business but also with a partner to share the risk.

The Question of Entry Barriers The second question to ask is whether entry barriers would prevent a new entrant from gaining a foothold and succeeding in the industry. If entry barriers are low and the industry is populated by small firms, internal development may be the preferred mode of entry. If entry barriers are high, the company may still be able to enter with ease if it has the requisite resources and capabilities for overcoming high barriers. For example, entry barriers due to reputational advantages may be surmounted by a diversified company with a widely known and trusted corporate name. But if the entry barriers cannot be overcome readily, then the only feasible entry route may be through acquisition of a well-established company. While entry barriers may also be overcome with a strong complementary joint venture, this mode is the more uncertain choice due to the lack of industry experience.

The Question of Speed Speed is another determining factor in deciding how to go about entering a new business. Acquisition is a favored mode of entry when speed is of the essence, as is the case in rapidly changing industries where fast movers can secure long-term positioning advantages. Speed is important in industries where early movers gain experience-based advantages that grow ever larger over time as they move down the learning curve. It is also important in technology-based industries where there is a race to establish an industry standard or leading technological platform. But in other cases it can be better to enter a market after the uncertainties about technology or consumer preferences have been resolved and learn from the missteps of early entrants. In these cases, joint venture or internal development may be preferred.

> **CORE CONCEPT**
>
> **Transaction costs** are the costs of completing a business agreement or deal, over and above the price of the deal. They can include the costs of searching for an attractive target, the costs of evaluating its worth, bargaining costs, and the costs of completing the transaction.

The Question of Comparative Cost The question of which mode of entry is most cost-effective is a critical one, given the need for a diversification strategy to pass the cost of entry test. Acquisition can be a high-cost mode of entry due to the need to pay a premium over the share price of the target company. When the premium is high, the price of the deal will exceed the worth of the acquired company as a stand-alone business by a substantial amount. Whether it is worth it to pay that high a price will depend on how much extra value will be created by the new combination of companies in the form of synergies. Moreover, the true cost of an acquisition must include the **transaction costs** of identifying and evaluating potential targets, negotiating a price, and completing other aspects of deal making. In addition, the true cost must take into account the costs of integrating the acquired company into the parent company's portfolio of businesses.

Joint ventures may provide a way to conserve on such entry costs. But even here, there are organizational coordination costs and transaction costs that must be considered, including settling on the terms of the arrangement. If the partnership doesn't proceed smoothly and is not founded on trust, these costs may be significant.

CHOOSING THE DIVERSIFICATION PATH: RELATED VERSUS UNRELATED BUSINESSES

Once a company decides to diversify, it faces the choice of whether to diversify into **related businesses, unrelated businesses,** or some mix of both. Businesses are said to be *related* when their value chains exhibit competitively important cross-business commonalities. By this, we mean that there is a close correspondence between the businesses in terms of *how they perform* key value chain activities and *the resources and capabilities each needs* to perform those activities. The big appeal of related diversification is the opportunity to build shareholder value by leveraging these cross-business commonalities into competitive advantages, thus allowing the company as a whole to perform better than just the sum of its individual businesses. Businesses are said to be *unrelated* when the resource requirements and key value chain activities are so dissimilar that no competitively important cross-business commonalities exist.

The next two sections explore the ins and outs of related and unrelated diversification.

CORE CONCEPT

Related businesses possess competitively valuable cross-business value chain and resource commonalities; **unrelated businesses** have dissimilar value chains and resource requirements, with no competitively important cross-business commonalities at the value chain level.

DIVERSIFICATION INTO RELATED BUSINESSES

LO 2

How related diversification strategies can produce cross-business strategic fit capable of delivering competitive advantage.

A related diversification strategy involves building the company around businesses where there is good *strategic fit across corresponding value chain activities.* **Strategic fit** exists whenever one or more activities constituting the value chains of different businesses are sufficiently similar to present opportunities for cross-business sharing or transferring of the resources and capabilities that enable these activities.[8] Prime examples of such opportunities include:

- *Transferring specialized expertise, technological know-how, or other competitively valuable strategic assets from one business's value chain to another's.* Google's ability to transfer software developers and other information technology specialists from other business applications to the development of its Android mobile operating system and Chrome operating system for PCs aided considerably in the success of these new internal ventures.
- *Sharing costs between businesses by combining their related value chain activities into a single operation.* For instance, it is often feasible to manufacture the products of different businesses in a single plant, use the same warehouses for shipping and distribution, or have a single sales force for the products of different businesses if they are marketed to the same types of customers.

CORE CONCEPT

Strategic fit exists whenever one or more activities constituting the value chains of different businesses are sufficiently similar to present opportunities for cross-business sharing or transferring of the resources and capabilities that enable these activities.

- *Exploiting the common use of a well-known brand name.* For example, Yamaha's name in motorcycles gave the company instant credibility and recognition in entering the personal-watercraft business, allowing it to achieve a significant market share without spending large sums on advertising to establish a brand identity for the WaveRunner. Likewise, Apple's reputation for producing easy-to-operate computers was a competitive asset that facilitated the company's diversification into digital music players and smartphones.
- *Sharing other resources (besides brands) that support corresponding value chain activities across businesses.* When Disney acquired Marvel Comics, management saw to it that Marvel's iconic characters, such as Spiderman, Iron Man, and Captain America, were shared with many of the other Disney businesses, including its theme parks, retail stores, and video game business. (Disney's characters, starting with Mickey Mouse, have always been among the most valuable of its resources.) Automobile companies like Ford share resources such as their relationships with suppliers and dealer networks across their lines of business.
- *Engaging in cross-business collaboration and knowledge sharing to create new competitively valuable resources and capabilities.* Businesses performing closely related value chain activities may seize opportunities to join forces, share knowledge and talents, and collaborate to create altogether new capabilities (such as virtually defect-free assembly methods or increased ability to speed new products to market) that will be mutually beneficial in improving their competitiveness and business performance.

Related diversification is based on value chain matchups with respect to *key* value chain activities—those that play a central role in each business's strategy and that link to its industry's key success factors. Such matchups facilitate the sharing or transfer of the resources and capabilities that enable the performance of these activities and underlie each business's quest for competitive advantage. By facilitating the sharing or transferring of such important competitive assets, related diversification can elevate each business's prospects for competitive success.

CORE CONCEPT

Related diversification involves sharing or transferring *specialized* resources and capabilities. **Specialized resources and capabilities** have very specific applications and their use is limited to a restricted range of industry and business types, in contrast to **general resources and capabilities** that can be widely applied and can be deployed across a broad range of industry and business types.

The resources and capabilities that are leveraged in related diversification are **specialized resources and capabilities.** By this, we mean that they have very *specific* applications; their use is restricted to a limited range of business contexts in which these applications are competitively relevant. Because they are adapted for particular applications, specialized resources and capabilities must be utilized by particular types of businesses operating in specific kinds of industries to have value; they have limited utility outside this designated range of industry and business applications. This is in contrast to **general resources and capabilities** (such as general management capabilities, human resource management capabilities, and general accounting services), which can be applied usefully across a wide range of industry and business types.

L'Oréal is the world's largest beauty products company, with more than $30 billion in revenues and a successful strategy of related diversification built upon leveraging a highly specialized set of resources and capabilities. These include 22 dermatologic and cosmetic research centers, R&D capabilities and scientific knowledge concerning skin and hair care, patents and secret formulas for hair and skin care products, and robotic applications developed specifically for testing the safety of hair and skin care products. These resources and capabilities are highly valuable for businesses focused on products for human skin and hair—they are *specialized* to such applications, and, in consequence, they are of little or no value beyond this restricted range of applications. To leverage these resources in a way that maximizes their potential value, L'Oréal has diversified into cosmetics, hair care products, skin care products, and fragrances (but not food, transportation, industrial services, or any application area far from the narrow domain in which its specialized resources are competitively relevant). L'Oréal's businesses are related to one another on the basis of its value-generating specialized resources and capabilities and the cross-business linkages among the value chain activities that they enable.

Corning's most competitively valuable resources and capabilities are specialized to applications concerning fiber optics and specialty glass and ceramics. Over the course of its 150-year history, it has developed an unmatched understanding of fundamental glass science and related technologies in the field of optics. Its capabilities now span a variety of sophisticated technologies and include expertise in domains such as custom glass composition, specialty glass melting and forming, precision optics, high-end transmissive coatings, and optomechanical materials. Corning has leveraged these specialized capabilities into a position of global leadership in five related market segments: display technologies based on glass substrates, environmental technologies using ceramic substrates and filters, optical fibers and cables for telecommunications, optical biosensors for drug discovery, and specialty materials employing advanced optics and specialty glass solutions. The market segments into which Corning has diversified are all related by their reliance on Corning's specialized capability set and by the many value chain activities that they have in common as a result.

General Mills has diversified into a closely related set of food businesses on the basis of its capabilities in the realm of "kitchen chemistry" and food production technologies. Its businesses include General Mills cereals, Pillsbury and Betty Crocker baking products, yogurts, organic foods, dinner mixes, canned goods, and snacks. Earlier it had diversified into restaurant businesses on the mistaken notion that all food businesses were related. By exiting these businesses in the mid-1990s, the company was able to improve its overall profitability and strengthen its position in its remaining businesses. The lesson from its experience—and a takeaway for the managers of any diversified company—is that *it is not product relatedness that defines a well-crafted related diversification strategy.* Rather, *the businesses must be related in terms of their key value chain activities and the specialized resources and capabilities that enable these activities.*[9] An example is Citizen Holdings Company, whose products appear to be different (watches, miniature card calculators, handheld televisions) but are related in terms of their common reliance on miniaturization know-how and advanced precision technologies.

While companies pursuing related diversification strategies may also have opportunities to share or transfer their *general* resources and capabilities (e.g., information systems; human resource management practices; accounting and tax services; budgeting, planning, and financial reporting systems; expertise in legal and regulatory affairs; and fringe-benefit management systems), *the most competitively valuable opportunities for resource sharing or transfer always come from leveraging their specialized resources and capabilities.* The reason for this is that specialized resources and capabilities drive the key value-creating activities that both connect the businesses (at points along their value chains where there is strategic fit) and link to the key success factors in the markets where they are competitively relevant. Figure 8.1 illustrates the range of opportunities to share and/or transfer specialized resources and capabilities among the value chain activities of related businesses. It is important to recognize that *even though general resources and capabilities may be shared by multiple business units, such resource sharing alone cannot form the backbone of a strategy keyed to related diversification.*

FIGURE 8.1 Related Businesses Provide Opportunities to Benefit from Competitively Valuable Strategic Fit

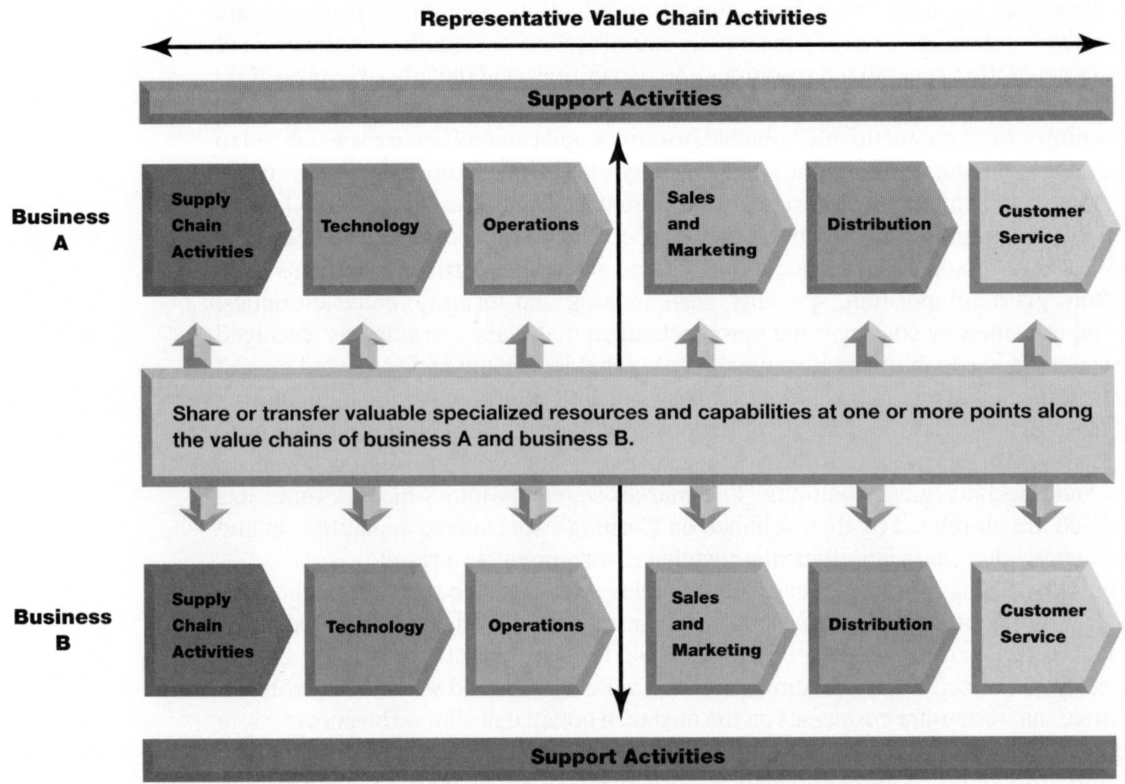

Identifying Cross-Business Strategic Fit along the Value Chain

Cross-business strategic fit can exist anywhere along the value chain—in R&D and technology activities, in supply chain activities and relationships with suppliers, in manufacturing, in sales and marketing, in distribution activities, or in customer service activities.[10]

Strategic Fit in Supply Chain Activities Businesses with strategic fit with respect to their supply chain activities can perform better together because of the potential for transferring skills in procuring materials, sharing resources and capabilities in logistics, collaborating with common supply chain partners, and/or increasing leverage with shippers in securing volume discounts on incoming parts and components. Dell Computer's strategic partnerships with leading suppliers of microprocessors, circuit boards, disk drives, memory chips, flat-panel displays, wireless capabilities, long-life batteries, and other PC-related components have been an important element of the company's strategy to diversify into servers, data storage devices, networking components, and LED TVs—products that include many components common to PCs and that can be sourced from the same strategic partners that provide Dell with PC components.

Strategic Fit in R&D and Technology Activities Businesses with strategic fit in R&D or technology development perform better together than apart because of potential cost savings in R&D, shorter times in getting new products to market, and more innovative products or processes. Moreover, technological advances in one business can lead to increased sales for both. Technological innovations have been the driver behind the efforts of cable TV companies to diversify into high-speed Internet access (via the use of cable modems) and, further, to explore providing local and long-distance telephone service to residential and commercial customers either through a single wire or by means of Voice over Internet Protocol (VoIP) technology.

Manufacturing-Related Strategic Fit Cross-business strategic fit in manufacturing-related activities can be exploited when a diversifier's expertise in quality control and cost-efficient production methods can be transferred to another business. When Emerson Electric diversified into the chain-saw business, it transferred its expertise in low-cost manufacture to its newly acquired Beaird-Poulan business division. The transfer drove Beaird-Poulan's new strategy—to be the low-cost provider of chain-saw products—and fundamentally changed the way Beaird-Poulan chain saws were designed and manufactured. Another benefit of production-related value chain commonalities is the ability to consolidate production into a smaller number of plants and significantly reduce overall production costs. When snowmobile maker Bombardier diversified into motorcycles, it was able to set up motorcycle assembly lines in the manufacturing facility where it was assembling snowmobiles. When Smucker's acquired Procter & Gamble's Jif peanut butter business, it was able to combine the manufacture of the two brands of peanut butter products while gaining greater leverage with vendors in purchasing its peanut supplies.

Strategic Fit in Sales and Marketing Activities Various cost-saving opportunities spring from diversifying into businesses with closely related sales and marketing activities. When the products are sold directly to the same customers, sales costs can often be reduced by using a single sales force instead of having two different salespeople call on the same customer. The products of related businesses can be promoted at the same website and included in the same media ads and sales brochures. There may be opportunities to reduce costs by consolidating order processing and billing and by using common promotional tie-ins. When global power-tool maker Black & Decker acquired Vector Products, it was able to use its own global sales force to sell the newly acquired Vector power inverters, vehicle battery chargers, and rechargeable spotlights because the types of customers that carried its power tools (discounters like Kmart, home centers, and hardware stores) also stocked the types of products produced by Vector.

A second category of benefits arises when different businesses use similar sales and marketing approaches. In such cases, there may be competitively valuable opportunities to transfer selling, merchandising, advertising, and product differentiation skills from one business to another. Procter & Gamble's product lineup includes Pampers diapers, Olay beauty products, Tide laundry detergent, Crest toothpaste, Charmin toilet tissue, Gillette razors and blades, Duracell batteries, Oral-B toothbrushes, and Head & Shoulders shampoo. All of these have different competitors and different supply chain and production requirements, but they all move through the same wholesale distribution systems, are sold in common retail settings to the same shoppers, and require the same marketing and merchandising skills.

Distribution-Related Strategic Fit Businesses with closely related distribution activities can perform better together than apart because of potential cost savings in sharing the same distribution facilities or using many of the same wholesale distributors and retail dealers. When Conair Corporation acquired Allegro Manufacturing's travel bag and travel accessory business, it was able to consolidate its own distribution centers for hair dryers and curling irons with those of Allegro, thereby generating cost savings for both businesses. Likewise, since Conair products and Allegro's neck rests, ear plugs, luggage tags, and toiletry kits were sold by the same types of retailers (discount stores, supermarket chains, and drugstore chains), Conair was able to convince many of the retailers not carrying Allegro products to take on the line.

Strategic Fit in Customer Service Activities Strategic fit with respect to customer service activities can enable cost savings or differentiation advantages, just as it does along other points of the value chain. For example, cost savings may come from consolidating after-sale service and repair organizations for the products of closely related businesses into a single operation. Likewise, different businesses can often use the same customer service infrastructure. For instance, an electric utility that diversifies into natural gas, water, appliance repair services, and home security services can use the same customer data network, the same call centers and local offices, the same billing and accounting systems, and the same customer service infrastructure to support all of its products and services. Through the transfer of best practices in customer service across a set of related businesses or through the sharing of resources such as proprietary information about customer preferences, a multibusiness company can also create a differentiation advantage through higher-quality customer service.

Strategic Fit, Economies of Scope, and Competitive Advantage

What makes related diversification an attractive strategy is the opportunity to convert cross-business strategic fit into a competitive advantage over business rivals whose operations do not offer comparable strategic-fit benefits. The greater the relatedness among a diversified company's businesses, the bigger a company's window for converting strategic fit into competitive advantage via (1) transferring skills or knowledge, (2) combining related value chain activities to achieve lower costs, (3) leveraging the use of a well-respected brand name, (4) sharing other valuable resources, and (5) using cross-business collaboration and knowledge sharing to create new resources and capabilities and drive innovation.

CORE CONCEPT

Economies of scope are cost reductions that flow from operating in multiple businesses (a *larger scope* of operation). This is in contrast to *economies of scale*, which accrue from a *larger-sized* operation.

Strategic Fit and Economies of Scope Strategic fit in the value chain activities of a diversified corporation's different businesses opens up opportunities for **economies of scope**—a concept distinct from *economies of scale*. Economies of *scale* are cost savings that accrue directly from a larger-sized operation—for example, unit costs may be lower in a large plant than in a small plant. Economies of *scope*, however, *stem directly from strategic fit along the value chains of related businesses*, which in turn enables the businesses to share resources or to transfer them from business to business at low cost. Such economies are open only to firms engaged in related diversification, since they are the result of related businesses performing R&D together, transferring managers from one business to another, using common manufacturing or distribution facilities, sharing a common sales force or dealer network, using the same established brand name, and the like. *The greater the cross-business economies associated with resource* *sharing and transfer, the greater the potential for a related diversification strategy to give a multibusiness enterprise a cost advantage over rivals.*

From Strategic Fit to Competitive Advantage, Added Profitability, and Gains in Shareholder Value The cost advantage from economies of scope is due to the fact that resource sharing allows a multibusiness firm to spread resource costs across its businesses and to avoid the expense of having to acquire and maintain duplicate sets of resources—one for each business. But related diversified companies can benefit from strategic fit in other ways as well.

Sharing or transferring valuable specialized assets among the company's businesses can help each business perform its value chain activities more proficiently. This translates into competitive advantage for the businesses in one or two basic ways: (1) The businesses can contribute to greater efficiency and lower costs relative to their competitors, and/or (2) they can provide a basis for differentiation so that customers are willing to pay relatively more for the businesses' goods and services. In either or both of these ways, a firm with a well-executed related diversification strategy can boost the chances of its businesses attaining a competitive advantage.

The competitive advantage potential that flows from the capture of strategic-fit benefits is what enables a company pursuing related diversification to achieve 1 + 1 = 3 financial performance and the hoped-for gains in shareholder value. The greater the relatedness among a diversified company's businesses, the bigger a company's window for converting strategic fit into competitive advantage. The strategic and business logic is compelling: Capturing the benefits of strategic fit along the value chains of its related businesses gives a diversified company a clear path to achieving competitive advantage over undiversified competitors and competitors whose own diversification efforts don't offer equivalent strategic-fit benefits.[11] Such competitive advantage potential provides a company with a dependable basis for earning profits and a return on investment that exceeds what the company's businesses could earn as stand-alone enterprises. Converting the competitive advantage potential into greater profitability is what fuels 1 + 1 = 3 gains in shareholder value—the necessary outcome for satisfying the *better-off test* and proving the business merit of a company's diversification effort.

Diversifying into related businesses where competitively valuable strategic-fit benefits can be captured puts a company's businesses in position to perform better financially as part of the company than they could have performed as independent enterprises, thus providing a clear avenue for increasing shareholder value and satisfying the *better-off test*.

There are five things to bear in mind here:

1. Capturing cross-business strategic-fit benefits via a strategy of related diversification builds shareholder value in ways that shareholders cannot undertake by simply owning a portfolio of stocks of companies in different industries.
2. The capture of cross-business strategic-fit benefits is possible only via a strategy of related diversification.
3. The greater the relatedness among a diversified company's businesses, the bigger the company's window for converting strategic fit into competitive advantage.
4. The benefits of cross-business strategic fit come from the transferring or sharing of competitively valuable resources and capabilities among the businesses—resources and capabilities that are *specialized* to certain applications and have value only in specific types of industries and businesses.
5. The benefits of cross-business strategic fit are not automatically realized when a company diversifies into related businesses; *the benefits materialize only after management has successfully pursued internal actions to capture them.*

Illustration Capsule 8.1 describes Microsoft's acquisition of Skype in pursuit of the strategic-fit benefits of a related diversification strategy.

ILLUSTRATION CAPSULE 8.1 Microsoft's Acquisition of Skype: Pursuing the Benefits of Cross-Business Strategic Fit

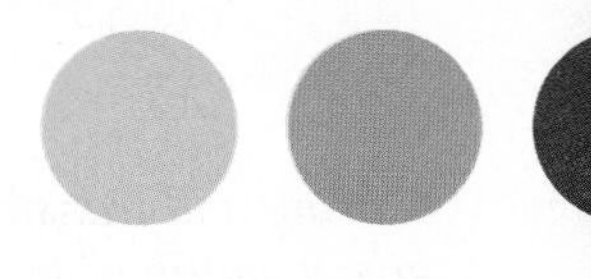

From humble beginnings in Gates's family garage, Microsoft has grown to exceed $77.85 billion of revenue in 2013 and offer a product line extending from gaming (Xbox) and Internet services (Internet Explorer and Bing) to mobile devices (Windows Phones). In 2011, Microsoft diversified its product line yet again through acquiring Skype Global for $8.5 billion in cash. Although Microsoft had previously ventured into the Internet communications industry with Windows Live Messenger, Skype offered Microsoft broader device support, mobile video calling, and access to over 170 million Skype users, potential new clients for Microsoft's existing products.

Microsoft considered Skype a valuable acquisition due to the strategic fit between the value chain activities of the two companies. Moreover, Skype's communication expertise combined with Microsoft's market reach offered an opportunity to generate new competitively valuable resources and capabilities. With the communications industry gradually shifting toward more face-to-face calling, Skype gave Microsoft an already-established visual communications platform to complement its existing Xbox Live services, Office Suite, and new Windows 8 software. In turn, as the leading operating system (OS) software developer in the world, Microsoft could expand Skype's scope and reach by prepackaging future Windows OS releases with Skype software.

In addition to offering cross-business collaboration and value chain-supporting opportunities, Skype also offered several immediate resources. Skype CEO Tony Bates possessed extensive knowledge of the Internet communications market and could ensure the long-term operational and strategic continuity of Skype.

Recognizing Bates's specialized expertise and experience, Microsoft retained Bates as head of its newly formed Microsoft Skype Division. Additionally, Microsoft gained access to over 50 Skype communications patents and the already-established relationships with many of Skype's previous partners (and Microsoft competitors), including Facebook, Sony, and Verizon. Moreover, by keeping the Skype name and opting to replace its Windows Live Messenger client, Microsoft could exploit the well-known Skype brand for its history of reliability and quality. With such a rich set of opportunities for the cross-business sharing and transferring of resources and capabilities, Microsoft believed that its acquisition of Skype would generate synergies and increase its competitiveness.

Only time will tell, but given Skype's growth and Microsoft's plans to incorporate Skype in its Windows 8 platform and Xbox Live services, the outcome of this related diversification move seems promising.

Note: Developed with Sean Zhang.

Sources: Company websites; www.cbsnews.com/8301-505124_162-42340380/with-verizon-and-facebook-partnerships-skype-positions-itself-for-app-world-dominance/; dealbook.nytimes.com/2011/05/10/microsoft-to-buy-skype-for-8-5-billion/; and www.nytimes.com/2012/05/29/technology/microsoft-at-work-on-meshing-its-products-with-skype.html?pagewanted=all&_r=1& (accessed February 21, 2013).

DIVERSIFICATION INTO UNRELATED BUSINESSES

LO 3

The merits and risks of unrelated diversification strategies.

Achieving cross-business strategic fit is not a motivation for unrelated diversification. Companies that pursue a strategy of unrelated diversification generally exhibit a willingness to diversify into *any business in any industry* where senior managers see an opportunity to realize consistently good financial results. Such companies are frequently labeled *conglomerates* because their business interests range broadly across diverse industries. Companies engaged in unrelated diversification nearly always enter new businesses by acquiring an established company rather than by forming a startup subsidiary within their own corporate structures or participating in joint ventures.

With a strategy of unrelated diversification, an acquisition is deemed to have potential if it passes the industry-attractiveness and cost of entry tests and if it has good prospects for attractive financial performance. Thus, with an unrelated diversification strategy, company managers spend much time and effort screening acquisition candidates and evaluating the pros and cons of keeping or divesting existing businesses, using such criteria as:

- Whether the business can meet corporate targets for profitability and return on investment.
- Whether the business is in an industry with attractive growth potential.
- Whether the business is big enough to contribute *significantly* to the parent firm's bottom line.

But the key to successful unrelated diversification is to go beyond these considerations and *ensure that the strategy passes the better-off test as well.* This test requires more than just growth in revenues; it requires *growth in profits*—beyond what could be achieved by a mutual fund or a holding company that owns shares of the businesses without adding any value. Unless the combination of businesses is more profitable together under the corporate umbrella than they are apart as independent businesses, *the strategy cannot create economic value for shareholders.* And unless it does so, there is *no real justification for unrelated diversification,* since top executives have a fiduciary responsibility to maximize long-term shareholder value for the company's owners (its shareholders).

Building Shareholder Value via Unrelated Diversification

Given the absence of cross-business strategic fit with which to create competitive advantages, building shareholder value via unrelated diversification ultimately hinges on the ability of the parent company to improve its businesses (and make the combination *better off*) via other means. Critical to this endeavor is the role that the parent company plays as a *corporate parent.*[12] To the extent that a company has strong *parenting capabilities*—capabilities that involve nurturing, guiding, grooming, and governing constituent businesses—a corporate parent can propel its businesses forward and help them gain ground over their market rivals. Corporate parents also contribute to the competitiveness of their unrelated businesses by sharing or transferring *general resources and capabilities* across the businesses—competitive assets that have utility in *any type* of industry and that can be leveraged across a wide range of business types as a result. Examples of the kinds of general resources that a corporate parent leverages in unrelated diversification include the corporation's reputation, credit rating, and access to financial markets; governance mechanisms; management training programs; a corporate ethics program; a central data and communications center; shared administrative resources such as public relations and legal services; and common systems for functions such as budgeting, financial reporting, and quality control.

The Benefits of Astute Corporate Parenting One of the most important ways that corporate parents contribute to the success of their businesses is by offering high-level oversight and guidance.[13] The top executives of a large diversified corporation have among them many years of accumulated experience in a variety of business settings and can often contribute expert problem-solving skills, creative strategy suggestions, and first-rate advice and guidance on how to improve competitiveness and financial performance to the heads of the company's various business subsidiaries. This is especially true in the case of newly acquired, smaller businesses. Particularly astute high-level guidance from corporate executives can help the subsidiaries perform better than they would otherwise be able to do through the efforts of the business unit heads alone. The outstanding leadership of Royal Little, the founder of Textron, was a major reason that the company became an exemplar of the unrelated diversification strategy while he was CEO. Little's bold moves transformed the company from its origins as a small textile manufacturer into a global powerhouse known for its Bell helicopters, Cessna aircraft, and host of other strong brands in a wide array of industries. Norm Wesley, a former CEO of the conglomerate Fortune Brands, is similarly credited with driving the sharp rise in the company's stock price while he was at the helm. Under his leadership, Fortune Brands became the $7 billion maker of products ranging from spirits (e.g., Jim Beam bourbon and rye, Gilbey's gin and vodka, Courvoisier cognac) to golf products (e.g., Titleist golf balls and clubs, FootJoy golf shoes and apparel, Scotty Cameron putters) to hardware (e.g., Moen faucets, American Lock security devices). (Fortune Brands has since been converted into two separate entities, Beam Inc. and Fortune Brands Home & Security.)

CORE CONCEPT

Corporate parenting refers to the role that a diversified corporation plays in nurturing its component businesses through the provision of top management expertise, disciplined control, financial resources, and other types of *general resources and capabilities* such as long-term planning systems, business development skills, management development processes, and incentive systems.

Corporate parents can also create added value for their businesses by providing them with other types of general resources that lower the operating costs of the individual businesses or that enhance their operating effectiveness. The administrative resources located at a company's corporate headquarters are a prime example. They typically include legal services, accounting expertise and tax services, and other elements of the administrative infrastructure, such as risk management capabilities, information technology resources, and public relations capabilities. Providing individual businesses with general support resources such as these creates value by *lowering companywide overhead costs,* since each business would otherwise have to duplicate the centralized activities.

An **umbrella brand** is a corporate brand name that can be applied to a wide assortment of business types. As such, it is a type of *general resource* that can be leveraged in unrelated diversification.

Corporate brands that do not connote any specific type of product are another type of general corporate resource that can be shared among unrelated businesses. GE's brand is an example, having been applied to businesses as diverse as financial services (GE Capital), medical imaging (GE medical diagnostics), and lighting (GE lightbulbs). Corporate brands that are applied in this fashion are sometimes called **umbrella brands.** Utilizing a well-known corporate name (GE) in a diversified company's individual businesses has the potential not only to lower costs (by spreading the fixed cost of developing and maintaining the brand over many businesses) but also to enhance each business's customer value proposition by linking its products to a name that consumers trust. In similar fashion, a corporation's reputation for well-crafted products, for product reliability, or for trustworthiness can lead to greater customer willingness to purchase the products of a wider range of a diversified company's businesses. Incentive systems, financial control systems, and a company's culture are other types of general corporate resources that may prove useful in enhancing the daily operations of a diverse set of businesses.

We discuss two other commonly employed ways for corporate parents to add value to their unrelated businesses next.

Judicious Cross-Business Allocation of Financial Resources

By reallocating surplus cash flows from some businesses to fund the capital requirements of other businesses—in essence, having the company serve as an *internal capital market*—corporate parents may also be able to create value. Such actions can be particularly important in times when credit is unusually tight (such as in the wake of the worldwide banking crisis that began in 2008) or in economies with less well developed capital markets. Under these conditions, with strong financial resources a corporate parent can add value by shifting funds from business units generating excess cash (more than they need to fund their own operating requirements and new capital investment opportunities) to other, cash-short businesses with appealing growth prospects. A parent company's ability to function as its own internal capital market enhances overall corporate performance and increases shareholder value to the extent that (1) its top managers have better access to information about investment opportunities internal to the firm than do external financiers or (2) it can provide funds that would otherwise be unavailable due to poor financial market conditions.

Acquiring and Restructuring Undervalued Companies Another way for parent companies to add value to unrelated businesses is by acquiring weakly performing companies at a bargain price and then *restructuring* their operations in ways that produce sometimes dramatic increases in profitability. **Restructuring** refers to overhauling and streamlining the operations of a business—combining plants with excess capacity, selling off underutilized assets, reducing unnecessary expenses, revamping its product offerings, consolidating administrative functions to reduce overhead costs, and otherwise improving the operating efficiency and profitability of a company. Restructuring generally involves transferring seasoned managers to the newly acquired business, either to replace the top layers of management or to step in temporarily until the business is returned to profitability or is well on its way to becoming a major market contender.

> **CORE CONCEPT**
>
> **Restructuring** refers to overhauling and streamlining the activities of a business—combining plants with excess capacity, selling off underutilized assets, reducing unnecessary expenses, and otherwise improving the productivity and profitability of a company.

Restructuring is often undertaken when a diversified company acquires a new business that is performing well below levels that the corporate parent believes are achievable. Diversified companies that have capabilities in restructuring (sometimes called *turnaround capabilities*) are able to significantly boost the performance of weak businesses in a relatively wide range of industries. Newell Rubbermaid (whose diverse product line includes Sharpie pens, Levolor window treatments, Goody hair accessories, Calphalon cookware, and Lenox power and hand tools) developed such a strong set of turnaround capabilities that the company was said to "Newellize" the businesses it acquired.

Successful unrelated diversification strategies based on restructuring require the parent company to have considerable expertise in identifying underperforming target companies and in negotiating attractive acquisition prices so that each acquisition passes the cost of entry test. The capabilities in this regard of Lord James Hanson and Lord Gordon White, who headed up the storied British conglomerate Hanson Trust, played a large part in Hanson Trust's impressive record of profitability.

The Path to Greater Shareholder Value through Unrelated Diversification

For a strategy of unrelated diversification to produce companywide financial results above and beyond what the businesses could generate operating as stand-alone entities, corporate executives must do three things to pass the three tests of corporate advantage:

1. Diversify into industries where the businesses can produce consistently good earnings and returns on investment (to satisfy the industry-attractiveness test).
2. Negotiate favorable acquisition prices (to satisfy the cost of entry test).
3. Do a superior job of corporate parenting via high-level managerial oversight and resource sharing, financial resource allocation and portfolio management, and/or the restructuring of underperforming businesses (to satisfy the better-off test).

CORE CONCEPT

A diversified company has a **parenting advantage** when it is more able than other companies to boost the combined performance of its individual businesses through high-level guidance, general oversight, and other corporate-level contributions.

The best corporate parents understand the nature and value of the kinds of resources at their command and know how to leverage them effectively across their businesses. Those that are able to create more value in their businesses than other diversified companies have what is called a **parenting advantage.** When a corporation has a parenting advantage, its top executives have the best chance of being able to craft and execute an unrelated diversification strategy that can satisfy all three tests of corporate advantage and truly enhance long-term economic shareholder value.

The Drawbacks of Unrelated Diversification

Unrelated diversification strategies have two important negatives that undercut the pluses: very demanding managerial requirements and limited competitive advantage potential.

Demanding Managerial Requirements Successfully managing a set of fundamentally different businesses operating in fundamentally different industry and competitive environments is a challenging and exceptionally difficult proposition.[14] Consider, for example, that corporations like General Electric, ITT, Mitsubishi, and Bharti Enterprises have dozens of business subsidiaries making hundreds and sometimes thousands of products. While headquarters executives can glean information about an industry from third-party sources, ask lots of questions when making occasional visits to the operations of the different businesses, and do their best to learn about the company's different businesses, they still remain heavily dependent on briefings from business unit heads and on "managing by the numbers"—that is, keeping a close track on the financial and operating results of each subsidiary. Managing by the numbers works well enough when business conditions are normal and the heads of the various business units are capable of consistently meeting their numbers. But problems arise if things start to go awry in a business and corporate management has to get deeply involved in the problems of a business it does not know much about. Because every business tends to encounter rough sledding at some juncture, unrelated diversification is thus a somewhat risky strategy from a managerial perspective.[15] Just one or two unforeseen problems or big strategic mistakes—which are much more likely without close corporate oversight—can cause a precipitous drop in corporate earnings and crash the parent company's stock price.

Hence, competently overseeing a set of widely diverse businesses can turn out to be much harder than it sounds. In practice, comparatively few companies have proved that they have top-management capabilities that are up to the task. There are far more companies whose corporate executives have failed at delivering consistently good financial results with an unrelated diversification strategy than there are companies with corporate executives who have been successful.[16] Unless a company truly has a parenting advantage, the odds are that the result of unrelated diversification will be 1 + 1 = 2 or even less.

Limited Competitive Advantage Potential The second big negative is that *unrelated diversification offers only a limited potential for competitive advantage beyond what each individual business can generate on its own.* Unlike a related diversification strategy, unrelated diversification provides no cross-business strategic-fit benefits that allow each business to perform its key value chain activities in a more efficient and effective manner. A cash-rich corporate parent pursuing unrelated diversification can provide its subsidiaries with much-needed capital, may achieve economies of scope in activities relying on general corporate resources, and may even offer some managerial know-how to help resolve problems in particular business units, but otherwise it has little to offer in the way of enhancing the competitive strength of its individual business units. In comparison to the highly specialized resources that facilitate related diversification, the general resources that support unrelated diversification tend to be relatively low value, for the simple reason that they are more common. Unless they are of exceptionally high quality (such as GE's world-renowned general management capabilities or Newell Rubbermaid's turnaround capabilities), resources and capabilities that are general in nature are less likely to provide a source of competitive advantage for diversified companies. Without the competitive advantage potential of strategic fit in competitively important value chain activities, consolidated performance of an unrelated group of businesses stands to be little more than the sum of what the individual business units could achieve if they were independent, in most circumstances.

Relying solely on leveraging general resources and the expertise of corporate executives to wisely manage a set of unrelated businesses is *a much weaker foundation for enhancing shareholder value* than is a strategy of related diversification.

Misguided Reasons for Pursuing Unrelated Diversification

Companies sometimes pursue unrelated diversification for reasons that are misguided. These include the following:

- *Risk reduction.* Spreading the company's investments over a set of diverse industries to spread risk cannot create long-term shareholder value since the company's shareholders can more flexibly (and more efficiently) reduce their exposure to risk by investing in a diversified portfolio of stocks and bonds.
- *Growth.* While unrelated diversification may enable a company to achieve rapid or continuous growth, firms that pursue growth for growth's sake are unlikely to maximize shareholder value. Only *profitable growth*—the kind that comes from creating added value for shareholders—can justify a strategy of unrelated diversification.
- *Stabilization.* Managers sometimes pursue broad diversification in the hope that market downtrends in some of the company's businesses will be partially offset by cyclical upswings in its other businesses, thus producing somewhat less earnings volatility. In actual practice, however, there's no convincing evidence that the consolidated profits of firms with unrelated diversification strategies are more stable or less subject to reversal in periods of recession and economic stress than the profits of firms with related diversification strategies.
- *Managerial motives.* Unrelated diversification can provide benefits to managers such as higher compensation (which tends to increase with firm size and degree

Only *profitable growth*—the kind that comes from creating added value for shareholders—can justify a strategy of unrelated diversification.

of diversification) and reduced unemployment risk. Pursuing diversification for these reasons will likely reduce shareholder value and violate managers' fiduciary responsibilities.

Because unrelated diversification strategies *at their best* have only a limited potential for creating long-term economic value for shareholders, it is essential that managers not compound this problem by taking a misguided approach toward unrelated diversification, in pursuit of objectives that are more likely to destroy shareholder value than create it.

COMBINATION RELATED-UNRELATED DIVERSIFICATION STRATEGIES

There's nothing to preclude a company from diversifying into both related and unrelated businesses. Indeed, in actual practice the business makeup of diversified companies varies considerably. Some diversified companies are really *dominant-business enterprises*—one major "core" business accounts for 50 to 80 percent of total revenues and a collection of small related or unrelated businesses accounts for the remainder. Some diversified companies are *narrowly diversified* around a few (two to five) related or unrelated businesses. Others are *broadly diversified* around a wide-ranging collection of related businesses, unrelated businesses, or a mixture of both. A number of multibusiness enterprises have diversified into unrelated areas but have a collection of related businesses within each area—thus giving them a business portfolio consisting of *several unrelated groups of related businesses.* There's ample room for companies to customize their diversification strategies to incorporate elements of both related and unrelated diversification, as may suit their own competitive asset profile and strategic vision. *Combination related-unrelated diversification strategies have particular appeal for companies with a mix of valuable competitive assets, covering the spectrum from general to specialized resources and capabilities.*

Figure 8.2 shows the range of alternatives for companies pursuing diversification.

EVALUATING THE STRATEGY OF A DIVERSIFIED COMPANY

LO 4

The analytic tools for evaluating a company's diversification strategy.

Strategic analysis of diversified companies builds on the concepts and methods used for single-business companies. But there are some additional aspects to consider and a couple of new analytic tools to master. The procedure for evaluating the pluses and minuses of a diversified company's strategy and deciding what actions to take to improve the company's performance involves six steps:

1. Assessing the attractiveness of the industries the company has diversified into, both individually and as a group.
2. Assessing the competitive strength of the company's business units and drawing a nine-cell matrix to simultaneously portray industry attractiveness and business unit competitive strength.
3. Evaluating the extent of cross-business strategic fit along the value chains of the company's various business units.

FIGURE 8.2 Three Strategy Options for Pursuing Diversification

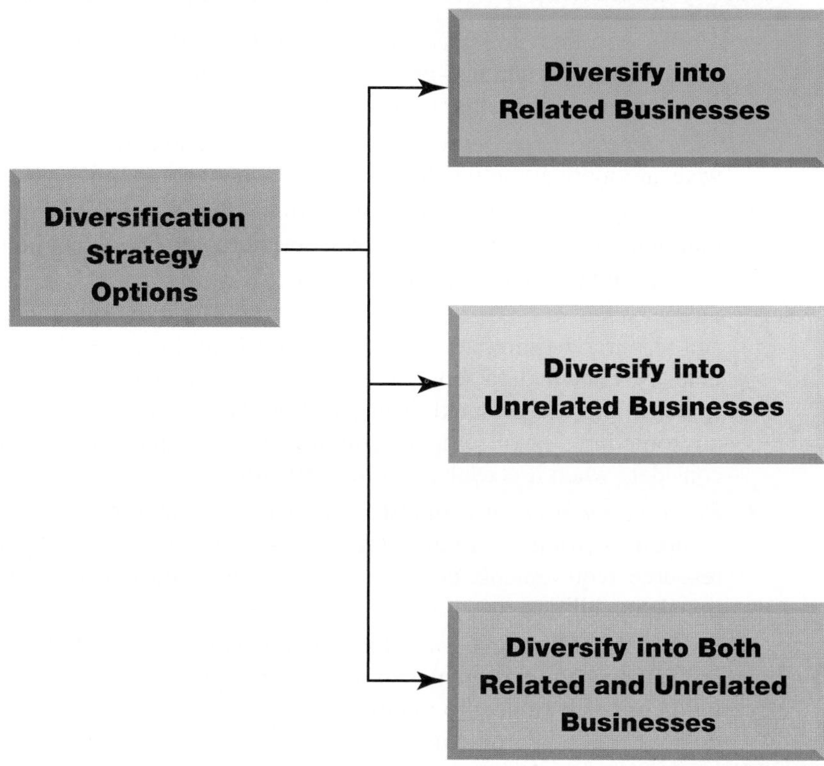

4. Checking whether the firm's resources fit the requirements of its present business lineup.
5. Ranking the performance prospects of the businesses from best to worst and determining what the corporate parent's priorities should be in allocating resources to its various businesses.
6. Crafting new strategic moves to improve overall corporate performance.

The core concepts and analytic techniques underlying each of these steps merit further discussion.

Step 1: Evaluating Industry Attractiveness

A principal consideration in evaluating the caliber of a diversified company's strategy is the attractiveness of the industries in which it has business operations. Several questions arise:

1. Does each industry the company has diversified into represent a good market for the company to be in—does it pass the industry-attractiveness test?
2. Which of the company's industries are most attractive, and which are least attractive?
3. How appealing is the whole group of industries in which the company has invested?

The more attractive the industries (both individually and as a group) that a diversified company is in, the better its prospects for good long-term performance.

Calculating Industry-Attractiveness Scores A simple and reliable analytic tool for gauging industry attractiveness involves calculating quantitative industry-attractiveness scores based on the following measures:

- *Market size and projected growth rate.* Big industries are more attractive than small industries, and fast-growing industries tend to be more attractive than slow-growing industries, other things being equal.
- *The intensity of competition.* Industries where competitive pressures are relatively weak are more attractive than industries where competitive pressures are strong.
- *Emerging opportunities and threats.* Industries with promising opportunities and minimal threats on the near horizon are more attractive than industries with modest opportunities and imposing threats.
- *The presence of cross-industry strategic fit.* The more one industry's value chain and resource requirements match up well with the value chain activities of other industries in which the company has operations, the more attractive the industry is to a firm pursuing related diversification. However, cross-industry strategic fit is not something that a company committed to a strategy of unrelated diversification considers when it is evaluating industry attractiveness.
- *Resource requirements.* Industries in which resource requirements are within the company's reach are more attractive than industries in which capital and other resource requirements could strain corporate financial resources and organizational capabilities.
- *Social, political, regulatory, and environmental factors.* Industries that have significant problems in such areas as consumer health, safety, or environmental pollution or those subject to intense regulation are less attractive than industries that do not have such problems.
- *Industry profitability.* Industries with healthy profit margins and high rates of return on investment are generally more attractive than industries with historically low or unstable profits.

Each attractiveness measure is then assigned a weight reflecting its relative importance in determining an industry's attractiveness, since not all attractiveness measures are equally important. The intensity of competition in an industry should nearly always carry a high weight (say, 0.20 to 0.30). Strategic-fit considerations should be assigned a high weight in the case of companies with related diversification strategies; but for companies with an unrelated diversification strategy, strategic fit with other industries may be dropped from the list of attractiveness measures altogether. The importance weights must add up to 1.

Finally, each industry is rated on each of the chosen industry-attractiveness measures, using a rating scale of 1 to 10 (where a *high* rating signifies *high* attractiveness, and a *low* rating signifies *low* attractiveness). *Keep in mind here that the more intensely competitive an industry is, the lower the attractiveness rating for that industry.* Likewise, the more the resource requirements associated with being in a particular industry are beyond the parent company's reach, the lower the attractiveness rating. On the other hand, the presence of good cross-industry strategic fit should be given a very high attractiveness rating, since there is good potential for competitive advantage and added shareholder value. Weighted attractiveness scores are then calculated by multiplying the industry's rating on each measure by the corresponding weight. For example, a rating of 8 times a weight of 0.25 gives a weighted attractiveness score of 2. The sum of the weighted scores for all the attractiveness measures provides an overall industry-attractiveness score. This procedure is illustrated in Table 8.1.

TABLE 8.1 Calculating Weighted Industry-Attractiveness Scores

		Industry-Attractiveness Assessments					
		Industry A		Industry B		Industry C	
Industry-Attractiveness Measure	Importance Weight	Attractiveness Rating*	Weighted Score	Attractiveness Rating*	Weighted Score	Attractiveness Rating*	Weighted Score
Market size and projected growth rate	0.10	8	0.80	3	0.30	5	0.50
Intensity of competition	0.25	8	2.00	2	0.50	5	1.25
Emerging opportunities and threats	0.10	6	0.60	5	0.50	4	0.40
Cross-industry strategic fit	0.30	8	2.40	2	0.60	3	0.90
Resource requirements	0.10	5	0.50	5	0.50	4	0.40
Social, political, regulatory, and environmental factors	0.05	8	0.40	3	0.15	7	1.05
Industry profitability	0.10	5	0.50	4	0.40	6	0.60
Sum of importance weights	**1.00**						
Weighted overall industry-attractiveness scores			**7.20**		**2.95**		**5.10**

**Rating scale:* 1 = very unattractive to company; 10 = very attractive to company.

Interpreting the Industry-Attractiveness Scores Industries with a score much below 5 probably do not pass the attractiveness test. If a company's industry-attractiveness scores are all above 5, it is probably fair to conclude that the group of industries the company operates in is attractive as a whole. But the group of industries takes on a decidedly lower degree of attractiveness as the number of industries with scores below 5 increases, especially if industries with low scores account for a sizable fraction of the company's revenues.

For a diversified company to be a strong performer, a substantial portion of its revenues and profits must come from business units with relatively high attractiveness scores. It is particularly important that a diversified company's principal businesses be in industries with a good outlook for growth and above-average profitability. Having a big fraction of the company's revenues and profits come from industries with slow growth, low profitability, or intense competition tends to drag overall company performance down. Business units in the least attractive industries are potential candidates for divestiture, unless they are positioned strongly enough to overcome the unattractive aspects of their industry environments or they are a strategically important component of the company's business makeup.

Step 2: Evaluating Business Unit Competitive Strength

The second step in evaluating a diversified company is to appraise the competitive strength of each business unit in its respective industry. Doing an appraisal of each business unit's strength and competitive position in its industry not only reveals its chances for success in its industry but also provides a basis for ranking the units from competitively strongest to competitively weakest and sizing up the competitive strength of all the business units as a group.

Calculating Competitive-Strength Scores for Each Business Unit Quantitative measures of each business unit's competitive strength can be calculated using a procedure similar to that for measuring industry attractiveness. The following factors are used in quantifying the competitive strengths of a diversified company's business subsidiaries:

- *Relative market share.* A business unit's *relative market share* is defined as the ratio of its market share to the market share held by the largest rival firm in the industry, with market share measured in unit volume, not dollars. For instance, if business A has a market-leading share of 40 percent and its largest rival has 30 percent, A's relative market share is 1.33. (Note that only business units that are market share leaders in their respective industries can have relative market shares greater than 1.) If business B has a 15 percent market share and B's largest rival has 30 percent, B's relative market share is 0.5. *The further below 1 a business unit's relative market share is, the weaker its competitive strength and market position vis-à-vis rivals.*
- *Costs relative to competitors' costs.* Business units that have low costs relative to those of key competitors tend to be more strongly positioned in their industries than business units struggling to maintain cost parity with major rivals. The only time a business unit's competitive strength may not be undermined by having higher costs than rivals is when it has incurred the higher costs to strongly differentiate its product offering and its customers are willing to pay premium prices for the differentiating features.
- *Ability to match or beat rivals on key product attributes.* A company's competitiveness depends in part on being able to satisfy buyer expectations with regard to features, product performance, reliability, service, and other important attributes.
- *Brand image and reputation.* A widely known and respected brand name is a valuable competitive asset in most industries.
- *Other competitively valuable resources and capabilities.* Valuable resources and capabilities, including those accessed through collaborative partnerships, enhance a company's ability to compete successfully and perhaps contend for industry leadership.
- *Ability to benefit from strategic fit with other business units.* Strategic fit with other businesses within the company enhances a business unit's competitive strength and may provide a competitive edge.

- *Ability to exercise bargaining leverage with key suppliers or customers.* Having bargaining leverage signals competitive strength and can be a source of competitive advantage.
- *Profitability relative to competitors.* Above-average profitability on a consistent basis is a signal of competitive advantage, while consistently below-average profitability usually denotes competitive disadvantage.

After settling on a set of competitive-strength measures that are well matched to the circumstances of the various business units, the company needs to assign weights indicating each measure's importance. As in the assignment of weights to industry-attractiveness measures, the importance weights must add up to 1. Each business unit is then rated on each of the chosen strength measures, using a rating scale of 1 to 10 (where a *high* rating signifies competitive *strength,* and a *low* rating signifies competitive *weakness*). In the event that the available information is too limited to confidently assign a rating value to a business unit on a particular strength measure, it is usually best to use a score of 5—this avoids biasing the overall score either up or down. Weighted strength ratings are calculated by multiplying the business unit's rating on each strength measure by the assigned weight. For example, a strength score of 6 times a weight of 0.15 gives a weighted strength rating of 0.90. The sum of the weighted ratings across all the strength measures provides a quantitative measure of a business unit's overall market strength and competitive standing. Table 8.2 provides sample calculations of competitive-strength ratings for three businesses.

Interpreting the Competitive-Strength Scores Business units with competitive-strength ratings above 6.7 (on a scale of 1 to 10) are strong market contenders in their industries. Businesses with ratings in the 3.3-to-6.7 range have moderate competitive strength vis-à-vis rivals. Businesses with ratings below 3.3 are in competitively weak market positions. If a diversified company's business units all have competitive-strength scores above 5, it is fair to conclude that its business units are all fairly strong market contenders in their respective industries. But as the number of business units with scores below 5 increases, there's reason to question whether the company can perform well with so many businesses in relatively weak competitive positions. This concern takes on even more importance when business units with low scores account for a sizable fraction of the company's revenues.

Using a Nine-Cell Matrix to Simultaneously Portray Industry Attractiveness and Competitive Strength The industry-attractiveness and business-strength scores can be used to portray the strategic positions of each business in a diversified company. Industry attractiveness is plotted on the vertical axis and competitive strength on the horizontal axis. A nine-cell grid emerges from dividing the vertical axis into three regions (high, medium, and low attractiveness) and the horizontal axis into three regions (strong, average, and weak competitive strength). As shown in Figure 8.3, scores of 6.7 or greater on a rating scale of 1 to 10 denote high industry attractiveness, scores of 3.3 to 6.7 denote medium attractiveness, and scores below 3.3 signal low attractiveness. Likewise, high competitive strength is defined as scores greater than 6.7, average strength as scores of 3.3 to 6.7, and low strength as scores below 3.3. *Each business unit is plotted on the nine-cell matrix according to its overall attractiveness score and strength score, and then it is shown as a "bubble."*

TABLE 8.2 Calculating Weighted Competitive-Strength Scores for a Diversified Company's Business Units

		Competitive-Strength Assessments					
		Business A in Industry A		Business B in Industry B		Business C in Industry C	
Competitive-Strength Measures	**Importance Weight**	**Strength Rating***	**Weighted Score**	**Strength Rating***	**Weighted Score**	**Strength Rating***	**Weighted Score**
Relative market share	0.15	10	1.50	2	0.30	6	0.90
Costs relative to competitors' costs	0.20	7	1.40	4	0.80	5	1.00
Ability to match or beat rivals on key product attributes	0.05	9	0.45	5	0.25	8	0.40
Ability to benefit from strategic fit with sister businesses	0.20	8	1.60	4	0.80	8	0.80
Bargaining leverage with suppliers/customers	0.05	9	0.45	2	0.10	6	0.30
Brand image and reputation	0.10	9	0.90	4	0.40	7	0.70
Competitively valuable capabilities	0.15	7	1.05	2	0.30	5	0.75
Profitability relative to competitors	0.10	5	0.50	2	0.20	4	0.40
Sum of importance weights	**1.00**						
Weighted overall competitive strength scores			**7.85**		**3.15**		**5.25**

**Rating scale:* 1 = very weak; 10 = very strong.

The size of each bubble is scaled to the percentage of revenues the business generates relative to total corporate revenues. The bubbles in Figure 8.3 were located on the grid using the three industry-attractiveness scores from Table 8.1 and the strength scores for the three business units in Table 8.2.

The locations of the business units on the attractiveness–strength matrix provide valuable guidance in deploying corporate resources. In general, *a diversified company's best prospects for good overall performance involve concentrating corporate resources on business units having the greatest competitive strength and industry attractiveness.* Businesses plotted in the three cells in the upper left portion of the attractiveness–strength matrix have both favorable industry attractiveness and

FIGURE 8.3 A Nine-Cell Industry-Attractiveness-Competitive-Strength Matrix

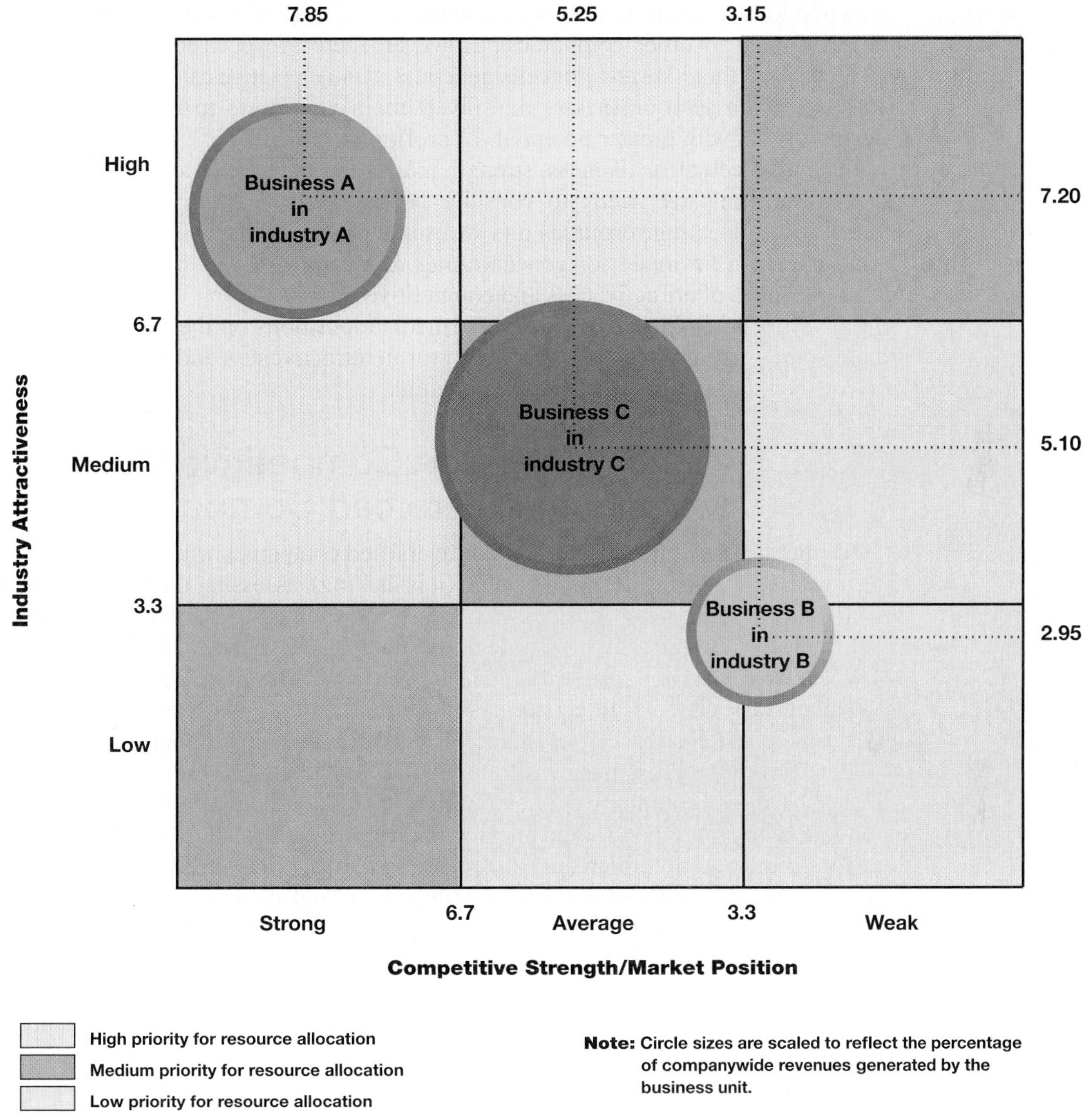

competitive strength and should receive a high investment priority. Business units plotted in these three cells (like business A) are referred to as "grow and build" businesses because of their capability to drive future increases in shareholder value.

Next in priority come businesses positioned in the three diagonal cells stretching from the lower left to the upper right (like business C). Such businesses usually merit intermediate priority in the parent's resource allocation ranking. However, some businesses in the medium-priority diagonal cells may have brighter or dimmer prospects than others. For example, a small business in the upper right cell of the matrix, despite being in a highly attractive industry, may occupy too weak a competitive position in its industry to justify the investment and resources needed to turn it into a strong market contender.

Businesses in the three cells in the lower right corner of the matrix (like business B) have comparatively low industry attractiveness and minimal competitive strength, making them weak performers with little potential for improvement. At best, they have the lowest claim on corporate resources and may be good candidates for being divested (sold to other companies). However, there are occasions when a business located in the three lower-right cells generates sizable positive cash flows. It may make sense to retain such businesses and divert their cash flows to finance expansion of business units with greater potential for profit growth.

The nine-cell attractiveness–strength matrix provides clear, strong logic for why a diversified company needs to consider both industry attractiveness and business strength in allocating resources and investment capital to its different businesses. A good case can be made for concentrating resources in those businesses that enjoy higher degrees of attractiveness and competitive strength, being very selective in making investments in businesses with intermediate positions on the grid, and withdrawing resources from businesses that are lower in attractiveness and strength unless they offer exceptional profit or cash flow potential.

The greater the value of cross-business strategic fit in enhancing the performance of a diversified company's businesses, the more competitively powerful is the company's related diversification strategy.

Step 3: Determining the Competitive Value of Strategic Fit in Diversified Companies

While this step can be bypassed for diversified companies whose businesses are all unrelated (since, by design, strategic fit is lacking), assessing the degree of strategic fit across a company's businesses is central to evaluating its related diversification strategy. But more than just strategic-fit identification is needed. *The real question is how much competitive value can be generated from strategic fit.* Are the cost savings associated with economies of scope likely to give one or more individual businesses a cost-based advantage over rivals? How much competitive value will come from the cross-business transfer of skills, technology, or intellectual capital or the sharing of competitive assets? Will leveraging a potent umbrella brand or corporate image strengthen the businesses and increase sales significantly? Will cross-business collaboration to create new competitive capabilities lead to significant gains in performance? Without significant strategic fit and dedicated company efforts to capture the benefits, one has to be skeptical about the potential for a diversified company's businesses to perform better together than apart.

Figure 8.4 illustrates the process of comparing the value chains of a company's businesses and identifying opportunities to exploit competitively valuable cross-business strategic fit.

CORE CONCEPT

A company pursuing related diversification exhibits **resource fit** when its businesses have matching specialized resource requirements along their value chains; a company pursuing unrelated diversification has resource fit when the parent company has adequate corporate resources (parenting and general resources) to support its businesses' needs and add value.

Step 4: Checking for Resource Fit

The businesses in a diversified company's lineup need to exhibit good **resource fit.** In firms with a related diversification strategy, resource fit exists *when the firm's businesses have matching specialized resource requirements at points along their value chains* that are critical for the businesses' market success. Matching resource requirements are important in related diversification because they facilitate resource sharing and low-cost resource transfer. In companies pursuing unrelated diversification, resource fit exists when the company has solid *parenting capabilities or resources of a general nature that it can share or transfer to its component businesses.* Firms pursuing related diversification and firms with combination related-unrelated diversification strategies can also benefit from leveraging

FIGURE 8.4 Identifying the Competitive Advantage Potential of Cross-Business Strategic Fit

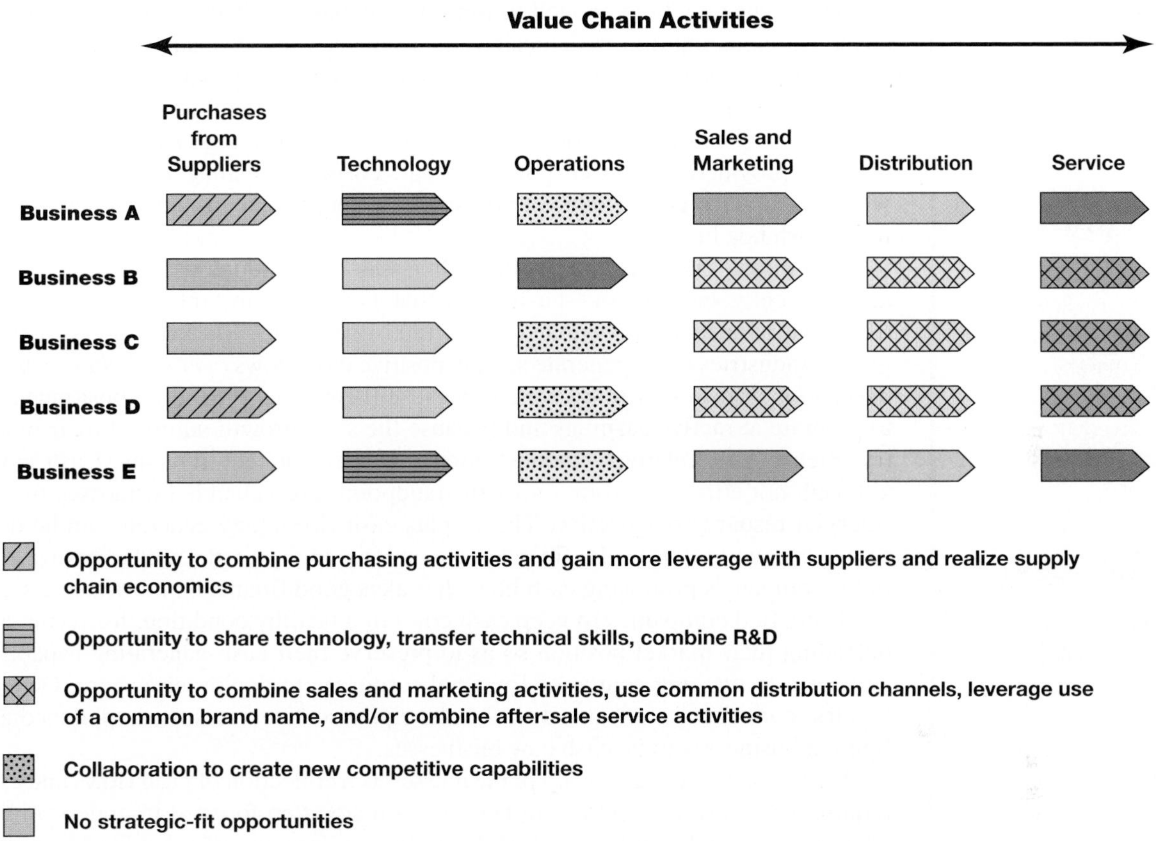

corporate parenting capabilities and other general resources. Another dimension of resource fit that concerns all types of multibusiness firms is whether they have resources sufficient to support their group of businesses without being spread too thin.

Financial Resource Fit One dimension of resource fit concerns whether a diversified company can generate the internal cash flows sufficient to fund the capital requirements of its businesses, pay its dividends, meet its debt obligations, and otherwise remain financially healthy. (Financial resources, including the firm's ability to borrow or otherwise raise funds, are a type of general resource.) While additional capital can usually be raised in financial markets, it is important for a diversified firm to have a healthy **internal capital market** that can support the financial requirements of its business lineup. The greater the extent to which a diversified company is able to fund investment in its businesses through internally generated cash flows rather than from equity issues or borrowing, the more powerful its financial resource fit and the less dependent the firm is on external financial resources. This can provide a competitive advantage over single business rivals when credit market conditions are tight, as they have been in the United States and abroad in recent years.

> **CORE CONCEPT**
>
> A strong **internal capital market** allows a diversified company to add value by shifting capital from business units generating *free cash flow* to those needing additional capital to expand and realize their growth potential.

CORE CONCEPT

A **portfolio approach** to ensuring financial fit among a firm's businesses is based on the fact that different businesses have different cash flow and investment characteristics.

CORE CONCEPT

A **cash hog** business generates cash flows that are too small to fully fund its growth; it thereby requires cash infusions to provide additional working capital and finance new capital investment.

CORE CONCEPT

A **cash cow** business generates cash flows over and above its internal requirements, thus providing a corporate parent with funds for investing in cash hog businesses, financing new acquisitions, or paying dividends.

A **portfolio approach** to ensuring financial fit among a firm's businesses is based on the fact that different businesses have different cash flow and investment characteristics. For example, business units in rapidly growing industries are often **cash hogs**—so labeled because the cash flows they are able to generate from internal operations aren't big enough to fund their expansion. To keep pace with rising buyer demand, rapid-growth businesses frequently need sizable annual capital investments—for new facilities and equipment, for new product development or technology improvements, and for additional working capital to support inventory expansion and a larger base of operations. Because a cash hog's financial resources must be provided by the corporate parent, corporate managers have to decide whether it makes good financial and strategic sense to keep pouring new money into a cash hog business.

In contrast, business units with leading market positions in mature industries are frequently **cash cows**—businesses that generate substantial cash surpluses over what is needed to adequately fund their operations. Market leaders in slow-growth industries often generate sizable positive cash flows *over and above what is needed for growth and reinvestment* because their industry-leading positions tend to generate attractive earnings and because the slow-growth nature of their industry often entails relatively modest annual investment requirements. Cash cows, although not attractive from a growth standpoint, are valuable businesses from a financial resource perspective. The surplus cash flows they generate can be used to pay corporate dividends, finance acquisitions, and provide funds for investing in the company's promising cash hogs. It makes good financial and strategic sense for diversified companies to keep cash cows in a healthy condition, fortifying and defending their market position so as to preserve their cash-generating capability and have an ongoing source of financial resources to deploy elsewhere. General Electric considers its advanced materials, equipment services, and appliance and lighting businesses to be cash cow businesses.

Viewing a diversified group of businesses as a collection of cash flows and cash requirements (present and future flows) is a major step forward in understanding what the financial ramifications of diversification are and why having businesses with good financial resource fit can be important. For instance, *a diversified company's businesses exhibit good financial resource fit when the excess cash generated by its cash cow businesses is sufficient to fund the investment requirements of promising cash hog businesses.* Ideally, investing in promising cash hog businesses over time results in growing the hogs into self-supporting *star businesses* that have strong or market-leading competitive positions in attractive, high-growth markets and high levels of profitability. Star businesses are often the cash cows of the future. When the markets of star businesses begin to mature and their growth slows, their competitive strength should produce self-generated cash flows that are more than sufficient to cover their investment needs. The "success sequence" is thus cash hog to young star (but perhaps still a cash hog) to self-supporting star to cash cow. While the practice of viewing a diversified company in terms of cash cows and cash hogs has declined in popularity, it illustrates one approach to analyzing financial resource fit and allocating financial resources across a portfolio of different businesses.

Aside from cash flow considerations, there are two other factors to consider in assessing whether a diversified company's businesses exhibit good financial fit:

- *Does each of the individual businesses adequately contribute to achieving companywide performance targets?* A business exhibits poor financial fit if it soaks up a disproportionate share of the company's financial resources, while making subpar or insignificant contributions to the bottom line. Too many underperforming businesses reduce the company's overall performance and ultimately limit growth in shareholder value.

- *Does the corporation have adequate financial strength to fund its different businesses and maintain a healthy credit rating?* A diversified company's strategy fails the resource-fit test when the resource needs of its portfolio unduly stretch the company's financial health and threaten to impair its credit rating. Many of the world's largest banks, including Royal Bank of Scotland, Citigroup, and HSBC, recently found themselves so undercapitalized and financially overextended that they were forced to sell off some of their business assets to meet regulatory requirements and restore public confidence in their solvency.

Nonfinancial Resource Fit Just as a diversified company must have adequate financial resources to support its various individual businesses, it must also have a big enough and deep enough pool of managerial, administrative, and competitive capabilities to support all of its different businesses. The following two questions help reveal whether a diversified company has sufficient nonfinancial resources:

- *Does the company have (or can it develop) the specific resources and capabilities needed to be successful in each of its businesses?* Sometimes the resources a company has accumulated in its core business prove to be a poor match with the competitive capabilities needed to succeed in the businesses into which it has diversified. For instance, BTR, a multibusiness company in Great Britain, discovered that the company's resources and managerial skills were quite well suited for parenting its industrial manufacturing businesses but not for parenting its distribution businesses (National Tyre Services and Texas-based Summers Group). As a result, BTR decided to divest its distribution businesses and focus exclusively on diversifying around small industrial manufacturing. For companies pursuing related diversification strategies, a mismatch between the company's competitive assets and the key success factors of an industry can be serious enough to warrant divesting businesses in that industry or not acquiring a new business. In contrast, when a company's resources and capabilities are a good match with the key success factors of industries it is not presently in, it makes sense to take a hard look at acquiring companies in these industries and expanding the company's business lineup.
- *Are the company's resources being stretched too thinly by the resource requirements of one or more of its businesses?* A diversified company must guard against overtaxing its resources and capabilities, a condition that can arise when (1) it goes on an acquisition spree and management is called on to assimilate and oversee many new businesses very quickly or (2) it lacks sufficient resource depth to do a creditable job of transferring skills and competencies from one of its businesses to another. The broader the diversification, the greater the concern about whether corporate executives are overburdened by the demands of competently parenting so many different businesses. Plus, the more a company's diversification strategy is tied to transferring know-how or technologies from existing businesses to newly acquired businesses, the more it has to develop a deep-enough resource pool to supply these businesses with the resources and capabilities they need to be successful.[17] Otherwise, its competitive assets end up being spread too thinly across many businesses, and the opportunity for achieving 1 + 1 = 3 outcomes slips through the cracks.

Step 5: Ranking Business Units and Assigning a Priority for Resource Allocation

Once a diversified company's strategy has been evaluated from the perspective of industry attractiveness, competitive strength, strategic fit, and resource fit, the next step is to use this information to rank the performance prospects of the businesses from best to worst. Such ranking helps top-level executives assign each business a priority for resource support and capital investment.

The locations of the different businesses in the nine-cell industry-attractiveness–competitive-strength matrix provide a solid basis for identifying high-opportunity businesses and low-opportunity businesses. Normally, competitively strong businesses in attractive industries have significantly better performance prospects than competitively weak businesses in unattractive industries. Also, the revenue and earnings outlook for businesses in fast-growing industries is normally better than for businesses in slow-growing industries. As a rule, *business subsidiaries with the brightest profit and growth prospects, attractive positions in the nine-cell matrix, and solid strategic and resource fit should receive top priority for allocation of corporate resources.* However, in ranking the prospects of the different businesses from best to worst, it is usually wise to also take into account each business's past performance in regard to sales growth, profit growth, contribution to company earnings, return on capital invested in the business, and cash flow from operations. While past performance is not always a reliable predictor of future performance, it does signal whether a business is already performing well or has problems to overcome.

Allocating Financial Resources Figure 8.5 shows the chief strategic and financial options for allocating a diversified company's financial resources. Divesting businesses with the weakest future prospects and businesses that lack adequate strategic fit and/or resource fit is one of the best ways of generating additional funds for redeployment to businesses with better opportunities and better strategic and resource fit. Free cash flows from cash cow businesses also add to the pool of funds that can be usefully redeployed. *Ideally,* a diversified company will have sufficient financial resources to strengthen or grow its existing businesses, make any new acquisitions that are desirable, fund other promising business opportunities, pay off existing debt, and periodically increase dividend payments to shareholders and/or repurchase shares of stock. But, as a practical matter, a company's financial resources are limited. Thus, to make the best use of the available funds, top executives must steer resources to those businesses with the best prospects and either divest or allocate minimal resources to businesses with marginal prospects—this is why ranking the performance prospects of the various businesses from best to worst is so crucial. Strategic uses of corporate resources should usually take precedence over financial options (see Figure 8.5) unless there is a compelling reason to strengthen the firm's balance sheet or better reward shareholders.

LO 5

What four main corporate strategy options a diversified company can employ for solidifying its strategy and improving company performance.

Step 6: Crafting New Strategic Moves to Improve Overall Corporate Performance

The conclusions flowing from the five preceding analytic steps set the agenda for crafting strategic moves to improve a diversified company's overall performance. The strategic options boil down to four broad categories of actions (see Figure 8.6):

FIGURE 8.5 The Chief Strategic and Financial Options for Allocating a Diversified Company's Financial Resources

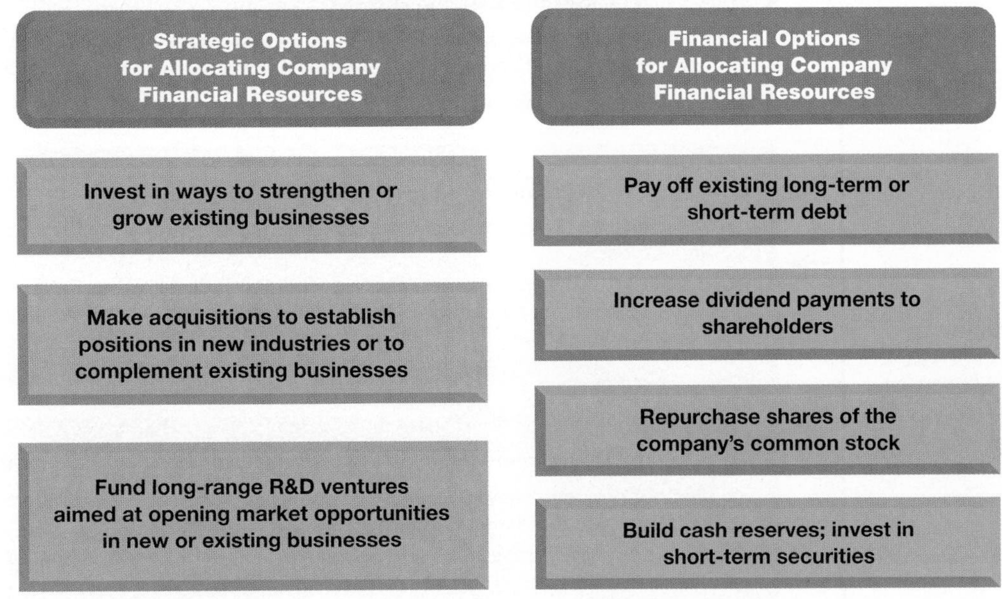

1. Sticking closely with the existing business lineup and pursuing the opportunities these businesses present.
2. Broadening the company's business scope by making new acquisitions in new industries.
3. Divesting certain businesses and retrenching to a narrower base of business operations.
4. Restructuring the company's business lineup and putting a whole new face on the company's business makeup.

Sticking Closely with the Present Business Lineup The option of sticking with the current business lineup makes sense when the company's existing businesses offer attractive growth opportunities and can be counted on to create economic value for shareholders. As long as the company's set of existing businesses have good prospects and are in alignment with the company's diversification strategy, then major changes in the company's business mix are unnecessary. Corporate executives can concentrate their attention on getting the best performance from each of the businesses, steering corporate resources into the areas of greatest potential and profitability. The specifics of "what to do" to wring better performance from the present business lineup have to be dictated by each business's circumstances and the preceding analysis of the corporate parent's diversification strategy.

Broadening a Diversified Company's Business Base Diversified companies sometimes find it desirable to build positions in new industries, whether related or unrelated. Several motivating factors are in play. One is sluggish growth that makes the potential revenue and profit boost of a newly acquired business look

FIGURE 8.6 A Company's Four Main Strategic Alternatives after It Diversifies

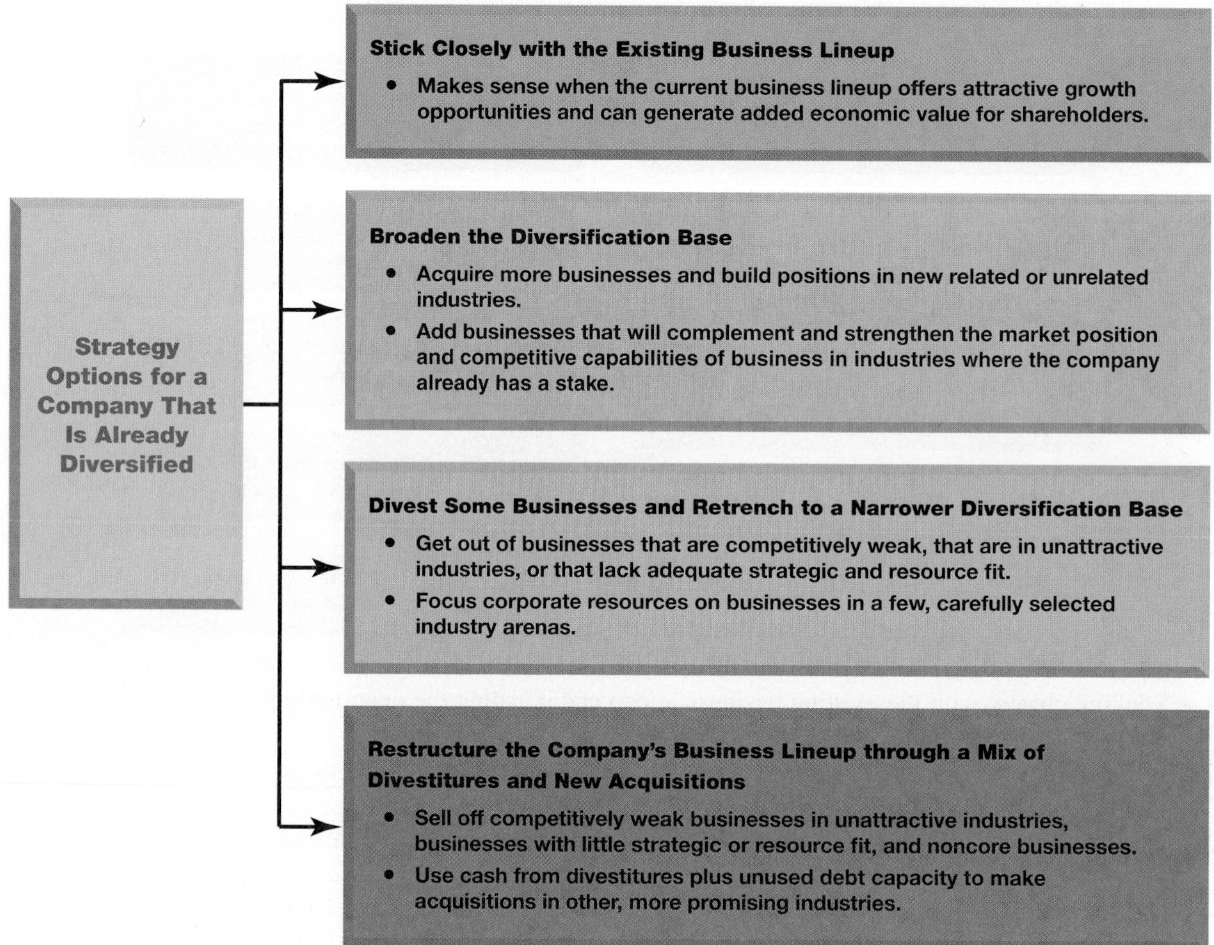

attractive. A second is the potential for transferring resources and capabilities to other related or complementary businesses. A third is rapidly changing conditions in one or more of a company's core businesses, brought on by technological, legislative, or demographic changes. For instance, the passage of legislation in the United States allowing banks, insurance companies, and stock brokerages to enter each other's businesses spurred a raft of acquisitions and mergers to create full-service financial enterprises capable of meeting the multiple financial needs of customers. A fourth, and very important, motivating factor for adding new businesses is to complement and strengthen the market position and competitive capabilities of one or more of the company's present businesses. Procter & Gamble's acquisition of Gillette strengthened and extended P&G's reach into personal care and household products—Gillette's businesses included Oral-B toothbrushes, Gillette razors and razor blades, Duracell batteries, and Braun shavers and small appliances.

Another important avenue for expanding the scope of a diversified company is to grow by extending the operations of existing businesses into additional country markets, as discussed in Chapter 7. Expanding a company's geographic scope may offer an exceptional competitive advantage potential by facilitating the full capture of economies of scale and learning- and experience-curve effects. In some businesses, the volume of sales needed to realize full economies of scale and/or benefit fully from experience-curve effects exceeds the volume that can be achieved by operating within the boundaries of just one or several country markets, especially small ones.

Retrenching to a Narrower Diversification Base A number of diversified firms have had difficulty managing a diverse group of businesses and have elected to exit some of them. Selling a business outright to another company is far and away the most frequently used option for divesting a business. In 2012, Sara Lee Corporation sold its International Coffee and Tea business to J.M. Smucker, while Nike sold its Umbro and Cole Haan brands to focus on brands like Jordan and Converse that are more complementary to the Nike brand. But sometimes a business selected for divestiture has ample resources and capabilities to compete successfully on its own. In such cases, a corporate parent may elect to spin the unwanted business off as a financially and managerially independent company, either by selling shares to the public via an initial public offering or by distributing shares in the new company to shareholders of the corporate parent. Darden Restaurants, owner of the Olive Garden chain, expects to complete a spin-off of its Red Lobster chain in 2015 and distribute the new shares of Red Lobster to Darden shareholders. Kimberly-Clark, a global health and hygiene consumer products company, spun off its health care business, K-C Health Care, in 2014.

Retrenching to a narrower diversification base is usually undertaken when top management concludes that its diversification has ranged too far afield and that the company can improve long-term performance by concentrating on a smaller number of businesses. But there are other important reasons for divesting one or more of a company's present businesses. Sometimes divesting a business has to be considered because market conditions in a once-attractive industry have badly deteriorated. A business can become a prime candidate for divestiture because it lacks adequate strategic or resource fit, because it is a cash hog with questionable long-term potential, or because remedying its competitive weaknesses is too expensive relative to the likely gains in profitability. Sometimes a company acquires businesses that, down the road, just do not work out as expected even though management has tried its best. Subpar performance by some business units is bound to occur, thereby raising questions of whether to divest them or keep them and attempt a turnaround. Other business units, despite adequate financial performance, may not mesh as well with the rest of the firm as was originally thought. For instance, PepsiCo divested its group of fast-food restaurant businesses to focus on its core soft-drink and snack-food businesses, where their specialized resources and capabilities could add more value.

A **spin-off** is an independent company created when a corporate parent divests a business either by selling shares to the public via an initial public offering or by distributing shares in the new company to shareholders of the corporate parent.

On occasion, a diversification move that seems sensible from a strategic-fit standpoint turns out to be a poor *cultural fit.*[18] When several pharmaceutical companies diversified into cosmetics and perfume, they discovered their personnel had little respect for the "frivolous" nature of such products compared to the far nobler task of developing miracle drugs to cure the ill. The absence of shared values and cultural compatibility between the medical research and chemical-compounding expertise of the pharmaceutical companies and the fashion and marketing orientation of the cosmetics business was the undoing of what otherwise was diversification into businesses with technology-sharing potential, product development fit, and some overlap in distribution channels.

Diversified companies need to divest low-performing businesses or businesses that don't fit in order to concentrate on expanding existing businesses and entering new ones where opportunities are more promising.

A useful guide to determine whether or when to divest a business subsidiary is to ask, "If we were not in this business today, would we want to get into it now?" When the answer is no or probably not, divestiture should be considered. Another signal that a business should be divested occurs when it is worth more to another company than to the present parent; in such cases, shareholders would be well served if the company sells the business and collects a premium price from the buyer for whom the business is a valuable fit.

Restructuring a Diversified Company's Business Lineup

CORE CONCEPT

Companywide restructuring *(corporate restructuring)* involves making major changes in a diversified company by divesting some businesses and/or acquiring others, so as to put a whole new face on the company's business lineup.

Restructuring a diversified company on a companywide basis *(corporate restructuring)* involves divesting some businesses and/or acquiring others, so as to put a whole new face on the company's business lineup.[19] Performing radical surgery on a company's business lineup is appealing when its financial performance is being squeezed or eroded by:

- A serious mismatch between the company's resources and capabilities and the type of diversification that it has pursued.
- Too many businesses in slow-growth, declining, low-margin, or otherwise unattractive industries.
- Too many competitively weak businesses.
- The emergence of new technologies that threaten the survival of one or more important businesses.
- Ongoing declines in the market shares of one or more major business units that are falling prey to more market-savvy competitors.
- An excessive debt burden with interest costs that eat deeply into profitability.
- Ill-chosen acquisitions that haven't lived up to expectations.

On occasion, corporate restructuring can be prompted by special circumstances—such as when a firm has a unique opportunity to make an acquisition so big and important that it has to sell several existing business units to finance the new acquisition or when a company needs to sell off some businesses in order to raise the cash for entering a potentially big industry with wave-of-the-future technologies or products. As businesses are divested, corporate restructuring generally involves aligning the remaining business units into groups with the best strategic fit and then redeploying the cash flows from the divested businesses to either pay down debt or make new acquisitions to strengthen the parent company's business position in the industries it has chosen to emphasize.

Over the past decade, corporate restructuring has become a popular strategy at many diversified companies, especially those that had diversified broadly into many different industries and lines of business. VF Corporation, maker of North Face and other popular "lifestyle" apparel brands, has used a restructuring strategy to provide its shareholders with returns that are more than five times greater than shareholder returns for competing apparel makers. Since its acquisition and turnaround of North Face in 2000, VF has spent nearly $5 billion to acquire 19 additional businesses, including about $2 billion in 2011 for Timberland. New apparel brands acquired by VF Corporation include 7 For All Mankind sportswear, Vans skateboard shoes, Nautica, John Varvatos, Reef surf wear, and Lucy athletic wear. By 2014, VF Corporation had become an $11 billion powerhouse—one of the largest and most profitable apparel and footwear companies in the world. It was listed as number 250 on *Fortune*'s 2013 list of the 500 largest U.S. companies.

Illustration Capsule 8.2 discusses how Kraft Foods has been pursuing long-term growth and increased shareholder value by restructuring its operations.

ILLUSTRATION CAPSULE 8.2 Growth through Restructuring at Kraft Foods

In 2012, Kraft Foods, the 90-year-old darling of the consumer packaged-goods industry, moved to improve its long-term performance by *restructuring* the corporation—the latest move by CEO Irene Rosenfeld, who was brought in to turn around the company's performance. In addition to trimming operations, the restructuring plan called for spinning off the North American grocery unit that included Kraft Macaroni and Cheese, Oscar Meyer, and other nonsnack brands from the $32 billion fast-growing global snacks business that included Oreo and Cadbury (the British confectionary acquired in 2010). While the grocery business would retain the name Kraft, the star of this strategic separation was the core snack business, renamed Mondelez. With this radical new operational structure in place, Kraft hoped to improve its ability to focus on new opportunities and pursue profitable growth.

Managing these two large and very different businesses jointly had made it difficult for Kraft to act nimbly and adapt to changing market conditions. It also inhibited the company from executing new strategies free from significant portfolio-wide considerations. In announcing her intention to split the company in September 2011, CEO Irene Rosenfeld said, "Simply put, we have now reached a point where North American Grocery and Global Snacks will each benefit from standing on its own and focusing on its unique drivers for success." She noted that as separate businesses, "each will have the leadership, resources, and mandate to realize its full potential."

As part of the restructuring effort, Rosenfeld reduced the number of management centers and sold off some underperforming brands. More recently, the new North American grocery business Kraft Foods Group has undertaken further restructuring to streamline its organizational structure and brand identity. Although in refashioning the company, Rosenfeld sacrificed some of the operational benefits the company enjoyed as a single entity, managers and investors have already begun to see some of the positive effects of appropriately scaled focus.

Note: Developed with Maximilian A. Pinto and Harold W. Greenstone.

Sources: S. Webb, "New Reality Makes Kraft Split Vital," *Food Global News,* September 2011; J. Jannarone, "Mondelez Can Slim Way to Success," *The Wall Street Journal* Online, May 28, 2013 (accessed March 31, 2014); M. J. de la Merced, "Kraft Foods, in Split, Is Keeping Oreos but Not Velveeta," *The New York Times Dealbook* Online, August 4, 2011 (accessed March 31, 2014); E. J. Schultz, "Kraft Restructures as It Eyes More Brand-Building," *Advertising Age* Online, June 14, 2013 (accessed March 31, 2014); E. J. Schultz, "Could Kraft Split Be a Blueprint for Blue Chips?" *Advertising Age,* August 2011; www.nytimes.com/2007/02/21/business/21kraft.html (accessed March 2, 2012); and stocks.investopedia.com/ (accessed March 2, 2012).

KEY POINTS

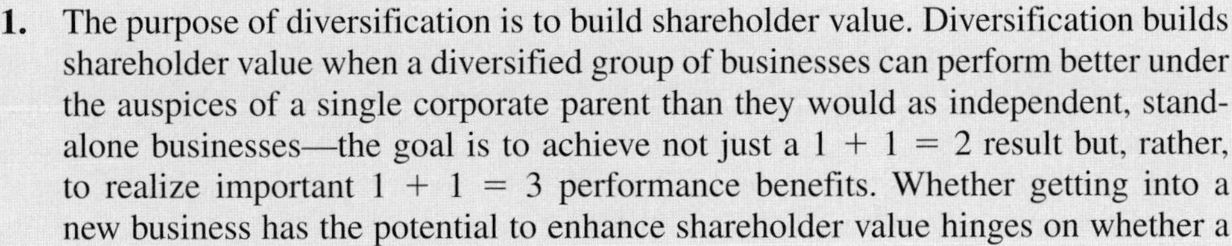

1. The purpose of diversification is to build shareholder value. Diversification builds shareholder value when a diversified group of businesses can perform better under the auspices of a single corporate parent than they would as independent, stand-alone businesses—the goal is to achieve not just a 1 + 1 = 2 result but, rather, to realize important 1 + 1 = 3 performance benefits. Whether getting into a new business has the potential to enhance shareholder value hinges on whether a

company's entry into that business can pass the three tests of corporate advantage: the industry-attractiveness test, the cost of entry test, and the better-off test.

2. Entry into new businesses can take any of three forms: acquisition, internal startup, or joint venture. The choice of which is best depends on the firm's resources and capabilities, the industry's entry barriers, the importance of speed, and relative costs.
3. There are two fundamental approaches to diversification—into related businesses and into unrelated businesses. The rationale for *related* diversification is to benefit from *strategic fit:* Diversify into businesses with commonalities across their respective value chains, and then capitalize on the strategic fit by sharing or transferring the resources and capabilities across matching value chain activities to gain competitive advantages.
4. *Unrelated* diversification strategies surrender the competitive advantage potential of strategic fit at the value chain level in return for the potential that can be realized from superior corporate parenting or the sharing and transfer of general resources and capabilities. An outstanding corporate parent can benefit its businesses through (1) providing high-level oversight and making available other corporate resources, (2) allocating financial resources across the business portfolio, and (3) restructuring underperforming acquisitions.
5. Related diversification provides a stronger foundation for creating shareholder value than does unrelated diversification, since the *specialized resources and capabilities* that are leveraged in related diversification tend to be more valuable competitive assets than the *general resources and capabilities* underlying unrelated diversification, which in most cases are relatively common and easier to imitate.
6. Analyzing how good a company's diversification strategy is consists of a six-step process:

   Step 1: *Evaluate the long-term attractiveness of the industries into which the firm has diversified.* Determining industry attractiveness involves developing a list of industry-attractiveness measures, each of which might have a different importance weight.

   Step 2: *Evaluate the relative competitive strength of each of the company's business units.* The purpose of rating the competitive strength of each business is to gain a clear understanding of which businesses are strong contenders in their industries, which are weak contenders, and what the underlying reasons are for their strength or weakness. The conclusions about industry attractiveness can be joined with the conclusions about competitive strength by drawing a nine-cell industry-attractiveness–competitive-strength matrix that helps identify the prospects of each business and the level of priority each business should be given in allocating corporate resources and investment capital.

   Step 3: *Check for cross-business strategic fit.* A business is more attractive strategically when it has value chain relationships with the other business units that offer the potential to (1) combine operations to realize economies of scope, (2) transfer technology, skills, know-how, or other resource capabilities from one business to another, (3) leverage the use of a trusted brand name or other resources that enhance differentiation, (4) share other competitively valuable resources among the company's businesses, and (5) build new resources and competitive capabilities via cross-business collaboration. Cross-business strategic fit represents a significant avenue for producing competitive advantage beyond what any one business can achieve on its own.

Step 4: *Check whether the firm's resources fit the resource requirements of its present business lineup.* In firms with a related diversification strategy, resource fit exists when the firm's businesses have matching resource requirements at points along their value chains that are critical for the businesses' market success. In companies pursuing unrelated diversification, resource fit exists when the company has solid parenting capabilities or resources of a general nature that it can share or transfer to its component businesses. When there is financial resource fit among the businesses of any type of diversified company, the company can generate internal cash flows sufficient to fund the capital requirements of its businesses, pay its dividends, meet its debt obligations, and otherwise remain financially healthy.

Step 5: *Rank the performance prospects of the businesses from best to worst, and determine what the corporate parent's priority should be in allocating resources to its various businesses.* The most important considerations in judging business unit performance are sales growth, profit growth, contribution to company earnings, and the return on capital invested in the business. Normally, strong business units in attractive industries should head the list for corporate resource support.

Step 6: *Craft new strategic moves to improve overall corporate performance.* This step entails using the results of the preceding analysis as the basis for selecting one of four different strategic paths for improving a diversified company's performance: (1) Stick closely with the existing business lineup and pursue opportunities presented by these businesses, (2) broaden the scope of diversification by entering additional industries, (3) retrench to a narrower scope of diversification by divesting poorly performing businesses, or (4) broadly restructure the business lineup with multiple divestitures and/or acquisitions.

ASSURANCE OF LEARNING EXERCISES

connect
LO 1, LO 2, LO 3, LO 4

1. See if you can identify the value chain relationships that make the businesses of the following companies related in competitively relevant ways. In particular, you should consider whether there are cross-business opportunities for (1) transferring skills and technology, (2) combining related value chain activities to achieve economies of scope, and/or (3) leveraging the use of a well-respected brand name or other resources that enhance differentiation.

Bloomin' Brands

- Outback Steakhouse
- Carrabba's Italian Grill
- Roy's Restaurant (Hawaiian fusion cuisine)
- Bonefish Grill (market-fresh fine seafood)
- Fleming's Prime Steakhouse & Wine Bar

L'Oréal

- Maybelline, Lancôme, Helena Rubinstein cosmetics
- L'Oréal, Garnier, and SoftSheen-Carson hair care products
- Redken, Matrix, L'Oréal Professional, Kiehl's, and Kérastase professional hair care and skin care products
- Ralph Lauren, Yves Saint Laurent, and Giorgio Armani fragrances
- La Roche-Posay, Vichy Laboratories, Dermablend, and SkinCeuticals dermocosmetics

Johnson & Johnson

- Baby products (powder, shampoo, oil, lotion)
- Band-Aids and other first-aid products
- Women's health and personal care products
- Neutrogena, Lubriderm, and Aveeno skin care products
- Nonprescription drugs (Tylenol, Motrin, Pepcid AC, Mylanta, Benadryl)
- Prescription drugs
- Oral health care (Listerine, Rembrandt)
- Nutritionals (Splenda, Lactaid)
- Prosthetic and other medical devices
- Surgical and hospital products
- Vision care (Acuvue contact lenses, Visine)

LO 1, LO 2, LO 3, LO 4

2. Peruse the business group listings for United Technologies shown below and listed at its website (www.utc.com). How would you characterize the company's corporate strategy—related diversification, unrelated diversification, or a combination related-unrelated diversification strategy? Explain your answer.
   - Carrier—the world's largest provider of air-conditioning, heating, and refrigeration solutions.
   - Hamilton Sundstrand—a provider of technologically advanced aerospace and industrial products.
   - Otis—the world's leading manufacturer, installer, and maintainer of elevators, escalators, and moving walkways.
   - Pratt & Whitney—a global leader in the design, manufacture, service, and support of aircraft engines, industrial gas turbines, and space propulsion systems.
   - Sikorsky—a world leader in helicopter design, manufacture, and service.
   - UTC Fire & Security—a supplier of fire and security systems developed for commercial, industrial, and residential customers.
   - UTC Power—a full-service provider of environmentally advanced power solutions.

connect

LO 1, LO 2, LO 3, LO 4, LO 5

3. ITT is a technology-oriented engineering and manufacturing company with the following business divisions and products:
   - Industrial Process Division—industrial pumps, valves, and monitoring and control systems; aftermarket services for the chemical, oil and gas, mining, pulp and paper, power, and biopharmaceutical markets.

- Motion Technologies Division—durable brake pads, shock absorbers, and damping technologies for the automotive and rail markets.
- Interconnect Solutions—connectors and fittings for the production of automobiles, aircraft, railcars and locomotives, oil field equipment, medical equipment, and industrial equipment.
- Control Technologies—energy absorption and vibration dampening equipment, transducers and regulators, and motion controls used in the production of robotics, medical equipment, automobiles, subsea equipment, industrial equipment, aircraft, and military vehicles.

Based on the above listing, would you say that ITT's business lineup reflects a strategy of related diversification, unrelated diversification, or a combination of related and unrelated diversification? What benefits are generated from any strategic fit existing between ITT's businesses? Also, what types of companies should ITT consider acquiring that might improve shareholder value? Justify your answer.

EXERCISE FOR SIMULATION PARTICIPANTS

1. In the event that your company has the opportunity to diversify into other products or businesses of your choosing, would you opt to pursue related diversification, unrelated diversification, or a combination of both? Explain why. **LO 1, LO 2, LO 3**
2. What specific resources and capabilities does your company possess that would make diversifying into related businesses attractive? Indicate what kinds of strategic-fit benefits could be captured by transferring these resources and competitive capabilities to newly acquired related businesses. **LO 1, LO 2**
3. If your company opted to pursue a strategy of related diversification, what industries or product categories could it diversify into that would allow it to achieve economies of scope? Name at least two or three such industries or product categories, and indicate the specific kinds of cost savings that might accrue from entry into each. **LO 1, LO 2**
4. If your company opted to pursue a strategy of unrelated diversification, what industries or product categories could it diversify into that would allow it to capitalize on using its present brand name and corporate image to good advantage in the newly entered businesses or product categories? Name at least two or three such industries or product categories, and indicate the *specific benefits* that might be captured by transferring your company's umbrella brand name to each. **LO 1, LO 3**

ENDNOTES

[1] Michael E. Porter, "From Competitive Advantage to Corporate Strategy," *Harvard Business Review* 45, no. 3 (May–June 1987), pp. 46–49.

[2] www.zerohedge.com/news/2013-02-14/heinz-confirms-it-will-be-acquired-buffett-28-billion-transaction-7250share (accessed February 2, 2014).

[3] finance.fortune.cnn.com/2012/07/31/companies-are-paying-up-for-deals/; blogs.wsj.com/cfo/2013/11/26/why-are-takeover-prices-plummeting/ (accessed February 2, 2014).

[4] A. Shleifer and R. Vishny, "Takeovers in the 60s and the 80s—Evidence and Implications," *Strategic Management Journal* 12 (Winter 1991), pp. 51–59; T. Brush, "Predicted Change in Operational Synergy and Post-Acquisition Performance of Acquired Businesses," *Strategic Management Journal* 17, no. 1 (1996), pp. 1–24; J. P. Walsh, "Top Management Turnover Following Mergers and Acquisitions," *Strategic Management Journal* 9, no. 2 (1988), pp. 173–183; A. Cannella and D. Hambrick, "Effects of Executive Departures on the Performance of Acquired Firms," *Strategic Management Journal* 14 (Summer 1993), pp. 137–152; R. Roll, "The Hubris Hypothesis of

Corporate Takeovers," *Journal of Business* 59, no. 2 (1986), pp. 197–216; P. Haspeslagh and D. Jemison, *Managing Acquisitions* (New York: Free Press, 1991).

[5] M.L.A. Hayward, "When Do Firms Learn from Their Acquisition Experience? Evidence from 1990–1995," *Strategic Management Journal* 23, no. 1 (2002), pp. 21–29; G. Ahuja and R. Katila, "Technological Acquisitions and the Innovation Performance of Acquiring Firms: A Longitudinal Study," *Strategic Management Journal* 22, no. 3 (2001), pp. 197–220; H. Barkema and F. Vermeulen, "International Expansion through Start-Up or Acquisition: A Learning Perspective," *Academy of Management Journal* 41, no. 1 (1998), pp. 7–26.

[6] Yves L. Doz and Gary Hamel, *Alliance Advantage: The Art of Creating Value through Partnering* (Boston: Harvard Business School Press, 1998), chaps. 1 and 2.

[7] J. Glover, "The Guardian," March 23, 1996, www.mcspotlight.org/media/press/guardpizza_23mar96.html.

[8] Michael E. Porter, *Competitive Advantage* (New York: Free Press, 1985), pp. 318–319, 337–353; Porter, "From Competitive Advantage to Corporate Strategy," pp. 53–57; Constantinos C. Markides and Peter J. Williamson, "Corporate Diversification and Organization Structure: A Resource-Based View," *Academy of Management Journal* 39, no. 2 (April 1996), pp. 340–367.

[9] David J. Collis and Cynthia A. Montgomery, "Creating Corporate Advantage," *Harvard Business Review* 76, no. 3 (May–June 1998), pp. 72–80; Markides and Williamson, "Corporate Diversification and Organization Structure."

[10] Jeanne M. Liedtka, "Collaboration across Lines of Business for Competitive Advantage," *Academy of Management Executive* 10, no. 2 (May 1996), pp. 20–34.

[11] Kathleen M. Eisenhardt and D. Charles Galunic, "Coevolving: At Last, a Way to Make Synergies Work," *Harvard Business Review* 78, no. 1 (January–February 2000), pp. 91–101; Constantinos C. Markides and Peter J. Williamson, "Related Diversification, Core Competences and Corporate Performance," *Strategic Management Journal* 15 (Summer 1994), pp. 149–165.

[12] A. Campbell, M. Goold, and M. Alexander, "Corporate Strategy: The Quest for Parenting Advantage," *Harvard Business Review* 73, no. 2 (March–April 1995), pp. 120–132.

[13] Cynthia A. Montgomery and B. Wernerfelt, "Diversification, Ricardian Rents, and Tobin-Q," *RAND Journal of Economics* 19, no. 4 (1988), pp. 623–632.

[14] Patricia L. Anslinger and Thomas E. Copeland, "Growth through Acquisitions: A Fresh Look," *Harvard Business Review* 74, no. 1 (January–February 1996), pp. 126–135.

[15] M. Lubatkin and S. Chatterjee, "Extending Modern Portfolio Theory," *Academy of Management Journal* 37, no.1 (February 1994), pp. 109–136.

[16] Lawrence G. Franko, "The Death of Diversification? The Focusing of the World's Industrial Firms, 1980–2000," *Business Horizons* 47, no. 4 (July–August 2004), pp. 41–50.

[17] David J. Collis and Cynthia A. Montgomery, "Competing on Resources: Strategy in the 90s," *Harvard Business Review* 73, no. 4 (July–August 1995), pp. 118–128.

[18] Peter F. Drucker, *Management: Tasks, Responsibilities, Practices* (New York: Harper & Row, 1974), p. 709.

[19] Lee Dranikoff, Tim Koller, and Anton Schneider, "Divestiture: Strategy's Missing Link," *Harvard Business Review* 80, no. 5 (May 2002), pp. 74–83.

CHAPTER 9

Ethics, Corporate Social Responsibility, Environmental Sustainability, and Strategy

Learning Objectives

THIS CHAPTER WILL HELP YOU UNDERSTAND:

LO 1 How the standards of ethical behavior in business are no different from the ethical standards and norms of the larger society and culture in which a company operates.

LO 2 What drives unethical business strategies and behavior.

LO 3 The costs of business ethics failures.

LO 4 The concepts of corporate social responsibility and environmental sustainability and how companies balance these duties with economic responsibilities to shareholders.

Social obligation is much bigger than supporting worthy causes. It includes anything that impacts people and the quality of their lives.

William Ford Jr. – *Chairman of the Ford Motor Company*

Since most corporate competitors have the same problems with sustainability and social reputation, it's worth trying to solve them together.

Simon Mainwaring – *Founder and CEO of We First, Inc.*

The time is always right to do what is right.

Martin Luther King, Jr. – *Civil Rights Activist and Humanitarian*

Clearly, a company has a responsibility to make a profit and grow the business. Just as clearly, a company and its personnel have a duty to obey the law and play by the rules of fair competition. But does a company also have a duty to go beyond legal requirements and conform to the ethical norms of the societies in which it operates? Does it have an obligation to contribute to the betterment of society, independent of the needs and preferences of the customers it serves? Should a company display a social conscience and devote a portion of its resources to bettering society? Should its strategic initiatives be screened for possible negative effects on future generations of the world's population?

This chapter focuses on whether a company, in the course of trying to craft and execute a strategy that delivers value to both customers and shareholders, also has a duty to (1) act in an ethical manner, (2) be a committed corporate citizen and allocate some of its resources to improving the well-being of employees, the communities in which it operates, and society as a whole, and (3) adopt business practices that conserve natural resources, protect the interests of future generations, and preserve the well-being of the planet.

WHAT DO WE MEAN BY *BUSINESS ETHICS*?

Ethics concerns principles of right or wrong conduct. **Business ethics** is the application of ethical principles and standards to the actions and decisions of business organizations and the conduct of their personnel.[1] *Ethical principles in business are not materially different from ethical principles in general.* Why? Because business actions have to be judged in the context of society's standards of right and wrong, not with respect to a special set of ethical standards applicable only to business situations. If dishonesty is considered unethical and immoral, then dishonest behavior in business—whether it relates to customers, suppliers, employees, shareholders, competitors, or government—qualifies as equally unethical and immoral. If being ethical entails not deliberately harming others, then failing to recall

CORE CONCEPT

Business ethics deals with the application of general ethical principles to the actions and decisions of businesses and the conduct of their personnel.

LO 1

How the standards of ethical behavior in business are no different from the ethical standards and norms of the larger society and culture in which a company operates.

a defective or unsafe product swiftly, regardless of the cost, is likewise unethical. If society deems bribery unethical, then it is unethical for company personnel to make payoffs to government officials to win government contracts or bestow favors to customers to win or retain their business. In short, ethical behavior in business situations requires adhering to generally accepted norms about right or wrong conduct. As a consequence, company managers have an obligation—indeed, a duty—to observe ethical norms when crafting and executing strategy.

WHERE DO ETHICAL STANDARDS COME FROM—ARE THEY UNIVERSAL OR DEPENDENT ON LOCAL NORMS?

Notions of right and wrong, fair and unfair, moral and immoral are present in all societies and cultures. But there are three distinct schools of thought about the extent to which ethical standards travel across cultures and whether multinational companies can apply the same set of ethical standards in any and all locations where they operate.

The School of Ethical Universalism

CORE CONCEPT

The school of **ethical universalism** holds that the most fundamental conceptions of right and wrong are *universal* and apply to members of all societies, all companies, and all businesspeople.

According to the school of **ethical universalism,** the most fundamental conceptions of right and wrong are *universal* and transcend culture, society, and religion.[2] For instance, being truthful (not lying and not being deliberately deceitful) strikes a chord of what's right in the peoples of all nations. Likewise, demonstrating integrity of character, not cheating or harming people, and treating others with decency are concepts that resonate with people of virtually all cultures and religions.

Common moral agreement about right and wrong actions and behaviors across multiple cultures and countries gives rise to universal ethical standards that apply to members of all societies, all companies, and all businesspeople. These universal ethical principles set forth the traits and behaviors that are considered virtuous and that a good person is supposed to believe in and to display. Thus, adherents of the school of ethical universalism maintain that it is entirely appropriate to expect all businesspeople to conform to these universal ethical standards.[3] For example, people in most societies would concur that it is unethical for companies to knowingly expose workers to toxic chemicals and hazardous materials or to sell products known to be unsafe or harmful to the users.

The strength of ethical universalism is that it draws upon the collective views of multiple societies and cultures to put some clear boundaries on what constitutes ethical and unethical business behavior, regardless of the country or culture in which a company's personnel are conducting activities. This means that with respect to basic moral standards that do not vary significantly according to local cultural beliefs, traditions, or religious convictions, a multinational company can develop a code of ethics that it applies more or less evenly across its worldwide operations. It can avoid the slippery slope that comes from having different ethical standards for different company personnel depending on where in the world they are working.

The School of Ethical Relativism

While undoubtedly there are some universal moral prescriptions (like being truthful and trustworthy), there are also observable variations from one society to another as to what constitutes ethical or unethical behavior. Indeed, differing religious beliefs, social customs, traditions, core values, and behavioral norms frequently give rise to different standards about what is fair or unfair, moral or immoral, and ethically right or wrong. For instance, European and American managers often establish standards of business conduct that protect human rights such as freedom of movement and residence, freedom of speech and political opinion, and the right to privacy. In China, where societal commitment to basic human rights is weak, human rights considerations play a small role in determining what is ethically right or wrong in conducting business activities. In Japan, managers believe that showing respect for the collective good of society is a more important ethical consideration. In Muslim countries, managers typically apply ethical standards compatible with the teachings of Muhammad. Consequently, the school of **ethical relativism** holds that a "one-size-fits-all" template for judging the ethical appropriateness of business actions and the behaviors of company personnel is totally inappropriate. Rather, the underlying thesis of ethical relativism is that whether certain actions or behaviors are ethically right or wrong depends on the ethical norms of the country or culture in which they take place. For businesses, this implies that when there are cross-country or cross-cultural differences in ethical standards, it is appropriate for *local ethical standards to take precedence over what the ethical standards may be in a company's home market.*[4] In a world of ethical relativism, there are few absolutes when it comes to business ethics, and thus few ethical absolutes for consistently judging the ethical correctness of a company's conduct in various countries and markets.

CORE CONCEPT

The school of **ethical relativism** holds that differing religious beliefs, customs, and behavioral norms across countries and cultures give rise to *multiple sets of standards concerning what is ethically right or wrong.* These differing standards mean that whether business-related actions are right or wrong depends on the prevailing local ethical standards.

This need to contour local ethical standards to fit local customs, local notions of fair and proper individual treatment, and local business practices gives rise to multiple sets of ethical standards. It also poses some challenging ethical dilemmas. Consider the following two examples.

Under ethical relativism, there can be no one-size-fits-all set of authentic ethical norms against which to gauge the conduct of company personnel.

The Use of Underage Labor In industrialized nations, the use of underage workers is considered taboo. Social activists are adamant that child labor is unethical and that companies should neither employ children under the age of 18 as full-time employees nor source any products from foreign suppliers that employ underage workers. Many countries have passed legislation forbidding the use of underage labor or, at a minimum, regulating the employment of people under the age of 18. However, in Ethiopia, Zimbabwe, Pakistan, Afghanistan, Somalia, Burma, North Korea, and more than 50 other countries, it is customary to view children as potential, even necessary, workers. In other countries, like China, India, Russia, and Brazil, child labor laws are often poorly enforced.[5] As of 2012, the International Labor Organization estimated that there were about 215 million child laborers age 5 to 17 and that some 115 million of them were engaged in hazardous work.[6]

While exposing children to hazardous work and long work hours is unquestionably deplorable, the fact remains that poverty-stricken families in many poor countries cannot subsist without the work efforts of young family members; sending their children to school instead of having them work is not a realistic option. If such children are not permitted to work (especially those in the 12-to-17 age group)—due to pressures imposed by activist groups in industrialized nations—they may be forced to go out on the streets begging or to seek work in parts of the "underground" economy such as drug trafficking and prostitution.[7] So, if all businesses in countries where employing underage workers is common succumb to the pressures to stop employing underage labor, then have they served the best interests of the underage workers, their families, and society in general? Illustration Capsule 9.1 describes IKEA's approach to dealing with this issue regarding its global supplier network.

The Payment of Bribes and Kickbacks A particularly thorny area facing multinational companies is the degree of cross-country variability in paying bribes.[8] In many countries in eastern Europe, Africa, Latin America, and Asia, it is customary to pay bribes to government officials in order to win a government contract, obtain a license or permit, or facilitate an administrative ruling.[9] In some developing nations, it is difficult for any company, foreign or domestic, to move goods through customs without paying off low-level officials. Senior managers in China and Russia often use their power to obtain kickbacks when they purchase materials or other products for their companies.[10] Likewise, in many countries it is normal to make payments to prospective customers in order to win or retain their business. Some people stretch to justify the payment of bribes and kickbacks on grounds that bribing government officials to get goods through customs or giving kickbacks to customers to retain their business or win new orders is simply a payment for services rendered, in the same way that people tip for service at restaurants.[11] But while this is a clever rationalization, it rests on moral quicksand.

Companies that forbid the payment of bribes and kickbacks in their codes of ethical conduct and that are serious about enforcing this prohibition face a particularly vexing problem in countries where bribery and kickback payments are an entrenched local custom. Complying with the company's code of ethical conduct in these countries is very often tantamount to losing business to competitors that have no such scruples—an outcome that penalizes ethical companies and ethical company personnel (who may suffer lost sales commissions or bonuses). On the other hand, the payment of bribes or kickbacks not only undercuts the company's code of ethics but also risks breaking the law. The Foreign Corrupt Practices Act (FCPA) prohibits U.S. companies from paying bribes to government officials, political parties, political candidates, or others in all countries where they do business. The Organization for Economic Cooperation and Development (OECD) has antibribery standards that criminalize the bribery of foreign public officials in international business transactions—all 34 OECD member countries and 6 nonmember countries have adopted these standards.

Despite laws forbidding bribery to secure sales and contracts, the practice persists. As of December 2012, 221 individuals and 90 entities were sanctioned under criminal proceedings for foreign bribery by the OECD. At least 83 of the sanctioned individuals were sentenced to prison. In 2014, Alcoa agreed to pay $384 million to settle charges brought by the Justice Department and the Securities and Exchange Commission (SEC) that it used bribes to lock in lucrative contracts in Bahrain. French oil giant Total settled criminal charges for $398 million the prior year for similar behavior in Iran. Other well-known companies caught up in recent or ongoing bribery cases include Archer Daniels Midland, the global agribusiness trader; Swiss oil-field services firm Weatherford; Avon; and Walmart. In 2013, the Ralph Lauren Corporation struck a nonprosecution agreement with the SEC to forfeit illicit profits made due to bribes paid by a subsidiary in Argentina. When the parent company found the problem, it immediately reported it

ILLUSTRATION CAPSULE 9.1

IKEA's Global Supplier Standards: Maintaining Low Costs While Fighting the Root Causes of Child Labor

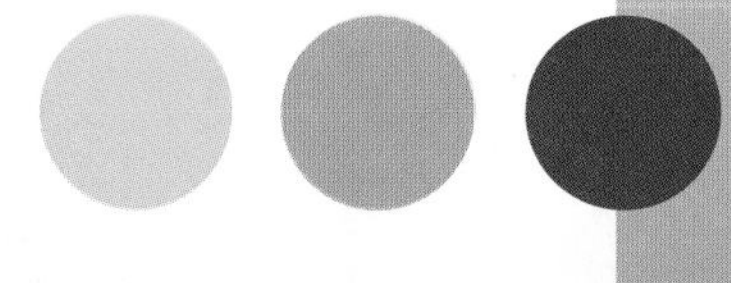

Known for its stylish ready-to-assemble home furnishings, IKEA has long relied on an extensive supplier network to manufacture its products and support its rapid global expansion. It has worked hard to develop a successful approach to encourage high ethical standards among its suppliers, including standards concerning the notoriously difficult issue of child labor.

IKEA's initial plan to combat the use of child labor by its suppliers involved (1) contracts that threatened immediate cancellation and (2) random audits by a third-party partner. Despite these safeguards, the company discovered that some of its Indian suppliers were still employing children. IKEA realized that this issue would crop up again and again if it continued to use low-cost suppliers in developing countries—a critical element in its cost-containment strategy.

To address this problem, IKEA developed and introduced its new code for suppliers, IWAY, that addresses social, safety, and environmental issues across its purchasing model. When faced with a supplier slip-up, IKEA works with the company to figure out and tackle the root cause of violations. Using child labor, for example, can signal bigger problems: production inefficiencies that require the lowest-cost labor, lack of alternative options for children like school or supervised community centers, family health or income challenges that mean children need to become breadwinners, and so on. IKEA takes action to provide technical expertise to improve working conditions and processes, offer financing help at reasonable rates, run training programs onsite, and help develop resources and infrastructure in areas where its suppliers are based. The IKEA foundation also began focusing on these issues through partnerships with UNICEF and Save the Children aimed at funding long-term community programs that support access to education, health care, and sustainable family incomes. It expects the programs will reach 15 million children by 2017.

IKEA's proactive approach has reduced some of the risks involved in relying on suppliers in developing countries. Through its approach, IKEA has been able to maintain its core strategic principles even when they seem to be at odds: low costs, great design, adherence to its ethical principles, and a commitment to a better world.

Note: Developed with Kiera O'Brien.

Sources: IKEA, "About the Company: This is IKEA," www.ikea.com/ms/en_US/this-is-ikea/people-and-planet/people-and-communities/ (accessed January 24, 2014); and Elain Cohen, "Banning Child Labor: The Symptom or the Cause?" *CSR Newswire,* www.csrwire.com/blog/posts/547-banning-child-labor-the-symptom-or-the-cause (accessed January 24, 2014).

---

to the SEC and provided substantial assistance with the investigation. The company paid only $882,000 in penalties (above the forfeited profits) as a result.

> Codes of conduct based on ethical relativism can be *ethically problematic* for multinational companies by creating a maze of conflicting ethical standards.

Using the Principle of Ethical Relativism to Create Ethical Standards Is Problematic for Multinational Companies Relying upon the principle of ethical relativism to determine what is right or wrong poses major problems for multinational companies trying to decide which ethical standards to enforce companywide. It is a slippery slope indeed to resolve such ethical diversity without any kind of higher-order moral compass. Consider, for example, the ethical inconsistency of a multinational company that, in the name of ethical relativism, declares it impermissible to engage in kickbacks unless such payments are customary and generally overlooked by legal authorities. It is likewise problematic for a multinational company to declare it ethically acceptable to use underage labor at its plants in those countries where child labor is allowed but ethically inappropriate to employ underage labor at its plants elsewhere. If a country's culture is accepting of environmental degradation or practices that expose workers to dangerous conditions (toxic chemicals or bodily harm), should a multinational company lower its ethical bar in that country but rule the very same actions to be ethically wrong in other countries?

Business leaders who rely upon the principle of ethical relativism to justify conflicting ethical standards for operating in different countries have little moral basis for establishing or enforcing ethical standards companywide. Rather, when a company's ethical standards vary from country to country, the clear message being sent to employees is that the company has no ethical standards or convictions of its own and prefers to let its standards of ethical right and wrong be governed by the customs and practices of the countries in which it operates. Applying multiple sets of ethical standards without some kind of higher-order moral compass is scarcely a basis for holding company personnel to high standards of ethical behavior. And it can lead to prosecutions of both companies and individuals alike when there are conflicting sets of laws.

Ethics and Integrative Social Contracts Theory

CORE CONCEPT

According to **integrated social contracts theory,** universal ethical principles based on the collective views of multiple societies form a "social contract" that all individuals and organizations have a duty to observe in all situations. *Within the boundaries of this social contract,* local cultures or groups can specify what *additional* actions may or may not be ethically permissible.

Integrative social contracts theory provides a middle position between the opposing views of ethical universalism and ethical relativism.[12] According to this theory, the ethical standards a company should try to uphold are governed by both (1) a limited number of universal ethical principles that are widely recognized as putting legitimate ethical boundaries on behaviors in *all* situations and (2) the circumstances of local cultures, traditions, and values that further prescribe what constitutes ethically permissible behavior. The universal ethical principles are based on the collective views of multiple cultures and societies and combine to form a "social contract" that all individuals, groups, organizations, and businesses in all situations have a duty to observe. *Within the boundaries of this social contract,* local cultures or groups can specify what *other* actions may or may not be ethically permissible. While this system leaves some "moral free space" for the people in a particular country (or local culture, or profession, or even a company) to make specific interpretations of what other actions may or may not be permissible, *universal ethical norms always take precedence.* Thus, local ethical standards can be *more* stringent than the universal ethical standards but *never less so.* For example, both the legal and medical professions have standards regarding what kinds of advertising are ethically permissible that extend beyond the universal norm that advertising not be false or misleading.

According to integrated social contracts theory, adherence to universal or "first-order" ethical norms should always take precedence over local or "second-order" norms.

The strength of integrated social contracts theory is that it accommodates the best parts of ethical universalism and ethical relativism. Moreover, integrative social contracts theory offers managers in multinational companies clear guidance in resolving cross-country ethical differences: Those parts of the company's code of ethics that involve universal ethical norms must be enforced worldwide, but within these boundaries there is room for ethical diversity and the opportunity for host-country cultures to exert *some* influence over the moral and ethical standards of business units operating in that country.

A good example of the application of integrative social contracts theory to business involves the payment of bribes and kickbacks. Yes, bribes and kickbacks seem to be common in some countries. But the fact that bribery flourishes in a country does not mean it is an authentic or legitimate ethical norm. Virtually all of the world's major religions (e.g., Buddhism, Christianity, Confucianism, Hinduism, Islam, Judaism, Sikhism, and Taoism) and all moral schools of thought condemn bribery and corruption. Therefore, a multinational company might reasonably conclude that there is a universal ethical principle to be observed in this case—one of refusing to condone bribery and kickbacks on the part of company personnel no matter what the local custom is and no matter what the sales consequences are.

In instances involving *universally applicable* ethical norms (like paying bribes), there can be *no compromise* on what is ethically permissible and what is not.

HOW AND WHY ETHICAL STANDARDS IMPACT THE TASKS OF CRAFTING AND EXECUTING STRATEGY

Many companies have acknowledged their ethical obligations in official codes of ethical conduct. In the United States, for example, the Sarbanes–Oxley Act, passed in 2002, requires that companies whose stock is publicly traded have a code of ethics or else explain in writing to the SEC why they do not. But there's a big difference between having a code of ethics because it is mandated and having ethical standards that truly provide guidance for a company's strategy and business conduct.[13] *The litmus test of whether a company's code of ethics is cosmetic is the extent to which it is embraced in crafting strategy and in operating the business day to day.*

It is up to senior executives to lead the way on compliance with the company's ethical code of conduct. They can do so by making it a point to consider three sets of questions whenever a new strategic initiative is under review:

- Is what we are proposing to do fully compliant with our code of ethical conduct? Are there any areas of ambiguity that may be of concern?
- Is it apparent that this proposed action is in harmony with our code? Are any conflicts or potential problems evident?
- Is there anything in the proposed action that could be considered ethically objectionable? Would our customers, employees, suppliers, stockholders, competitors, communities, the SEC, or the media view this action as ethically objectionable?

Unless questions of this nature are posed—either in open discussion or by force of habit in the minds of strategy makers—there's a risk that strategic initiatives will become disconnected from the company's code of ethics. If a company's executives believe strongly in living up to the company's ethical standards, they will unhesitatingly reject strategic initiatives and operating approaches that don't measure up. However, in companies with a cosmetic approach to ethics, any strategy–ethics linkage stems mainly from a desire to avoid the risk of embarrassment and possible disciplinary action for approving a strategic initiative that is deemed by society to be unethical and perhaps illegal.

While most company managers are careful to ensure that a company's strategy is within the bounds of what is *legal,* evidence indicates they are not always so careful to ensure that all elements of their strategies and operating activities are within the bounds of what is considered *ethical.* In recent years, there have been revelations of ethical misconduct on the part of managers at such companies as Koch Industries,

LO 2

What drives unethical business strategies and behavior.

casino giant Las Vegas Sands, Hewlett-Packard, GlaxoSmithKline, Marathon Oil Corporation, Kraft Foods Inc., Motorola Solutions, Pfizer, Oracle Corporation, several leading investment banking firms, and a host of mortgage lenders. The consequences of crafting strategies that cannot pass the test of moral scrutiny are manifested in sizable fines, devastating public relations hits, sharp drops in stock prices that cost shareholders billions of dollars, criminal indictments, and convictions of company executives. The fallout from all these scandals has resulted in heightened management attention to legal and ethical considerations in crafting strategy.

DRIVERS OF UNETHICAL BUSINESS STRATEGIES AND BEHAVIOR

Apart from the "business of business is business, not ethics" kind of thinking apparent in recent high-profile business scandals, three other main drivers of unethical business behavior also stand out:[14]

- Faulty oversight, enabling the unscrupulous pursuit of personal gain and self-interest.
- Heavy pressures on company managers to meet or beat short-term performance targets.
- A company culture that puts profitability and business performance ahead of ethical behavior.

Faulty Oversight, Enabling the Unscrupulous Pursuit of Personal Gain and Self-Interest People who are obsessed with wealth accumulation, power, status, and their own self-interest often push ethical principles aside in their quest for personal gain. Driven by greed and ambition, they exhibit few qualms in skirting the rules or doing whatever is necessary to achieve their goals. A general disregard for business ethics can prompt all kinds of unethical strategic maneuvers and behaviors at companies.

The U.S. government has been conducting a multiyear investigation of insider trading, the illegal practice of exchanging confidential information to gain an advantage in the stock market. Focusing on the hedge fund industry and nicknamed "Operation Perfect Hedge," the investigation has brought to light scores of violations and led to at least 79 guilty pleas or convictions by early 2014. Among the most prominent of those convicted was Raj Rajaratnam, the former head of Galleon Group, who was sentenced to 11 years in prison and fined $10 million. At SAC Capital, a $14 billion hedge fund, eight hedge fund managers were convicted of insider trading, in what has been called the most lucrative insider trading scheme in U.S. history. The company has agreed to pay $1.8 billion in penalties and has been forced to stop managing money for outside investors.[15] Since Operation Perfect Hedge began, abnormal jumps in the stock price of target firms (a sign of insider trading) have fallen 45 percent.

CORE CONCEPT

Self-dealing occurs when managers take advantage of their position to further their own private interests rather than those of the firm.

Responsible corporate governance and oversight by the company's corporate board is necessary to guard against self-dealing and the manipulation of information to disguise such actions by a company's managers. **Self-dealing** occurs when managers take advantage of their position to further their own private interests rather than those of the firm. As discussed in Chapter 2, the duty of the corporate board (and its compensation and audit committees in particular) is to guard against such actions. A strong, independent board is necessary to have proper oversight of the company's financial practices and to hold top managers accountable for their actions.

A particularly egregious example of the lack of proper oversight is the scandal over mortgage lending and banking practices that resulted in a crisis for the U.S. residential real estate market and heartrending consequences for many home buyers. This scandal stemmed from consciously unethical strategies at many banks and mortgage companies to boost the fees they earned on home mortgages by deliberately lowering lending standards to approve so-called subprime loans for home buyers whose incomes were insufficient to make their monthly mortgage payments. Once these lenders earned their fees on these loans, they repackaged the loans to hide their true nature and auctioned them off to unsuspecting investors, who later suffered huge losses when the high-risk borrowers began to default on their loan payments. (Government authorities later forced some of the firms that auctioned off these packaged loans to repurchase them at the auction price and bear the losses themselves.) A lawsuit by the attorneys general of 49 states charging widespread and systematic fraud ultimately resulted in a $26 billion settlement by the five largest U.S. banks (Bank of America, Citigroup, JPMorgan Chase, Wells Fargo, and Ally Financial). Included in the settlement were new rules designed to increase oversight and reform policies and practices among the mortgage companies. The settlement includes what are believed to be a set of robust monitoring and enforcement mechanisms that should help prevent such abuses in the future.[16]

Heavy Pressures on Company Managers to Meet Short-Term Performance Targets When key personnel find themselves scrambling to meet the quarterly and annual sales and profit expectations of investors and financial analysts, they often feel enormous pressure to *do whatever it takes* to protect their reputation for delivering good results. Executives at high-performing companies know that investors will see the slightest sign of a slowdown in earnings growth as a red flag and drive down the company's stock price. In addition, slowing growth or declining profits could lead to a downgrade of the company's credit rating if it has used lots of debt to finance its growth. The pressure to "never miss a quarter"—so as not to upset the expectations of analysts, investors, and creditors—prompts nearsighted managers to engage in short-term maneuvers to make the numbers, regardless of whether these moves are really in the best long-term interests of the company. Sometimes the pressure induces company personnel to continue to stretch the rules until the limits of ethical conduct are overlooked.[17] Once ethical boundaries are crossed in efforts to "meet or beat their numbers," the threshold for making more extreme ethical compromises becomes lower.

In 2014, the SEC charged Diamond Foods (maker of Pop Secret and Emerald Nuts) with accounting fraud, alleging that the company falsified costs in order to boost earnings and stock prices. The company has agreed to pay $5 million to settle SEC fraud charges, while its (now ousted) CEO must pay $125,000 to settle a separate charge of negligence and return $4 million in bonuses to the company. Litigation continues against its now former CFO. The real blow for the company was that its pending acquisition of potato chip giant Pringles fell apart as a result of the scandal, thwarting the company's dreams of becoming the second-largest snack company in the world.[18]

Company executives often feel pressured to hit financial performance targets because their compensation depends heavily on the company's performance. Over the last two decades, it has become fashionable for boards of directors to grant lavish bonuses, stock option awards, and other compensation benefits to executives for

CORE CONCEPT

Short-termism is the tendency for managers to focus excessively on short-term performance objectives at the expense of longer-term strategic objectives. It has negative implications for the likelihood of ethical lapses as well as company performance in the longer run.

meeting specified performance targets. So outlandishly large were these rewards that executives had strong personal incentives to bend the rules and engage in behaviors that allowed the targets to be met. Much of the accounting manipulation at the root of recent corporate scandals has entailed situations in which executives benefited enormously from misleading accounting or other shady activities that allowed them to hit the numbers and receive incentive awards ranging from $10 million to more than $1 billion for hedge fund managers.

The fundamental problem with **short-termism**—the tendency for managers to focus excessive attention on short-term performance objectives—is that it doesn't create value for customers or improve the firm's competitiveness in the marketplace; that is, it sacrifices the activities that are the most reliable drivers of higher profits and added shareholder value in the long run. Cutting ethical corners in the name of profits carries exceptionally high risk for shareholders—the steep stock price decline and tarnished brand image that accompany the discovery of scurrilous behavior leave shareholders with a company worth much less than before—and the rebuilding task can be arduous, taking both considerable time and resources.

A Company Culture That Puts Profitability and Business Performance Ahead of Ethical Behavior When a company's culture spawns an ethically corrupt or amoral work climate, people have a company-approved license to ignore "what's right" and engage in any behavior or strategy they think they can get away with. Such cultural norms as "Everyone else does it" and "It is okay to bend the rules to get the job done" permeate the work environment. At such companies, ethically immoral people are certain to play down observance of ethical strategic actions and business conduct. Moreover, cultural pressures to utilize unethical means if circumstances become challenging can prompt otherwise honorable people to behave unethically. A perfect example of a company culture gone awry on ethics is Enron, a now-defunct but infamous company found guilty of one of the most sprawling business frauds in U.S. history.[19]

Enron's leaders encouraged company personnel to focus on the current bottom line and to be innovative and aggressive in figuring out how to grow current earnings—regardless of the methods. Enron's annual "rank and yank" performance evaluation process, in which the lowest-ranking 15 to 20 percent of employees were let go, made it abundantly clear that bottom-line results were what mattered most. The name of the game at Enron became devising clever ways to boost revenues and earnings, even if this sometimes meant operating outside established policies. In fact, outside-the-lines behavior was celebrated if it generated profitable new business.

A high-performance–high-rewards climate came to pervade the Enron culture, as the best workers (determined by who produced the best bottom-line results) received impressively large incentives and bonuses. On Car Day at Enron, an array of luxury sports cars arrived for presentation to the most successful employees. Understandably, employees wanted to be seen as part of Enron's star team and partake in the benefits granted to Enron's best and brightest employees. The high monetary rewards, the ambitious and hard-driving people whom the company hired and promoted, and the competitive, results-oriented culture combined to give Enron a reputation not only for trampling competitors but also for internal ruthlessness. The company's win-at-all-costs mindset nurtured a culture that gradually and then more rapidly fostered the erosion of ethical standards, eventually making a mockery of the company's stated values of integrity and respect. When it became evident in fall 2001 that Enron was a house of cards propped up by deceitful accounting and myriad unsavory practices, the company imploded in a matter of weeks—one of the biggest bankruptcies of all time, costing investors $64 billion in losses.

In contrast, when high ethical principles are deeply ingrained in the corporate culture of a company, culture can function as a powerful mechanism for communicating ethical behavioral norms and gaining employee buy-in to the company's moral standards, business principles, and corporate values. In such cases, the ethical principles embraced in the company's code of ethics and/or in its statement of corporate values are seen as integral to the company's identity, self-image, and ways of operating. The message that ethics matters—and matters a lot—resounds loudly and clearly throughout the organization and in its strategy and decisions. Illustration Capsule 9.2 discusses Novo Nordisk's approach to building an ethical culture and putting its ethical principles into practice.

WHY SHOULD COMPANY STRATEGIES BE ETHICAL?

There are two reasons why a company's strategy should be ethical: (1) because a strategy that is unethical is morally wrong and reflects badly on the character of the company and its personnel, and (2) because an ethical strategy can be good business and serve the self-interest of shareholders.

The Moral Case for an Ethical Strategy

Managers do not dispassionately assess what strategic course to steer—how strongly committed they are to observing ethical principles and standards definitely comes into play in making strategic choices. Ethical strategy making is generally the product of managers who are of strong moral character (i.e., who are trustworthy, have integrity, and truly care about conducting the company's business honorably). Managers with high ethical principles are usually advocates of a corporate code of ethics and strong ethics compliance, and they are genuinely committed to upholding corporate values and ethical business principles. They demonstrate their commitment by displaying the company's stated values and living up to its business principles and ethical standards. They understand the difference between merely adopting value statements and codes of ethics and ensuring that they are followed strictly in a company's actual strategy and business conduct. As a consequence, ethically strong managers consciously opt for strategic actions that can pass the strictest moral scrutiny—they display no tolerance for strategies with ethically controversial components.

LO 3

The costs of business ethics failures.

The Business Case for Ethical Strategies

In addition to the moral reasons for adopting ethical strategies, there may be solid business reasons. Pursuing unethical strategies and tolerating unethical conduct not only damages a company's reputation but also may result in a wide-ranging set of other costly consequences. Figure 9.1 shows the kinds of costs a company can incur when unethical behavior on its part is discovered, the wrongdoings of company personnel are headlined in the media, and it is forced to make amends for its behavior. The more egregious are a company's ethical violations, the higher the costs and the bigger the damage to its reputation (and to the reputations of the company personnel involved). In high-profile instances, the costs of ethical misconduct can easily run into

ILLUSTRATION CAPSULE 9.2

How Novo Nordisk Puts Its Ethical Principles into Practice

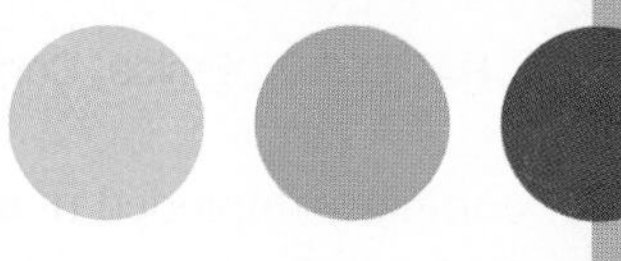

Novo Nordisk is a $13.8 billion global pharmaceutical company, known for its innovation and leadership in diabetes treatments. It is also known for its dedication to ethical business practices. In 2012, the company was listed as the global leader in business ethics by *Corporate Knights,* a corporate social responsibility advisory firm.

Novo Nordisk's company policies are explicit in their attention to both bioethics and business ethics. In the realm of bioethics, the company is committed to conducting its research involving people, animals, and gene technology in accordance with the highest global ethical standards. Moreover, the company requires that all of its suppliers and other external partners also adhere to Novo Nordisk's bioethical standards. In the realm of business ethics, the policies dictate (1) that high ethical standards be applied consistently across the company's value chain, (2) that all ethical dilemmas encountered be addressed transparently, and (3) that company officers and employees be held accountable for complying with all laws, regulations, and company rules.

Novo Nordisk's strong culture of responsibility helps to translate the company's policies into practice. At Novo Nordisk, every employee pledges to conduct himself or herself according to the Novo Nordisk Way, a set of behavioral norms that has come to define the company's culture. It's a culture that promotes teamwork, cooperation, respect for others, and fairness. The commitment to business ethics grew out of those values, which are promoted throughout the company by hiring practices, management leadership, and employee mobility to foster a global one-company culture.

As part of this process, Novo Nordisk has set up a business ethics board, composed of senior management. The board identifies key ethical challenges for the company, drafting guidelines and developing training programs. The training programs are rigorous: All Novo Nordisk employees are trained annually in business ethics. The board is also responsible for ensuring compliance. It has set up an anonymous hotline and conducts ethics audits. During 2012, 48 audits were conducted. The goal of the audits is to maintain a culture that promotes the principles of the Novo Nordisk Way.

Implementing a code of ethics across an organization of 26,000 employees is very difficult and lapses do occur. But such incidents are exceptional and are swiftly addressed by the company. For example, when insider trading allegations came to light against a corporate executive in 2008, the company immediately suspended and subsequently fired the employee.

Note: Developed with Dennis L. Huggins.

Sources: J. Edwards, "Novo Nordisk Exec Charged with Insider Trading; Cash Stashed in Caribbean," *CBS News,* September 2008, www.cbsnews.com (accessed February 19, 2012); company filings and website (accessed April 1, 2014); and Corporate Knights, "The 8th Annual Global 100," global100.org/ (accessed February 20, 2012).

FIGURE 9.1 The Costs Companies Incur When Ethical Wrongdoing Is Discovered

Visible Costs	Internal Administrative Costs	Intangible or Less Visible Costs
• Government fines and penalties • Civil penalties arising from class-action lawsuits and other litigation aimed at punishing the company for its offense and the harm done to others • The costs to shareholders in the form of a lower stock price (and possibly lower dividends)	• Legal and investigative costs incurred by the company • The costs of providing remedial education and ethics training to company personnel • The costs of taking corrective actions • Administrative costs associated with ensuring future compliance	• Customer defections • Loss of reputation • Lost employee morale and higher degrees of employee cynicism • Higher employee turnover • Higher recruiting costs and difficulty in attracting talented employees • Adverse effects on employee productivity • The costs of complying with often harsher government regulations

Source: Adapted from Terry Thomas, John R. Schermerhorn, and John W. Dienhart, "Strategic Leadership of Ethical Behavior," *Academy of Management Executive* 18, no. 2 (May 2004), p. 58.

the hundreds of millions and even billions of dollars, especially if they provoke widespread public outrage and many people were harmed. The penalties levied on executives caught in wrongdoing can skyrocket as well, as the 150-year prison term sentence of infamous financier and Ponzi scheme perpetrator Bernie Madoff illustrates.

Conducting business in an ethical fashion is not only morally right—it is in a company's enlightened self-interest.

The fallout of a company's ethical misconduct goes well beyond the costs of making amends for the misdeeds. Customers shun companies caught up in highly publicized ethical scandals. Rehabilitating a company's shattered reputation is time-consuming and costly. Companies known to have engaged in unethical conduct have difficulty in recruiting and retaining talented employees. Most ethically upstanding people are repulsed by a work environment where unethical behavior is condoned; they don't want to get entrapped in a compromising situation, nor do they want their personal reputations tarnished by the actions of an unsavory employer. Creditors are unnerved by the unethical actions of a borrower because of the potential business fallout and subsequent risk of default on loans.

Shareholders suffer major damage when a company's unethical behavior is discovered. Making amends for unethical business conduct is costly, and it takes years to rehabilitate a tarnished company reputation.

All told, a company's unethical behavior risks doing considerable damage to shareholders in the form of lost revenues, higher costs, lower profits, lower stock prices, and a diminished business reputation. To a significant degree, therefore, ethical strategies and ethical conduct are *good business.* Most companies understand the value of operating in a manner that wins the approval of suppliers, employees, investors, and society at large. Most businesspeople recognize the risks and adverse fallout attached to the discovery of unethical behavior. Hence, companies have an incentive to employ strategies that can pass the test of being ethical. Even if a company's managers are not personally committed to high ethical standards, they have good reason to operate within ethical bounds, if only to (1) avoid the risk of embarrassment, scandal, disciplinary action, fines, and possible jail time for unethical conduct on their part and (2) escape being held accountable for lax enforcement of ethical standards and unethical behavior by personnel under their supervision.

STRATEGY, CORPORATE SOCIAL RESPONSIBILITY, AND ENVIRONMENTAL SUSTAINABILITY

LO 4

The concepts of corporate social responsibility and environmental sustainability and how companies balance these duties with economic responsibilities to shareholders.

The idea that businesses have an obligation to foster social betterment, a much-debated topic over the past 50 years, took root in the 19th century when progressive companies in the aftermath of the industrial revolution began to provide workers with housing and other amenities. The notion that corporate executives should balance the interests of all stakeholders—shareholders, employees, customers, suppliers, the communities in which they operate, and society at large—began to blossom in the 1960s. Some years later, a group of chief executives of America's 200 largest corporations, calling themselves the Business Roundtable, came out in strong support of the concept of **corporate social responsibility (CSR):**

> Balancing the shareholder's expectations of maximum return against other priorities is one of the fundamental problems confronting corporate management. The shareholder must receive a good return but the legitimate concerns of other constituencies (customers, employees, communities, suppliers and society at large) also must have the appropriate attention. . . . [Leading managers] believe that by giving enlightened consideration to balancing the legitimate claims of all its constituents, a corporation will best serve the interest of its shareholders.

CORE CONCEPT

Corporate social responsibility (CSR) refers to a company's *duty* to operate in an honorable manner, provide good working conditions for employees, encourage workforce diversity, be a good steward of the environment, and actively work to better the quality of life in the local communities where it operates and in society at large.

Today, corporate social responsibility is a concept that resonates in western Europe, the United States, Canada, and such developing nations as Brazil and India.

The Concepts of Corporate Social Responsibility and Good Corporate Citizenship

The essence of socially responsible business behavior is that a company should balance strategic actions to benefit shareholders against the *duty* to be a good corporate citizen. The underlying thesis is that company managers should display a *social conscience* in operating the business and specifically take into account how management decisions and company actions affect the well-being of employees, local communities, the environment, and society at large.[20] Acting in a socially responsible manner thus encompasses more than just participating in community service projects and donating money to charities and other worthy causes. Demonstrating social responsibility also entails undertaking actions that earn trust and respect from all stakeholders—operating in an honorable and ethical manner, striving to make the company a great place to work, demonstrating genuine respect for the environment, and trying to make a difference in bettering society. As depicted in Figure 9.2, corporate responsibility programs commonly include the following elements:

- *Striving to employ an ethical strategy and observe ethical principles in operating the business.* A sincere commitment to observing ethical principles is a necessary

FIGURE 9.2 The Five Components of a Corporate Social Responsibility Strategy

Source: Adapted from material in Ronald Paul Hill, Debra Stephens, and Iain Smith, "Corporate Social Responsibility: An Examination of Individual Firm Behavior," *Business and Society Review* 108, no. 3 (September 2003), p. 348.

component of a CSR strategy simply because unethical conduct is incompatible with the concept of good corporate citizenship and socially responsible business behavior.

- *Making charitable contributions, supporting community service endeavors, engaging in broader philanthropic initiatives, and reaching out to make a difference in the lives of the disadvantaged.* Some companies fulfill their philanthropic obligations by spreading their efforts over a multitude of charitable and community activities—for instance, Wells Fargo and Google support a broad variety of community, art, and social welfare programs. Others prefer to focus their energies more narrowly. McDonald's, for example, concentrates on sponsoring the Ronald McDonald House program (which provides a home away from home for the families of seriously ill children receiving treatment at nearby hospitals). British Telecom gives 1 percent of its profits directly to communities, largely for education—teacher training, in-school workshops, and digital technology. Leading prescription drug maker GlaxoSmithKline and other pharmaceutical companies either donate or heavily discount medicines for distribution in the least developed nations. Companies frequently reinforce their philanthropic efforts by encouraging employees to support charitable causes and participate in community affairs, often through programs that match employee contributions.

- *Taking actions to protect the environment and, in particular, to minimize or eliminate any adverse impact on the environment stemming from the company's own business activities.* Corporate social responsibility as it applies to environmental protection entails actively striving to be a good steward of the environment. This means using the best available science and technology to reduce environmentally harmful aspects of the company's operations *below the levels required by prevailing environmental regulations.* It also means putting time and money into improving the environment in ways that extend beyond a company's own industry boundaries—such as participating in recycling projects, adopting energy conservation practices, and supporting efforts to clean up local water supplies. Retailers like Walmart and Home Depot in the United States and B&Q in the United Kingdom have pressured their suppliers to adopt stronger environmental protection practices in order to lower the carbon footprint of their entire supply chains.
- *Creating a work environment that enhances the quality of life for employees.* Numerous companies exert extra effort to enhance the quality of life for their employees at work and at home. This can include onsite day care, flexible work schedules, workplace exercise facilities, special leaves for employees to care for sick family members, work-at-home opportunities, career development programs and education opportunities, special safety programs, and the like.
- *Building a diverse workforce with respect to gender, race, national origin, and other aspects that different people bring to the workplace.* Most large companies in the United States have established workforce diversity programs, and some go the extra mile to ensure that their workplaces are attractive to ethnic minorities and inclusive of all groups and perspectives. At some companies, the diversity initiative extends to suppliers—sourcing items from small businesses owned by women or members of ethnic minorities, for example. The pursuit of workforce diversity can also be good business. At Coca-Cola, where strategic success depends on getting people all over the world to become loyal consumers of the company's beverages, efforts to build a public persona of inclusiveness for people of all races, religions, nationalities, interests, and talents have considerable strategic value.

The particular combination of socially responsible endeavors a company elects to pursue defines its **corporate social responsibility strategy.** Illustration Capsule 9.3 describes Burt's Bees' approach to corporate social responsibility—an approach that ensures that social responsibility is reflected in all of the company's actions and endeavors. As the Burt's Bees example shows, the specific components emphasized in a CSR strategy vary from company to company and are typically linked to a company's core values. General Mills, for example, centers its CSR strategy around three themes: nourishing lives (via healthier and easier-to-prepare foods), nourishing communities (via charitable donations to community causes and volunteerism for community service projects), and nourishing the environment (via efforts to conserve natural resources, reduce energy and water usage, promote recycling, and otherwise support environmental sustainability).[21] Starbucks's CSR strategy includes four main elements (ethical sourcing, community service, environmental

CORE CONCEPT

A company's **CSR strategy** is defined by the specific combination of socially beneficial activities the company opts to support with its contributions of time, money, and other resources.

ILLUSTRATION CAPSULE 9.3

Burt's Bees: A Strategy Based on Corporate Social Responsibility

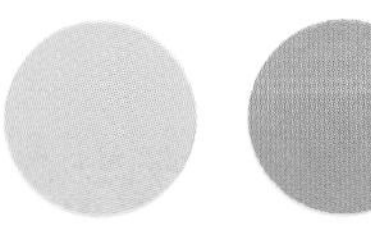
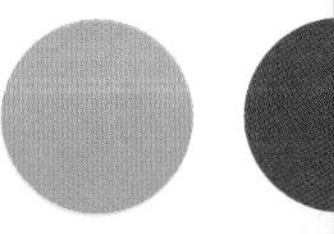

Burt's Bees is a leading company in natural personal care, offering nearly 200 products including its popular beeswax lip balms and skin care creams. The brand has enjoyed tremendous success as consumers have begun to embrace all-natural, environmentally friendly products, boosting Burt's Bees' revenues to over $250 million by 2012. Much of Burt's Bees' success can be attributed to its skillful use of corporate social responsibility (CSR) as a strategic tool to engage customers and differentiate itself from competitors.

While many companies have embraced corporate social responsibility, few companies have managed to integrate CSR as fully and seamlessly throughout their organizations as has Burt's Bees. The company's business model is centered on a principle Burt's Bees refers to as "The Greater Good," which specifies that all company practices must be socially responsible. The execution of this strategy is managed by a special committee dedicated to leading the organization to attain its CSR goals with respect to three primary areas: natural well-being, humanitarian responsibility, and environmental sustainability.

Natural well-being is focused on the ingredients used to create Burt's Bees products. Today, the average Burt's Bees product contains over 99 percent natural ingredients; by 2020, the brand expects to produce only 100 percent natural products.

Burt's Bees' humanitarian focus is centered on its relationships with employees and suppliers. A key part of this effort involves a mandatory employee training program that focuses on four key areas: outreach, wellness, world-class leadership, and the environment. Another is the company's Responsible Sourcing Mission, which lays out a carefully prescribed set of guidelines for sourcing responsible suppliers and managing supplier relationships.

A focus on caring for the environment is clearly interwoven into all aspects of Burt's Bees. By focusing on environmentally efficient processes, the company uses its in-house manufacturing capability as a point of strategic differentiation.

Burt's Bees faced some consumer backlash when it was purchased recently by The Clorox Company, whose traditional image is viewed in sharp contrast to Burt's Bees' values. But while Burt's Bees is still only a small part of Clorox's total revenue, it has become its fastest-growing division.

Note: Developed with Ross M. Templeton.

Sources: Company websites; Louise Story, "Can Burt's Bees Turn Clorox Green?" *The New York Times,* January 6, 2008; Bill Chameides, "Burt's Bees Are Busy on the Sustainability Front," *Huffington Post,* June 25, 2010; Katie Bird, "Burt's Bees' International Performance Weaker than Expected," *Cosmetics Design,* January 6, 2011, CosmeticsDesign.com; "Burt's Bees, Marks & Spencer Share Staff Engagement Tactics," *Environmental Leader,* May 31, 2011, EnvironmentalLeader.com; and blogs.newsobserver.com/ (accessed March 1, 2012).

stewardship, and farmer support), all of which have touch points with the way that the company procures its coffee—a key aspect of its product differentiation strategy. Some companies use other terms, such as *corporate citizenship, corporate responsibility,* or *sustainable responsible business (SRB)* to characterize their CSR initiatives.

Although there is wide variation in how companies devise and implement a CSR strategy, communities of companies concerned with corporate social responsibility (such as CSR Europe) have emerged to help companies share best CSR practices. Moreover, a number of reporting standards have been developed, including ISO 26000—a new internationally recognized standard for social responsibility set by the International Standards Organization (ISO).[22] Companies that exhibit a strong commitment to corporate social responsibility are often recognized by being included on lists such as *Corporate Responsibility* magazine's "100 Best Corporate Citizens" or *Corporate Knights* magazine's "Global 100 Most Sustainable Corporations."

Corporate Social Responsibility and the Triple Bottom Line CSR initiatives undertaken by companies are frequently directed at improving the company's *triple bottom line (TBL)*—a reference to three types of performance metrics: *economic, social,* and *environmental.* The goal is for a company to succeed simultaneously in all three dimensions, as illustrated in Figure 9.3.[23] The three dimensions of performance are often referred to in terms of the "three pillars" of "people, planet, and profit." The term *people* refers to the various social initiatives that make up CSR strategies, such as corporate giving, community involvement, and company efforts to improve the lives of its internal and external stakeholders. *Planet* refers to a firm's ecological impact and environmental practices. The term *profit* has a broader meaning with respect to the triple bottom line than it does otherwise. It encompasses not only the

FIGURE 9.3 The Triple Bottom Line: Excelling on Three Measures of Company Performance

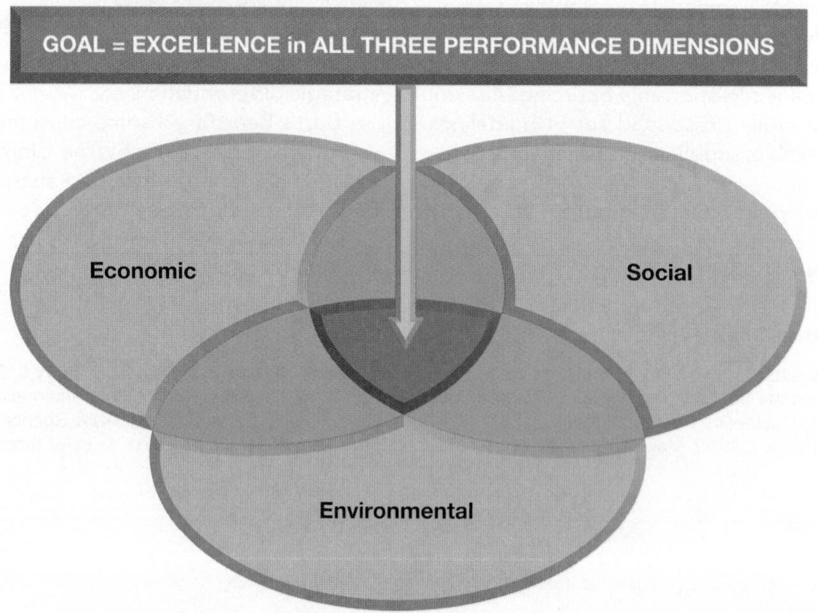

Source: Developed with help from Amy E. Florentino.

ILLUSTRATION CAPSULE 9.4

TOMS's Well-Balanced Triple Bottom Line

Having sold over 2 million pairs of shoes worldwide, self-designated "Chief Shoe Giver" Blake Mycoskie founded TOMS on the principle of "One for One." Operating under the belief that "the way you shop can change the world," TOMS donates a pair of shoes to a child in need in over 50 different countries for every pair purchased. Each pair is made with sustainable materials that include organic canvas and recycled materials that minimize TOMS's ecological footprint. TOMS has been recognized with the Award for Corporate Excellence by the Office of the Secretary of State, while *Fortune* magazine has named Mycoskie to its "40 under 40" list.

Mycoskie credits much of TOMS's growth not to success in traditional avenues of advertising but, rather, to the story behind the TOMS shoe as told by TOMS's customers. By focusing on the story behind its product and the importance of sustainable giving, TOMS generates brand awareness through motivated customers who share their feel-good purchases with friends and family. By utilizing user marketing rather than corporate marketing, TOMS successfully pitches a grassroots company-image and bundles a lifestyle with its product.

TOMS's environmental sustainability approach includes offering a line of vegan shoes, which contain no animal by-products, and maintaining its commitment to use earth and animal-friendly materials whenever possible. Its shoeboxes are made with 80 percent recycled waste and are printed with soy ink. Through these production considerations, TOMS caters to an environmentally conscious demographic with few established competitors and with loyal consumers who have helped TOMS experience sustained growth despite the global recession.

From Shoe Giving Trips to employee training on the importance of environmental sustainability, TOMS aspires to offer its employees "more than a 9-to-5" job. This commitment to a worthwhile cause creates not only happier employees but also more autonomous and creative global citizens who work together to inspire change. By attaining *economic* growth through an emphasis on *social* justice and *environmental* sustainability, TOMS has maintained a well-balanced triple bottom line.

Note: Developed with Sean Zhang.

Source: Keynote statements by Blake Mycoskie and other information posted at www.toms.com.

profit a firm earns for its shareholders but also the economic impact that the company has on society more generally, in terms of the overall value that it creates and the overall costs that it imposes on society. For example, Procter & Gamble's Swiffer cleaning system, one of the company's best-selling products, not only offers an earth-friendly design but also outperforms less ecologically friendly alternatives in terms of its broader economic impact: It reduces demands on municipal water sources, saves electricity that would be needed to heat mop water, and doesn't add to the amount of detergent making its way into waterways and waste treatment facilities. Nike sees itself as bringing people, planet, and profits into balance by producing innovative new products in a more sustainable way, recognizing that sustainability is key to its future profitability. TOMS shoes has built its strategy around maintaining a well-balanced triple bottom line, as explained in Illustration Capsule 9.4.

Many companies now make a point of citing the beneficial outcomes of their CSR strategies in press releases and issue special reports for consumers and investors to review. Staples, the world's largest office products company, makes reporting an important part of its commitment to corporate responsibility; the company posts a "Staples Soul Report" on its website that describes its initiatives and accomplishments in the areas of diversity, environment, community, and ethics. Triple-bottom-line reporting is emerging as an increasingly important way for companies to make the results of their CSR strategies apparent to stakeholders and for stakeholders to hold companies accountable for their impact on society. The use of standard reporting frameworks and metrics, such as those developed by the Global Reporting Initiative, promotes greater transparency and facilitates benchmarking CSR efforts across firms and industries.

Investment firms have created mutual funds consisting of companies that are excelling on the basis of the triple bottom line in order to attract funds from environmentally and socially aware investors. The Dow Jones Sustainability World Index is made up of the top 10 percent of the 2,500 companies listed in the Dow Jones World Index in terms of economic performance, environmental performance, and social performance. Companies are evaluated in these three performance areas, using indicators such as corporate governance, climate change mitigation, and labor practices. Table 9.1 shows a sampling of the companies selected for the Dow Jones Sustainability World Index in 2013.

TABLE 9.1 A Selection of Companies Recognized for Their Triple-Bottom-Line Performance in 2013

Name	Market Sector	Country
Volkswagen AG	Automobiles & Components	Germany
Australia & New Zealand Banking Group Ltd.	Banks	Australia
Siemens AG	Capital Goods	Germany
Adecco SA	Commercial & Professional Services	Switzerland
Panasonic Corp.	Consumer Durables & Apparel	Japan
Tabcorp Holdings Ltd.	Consumer Services	Australia
Citigroup Inc.	Diversified Financials	United States
BG Group PLC	Energy	United Kingdom
Woolworths Ltd.	Food & Staples Retailing	Australia
Nestlé SA	Food, Beverage, & Tobacco	Switzerland
Abbott Laboratories	Health Care Equipment & Services	United States
Henkel AG & Co. KGaA	Household & Personal Products	Germany
Allianz SE	Insurance	Germany
Akzo Nobel NV	Materials	Netherlands
Telenet Group Holding NV	Media	Belgium
Roche Holding AG	Pharmaceuticals, Biotechnology, & Life Sciences	Switzerland
Stockland	Real Estate	Australia

Name	Market Sector	Country
Lotte Shopping Co Ltd.	Retailing	Republic of Korea
Taiwan Semiconductor Manufacturing Co. Ltd.	Semiconductors & Semiconductor Equipment	Taiwan
SAP AG	Software & Services	Germany
Alcatel-Lucent	Technology Hardware & Equipment	France
KT Corp.	Telecommunication Services	Republic of Korea
Air France-KLM	Transportation	France
EDP—Energias de Portugal SA	Utilities	Portugal

Source: Reprinted with permission from RobecoSAM AG. www.sustainability-indices.com/review/industry-group-leaders-2013.jsp (accessed February 7, 2014).

What Do We Mean by *Sustainability* and *Sustainable Business Practices*?

The term *sustainability* is used in a variety of ways. In many firms, it is synonymous with corporate social responsibility; it is seen by some as a term that is gradually replacing CSR in the business lexicon. Indeed, sustainability reporting and TBL reporting are often one and the same, as illustrated by the Dow Jones Sustainability World Index, which tracks the same three types of performance measures that constitute the triple bottom line.

More often, however, the term takes on a more focused meaning, concerned with the relationship of a company to its *environment* and its use of *natural resources,* including land, water, air, plants, animals, minerals, fossil fuels, and biodiversity. It is widely recognized that the world's natural resources are finite and are being consumed and degraded at rates that threaten their capacity for renewal. Since corporations are the biggest users of natural resources, managing and maintaining these resources is critical for the long-term economic interests of corporations.

CORE CONCEPT

Sustainable business practices are those that meet the needs of the present without compromising the ability to meet the needs of the future.

For some companies, this issue has direct and obvious implications for the continued viability of their business model and strategy. Pacific Gas and Electric has begun measuring the full carbon footprint of its supply chain to become not only a "greener" company but a more efficient energy producer.[24] Beverage companies such as Coca-Cola and PepsiCo are having to rethink their business models because of the prospect of future worldwide water shortages. For other companies, the connection is less direct, but all companies are part of a business ecosystem whose economic health depends on the availability of natural resources. In response, most major companies have begun to change *how* they do business, emphasizing the use of **sustainable business practices,** defined as those capable of meeting the needs of the present without compromising the ability to meet the needs of the future. Many have also begun to incorporate a consideration of environmental sustainability into their strategy-making activities.

CORE CONCEPT

A company's **environmental sustainability strategy** consists of its deliberate actions to protect the environment, provide for the longevity of natural resources, maintain ecological support systems for future generations, and guard against ultimate endangerment of the planet.

Environmental sustainability strategies entail deliberate and concerted actions to operate businesses in a manner that protects natural resources and ecological support systems, guards against outcomes that will ultimately endanger the planet, and is therefore sustainable for centuries.[25] One aspect of environmental sustainability is keeping use of the Earth's natural resources within levels that can be replenished via the use of sustainable business practices. In the case of some resources (like crude oil, fresh water, and edible fish from the oceans), scientists say that use levels either are already unsustainable or will be soon, given the world's growing population and propensity to consume additional resources as incomes and living standards rise. Another aspect of sustainability concerns containing the adverse effects of greenhouse gases and other forms of air pollution so as to reduce their impact on undesirable climate and atmospheric changes. Other aspects of sustainability include greater reliance on sustainable energy sources, greater use of recyclable materials, the use of sustainable methods of growing foods (to reduce topsoil depletion and the use of pesticides, herbicides, fertilizers, and other chemicals that may be harmful to human health or ecological systems), habitat protection, environmentally sound waste management practices, and increased attempts to decouple environmental degradation and economic growth (according to scientists, economic growth has historically been accompanied by declines in the well-being of the environment).

Unilever, a diversified producer of processed foods, personal care, and home cleaning products, is among the many committed corporations pursuing sustainable business practices. The company tracks 11 sustainable agricultural indicators in its processed-foods business and has launched a variety of programs to improve the environmental performance of its suppliers. Examples of such programs include special low-rate financing for tomato suppliers choosing to switch to water-conserving irrigation systems and training programs in India that have allowed contract cucumber growers to reduce pesticide use by 90 percent while improving yields by 78 percent. Unilever has also reengineered many internal processes to improve the company's overall performance on sustainability measures. For example, the company's factories have reduced water usage by 63 percent and total waste by 67 percent since 1995 through the implementation of sustainability initiatives. Unilever has also redesigned packaging for many of its products to conserve natural resources and reduce the volume of consumer waste. For example, the company's Suave shampoo bottles were reshaped to save almost 150 tons of plastic resin per year, which is the equivalent of 15 million fewer empty bottles making it to landfills annually. As the producer of Lipton Tea, Unilever is the world's largest purchaser of tea leaves; the company has committed to sourcing all of its tea from Rainforest Alliance Certified farms by 2015, due to their comprehensive triple-bottom-line approach toward sustainable farm management.

Crafting Corporate Social Responsibility and Sustainability Strategies

While CSR and environmental sustainability strategies take many forms, those that both provide valuable social benefits *and* fulfill customer needs in a superior fashion may also contribute to a company's competitive advantage.[26] For example, while carbon emissions may be a generic social concern for financial institutions such as Wells Fargo, Ford's sustainability strategy for reducing carbon emissions has produced both competitive advantage and environmental benefits. Its Ford Fusion hybrid automobile not only is among the least polluting automobiles but also now ranks 1 out of 22 in hybrid cars, with exceptional fuel economy, a quiet powertrain, and a spacious cabin. It has gained the attention and loyalty of fuel-conscious buyers and given Ford a new green image. Green Mountain Coffee Roasters' commitment to protect the welfare of coffee growers and their families (in particular, making sure they receive a fair price) also meets its customers' wants and needs. In its dealings with suppliers at small farmer cooperatives in Peru, Mexico, and Sumatra, Green Mountain pays fair trade prices for coffee beans. Green Mountain also purchases about 29 percent of its coffee directly from farmers so as to cut out intermediaries and see that farmers realize a higher price for their efforts—coffee is the world's second most heavily traded commodity after oil, requiring the labor of some 20 million people, most of whom live at the poverty level.[27] Its consumers are aware of these efforts and purchase Green Mountain coffee, in part, to encourage such practices.

CSR strategies and environmental sustainability strategies that both provide valuable social benefits *and* fulfill customer needs in a superior fashion can lead to competitive advantage. Corporate social agendas that address only social issues may help boost a company's reputation for corporate citizenship but are unlikely to improve its competitive strength in the marketplace.

CSR strategies and environmental sustainability strategies are more likely to contribute to a company's competitive advantage if they are linked to a company's competitively important resources and capabilities or value chain activities. Thus, it is common for companies engaged in natural resource extraction, electric power production, forestry and paper products manufacture, motor vehicles production, and chemical production to place more emphasis on addressing environmental concerns than, say, software and electronics firms or apparel manufacturers. Companies whose business success is heavily dependent on maintaining high employee morale or attracting and retaining the best and brightest employees are somewhat more prone to stress the well-being of their employees and foster a positive, high-energy workplace environment that elicits the dedication and enthusiastic commitment of employees, thus putting real meaning behind the claim "Our people are our greatest asset." Ernst & Young, one of the four largest global accounting firms, stresses its "People First" workforce diversity strategy that is all about respecting differences, fostering individuality, and promoting inclusiveness so that its more than 175,000 employees in over 150 countries can feel valued, engaged, and empowered in developing creative ways to serve the firm's clients. Costco Wholesale, the warehouse club, credits its success to its treatment of its employees, who are paid an average of $20.89 an hour, not including overtime—far above the industry average. Eighty-eight percent of Costco's employees have company-sponsored insurance; CEO Craig Jelinek is committed to ensuring that his people make a living wage and receive health benefits, an approach that he says "also puts more money back into the economy. It's really that simple." Between 2009 and 2014, Costco sales grew 39 percent and stock prices doubled—an anomaly in an industry plagued by turmoil and downsizing.

At Whole Foods Market, a $12.9 billion supermarket chain specializing in organic and natural foods, its environmental sustainability strategy is evident in almost every segment of its company value chain and is a big part of its differentiation strategy. The company's procurement policies encourage stores to purchase fresh fruits and vegetables from local farmers and screen processed-food items for more than 400 common ingredients that the company considers unhealthy or environmentally unsound. Spoiled food items are sent to regional composting centers rather than landfills, and all cleaning products used in its stores are biodegradable. The company also has created the Animal Compassion Foundation to develop natural and humane ways of raising farm animals and has converted all of its vehicles to run on biofuels.

Not all companies choose to link their corporate environmental or social agendas to their value chain, their business model, or their industry. For example, the Clorox Company Foundation supports programs that serve youth, focusing its giving on nonprofit civic organizations, schools, and colleges. However, unless a company's social responsibility initiatives become part of the way it operates its business every day, the initiatives are unlikely to catch fire and be fully effective. As an executive at Royal Dutch/Shell put it, corporate social responsibility "is not a cosmetic; it must be rooted in our values. It must make a difference to the way we do business."[28] The same is true for environmental sustainability initiatives.

The Moral Case for Corporate Social Responsibility and Environmentally Sustainable Business Practices

Every action a company takes can be interpreted as a statement of what it stands for.

The moral case for why businesses should act in a manner that benefits all of the company's stakeholders—not just shareholders—boils down to "It's the right thing to do." Ordinary decency, civic-mindedness, and contributions to society's well-being should be expected of any business.[29] In today's social and political climate, most business leaders can be expected to acknowledge that socially responsible actions are important and that businesses have a duty to be good corporate citizens. But there is a complementary school of thought that business operates on the basis of an implied social contract with the members of society. According to this contract, society grants a business the right to conduct its business affairs and agrees not to unreasonably restrain its pursuit of a fair profit for the goods or services it sells. In return for this "license to operate," a business is obligated to act as a responsible citizen, do its fair share to promote the general welfare, and avoid doing any harm. Such a view clearly puts a moral burden on a company to operate honorably, provide good working conditions to employees, be a good environmental steward, and display good corporate citizenship.

The Business Case for Corporate Social Responsibility and Environmentally Sustainable Business Practices

Whatever the moral arguments for socially responsible business behavior and environmentally sustainable business practices, there are definitely good business reasons why companies should be public-spirited and devote time and resources to social responsibility initiatives, environmental sustainability, and good corporate citizenship:

- *Such actions can lead to increased buyer patronage.* A strong visible social responsibility or environmental sustainability strategy gives a company an edge in appealing to consumers who prefer to do business with companies that are good corporate citizens. Ben & Jerry's, Whole Foods Market, Stonyfield Farm, and The Body Shop have definitely expanded their customer bases because of their visible and well-publicized activities as socially conscious companies. More and more companies are also recognizing the cash register payoff of social responsibility strategies that reach out to people of all cultures and demographics (women, retirees, and ethnic groups).

The higher the public profile of a company or its brand, the greater the scrutiny of its activities and the higher the potential for it to become a target for pressure group action.

- *A strong commitment to socially responsible behavior reduces the risk of reputation-damaging incidents.* Companies that place little importance on operating in a socially responsible manner are more prone to scandal and embarrassment. Consumer, environmental, and human rights activist groups are quick to criticize businesses whose behavior they consider to be out of line, and they are adept at getting their message into the media and onto the Internet. Pressure groups can generate widespread adverse publicity, promote boycotts, and influence like-minded or sympathetic buyers to avoid an offender's products.

Research has shown that product boycott announcements are associated with a decline in a company's stock price.[30] When a major oil company suffered damage to its reputation on environmental and social grounds, the CEO repeatedly said that the most negative impact the company suffered—and the one that made him fear for the future of the company—was that bright young graduates were no longer attracted to working for the company. For many years, Nike received stinging criticism for not policing sweatshop conditions in the Asian factories that produced Nike footwear, a situation that caused Nike cofounder and chairman Phil Knight to observe that "Nike has become synonymous with slave wages, forced overtime, and arbitrary abuse."[31] In response, Nike began an extensive effort to monitor conditions in the 800 factories of the contract manufacturers that produced Nike shoes. As Knight said, "Good shoes come from good factories and good factories have good labor relations." Nonetheless, Nike has continually been plagued by complaints from human rights activists that its monitoring procedures are flawed and that it is not doing enough to correct the plight of factory workers. As this suggests, a damaged reputation is not easily repaired.

- *Socially responsible actions and sustainable business practices can lower costs and enhance employee recruiting and workforce retention.* Companies with deservedly good reputations for social responsibility and sustainable business practices are better able to attract and retain employees, compared to companies with tarnished reputations. Some employees just feel better about working for a company committed to improving society. This can contribute to lower turnover and better worker productivity. Other direct and indirect economic benefits include lower costs for staff recruitment and training. For example, Starbucks is said to enjoy much lower rates of employee turnover because of its full-benefits package for both full-time and part-time employees, management efforts to make Starbucks a great place to work, and the company's socially responsible practices. Sustainable business practices are often concomitant with greater operational efficiencies. For example, when a U.S. manufacturer of recycled paper, taking eco-efficiency to heart, discovered how to increase its fiber recovery rate, it saved the equivalent of 20,000 tons of waste paper—a factor that helped the company become the industry's lowest-cost producer. By helping two-thirds of its employees to stop smoking and by investing in a number of wellness programs for employees, Johnson & Johnson has saved $250 million on its health care costs over the past decade.[32]
- *Opportunities for revenue enhancement may also come from CSR and environmental sustainability strategies.* The drive for sustainability and social responsibility can spur innovative efforts that in turn lead to new products and opportunities for revenue enhancement. Electric cars such as the Chevy Volt and the Nissan Leaf are one example. In many cases, the revenue opportunities are tied to a company's core products. PepsiCo and Coca-Cola, for example, have expanded into the juice business to offer a healthier alternative to their carbonated beverages. General Electric has created a profitable new business in wind turbines. In other cases, revenue enhancement opportunities come from innovative ways to reduce waste and use the by-products of a company's production. Tyson Foods now produces jet fuel for B-52 bombers from the vast amount of animal waste resulting from its meat product business. Staples has become one of the largest nonutility corporate producers of renewable energy in the United States due to its installation of solar power panels in all of its outlets (and the sale of what it does not consume in renewable energy credit markets).

- *Well-conceived CSR strategies and sustainable business practices are in the best long-term interest of shareholders.* When CSR and sustainability strategies increase buyer patronage, offer revenue-enhancing opportunities, lower costs, increase productivity, and reduce the risk of reputation-damaging incidents, they contribute to the economic value created by a company and improve its profitability. A two-year study of leading companies found that improving environmental compliance and developing environmentally friendly products can enhance earnings per share, profitability, and the likelihood of winning contracts. The stock prices of companies that rate high on social and environmental performance criteria have been found to perform 35 to 45 percent better than the average of the 2,500 companies that constitute the Dow Jones Global Index.[33] A review of 135 studies indicated there is a positive, but small, correlation between good corporate behavior and good financial performance; only 2 percent of the studies showed that dedicating corporate resources to social responsibility harmed the interests of shareholders.[34] Furthermore, socially responsible business behavior helps avoid or preempt legal and regulatory actions that could prove costly and otherwise burdensome. In some cases, it is possible to craft corporate social responsibility strategies that contribute to competitive advantage and, at the same time, deliver greater value to society. For instance, Walmart, by working with its suppliers to reduce the use of packaging materials and revamping the routes of its delivery trucks to cut out 100 million miles of travel, saved $200 million in costs (which enhanced its cost competitiveness vis-à-vis rivals) and lowered carbon emissions.[35] Thus, a social responsibility strategy that packs some punch and is more than rhetorical flourish can produce outcomes that are in the best interest of shareholders.

Socially responsible strategies that create value for customers and lower costs can improve company profits and shareholder value at the same time that they address other stakeholder interests.

There's little hard evidence indicating shareholders are disadvantaged in any meaningful way by a company's actions to be socially responsible.

In sum, companies that take social responsibility and environmental sustainability seriously can improve their business reputations and operational efficiency while also reducing their risk exposure and encouraging loyalty and innovation. Overall, companies that take special pains to protect the environment (beyond what is required by law), are active in community affairs, and are generous supporters of charitable causes and projects that benefit society are more likely to be seen as good investments and as good companies to work for or do business with. Shareholders are likely to view the business case for social responsibility as a strong one, particularly when it results in the creation of more customer value, greater productivity, lower operating costs, and lower business risk—all of which should increase firm profitability and enhance shareholder value even as the company's actions address broader stakeholder interests.

Companies are, of course, sometimes rewarded for bad behavior—a company that is able to shift environmental and other social costs associated with its activities onto society as a whole can reap large short-term profits. The major cigarette producers for many years were able to earn greatly inflated profits by shifting the health-related costs of smoking onto others and escaping any responsibility for the harm their products caused to consumers and the general public. Only recently have they been facing the prospect of having to pay high punitive damages for their actions. Unfortunately, the cigarette makers are not alone in trying to evade paying for the social harms of their operations for as long as they can. Calling a halt to such actions usually hinges on (1) the effectiveness of activist social groups in publicizing the adverse consequences of a company's social irresponsibility and marshaling public opinion for something to be done, (2) the enactment of legislation or regulations to correct the inequity, and (3) decisions on the part of socially conscious buyers to take their business elsewhere.

KEY POINTS

1. Ethics concerns standards of right and wrong. Business ethics concerns the application of ethical principles to the actions and decisions of business organizations and the conduct of their personnel. Ethical principles in business are not materially different from ethical principles in general.
2. There are three schools of thought about ethical standards for companies with international operations:
   - According to the *school of ethical universalism,* common understandings across multiple cultures and countries about what constitutes right and wrong behaviors give rise to universal ethical standards that apply to members of all societies, all companies, and all businesspeople.
   - According to the *school of ethical relativism,* different societal cultures and customs have divergent values and standards of right and wrong. Thus, what is ethical or unethical must be judged in the light of local customs and social mores and can vary from one culture or nation to another.
   - According to the *integrated social contracts theory,* universal ethical principles based on the collective views of multiple cultures and societies combine to form a "social contract" that all individuals in all situations have a duty to observe. Within the boundaries of this social contract, local cultures or groups can specify what additional actions are not ethically permissible. However, universal norms always take precedence over local ethical norms.
3. Apart from the "business of business is business, not ethics" kind of thinking, three other factors contribute to unethical business behavior: (1) faulty oversight that enables the unscrupulous pursuit of personal gain, (2) heavy pressures on company managers to meet or beat short-term earnings targets, and (3) a company culture that puts profitability and good business performance ahead of ethical behavior. In contrast, culture can function as a powerful mechanism for promoting ethical business conduct when high ethical principles are deeply ingrained in the corporate culture of a company.
4. Business ethics failures can result in three types of costs: (1) visible costs, such as fines, penalties, and lower stock prices, (2) internal administrative costs, such as legal costs and costs of taking corrective action, and (3) intangible costs or less visible costs, such as customer defections and damage to the company's reputation.
5. The term *corporate social responsibility* concerns a company's *duty* to operate in an honorable manner, provide good working conditions for employees, encourage workforce diversity, be a good steward of the environment, and support philanthropic endeavors in local communities where it operates and in society at large. The particular combination of socially responsible endeavors a company elects to pursue defines its corporate social responsibility (CSR) strategy.
6. The triple bottom line refers to company performance in three realms: economic, social, and environmental. Increasingly, companies are reporting their performance with respect to all three performance dimensions.
7. *Sustainability* is a term that is used in various ways, but most often it concerns a firm's relationship to the environment and its use of natural resources. Sustainable business practices are those capable of meeting the needs of the present without

compromising the world's ability to meet future needs. A company's environmental sustainability strategy consists of its deliberate actions to protect the environment, provide for the longevity of natural resources, maintain ecological support systems for future generations, and guard against ultimate endangerment of the planet.

8. CSR strategies and environmental sustainability strategies that both provide valuable social benefits *and* fulfill customer needs in a superior fashion can lead to competitive advantage.
9. The moral case for corporate social responsibility and environmental sustainability boils down to a simple concept: It's the right thing to do. There are also solid reasons why CSR and environmental sustainability strategies may be good business—they can be conducive to greater buyer patronage, reduce the risk of reputation-damaging incidents, provide opportunities for revenue enhancement, and lower costs. Well-crafted CSR and environmental sustainability strategies are in the best long-term interest of shareholders, for the reasons just mentioned and because they can avoid or preempt costly legal or regulatory actions.

ASSURANCE OF LEARNING EXERCISES

LO 1, LO 4 1. Widely known as an ethical company, Dell recently committed itself to becoming a more environmentally sustainable business. After reviewing the About Dell section of its website (**www.dell.com/learn/us/en/uscorp1/about-dell**), prepare a list of 10 specific policies and programs that help the company achieve its vision of driving social and environmental change while still remaining innovative and profitable.

LO 2, LO 3 2. Prepare a one- to two-page analysis of a recent ethics scandal using your university library's access to LexisNexis or other Internet resources. Your report should (1) discuss the conditions that gave rise to unethical business strategies and behavior and (2) provide an overview of the costs resulting from the company's business ethics failure.

connect **LO 4** 3. Based on information provided in Illustration Capsule 9.3, explain how Burt's Bees' CSR strategy has contributed to its success in the marketplace. How are the company's various stakeholder groups affected by its commitment to social responsibility? How would you evaluate its triple-bottom-line performance?

connect **LO 4** 4. Go to **www.google.com/green/** and read about the company's latest initiatives surrounding sustainability. What are Google's key policies and actions that help it reduce its environmental footprint? How does the company integrate the idea of creating a "better web that's better for the environment" with its strategies for creating profit and value. How do these initiatives help build competitive advantage for Google?

EXERCISE FOR SIMULATION PARTICIPANTS

1. Is your company's strategy ethical? Why or why not? Is there anything that your company has done or is now doing that could legitimately be considered "shady" by your competitors? **LO 1**
2. In what ways, if any, is your company exercising corporate social responsibility? What are the elements of your company's CSR strategy? Are there any changes to this strategy that you would suggest? **LO 4**
3. If some shareholders complained that you and your co-managers have been spending too little or too much on corporate social responsibility, what would you tell them? **LO 3, LO 4**
4. Is your company striving to conduct its business in an environmentally sustainable manner? What specific *additional* actions could your company take that would make an even greater contribution to environmental sustainability? **LO 4**
5. In what ways is your company's environmental sustainability strategy in the best long-term interest of shareholders? Does it contribute to your company's competitive advantage or profitability? **LO 4**

ENDNOTES

[1] James E. Post, Anne T. Lawrence, and James Weber, *Business and Society: Corporate Strategy, Public Policy, Ethics,* 10th ed. (New York: McGraw-Hill, 2002).
[2] Mark S. Schwartz, "Universal Moral Values for Corporate Codes of Ethics," *Journal of Business Ethics* 59, no. 1 (June 2005), pp. 27–44.
[3] Mark S. Schwartz, "A Code of Ethics for Corporate Codes of Ethics," *Journal of Business Ethics* 41, no. 1–2 (November–December 2002), pp. 27–43.
[4] T. L. Beauchamp and N. E. Bowie, *Ethical Theory and Business* (Upper Saddle River, NJ: Prentice-Hall, 2001).
[5] www.cnn.com/2013/10/15/world/child-labor-index-2014/ (accessed February 6, 2014).
[6] U.S. Department of Labor, "The Department of Labor's 2012 Findings on the Worst Forms of Child Labor," www.dol.gov/ilab/programs/ocft/PDF/2012OCFTreport.pdf.
[7] W. M. Greenfield, "In the Name of Corporate Social Responsibility," *Business Horizons* 47, no. 1 (January–February 2004), p. 22.
[8] Rajib Sanyal, "Determinants of Bribery in International Business: The Cultural and Economic Factors," *Journal of Business Ethics* 59, no. 1 (June 2005), pp. 139–145.
[9] Transparency International, *Global Corruption Report,* www.globalcorruptionreport.org.
[10] Roger Chen and Chia-Pei Chen, "Chinese Professional Managers and the Issue of Ethical Behavior," *Ivey Business Journal* 69, no. 5 (May–June 2005), p. 1.
[11] Antonio Argandoa, "Corruption and Companies: The Use of Facilitating Payments," *Journal of Business Ethics* 60, no. 3 (September 2005), pp. 251–264.
[12] Thomas Donaldson and Thomas W. Dunfee, "Towards a Unified Conception of Business Ethics: Integrative Social Contracts Theory," *Academy of Management Review* 19, no. 2 (April 1994), pp. 252–284; Andrew Spicer, Thomas W. Dunfee, and Wendy J. Bailey, "Does National Context Matter in Ethical Decision Making? An Empirical Test of Integrative Social Contracts Theory," *Academy of Management Journal* 47, no. 4 (August 2004), p. 610.
[13] Lynn Paine, Rohit Deshpandé, Joshua D. Margolis, and Kim Eric Bettcher, "Up to Code: Does Your Company's Conduct Meet World-Class Standards?" *Harvard Business Review* 83, no. 12 (December 2005), pp. 122–133.
[14] John F. Veiga, Timothy D. Golden, and Kathleen Dechant, "Why Managers Bend Company Rules," *Academy of Management Executive* 18, no. 2 (May 2004).
[15] www.reuters.com/article/2014/02/06/us-sac-martoma-idUSBREA131TL20140206.
[16] Lorin Berlin and Emily Peck, "National Mortgage Settlement: States, Big Banks Reach $25 Billion Deal," *Huff Post Business,* February 9, 2012, www.huffingtonpost.com/2012/02/09/-national-mortgage-settlement_n_1265292.html (accessed February 15, 2012).
[17] Ronald R. Sims and Johannes Brinkmann, "Enron Ethics (Or: Culture Matters More than Codes)," *Journal of Business Ethics* 45, no. 3 (July 2003), pp. 244–246.
[18] www.sfgate.com/business/bottomline/article/SEC-charges-Diamond-Foods-with-accounting-fraud-5129129.php (accessed February 7, 2014).
[19] Kurt Eichenwald, *Conspiracy of Fools: A True Story* (New York: Broadway Books, 2005).
[20] Timothy M. Devinney, "Is the Socially Responsible Corporation a Myth? The Good, the Bad, and the Ugly of Corporate Social Responsibility," *Academy of Management Perspectives* 23, no. 2 (May 2009), pp. 44–56.
[21] Information posted at www.generalmills.com (accessed March 13, 2013).
[22] Adrian Henriques, "ISO 26000: A New Standard for Human Rights?" *Institute for Human Rights and Business,* March 23, 2010, www.institutehrb.org/blogs/guest/iso_26000_a_new_standard_for_human_rights.html?gclid=CJih7NjN2alCFVs65QodrVOdyQ (accessed July 7, 2010).
[23] Gerald I.J.M. Zetsloot and Marcel N. A. van Marrewijk, "From Quality to Sustainability," *Journal of Business Ethics* 55 (2004), pp. 79–82.
[24] Tilde Herrera, "PG&E Claims Industry First with Supply Chain Footprint Project," *GreenBiz.com*, June 30, 2010, www.greenbiz.com/news/2010/06/30/-pge—claims-industry-first-supply-chain-carbon-footprint-project.
[25] J. G. Speth, *The Bridge at the End of the World: Capitalism, the Environment, and Crossing from Crisis to Sustainability* (New Haven, CT: Yale University Press, 2008).
[26] Michael E. Porter and Mark R. Kramer, "Strategy & Society: The Link between Competitive Advantage and Corporate Social Responsibility," *Harvard Business Review* 84, no. 12 (December 2006), pp. 78–92.
[27] David Hess, Nikolai Rogovsky, and Thomas W. Dunfee, "The Next Wave of Corporate Community Involvement: Corporate Social Initiatives," *California Management Review* 44, no. 2 (Winter 2002), pp. 110–125; Susan Ariel Aaronson, "Corporate Responsibility in

the Global Village: The British Role Model and the American Laggard," *Business and Society Review* 108, no. 3 (September 2003), p. 323.

[28] N. Craig Smith, "Corporate Responsibility: Whether and How," *California Management Review* 45, no. 4 (Summer 2003), p. 63.

[29] Jeb Brugmann and C. K. Prahalad, "Cocreating Business's New Social Compact," *Harvard Business Review* 85, no. 2 (February 2007), pp. 80–90.

[30] Wallace N. Davidson, Abuzar El-Jelly, and Dan L. Worrell, "Influencing Managers to Change Unpopular Corporate Behavior through Boycotts and Divestitures: A Stock Market Test," *Business and Society* 34, no. 2 (1995), pp. 171–196.

[31] Tom McCawley, "Racing to Improve Its Reputation: Nike Has Fought to Shed Its Image as an Exploiter of Third-World Labor Yet It Is Still a Target of Activists," *Financial Times*, December 2000, p. 14.

[32] Michael E. Porter and Mark Kramer, "Creating Shared Value," *Harvard Business Review* 89, no. 1–2 (January–February 2011).

[33] James C. Collins and Jerry I. Porras, *Built to Last: Successful Habits of Visionary Companies*, 3rd ed. (London: HarperBusiness, 2002).

[34] Joshua D. Margolis and Hillary A. Elfenbein, "Doing Well by Doing Good: Don't Count on It," *Harvard Business Review* 86, no. 1 (January 2008), pp. 19–20; Lee E. Preston, Douglas P. O'Bannon, Ronald M. Roman, Sefa Hayibor, and Bradley R. Agle, "The Relationship between Social and Financial Performance: Repainting a Portrait," *Business and Society* 38, no. 1 (March 1999), pp. 109–125.

[35] Leonard L. Berry, Ann M. Mirobito, and William B. Baun, "What's the Hard Return on Employee Wellness Programs?" *Harvard Business Review* 88, no. 12 (December 2010), p. 105.

CHAPTER 10

Building an Organization Capable of Good Strategy Execution

People, Capabilities, and Structure

Learning Objectives

THIS CHAPTER WILL HELP YOU UNDERSTAND:

LO 1 What managers must do to execute strategy successfully.

LO 2 Why hiring, training, and retaining the right people constitute a key component of the strategy execution process.

LO 3 That good strategy execution requires continuously building and upgrading the organization's resources and capabilities.

LO 4 What issues to consider in establishing a strategy-supportive organizational structure and organizing the work effort.

LO 5 The pros and cons of centralized and decentralized decision making in implementing the chosen strategy.

Any strategy, however brilliant, needs to be implemented properly if it is to deliver the desired results.

Costas Markides – *London Business School Professor and Consultant*

Teamwork is the ability to direct individual accomplishments toward organizational objectives. It is the fuel that allows common people to attain uncommon results.

Andrew Carnegie – *Steel Industry Magnate and Philanthropist*

Coming together is a beginning. Keeping together is progress. Working together is success.

Henry Ford – *Founder of the Ford Motor Company*

Once managers have decided on a strategy, the emphasis turns to converting it into actions and good results. Putting the strategy into place and getting the organization to execute it well call for different sets of managerial skills. Whereas crafting strategy is largely an analysis-driven activity focused on market conditions and the company's resources and capabilities, executing strategy is primarily operations-driven, revolving around the management of people, business processes, and organizational structure. Successful strategy execution depends on doing a good job of working with and through others; building and strengthening competitive capabilities; creating an appropriate organizational structure; allocating resources; instituting strategy-supportive policies, processes, and systems; and instilling a discipline of getting things done. Executing strategy is an action-oriented, make-things-happen task that tests a manager's ability to direct organizational change, achieve continuous improvement in operations and business processes, create and nurture a strategy-supportive culture, and consistently meet or beat performance targets.

Experienced managers are well aware that it is much easier to develop a sound strategic plan than it is to execute the plan and achieve targeted outcomes. According to one executive, "It's been rather easy for us to decide where we wanted to go. The hard part is to get the organization to act on the new priorities."[1] It takes adept managerial leadership to convincingly communicate a new strategy and the reasons for it, overcome pockets of doubt, secure the commitment of key personnel, build consensus for how to implement the strategy, and move forward to get all the pieces into place and deliver results. *Just because senior managers announce a new strategy doesn't mean that organization members will embrace it and move forward enthusiastically to implement it.* Company personnel must understand—in their heads and hearts—why a new strategic direction is necessary and where the new strategy is taking them.[2] Instituting change is, of course, easier when the problems with the old strategy have become obvious and/or the company has spiraled into a financial crisis.

But the challenge of successfully implementing new strategic initiatives goes well beyond managerial adeptness in overcoming resistance to change. What really makes executing strategy a tougher, more time-consuming management challenge than crafting strategy are the wide array of managerial activities that must be attended to, the many ways to put new strategic initiatives in place and keep things moving, and the number of bedeviling issues that always crop up and have to be resolved. It takes first-rate "managerial smarts" to zero in on what exactly needs to be done and how to get good results in a timely manner. Excellent people-management skills and perseverance are required to get a variety of initiatives launched and to integrate the efforts of many different work groups into a smoothly functioning whole. Depending on how much consensus building and organizational change is involved, the process of implementing strategy changes can take several months to several years. Achieving *real proficiency* in executing the strategy can take even longer.

Like crafting strategy, *executing strategy is a job for a company's whole management team—not just a few senior managers.* While the chief executive officer and the heads of major units (business divisions, functional departments, and key operating units) are ultimately responsible for seeing that strategy is executed successfully, the process typically affects every part of the firm—all value chain activities and all work groups. Top-level managers must rely on the active support of middle and lower managers to institute whatever new operating practices are needed in the various operating units to achieve proficient strategy execution. Middle and lower-level managers must ensure that frontline employees perform strategy-critical value chain activities well and produce operating results that allow companywide performance targets to be met. Consequently, *all company personnel are actively involved in the strategy execution process in one way or another.*

A FRAMEWORK FOR EXECUTING STRATEGY

CORE CONCEPT

Good strategy execution requires a *team effort.* All managers have strategy-executing responsibility in their areas of authority, and all employees are active participants in the strategy execution process.

The managerial approach to implementing and executing a strategy always has to be customized to fit the particulars of a company's situation. Making minor changes in an existing strategy differs from implementing radical strategy changes. The techniques for successfully executing a low-cost provider strategy are different from those for executing a high-end differentiation strategy. Implementing a new strategy for a struggling company in the midst of a financial crisis is a different job from improving strategy execution in a company that is doing relatively well. Moreover, some managers are more adept than others at using particular approaches to achieving certain kinds of organizational changes. Hence, there's no definitive managerial recipe for successful strategy execution that cuts across all company situations and all strategies or that works for all managers. Rather, the specific actions required to execute a strategy—the "to-do list" that constitutes management's action agenda—always represent management's judgment about how best to proceed in light of prevailing circumstances.

LO 1

What managers must do to execute strategy successfully.

The Principal Components of the Strategy Execution Process

Despite the need to tailor a company's strategy-executing approaches to the particulars of the situation at hand, certain managerial bases must be covered no matter what the circumstances. These include 10 basic managerial tasks (see Figure 10.1):

1. Staffing the organization with managers and employees capable of executing the strategy well.
2. Developing the resources and organizational capabilities required for successful strategy execution.
3. Creating a strategy-supportive organizational structure.
4. Allocating sufficient resources (budgetary and otherwise) to the strategy execution effort.
5. Instituting policies and procedures that facilitate strategy execution.

6. Adopting best practices and business processes to drive continuous improvement in strategy execution activities.
7. Installing information and operating systems that enable company personnel to carry out their strategic roles proficiently.
8. Tying rewards and incentives directly to the achievement of strategic and financial targets.
9. Instilling a corporate culture that promotes good strategy execution.
10. Exercising the internal leadership needed to propel strategy implementation forward.

When strategies fail, it is often because of poor execution. Strategy execution is therefore a critical managerial endeavor.

How well managers perform these 10 tasks has a decisive impact on whether the outcome of the strategy execution effort is a spectacular success, a colossal failure, or something in between.

The two best signs of good strategy execution are whether a company is meeting or beating its performance targets and whether it is performing value chain activities in a manner that is conducive to companywide operating excellence.

In devising an action agenda for executing strategy, managers should start by conducting *a probing assessment of what the organization must do differently to carry out the strategy successfully.* Each manager needs to ask the question "What needs to be done in my area of responsibility to implement our part of the company's strategy, and what should I do to get these things accomplished?" It is then incumbent on every manager to determine *precisely how to make the necessary internal changes.* Successful strategy implementers have a knack for diagnosing what their organizations need to do to execute the chosen strategy well and figuring out how to get these things done efficiently. They are masters in promoting results-oriented behaviors on the part of company personnel and following through on making the right things happen in a timely fashion.[3]

In big organizations with geographically scattered operating units, senior executives' action agenda mostly involves communicating the case for change, building consensus for how to proceed, installing strong managers to move the process forward in key organizational units, directing resources to the right places, establishing deadlines and measures of progress, rewarding those who achieve implementation milestones, and personally leading the strategic change process. Thus, the bigger the organization, the more that successful strategy execution depends on the cooperation and implementation skills of operating managers who can promote needed changes at the lowest organizational levels and deliver results. In small organizations, top managers can deal directly with frontline managers and employees, personally orchestrating the action steps and implementation sequence, observing firsthand how implementation is progressing, and deciding how hard and how fast to push the process along. Whether the organization is large or small and whether strategy implementation involves sweeping or minor changes, effective leadership requires a keen grasp of what to do and how to do it in light of the organization's circumstances. Then it remains for company personnel in strategy-critical areas to step up to the plate and produce the desired results.

What's Covered in Chapters 10, 11, and 12 In the remainder of this chapter and in the next two chapters, we discuss what is involved in performing the 10 key managerial tasks that shape the process of executing strategy. This chapter explores the first three of these tasks (highlighted in blue in Figure 10.1): (1) staffing the organization with people capable of executing the strategy well, (2) developing the resources and building the organizational capabilities needed for successful strategy execution, and (3) creating an organizational structure supportive of the strategy execution process. Chapter 11 concerns the tasks of allocating resources, instituting strategy-facilitating policies and procedures, employing business process management

FIGURE 10.1 The 10 Basic Tasks of the Strategy Execution Process

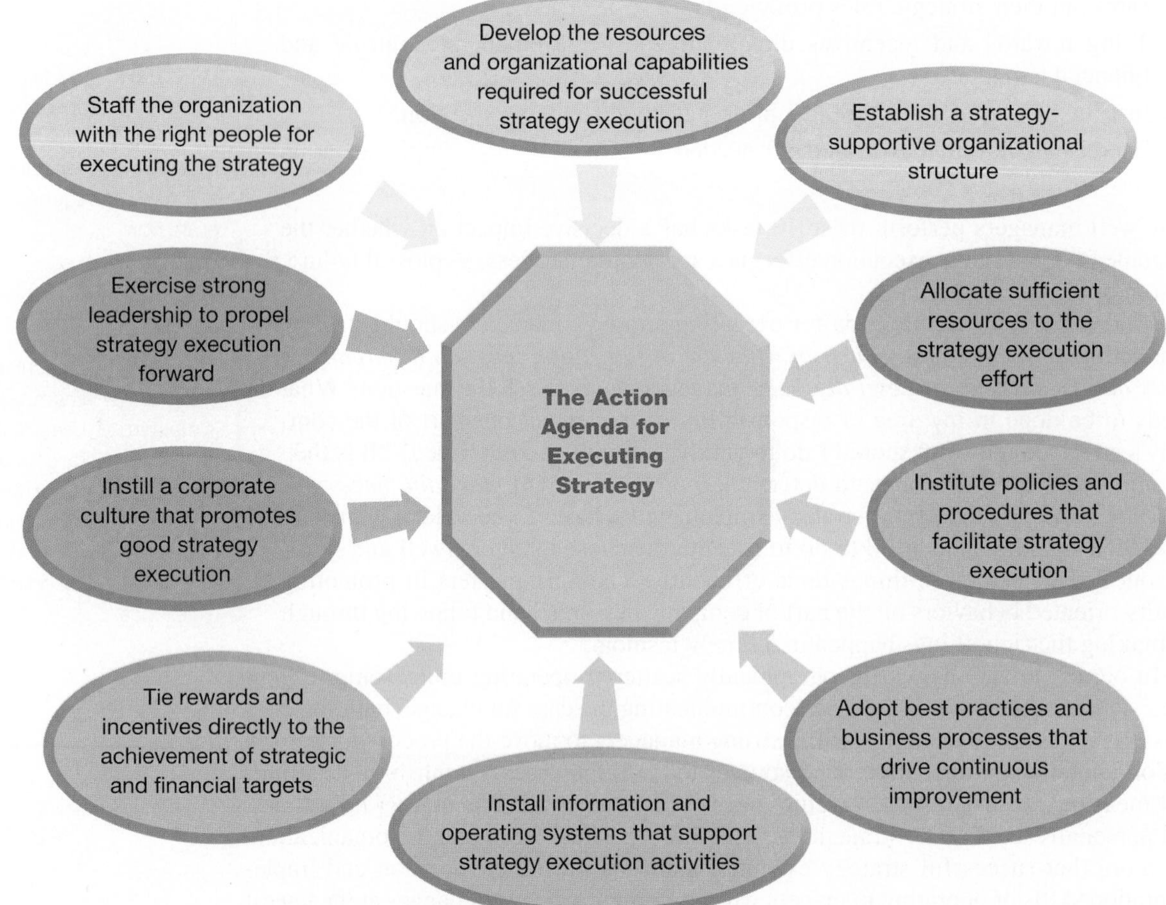

tools and best practices, installing operating and information systems, and tying rewards to the achievement of good results (highlighted in green in Figure 10.1). Chapter 12 deals with the two remaining tasks: creating a strategy-supportive corporate culture and exercising the leadership needed to drive the execution process forward (highlighted in purple).

BUILDING AN ORGANIZATION CAPABLE OF GOOD STRATEGY EXECUTION: THREE KEY ACTIONS

Proficient strategy execution depends foremost on having in place an organization capable of the tasks demanded of it. Building an execution-capable organization is thus always a top priority. As shown in Figure 10.2, three types of organization-building actions are paramount:

1. *Staffing the organization*—putting together a strong management team, and recruiting and retaining employees with the needed experience, technical skills, and intellectual capital.

FIGURE 10.2 Building an Organization Capable of Proficient Strategy Execution: Three Key Actions

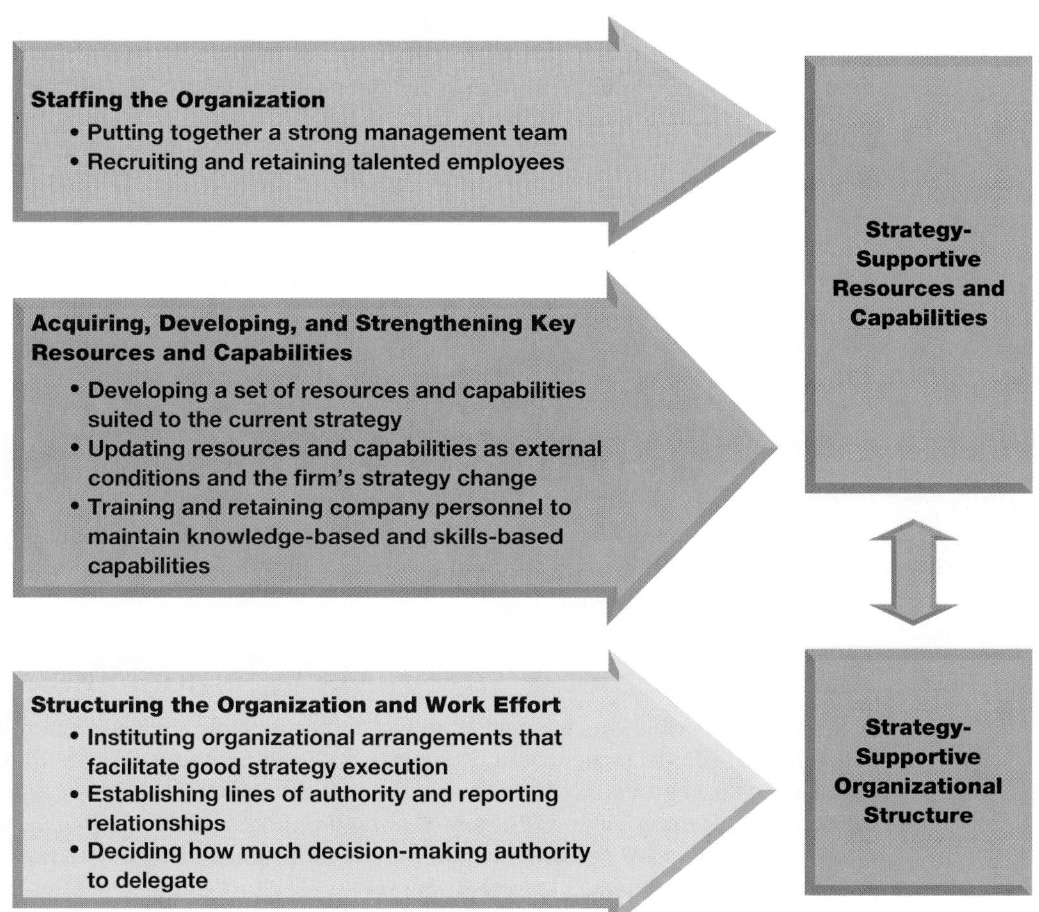

2. *Acquiring, developing, and strengthening the resources and capabilities required for good strategy execution*—accumulating the required resources, developing proficiencies in performing strategy-critical value chain activities, and updating the company's capabilities to match changing market conditions and customer expectations.
3. *Structuring the organization and work effort*—organizing value chain activities and business processes, establishing lines of authority and reporting relationships, and deciding how much decision-making authority to delegate to lower-level managers and frontline employees.

Implementing a strategy depends critically on ensuring that strategy-supportive resources and capabilities are in place, ready to be deployed. These include the skills, talents, experience, and knowledge of the company's human resources (managerial and otherwise)—see Figure 10.2. Proficient strategy execution depends heavily on competent personnel of all types, but because of the many managerial tasks involved and the role of leadership in strategy execution, assembling a strong management team is especially important.

If the strategy being implemented is a new strategy, the company may need to add to its resource and capability mix in other respects as well. But renewing, upgrading, and revising the organization's resources and capabilities is a part of the strategy execution process even if the strategy is fundamentally the same, since strategic assets depreciate and conditions are always changing. Thus, augmenting and strengthening the firm's core competencies and seeing that they are suited to the current strategy are also top priorities.

Structuring the organization and work effort is another critical aspect of building an organization capable of good strategy execution. An organization structure that is well matched to the strategy can help facilitate its implementation; one that is not well suited can lead to higher bureaucratic costs and communication or coordination breakdowns.

STAFFING THE ORGANIZATION

LO 2

Why hiring, training, and retaining the right people constitute a key component of the strategy execution process.

No company can hope to perform the activities required for successful strategy execution without attracting and retaining talented managers and employees with suitable skills and *intellectual capital.*

Putting Together a Strong Management Team

Assembling a capable management team is a cornerstone of the organization-building task.[4] While different strategies and company circumstances sometimes call for different mixes of backgrounds, experiences, management styles, and know-how, *the most important consideration is to fill key managerial slots with smart people who are clear thinkers, good at figuring out what needs to be done, skilled in managing people, and accomplished in delivering good results.*[5] The task of implementing challenging strategic initiatives must be assigned to executives who have the skills and talents to handle them and who can be counted on to get the job done well. Without a capable, results-oriented management team, the implementation process is likely to be hampered by missed deadlines, misdirected or wasteful efforts, and managerial ineptness. Weak executives are serious impediments to getting optimal results because they are unable to differentiate between ideas that have merit and those that are misguided—the caliber of work done under their supervision suffers.[6] In contrast, managers with strong strategy implementation capabilities have a talent for asking tough, incisive questions. They know enough about the details of the business to be able to ensure the soundness of the decisions of the people around them, and they can discern whether the resources people are asking for to put the strategy in place make sense. They are good at getting things done through others, partly by making sure they have the right people under them, assigned to the right jobs. They consistently follow through on issues, monitor progress carefully, make adjustments when needed, and keep important details from slipping through the cracks. In short, they understand how to drive organizational change, and they have the managerial discipline requisite for first-rate strategy execution.

Sometimes a company's existing management team is up to the task. At other times it may need to be strengthened by promoting qualified people from within or by bringing in outsiders whose experiences, talents, and leadership styles better suit the situation. In turnaround and rapid-growth situations, and in instances when a company doesn't have insiders with the requisite know-how, filling key management slots from the outside is a standard organization-building approach. In addition, it is important to identify and replace managers who are incapable, for whatever reason, of making the required changes in a timely and cost-effective manner. For a management team to be truly effective at strategy execution, it must be composed of managers who recognize that organizational changes are needed and who are ready to get on with the process.

Putting together a talented management team with the right mix of experiences, skills, and abilities to get things done is one of the first steps to take in launching the strategy-executing process.

The overriding aim in building a management team should be to assemble a *critical mass* of talented managers who can function as agents of change and oversee top-notch strategy execution. Every manager's success is enhanced (or limited) by the quality of his or her managerial colleagues and the degree to which they freely exchange ideas, debate ways to make operating improvements, and join forces to tackle issues and solve problems. When a first-rate manager enjoys the help and support of other first-rate managers, it's possible to create a managerial whole that is greater than the sum of individual efforts—talented managers who work well together as a team can produce organizational results that are dramatically better than what one or two star managers acting individually can achieve.[7]

Illustration Capsule 10.1 describes Deloitte's highly effective approach to developing employee talent and a top-caliber management team.

Recruiting, Training, and Retaining Capable Employees

Assembling a capable management team is not enough. Staffing the organization with the right kinds of people must extend to all kinds of company personnel for value chain activities to be performed competently. *The quality of an organization's people is always an essential ingredient of successful strategy execution—knowledgeable, engaged employees are a company's best source of creative ideas for the nuts-and-bolts operating improvements that lead to operating excellence.* Companies like Google, SAS, The Boston Consulting Group, Edward Jones, Quicken Loans, Genentech, Intuit, Salesforce.com, and Goldman Sachs make a concerted effort to recruit the best and brightest people they can find and then retain them with excellent compensation packages, opportunities for rapid advancement and professional growth, and interesting assignments. Having a pool of "A players" with strong skill sets and lots of brainpower is essential to their business.

In many industries, adding to a company's talent base and building intellectual capital are more important to good strategy execution than are additional investments in capital projects.

Facebook makes a point of hiring the very brightest and most talented programmers it can find and motivating them with both good monetary incentives and the challenge of working on cutting-edge technology projects. McKinsey & Company, one of the world's premier management consulting firms, recruits only cream-of-the-crop MBAs at the nation's top-10 business schools; such talent is essential to McKinsey's strategy of performing high-level consulting for the world's top corporations. The leading global accounting firms screen candidates not only on the basis of their accounting expertise but also on whether they possess the people skills needed to relate well with clients and colleagues. Southwest Airlines goes to considerable lengths to hire people who can have fun and be fun on the job; it uses special interviewing and screening methods to gauge whether applicants for customer-contact jobs have outgoing personality traits that match its strategy of creating a high-spirited, fun-loving in-flight atmosphere for passengers. Southwest Airlines is so selective that only about 3 percent of the people who apply are offered jobs.

ILLUSTRATION CAPSULE 10.1

Management Development at Deloitte Touche Tohmatsu Limited

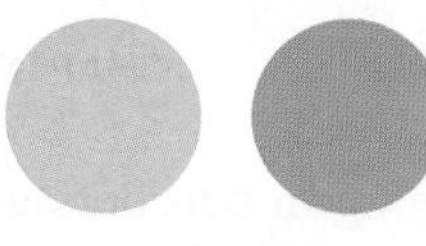

EXHIBIT 1

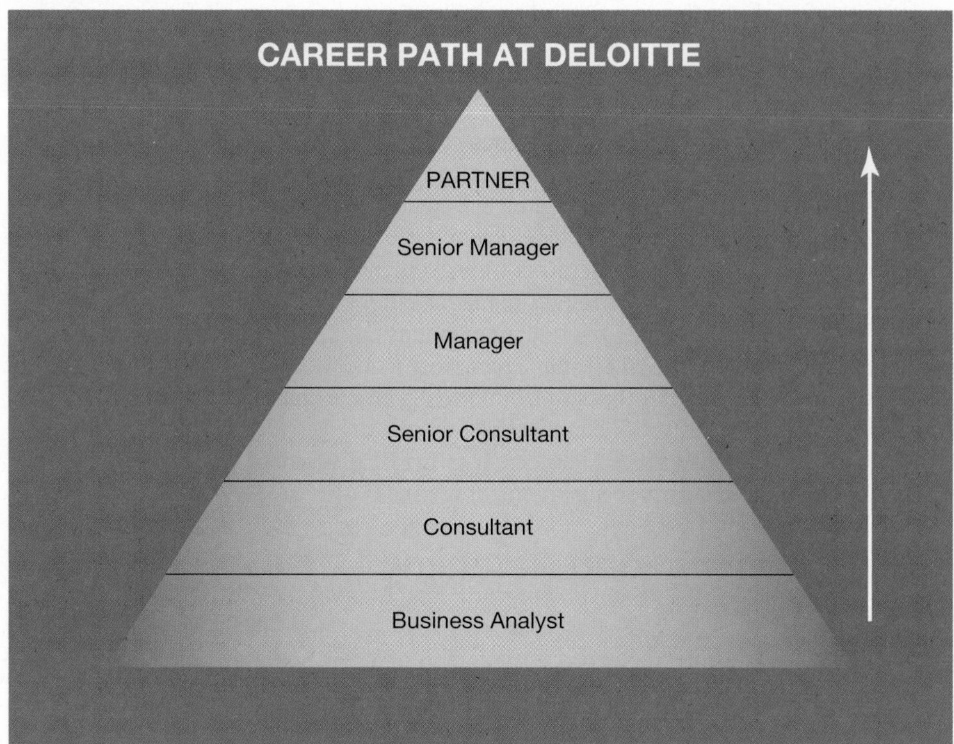

Source: mycareer.deloitte.com/us/en/students/programsinternships/graduates/businesstechnology/wherecanigofromhere

Hiring, retaining, and cultivating talent are critical activities at Deloitte, the world's largest professional services firm. By offering robust learning and development programs, Deloitte has been able to create a strong talent pipeline to the firm's partnership. Deloitte's emphasis on learning and development, across all stages of the employee life cycle, has led to recognitions such as being ranked number one on *Chief Executives'* list of "Best Private Companies for Leaders" and being listed among *Fortune*'s "100 Best Companies to Work For." The following programs contribute to Deloitte's successful execution of its talent strategy:

- *Clear path to partnership.* During the initial recruiting phase and then throughout an employee's tenure at the firm, Deloitte lays out a clear career path. The path indicates the expected timeline for promotion to each of the firm's hierarchy levels, along with the competencies and experience required. Deloitte's transparency on career paths, coupled with its in-depth performance management process, helps employees clearly understand their performance. This serves as a motivational tool for top performers, often leading to career acceleration. (See Exhibit 1.)
- *Formal training programs.* Like other leading organizations, Deloitte has a program to ensure that recent college graduates are equipped with the necessary training and tools for succeeding on the job. Yet Deloitte's commitment to formal training is evident at all levels within the organization. Each time an employee is promoted, he or she attends "milestone" school, a weeklong simulation that replicates true business situations employees would face as they transition to new stages of career development. In addition, Deloitte institutes mandatory training hours for all of its employees to ensure that individuals continue to further their professional development.
- *Special programs for high performers.* Deloitte also offers fellowships and programs to help employees acquire new skills and enhance their leadership development. For example, the Global Fellows program helps top performers work with senior leaders in the organization to focus on the realities of delivering client service across borders. Deloitte has also established the

Emerging Leaders Development program, which utilizes skill building, 360-degree feedback, and one-on-one executive coaching to help top-performing managers and senior managers prepare for partnership.

- *Sponsorship, not mentorship.* To train the next generation of leaders, Deloitte has implemented formal mentorship programs to provide leadership development support. Deloitte, however, uses the term *sponsorship* to describe this initiative. A sponsor is tasked with taking a vested interest in an individual and advocating on his or her behalf. Sponsors help rising leaders navigate the firm, develop new competencies, expand their network, and hone the skills needed to accelerate their career.

Note: Developed with Heather Levy.

Sources: Company websites; www.accountingweb.com/article/leadership-development-community-service-integral-deloitte-university/220845 (accessed February 2014).

In high-tech companies, the challenge is to staff work groups with gifted, imaginative, and energetic people who can bring life to new ideas quickly and inject into the organization what one Dell executive calls "hum."[8] The saying "People are our most important asset" may seem trite, but it fits high-technology companies precisely. Besides checking closely for functional and technical skills, Dell tests applicants for their tolerance of ambiguity and change, their capacity to work in teams, and their ability to learn on the fly. Companies like Zappos, Amazon.com, Google, and Cisco Systems have broken new ground in recruiting, hiring, cultivating, developing, and retaining talented employees—almost all of whom are in their 20s and 30s. Cisco goes after the top 10 percent, raiding other companies and endeavoring to retain key people at the companies it acquires. Cisco executives believe that a cadre of star engineers, programmers, managers, salespeople, and support personnel is the backbone of the company's efforts to execute its strategy and remain the world's leading provider of Internet infrastructure products and technology.

The best companies make a point of recruiting and retaining talented employees—the objective is to make the company's entire workforce (managers and rank-and-file employees) a genuine competitive asset.

In recognition of the importance of a talented and energetic workforce, companies have instituted a number of practices aimed at staffing jobs with the best people they can find:

1. Spending considerable effort on screening and evaluating job applicants—selecting only those with suitable skill sets, energy, initiative, judgment, aptitude for learning, and personality traits that mesh well with the company's work environment and culture.
2. Providing employees with training programs that continue throughout their careers.
3. Offering promising employees challenging, interesting, and skill-stretching assignments.
4. Rotating people through jobs that span functional and geographic boundaries. Providing people with opportunities to gain experience in a variety of international settings is increasingly considered an essential part of career development in multinational companies.
5. Making the work environment stimulating and engaging so that employees will consider the company a great place to work.
6. Encouraging employees to challenge existing ways of doing things, to be creative and innovative in proposing better ways of operating, and to push their ideas for new products or businesses. Progressive companies work hard at creating an environment in which employees are made to feel that their views and suggestions count.

7. Striving to retain talented, high-performing employees via promotions, salary increases, performance bonuses, stock options and equity ownership, benefit packages including health insurance and retirement packages, and other perks, such as flexible work hours and onsite day care.
8. Coaching average performers to improve their skills and capabilities, while weeding out underperformers.

DEVELOPING AND BUILDING CRITICAL RESOURCES AND CAPABILITIES

LO 3

That good strategy execution requires continuously building and upgrading the organization's resources and capabilities.

High among the organization-building priorities in the strategy execution process is the need to build and strengthen competitively valuable resources and capabilities. As explained in Chapter 4, a company's ability to perform value-creating activities and realize its strategic objectives depends upon its resources and capabilities. In the course of crafting strategy, it is important for managers to identify the resources and capabilities that will enable the firm's strategy to succeed. Good strategy execution requires putting those resources and capabilities into place, strengthening them as needed, and then modifying them as market conditions evolve.

If the strategy being implemented is new, company managers may have to acquire new resources, significantly broaden or deepen certain capabilities, or even add entirely new competencies in order to put the strategic initiatives in place and execute them proficiently. But even if the strategy has not changed materially, good strategy execution involves refreshing and strengthening the firm's resources and capabilities to keep them in top form.

Three Approaches to Building and Strengthening Capabilities

Building new competencies and capabilities is a multistage process that occurs over a period of months and years. It is not something that is accomplished overnight.

Building core competencies and competitive capabilities is a time-consuming, managerially challenging exercise. While some assist can be gotten from discovering how best-in-industry or best-in-world companies perform a particular activity, trying to replicate and then improve on the capabilities of others is easier said than done—for the same reasons that one is unlikely to ever become a world-class slopestyle snowboarder just by studying what Olympic gold medalist Jamie Anderson does.

With deliberate effort, well-orchestrated organizational actions, and continued practice, however, it is possible for a firm to become proficient at capability building despite the difficulty. Indeed, by making capability-building activities a *routine* part of their strategy execution endeavors, some firms are able to develop *dynamic capabilities* that assist them in managing resource and capability change, as discussed in Chapter 4. The most common approaches to capability building include (1) developing capabilities internally, (2) acquiring capabilities through mergers and acquisitions, and (3) accessing capabilities via collaborative partnerships.

Developing Capabilities Internally Capabilities develop incrementally along an evolutionary development path as organizations search for solutions to their problems. The process is a complex one, since capabilities are the product of *bundles of skills and know-how that are integrated into organizational routines* and *deployed* *within activity systems* through the combined efforts of teams that are often cross-functional in nature, spanning a variety of departments and locations. For instance, the capability of speeding new products to market involves the *collaborative efforts* of personnel in R&D, engineering and design, purchasing, production, marketing, and distribution. Similarly, the capability to provide superior customer service is a team effort among people in customer call centers (where orders are taken and inquiries are answered), shipping and delivery, billing and accounts receivable, and after-sale support. The process of building a capability begins when managers set an objective of developing a particular capability and organize activity around that objective.[9] Managers can ignite the process by having high aspirations and setting "stretch objectives" for the organization, as described in Chapter 2.[10]

Because the process is incremental, the first step is to develop the *ability* to do something, however imperfectly or inefficiently. This entails selecting people with the requisite skills and experience, upgrading or expanding individual abilities as needed, and then molding the efforts of individuals into a joint effort to create an organizational ability. At this stage, progress can be fitful since it depends on experimenting, actively searching for alternative solutions, and learning through trial and error.[11]

A company's capabilities must be continually refreshed and renewed to remain aligned with changing customer expectations, altered competitive conditions, and new strategic initiatives.

As experience grows and company personnel learn how to perform the activities consistently well and at an acceptable cost, the ability *evolves* into a tried-and-true competence. Getting to this point requires a *continual investment* of resources and *systematic efforts* to improve processes and solve problems creatively as they arise. Improvements in the functioning of a capability come from task repetition and the resulting *learning by doing* of individuals and teams. But the process can be accelerated by making learning a more deliberate endeavor and providing the incentives that will motivate company personnel to achieve the desired ends.[12] This can be critical to successful strategy execution when market conditions are changing rapidly.

It is generally much easier and less time-consuming to update and remodel a company's existing capabilities as external conditions and company strategy change than it is to create them from scratch. Maintaining capabilities in top form may simply require exercising them continually and fine-tuning them as necessary. Refreshing and updating capabilities require only a limited set of modifications to a set of routines that is otherwise in place. Phasing out an existing capability takes significantly less effort than adding a brand new one. Replicating a company capability, while not an easy process, still begins with an *established template*.[13] Even the process of augmenting a capability may require less effort if it involves the recombination of well-established company capabilities and draws on existing company resources.[14] Companies like Cray in large computers and Honda in gasoline engines, for example, have leveraged the expertise of their talent pool by frequently re-forming high-intensity teams and reusing key people on special projects designed to augment their capabilities. Canon combined miniaturization capabilities that it developed in producing calculators with its existing capabilities in precision optics to revolutionize the 35-mm camera market.[15] Toyota, en route to overtaking General Motors as the global leader in motor vehicles, aggressively upgraded its capabilities in fuel-efficient hybrid engine technology and constantly fine-tuned its famed Toyota Production System to enhance its already proficient capabilities in manufacturing top-quality vehicles at relatively low costs.

Managerial actions to develop core competencies and competitive capabilities generally take one of two forms: either strengthening the company's base of skills, knowledge, and experience or coordinating and integrating the efforts of the various work groups and departments. Actions of the first sort can be undertaken at all managerial levels, but actions of the second sort are best orchestrated by senior managers who not only appreciate the strategy-executing significance of strong capabilities but also have the clout to enforce the necessary cooperation and coordination among individuals, groups, and departments.[16]

Acquiring Capabilities through Mergers and Acquisitions Sometimes the best way for a company to upgrade its portfolio of capabilities is by acquiring (or merging with) another company with attractive resources and capabilities.[17] An acquisition aimed at building a stronger portfolio of resources and capabilities can be every bit as valuable as an acquisition aimed at adding new products or services to the company's lineup of offerings. The advantage of this mode of acquiring new capabilities is primarily one of speed, since developing new capabilities internally can, at best, take many years of effort and, at worst, come to naught. Capabilities-motivated acquisitions are essential (1) when the company does not have the ability to create the needed capability internally (perhaps because it is too far afield from its existing capabilities) and (2) when industry conditions, technology, or competitors are moving at such a rapid clip that time is of the essence.

At the same time, acquiring capabilities in this way is not without difficulty. Capabilities involve tacit knowledge and complex routines that cannot be transferred readily from one organizational unit to another. This may limit the extent to which the new capability can be utilized. For example, the Newell Company acquired Rubbermaid in part for its famed product innovation capabilities. Transferring these capabilities to other parts of the Newell organization proved easier said than done, however, contributing to a slump in the firm's stock prices that lasted for some time. Integrating the capabilities of two firms involved in a merger or acquisition may pose an additional challenge, particularly if there are underlying incompatibilities in their supporting systems or processes. Moreover, since internal fit is important, there is always the risk that under new management the acquired capabilities may not be as productive as they had been. In a worst-case scenario, the acquisition process may end up damaging or destroying the very capabilities that were the object of the acquisition in the first place.

Accessing Capabilities through Collaborative Partnerships A third way of obtaining valuable resources and capabilities is to form collaborative partnerships with suppliers, competitors, or other companies having the cutting-edge expertise. There are three basic ways to pursue this course of action:

1. *Outsource the function in which the company's capabilities are deficient to a key supplier or another provider.* Whether this is a wise move depends on what can be safely delegated to outside suppliers or allies and which internal capabilities are key to the company's long-term success. As discussed in Chapter 6, outsourcing has the advantage of conserving resources so that the firm can focus its energies on those activities most central to its strategy. It may be a good choice for firms that are too small and resource-constrained to execute all the parts of their strategy internally.
2. *Collaborate with a firm that has complementary resources and capabilities in a joint venture, strategic alliance, or other type of partnership established for the purpose of achieving a shared strategic objective.* This requires launching initiatives to identify the most attractive potential partners and to establish collaborative working relationships. Since the success of the venture will depend on how well the partners work together, potential partners should be selected as much for their management style, culture, and goals as for their resources and capabilities.

3. *Engage in a collaborative partnership for the purpose of learning how the partner does things, internalizing its methods and thereby acquiring its capabilities.* This may be a viable method when each partner has something to learn from the other and can achieve an outcome *beneficial to both partners.* For example, firms sometimes enter into collaborative marketing arrangements whereby each partner is granted access to the other's dealer network for the purpose of expanding sales in geographic areas where the firms lack dealers. BMW and Continental Tire recently teamed up to develop self-driving car technology and prototype vehicles capable of highly automated driving on freeways. But if the intended gains are only one-sided, the arrangement more likely involves an abuse of trust. In consequence, it not only puts the cooperative venture at risk but also encourages the firm's partner to treat the firm similarly or refuse further dealings with the firm.

The Strategic Role of Employee Training

Training and retraining are important when a company shifts to a strategy requiring different skills, competitive capabilities, and operating methods. Training is also strategically important in organizational efforts to build skill-based competencies. And it is a key activity in businesses where technical know-how is changing so rapidly that a company loses its ability to compete unless its employees have cutting-edge knowledge and expertise. Successful strategy implementers see to it that the training function is both adequately funded and effective. If better execution of the chosen strategy calls for new skills, deeper technological capability, or the building and using of new capabilities, training efforts need to be placed near the top of the action agenda.

The strategic importance of training has not gone unnoticed. Over 600 companies have established internal "universities" to lead the training effort, facilitate continuous organizational learning, and upgrade their company's knowledge resources. Many companies conduct orientation sessions for new employees, fund an assortment of competence-building training programs, and reimburse employees for tuition and other expenses associated with obtaining additional college education, attending professional development courses, and earning professional certification of one kind or another. A number of companies offer online, just-in-time training courses to employees around the clock. Increasingly, employees at all levels are expected to take an active role in their own professional development and assume responsibility for keeping their skills up to date and in sync with the company's needs.

Strategy Execution Capabilities and Competitive Advantage

As firms get better at executing their strategies, they develop capabilities in the domain of strategy execution much as they build other organizational capabilities. Superior strategy execution capabilities allow companies to get the most from their other organizational resources and competitive capabilities. In this way they contribute to the success of a firm's business model. But excellence in strategy execution can also be a more direct source of competitive advantage, since more efficient and effective strategy execution can lower costs and permit firms to deliver more value to customers. Superior strategy execution capabilities may also enable a company to react more quickly to market changes and beat other firms to the market with new products and services. This can allow a company to profit from a period of uncontested market

ILLUSTRATION CAPSULE 10.2 Zara's Strategy Execution Capabilities

Zara, a member of Inditex Group, is a "fast fashion" retailer. As soon as designs are seen in high-end fashion houses such as Prada, Zara's design team sets to work altering the clothing designs so that they can produce high fashion at mass-retailing prices. Zara's strategy is clever, but by no means unique. The company's competitive advantage is in strategy execution. Every step of Zara's value chain execution is geared toward putting fashionable clothes in stores quickly, realizing high turnover, and strategically driving traffic.

The first key lever is a quick production process. Zara's design team uses inspiration from high fashion and nearly real-time feedback from stores to create up-to-the-minute pieces. Manufacturing largely occurs in factories close to headquarters in Spain, northern Africa, and Turkey, all areas considered to have a high cost of labor. Placing the factories strategically close allows for more flexibility and greater responsiveness to market needs, thereby outweighing the additional labor costs. The entire production process, from design to arrival at stores, takes only two weeks, while other retailers take six months. While traditional retailers commit up to 80 percent of their lines by the start of the season, Zara commits only 50 to 60 percent, meaning that up to half of the merchandise to hit stores is designed and manufactured during the season. Zara purposefully manufactures in small lot sizes to avoid discounting later on and also to encourage impulse shopping, as a particular item could be gone in a few days. From start to finish, Zara has engineered its production process to maximize turnover and turnaround time, creating a true advantage in this step of strategy execution.

Zara also excels at driving traffic to stores. First, the small lot sizes and frequent shipments (up to twice a week per store) drive customers to visit often and purchase quickly. Zara shoppers average 17 visits per year, versus 4 to 5 for The Gap. On average, items stay in a Zara store only 11 days. Second, Zara spends no money on advertising, but it occupies some of the most expensive retail space in town, always near the high-fashion houses it imitates. Proximity reinforces the high-fashion association, while the busy street drives significant foot traffic. Overall, Zara has managed to create competitive advantage in every level of strategy execution by tightly aligning design, production, advertising, and real estate with the overall strategy of fast fashion: extremely fast and extremely flexible.

Note: Developed with Sara Paccamonti.

Sources: Suzy Hansen, "How Zara Grew into the World's Largest Fashion Retailer," *The New York Times,* November 9, 2012, www.nytimes.com/2012/11/11/magazine/how-zara-grew-into-the-worlds-largest-fashion-retailer.html?pagewanted=all (accessed February 5, 2014); and Seth Stevenson, "Polka Dots Are In? Polka Dots It Is!" *Slate,* June 21, 2012, www.slate.com/articles/arts/operations/2012/06/zara_s_fast_fashion_how_the_company_gets_new_styles_to_stores_so_quickly_.html (accessed February 5, 2014).

Superior strategy execution capabilities are the only source of sustainable competitive advantage when strategies are easy for rivals to copy.

dominance. See Illustration Capsule 10.2 for an example of Zara's route to competitive advantage.

Because strategy execution capabilities are socially complex capabilities that develop with experience over long periods of time, they are hard to imitate. And there is no substitute for good strategy execution. (Recall the tests of resource advantage from Chapter 4.) As such, they may be as important a source of sustained competitive advantage as the core competencies that drive a firm's strategy. Indeed, they may be a far more important avenue for securing a competitive edge over rivals in situations where it is relatively easy for rivals to copy promising strategies. In such cases, the only way for firms to achieve lasting competitive advantage is to *out-execute* their competitors.

MATCHING ORGANIZATIONAL STRUCTURE TO THE STRATEGY

While there are few hard-and-fast rules for organizing the work effort to support good strategy execution, there is one: A firm's organizational structure should be *matched* to the particular requirements of implementing the firm's strategy. Every company's strategy is grounded in its own set of organizational capabilities and value chain activities. Moreover, every firm's organization chart is partly a product of its particular situation, reflecting prior organizational patterns, varying internal circumstances, executive judgments about reporting relationships, and the politics of who gets which assignments. Thus, the determinants of the fine details of each firm's organizational structure are unique. But some considerations in organizing the work effort are common to all companies. These are summarized in Figure 10.3 and discussed in the following sections.

LO 4

What issues to consider in establishing a strategy-supportive organizational structure and organizing the work effort.

A company's organizational structure should be matched to the particular requirements of implementing the firm's strategy.

Deciding Which Value Chain Activities to Perform Internally and Which to Outsource

Aside from the fact that an outsider, because of its expertise and specialized know-how, may be able to perform certain value chain activities better or cheaper than a company can perform them internally (as discussed in Chapter 6), outsourcing can also sometimes make a positive contribution to strategy execution. Outsourcing

FIGURE 10.3 Structuring the Work Effort to Promote Successful Strategy Execution

Decide which value chain activities to perform internally and which ones to outsource

Align the organizational structure with the strategy

Decide how much authority to centralize at the top and how much to delegate to down-the-line managers and employees

Facilitate collaboration with external partners and strategic allies

An Organizational Structure Matched to the Requirements of Successful Strategy Execution

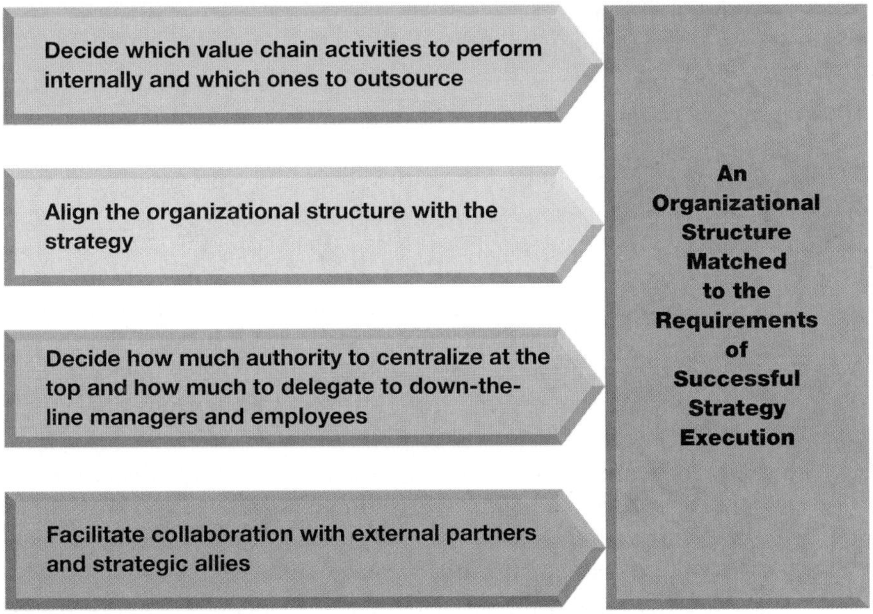

Wisely choosing which activities to perform internally and which to outsource can lead to several strategy-executing advantages—lower costs, heightened strategic focus, less internal bureaucracy, speedier decision making, and a better arsenal of organizational capabilities.

the performance of selected activities to outside vendors enables a company to heighten its strategic focus and *concentrate its full energies on performing those value chain activities that are at the core of its strategy, where it can create unique value.* For example, E. & J. Gallo Winery outsources 95 percent of its grape production, letting farmers take on weather-related and other grape-growing risks while it concentrates its full energies on wine production and sales.[18] Broadcom, a global leader in chips for broadband communication systems, outsources the manufacture of its chips to Taiwan Semiconductor, thus freeing company personnel to focus their full energies on R&D, new chip design, and marketing. Nike concentrates on design, marketing, and distribution to retailers, while outsourcing virtually all production of its shoes and sporting apparel. Illustration Capsule 10.3 describes Apple's decisions about which activities to outsource and which to perform in-house.

Such heightened focus on performing strategy-critical activities can yield three important execution-related benefits:

- *The company improves its chances for outclassing rivals in the performance of strategy-critical activities and turning a competence into a distinctive competence.* At the very least, the heightened focus on performing a select few value chain activities should promote more effective performance of those activities. This could materially enhance competitive capabilities by either lowering costs or improving product or service quality. Whirlpool, ING Insurance, Hugo Boss, Japan Airlines, and Chevron have outsourced their data processing activities to computer service firms, believing that outside specialists can perform the needed services at lower costs and equal or better quality. A relatively large number of companies outsource the operation of their websites to web design and hosting enterprises. Many businesses that get a lot of inquiries from customers or that have to provide 24/7 technical support to users of their products around the world have found that it is considerably less expensive to outsource these functions to specialists (often located in foreign countries where skilled personnel are readily available and worker compensation costs are much lower) than to operate their own call centers. NOVO1 is a company that specializes in call center operation, with five such centers located in the United States.
- *The streamlining of internal operations that flows from outsourcing often acts to decrease internal bureaucracies, flatten the organizational structure, speed internal decision making, and shorten the time it takes to respond to changing market conditions.* In consumer electronics, where advancing technology drives new product innovation, organizing the work effort in a manner that expedites getting next-generation products to market ahead of rivals is a critical competitive capability. The world's motor vehicle manufacturers have found that they can shorten the cycle time for new models by outsourcing the production of many parts and components to independent suppliers. They then work closely with the suppliers to swiftly incorporate new technology and to better integrate individual parts and components to form engine cooling systems, transmission systems, electrical systems, and so on.
- *Partnerships can add to a company's arsenal of capabilities and contribute to better strategy execution.* By building, continually improving, and then leveraging partnerships, a company enhances its overall organizational capabilities and strengthens its competitive assets—assets that deliver more value to customers and consequently pave the way for competitive success. Soft-drink and beer

ILLUSTRATION CAPSULE 10.3 Which Value Chain Activities Does Apple Outsource and Why?

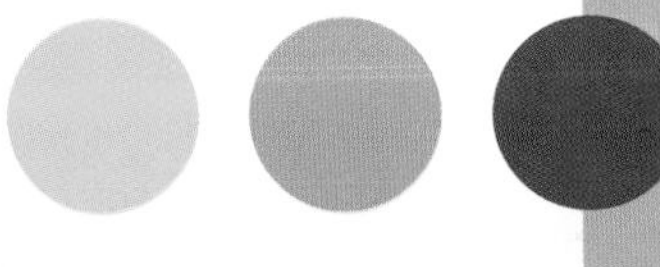

Innovation and design are core competencies for Apple and the drivers behind the creation of winning products such as the iPod, iPhone, and iPad. In consequence, all activities directly related to new product development and product design are performed internally. For example, Apple's Industrial Design Group is responsible for creating the look and feel of all Apple products—from the MacBook Air to the iPhone, and beyond to future products.

Producing a continuing stream of great new products and product versions is key to the success of Apple's strategy. But executing this strategy takes more than innovation and design capabilities. Manufacturing flexibility and speed are imperative in the production of Apple products to ensure that the latest ideas are reflected in the products and that the company meets the high demand for its products—especially around launch.

For these capabilities, Apple turns to outsourcing, as do the majority of its competitors in the consumer electronics space. Apple outsources the manufacturing of products like its iPhone to Asia, where contract manufacturing organizations (CMOs) create value through their vast scale, high flexibility, and low cost. Perhaps no company better epitomizes the Asian CMO value proposition than Foxconn, a company that assembles not only for Apple but for Hewlett-Packard, Motorola, Amazon.com, and Samsung as well. Foxconn's scale is incredible, with its largest facility (Foxconn City in Shenzhen, China) employing over 230,000 workers. Such scale offers companies a significant degree of flexibility, as Foxconn has the ability to hire 3,000 employees on practically a moment's notice. Apple, more so than its competitors, is able to capture CMO value creation by leveraging its immense sales volume and strong cash position to receive preferred treatment.

Note: Developed with Margaret W. Macauley.

Sources: Company website; and Charles Duhigg and Keith Bradsher, "How the U.S. Lost Out on iPhone Work," *The New York Times,* January 21, 2012, www.nytimes.com/2012/01/22/business/apple-america-and-a-squeezed-middle-class.html?pagewanted=all&_r=0 (accessed March 5, 2012).

manufacturers cultivate their relationships with their bottlers and distributors to strengthen access to local markets and build loyalty, support, and commitment for corporate marketing programs, without which their own sales and growth would be weakened. Similarly, fast-food enterprises like Wendy's and Burger King find it essential to work hand in hand with franchisees on outlet cleanliness, consistency of product quality, in-store ambience, courtesy and friendliness of store personnel, and other aspects of store operations. Unless franchisees continuously deliver sufficient customer satisfaction to attract repeat business, a fast-food chain's sales and competitive standing will quickly suffer. Companies like Boeing, Aerospatiale, Verizon Communications, and Dell have learned that their central R&D groups cannot begin to match the innovative capabilities of a well-managed network of supply chain partners.

However, as emphasized in Chapter 6, a company must guard against going overboard on outsourcing and becoming overly dependent on outside suppliers. A company cannot be the master of its own destiny unless it maintains expertise and resource depth in performing those value chain activities that underpin its long-term competitive success.[19] As a general rule, therefore, it is the strategically less important activities for which outsourcing is likely to make the most strategic sense—activities like handling customer inquiries and providing technical support, doing the payroll, administering employee benefit programs, providing corporate security, maintaining fleet vehicles, operating the company's website, conducting employee training, and performing an assortment of information and data processing functions.

Aligning the Firm's Organizational Structure with Its Strategy

CORE CONCEPT

A firm's **organizational structure** comprises the formal and informal arrangement of tasks, responsibilities, lines of authority, and reporting relationships by which the firm is administered.

The design of the firm's **organizational structure** is a critical aspect of the strategy execution process. The organizational structure comprises the formal and informal arrangement of tasks, responsibilities, and lines of authority and communication by which the firm is administered.[20] It specifies the linkages among parts of the organization, the reporting relationships, the direction of information flows, and the decision-making processes. It is a key factor in strategy implementation since it exerts a strong influence on how well managers can coordinate and control the complex set of activities involved.[21]

A well-designed organizational structure is one in which the various parts (e.g., decision-making rights, communication patterns) are aligned with one another and also matched to the requirements of the strategy. With the right structure in place, managers can orchestrate the various aspects of the implementation process with an even hand and a light touch. Without a supportive structure, strategy execution is more likely to become bogged down by administrative confusion, political maneuvering, and bureaucratic waste.

Good organizational design may even contribute to the firm's ability to create value for customers and realize a profit. By enabling lower bureaucratic costs and facilitating operational efficiency, it can lower a firm's operating costs. By facilitating the coordination of activities within the firm, it can improve the capability-building process, leading to greater differentiation and/or lower costs. Moreover, by improving the speed with which information is communicated and activities are coordinated, it can enable the firm to beat rivals to the market and profit from a period of unrivaled advantage.

Making Strategy-Critical Activities the Main Building Blocks of the Organizational Structure In any business, some activities in the value chain are always more critical to successful strategy execution than others. For instance, ski apparel companies like Sport Obermeyer, Arc'teryx, and Spyder must be good at styling and design, low-cost manufacturing, distribution (convincing an attractively large number of dealers to stock and promote the company's brand), and marketing and advertising (building a brand image that generates buzz and appeal among ski enthusiasts). For discount stockbrokers, like Scottrade and TD Ameritrade, the strategy-critical activities are fast access to information, accurate order execution, efficient record keeping and transaction processing, and good customer service. With respect to such core value chain activities, it is important for management to build its organizational structure around proficient performance of these activities, making them the centerpieces or main building blocks in the enterprise's organizational structure.

The rationale is compelling: If activities crucial to strategic success are to have the resources, decision-making influence, and organizational impact they need, they must be centerpieces in the enterprise's organizational scheme. Making them the focus of structuring efforts will also facilitate their coordination and promote good internal fit—an essential attribute of a winning strategy, as summarized in Chapter 1 and elaborated in Chapter 4. To the extent that implementing a new strategy entails new or altered key activities or capabilities, different organizational arrangements may be required.

Matching Type of Organizational Structure to Strategy Execution Requirements Organizational structures can be classified into a limited number of standard types. The type that is most suitable for a given firm will depend on the firm's size and complexity as well as its strategy. As firms grow and their needs for structure evolve, their structural form is likely to evolve from one type to another. The four basic types are the *simple structure,* the *functional structure,* the *multidivisional structure,* and the *matrix structure,* as described next.

1. Simple Structure A **simple structure** is one in which a central executive (often the owner-manager) handles all major decisions and oversees the operations of the organization with the help of a small staff.[22] Simple structures are also known as *line-and-staff structures,* since a central administrative staff supervises line employees who conduct the operations of the firm, or *flat structures,* since there are few levels of hierarchy. The simple structure is characterized by limited task specialization; few rules; informal relationships; minimal use of training, planning, and liaison devices; and a lack of sophisticated support systems. It has all the advantages of simplicity, including low administrative costs, ease of coordination, flexibility, quick decision making, adaptability, and responsiveness to change. Its informality and lack of rules may foster creativity and heightened individual responsibility.

CORE CONCEPT

A **simple structure** consists of a central executive (often the owner-manager) who handles all major decisions and oversees all operations with the help of a small staff. Simple structures are also called *line-and-staff structures* or *flat structures.*

Simple organizational structures are typically employed by small firms and entrepreneurial startups. The simple structure is the most common type of organizational structure since small firms are the most prevalent type of business. As an organization grows, however, this structural form becomes inadequate to the demands that come with size and complexity. In response, growing firms tend to alter their organizational structure from a simple structure to a *functional structure.*

CORE CONCEPT

A **functional structure** is organized into functional departments, with departmental managers who report to the CEO and small corporate staff. Functional structures are also called *departmental structures* and *unitary structures* or *U-forms.*

2. Functional Structure A **functional structure** is one that is organized along functional lines, where a function represents a major component of the firm's value chain, such as R&D, engineering and design, manufacturing, sales and marketing, logistics, and customer service. Each functional unit is supervised by functional line managers who report to the chief executive officer and a corporate staff. This arrangement allows functional managers to focus on their area of responsibility, leaving it to the CEO and headquarters to provide direction and ensure that the activities of the functional managers are coordinated and integrated. Functional structures are also known as *departmental structures,* since the functional units are commonly called departments, and *unitary structures* or *U-forms,* since a single unit is responsible for each function.

In large organizations, functional structures lighten the load on top management, in comparison to simple structures, and enable more efficient use of managerial resources. Their primary advantage, however, is greater *task specialization,* which promotes learning, enables the realization of scale economies, and offers productivity advantages not otherwise available. Their chief disadvantage is that the departmental boundaries can inhibit the flow of information and limit the opportunities for cross-functional cooperation and coordination.

The primary advantage of a functional structure is greater *task specialization,* which promotes learning, enables the realization of scale economies, and offers productivity advantages not otherwise available.

It is generally agreed that a functional structure is the best organizational arrangement when a company is in just one particular business (irrespective of which of the five generic competitive strategies it opts to pursue). For instance, a technical instruments manufacturer may be organized around research and development, engineering, supply chain management, assembly, quality control, marketing, and technical services. A discount retailer, such as Dollar General or Kmart, may organize around such functional units as purchasing, warehousing, distribution logistics, store operations, advertising, merchandising and promotion, and customer service. Functional structures can also be appropriate for firms with high-volume production, products that are closely related, and a limited degree of vertical integration. For example, General Motors now manages all of its brands (Cadillac, GMC, Chevrolet, Buick, etc.) under a common functional structure designed to promote technical transfer and capture economies of scale.

As firms continue to grow, they often become more diversified and complex, placing a greater burden on top management. At some point, the centralized control that characterizes the functional structure becomes a liability, and the advantages of functional specialization begin to break down. To resolve these problems and address a growing need for coordination across functions, firms generally turn to the *multidivisional structure*.

CORE CONCEPT

A **multidivisional structure** is a decentralized structure consisting of a set of operating divisions organized along business, product, customer group, or geographic lines and a central corporate headquarters that allocates resources, provides support functions, and monitors divisional activities. Multidivisional structures are also called *divisional structures* or *M-forms*.

3. Multidivisional Structure A **multidivisional structure** is a decentralized structure consisting of a set of operating divisions organized along market, customer, product, or geographic lines, along with a central corporate headquarters, which monitors divisional activities, allocates resources, performs assorted support functions, and exercises overall control. Since each division is essentially a business (often called a *single business unit* or *SBU*), the divisions typically operate as independent profit centers (i.e., with profit and loss responsibility) and are organized internally along functional lines. Division managers oversee day-to-day operations and the development of business-level strategy, while corporate executives attend to overall performance and corporate strategy, the elements of which were described in Chapter 8. Multidivisional structures are also called *divisional structures* or *M-forms,* in contrast with U-form (functional) structures.

Multidivisional structures are common among companies pursuing some form of diversification strategy or international strategy, with operations in a number of businesses or countries. When the strategy is one of unrelated diversification, as in a conglomerate, the divisions generally represent businesses in separate industries. When the strategy is based on related diversification, the divisions may be organized according to industries, customer groups, product lines, geographic regions, or technologies. In this arrangement, the decision about where to draw the divisional lines depends foremost on the nature of the relatedness and the strategy-critical building blocks, in terms of which businesses have key value chain activities in common. For example, a company selling closely related products to business customers as well as two types of end consumers—online buyers and in-store buyers—may organize its divisions according to customer groups since the value chains involved in serving the three groups differ. Another company may organize by product line due to commonalities in product development and production within each product line. Multidivisional structures are also common among vertically integrated firms. There the major building blocks are often divisional units performing one or more of the major processing steps along the value chain (e.g., raw-material production, components manufacture, assembly, wholesale distribution, retail store operations).

Multidivisional structures offer significant advantages over functional structures in terms of facilitating the management of a complex and diverse set of operations.[23] Putting business-level strategy in the hands of division managers while leaving corporate strategy to top executives reduces the potential for information overload and improves the quality of decision making in each domain. This also minimizes the costs of coordinating divisionwide activities while enhancing top management's ability to control a diverse and complex operation. Moreover, multidivisional structures can help align individual incentives with the goals of the corporation and spur productivity by encouraging competition for resources among the different divisions.

But a multidivisional structure can also present some problems to a company pursuing related diversification, because having independent business units—each running its own business in its own way—inhibits cross-business collaboration and the capture of cross-business synergies, which are critical for the success of a related diversification strategy, as Chapter 8 explains. To solve this type of problem, firms turn to more complex structures, such as the matrix structure.

4. Matrix Structure A **matrix structure** is a combination structure in which the organization is organized along two or more dimensions at once (e.g., business, geographic area, value chain function) for the purpose of enhancing cross-unit communication, collaboration, and coordination. In essence, it overlays one type of structure onto another type. Matrix structures are managed through multiple reporting relationships, so a middle manager may report to several bosses. For instance, in a matrix structure based on product line, region, and function, a sales manager for plastic containers in Georgia might report to the manager of the plastics division, the head of the southeast sales region, and the head of marketing.

CORE CONCEPT

A **matrix structure** is a combination structure that overlays one type of structure onto another type, with multiple reporting relationships. It is used to foster cross-unit collaboration. Matrix structures are also called *composite structures* or *combination structures*.

Matrix organizational structures have evolved from the complex, overformalized structures that were popular in the 1960s, 70s, and 80s but often produced inefficient, unwieldy bureaucracies. The modern incarnation of the matrix structure is generally a more flexible arrangement, with a single primary reporting relationship that can be overlaid with a *temporary* secondary reporting relationship as need arises. For example, a software company that is organized into functional departments (software design, quality control, customer relations) may assign employees from those departments to different projects on a temporary basis, so an employee reports to a project manager as well as to his or her primary boss (the functional department head) for the duration of a project.

Matrix structures are also called *composite structures* or *combination structures*. They are often used for project-based, process-based, or team-based management. Such approaches are common in businesses involving projects of limited duration, such as consulting, architecture, and engineering services. The type of close cross-unit collaboration that a flexible matrix structure supports is also needed to build competitive capabilities in strategically important activities, such as speeding new products to market, that involve employees scattered across several organizational units.[24] Capabilities-based matrix structures that combine process departments (like new product development) with more traditional functional departments provide a solution.

An advantage of matrix structures is that they facilitate the sharing of plant and equipment, specialized knowledge, and other key resources. Thus, they lower costs by enabling the realization of economies of scope. They also have the advantage of flexibility in form and may allow for better oversight since supervision is provided from more than one perspective. A disadvantage is that they add another layer of management, thereby increasing bureaucratic costs and possibly decreasing response time to new situations.[25] In addition, there is a potential for confusion among employees due to dual reporting relationships and divided loyalties. While there is some controversy over the utility of matrix structures, the modern approach to matrix structures does much to minimize their disadvantages.[26]

LO 5

The pros and cons of centralized and decentralized decision making in implementing the chosen strategy.

Determining How Much Authority to Delegate

Under any organizational structure, there is room for considerable variation in how much authority top managers retain and how much is delegated to down-the-line managers and employees. In executing strategy and conducting daily operations, companies must decide how much authority to delegate to the managers of each organizational unit—especially the heads of divisions, functional departments, plants, and other operating units—and how much decision-making latitude to give individual employees in performing their jobs. The two extremes are to *centralize decision making* at the top or to *decentralize decision making* by giving managers and employees at all levels considerable decision-making latitude in their areas of responsibility. As shown in Table 10.1, the two approaches are based on sharply different underlying principles and beliefs, with each having its pros and cons.

TABLE 10.1 Advantages and Disadvantages of Centralized versus Decentralized Decision Making

Centralized Organizational Structures	Decentralized Organizational Structures
Basic tenets • Decisions on most matters of importance should be in the hands of top-level managers who have the experience, expertise, and judgment to decide what is the best course of action. • Lower-level personnel have neither the knowledge, time, nor inclination to properly manage the tasks they are performing. • Strong control from the top is a more effective means for coordinating company actions.	**Basic tenets** • Decision-making authority should be put in the hands of the people closest to, and most familiar with, the situation. • Those with decision-making authority should be trained to exercise good judgment. • A company that draws on the combined intellectual capital of all its employees can outperform a command-and-control company.
Chief advantages • Fixes accountability through tight control from the top. • Eliminates potential for conflicting goals and actions on the part of lower-level managers. • Facilitates quick decision making and strong leadership under crisis situations.	**Chief advantages** • Encourages company employees to exercise initiative and act responsibly. • Promotes greater motivation and involvement in the business on the part of more company personnel. • Spurs new ideas and creative thinking. • Allows for fast response to market change. • Entails fewer layers of management.
Primary disadvantages • Lengthens response times by those closest to the market conditions because they must seek approval for their actions. • Does not encourage responsibility among lower-level managers and rank-and-file employees. • Discourages lower-level managers and rank-and-file employees from exercising any initiative.	**Primary disadvantages** • May result in higher-level managers being unaware of actions taken by empowered personnel under their supervision. • Can lead to inconsistent or conflicting approaches by different managers and employees. • Can impair cross-unit collaboration.

Centralized Decision Making: Pros and Cons In a highly centralized organizational structure, *top executives retain authority for most strategic and operating decisions* and keep a tight rein on business unit heads, department heads, and the managers of key operating units. Comparatively little discretionary authority is granted to frontline supervisors and rank-and-file employees. The command-and-control paradigm of centralized structures is based on the underlying assumptions that frontline personnel have neither the time nor the inclination to direct and properly control the work they are performing and that they lack the knowledge and judgment to make wise decisions about how best to do it—hence the need for managerially prescribed policies and procedures, close supervision, and tight control. The thesis underlying centralized structures is that strict enforcement of detailed procedures backed by rigorous managerial oversight is the most reliable way to keep the daily execution of strategy on track.

One advantage of a centralized structure, with tight control by the manager in charge, is that it is easy to know who is accountable when things do not go well. This structure can also reduce the potential for conflicting decisions and actions among lower-level managers who may have differing perspectives and ideas about how to tackle certain tasks or resolve particular issues. For example, a manager in charge of an engineering department may be more interested in pursuing a new technology than is a marketing manager who doubts that customers will value the technology as highly. Another advantage of a command-and-control structure is that it can facilitate strong leadership from the top in a crisis situation that affects the organization as a whole and can enable a more uniform and swift response.

But there are some serious disadvantages as well. Hierarchical command-and-control structures do not encourage responsibility and initiative on the part of lower-level managers and employees. They can make a large organization with a complex structure sluggish in responding to changing market conditions because of the time it takes for the review-and-approval process to run up all the layers of the management bureaucracy. Furthermore, to work well, centralized decision making requires top-level managers to gather and process whatever information is relevant to the decision. When the relevant knowledge resides at lower organizational levels (or is technical, detailed, or hard to express in words), it is difficult and time-consuming to get all the facts in front of a high-level executive located far from the scene of the action—full understanding of the situation cannot be readily copied from one mind to another. Hence, centralized decision making is often impractical—the larger the company and the more scattered its operations, the more that decision-making authority must be delegated to managers closer to the scene of the action.

Decentralized Decision Making: Pros and Cons In a highly decentralized organization, *decision-making authority is pushed down to the lowest organizational level capable of making timely, informed, competent decisions.* The objective is to put adequate decision-making authority in the hands of the people closest to and most familiar with the situation and train them to weigh all the factors and exercise good judgment. At Starbucks, for example, employees are encouraged to exercise initiative in promoting customer satisfaction—there's the oft-repeated story of a store employee who, when the computerized cash register system went offline, offered free coffee to waiting customers, thereby avoiding customer displeasure and damage to Starbucks's reputation.[27]

The ultimate goal of decentralized decision making is to put authority in the hands of those persons closest to and most knowledgeable about the situation.

The case for empowering down-the-line managers and employees to make decisions related to daily operations and strategy execution is based on the belief that a company that draws on the combined intellectual capital of all its employees can outperform a command-and-control company.[28] The challenge in a decentralized system is maintaining adequate control. With decentralized decision making, top management maintains control by placing limits on the authority granted to company personnel, installing companywide strategic control systems, holding people accountable for their decisions, instituting compensation incentives that reward people for doing their jobs well, and creating a corporate culture where there's strong peer pressure on individuals to act responsibly.[29]

Decentralized organizational structures have much to recommend them. Delegating authority to subordinate managers and rank-and-file employees encourages them to take responsibility and exercise initiative. It shortens organizational response times to market changes and spurs new ideas, creative thinking, innovation, and greater involvement on the part of all company personnel. In worker-empowered structures, jobs can be defined more broadly, several tasks can be integrated into a single job, and people can direct their own work. Fewer managers are needed because deciding how to do things becomes part of each person's or team's job. Further, today's online communication systems and smartphones make it easy and relatively inexpensive for people at all organizational levels to have direct access to data, other employees, managers, suppliers, and customers. They can access information quickly (via the Internet or company network), readily check with superiors or whomever else as needed, and take responsible action. Typically, there are genuine gains in morale and productivity when people are provided with the tools and information they need to operate in a self-directed way.

But decentralization also has some disadvantages. Top managers lose an element of control over what goes on and may thus be unaware of actions being taken by personnel under their supervision. Such lack of control can be problematic in the event that empowered employees make decisions that conflict with those of others or that serve their unit's interests at the expense of other parts of the company. Moreover, because decentralization gives organizational units the authority to act independently, there is risk of too little collaboration and coordination between different units.

Many companies have concluded that the advantages of decentralization outweigh the disadvantages. Over the past several decades, there's been a decided shift from centralized, hierarchical structures to flatter, more decentralized structures that stress employee empowerment. This shift reflects a strong and growing consensus that authoritarian, hierarchical organizational structures are not well suited to implementing and executing strategies in an era when extensive information and instant communication are the norm and when a big fraction of the organization's most valuable assets consists of intellectual capital that resides in its employees' capabilities.

Capturing Cross-Business Strategic Fit in a Decentralized Structure Diversified companies striving to capture the benefits of synergy between separate businesses must beware of giving business unit heads full rein to operate independently. Cross-business strategic fit typically must be captured either by enforcing close cross-business collaboration or by centralizing the performance of functions requiring close coordination at the corporate level.[30] For example, if businesses with overlapping process and product technologies have their own independent R&D departments—each pursuing its own priorities, projects, and strategic agendas—it's hard for the corporate parent to prevent duplication of effort, capture either economies of scale or economies of scope, or encourage more collaborative R&D efforts. Where cross-business strategic fit with respect to R&D is important, the best solution is usually to centralize the R&D function and have a coordinated corporate R&D effort that serves the interests of both the individual businesses and

Efforts to decentralize decision making and give company personnel some leeway in conducting operations must be tempered with the need to maintain adequate control and cross-unit coordination.

the company as a whole. Likewise, centralizing the related activities of separate businesses makes sense when there are opportunities to share a common sales force, use common distribution channels, rely on a common field service organization, use common e-commerce systems, and so on.

Facilitating Collaboration with External Partners and Strategic Allies

Organizational mechanisms—whether formal or informal—are also required to ensure effective working relationships with each major outside constituency involved in strategy execution. Strategic alliances, outsourcing arrangements, joint ventures, and cooperative partnerships can contribute little of value without active management of the relationship. Unless top management sees that constructive organizational bridge building with external partners occurs and that productive working relationships emerge, the potential value of cooperative relationships is lost and the company's power to execute its strategy is weakened. For example, if close working relationships with suppliers are crucial, then supply chain management must enter into considerations of how to create an effective organizational structure. If distributor, dealer, or franchisee relationships are important, then someone must be assigned the task of nurturing the relationships with such forward-channel allies.

Building organizational bridges with external partners and strategic allies can be accomplished by appointing "relationship managers" with responsibility for making particular strategic partnerships generate the intended benefits. Relationship managers have many roles and functions: getting the right people together, promoting good rapport, facilitating the flow of information, nurturing interpersonal communication and cooperation, and ensuring effective coordination.[31] Multiple cross-organization ties have to be established and kept open to ensure proper communication and coordination. There has to be enough information sharing to make the relationship work and periodic frank discussions of conflicts, trouble spots, and changing situations.

Organizing and managing a network structure provides a mechanism for encouraging more effective collaboration and cooperation among external partners. A **network structure** is the arrangement linking a number of independent organizations involved in some common undertaking. A well-managed network structure typically includes one firm in a more central role, with the responsibility of ensuring that the right partners are included and the activities across the network are coordinated. The high-end Italian motorcycle company Ducati operates in this manner, assembling its motorcycles from parts obtained from a hand-picked integrated network of parts suppliers.

CORE CONCEPT

A **network structure** is the arrangement linking a number of independent organizations involved in some common undertaking, with one firm typically in a more central role.

Further Perspectives on Structuring the Work Effort

All organizational designs have their strategy-related strengths and weaknesses. To do a good job of matching structure to strategy, strategy implementers first have to pick a basic organizational design and modify it as needed to fit the company's particular business lineup. They must then (1) supplement the design with appropriate coordinating mechanisms (cross-functional task forces, special project teams, self-contained work teams, etc.) and (2) institute whatever networking and communications arrangements are necessary to support effective execution of the firm's strategy. Some companies may avoid setting up "ideal" organizational arrangements because they do not want to disturb existing reporting relationships or because they need to accommodate other situational idiosyncrasies, yet they must still work toward the goal of building a competitively capable organization.

What can be said unequivocally is that building a capable organization entails a process of consciously knitting together the efforts of individuals and groups. Organizational capabilities emerge from establishing and nurturing cooperative working relationships among people and groups to perform activities in a more efficient, value-creating fashion. While an appropriate organizational structure can facilitate this, organization building is a task in which senior management must be deeply involved. Indeed, effectively managing both internal organizational processes and external collaboration to create and develop competitively valuable organizational capabilities remains a top challenge for senior executives in today's companies.

KEY POINTS

1. Executing strategy is an action-oriented, operations-driven activity revolving around the management of people, business processes, and organizational structure. In devising an action agenda for executing strategy, managers should start by conducting a probing assessment of what the organization must do differently to carry out the strategy successfully. They should then consider precisely *how* to make the necessary internal changes.
2. Good strategy execution requires a *team effort.* All managers have strategy-executing responsibility in their areas of authority, and all employees are active participants in the strategy execution process.
3. Ten managerial tasks are part of every company effort to execute strategy: (1) staffing the organization with the right people, (2) developing the resources and building the necessary organizational capabilities, (3) creating a supportive organizational structure, (4) allocating sufficient resources, (5) instituting supportive policies and procedures, (6) adopting processes for continuous improvement, (7) installing systems that enable proficient company operations, (8) tying incentives to the achievement of desired targets, (9) instilling the right corporate culture, and (10) exercising internal leadership to propel strategy execution forward.
4. The two best signs of good strategy execution are that a company is meeting or beating its performance targets and is performing value chain activities in a manner that is conducive to companywide operating excellence. *Shortfalls in performance signal weak strategy, weak execution, or both.*
5. Building an organization capable of good strategy execution entails three types of actions: (1) *staffing the organization*—assembling a talented management team and recruiting and retaining employees with the needed experience, technical skills, and intellectual capital; (2) *acquiring, developing, and strengthening strategy-supportive resources and capabilities*—accumulating the required resources, developing proficiencies in performing strategy-critical value chain activities, and updating the company's capabilities to match changing market conditions and customer expectations; and (3) *structuring the organization and work effort*—instituting organizational arrangements that facilitate good strategy execution,

deciding how much decision-making authority to delegate, and managing external relationships.

6. Building core competencies and competitive capabilities is a time-consuming, managerially challenging exercise that can be approached in three ways: (1) developing capabilities internally, (2) acquiring capabilities through mergers and acquisitions, and (3) accessing capabilities via collaborative partnerships.
7. In building capabilities internally, the first step is to develop the *ability* to do something, through experimenting, actively searching for alternative solutions, and learning by trial and error. As experience grows and company personnel learn how to perform the activities consistently well and at an acceptable cost, the ability evolves into a tried-and-true capability. The process can be accelerated by making learning a more deliberate endeavor and providing the incentives that will motivate company personnel to achieve the desired ends.
8. As firms get better at executing their strategies, they develop capabilities in the domain of strategy execution. Superior strategy execution capabilities allow companies to get the most from their organizational resources and capabilities. But excellence in strategy execution can also be a more direct source of competitive advantage, since more efficient and effective strategy execution can lower costs and permit firms to deliver more value to customers. Because they are socially complex capabilities, superior strategy execution capabilities are hard to imitate and have no good substitutes. As such, they can be an important source of *sustainable* competitive advantage. Any time rivals can readily duplicate successful strategies, making it impossible to *out-strategize* rivals, the chief way to achieve lasting competitive advantage is to *out-execute* them.
9. Structuring the organization and organizing the work effort in a strategy-supportive fashion has four aspects: (1) deciding which value chain activities to perform internally and which ones to outsource; (2) aligning the firm's organizational structure with its strategy; (3) deciding how much authority to centralize at the top and how much to delegate to down-the-line managers and employees; and (4) facilitating the necessary collaboration and coordination with external partners and strategic allies.
10. To align the firm's organizational structure with its strategy, it is important to make strategy-critical activities the main building blocks. There are four basic types of organizational structures: the simple structure, the functional structure, the multidivisional structure, and the matrix structure. Which is most appropriate depends on the firm's size, complexity, and strategy.

ASSURANCE OF LEARNING EXERCISES

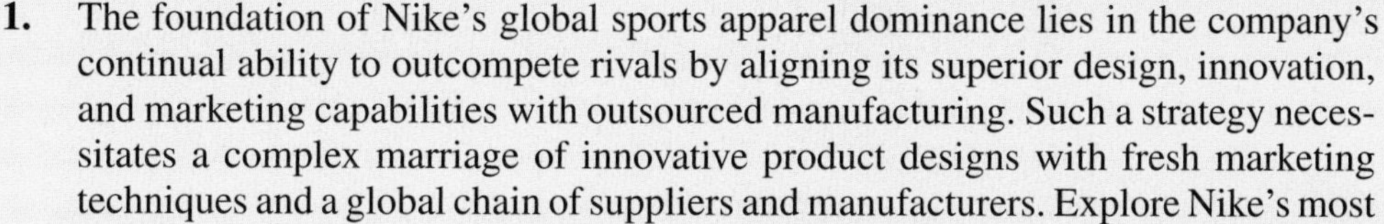

1. The foundation of Nike's global sports apparel dominance lies in the company's continual ability to outcompete rivals by aligning its superior design, innovation, and marketing capabilities with outsourced manufacturing. Such a strategy necessitates a complex marriage of innovative product designs with fresh marketing techniques and a global chain of suppliers and manufacturers. Explore Nike's most

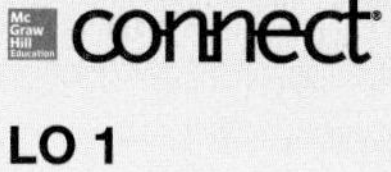

LO 1

recent strategic management changes (**nikeinc.com/news/nike-announces-strategic-leadership-changes**). How well do these changes reflect the company's focus on innovative design and marketing strategies? Has the company's relentless focus on apparel innovation affected its supply chain management? Do these changes—or Nike's strategy, more broadly—reflect the company's ubiquitous Swoosh logo and "Just Do It" slogan? Visit Nike's corporate website for more in-depth information: **nikeinc.com/pages/about-nike-inc**.

connect

LO 2

2. Search online to read about Jeff Bezos's management of his new executives. Specifically, explore Amazon.com's "S-Team" meetings (**management.fortune.cnn.com/2012/11/16/jeff-bezos-amazon/**). Why does Bezos begin meetings of senior executives with 30 minutes of silent reading? How does this focus the group? Why does Bezos insist new ideas must be written and presented in memo form? How does this reflect the founder's insistence on clear, concise, and innovative thinking in his company? And does this exercise work as a de facto crash course for new Amazon executives? Explain why this small but crucial management strategy reflects Bezos's overriding goal of cohesive and clear idea presentation.

LO 2, LO 3

3. Review Facebook's Careers page (**www.Facebook.com/careers/**). The page emphasizes Facebook's core values and explains how potential employees could fit that mold. Bold and decisive thinking and a commitment to transparency and social connectivity drive the page and the company as a whole. Then research Facebook's internal management training programs, called "employee boot camps," using a search engine like Google or Bing. How do these programs integrate the traits and stated goals on the Careers page into specific and tangible construction of employee capabilities? Boot camps are open to all Facebook employees, not just engineers. How does this internal training prepare Facebook employees of all types to "move fast and break things"?

LO 4

4. Review Valve Corporation's company handbook online: **www.valvesoftware.com/company/Valve_Handbook_LowRes.pdf**. Specifically, focus on Valve's corporate structure. Valve has hundreds of employees but no managers or bosses at all. Valve's gaming success hinges on innovative and completely original experiences like Portal and Half-Life. Does it seem that Valve's corporate structure uniquely promotes this type of gaming innovation? Why or why not? How would you characterize Valve's organizational structure? Is it completely unique, or could it be characterized as a multidivisional, matrix, or functional structure? Explain your answer.

LO 5

5. Keep Valve's unique structure in mind. Using Google Scholar or your university's access to online databases, do a search for recent writings on decentralized decision making and employee empowerment. According to these articles, under which conditions should a company strive for more centralization? Can employee empowerment ever backfire, and, if so, how should companies build and impose a more effective organizational structure?

EXERCISE FOR SIMULATION PARTICIPANTS

1. How would you describe the organization of your company's top-management team? Is some decision making decentralized and delegated to individual managers? If so, explain how the decentralization works. Or are decisions made more by consensus, with all co-managers having input? What do you see as the advantages and disadvantages of the decision-making approach your company is employing? **LO 5**
2. What specific actions have you and your co-managers taken to develop core competencies or competitive capabilities that can contribute to good strategy execution and potential competitive advantage? If no actions have been taken, explain your rationale for doing nothing. **LO 3**
3. What value chain activities are most crucial to good execution of your company's strategy? Does your company have the ability to outsource any value chain activities? If so, have you and your co-managers opted to engage in outsourcing? Why or why not? **LO 1, LO 4**

ENDNOTES

[1] Steven W. Floyd and Bill Wooldridge, "Managing Strategic Consensus: The Foundation of Effective Implementation," *Academy of Management Executive* 6, no. 4 (November 1992), p. 27.

[2] Jack Welch with Suzy Welch, *Winning* (New York: HarperBusiness, 2005).

[3] Larry Bossidy and Ram Charan, *Execution: The Discipline of Getting Things Done* (New York: Crown Business, 2002).

[4] Christopher A. Bartlett and Sumantra Ghoshal, "Building Competitive Advantage through People," *MIT Sloan Management Review* 43, no. 2 (Winter 2002), pp. 34–41.

[5] Justin Menkes, "Hiring for Smarts," *Harvard Business Review* 83, no. 11 (November 2005), pp. 100–109; Justin Menkes, *Executive Intelligence* (New York: HarperCollins, 2005).

[6] Menkes, *Executive Intelligence,* pp. 68, 76.

[7] Jim Collins, *Good to Great* (New York: HarperBusiness, 2001).

[8] John Byrne, "The Search for the Young and Gifted," *Businessweek,* October 4, 1999, p. 108.

[9] C. Helfat and M. Peteraf, "The Dynamic Resource-Based View: Capability Lifecycles," *Strategic Management Journal* 24, no. 10 (October 2003), pp. 997–1010.

[10] G. Hamel and C. K. Prahalad, "Strategy as Stretch and Leverage," *Harvard Business Review* 71, no. 2 (March–April 1993), pp. 75–84.

[11] G. Dosi, R. Nelson, and S. Winter (eds.), *The Nature and Dynamics of Organizational Capabilities* (Oxford, England: Oxford University Press, 2001).

[12] S. Winter, "The Satisficing Principle in Capability Learning," *Strategic Management Journal* 21, no. 10–11 (October–November 2000), pp. 981–996; M. Zollo and S. Winter, "Deliberate Learning and the Evolution of Dynamic Capabilities," *Organization Science* 13, no. 3 (May–June 2002), pp. 339–351.

[13] G. Szulanski and S. Winter, "Getting It Right the Second Time," *Harvard Business Review* 80 (January 2002), pp. 62–69.

[14] B. Kogut and U. Zander, "Knowledge of the Firm, Combinative Capabilities, and the Replication of Technology," *Organization Science* 3, no. 3 (August 1992), pp. 383–397.

[15] C. Helfat and R. Raubitschek, "Product Sequencing: Co-evolution of Knowledge, Capabilities and Products," *Strategic Management Journal* 21, no. 10–11 (October–November 2000), pp. 961–980.

[16] Robert H. Hayes, Gary P. Pisano, and David M. Upton, *Strategic Operations: Competing through Capabilities* (New York: Free Press, 1996); Jonas Ridderstrale, "Cashing In on Corporate Competencies," *Business Strategy Review* 14, no. 1 (Spring 2003), pp. 27–38; Danny Miller, Russell Eisenstat, and Nathaniel Foote, "Strategy from the Inside Out: Building Capability-Creating Organizations," *California Management Review* 44, no. 3 (Spring 2002), pp. 37–55.

[17] S. Karim and W. Mitchell, "Path-Dependent and Path-Breaking Change: Reconfiguring Business Resources Following Acquisitions in the US Medical Sector, 1978–1995," *Strategic Management Journal* 21, no. 10–11 (October–November 2000), pp. 1061–1082; L. Capron, P. Dussauge, and W. Mitchell, "Resource Redeployment Following Horizontal Acquisitions in Europe and North America, 1988–1992," *Strategic Management Journal* 19, no. 7 (July 1998), pp. 631–662.

[18] J. B. Quinn, *Intelligent Enterprise* (New York: Free Press, 1992).

[19] Gary P. Pisano and Willy C. Shih, "Restoring American Competitiveness," *Harvard Business Review* 87, no. 7–8 (July–August 2009), pp. 114–125.

[20] A. Chandler, *Strategy and Structure* (Cambridge, MA: MIT Press, 1962).

[21] E. Olsen, S. Slater, and G. Hult, "The Importance of Structure and Process to Strategy Implementation," *Business Horizons* 48, no. 1 (2005), pp. 47–54; H. Barkema, J. Baum, and E. Mannix, "Management Challenges in a New Time," *Academy of Management Journal* 45, no. 5 (October 2002), pp. 916–930.

[22] H. Mintzberg, *The Structuring of Organizations* (Englewood Cliffs, NJ: Prentice Hall, 1979); C. Levicki, *The Interactive Strategy Workout,* 2nd ed. (London: Prentice Hall, 1999).

[23] O. Williamson, *Market and Hierarchies* (New York: Free Press, 1975); R. M. Burton and B. Obel, "A Computer Simulation Test of the M-Form Hypothesis," *Administrative Science Quarterly* 25 (1980), pp. 457–476.

[24] J. Baum and S. Wally, "Strategic Decision Speed and Firm Performance," *Strategic Management Journal* 24 (2003), pp. 1107–1129.

[25] C. Bartlett and S. Ghoshal, "Matrix Management: Not a Structure, a Frame of Mind," *Harvard Business Review,* July–August 1990, pp. 138–145.

[26] M. Goold and A. Campbell, "Structured Networks: Towards the Well Designed Matrix," *Long Range Planning* 36, no. 5 (2003), pp. 427–439.

[27] Iain Somerville and John Edward Mroz, "New Competencies for a New World," in Frances Hesselbein, Marshall Goldsmith, and Richard Beckard (eds.), *The Organization of the Future* (San Francisco: Jossey-Bass, 1997), p. 70.

[28] Stanley E. Fawcett, Gary K. Rhoads, and Phillip Burnah, "People as the Bridge to Competitiveness: Benchmarking the 'ABCs' of an Empowered Workforce," *Benchmarking: An International Journal* 11, no. 4 (2004), pp. 346–360.

[29] Robert Simons, "Control in an Age of Empowerment," *Harvard Business Review* 73 (March–April 1995), pp. 80–88.

[30] Jeanne M. Liedtka, "Collaboration across Lines of Business for Competitive Advantage," *Academy of Management Executive* 10, no. 2 (May 1996), pp. 20–34.

[31] Rosabeth Moss Kanter, "Collaborative Advantage: The Art of the Alliance," *Harvard Business Review* 72, no. 4 (July–August 1994), pp. 96–108.

CHAPTER 11

Managing Internal Operations

Actions That Promote Good Strategy Execution

Learning Objectives

THIS CHAPTER WILL HELP YOU UNDERSTAND:

LO 1 Why resource allocation should always be based on strategic priorities.

LO 2 How well-designed policies and procedures can facilitate good strategy execution.

LO 3 How best practices and process management tools drive continuous improvement in the performance of value chain activities and promote superior strategy execution.

LO 4 The role of information and operating systems in enabling company personnel to carry out their strategic roles proficiently.

LO 5 How and why the use of well-designed incentives and rewards can be management's single most powerful tool for promoting adept strategy execution.

Adhering to budgeting rules shouldn't trump good decision-making.

Emily Oster – *Economist and Author*

Pay your people the least possible and you'll get the same from them.

Malcolm Forbes – *Late Publisher of* Forbes *Magazine*

Apple is a very disciplined company, and we have great processes. But that's not what it's about. Process makes you more efficient.

Steve Jobs – *Cofounder of Apple, Inc.*

In Chapter 10, we emphasized that proficient strategy execution begins with three types of managerial actions: staffing the organization with the right people; acquiring, developing, and strengthening the firm's resources and capabilities; and structuring the organization in a manner supportive of the strategy execution effort.

In this chapter, we discuss five additional managerial actions that advance the cause of good strategy execution:

- Allocating ample resources to execution-critical value chain activities.
- Instituting policies and procedures that facilitate strategy execution.
- Employing process management tools to drive continuous improvement in how value chain activities are performed.
- Installing information and operating systems that enable company personnel to carry out their strategic roles proficiently.
- Using rewards and incentives to promote better strategy execution and the achievement of strategic and financial targets.

ALLOCATING RESOURCES TO THE STRATEGY EXECUTION EFFORT

LO 1

Why resource allocation should always be based on strategic priorities.

Early in the strategy implementation process, managers must determine what resources (in terms of funding, people, and so on) will be required and how they should be distributed across the company's various organizational units. This includes carefully screening requests for more people and new facilities and equipment, approving those that will contribute to the strategy execution effort, and turning down those that don't. Should internal cash flows prove insufficient to fund the planned strategic initiatives, then management must raise additional funds through borrowing or selling additional shares of stock to investors.

A company's ability to marshal the resources needed to support new strategic initiatives has a major impact on the strategy execution process. Too little funding and an insufficiency of other types of resources slow progress and impede the efforts of organizational units to execute their pieces of the strategic plan proficiently. Too much funding and an overabundance of other resources waste organizational resources and reduce financial performance. Both outcomes argue for managers to be deeply involved in reviewing budget proposals and directing the proper kinds and amounts of resources to strategy-critical organizational units.

A change in strategy nearly always calls for budget reallocations and resource shifting. Previously important units with a lesser role in the new strategy may need downsizing. Units that now have a bigger strategic role may need more people, new equipment, additional facilities, and above-average increases in their operating budgets. Implementing a new strategy requires managers to take an active and sometimes forceful role in shifting resources, not only to amply support activities with a critical role in the new strategy but also to find opportunities to execute the strategy more cost-effectively. This requires putting enough resources behind new strategic initiatives to fuel their success and making the tough decisions to kill projects and activities that are no longer justified. Google's strong support of R&D activities helped it to grow to a $350 billion giant in just 16 years. It was named the world's most innovative company by *Fast Company* magazine in 2014, for innovations such as Google Glass wearable computers, self-driving automobiles, and Shopping Express, an experimental same-day delivery service from stores such as Whole Foods, Target, and Office Depot. In 2013, however, Google decided to kill its 20 percent time policy, which allowed its staff to work on side projects of their choice one day a week. While this program gave rise to many innovations, such as Gmail and AdSense (a big contributor to Google's revenues), it also meant that fewer resources were available to projects that were deemed closer to the core of Google's mission.

The funding requirements of good strategy execution must drive how capital allocations are made and the size of each unit's operating budget. Underfunding organizational units and activities pivotal to the strategy impedes successful strategy implementation.

A company's operating budget must be *strategy-driven* (in order to amply fund the performance of key value chain activities).

Visible actions to reallocate operating funds and move people into new organizational units signal a determined commitment to strategic change. Such actions can catalyze the implementation process and give it credibility. Microsoft has made a practice of regularly shifting hundreds of programmers to new high-priority programming initiatives within a matter of weeks or even days. Fast-moving developments in many markets are prompting companies to abandon traditional annual budgeting and resource allocation cycles in favor of resource allocation processes supportive of more rapid adjustments in strategy. In response to rapid technological change in the communications industry, AT&T has prioritized investments and acquisitions that have allowed it to offer its enterprise customers faster, more flexible networks and provide innovative new customer services, such as its Sponsored Data plan.

Merely fine-tuning the execution of a company's existing strategy seldom requires big shifts of resources from one area to another. In contrast, new strategic initiatives generally require not only big shifts in resources but a larger allocation of resources to the effort as well. However, there are times when strategy changes or new execution initiatives need to be made without adding to total company expenses. In such circumstances, managers have to work their way through the existing budget line by line and activity by activity, looking for ways to trim costs and shift resources to activities that are higher-priority in the strategy execution effort. In the event that a company needs to make significant cost cuts during the course of launching new strategic initiatives, managers must be especially creative in finding ways to do more with less. Indeed, it is not unusual for strategy changes and the drive for good strategy execution to be aimed at achieving considerably higher levels of operating efficiency and, at the same time, making sure critical value chain activities are performed as effectively as possible.

INSTITUTING POLICIES AND PROCEDURES THAT FACILITATE STRATEGY EXECUTION

A company's policies and procedures can either support or hinder good strategy execution. Anytime a company moves to put new strategy elements in place or improve its strategy execution capabilities, some changes in work practices are usually needed. Managers are thus well advised to carefully review existing policies and procedures and to revise or discard those that are out of sync.

LO 2

How well-designed policies and procedures can facilitate good strategy execution.

As shown in Figure 11.1, well-conceived policies and operating procedures facilitate strategy execution in three ways:

1. *By providing top-down guidance regarding how things need to be done.* Policies and procedures provide company personnel with a set of guidelines for how to perform organizational activities, conduct various aspects of operations, solve problems as they arise, and accomplish particular tasks. In essence, they represent a store of organizational or managerial knowledge about efficient and effective ways of doing things—a set of well-honed *routines* for running the company. They clarify uncertainty about how to proceed in executing strategy and align the actions and behavior of company personnel with the requirements for good strategy execution. Moreover, they place limits on ineffective

A company's policies and procedures provide a set of well-honed *routines* for running the company and executing the strategy.

FIGURE 11.1 How Policies and Procedures Facilitate Good Strategy Execution

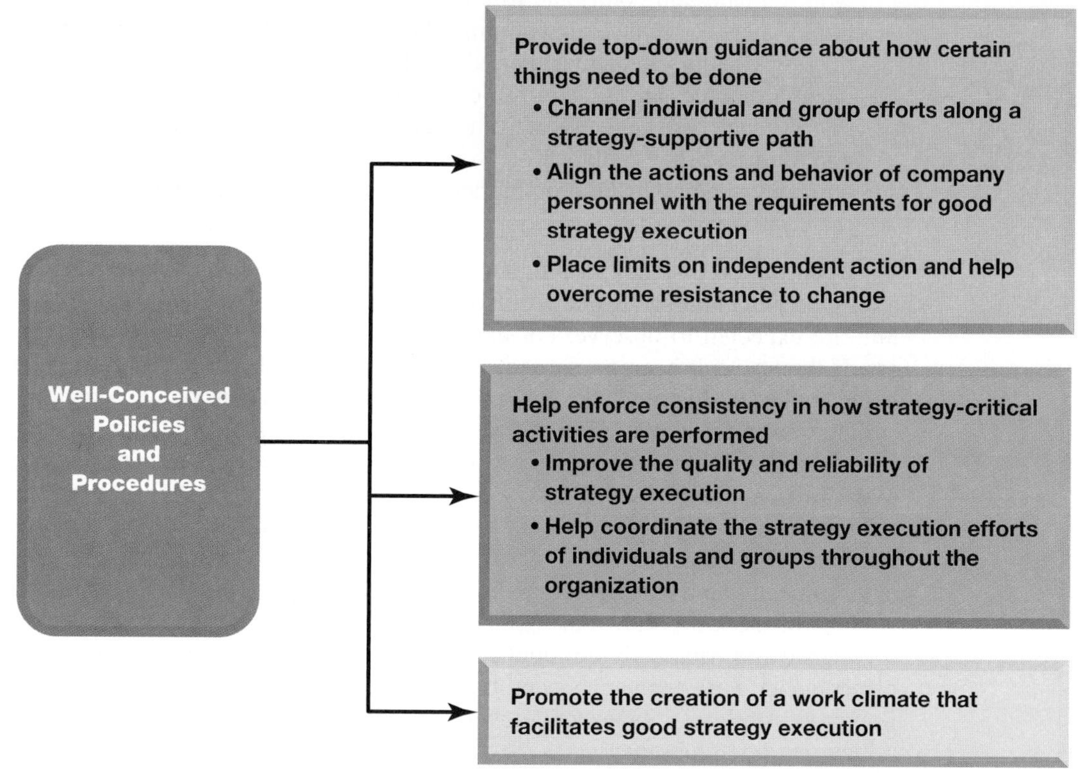

independent action. When they are well matched with the requirements of the strategy implementation plan, they channel the efforts of individuals along a path that supports the plan. When existing ways of doing things pose a barrier to strategy execution initiatives, actions and behaviors have to be changed. Under these conditions, the managerial role is to establish and enforce new policies and operating practices that are more conducive to executing the strategy appropriately. Policies are a particularly useful way to counteract tendencies for some people to resist change. People generally refrain from violating company policy or going against recommended practices and procedures without gaining clearance or having strong justification.

2. *By helping ensure consistency in how execution-critical activities are performed.* Policies and procedures serve to standardize the way that activities are performed. This can be important for ensuring the quality and reliability of the strategy execution process. It helps align and coordinate the strategy execution efforts of individuals and groups throughout the organization—a feature that is particularly beneficial when there are geographically scattered operating units. For example, eliminating significant differences in the operating practices of different plants, sales regions, or customer service centers or in the individual outlets in a chain operation helps a company deliver consistent product quality and service to customers. Good strategy execution nearly always entails an ability to replicate product quality and the caliber of customer service at every location where the company does business—anything less blurs the company's image and lowers customer satisfaction.
3. *By promoting the creation of a work climate that facilitates good strategy execution.* A company's policies and procedures help to set the tone of a company's work climate and contribute to a common understanding of "how we do things around here." Because abandoning old policies and procedures in favor of new ones invariably alters the internal work climate, managers can use the policy-changing process as a powerful lever for changing the corporate culture in ways that produce a stronger fit with the new strategy. The trick here, obviously, is to come up with new policies or procedures that catch the immediate attention of company personnel and prompt them to quickly shift their actions and behavior in the desired direction.

To ensure consistency in product quality and service behavior patterns, McDonald's policy manual spells out detailed procedures that personnel in each McDonald's unit are expected to observe. For example, "Cooks must turn, never flip, hamburgers. If they haven't been purchased, Big Macs must be discarded in 10 minutes after being cooked and French fries in 7 minutes. Cashiers must make eye contact with and smile at every customer." Retail chain stores and other organizational chains (e.g., hotels, hospitals, child care centers) similarly rely on detailed policies and procedures to ensure consistency in their operations and reliable service to their customers. Video game developer Valve Corporation prides itself on a lack of rigid policies and procedures; its 37-page handbook for new employees details how things get done in such an environment—an ironic tribute to the fact that all types of companies need policies.

One of the big policy-making issues concerns what activities need to be strictly prescribed and what activities ought to allow room for independent action on the part of personnel. Few companies need thick policy manuals to direct the strategy execution process or prescribe exactly how daily operations are to be conducted. Too much policy can be as obstructive as wrong policy and as confusing as no policy. There is wisdom in a middle approach: *Prescribe enough policies to give organization members clear direction and to place reasonable boundaries on their actions; then empower them to act within these boundaries in pursuit of company goals.* Allowing company personnel to act with some degree of freedom is especially appropriate when individual creativity and initiative are more essential to good strategy execution than are standardization and strict conformity. Instituting policies that facilitate strategy execution can therefore mean policies that require things be done according to a precisely defined standard or policies that give employees substantial leeway to do activities the way they think best.

There is wisdom in a middle-ground approach: Prescribe enough policies to give organization members clear direction and to place reasonable boundaries on their actions; then empower them to act within these boundaries in pursuit of company goals.

ADOPTING BEST PRACTICES AND EMPLOYING PROCESS MANAGEMENT TOOLS

LO 3

How best practices and process management tools drive continuous improvement in the performance of value chain activities and promote superior strategy execution.

Company managers can significantly advance the cause of competent strategy execution by adopting best practices and using process management tools to drive continuous improvement in how internal operations are conducted. One of the most widely used methods for gauging how well a company is executing its strategy entails benchmarking the company's performance of particular activities and business processes against "best-in-industry" and "best-in-world" performers.[1] It can also be useful to look at "best-in-company" performers of an activity if a company has a number of different organizational units performing much the same function at different locations. Identifying, analyzing, and understanding how top-performing companies or organizational units conduct particular value chain activities and business processes provide useful yardsticks for judging the effectiveness and efficiency of internal operations and setting performance standards for organizational units to meet or beat.

How the Process of Identifying and Incorporating Best Practices Works

As discussed in Chapter 4, *benchmarking* is the backbone of the process of identifying, studying, and implementing *best practices.* The role of benchmarking is to look outward to find best practices and then to develop the data for measuring how well a company's own performance of an activity stacks up against the best-practice standard. However, benchmarking is more complicated than simply identifying which companies are the best performers of an activity and then trying to imitate their approaches—especially if these companies are in other industries. Normally, the best practices of other organizations must be *adapted* to fit the specific circumstances of a company's own business, strategy, and operating requirements. Since each organization is unique, the telling part of any best-practice initiative is how well the company puts its own version of the best practice into place and makes it work. Indeed, a best practice remains little more than another company's interesting success story unless company personnel buy into the task of translating what can be learned from other companies into real action and results. The agents of change must be frontline employees who are convinced of the need to abandon the old ways of doing things and switch to a best-practice mindset.

Wide-scale use of best practices across a company's entire value chain promotes operating excellence and good strategy execution.

As shown in Figure 11.2, to the extent that a company is able to successfully adapt a best practice pioneered elsewhere to fit its circumstances, it is likely to improve its performance of the activity, perhaps dramatically—an outcome that promotes better strategy execution. It follows that a company can make giant strides toward excellent strategy execution by adopting a best-practice mindset and successfully *implementing the use of best practices across more of its value chain activities*. The more that organizational units use best practices in performing their work, the closer a company moves toward performing its value chain activities more effectively and efficiently. This is what operational excellence is all about. Employing best practices to improve internal operations and strategy execution has powerful appeal—legions of companies across the world are now making concerted efforts to employ best practices in performing many value chain activities, and they regularly benchmark their performance of these activities against best-in-industry or best-in-world performers.

Business Process Reengineering, Total Quality Management, and Six Sigma Quality Programs: Tools for Promoting Operating Excellence

Three other powerful management tools for promoting operating excellence and better strategy execution are business process reengineering, total quality management (TQM) programs, and Six Sigma quality control programs. Each of these merits discussion since many companies around the world use these tools to help execute strategies tied to cost reduction, defect-free manufacture, superior product quality, superior customer service, and total customer satisfaction.

Business Process Reengineering Companies searching for ways to improve their operations have sometimes discovered that the execution of strategy-critical activities is hampered by a disconnected organizational arrangement whereby pieces of an activity are performed in several different functional departments, with no one manager or group being accountable for optimal performance of the entire activity.

FIGURE 11.2 From Benchmarking and Best-Practice Implementation to Operational Excellence in Strategy Execution

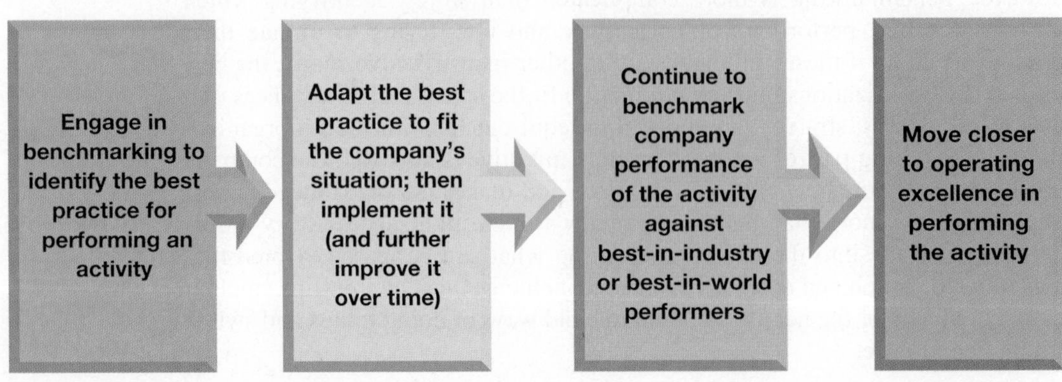

This can easily occur in such inherently cross-functional activities as customer service (which can involve personnel in order filling, warehousing and shipping, invoicing, accounts receivable, after-sale repair, and technical support), particularly for companies with a functional organizational structure.

To address the suboptimal performance problems that can arise from this type of situation, a company can *reengineer the work effort,* pulling the pieces of an activity out of different departments and creating a single department or cross-functional work group to take charge of the whole process. The use of cross-functional teams has been popularized by the practice of **business process reengineering,** which involves radically redesigning and streamlining the workflow (often enabled by cutting-edge use of online technology and information systems), with the goal of achieving quantum gains in performance of the activity.[2]

CORE CONCEPT

Business process reengineering involves radically redesigning and streamlining how an activity is performed, with the intent of achieving quantum improvements in performance.

The reengineering of value chain activities has been undertaken at many companies in many industries all over the world, with excellent results being achieved at some firms.[3] Hallmark reengineered its process for developing new greeting cards, creating teams of mixed-occupation personnel (artists, writers, lithographers, merchandisers, and administrators) to work on a single holiday or greeting card theme. The reengineered process speeded development times for new lines of greeting cards by up to 24 months, was more cost-efficient, and increased customer satisfaction.[4] In the order-processing section of General Electric's circuit breaker division, elapsed time from order receipt to delivery was cut from three weeks to three days by consolidating six production units into one, reducing a variety of former inventory and handling steps, automating the design system to replace a human custom-design process, and cutting the organizational layers between managers and workers from three to one. Productivity rose 20 percent in one year, and unit manufacturing costs dropped 30 percent. Northwest Water, a British utility, used process reengineering to eliminate 45 work depots that served as home bases to crews who installed and repaired water and sewage lines and equipment. Under the reengineered arrangement, crews worked directly from their vehicles, receiving assignments and reporting work completion from computer terminals in their trucks. Crew members became contractors to Northwest Water rather than employees, a move that not only eliminated the need for the work depots but also allowed Northwest Water to eliminate a big percentage of the bureaucratic personnel and supervisory organization that managed the crews.[5]

While business process reengineering has been criticized as an excuse for downsizing, it has nonetheless proved itself a useful tool for streamlining a company's work effort and moving closer to operational excellence. It has also inspired more technologically based approaches to integrating and streamlining business processes, such as *enterprise resource planning,* a software-based system implemented with the help of consulting companies such as SAP (the leading provider of business software).

Total Quality Management Programs **Total quality management (TQM)** is a comprehensive, structured approach to management that emphasizes continuous improvement in all phases of operations, 100 percent accuracy in performing tasks, involvement and empowerment of employees at all levels, team-based work design, benchmarking, and total customer satisfaction.[6] While TQM concentrates on producing quality goods and fully satisfying customer expectations, it achieves its biggest successes when it is extended to employee efforts in *all departments*—human resources, billing, accounting, and information systems—that may lack pressing, customer-driven incentives to improve. It involves reforming the corporate culture and shifting to a continuous-improvement business

CORE CONCEPT

Total quality management (TQM) entails creating a total quality culture, involving managers and employees at all levels, bent on continuously improving the performance of every value chain activity.

philosophy that permeates every facet of the organization.[7] TQM aims at instilling enthusiasm and commitment to doing things right from the top to the bottom of the organization. Management's job is to kindle an organizationwide search for ways to improve that involves all company personnel exercising initiative and using their ingenuity. TQM doctrine preaches that there's no such thing as "good enough" and that everyone has a responsibility to participate in continuous improvement. TQM is thus a race without a finish. Success comes from making little steps forward each day, a process that the Japanese call *kaizen.*

TQM takes a fairly long time to show significant results—very little benefit emerges within the first six months. The long-term payoff of TQM, if it comes, depends heavily on management's success in implanting a culture within which the TQM philosophy and practices can thrive. But it is a management tool that has attracted numerous users and advocates over several decades, and it can deliver good results when used properly.

CORE CONCEPT

Six Sigma programs utilize advanced statistical methods to improve quality by reducing defects and variability in the performance of business processes.

Six Sigma Quality Control Programs **Six Sigma programs** offer another way to drive continuous improvement in quality and strategy execution. This approach entails the use of advanced statistical methods to identify and remove the causes of defects (errors) and undesirable variability in performing an activity or business process. When performance of an activity or process reaches "Six Sigma quality," there are *no more than 3.4 defects per million iterations* (equal to 99.9997 percent accuracy).[8]

There are two important types of Six Sigma programs. The Six Sigma process of define, measure, analyze, improve, and control (DMAIC, pronounced "de-may-ic") is an improvement system for existing processes falling below specification and needing incremental improvement. The Six Sigma process of define, measure, analyze, design, and verify (DMADV, pronounced "de-mad-vee") is used to develop *new* processes or products at Six Sigma quality levels. DMADV is sometimes referred to as Design for Six Sigma, or DFSS. Both Six Sigma programs are overseen by personnel who have completed Six Sigma "master black belt" training, and they are executed by personnel who have earned Six Sigma "green belts" and Six Sigma "black belts." According to the Six Sigma Academy, personnel with black belts can save companies approximately $230,000 per project and can complete four to six projects a year.[9]

The statistical thinking underlying Six Sigma is based on the following three principles: (1) All work is a process, (2) all processes have variability, and (3) all processes create data that explain variability.[10] Six Sigma's DMAIC process is a particularly good vehicle for improving performance when there are *wide variations* in how well an activity is performed. For instance, airlines striving to improve the on-time performance of their flights have more to gain from actions to curtail the number of flights that are late by more than 30 minutes than from actions to reduce the number of flights that are late by less than 5 minutes. Six Sigma quality control programs are of particular interest for large companies, which are better able to shoulder the cost of the large investment required in employee training, organizational infrastructure, and consulting services. For example, to realize a cost savings of $4.4 billion from rolling out its Six Sigma program, GE had to invest $1.6 billion and suffer losses from the program during its first year.[11]

Since the programs were first introduced, thousands of companies and nonprofit organizations around the world have used Six Sigma to promote operating excellence. For companies at the forefront of this movement, such as Motorola, GE, Ford, and Honeywell (Allied Signal), the cost savings as a percentage of revenue varied from

1.2 to 4.5 percent, according to data analysis conducted by iSixSigma (an organization that provides free articles, tools, and resources concerning Six Sigma). More recently, there has been a resurgence of interest in Six Sigma practices, with companies such as Coca-Cola, Ocean Spray, GEICO, and Merrill Lynch turning to Six Sigma as a vehicle to improve their bottom lines. The use of Six Sigma at Bank of America has helped the bank reap about $2 billion in revenue gains and cost savings. The bank holds an annual "Best of Six Sigma Expo" to celebrate the teams that help it succeed.

Six Sigma has also been used to improve processes in health care. A Milwaukee hospital used Six Sigma to improve the accuracy of administering the proper drug doses to patients. DMAIC analysis of the three-stage process by which prescriptions were written by doctors, filled by the hospital pharmacy, and then administered to patients by nurses revealed that most mistakes came from misreading the doctors' handwriting. The hospital implemented a program requiring doctors to enter the prescription on the hospital's computers, which slashed the number of errors dramatically. In recent years, Pfizer embarked on 85 Six Sigma projects to streamline its R&D process and lower the cost of delivering medicines to patients in its pharmaceutical sciences division.

Illustration Capsule 11.1 describes Whirlpool's use of Six Sigma in its appliance business.

Despite its potential benefits, Six Sigma is not without its problems. There is evidence, for example, that Six Sigma techniques can stifle innovation and creativity. The essence of Six Sigma is to reduce variability in processes, but creative processes, by nature, include quite a bit of variability. In many instances, breakthrough innovations occur only after thousands of ideas have been abandoned and promising ideas have gone through multiple iterations and extensive prototyping. Google's chairman, Eric Schmidt, has declared that applying Six Sigma measurement and control principles to creative activities at Google would choke off innovation altogether.[12]

A blended approach to Six Sigma implementation that is gaining in popularity pursues incremental improvements in operating efficiency, while R&D and other processes that allow the company to develop new ways of offering value to customers are given freer rein. Managers of these **ambidextrous organizations** are adept at employing continuous improvement in operating processes but allowing R&D to operate under a set of rules that allows for exploration and the development of breakthrough innovations. However, the two distinctly different approaches to managing employees must be carried out by tightly integrated senior managers to ensure that the separate and diversely oriented units operate with a common purpose. Ciba Vision, a global leader in contact lenses, has dramatically reduced operating expenses through the use of continuous-improvement programs, while simultaneously and harmoniously developing a new series of contact lens products that have allowed its revenues to increase by 300 percent over a 10-year period.[13] An enterprise that systematically and wisely applies Six Sigma methods to its value chain, activity by activity, can make major strides in improving the proficiency with which its strategy is executed without sacrificing innovation. As is the case with TQM, obtaining managerial commitment, establishing a quality culture, and fully involving employees are all of critical importance to the successful implementation of Six Sigma quality programs.[14]

Ambidextrous organizations are adept at employing continuous improvement in operating processes but allowing R&D to operate under a set of rules that allows for exploration and the development of breakthrough innovations.

The Difference between Business Process Reengineering and Continuous-Improvement Programs like Six Sigma and TQM Whereas business process reengineering aims at *quantum gains* on the

ILLUSTRATION CAPSULE 11.1 Whirlpool's Use of Six Sigma to Promote Operating Excellence

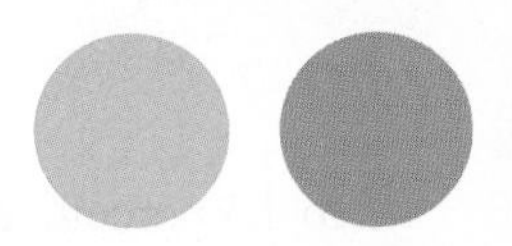

Top management at Whirlpool Corporation (with 59 manufacturing and technology centers around the world and sales in some 170 countries totaling $19 billion in 2013) has a vision of Whirlpool appliances in "Every Home . . . Everywhere with Pride, Passion, and Performance." One of management's chief objectives in pursuing this vision is to build unmatched customer loyalty to the Whirlpool brand. Whirlpool's strategy to win the hearts and minds of appliance buyers the world over has been to produce and market appliances with top-notch quality and innovative features that users will find appealing. In addition, Whirlpool's strategy has been to offer a wide selection of models (recognizing that buyer tastes and needs differ) and to strive for low-cost production efficiency, thereby enabling Whirlpool to price its products very competitively. Executing this strategy at Whirlpool's operations in North America (where it is the market leader), Latin America (where it is also the market leader), Europe (where it ranks third), and Asia (where it is number one in India and has a foothold with huge growth opportunities elsewhere) has involved a strong focus on continuous improvement, lean manufacturing capabilities, and operating excellence. To marshal the efforts of its 69,000 employees in executing the strategy successfully, management developed a comprehensive Operational Excellence program with Six Sigma as one of the centerpieces.

The Operational Excellence initiative, which began in the 1990s, incorporated Six Sigma techniques to improve the quality of Whirlpool products and, at the same time, lower costs and trim the time it took to get product innovations to the marketplace. The Six Sigma program helped Whirlpool save $175 million in manufacturing costs in its first three years.

To sustain the productivity gains and cost savings, Whirlpool embedded Six Sigma practices within each of its manufacturing facilities worldwide and instilled a culture based on Six Sigma and lean manufacturing skills and capabilities. In 2002, each of Whirlpool's operating units began taking the Six Sigma initiative to a higher level by first placing the needs of the customer at the center of every function—R&D, technology, manufacturing, marketing, and administrative support—and then striving to consistently improve quality levels while eliminating all unnecessary costs. The company systematically went through every aspect of its business with the view that company personnel should perform every activity at every level in a manner that delivers value to the customer and leads to continuous improvement on how things are done.

Whirlpool management believes that the company's Operational Excellence process has been a major contributor in sustaining the company's position as the leading global manufacturer and marketer of home appliances.

Sources: www.whirlpool.com and LexisNexis-Edgar Online (accessed April 3, 2014).

Business process reengineering aims at one-time quantum improvement, while continuous-improvement programs like TQM and Six Sigma aim at ongoing incremental improvements.

order of 30 to 50 percent or more, total quality programs like TQM and Six Sigma stress *ongoing incremental progress,* striving for inch-by-inch gains again and again in a never-ending stream. The two approaches to improved performance of value chain activities and operating excellence are not mutually exclusive; it makes sense to use them in tandem. Reengineering can be used first to produce a good basic design that yields quick, dramatic improvements in performing a business process. Total quality or Six Sigma programs can then be used as a follow-on to reengineering and best-practice implementation to deliver continuing improvements over a longer period of time.

Capturing the Benefits of Initiatives to Improve Operations

The biggest beneficiaries of benchmarking and best-practice initiatives, reengineering, TQM, and Six Sigma are companies that view such programs not as ends in themselves but as tools for implementing company strategy more effectively. The least rewarding payoffs occur when company managers seize on the programs as novel ideas that might be worth a try. In most such instances, they result in strategy-blind efforts to simply manage better.

There's an important lesson here. Business process management tools all need to be linked to a company's strategic priorities to contribute effectively to improving the strategy's execution. Only strategy can point to which value chain activities matter and what performance targets make the most sense. Without a strategic framework, managers lack the context in which to fix things that really matter to business unit performance and competitive success.

To get the most from initiatives to execute strategy more proficiently, managers must have a clear idea of what specific outcomes really matter. Is it high on-time delivery, lower overall costs, fewer customer complaints, shorter cycle times, a higher percentage of revenues coming from recently introduced products, or something else? Benchmarking best-in-industry and best-in-world performance of targeted value chain activities provides a realistic basis for setting internal performance milestones and longer-range targets. Once initiatives to improve operations are linked to the company's strategic priorities, then comes the managerial task of building a total quality culture that is genuinely committed to achieving the performance outcomes that strategic success requires.[15]

Managers can take the following action steps to realize full value from TQM or Six Sigma initiatives and promote a culture of operating excellence:[16]

1. Demonstrating visible, unequivocal, and unyielding commitment to total quality and continuous improvement, including specifying measurable objectives for increasing quality and making continual progress.
2. Nudging people toward quality-supportive behaviors by:
   a. Screening job applicants rigorously and hiring only those with attitudes and aptitudes that are right for quality-based performance.
   b. Providing quality training for employees.
   c. Using teams and team-building exercises to reinforce and nurture individual effort. (The creation of a quality culture is facilitated when teams become more cross-functional, multitask-oriented, and increasingly self-managed.)
   d. Recognizing and rewarding individual and team efforts to improve quality regularly and systematically.
   e. Stressing prevention (doing it right the first time), not correction (instituting ways to undo or overcome mistakes).
3. Empowering employees so that authority for delivering great service or improving products is in the hands of the doers rather than the overseers—*improving quality has to be seen as part of everyone's job.*
4. Using online systems to provide all relevant parties with the latest best practices, thereby speeding the diffusion and adoption of best practices throughout the organization. Online systems can also allow company personnel to exchange data and opinions about how to upgrade the prevailing best-in-company practices.
5. Emphasizing that performance can and must be improved, because competitors are not resting on their laurels and customers are always looking for something better.

The purpose of using benchmarking, best practices, business process reengineering, TQM, and Six Sigma programs is to improve the performance of strategy-critical activities and thereby enhance strategy execution.

In sum, benchmarking, the adoption of best practices, business process reengineering, TQM, and Six Sigma techniques all need to be seen and used as part of a bigger-picture effort to execute strategy proficiently. Used properly, all of these tools are capable of improving the proficiency with which an organization performs its value chain activities. Not only do improvements from such initiatives add up over time and strengthen organizational capabilities, but they also help build a culture of operating excellence. All this lays the groundwork for gaining a competitive advantage.[17] While it is relatively easy for rivals to also implement process management tools, it is much more difficult and time-consuming for them to instill a deeply ingrained culture of operating excellence (as occurs when such techniques are religiously employed and top management exhibits lasting commitment to operational excellence throughout the organization).

INSTALLING INFORMATION AND OPERATING SYSTEMS

LO 4

The role of information and operating systems in enabling company personnel to carry out their strategic roles proficiently.

Company strategies can't be executed well without a number of internal systems for business operations. Qantas Airways, JetBlue, Ryanair, British Airways, and other successful airlines cannot hope to provide passenger-pleasing service without a user-friendly online reservation system, an accurate and speedy baggage-handling system, and a strict aircraft maintenance program that minimizes problems requiring at-the-gate service that delay departures. FedEx has internal communication systems that allow it to coordinate its over 90,000 vehicles in handling a daily average of 10 million shipments to 220 countries. Its leading-edge flight operations systems allow a single controller to direct as many as 200 of FedEx's aircraft simultaneously, overriding their flight plans should weather problems or other special circumstances arise. In addition, FedEx has created a series of e-business tools for customers that allow them to ship and track packages online, create address books, review shipping history, generate custom reports, simplify customer billing, reduce internal warehousing and inventory management costs, purchase goods and services from suppliers, and respond to their own quickly changing customer demands. All of FedEx's systems support the company's strategy of providing businesses and individuals with a broad array of package delivery services and enhancing its competitiveness against United Parcel Service, DHL, and the U.S. Postal Service.

Amazon.com ships customer orders of books, CDs, and myriad other items from a global network of some 94 warehouses (in 2014). The warehouses are so technologically sophisticated that they require about as many lines of code to run as Amazon's website does. Using complex picking algorithms, computers initiate the order-picking process by sending signals to workers' wireless receivers, telling them which items to pick off the shelves in which order. Computers also generate data on mix-boxed items, chute backup times, line speed, worker productivity, and shipping weights on orders. Systems are upgraded regularly, and productivity improvements are aggressively pursued. Amazon's warehouse efficiency and cost per order filled are so low that one of the fastest-growing and most profitable parts of Amazon's business is using its warehouses to run the e-commerce operations of large retail chains such as Target.

Otis Elevator, the world's largest manufacturer of elevators, with more than 2.5 million elevators and escalators installed worldwide, has a 24/7 remote electronic monitoring system that can detect when an elevator or escalator installed on a customer's site has any of 325 problems.[18] If the monitoring system detects a problem, it analyzes and diagnoses the cause and location, then makes the service call to an Otis mechanic at the nearest location, and helps the mechanic (who is equipped with a web-enabled cell phone) identify the component causing the problem. The company's maintenance system helps keep outage times under three hours. All trouble-call data are relayed to design and manufacturing personnel, allowing them to quickly alter design specifications or manufacturing procedures when needed to correct recurring problems. All customers have online access to performance data on each of their Otis elevators and escalators.

Well-conceived state-of-the-art operating systems not only enable better strategy execution but also strengthen organizational capabilities—enough at times to provide a competitive edge over rivals. For example, a company with a differentiation strategy based on superior quality has added capability if it has systems for training personnel in quality techniques, tracking product quality at each production step, and ensuring that all goods shipped meet quality standards. If the systems it employs are advanced systems that have not yet been adopted by rivals, the systems may provide the company with a competitive advantage as long as the costs of deploying the systems do not outweigh their benefits. Similarly, a company striving to be a low-cost provider is competitively stronger if it has an unrivaled benchmarking system that identifies opportunities to implement best practices and drive costs out of the business faster than others can. Fast-growing companies get an important assist from having capabilities in place to recruit and train new employees in large numbers and from investing in infrastructure that gives them the capability to handle rapid growth as it occurs, rather than having to scramble to catch up to customer demand.

Instituting Adequate Information Systems, Performance Tracking, and Controls

Accurate and timely information about daily operations is essential if managers are to gauge how well the strategy execution process is proceeding. Companies everywhere are capitalizing on today's technology to install real-time data-generating capability. Most retail companies now have automated online systems that generate daily sales reports for each store and maintain up-to-the-minute inventory and sales records on each item. Manufacturing plants typically generate daily production reports and track labor productivity on every shift. Transportation companies have elaborate information systems to provide real-time arrival information for buses and trains that is automatically sent to digital message signs and platform audio address systems.

Siemens Healthcare, one of the largest suppliers to the health care industry, uses a cloud-based business activity monitoring (BAM) system to continuously monitor and improve the company's processes across more than 125 countries. Customer satisfaction is one of Siemens's most important business objectives, so the reliability of its order management and services is crucial. Prezi is a presentation software company that uses the business intelligence platform GoodData to access companywide data in a quick, meaningful way. Data dashboards are constantly being updated so that Prezi teams can see how product development and sales strategies are working in real time. Companies that rely on customer-contact personnel to act promptly and creatively in pleasing customers have installed online information systems that make essential customer data accessible to such personnel through a few keystrokes; this enables them to respond more effectively to customer inquiries and to deliver personalized customer service.

Information systems need to cover five broad areas: (1) customer data, (2) operations data, (3) employee data, (4) supplier and/or strategic partner data, and (5) financial performance data. All key strategic performance indicators must be tracked and reported in real time whenever possible. Real-time information systems permit company managers to stay on top of implementation initiatives and daily operations and to intervene if things seem to be drifting off course. Tracking key performance indicators, gathering information from operating personnel, quickly identifying and diagnosing problems, and taking corrective actions are all integral pieces of the process of managing strategy execution and overseeing operations.

Having state-of-the-art operating systems, information systems, and real-time data is integral to superior strategy execution and operating excellence.

Statistical information gives managers a feel for the numbers, briefings and meetings provide a feel for the latest developments and emerging issues, and personal contacts add a feel for the people dimension. All are good barometers of how well things are going and what operating aspects need management attention. Managers must identify problem areas and deviations from plans before they can take action to get the organization back on course, by either improving the approaches to strategy execution or fine-tuning the strategy. Jeff Bezos, Amazon.com's CEO, is an ardent proponent of managing by the numbers. As he puts it, "Math-based decisions always trump opinion and judgment. The trouble with most corporations is that they make judgment-based decisions when data-based decisions could be made."[19]

Monitoring Employee Performance Information systems also provide managers with a means for monitoring the performance of empowered workers to see that they are acting within the specified limits.[20] Leaving empowered employees to their own devices in meeting performance standards without appropriate checks and balances can expose an organization to excessive risk.[21] Instances abound of employees' decisions or behavior going awry, sometimes costing a company huge sums or producing lawsuits and reputation-damaging publicity.

Scrutinizing daily and weekly operating statistics is one of the ways in which managers can monitor the results that flow from the actions of subordinates without resorting to constant over-the-shoulder supervision; if the operating results look good, then it is reasonable to assume that empowerment is working. But close monitoring of operating performance is only one of the control tools at management's disposal. Another valuable lever of control in companies that rely on empowered employees, especially in those that use self-managed work groups or other such teams, is peer-based control. Because peer evaluation is such a powerful control device, companies organized into teams can remove some layers of the management hierarchy and rely on strong peer pressure to keep team members operating between the white lines. This is especially true when a company has the information systems capability to monitor team performance daily or in real time.

USING REWARDS AND INCENTIVES TO PROMOTE BETTER STRATEGY EXECUTION

It is essential that company personnel be enthusiastically committed to executing strategy successfully and achieving performance targets. Enlisting such commitment typically requires use of an assortment of motivational techniques and rewards. Indeed, *an effectively designed reward structure is the single most powerful tool management has for mobilizing employee commitment to successful strategy execution.* But incentives and rewards do more than just strengthen the resolve of company personnel to succeed—they also focus employees' attention on the accomplishment of specific strategy execution objectives. Not only do they spur the efforts of individuals to achieve those aims, but they also help to coordinate the activities of individuals throughout the organization by aligning their personal motives with the goals of the organization. In this manner, reward systems serve as an indirect type of control mechanism that conserves on the more costly control mechanism of supervisory oversight.

To win employees' sustained, energetic commitment to the strategy execution process, management must be resourceful in designing and using motivational incentives—both monetary and nonmonetary. The more a manager understands what motivates subordinates and the more he or she relies on motivational incentives as a tool for achieving the targeted strategic and financial results, the greater will be employees' commitment to good day-in, day-out strategy execution and the achievement of performance targets.[22]

LO 5

How and why the use of well-designed incentives and rewards can be management's single most powerful tool for promoting adept strategy execution.

Incentives and Motivational Practices That Facilitate Good Strategy Execution

Financial incentives generally head the list of motivating tools for gaining wholehearted employee commitment to good strategy execution and focusing attention on strategic priorities. Generous financial rewards always catch employees' attention and produce *high-powered incentives* for individuals to exert their best efforts. A company's package of monetary rewards typically includes some combination of base-pay increases, performance bonuses, profit-sharing plans, stock awards, company contributions to employee 401(k) or retirement plans, and piecework incentives (in the case of production workers). But most successful companies and managers also make extensive use of nonmonetary incentives. Some of the most important nonmonetary approaches companies can use to enhance employee motivation include the following:[23]

A properly designed reward structure is management's single most powerful tool for mobilizing employee commitment to successful strategy execution and aligning efforts throughout the organization with strategic priorities.

CORE CONCEPT

Financial rewards provide **high-powered incentives** when rewards are tied to specific outcome objectives.

- *Providing attractive perks and fringe benefits.* The various options include coverage of health insurance premiums, wellness programs, college tuition reimbursement, generous paid vacation time, onsite child care, onsite fitness centers and massage services, opportunities for getaways at company-owned recreational facilities, personal concierge services, subsidized cafeterias and free lunches, casual dress every day, personal travel services, paid sabbaticals, maternity and paternity leaves, paid leaves to care for ill family members, telecommuting, compressed workweeks (four 10-hour days instead of five 8-hour days), flextime (variable work schedules that accommodate individual needs), college scholarships for children, and relocation services.
- *Giving awards and public recognition to high performers and showcasing company successes.* Many companies hold award ceremonies to honor top-performing individuals, teams, and organizational units and to celebrate important company milestones and achievements. Others make a special point of recognizing the outstanding accomplishments of individuals, teams, and organizational units at informal company gatherings or in the company newsletter. Such actions foster a positive *esprit de corps* within the organization and may also act to spur healthy competition among units and teams within the company.
- *Relying on promotion from within whenever possible.* This practice helps bind workers to their employer, and employers to their workers. Moreover, it provides strong incentives for good performance. Promoting from within also helps ensure that people in positions of responsibility have knowledge specific to the business, technology, and operations they are managing.

- *Inviting and acting on ideas and suggestions from employees.* Many companies find that their best ideas for nuts-and-bolts operating improvements come from the suggestions of employees. Moreover, research indicates that giving decision-making power to down-the-line employees increases their motivation and satisfaction as well as their productivity. The use of self-managed teams has much the same effect.
- *Creating a work atmosphere in which there is genuine caring and mutual respect among workers and between management and employees.* A "family" work environment where people are on a first-name basis and there is strong camaraderie promotes teamwork and cross-unit collaboration.
- *Stating the strategic vision in inspirational terms that make employees feel they are a part of something worthwhile in a larger social sense.* There's strong motivating power associated with giving people a chance to be part of something exciting and personally satisfying. Jobs with a noble purpose tend to inspire employees to give their all. As described in Chapter 9, this not only increases productivity but reduces turnover and lowers costs for staff recruitment and training as well.
- *Sharing information with employees about financial performance, strategy, operational measures, market conditions, and competitors' actions.* Broad disclosure and prompt communication send the message that managers trust their workers and regard them as valued partners in the enterprise. Keeping employees in the dark denies them information useful to performing their jobs, prevents them from being intellectually engaged, saps their motivation, and detracts from performance.
- *Providing a comfortable and attractive working environment.* An appealing workplace environment can have decidedly positive effects on employee morale and productivity. Providing a comfortable work environment, designed with ergonomics in mind, is particularly important when workers are expected to spend long hours at work.

For specific examples of the motivational tactics employed by several prominent companies (many of which appear on *Fortune*'s list of the 100 best companies to work for in America), see Illustration Capsule 11.2.

Striking the Right Balance between Rewards and Punishment

While most approaches to motivation, compensation, and people management accentuate the positive, companies also make it clear that lackadaisical or indifferent effort and subpar performance can result in negative consequences. At General Electric, McKinsey & Company, several global public accounting firms, and other companies that look for and expect top-notch individual performance, there's an "up-or-out" policy—managers and professionals whose performance is not good enough to warrant promotion are first denied bonuses and stock awards and eventually weeded out. At most companies, senior executives and key personnel in underperforming units are pressured to raise performance to acceptable levels and keep it there or risk being replaced.

As a general rule, it is unwise to take off the pressure for good performance or play down the adverse consequences of shortfalls in performance. There is scant evidence that a no-pressure, no-adverse-consequences work environment leads to superior strategy execution or operating excellence. As the CEO of a major bank put it, "There's a deliberate policy here to create a level of anxiety. Winners usually play like

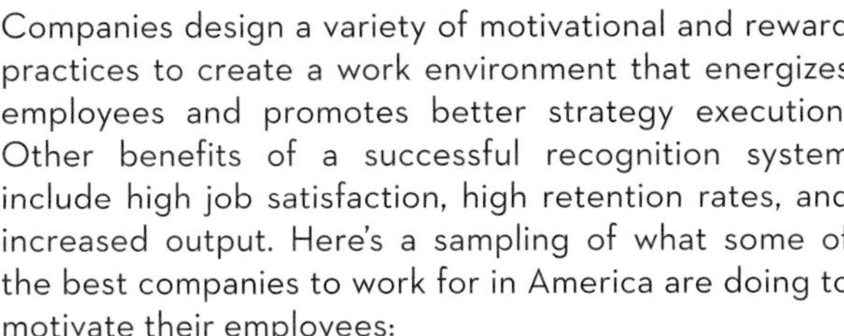

ILLUSTRATION CAPSULE 11.2

How the Best Companies to Work for Motivate and Reward Employees

Companies design a variety of motivational and reward practices to create a work environment that energizes employees and promotes better strategy execution. Other benefits of a successful recognition system include high job satisfaction, high retention rates, and increased output. Here's a sampling of what some of the best companies to work for in America are doing to motivate their employees:

- Software developer SAS prioritizes work-life balance and mental health for its workforce of 7,000. The onsite health center it hosts for families of all employees maintains a staff of 53 medical and support personnel, including nurses, registered dietitians, lab technicians, and clinical psychologists. The sprawling headquarters also has a Frisbee golf course, indoor swimming pool, and walking and biking trails decorated with sculptures from the company's 4,000-item art collection. With such an environment, it should come as no surprise that 95 percent of employees report looking forward to heading to the office every day.
- Salesforce.com Inc., a global cloud-computing company based in San Francisco, has been listed by *Forbes* magazine as the most innovative company in America. Doubling its workforce from 5,000 to 10,000 in the past two years, Salesforce.com incentivizes new hires to work cooperatively with existing teams. The company's recognition programs include rewards for achievement both in the office and in the larger community. For example, in 2013, top sellers were awarded two-week trips to Bhutan for their dedication and results.
- DPR Construction is one of the nation's top-50 general contractors, serving clients like Facebook, Pixar, and Genentech. The company fosters teamwork and equality across levels with features like open-office floor plans, business cards with no titles, and a bonus plan for employees. DPR also prioritizes safety for its employees. In 1999, a craftsperson who reached 30,000 consecutive safe work hours was rewarded with a new Ford F-150 truck. Management created a new safety award in his name that includes a plaque, a $2,000 trip, a 40-hour week off with pay, and a safety jacket with hours printed on it. In 2013, thirteen craftspeople received this generous award for their dedication to safety.
- Hilcorp, an oil and gas exploration company, made headlines in 2011 for its shocking generosity. After reaching its five-year goal to double in size, the company gave every employee a $50,000 dream car voucher (or $35,000 in cash). Building on this success, later that year Hilcorp announced an incentive program called Dream 2015. This plan promises to award every person in the company $100,000 in 2015 if certain goals are met.

Note: Developed with Meghan L. Cooney.

Sources: "100 Best Companies to Work For, 2014," *Fortune,* money.cnn.com/magazines/fortune/best-companies/ (accessed February 15, 2014); and company profiles, *GreatRated!* us.greatrated.com/sas (accessed February 24, 2014).

they're one touchdown behind."[24] A number of companies deliberately give employees heavy workloads and tight deadlines to test their mettle—personnel are pushed hard to achieve "stretch" objectives and are expected to put in long hours (nights and weekends if need be). High-performing organizations nearly always have a cadre of ambitious people who relish the opportunity to climb the ladder of success, love a challenge, thrive in a performance-oriented environment, and find some competition and pressure useful to satisfy their own drives for personal recognition, accomplishment, and self-satisfaction.

However, if an organization's motivational approaches and reward structure induce too much stress, internal competitiveness, job insecurity, and fear of unpleasant consequences, the impact on workforce morale and strategy execution can be counterproductive. Evidence shows that managerial initiatives to improve strategy execution should incorporate more positive than negative motivational elements because when cooperation is positively enlisted and rewarded, rather than coerced by orders and threats (implicit or explicit), people tend to respond with more enthusiasm, dedication, creativity, and initiative.[25]

Linking Rewards to Achieving the Right Outcomes

To create a strategy-supportive system of rewards and incentives, a company must reward people for accomplishing results, not for just dutifully performing assigned tasks. Showing up for work and performing assignments do not, by themselves, guarantee results. To make the work environment results-oriented, managers need to focus jobholders' attention and energy on what to *achieve* as opposed to what to *do*.[26] Employee productivity among employees at Best Buy's corporate headquarters rose by 35 percent after the company began to focus on the results of each employee's work rather than on employees' willingness to come to work early and stay late.

Incentives must be based on accomplishing the right results, not on dutifully performing assigned tasks.

Ideally, every organizational unit, every manager, every team or work group, and perhaps every employee should be held accountable for achieving outcomes that contribute to good strategy execution and business performance. If the company's strategy is to be a low-cost provider, the incentive system must reward actions and achievements that result in lower costs. If the company has a differentiation strategy focused on delivering superior quality and service, the incentive system must reward such outcomes as Six Sigma defect rates, infrequent customer complaints, speedy order processing and delivery, and high levels of customer satisfaction. If a company's growth is predicated on a strategy of new product innovation, incentives should be tied to such factors as the percentages of revenues and profits coming from newly introduced products.

The key to creating a reward system that promotes good strategy execution is to make measures of good business performance and good strategy execution the *dominating basis* for designing incentives, evaluating individual and group efforts, and handing out rewards.

Incentive compensation for top executives is typically tied to such financial measures as revenue and earnings growth, stock price performance, return on investment, and creditworthiness or to strategic measures such as market share growth. However, incentives for department heads, teams, and individual workers may be tied to performance outcomes more closely related to their strategic area of responsibility. In manufacturing, incentive compensation may be tied to unit manufacturing costs, on-time production and shipping, defect rates, the number and extent of work stoppages due to equipment breakdowns, and so on. In sales and marketing, there may be incentives for achieving dollar sales or unit volume targets, market share, sales penetration of each target customer group, the fate of newly introduced products, the frequency of customer complaints, the number of new accounts acquired, and customer satisfaction. Which performance measures to base incentive compensation on depends on the situation—the priority placed on various financial and strategic objectives, the requirements for strategic and competitive success, and the specific results needed to keep strategy execution on track.

Illustration Capsule 11.3 provides a vivid example of how one company has designed incentives linked directly to outcomes reflecting good execution.

ILLUSTRATION CAPSULE 11.3 Nucor Corporation: Tying Incentives Directly to Strategy Execution

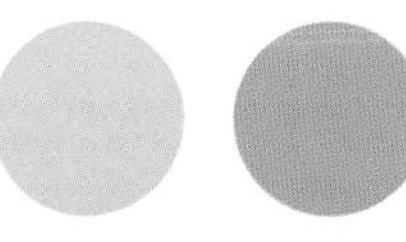

The strategy at Nucor Corporation, one of the three largest steel producers in the United States, is to be *the* low-cost producer of steel products. Because labor costs are a significant fraction of total cost in the steel business, successful implementation of Nucor's low-cost leadership strategy entails achieving lower labor costs per ton of steel than competitors' costs. Nucor management uses an incentive system to promote high worker productivity and drive labor costs per ton below those of rivals. Each plant's workforce is organized into production teams (each assigned to perform particular functions), and weekly production targets are established for each team. Base-pay scales are set at levels comparable to wages for similar manufacturing jobs in the local areas where Nucor has plants, but workers can earn a 1 percent bonus for each 1 percent that their output exceeds target levels. If a production team exceeds its weekly production target by 10 percent, team members receive a 10 percent bonus in their next paycheck; if a team exceeds its quota by 20 percent, team members earn a 20 percent bonus. Bonuses, paid every two weeks, are based on the prior two weeks' actual production levels measured against the targets.

Nucor's piece-rate incentive plan has produced impressive results. The production teams put forth exceptional effort; it is not uncommon for most teams to beat their weekly production targets by 20 to 50 percent. When added to employees' base pay, the bonuses earned by Nucor workers make Nucor's workforce among the highest-paid in the U.S. steel industry. From a management perspective, the incentive system has resulted in Nucor having labor productivity levels 10 to 20 percent above the average of the unionized workforces at several

of its largest rivals, which in turn has given Nucor a significant labor cost advantage over most rivals.

After years of record-setting profits, Nucor struggled in the economic downturn of 2008–2010, along with the manufacturers and builders who buy its steel. But while bonuses have dwindled, Nucor showed remarkable loyalty to its production workers, avoiding layoffs by having employees get ahead on maintenance, perform work formerly done by contractors, and search for cost savings. Morale at the company remained high, and Nucor's CEO at the time, Daniel DiMicco, was inducted into *IndustryWeek* magazine's Manufacturing Hall of Fame because of his no-layoff policies. As industry growth has resumed, Nucor has retained a well-trained workforce, more committed than ever to achieving the kind of productivity for which Nucor is justifiably famous. DiMicco had good reason to expect Nucor to be "first out of the box" following the crisis, and although he has since stepped aside, the company's culture of making its employees think like owners has not changed.

Sources: Company website (accessed March 2012); N. Byrnes, "Pain, but No Layoffs at Nucor," *Bloomberg Businessweek,* March 26, 2009; and J. McGregor, "Nucor's CEO Is Stepping Aside, but Its Culture Likely Won't," *The Washington Post* Online, November 20, 2012 (accessed April 3, 2014).

> The first principle in designing an effective incentive compensation system is to tie rewards to performance outcomes directly linked to good strategy execution and the achievement of financial and strategic objectives.

Additional Guidelines for Designing Incentive Compensation Systems The first principle in designing an effective incentive compensation system is to tie rewards to performance outcomes directly linked to good strategy execution and targeted strategic and financial objectives, as explained earlier. But for a company's reward system to truly motivate organization members, inspire their best efforts, and sustain high levels of productivity, it is equally important to observe the following additional guidelines in designing and administering the reward system:

- *Make the performance payoff a major, not minor, piece of the total compensation package.* Performance bonuses must be at least 10 to 12 percent of base salary to have much impact. Incentives that amount to 20 percent or more of total compensation are big attention-getters, likely to really drive individual or team efforts. Incentives amounting to less than 5 percent of total compensation have a comparatively weak motivational impact. Moreover, the payoff for high-performing individuals and teams must be meaningfully greater than the payoff for average performers, and the payoff for average performers meaningfully bigger than that for below-average performers.

- *Have incentives that extend to all managers and all workers, not just top management.* It is a gross miscalculation to expect that lower-level managers and employees will work their hardest to hit performance targets just so a few senior executives can get lucrative rewards.
- *Administer the reward system with scrupulous objectivity and fairness.* If performance standards are set unrealistically high or if individual and group performance evaluations are not accurate and well documented, dissatisfaction with the system will overcome any positive benefits.
- *Ensure that the performance targets set for each individual or team involve outcomes that the individual or team can personally affect.* The role of incentives is to enhance individual commitment and channel behavior in beneficial directions. This role is not well served when the performance measures by which company personnel are judged are outside their arena of influence.
- *Keep the time between achieving the performance target and receiving the reward as short as possible.* To combat problems with late-arriving flights, Continental pays employees a cash bonus each month whenever actual on-time flight performance meets or beats the monthly on-time target. Annual bonus payouts work best for higher-level managers and for situations where the outcome target relates to overall company profitability.
- *Avoid rewarding effort rather than results.* While it is tempting to reward people who have tried hard, gone the extra mile, and yet fallen short of achieving performance targets because of circumstances beyond their control, it is ill advised to do so. The problem with making exceptions for unknowable, uncontrollable, or unforeseeable circumstances is that once "good excuses" start to creep into justifying rewards for subpar results, the door opens to all kinds of reasons why actual performance has failed to match targeted performance. A "no excuses" standard is more evenhanded, easier to administer, and more conducive to creating a results-oriented work climate.

The unwavering standard for judging whether individuals, teams, and organizational units have done a good job must be whether they meet or beat performance targets that reflect good strategy execution.

For an organization's incentive system to work well, the details of the reward structure must be communicated and explained. Everybody needs to understand how his or her incentive compensation is calculated and how individual and group performance targets contribute to organizational performance targets. The pressure to achieve the targeted financial and strategic performance objectives and continuously improve on strategy execution should be unrelenting. People at all levels must be held accountable for carrying out their assigned parts of the strategic plan, and they must understand that their rewards are based on the caliber of results achieved. But with the pressure to perform should come meaningful rewards. Without an attractive payoff, the system breaks down, and managers are left with the less workable options of issuing orders, trying to enforce compliance, and depending on the goodwill of employees.

KEY POINTS

1. Implementing a new or different strategy calls for managers to identify the resource requirements of each new strategic initiative and then consider whether the current pattern of resource allocation and the budgets of the various subunits are suitable.
2. Company policies and procedures facilitate strategy execution when they are designed to fit the strategy and its objectives. Anytime a company alters its strategy, managers should review existing policies and operating procedures and replace those that are out of sync. Well-conceived policies and procedures aid the task of strategy execution by (1) providing top-down guidance to company personnel regarding how things need to be done and what the limits are on independent actions, (2) enforcing consistency in the performance of strategy-critical activities, thereby improving the quality of the strategy execution effort and coordinating the efforts of company personnel, however widely dispersed, and (3) promoting the creation of a work climate conducive to good strategy execution.
3. Competent strategy execution entails visible unyielding managerial commitment to best practices and continuous improvement. Benchmarking, best-practice adoption, business process reengineering, total quality management (TQM), and Six Sigma programs are important process management tools for promoting better strategy execution.
4. Company strategies can't be implemented or executed well without a number of support systems to carry on business operations. Real-time information systems and control systems further aid the cause of good strategy execution.
5. Strategy-supportive motivational practices and reward systems are powerful management tools for gaining employee commitment and focusing their attention on the strategy execution goals. The key to creating a reward system that promotes good strategy execution is to make measures of good business performance and good strategy execution the *dominating basis* for designing incentives, evaluating individual and group efforts, and handing out rewards. Positive motivational practices generally work better than negative ones, but there is a place for both. While financial rewards provide high-powered incentives, nonmonetary incentives are also important. For an incentive compensation system to work well, (1) the performance payoff should be a major percentage of the compensation package, (2) the use of incentives should extend to all managers and workers, (3) the system should be administered with objectivity and fairness, (4) each individual's performance targets should involve outcomes the person can personally affect, (5) rewards should promptly follow the achievement of performance targets, and (6) rewards should be given for results and not just effort.

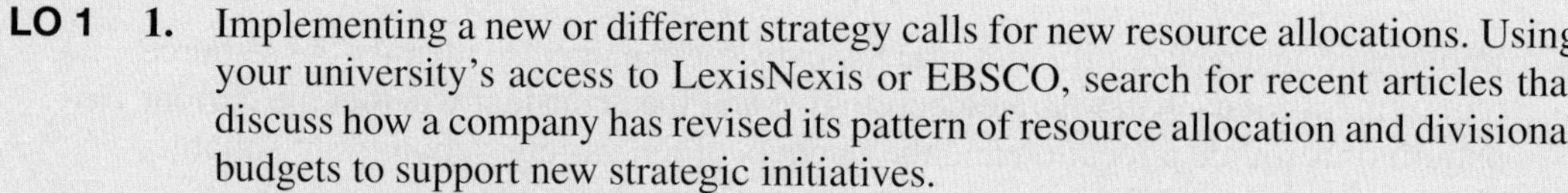

ASSURANCE OF LEARNING EXERCISES

LO 1 **1.** Implementing a new or different strategy calls for new resource allocations. Using your university's access to LexisNexis or EBSCO, search for recent articles that discuss how a company has revised its pattern of resource allocation and divisional budgets to support new strategic initiatives.

LO 2 **2.** Policies and procedures facilitate strategy execution when they are designed to fit the company's strategy and objectives. Using your university's access to LexisNexis or EBSCO, search for recent articles that discuss how a company has revised its policies and procedures to provide better top-down guidance to company personnel on how to conduct their daily activities and responsibilities.

LO 3 **3.** Illustration Capsule 11.1 discusses Whirlpool Corporation's Operational Excellence initiative and its use of Six Sigma practices. How did the implementation of the program change the culture and mindset of the company's personnel? List three tangible benefits provided by the program. Explain why a commitment to quality control is important in the appliance industry?

connect

LO 3 **4.** Read some of the recent Six Sigma articles posted at **www.isixsigma.com**. Prepare a one-page report to your instructor detailing how Six Sigma is being used in two companies and what benefits the companies are reaping as a result. Further, discuss two to three criticisms of, or potential difficulties with, Six Sigma implementation.

LO 4 **5.** Company strategies can't be executed well without a number of support systems to carry on business operations. Using your university's access to LexisNexis or EBSCO, search for recent articles that discuss how a company has used real-time information systems and control systems to aid the cause of good strategy execution.

LO 5 **6.** Illustration Capsule 11.2 provides a sampling of motivational tactics employed by several prominent companies (many of which appear on *Fortune*'s list of the 100 best companies to work for in America). Discuss how rewards at SAS, Salesforce.com, DPR Construction, and Hilcorp aid in the strategy execution efforts of each company.

connect

EXERCISE FOR SIMULATION PARTICIPANTS

LO 1 **1.** Have you and your co-managers allocated ample resources to strategy-critical areas? If so, explain how these investments have contributed to good strategy execution and improved company performance.

LO 2, LO 3, LO 4 **2.** What actions, if any, is your company taking to pursue continuous improvement in how it performs certain value chain activities?

LO 3 **3.** Is benchmarking data available in the simulation exercise in which you are participating? If so, do you and your co-managers regularly study the benchmarking data to see how well your company is doing? Do you consider the benchmarking information provided to be valuable? Why or why not? Cite three recent instances in which your examination of the benchmarking statistics has caused you and your co-managers to take corrective actions to boost company performance.

4. What hard evidence can you cite that indicates your company's management team is doing a *better* or *worse* job of achieving operating excellence and executing strategy than are the management teams at rival companies? **LO 3**

5. Are you and your co-managers consciously trying to achieve operating excellence? Explain how you are doing this and how you will track the progress you are making. **LO 2, LO 3, LO 4**

6. Does your company have opportunities to use incentive compensation techniques? If so, explain your company's approach to incentive compensation. Is there any hard evidence you can cite that indicates your company's use of incentive compensation techniques has worked? For example, have your company's compensation incentives actually increased productivity? Can you cite evidence indicating that the productivity gains have resulted in lower labor costs? If the productivity gains have *not* translated into lower labor costs, is it fair to say that your company's use of incentive compensation is a failure? **LO 5**

ENDNOTES

[1] Christopher E. Bogan and Michael J. English, *Benchmarking for Best Practices: Winning through Innovative Adaptation* (New York: McGraw-Hill, 1994); Mustafa Ungan, "Factors Affecting the Adoption of Manufacturing Best Practices," *Benchmarking: An International Journal* 11, no. 5 (2004), pp. 504–520; Paul Hyland and Ron Beckett, "Learning to Compete: The Value of Internal Benchmarking," *Benchmarking: An International Journal* 9, no. 3 (2002), pp. 293–304; Yoshinobu Ohinata, "Benchmarking: The Japanese Experience," *Long-Range Planning* 27, no. 4 (August 1994), pp. 48–53.

[2] M. Hammer and J. Champy, *Reengineering the Corporation: A Manifesto for Business Revolution* (New York: HarperCollins, 1993).

[3] James Brian Quinn, *Intelligent Enterprise* (New York: Free Press, 1992); Ann Majchrzak and Qianwei Wang, "Breaking the Functional Mind-Set in Process Organizations," *Harvard Business Review* 74, no. 5 (September–October 1996), pp. 93–99; Stephen L. Walston, Lawton R. Burns, and John R. Kimberly, "Does Reengineering Really Work? An Examination of the Context and Outcomes of Hospital Reengineering Initiatives," *Health Services Research* 34, no. 6 (February 2000), pp. 1363–1388; Allessio Ascari, Melinda Rock, and Soumitra Dutta, "Reengineering and Organizational Change: Lessons from a Comparative Analysis of Company Experiences," *European Management Journal* 13, no. 1 (March 1995), pp. 1–13; Ronald J. Burke, "Process Reengineering: Who Embraces It and Why?" *The TQM Magazine* 16, no. 2 (2004), pp. 114–119.

[4] www.answers.com (accessed July 8, 2009); "Reengineering: Beyond the Buzzword," *Businessweek,* May 24, 1993, www.businessweek.com (accessed July 8, 2009).

[5] Gene Hall, Jim Rosenthal, and Judy Wade, "How to Make Reengineering Really Work," *Harvard Business Review* 71, no. 6 (November–December 1993), pp. 119–131.

[6] M. Walton, *The Deming Management Method* (New York: Pedigree, 1986); J. Juran, *Juran on Quality by Design* (New York: Free Press, 1992); Philip Crosby, *Quality Is Free: The Act of Making Quality Certain* (New York: McGraw-Hill, 1979); S. George, *The Baldrige Quality System* (New York: Wiley, 1992); Mark J. Zbaracki, "The Rhetoric and Reality of Total Quality Management," *Administrative Science Quarterly* 43, no. 3 (September 1998), pp. 602–636.

[7] Robert T. Amsden, Thomas W. Ferratt, and Davida M. Amsden, "TQM: Core Paradigm Changes," *Business Horizons* 39, no. 6 (November–December 1996), pp. 6–14.

[8] Peter S. Pande and Larry Holpp, *What Is Six Sigma?* (New York: McGraw-Hill, 2002); Jiju Antony, "Some Pros and Cons of Six Sigma: An Academic Perspective," *TQM Magazine* 16, no. 4 (2004), pp. 303–306; Peter S. Pande, Robert P. Neuman, and Roland R. Cavanagh, *The Six Sigma Way: How GE, Motorola and Other Top Companies Are Honing Their Performance* (New York: McGraw-Hill, 2000); Joseph Gordon and M. Joseph Gordon, Jr., *Six Sigma Quality for Business and Manufacture* (New York: Elsevier, 2002); Godecke Wessel and Peter Burcher, "Six Sigma for Small and Medium-Sized Enterprises," *TQM Magazine* 16, no. 4 (2004), pp. 264–272.

[9] www.isixsigma.com (accessed November 4, 2002); www.villanovau.com/certificate-programs/six-sigma-training.aspx (accessed February 16, 2012).

[10] Kennedy Smith, "Six Sigma for the Service Sector," *Quality Digest Magazine,* May 2003; www.qualitydigest.com (accessed September 28, 2003).

[11] www.isixsigma.com/implementation/financial-analysis/six-sigma-costs-and-savings/ (accessed February 23, 2012).

[12] "A Dark Art No More," *The Economist* 385, no. 8550 (October 13, 2007), p. 10; Brian Hindo, "At 3M, a Struggle between Efficiency and Creativity," *Businessweek,* June 11, 2007, pp. 8–16.

[13] Charles A. O'Reilly and Michael L. Tushman, "The Ambidextrous Organization," *Harvard Business Review* 82, no. 4 (April 2004), pp. 74–81.

[14] Terry Nels Lee, Stanley E. Fawcett, and Jason Briscoe, "Benchmarking the Challenge to Quality Program Implementation," *Benchmarking: An International Journal* 9, no. 4 (2002), pp. 374–387.

[15] Milan Ambrož, "Total Quality System as a Product of the Empowered Corporate Culture,"

TQM Magazine 16, no. 2 (2004), pp. 93–104; Nick A. Dayton, "The Demise of Total Quality Management," *TQM Magazine* 15, no. 6 (2003), pp. 391–396.

[16] Judy D. Olian and Sara L. Rynes, "Making Total Quality Work: Aligning Organizational Processes, Performance Measures, and Stakeholders," *Human Resource Management* 30, no. 3 (Fall 1991), pp. 310–311; Paul S. Goodman and Eric D. Darr, "Exchanging Best Practices Information through Computer-Aided Systems," *Academy of Management Executive* 10, no. 2 (May 1996), p. 7.

[17] Thomas C. Powell, "Total Quality Management as Competitive Advantage," *Strategic Management Journal* 16 (1995), pp. 15–37; Richard M. Hodgetts, "Quality Lessons from America's Baldrige Winners," *Business Horizons* 37, no. 4 (July–August 1994), pp. 74–79; Richard Reed, David J. Lemak, and Joseph C. Montgomery, "Beyond Process: TQM Content and Firm Performance," *Academy of Management Review* 21, no. 1 (January 1996), pp. 173–202.

[18] www.otiselevator.com (accessed February 16, 2012).

[19] Fred Vogelstein, "Winning the Amazon Way," *Fortune* 147, no. 10 (May 26, 2003), pp. 60–69.

[20] Robert Simons, "Control in an Age of Empowerment," *Harvard Business Review* 73 (March–April 1995), pp. 80–88.

[21] David C. Band and Gerald Scanlan, "Strategic Control through Core Competencies," *Long Range Planning* 28, no. 2 (April 1995), pp. 102–114.

[22] Stanley E. Fawcett, Gary K. Rhoads, and Phillip Burnah, "People as the Bridge to Competitiveness: Benchmarking the 'ABCs' of an Empowered Workforce," *Benchmarking: An International Journal* 11, no. 4 (2004), pp. 346–360.

[23] Jeffrey Pfeffer and John F. Veiga, "Putting People First for Organizational Success," *Academy of Management Executive* 13, no. 2 (May 1999), pp. 37–45; Linda K. Stroh and Paula M. Caliguiri, "Increasing Global Competitiveness through Effective People Management," *Journal of World Business* 33, no. 1 (Spring 1998), pp. 1–16; articles in *Fortune* on the 100 best companies to work for (various issues).

[24] As quoted in John P. Kotter and James L. Heskett, *Corporate Culture and Performance* (New York: Free Press, 1992), p. 91.

[25] Clayton M. Christensen, Matt Marx, and Howard Stevenson, "The Tools of Cooperation and Change," *Harvard Business Review* 84, no. 10 (October 2006), pp. 73–80.

[26] Steven Kerr, "On the Folly of Rewarding A While Hoping for B," *Academy of Management Executive* 9, no. 1 (February 1995), pp. 7–14; Doran Twer, "Linking Pay to Business Objectives," *Journal of Business Strategy* 15, no. 4 (July–August 1994), pp. 15–18.

CHAPTER 12

Corporate Culture and Leadership

Keys to Good Strategy Execution

Learning Objectives

THIS CHAPTER WILL HELP YOU UNDERSTAND:

LO 1 The key features of a company's corporate culture and the role of a company's core values and ethical standards in building corporate culture.

LO 2 How and why a company's culture can aid the drive for proficient strategy execution.

LO 3 The kinds of actions management can take to change a problem corporate culture.

LO 4 What constitutes effective managerial leadership in achieving superior strategy execution.

The key to successful leadership today is influence, not authority.

Kenneth Blanchard – *Author and Management Expert*

As we look ahead into the next century, leaders will be those who empower others.

Bill Gates – *Cofounder and Former CEO and Chairman of Microsoft*

If you want to change the culture, you will have to start by changing the organization.

Mary Douglas – *Social Anthropologist and Expert on Culture*

In the previous two chapters, we examined eight of the managerial tasks that drive good strategy execution: staffing the organization, acquiring the needed resources and capabilities, designing the organizational structure, allocating resources, establishing policies and procedures, employing process management tools, installing operating systems, and providing the right incentives. In this chapter, we explore the two remaining managerial tasks that contribute to good strategy execution: creating a strategy-supportive corporate culture and exerting the internal leadership needed to drive the implementation of strategic initiatives forward.

INSTILLING A CORPORATE CULTURE CONDUCIVE TO GOOD STRATEGY EXECUTION

Every company has its own unique **corporate culture**—the shared values, ingrained attitudes, and company traditions that determine norms of behavior, accepted work practices, and styles of operating.[1] The character of a company's culture is a product of the core values and beliefs that executives espouse, the standards of what is ethically acceptable and what is not, the "chemistry" and the "personality" that permeate the work environment, the company's traditions, and the stories that get told over and over to illustrate and reinforce the company's shared values, business practices, and traditions. In a very real sense, the culture is the company's automatic, self-replicating "operating system" that defines "how we do things around here."[2] It can be thought of as the company's psyche or *organizational DNA*.[3] A company's culture is important because it influences the organization's actions and approaches to conducting business. As such, it plays an important role in strategy execution and may have an appreciable effect on business performance as well.

CORE CONCEPT

Corporate culture refers to the shared values, ingrained attitudes, core beliefs, and company traditions that determine norms of behavior, accepted work practices, and styles of operating.

Corporate cultures vary widely. For instance, the bedrock of Walmart's culture is zealous pursuit of low costs and frugal operating practices, a strong work ethic,

LO 1

The key features of a company's corporate culture and the role of a company's core values and ethical standards in building corporate culture.

ritualistic headquarters meetings to exchange ideas and review problems, and company executives' commitment to visiting stores, listening to customers, and soliciting suggestions from employees. The culture of General Electric (GE) under CEO Jeff Immelt entails a commitment to creativity and bold innovation that wires the company for growth. It drives a willingness to accept the risk of embracing new ventures with the potential to grow GE revenues by at least $100 million, real prowess in improving customer service, pressure to produce good business results, and cross-business sharing of ideas, best practices, and learning.[4] At Publix, the most profitable grocery store chain in the United States, corporate culture is centered on delivering exceptional service to customers; the company's reputation for never disappointing its customers is "legendary in the industry."[5] Its "people first" culture is focused not only on its customers but on its employees as well, who are also the company's largest collective shareholders.[6] Publix makes a point of promoting employees from within so that they are motivated not only by an ownership stake in the company but by opportunities for advancement in the company as well. Illustration Capsule 12.1 describes the corporate culture of another exemplar company—W. L. Gore & Associates, the inventor of GORE-TEX.

Identifying the Key Features of a Company's Corporate Culture

A company's corporate culture is mirrored in the character or "personality" of its work environment—the features that describe how the company goes about its business and the workplace behaviors that are held in high esteem. Some of these features are readily apparent, and others operate quite subtly. The chief things to look for include:

- The values, business principles, and ethical standards that management preaches and *practices*—these are the key to a company's culture, but actions speak much louder than words here.
- The company's approach to people management and the official policies, procedures, and operating practices that provide guidelines for the behavior of company personnel.
- The atmosphere and spirit that pervades the work climate—whether the workplace is competitive or cooperative, innovative or resistant to change, political or collegial, all business or fun-loving, and the like.
- The way managers and employees interact and relate to one another—whether and to what extent good camaraderie exists, whether people tend to work independently or collaboratively, whether communications among employees are free-flowing or infrequent, whether people are called by their first names, whether co-workers spend little or lots of time together outside the workplace, and so on.
- The strength of peer pressure to do things in particular ways and conform to expected norms.
- The actions and behaviors that management explicitly encourages and rewards and those that are frowned upon.
- The company's revered traditions and oft-repeated stories about "heroic acts" and "how we do things around here."
- The manner in which the company deals with external stakeholders—whether it treats suppliers as business partners or prefers hard-nosed, arm's-length business arrangements and whether its commitment to corporate citizenship and environmental sustainability is strong and genuine.

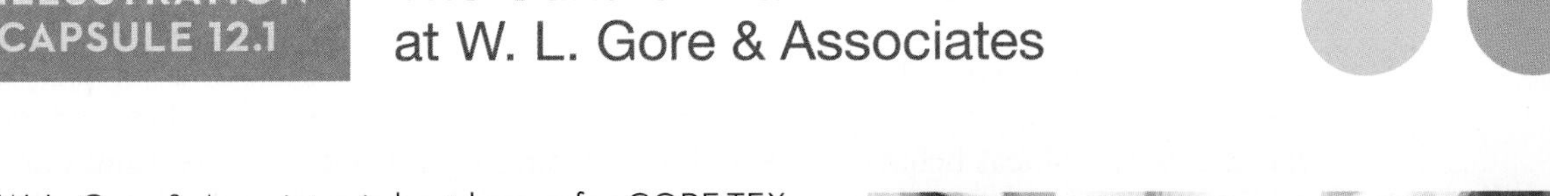

ILLUSTRATION CAPSULE 12.1 The Culture That Drives Innovation at W. L. Gore & Associates

W. L. Gore & Associates is best known for GORE-TEX, the waterproof, breathable fabric highly prized by outdoor enthusiasts. But the company has developed a wide variety of other revolutionary products, including Elixir guitar strings, Ride-On bike cables, and a host of medical devices such as cardiovascular patches and synthetic blood vessels. As a result, it is now one of the largest privately held companies in the United States, with more than $3 billion in revenue and 10,000 employees in 30 countries worldwide.

When Gore developed the core technology on which most of its more than 2,000 worldwide patents is based, the company's unique culture played a crucial role in allowing Gore to pursue multiple end-market applications simultaneously, enabling rapid growth from a niche business into a diversified multinational company. The company's culture is team-based and designed to foster personal initiative. It is described on the company's website as follows:

> There are no traditional organizational charts, no chains of command, nor predetermined channels of communication. Instead, we communicate directly with each other and are accountable to fellow members of our multi-discipline teams. We encourage hands-on innovation, involving those closest to a project in decision making. Teams organize around opportunities and leaders emerge.

Personal stories posted on the website describe the discovery process behind a number of breakthrough products developed by particular teams at W. L. Gore & Associates. Employees are encouraged to use 10 percent of their time to tinker with new ideas and to take

the long view regarding the idea's development. Promising ideas attract more people who are willing to work on them without orders from higher-ups. Instead, self-managing associates operating in self-developed teams are simply encouraged to pursue novel applications of Gore technology until these applications are fully commercialized or have had their potential exhausted. The encouragement comes both from the culture (norms and practices) of the organization and from a profit-sharing arrangement that allows employees to benefit directly from their successes.

This approach makes Gore a great place to work and has helped it attract, retain, and motivate top talent globally. Gore has been on *Fortune* magazine's list of the 100 best companies to work for in the United States for the last 17 years. Gore places similarly on the lists of other countries in which it operates, such as the United Kingdom, Germany, France, Italy, and Sweden.

Note: Developed with Kenneth P. Fraser.

Sources: Company websites; www.gore.com/en_xx/news/FORTUNE-2011.html; www.director.co.uk/magazine/2010/2_Feb/WLGore_63_06.html; and www.fastcompany.com/magazine/89/open_gore.html (accessed March 10, 2012).

The values, beliefs, and practices that undergird a company's culture can come from anywhere in the organizational hierarchy. Typically, key elements of the culture originate with a founder or certain strong leaders who articulated them as a set of business principles, company policies, operating approaches, and ways of dealing with employees, customers, vendors, shareholders, and local communities where the company has operations. They also stem from exemplary actions on the part of company personnel and evolving consensus about "how we ought to do things around here."[7] Over time, these cultural underpinnings take root, come to be accepted by company managers and employees alike, and become ingrained in the way the company conducts its business.

The Role of Core Values and Ethics The foundation of a company's corporate culture nearly always resides in its dedication to certain core values and the bar it sets for ethical behavior. The culture-shaping significance of core values and ethical behaviors accounts for why so many companies have developed a formal value statement and a code of ethics. Of course, sometimes a company's stated core values and code of ethics are cosmetic, existing mainly to impress outsiders and help create a positive company image. But usually they have been developed to purposely mold the culture and communicate the kinds of actions and behavior that are expected of all company personnel. Many executives want the work climate at their companies to mirror certain values and ethical standards, partly because of personal convictions but mainly because they are convinced that adherence to such principles will promote better strategy execution, make the company a better performer, and positively impact its reputation.[8] Not incidentally, strongly ingrained values and ethical standards reduce the likelihood of lapses in ethical and socially approved behavior that mar a company's public image and put its financial performance and market standing at risk.

A company's culture is grounded in and shaped by its core values and ethical standards.

As depicted in Figure 12.1, a company's stated core values and ethical principles have two roles in the culture-building process. First, a company that works hard at putting its stated core values and ethical principles into practice fosters a work climate in which company personnel share strongly held convictions about how the company's business is to be conducted. Second, the stated values and ethical principles provide company personnel with guidance about the manner in which they are to do their jobs—which behaviors and ways of doing things are approved (and expected) and which are out-of-bounds. These value-based and ethics-based cultural norms serve as yardsticks for gauging the appropriateness of particular actions, decisions, and behaviors, thus helping steer company personnel toward both doing things right and doing the right thing.

A company's value statement and code of ethics communicate expectations of how employees should conduct themselves in the workplace.

FIGURE 12.1 The Two Culture-Building Roles of a Company's Core Values and Ethical Standards

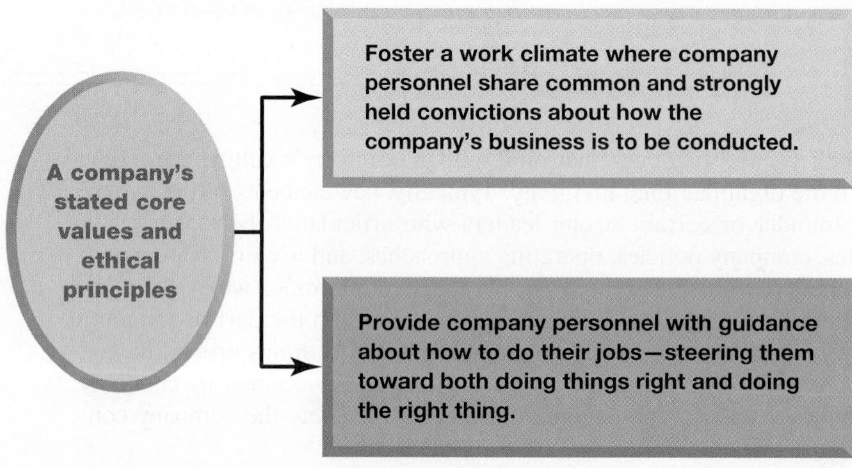

Embedding Cultural Norms in the Organization and Perpetuating the Culture Once values and ethical standards have been formally adopted, they must be institutionalized in the company's policies and practices and embedded in the conduct of company personnel. This can be done in a number of different ways.[9] Tradition-steeped companies with a rich folklore rely heavily on word-of-mouth indoctrination and the power of tradition to instill values and enforce ethical conduct. But most companies employ a variety of techniques, drawing on some or all of the following:

1. Screening applicants and hiring those who will mesh well with the culture.
2. Incorporating discussions of the company's culture and behavioral norms into orientation programs for new employees and training courses for managers and employees.
3. Having senior executives frequently reiterate the importance and role of company values and ethical principles at company events and in internal communications to employees.
4. Expecting managers at all levels to be cultural role models and exhibit the advocated cultural norms in their own behavior.
5. Making the display of cultural norms a factor in evaluating each person's job performance, granting compensation increases, and deciding who to promote.
6. Stressing that line managers all the way down to first-level supervisors give ongoing attention to explaining the desired cultural traits and behaviors in their areas and clarifying why they are important.
7. Encouraging company personnel to exert strong peer pressure on co-workers to conform to expected cultural norms.
8. Holding periodic ceremonies to honor people who excel in displaying the company values and ethical principles.

To deeply ingrain the stated core values and high ethical standards, companies must turn them into *strictly enforced cultural norms.* They must make it unequivocally clear that living up to the company's values and ethical standards has to be "a way of life" at the company and that there will be little toleration for errant behavior.

The Role of Stories Frequently, a significant part of a company's culture is captured in the stories that get told over and over again to illustrate to newcomers the importance of certain values and the depth of commitment that various company personnel have displayed. One of the folktales at Zappos, known for its outstanding customer service, is about a customer who ordered shoes for her ill mother from Zappos, hoping they would remedy her mother's foot pain and numbness. When the shoes didn't work, the mother called the company to ask how to return them and explain why she was returning them. Two days later, she received a large bouquet of flowers from the company, along with well wishes and a customer upgrade giving her free expedited service on all future orders. Specialty food market Trader Joe's is similarly known for its culture of going beyond the call of duty for its customers. When a World War II veteran was snowed in without any food for meals, his daughter called several supermarkets to see if they offered grocery delivery. Although Trader Joe's technically doesn't offer delivery, it graciously helped the veteran, even recommending items for his low-sodium diet. When the store delivered the groceries, the veteran wasn't charged for either the groceries or the delivery. When Apple's iPad 2 was launched, one was returned to the company almost immediately, with a note attached that said

"Wife said No!"[10] Apple sent the customer a refund, but it also sent back the device with a note reading "Apple says Yes!" Such stories serve the valuable purpose of illustrating the kinds of behavior the company reveres and inspiring company personnel to perform similarly. Moreover, each retelling of a legendary story puts a bit more peer pressure on company personnel to display core values and do their part in keeping the company's traditions alive.

Forces That Cause a Company's Culture to Evolve Despite the role of time-honored stories and long-standing traditions in perpetuating a company's culture, cultures are far from static—just like strategy and organizational structure, they evolve. New challenges in the marketplace, revolutionary technologies, and shifting internal conditions—especially an internal crisis, a change in company direction, or top-executive turnover—tend to breed new ways of doing things and, in turn, drive cultural evolution. An incoming CEO who decides to shake up the existing business and take it in new directions often triggers a cultural shift, perhaps one of major proportions. Likewise, diversification into new businesses, expansion into foreign countries, rapid growth that brings an influx of new employees, and the merger with or acquisition of another company can all precipitate significant cultural change.

Strong versus Weak Cultures

Company cultures vary widely in strength and influence. Some are strongly embedded and have a big influence on a company's operating practices and the behavior of company personnel. Others are weakly ingrained and have little effect on behaviors and how company activities are conducted.

CORE CONCEPT

In a **strong-culture company,** deeply rooted values and norms of behavior are widely shared and regulate the conduct of the company's business.

Strong-Culture Companies The hallmark of a **strong-culture company** is the dominating presence of certain deeply rooted values and behavioral norms that "regulate" the conduct of company personnel as they go about the company's business.[11] Strong cultures enable a company to operate like a well-oiled machine, smoothly operating without a lot of intervention from management. Senior managers in strong-culture companies embody the cultural norms in their own actions and expect the same of others within the company. An unequivocal expectation that company personnel will act and behave in accordance with the adopted values and ways of doing business leads to two important outcomes: (1) Over time, the values come to be widely shared by rank-and-file employees—people who dislike the culture tend to leave—and (2) individuals encounter strong peer pressure from co-workers to observe the culturally approved norms and behaviors. Hence, a strongly implanted corporate culture ends up having a powerful influence on behavior because so many company personnel are accepting of cultural traditions and because this acceptance is reinforced by both management expectations and co-worker peer pressure to conform to cultural norms.

Strong cultures emerge only after a period of deliberate and rather intensive culture building that generally takes years (sometimes decades). Two factors contribute to the development of strong cultures: (1) a founder or strong leader who established core values, principles, and practices that are viewed as having contributed to the success of the company, and (2) a sincere, long-standing company commitment to operating the business according to these established traditions and values. Continuity of leadership, low workforce turnover, geographic concentration, and considerable organizational success all contribute to the emergence and sustainability of a strong culture.[12]

In strong-culture companies, values and behavioral norms are so ingrained that they can endure leadership changes at the top—although their strength can erode over time if new CEOs cease to nurture them or move aggressively to institute cultural adjustments. The cultural norms in a strong-culture company typically do not change much as strategy evolves, either because the culture constrains the choice of new strategies or because the dominant traits of the culture are somewhat strategy-neutral and compatible with evolving versions of the company's strategy. As a consequence, *strongly implanted cultures provide a huge assist in executing strategy* because company managers can use the traditions, beliefs, values, common bonds, or behavioral norms as levers to mobilize commitment to executing the chosen strategy.

Weak-Culture Companies In direct contrast to strong-culture companies, weak-culture companies lack widely shared and strongly held values and principles. As a result, they also lack cultural mechanisms for aligning, constraining, and regulating the actions, decisions, and behaviors of company personnel. In the absence of any long-standing top management commitment to particular values, beliefs, operating practices, and behavioral norms, individuals encounter little pressure to do things in particular ways. Such a dearth of companywide cultural influences and revered traditions produces a work climate where there is no strong employee allegiance to what the company stands for or to operating the business in well-defined ways. While individual employees may well have some bonds of identification with and loyalty toward their department, their colleagues, their union, or their immediate boss, there's neither passion about the company nor emotional commitment to what it is trying to accomplish—a condition that often results in many employees' viewing their company as just a place to work and their job as just a way to make a living.

As a consequence, *weak cultures provide little or no assistance in executing strategy* because there are no traditions, beliefs, values, common bonds, or behavioral norms that management can use as levers to mobilize commitment to executing the chosen strategy. Without a work climate that channels organizational energy in the direction of good strategy execution, managers are left with the options of either using compensation incentives and other motivational devices to mobilize employee commitment, supervising and monitoring employee actions more closely, or trying to establish cultural roots that will in time start to nurture the strategy execution process.

Why Corporate Cultures Matter to the Strategy Execution Process

LO 2

How and why a company's culture can aid the drive for proficient strategy execution.

Even if a company has a strong culture, the culture and work climate may or may not be compatible with what is needed for effective implementation of the chosen strategy. When a company's present culture promotes attitudes, behaviors, and ways of doing things that are *in sync with the chosen strategy* and conducive to first-rate strategy execution, the culture functions as a valuable ally in the strategy execution process. For example, a corporate culture characterized by frugality and thrift prompts employee actions to identify cost-saving opportunities—the very behavior needed for successful execution of a low-cost leadership strategy. A culture that celebrates taking initiative, exhibiting creativity, taking risks, and embracing change is conducive to successful execution of product innovation and technological leadership strategies.[13]

A culture that is grounded in actions, behaviors, and work practices that are conducive to good strategy implementation supports the strategy execution effort in three ways:

1. *A culture that is well matched to the chosen strategy and the requirements of the strategy execution effort focuses the attention of employees on what is most important to this effort.* Moreover, it directs their behavior and serves as a guide to their decision making. In this manner, it can align the efforts and decisions of employees throughout the firm and minimize the need for direct supervision.
2. *Culture-induced peer pressure further induces company personnel to do things in a manner that aids the cause of good strategy execution.* The stronger the culture (the more widely shared and deeply held the values), the more effective peer pressure is in shaping and supporting the strategy execution effort. Research has shown that strong group norms can shape employee behavior even more powerfully than can financial incentives.
3. *A company culture that is consistent with the requirements for good strategy execution can energize employees, deepen their commitment to execute the strategy flawlessly, and enhance worker productivity in the process.* When a company's culture is grounded in many of the needed strategy-executing behaviors, employees feel genuinely better about their jobs, the company they work for, and the merits of what the company is trying to accomplish. Greater employee buy-in for what the company is trying to accomplish boosts motivation and marshals organizational energy behind the drive for good strategy execution. An energized workforce enhances the chances of achieving execution-critical performance targets and good strategy execution.

A strong culture that encourages actions, behaviors, and work practices that are in sync with the chosen strategy and conducive to good strategy execution is a valuable ally in the strategy execution process.

In sharp contrast, when a culture is in conflict with the chosen strategy or what is required to execute the company's strategy well, the culture becomes a stumbling block.[14] Some of the very behaviors needed to execute the strategy successfully run contrary to the attitudes, behaviors, and operating practices embedded in the prevailing culture. Such a clash poses a real dilemma for company personnel. Should they be loyal to the culture and company traditions (to which they are likely to be emotionally attached) and thus resist or be indifferent to actions that will promote better strategy execution—a choice that will certainly weaken the drive for good strategy execution? Alternatively, should they go along with management's strategy execution effort and engage in actions that run counter to the culture—a choice that will likely impair morale and lead to a less-than-wholehearted commitment to good strategy execution? Neither choice leads to desirable outcomes. Culture-bred resistance to the actions and behaviors needed for good strategy execution, particularly if strong and widespread, poses a formidable hurdle that must be cleared for a strategy's execution to be successful.

It is in management's best interest to dedicate considerable effort to establishing a corporate culture that encourages behaviors and work practices conducive to good strategy execution.

The consequences of having—or not having—an execution-supportive corporate culture says something important about the task of managing the strategy execution process: *Closely aligning corporate culture with the requirements for proficient strategy execution merits the full attention of senior executives.* The culture-building objective is to create a work climate and style of operating that mobilize the energy of company personnel squarely behind efforts to execute strategy competently. The more deeply management can embed execution-supportive ways of doing things, the more management can rely on the culture to automatically steer company personnel toward behaviors and work practices that aid good strategy execution and veer from doing things that impede it. Moreover, culturally astute managers understand that nourishing the right cultural environment not only adds power to their push for proficient strategy execution but also promotes strong employee identification with, and commitment to, the company's vision, performance targets, and strategy.

Healthy Cultures That Aid Good Strategy Execution

A strong culture, provided it fits the chosen strategy and embraces execution-supportive attitudes, behaviors, and work practices, is definitely a healthy culture. Two other types of cultures exist that tend to be healthy and largely supportive of good strategy execution: high-performance cultures and adaptive cultures.

High-Performance Cultures Some companies have so-called "high-performance" cultures where the standout traits are a "can-do" spirit, pride in doing things right, no-excuses accountability, and a pervasive results-oriented work climate in which people go all out to meet or beat stretch objectives.[15] In high-performance cultures, there's a strong sense of involvement on the part of company personnel and emphasis on individual initiative and effort. Performance expectations are clearly delineated for the company as a whole, for each organizational unit, and for each individual. Issues and problems are promptly addressed; there's a razor-sharp focus on what needs to be done. The clear and unyielding expectation is that all company personnel, from senior executives to frontline employees, will display high-performance behaviors and a passion for making the company successful. Such a culture—permeated by a spirit of achievement and constructive pressure to achieve good results—is a valuable contributor to good strategy execution and operating excellence.[16]

The challenge in creating a high-performance culture is to inspire high loyalty and dedication on the part of employees, such that they are energized to put forth their very best efforts. Managers have to take pains to reinforce constructive behavior, reward top performers, and purge habits and behaviors that stand in the way of high productivity and good results. They must work at knowing the strengths and weaknesses of their subordinates, so as to better match talent with task and enable people to make meaningful contributions by doing what they do best. They have to stress learning from mistakes and must put an unrelenting emphasis on moving forward and making good progress—in effect, there has to be a disciplined, performance-focused approach to managing the organization.

Adaptive Cultures The hallmark of adaptive corporate cultures is willingness on the part of organization members to accept change and take on the challenge of introducing and executing new strategies. Company personnel share a feeling of confidence that the organization can deal with whatever threats and opportunities arise; they are receptive to risk taking, experimentation, innovation, and changing strategies and practices. The work climate is supportive of managers and employees who propose or initiate useful change. Internal entrepreneurship (often called *intrapreneurship*) on the part of individuals and groups is encouraged and rewarded. Senior executives seek out, support, and promote individuals who exercise initiative, spot opportunities for improvement, and display the skills to implement them. Managers openly evaluate ideas and suggestions, fund initiatives to develop new or better products, and take prudent risks to pursue emerging market opportunities. As in high-performance cultures, the company exhibits a proactive approach to identifying issues, evaluating the implications and options, and moving ahead quickly with workable solutions. Strategies and traditional operating practices are modified as needed to adjust to, or take advantage of, changes in the business environment.

As a company's strategy evolves, an adaptive culture is a definite ally in the strategy-implementing, strategy-executing process as compared to cultures that are resistant to change.

But why is change so willingly embraced in an adaptive culture? Why are organization members not fearful of how change will affect them? Why does an adaptive culture not break down from the force of ongoing changes in strategy, operating practices, and behavioral norms? The answers lie in two distinctive and dominant traits of an adaptive culture: (1) Changes in operating practices and behaviors must *not* compromise core values and long-standing business principles (since they are at the root of the culture), and (2) changes that are instituted must satisfy the legitimate interests of key constituencies—customers, employees, shareholders, suppliers, and the communities where the company operates. In other words, what sustains an adaptive culture is that organization members perceive the changes that management is trying to institute as *legitimate,* in keeping with the core values, and in the overall best interests of stakeholders.[17] Not surprisingly, company personnel are usually more receptive to change when their employment security is not threatened and when they view new duties or job assignments as part of the process of adapting to new conditions. Should workforce downsizing be necessary, it is important that layoffs be handled humanely and employee departures be made as painless as possible.

Technology companies, software companies, and Internet-based companies are good illustrations of organizations with adaptive cultures. Such companies thrive on change—driving it, leading it, and capitalizing on it. Companies like Facebook, Twitter, Adobe, Groupon, Cisco Systems, Google, Yahoo, and Yelp cultivate the capability to act and react rapidly. They are avid practitioners of entrepreneurship and innovation, with a demonstrated willingness to take bold risks to create altogether new products, new businesses, and new industries. To create and nurture a culture that can adapt rapidly to shifting business conditions, they make a point of staffing their organizations with people who are flexible, who rise to the challenge of change, and who have an aptitude for adapting well to new circumstances.

In fast-changing business environments, a corporate culture that is receptive to altering organizational practices and behaviors is a virtual necessity. However, adaptive cultures work to the advantage of all companies, not just those in rapid-change environments. Every company operates in a market and business climate that is changing to one degree or another and that, in turn, requires internal operating responses and new behaviors on the part of organization members.

Unhealthy Cultures That Impede Good Strategy Execution

The distinctive characteristic of an unhealthy corporate culture is the presence of counterproductive cultural traits that adversely impact the work climate and company performance. Five particularly unhealthy cultural traits are hostility to change, heavily politicized decision making, insular thinking, unethical and greed-driven behaviors, and the presence of incompatible, clashing subcultures.

Change-Resistant Cultures Change-resistant cultures—where skepticism about the importance of new developments and a fear of change are the norm—place a premium on not making mistakes, prompting managers to lean toward safe, conservative options intended to maintain the status quo, protect their power base, and guard their immediate interests. When such companies encounter business environments with accelerating change, going slow on altering traditional ways of doing things can be a serious liability. Under these conditions, change-resistant cultures encourage a number of unhealthy behaviors—avoiding risks, not capitalizing on emerging opportunities, taking a lax approach to both product innovation and continuous improvement in performing value chain activities, and responding more slowly than is warranted to market change. In change-resistant cultures, word quickly gets around that proposals to do things differently face an uphill battle and that people who champion them may be seen as something of a nuisance or a troublemaker. Executives who don't value managers or employees with initiative and new ideas put a damper on product innovation, experimentation, and efforts to improve.

Hostility to change is most often found in companies with stodgy bureaucracies that have enjoyed considerable market success in years past and that are wedded to the "We have done it this way for years" syndrome. Blockbuster, Yahoo, Toys 'R Us, Sears, and Eastman Kodak are classic examples of companies whose change-resistant bureaucracies have damaged their market standings and financial performance; clinging to what made them successful, they were reluctant to alter operating practices and modify their business approaches when signals of market change first sounded. As strategies of gradual change won out over bold innovation, all four lost market share to rivals that quickly moved to institute changes more in tune with evolving market conditions and buyer preferences. While IBM and GM have made strides in building a culture needed for market success, Sears and Kodak are still struggling to recoup lost ground.

Politicized Cultures What makes a politicized internal environment so unhealthy is that political infighting consumes a great deal of organizational energy, often with the result that what's best for the company takes a backseat to political maneuvering. In companies where internal politics pervades the work climate, empire-building managers pursue their own agendas and operate the work units under their supervision as autonomous "fiefdoms." The positions they take on issues are usually aimed at protecting or expanding their own turf. Collaboration with other organizational units is viewed with suspicion, and cross-unit cooperation occurs grudgingly. The support or opposition of politically influential executives and/or coalitions among departments with vested interests in a particular outcome tends to shape what actions the company takes. All this political maneuvering takes away from efforts to execute strategy with real proficiency and frustrates company personnel who are less political and more inclined to do what is in the company's best interests.

Insular, Inwardly Focused Cultures Sometimes a company reigns as an industry leader or enjoys great market success for so long that its personnel start to believe they have all the answers or can develop them on their own. There is a strong tendency to neglect what customers are saying and how their needs and expectations are changing. Such confidence in the correctness of how the company does things and an unflinching belief in its competitive superiority breed arrogance, prompting company personnel to discount the merits of what outsiders are doing and to see little payoff from studying best-in-class performers. Insular thinking, internally driven solutions, and a must-be-invented-here mindset come to permeate the corporate culture. An inwardly focused corporate culture gives rise to managerial inbreeding and a failure to recruit people who can offer fresh thinking and outside perspectives. The big risk of insular cultural thinking is that the company can underestimate the capabilities and accomplishments of rival companies while overestimating its own—all of which diminishes a company's competitiveness over time.

Unethical and Greed-Driven Cultures Companies that have little regard for ethical standards or are run by executives driven by greed and ego gratification are scandals waiting to happen. Executives exude the negatives of arrogance, ego, greed, and an "ends-justify-the-means" mentality in pursuing overambitious revenue and profitability targets.[18] Senior managers wink at unethical behavior and may cross over the line to unethical (and sometimes criminal) behavior themselves. They are prone to adopt accounting principles that make financial performance look better than it really is. Legions of companies have fallen prey to unethical behavior and greed, most notably Enron, Rite Aid, Xerox, Olympus, Peregrine Financial Group, Pilot Flying J, Marsh & McLennan, Siemens, Countrywide Financial, and JPMorgan Chase, with executives being indicted and/or convicted of criminal behavior.

Incompatible Subcultures Although it is common to speak about corporate culture in the singular, it is not unusual for companies to have multiple cultures (or subcultures). Values, beliefs, and practices within a company sometimes vary significantly by department, geographic location, division, or business unit. As long as the subcultures are compatible with the overarching corporate culture and are supportive of the strategy execution efforts, this is not problematic. Multiple cultures pose an unhealthy situation when they are composed of incompatible subcultures that embrace conflicting business philosophies, support inconsistent approaches to strategy execution, and encourage incompatible methods of people management. Clashing subcultures can prevent a company from coordinating its efforts to craft and execute strategy and can distract company personnel from the business of business. Internal jockeying among the subcultures for cultural dominance impedes teamwork among the company's various organizational units and blocks the emergence of a collaborative approach to strategy execution. Such a lack of consensus about how to proceed is likely to result in fragmented or inconsistent approaches to implementing new strategic initiatives and in limited success in executing the company's overall strategy.

Changing a Problem Culture

LO 3

The kinds of actions management can take to change a problem corporate culture.

When a strong culture is unhealthy or otherwise out of sync with the actions and behaviors needed to execute the strategy successfully, the culture must be changed as rapidly as can be managed. This means eliminating any unhealthy or dysfunctional cultural traits as fast as possible and aggressively striving to ingrain new behaviors and work practices that will enable first-rate strategy execution. The more entrenched the unhealthy or mismatched aspects of a company culture, the more likely the culture will impede strategy execution and the greater the need for change.

Changing a problem culture is among the toughest management tasks because of the heavy anchor of ingrained behaviors and attitudes. It is natural for company personnel to cling to familiar practices and to be wary of change, if not hostile to new approaches concerning how things are to be done. Consequently, it takes concerted management action over a period of time to root out unwanted behaviors and replace an unsupportive culture with more effective ways of doing things. *The single most visible factor that distinguishes successful culture-change efforts from failed attempts is competent leadership at the top.* Great power is needed to force major cultural change and overcome the stubborn resistance of entrenched cultures—and great power is possessed only by the most senior executives, especially the CEO. However, while top management must lead the change effort, the tasks of marshaling support for a new culture and instilling the desired cultural behaviors must involve a company's whole management team. Middle managers and frontline supervisors play a key role in implementing the new work practices and operating approaches, helping win rank-and-file acceptance of and support for changes, and instilling the desired behavioral norms.

As shown in Figure 12.2, the first step in fixing a problem culture is for top management to identify those facets of the present culture that are dysfunctional and pose obstacles to executing strategic initiatives. Second, managers must clearly define the desired new behaviors and features of the culture they want to create. Third, they must convince company personnel of why the present culture poses problems and why and how new behaviors and operating approaches will improve company performance—the case for cultural reform has to be persuasive. Finally, and most important, all the talk about remodeling the present culture must be followed swiftly by visible, forceful actions to promote the desired new behaviors and work practices—actions that company personnel will interpret as a determined top-management commitment to bringing about a different work climate and new ways of operating. The actions to implant the new culture must be both substantive and symbolic.

Making a Compelling Case for Culture Change The way for management to begin a major remodeling of the corporate culture is by selling company personnel on the need for new-style behaviors and work practices. This means making a compelling case for why the culture-remodeling efforts are in the organization's best interests and why company personnel should wholeheartedly join the effort to do things somewhat differently. This can be done by:

- Explaining why and how certain behaviors and work practices in the current culture pose obstacles to good strategy execution.
- Explaining how new behaviors and work practices will be more advantageous and produce better results. Effective culture-change leaders are good at telling stories

FIGURE 12.2 Changing a Problem Culture

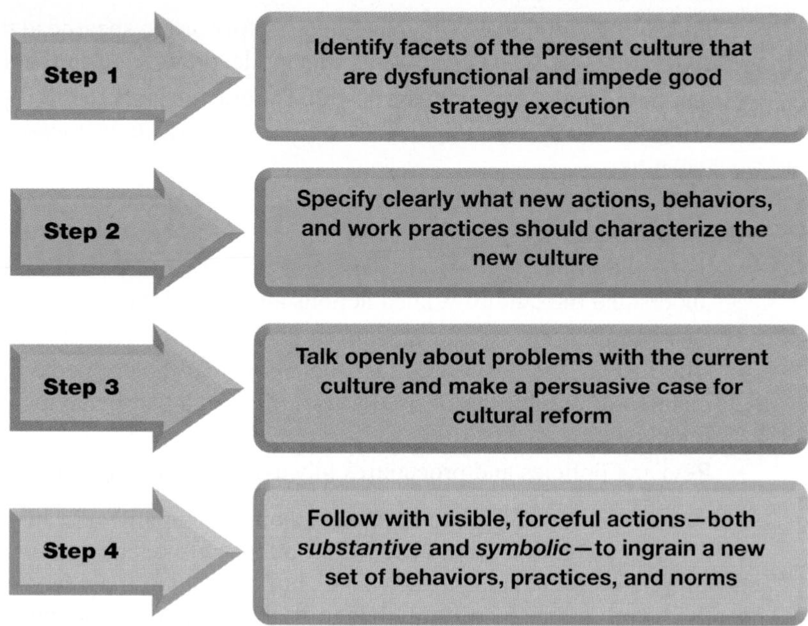

to describe the new values and desired behaviors and connect them to everyday practices.

- Citing reasons why the current strategy has to be modified, if the need for cultural change is due to a change in strategy. This includes explaining why the new strategic initiatives will bolster the company's competitiveness and performance and how a change in culture can help in executing the new strategy.

It is essential for the CEO and other top executives to talk personally to personnel all across the company about the reasons for modifying work practices and culture-related behaviors. For the culture-change effort to be successful, frontline supervisors and employee opinion leaders must be won over to the cause, which means convincing them of the merits of *practicing* and *enforcing* cultural norms at every level of the organization, from the highest to the lowest. Arguments for new ways of doing things and new work practices tend to be embraced more readily if employees understand how they will benefit company stakeholders (particularly customers, employees, and shareholders). Until a large majority of employees accept the need for a new culture and agree that different work practices and behaviors are called for, there's more work to be done in selling company personnel on the whys and wherefores of culture change. Building widespread organizational support requires taking every opportunity to repeat the message of why the new work practices, operating approaches, and behaviors are good for company stakeholders and essential for the company's future success.

Substantive Culture-Changing Actions No culture-change effort can get very far when leaders merely talk about the need for different actions, behaviors, and work practices. Company executives must give the culture-change effort some teeth by initiating *a series of actions* that company personnel will see as unmistakably indicative of the seriousness of management's commitment to cultural change. The strongest signs that management is truly committed to instilling a new culture include:

- Replacing key executives who are resisting or obstructing needed organizational and cultural changes.
- Promoting individuals who have stepped forward to spearhead the shift to a different culture and who can serve as role models for the desired cultural behavior.
- Appointing outsiders with the desired cultural attributes to high-profile positions—bringing in new-breed managers sends an unambiguous message that a new era is dawning.
- Screening all candidates for new positions carefully, hiring only those who appear to fit in with the new culture.
- Mandating that all company personnel attend culture-training programs to better understand the culture-related actions and behaviors that are expected.
- Designing compensation incentives that boost the pay of teams and individuals who display the desired cultural behaviors. Company personnel are much more inclined to exhibit the desired kinds of actions and behaviors when it is in their financial best interest to do so.
- Revising policies and procedures in ways that will help drive cultural change.

Executives must take care to launch enough companywide culture-change actions at the outset so as to leave no room for doubt that management is dead serious about changing the present culture and that a cultural transformation is inevitable. Management's commitment to cultural change in the company must be made credible. The series of actions initiated by top management must command attention, get the change process off to a fast start, and be followed by unrelenting efforts to firmly establish the new work practices, desired behaviors, and style of operating as "standard."

Symbolic Culture-Changing Actions There's also an important place for symbolic managerial actions to alter a problem culture and tighten the strategy–culture fit. The most important symbolic actions are those that top executives take to *lead by example.* For instance, if the organization's strategy involves a drive to become the industry's low-cost producer, senior managers must display frugality in their own actions and decisions. Examples include inexpensive decorations in the executive suite, conservative expense accounts and entertainment allowances, a lean staff in the corporate office, scrutiny of budget requests, few executive perks, and so on. At Walmart, all the executive offices are simply decorated; executives are habitually frugal in their own actions, and they are zealous in their efforts to control costs and promote greater efficiency. At Nucor, one of the world's low-cost producers of steel products, executives fly coach class and use taxis at airports rather than limousines. Top executives must be alert to the fact that company personnel will be watching their behavior to see if their actions match their rhetoric. Hence, they need to make sure their current decisions and actions will be construed as consistent with the new-culture values and norms.[19]

Another category of symbolic actions includes holding ceremonial events to single out and honor people whose actions and performance exemplify what is called for in the new culture. Such events also provide an opportunity to celebrate each culture-change success. Executives sensitive to their role in promoting strategy–culture fit make a habit of appearing at ceremonial functions to praise individuals and groups that exemplify the desired behaviors. They show up at employee training programs to stress strategic priorities, values, ethical principles, and cultural norms. Every group gathering is seen as an opportunity to repeat and ingrain values, praise good deeds, expound on the merits of the new culture, and cite instances of how the new work practices and operating approaches have produced the desired results.

The use of symbols in culture building is widespread. Numerous businesses have employee-of-the-month awards. The military has a long-standing custom of awarding ribbons and medals for exemplary actions. Mary Kay Cosmetics awards an array of prizes ceremoniously to its beauty consultants for reaching various sales plateaus, including the iconic pink Cadillac.

How Long Does It Take to Change a Problem Culture? Planting the seeds of a new culture and helping the culture grow strong roots require a determined, sustained effort by the chief executive and other senior managers. Changing a problem culture is never a short-term exercise; it takes time for a new culture to emerge and take root. And it takes even longer for a new culture to become deeply embedded. The bigger the organization and the greater the cultural shift needed to produce an execution-supportive fit, the longer it takes. In large companies, fixing a problem culture and instilling a new set of attitudes and behaviors can take two to five years. In fact, it is usually tougher to reform an entrenched problematic culture than it is to instill a strategy-supportive culture from scratch in a brand new organization.

Illustration Capsule 12.2 discusses the approaches used at America Latina Logistica (ALL) to change a culture that was grounded in antiquated practices and bureaucratic management.

ILLUSTRATION CAPSULE 12.2 Culture Transformation at America Latina Logistica

For many, a steam-engine locomotive's stocky profile, billowing exhaust, and hiss evoke nostalgia for a bygone era. For the managers at America Latina Logistica (ALL), which had just acquired the southern freight lines of the Brazilian Rail Network (RFFSA), such antiquated locomotives represented the difficulties they faced in fixing their ailing railroad.

When ALL assumed control of the RFFSA's Southern Line in 1997, it was losing money, struggling from decades of underinvestment, and encumbered by bureaucratic management. Half the network's bridges required repairs, over three-quarters of its rails were undersized for supporting standard-sized loads, and the system still relied on 20 steam-engine locomotives to move industrial customers' cargo.

CEO Alexandre Behring's priority was to transform ALL into a performance-oriented organization with the strong cost discipline necessary to support an overdue modernization program. He decided that this would require a complete cultural transformation for the company. His first step was to recruit a new management team and fire the dozens of political appointees previously administering the railroad. In his first 10 days, he and his COO interviewed the top-150 managers to evaluate their suitability. They selected 30 for additional responsibility and removed those who did not embrace the new direction. The company established a trainee program, and in four years hired 500 recent college graduates. In Behring's first year, he introduced a performance-based bonus program; in his second year, the company began comparing performance on operational indicators like car utilization and on-time delivery between divisions.

The top managers also took symbolic steps to demonstrate their commitment to the new culture and to reinforce the personnel and process changes they implemented. They sold cars previously reserved for officers' use and fired the chauffeurs retained to drive them. Behring became certified as a train conductor and spent a week each month working in the field, wearing the conductor uniform. For the first time, managers visited injured workers at home. The company created the "Diesel Cup" to recognize conductors who most effectively reduced fuel consumption.

Behring's new direction energized the company's middle managers and line employees, who had been demoralized after years of political interference and ineffectual leadership. In three years Behring transformed a company that hadn't made a hire in over a decade into one of the most desirable employers in Brazil, attracting 9,000 applications for 18 trainee positions. In 2000 ALL achieved profitability, enabled by the company's cultural transformation.

Note: Developed with Peter Jacobson.

Sources: Company website, pt.all-logistica.com; www.strategy-business.com/article/ac00012?pg=1; blogs.hbr.org/2012/09/shape-strategy-with-simple-rul/; and Donald N. Sull, Fernando Martins, and Andre Delbin Silva, "America Latina Logistica," Harvard Business School case 9-804-139, January 14, 2004.

LEADING THE STRATEGY EXECUTION PROCESS

For an enterprise to execute its strategy in truly proficient fashion, top executives must take the lead in the strategy implementation process and personally drive the pace of progress. They have to be out in the field, seeing for themselves how well operations are going, gathering information firsthand, and gauging the progress being made. Proficient strategy execution requires company managers to be diligent and adept in spotting problems, learning what obstacles lay in the path of good execution, and then clearing the way for progress—the goal must be to produce better results speedily and productively. There must be constructive, but unrelenting, pressure on organizational units to (1) demonstrate excellence in all dimensions of strategy execution and (2) do so on a consistent basis—ultimately, that's what will enable a well-crafted strategy to achieve the desired performance results.

LO 4

What constitutes effective managerial leadership in achieving superior strategy execution.

The specifics of how to implement a strategy and deliver the intended results must start with understanding the requirements for good strategy execution. Afterward comes a diagnosis of the organization's preparedness to execute the strategic initiatives and decisions on how to move forward and achieve the targeted results.[20] In general, leading the drive for good strategy execution and operating excellence calls for three actions on the part of the managers in charge:

- Staying on top of what is happening and closely monitoring progress.
- Putting constructive pressure on the organization to execute the strategy well and achieve operating excellence.
- Initiating corrective actions to improve strategy execution and achieve the targeted performance results.

Staying on Top of How Well Things Are Going

To stay on top of how well the strategy execution process is going, senior executives have to tap into information from a wide range of sources. In addition to communicating regularly with key subordinates and reviewing the latest operating results, watching the competitive reactions of rival firms, and visiting with key customers and suppliers to get their perspectives, they usually visit various company facilities and talk with many different company personnel at many different organizational levels—a technique often labeled **managing by walking around (MBWA).** Most managers attach great importance to spending time with people at company facilities, asking questions, listening to their opinions and concerns, and gathering firsthand information about how well aspects of the strategy execution process are going. Facilities tours and face-to-face contacts with operating-level employees give executives a good grasp of what progress is being made, what problems are being encountered, and whether additional resources or different approaches may be needed. Just as important, MBWA provides opportunities to give encouragement, lift spirits, shift attention from the old to the new priorities, and create some excitement—all of which generate positive energy and help boost strategy execution efforts.

CORE CONCEPT

Management by walking around (MBWA) is one of the techniques that effective leaders use to stay informed about how well the strategy execution process is progressing.

Jeff Bezos, Amazon.com's CEO, is noted for his practice of MBWA, firing off a battery of questions when he tours facilities and insisting that Amazon managers spend time in the trenches with their people to prevent getting disconnected from the reality of what's happening.[21] Walmart executives have had a long-standing practice of spending two to three days every week visiting Walmart's stores and talking with store managers and employees. Sam Walton, Walmart's founder, insisted, "The key is to get out into the store and listen to what the associates have to say." Jack Welch, the highly effective former CEO of General Electric, not only spent several days each month personally visiting GE operations and talking with major customers but also arranged his schedule so that he could spend time exchanging information and ideas with GE managers from all over the world who were attending classes at the company's leadership development center near GE's headquarters.

Many manufacturing executives make a point of strolling the factory floor to talk with workers and meeting regularly with union officials. Some managers operate out of open cubicles in big spaces filled with open cubicles for other personnel so that they can interact easily and frequently with co-workers. Managers at some companies host weekly get-togethers (often on Friday afternoons) to create a regular opportunity for information to flow freely between down-the-line employees and executives.

Mobilizing the Effort for Excellence in Strategy Execution

Part of the leadership task in mobilizing organizational energy behind the drive for good strategy execution entails nurturing a results-oriented work climate, where performance standards are high and a spirit of achievement is pervasive. Successfully leading the effort is typically characterized by such leadership actions and managerial practices as:

- *Treating employees as valued partners.* Some companies symbolize the value of individual employees and the importance of their contributions by referring to them as cast members (Disney), crew members (McDonald's), job owners (Graniterock), partners (Starbucks), or associates (Walmart, LensCrafters, W. L. Gore, Edward Jones, Publix Supermarkets, and Marriott International). Very often, there is a strong company commitment to training each employee thoroughly, offering attractive compensation and benefits, emphasizing promotion from within and promising career opportunities, providing a high degree of job security, and otherwise making employees feel well treated and valued.
- *Fostering an esprit de corps that energizes organization members.* The task here is to skillfully use people-management practices calculated to build morale, foster pride in working for the company, promote teamwork and collaborative group effort, win the emotional commitment of individuals and organizational units to what the company is trying to accomplish, and inspire company personnel to do their best in achieving good results.[22]
- *Using empowerment to help create a fully engaged workforce.* Top executives—and, to some degree, the enterprise's entire management team—must seek to engage the full organization in the strategy execution effort. A fully engaged workforce, where individuals bring their best to work every day, is necessary to produce great results.[23] So is having a group of dedicated managers committed to making a difference in their organization. The two best things top-level executives can do to create a fully engaged organization are (1) delegate authority to middle and lower-level managers to get the strategy execution process moving and (2) empower rank-and-file employees to act on their own initiative. Operating excellence requires that everybody contribute ideas, exercise initiative and creativity in performing his or her work, and have a desire to do things in the best possible manner.
- *Setting stretch objectives and clearly communicating an expectation that company personnel are to give their best in achieving performance targets.* Stretch objectives—those beyond an organization's current capacities—can sometimes spur organization members to increase their resolve and redouble their efforts to execute the strategy flawlessly and ultimately reach the stretch objectives. When stretch objectives are met, the satisfaction of achievement and boost to employee morale can result in an even higher level of organizational drive.
- *Using the tools of benchmarking, best practices, business process reengineering, TQM, and Six Sigma to focus attention on continuous improvement.* These are proven approaches to getting better operating results and facilitating better strategy execution.

- *Using the full range of motivational techniques and compensation incentives to inspire company personnel, nurture a results-oriented work climate, and reward high performance.* Managers cannot mandate innovative improvements by simply exhorting people to "be creative," nor can they make continuous progress toward operating excellence with directives to "try harder." Rather, they must foster a culture where innovative ideas and experimentation with new ways of doing things can blossom and thrive. Individuals and groups should be strongly encouraged to brainstorm, let their imaginations fly in all directions, and come up with proposals for improving the way that things are done. This means giving company personnel enough autonomy to stand out, excel, and contribute. And it means that the rewards for successful champions of new ideas and operating improvements should be large and visible. It is particularly important that people who champion an unsuccessful idea are not punished or sidelined but, rather, encouraged to try again. Finding great ideas requires taking risks and recognizing that many ideas won't pan out.
- *Celebrating individual, group, and company successes.* Top management should miss no opportunity to express respect for individual employees and appreciation of extraordinary individual and group effort.[24] Companies like Google, Tupperware, and McDonald's actively seek out reasons and opportunities to give pins, ribbons, buttons, badges, and medals for good showings by average performers—the idea being to express appreciation and give a motivational boost to people who stand out in doing ordinary jobs. Whole Foods, Cisco Systems, and 3M Corporation make a point of ceremoniously honoring individuals who believe so strongly in their ideas that they take it on themselves to hurdle the bureaucracy, maneuver their projects through the system, and turn them into improved services, new products, or even new businesses. Taj Hotels Resorts and Palaces credits its ability to deliver unprecedented levels of service to its guests to its Special Thanks and Recognition System (STARS) program, which rewards employees for exceptional effort, tracked on a yearly basis using a variety of metrics.[25]

While leadership efforts to instill a results-oriented, high-performance culture usually accentuate the positive, negative consequences for poor performance must be in play as well. Managers whose units consistently perform poorly must be replaced. Low-performing workers and people who reject the results-oriented cultural emphasis must be weeded out or at least employed differently. Average performers should be candidly counseled that they have limited career potential unless they show more progress in the form of additional effort, better skills, and improved ability to execute the strategy well and deliver good results.

Leading the Process of Making Corrective Adjustments

There comes a time at every company when managers have to fine-tune or overhaul the approaches to strategy execution since no action plan for executing strategy can foresee all the problems that will arise. Clearly, when a company's strategy execution effort is not delivering good results, it is the leader's responsibility to step forward and initiate corrective actions, although sometimes it must be recognized that unsatisfactory performance may be due as much or more to flawed strategy as to weak strategy execution.[26]

Success in making corrective actions hinges on (1) a thorough analysis of the situation, (2) the exercise of good business judgment in deciding what actions to take, and (3) good implementation of the corrective actions that are initiated. Successful managers are skilled in getting an organization back on track rather quickly. They (and their staffs) are good at discerning what actions to take and in bringing them to a successful conclusion. Managers who struggle to show measurable progress in implementing corrective actions in a timely fashion are candidates for being replaced.

The *process* of making corrective adjustments in strategy execution varies according to the situation. In a crisis, taking remedial action quickly is of the essence. But it still takes time to review the situation, examine the available data, identify and evaluate options (crunching whatever numbers may be appropriate to determine which options are likely to generate the best outcomes), and decide what to do. When the situation allows managers to proceed more deliberately in deciding when to make changes and what changes to make, most managers seem to prefer a process of incrementally solidifying commitment to a particular course of action.[27] The process that managers go through in deciding on corrective adjustments is essentially the same for both proactive and reactive changes: They sense needs, gather information, broaden and deepen their understanding of the situation, develop options and explore their pros and cons, put forth action proposals, strive for a consensus, and finally formally adopt an agreed-on course of action. The time frame for deciding what corrective changes to initiate can be a few hours, a few days, a few weeks, or even a few months if the situation is particularly complicated.

The challenges of making the right corrective adjustments and leading a successful strategy execution effort are, without question, substantial.[28] There's no generic, by-the-books procedure to follow. Because each instance of executing strategy occurs under different organizational circumstances, the managerial agenda for executing strategy always needs to be situation-specific. But the job is definitely doable. Although there is no prescriptive answer to the question of exactly what to do, any of several courses of action may produce good results. As we said at the beginning of Chapter 10, executing strategy is an action-oriented, make-the-right-things-happen task that challenges a manager's ability to lead and direct organizational change, create or reinvent business processes, manage and motivate people, and achieve performance targets. If you now better understand what the challenges are, what tasks are involved, what tools can be used to aid the managerial process of executing strategy, and why the action agenda for implementing and executing strategy sweeps across so many aspects of managerial work, then the discussions in Chapters 10, 11, and 12 have been a success.

A FINAL WORD ON LEADING THE PROCESS OF CRAFTING AND EXECUTING STRATEGY

In practice, it is hard to separate leading the process of executing strategy from leading the other pieces of the strategy process. As we emphasized in Chapter 2, the job of crafting and executing strategy consists of five interrelated and linked stages, with much looping and recycling to fine-tune and adjust the strategic vision, objectives, strategy, and implementation approaches to fit one another and to fit changing circumstances. The process is continuous, and the conceptually separate acts of crafting and executing strategy blur together in real-world situations. *The best tests of good strategic leadership are whether the company has a good strategy and business model, whether the strategy is being competently executed, and whether the enterprise is meeting or beating its performance targets.* If these three conditions exist, then there is every reason to conclude that the company has good strategic leadership and is a well-managed enterprise.

KEY POINTS

1. Corporate culture is the character of a company's internal work climate—the shared values, ingrained attitudes, core beliefs and company traditions that determine norms of behavior, accepted work practices, and styles of operating. A company's culture is important because it influences the organization's actions, its approaches to conducting business, and ultimately its performance in the marketplace. It can be thought of as the company's organizational DNA.
2. The key features of a company's culture include the company's values and ethical standards, its approach to people management, its work atmosphere and company spirit, how its personnel interact, the strength of peer pressure to conform to norms, the behaviors awarded through incentives (both financial and symbolic), the traditions and oft-repeated "myths," and its manner of dealing with stakeholders.
3. A company's culture is grounded in and shaped by its core values and ethical standards. Core values and ethical principles serve two roles in the culture-building process: (1) They foster a work climate in which employees share common and strongly held convictions about how company business is to be conducted, and (2) they provide company personnel with guidance about the manner in which they are to do their jobs—which behaviors and ways of doing things are approved (and expected) and which are out-of-bounds. They serve as yardsticks for gauging the appropriateness of particular actions, decisions, and behaviors.
4. Company cultures vary widely in strength and influence. Some cultures are *strong* and have a big impact on a company's practices and behavioral norms. Others are *weak* and have comparatively little influence on company operations.
5. Strong company cultures can have either positive or negative effects on strategy execution. When they are in sync with the chosen strategy and well matched to the behavioral requirements of the company's strategy implementation plan, they can be a powerful aid to strategy execution. A culture that is grounded in the types of actions and behaviors that are conducive to good strategy execution assists the effort in three ways:
   - By focusing employee attention on the actions that are most important in the strategy execution effort.
   - By inducing peer pressure for employees to contribute to the success of the strategy execution effort.
   - By energizing employees, deepening their commitment to the strategy execution effort, and increasing the productivity of their efforts

   It is thus in management's best interest to dedicate considerable effort to establishing a strongly implanted corporate culture that encourages behaviors and work practices conducive to good strategy execution.
6. Strong corporate cultures that are conducive to good strategy execution are healthy cultures. So are high-performance cultures and adaptive cultures. The latter are particularly important in dynamic environments. Strong cultures can also be unhealthy. The five types of unhealthy cultures are those that are (1) change-resistant, (2) heavily politicized, (3) insular and inwardly focused, (4) ethically unprincipled and infused with greed, and (5) composed of incompatible subcultures. All five impede good strategy execution.

7. Changing a company's culture, especially a strong one with traits that don't fit a new strategy's requirements, is a tough and often time-consuming challenge. Changing a culture requires competent leadership at the top. It requires making a compelling case for cultural change and employing both symbolic actions and substantive actions that unmistakably indicate serious and credible commitment on the part of top management. The more that culture-driven actions and behaviors fit what's needed for good strategy execution, the less managers must depend on policies, rules, procedures, and supervision to enforce what people should and should not do.
8. Leading the drive for good strategy execution and operating excellence calls for three actions on the part of the manager in charge:
   - Staying on top of what is happening and closely monitoring progress. This is often accomplished through managing by walking around (MBWA).
   - Mobilizing the effort for excellence in strategy execution by putting constructive pressure on the organization to execute the strategy well.
   - Initiating corrective actions to improve strategy execution and achieve the targeted performance results.

ASSURANCE OF LEARNING EXERCISES

connect
LO 1

1. Go to the company website for REI (**www.rei.com**). Click on the Stewardship tab, and then click on some of the tabs below to learn more about the company's culture and values. What are the key features of its culture? Do features of REI's culture influence the company's ethical practices? If so, how?

LO 2

2. Based on what you learned about REI from answering the previous question, how do you think the company's culture affects its ability to execute strategy and operate with excellence?

connect
LO 1, LO 2

3. Illustration Capsule 12.1 discusses W. L. Gore's strategy-supportive corporate culture. What are the standout features of Gore's corporate culture? How does Gore's culture contribute to innovation and creativity at the company? How does the company's culture make Gore a good place to work?

LO 3

4. If you were an executive at a company that had a pervasive yet problematic culture, what steps would you take to change it? Using Google Scholar or your university library's access to EBSCO, LexisNexis, or other databases, search for recent articles in business publications on "culture change." What role did the executives play in the culture change? How does this differ from what you would have done to change the culture?

LO 4

5. Leading the strategy execution process involves staying on top of the situation and monitoring progress, putting constructive pressure on the organization to achieve operating excellence, and initiating corrective actions to improve the execution effort. Using your university's access to business periodicals, discuss a recent example of how a company's managers have demonstrated the kind of effective internal leadership needed for superior strategy execution.

EXERCISE FOR SIMULATION PARTICIPANTS

1. If you were making a speech to company personnel, what would you tell employees about the kind of corporate culture you would like to have at your company? What specific cultural traits would you like your company to exhibit? Explain. **LO 1, LO 2**

2. What core values would you want to ingrain in your company's culture? Why? **LO 1**

3. Following each decision round, do you and your co-managers make corrective adjustments in either your company's strategy or the way the strategy is being executed? List at least three such adjustments you made in the most recent decision round. What hard evidence (in the form of results relating to your company's performance in the most recent year) can you cite that indicates that the various corrective adjustments you made either succeeded at improving or failed to improve your company's performance? **LO 3, LO 4**

4. What would happen to your company's performance if you and your co-managers stick with the status quo and fail to make any corrective adjustments after each decision round? **LO 4**

ENDNOTES

[1] Jennifer A. Chatham and Sandra E. Cha, "Leading by Leveraging Culture," *California Management Review* 45, no. 4 (Summer 2003), pp. 20–34; Edgar Shein, *Organizational Culture and Leadership: A Dynamic View* (San Francisco, CA: Jossey-Bass, 1992).

[2] T. E. Deal and A. A. Kennedy, *Corporate Cultures: The Rites and Rituals of Corporate Life* (Harmondsworth, UK: Penguin, 1982).

[3] Joanne Reid and Victoria Hubbell, "Creating a Performance Culture," *Ivey Business Journal* 69, no. 4 (March–April 2005), p. 1.

[4] Diane Brady, "The Immelt Revolution," *Businessweek,* March 27, 2005, www.businessweek.com (accessed April 4, 2013).

[5] www.publix.com/about/PublixHistory.do (accessed February 22, 2014).

[6] www.forbes.com/sites/briansolomon/2013/07/24/the-wal-mart-slayer-how-publixs-people-first-culture-is-winning-the-grocer-war/ (accessed February 22, 2014).

[7] John P. Kotter and James L. Heskett, *Corporate Culture and Performance* (New York: Free Press, 1992), p. 7. See also Robert Goffee and Gareth Jones, *The Character of a Corporation* (New York: HarperCollins, 1998).

[8] Joseph L. Badaracco, *Defining Moments: When Managers Must Choose between Right and Wrong* (Boston: Harvard Business School Press, 1997); Joe Badaracco and Allen P. Webb, "Business Ethics: A View from the Trenches," *California Management Review* 37, no. 2 (Winter 1995), pp. 8–28; Patrick E. Murphy, "Corporate Ethics Statements: Current Status and Future Prospects," *Journal of Business Ethics* 14 (1995), pp. 727–740; Lynn Sharp Paine, "Managing for Organizational Integrity," *Harvard Business Review* 72, no. 2 (March–April 1994), pp. 106–117.

[9] Emily F. Carasco and Jang B. Singh, "The Content and Focus of the Codes of Ethics of the World's Largest Transnational Corporations," *Business and Society Review* 108, no. 1 (January 2003), pp. 71–94; Patrick E. Murphy, "Corporate Ethics Statements: Current Status and Future Prospects," *Journal of Business Ethics* 14 (1995), pp. 727–740; John Humble, David Jackson, and Alan Thomson, "The Strategic Power of Corporate Values," *Long Range Planning* 27, no. 6 (December 1994), pp. 28–42; Mark S. Schwartz, "A Code of Ethics for Corporate Codes of Ethics," *Journal of Business Ethics* 41, no. 1–2 (November–December 2002), pp. 27–43.

[10] mentalfloss.com/article/30198/11-best-customer-service-stories-ever (accessed February 22, 2014).

[11] Terrence E. Deal and Allen A. Kennedy, *Corporate Cultures* (Reading, MA: Addison-Wesley, 1982); Terrence E. Deal and Allen A. Kennedy, *The New Corporate Cultures: Revitalizing the Workplace after Downsizing, Mergers, and Reengineering* (Cambridge, MA: Perseus, 1999).

[12] Vijay Sathe, *Culture and Related Corporate Realities* (Homewood, IL: Irwin, 1985).

[13] Avan R. Jassawalla and Hemant C. Sashittal, "Cultures That Support Product-Innovation Processes," *Academy of Management Executive* 16, no. 3 (August 2002), pp. 42–54.

[14] Kotter and Heskett, *Corporate Culture and Performance,* p. 5.

[15] Reid and Hubbell, "Creating a Performance Culture," pp. 1–5.

[16] Jay B. Barney and Delwyn N. Clark, *Resource-Based Theory: Creating and Sustaining Competitive Advantage* (New York: Oxford University Press, 2007), chap. 4.

[17] Rosabeth Moss Kanter, "Transforming Giants," *Harvard Business Review* 86, no. 1 (January 2008), pp. 43–52.

[18] Kurt Eichenwald, *Conspiracy of Fools: A True Story* (New York: Broadway Books, 2005).

[19] Judy D. Olian and Sara L. Rynes, "Making Total Quality Work: Aligning Organizational Processes, Performance Measures, and Stakeholders," *Human Resource Management* 30, no. 3 (Fall 1991), p. 324.

[20] Larry Bossidy and Ram Charan, *Confronting Reality: Doing What Matters to Get Things Right* (New York: Crown Business, 2004); Larry Bossidy and Ram Charan, *Execution: The Discipline of Getting Things Done* (New York: Crown Business, 2002); John P. Kotter, "Leading Change: Why Transformation Efforts Fail," *Harvard Business Review* 73, no. 2 (March–April 1995), pp. 59–67; Thomas M. Hout and John C. Carter, "Getting It Done: New Roles for Senior Executives," *Harvard Business Review* 73, no. 6 (November–December 1995), pp. 133–145; Sumantra Ghoshal and Christopher A. Bartlett, "Changing the Role of Top Management: Beyond Structure to Processes," *Harvard Business Review* 73, no. 1 (January–February 1995), pp. 86–96.

[21] Fred Vogelstein, "Winning the Amazon Way," *Fortune,* May 26, 2003, p. 64.

[22] For a more in-depth discussion of the leader's role in creating a results-oriented culture that nurtures success, see Benjamin Schneider, Sarah K. Gunnarson, and Kathryn Niles-Jolly, "Creating the Climate and Culture of Success," *Organizational Dynamics,* Summer 1994, pp. 17–29.

[23] Michael T. Kanazawa and Robert H. Miles, *Big Ideas to Big Results* (Upper Saddle River, NJ: FT Press, 2008).

[24] Jeffrey Pfeffer, "Producing Sustainable Competitive Advantage through the Effective Management of People," *Academy of Management Executive* 9, no.1 (February 1995), pp. 55–69.

[25] **www.forbes.com/sites/kevinkruse/2012/10/08/employee-recognition/**.

[26] Cynthia A. Montgomery, "Putting Leadership Back into Strategy," *Harvard Business Review* 86, no. 1 (January 2008), pp. 54–60.

[27] James Brian Quinn, *Strategies for Change: Logical Incrementalism* (Homewood, IL: Irwin, 1980).

[28] Daniel Goleman, "What Makes a Leader," *Harvard Business Review* 76, no. 6 (November–December 1998), pp. 92–102; Ronald A. Heifetz and Donald L. Laurie, "The Work of Leadership," *Harvard Business Review* 75, no. 1 (January–February 1997), pp. 124–134; Charles M. Farkas and Suzy Wetlaufer, "The Ways Chief Executive Officers Lead," *Harvard Business Review* 74, no. 3 (May–June 1996), pp. 110–122; Michael E. Porter, Jay W. Lorsch, and Nitin Nohria, "Seven Surprises for New CEOs," *Harvard Business Review* 82, no. 10 (October 2004), pp. 62–72.

PART 2

Readings in Crafting and Executing Strategy

READING 01

The Perils of Bad Strategy

Richard Rumelt
UCLA

Bad strategy abounds, says UCLA management professor Richard Rumelt. Senior executives who can spot it stand a much better chance of creating good strategies.

Horatio Nelson had a problem. The British admiral's fleet was outnumbered at Trafalgar by an armada of French and Spanish ships that Napoleon had ordered to disrupt Britain's commerce and prepare for a cross-channel invasion. The prevailing tactics in 1805 were for the two opposing fleets to stay in line, firing broadsides at each other. But Nelson had a strategic insight into how to deal with being outnumbered. He broke the British fleet into two columns and drove them at the Franco-Spanish fleet, hitting its line perpendicularly. The lead British ships took a great risk, but Nelson judged that the less-trained Franco-Spanish gunners would not be able to compensate for the heavy swell that day and that the enemy fleet, with its coherence lost, would be no match for the more experienced British captains and gunners in the ensuing melee. He was proved right: the French and Spanish lost 22 ships, two-thirds of their fleet. The British lost none.[1]

Nelson's victory is a classic example of good strategy, which almost always looks this simple and obvious in retrospect. It does not pop out of some strategic-management tool, matrix, triangle, or fill-in-the-blanks scheme. Instead, a talented leader has identified the one or two critical issues in a situation—the pivot points that can multiply the effectiveness of effort—and then focused and concentrated action and resources on them. A good strategy does more than urge us forward toward a goal or vision; it honestly acknowledges the challenges we face and provides an approach to overcoming them.

Too many organizational leaders say they have a strategy when they do not. Instead, they espouse what I call "bad strategy." Bad strategy ignores the power of choice and focus, trying instead to accommodate a multitude of conflicting demands and interests. Like a quarterback whose only advice to his teammates is "let's win," bad strategy covers up its failure to guide by embracing the language of broad goals, ambition, vision, and values. Each of these elements is, of course, an important part of human life. But, by themselves, they are not substitutes for the hard work of strategy.

In this article, I try to lay out the attributes of bad strategy and explain why it is so prevalent. Make no mistake: the creeping spread of bad strategy affects us all. Heavy with goals and slogans, governments have become less and less able to solve problems. Corporate boards sign off on strategic plans that are little more than wishful thinking. The US education system is rich with targets and standards but poor at comprehending and countering the sources of underperformance. The only remedy is for us to demand more from those who lead. More than charisma and vision, we must demand good strategy.

THE HALLMARKS OF BAD STRATEGY

I coined the term bad strategy in 2007 at a Washington, DC, seminar on national-security strategy. My role was to provide a business and corporate-strategy perspective. The participants expected, I think, that my remarks would detail the seriousness and growing competence with which business strategy was created. Using words and slides, I told the group that many businesses did have powerful, effective strategies. But in my personal experiences with corporate practice, I saw a growing profusion of bad strategy.

In the years since that seminar, I have had the opportunity to discuss the bad-strategy concept with a number of senior executives. In the process, I have condensed my list of its key hallmarks to four points: the failure to face the challenge, mistaking goals for strategy, bad strategic objectives, and fluff.

Failure to Face the Problem

A strategy is a way through a difficulty, an approach to overcoming an obstacle, a response to a challenge. If the challenge is not defined, it is difficult or impossible to assess the quality of the strategy. And, if you cannot assess that, you cannot reject a bad strategy or improve a good one.

International Harvester learned about this element of bad strategy the hard way. In July 1979, the company's strategic and financial planners produced a thick sheaf of paper titled "Corporate Strategic Plan: International Harvester." It was an amalgam of five separate strategic plans, each created by one of the operating divisions.

The strategic plan did not lack for texture and detail. Looking, for example, within the agricultural-equipment group—International Harvester's core, dating back to the McCormick reaper, which was a foundation of the company—there is information and discussion about each segment. The overall intent was to strengthen the dealer/distributor network and to reduce manufacturing costs. Market share in agricultural equipment was also projected to increase, from 16 percent to 20 percent.

The problem with all this was that the plan didn't even mention Harvester's grossly inefficient production facilities, especially in its agricultural-equipment business, or the fact that Harvester had the *worst* labor relations in US industry. As a result, the company's profit margin had been about one-half of its competitors' for a long time. As a corporation, International Harvester's main problem was its inefficient work organization—a problem that would not be solved by investing in new equipment or pressing managers to increase market share.

By cutting administrative overhead, Harvester boosted reported profits for a year or two. But following a disastrous six-month strike, the company quickly began to collapse. It sold off various businesses—including its agricultural-equipment business, to Tenneco. The truck division, renamed Navistar, is today a leading maker of heavy trucks and engines.

To summarize: if you fail to identify and analyze the obstacles, you don't have a strategy. Instead, you have a stretch goal or a budget or a list of things you wish would happen.

Mistaking Goals for Strategy

A few years ago, a CEO I'll call Chad Logan asked me to work with the management team of his graphic-arts company on "strategic thinking." Logan explained that his overall goal was simple—he called it the "20/20 plan." Revenues were to grow at 20 percent a year, and the profit margin was to be 20 percent or higher.

"This 20/20 plan is a very aggressive financial goal," I said. "What has to happen for it to be realized?" Logan tapped the plan with a blunt forefinger. "The thing I learned as a football player is that winning requires strength and skill, but more than anything it requires the will to win—the drive to

"The 'great pushes' during World War I led to the deaths of a generation of European youths. Maybe that's why motivational speakers are not the staple on the European management-lecture circuit that they are in the United States."

succeed. . . . Sure, 20/20 is a stretch, but the secret of success is setting your sights high. We are going to keep pushing until we get there."

That was typical of the overall strategy, which was to increase the company's share in each market, cut costs in each business, and thereby ramp up revenue and profit. A summary graph, showing past and forecast profit, forms an almost perfect hockey stick, with an immediate recovery from decline followed by a steady rise.

I tried again: "Chad, when a company makes the kind of jump in performance your plan envisions, there is usually a key strength you are building on or a change in the industry that opens up new opportunities. Can you clarify what the point of leverage might be here, in your company?"

Logan frowned and pressed his lips together, expressing frustration that I didn't understand him. He pulled a sheet of paper out of his briefcase and ran a finger under the highlighted text. "This is what Jack Welch says," he told me. The text read: "We have found that by reaching for what appears to be the impossible, we often actually do the impossible." (Logan's reading of Welch was, of course, highly selective. Yes, Welch believed in stretch goals. But he also said, "If you don't have a competitive advantage, don't compete.")

The reference to "pushing until we get there" triggered in my mind an association with the great pushes of 1915–17 during World War I, which led to the deaths of a generation of European youths. Maybe that's why motivational speakers are not the staple on the European management-lecture circuit that they are in the United States. For the slaughtered troops did not suffer from a lack of motivation. They suffered from a lack of competent strategic leadership. A leader may justly ask for "one last push," but the leader's job is more than that. The job of the leader—the strategist—is also to create the conditions that will make the push effective, to have a strategy worthy of the effort called upon.

Bad Strategic Objectives

Another sign of bad strategy is fuzzy strategic objectives. One form this problem can take is a scrambled mess of things to accomplish—a dog's dinner of goals. A long list of things to do, often mislabeled as strategies or objectives, is not a strategy. It is just a list of things to do. Such lists usually grow out of planning meetings in which a wide variety of stakeholders suggest things they would like to see accomplished. Rather than focus on a few important items, the group sweeps the whole day's collection into the strategic plan. Then, in recognition that it is a dog's dinner, the label "long term" is added, implying that none of these things need be done today. As a vivid example, I recently had the chance to discuss strategy with the mayor of a small city in the Pacific Northwest. His planning committee's strategic plan contained 47 strategies and 178 action items. Action item number 122 was "create a strategic plan."

A second type of weak strategic objective is one that is "blue sky"—typically a simple restatement of the desired state of affairs or of the challenge. It skips over the annoying fact that no one has a clue as to how to get there. A leader may successfully identify the key challenge and propose an overall approach to dealing with the challenge. But if the consequent strategic objectives are just as difficult to meet as the original challenge, the strategy has added little value.

Good strategy, in contrast, works by focusing energy and resources on one, or a very few, pivotal objectives whose accomplishment will lead to a cascade of favorable outcomes. It also builds a bridge between the critical challenge at the heart of the strategy and action—between desire and immediate objectives that lie within grasp. Thus, the objectives that a good strategy sets stand a good chance of being accomplished, given existing resources and competencies.

Fluff

A final hallmark of mediocrity and bad strategy is superficial abstraction—a flurry of fluff—designed to mask the absence of thought.

Fluff is a restatement of the obvious, combined with a generous sprinkling of buzzwords that masquerade as expertise. Here is a quote from a major retail bank's internal strategy memoranda: "Our fundamental strategy is one of customer-centric intermediation." Intermediation means that the company accepts deposits and then lends out the money. In other words, it is a bank. The buzzphrase "customer centric" could mean that the bank competes by offering better terms and service, but an examination of its policies does not reveal any distinction in this regard. The phrase "customer-centric intermediation" is pure fluff. Remove the fluff and you learn that the bank's fundamental strategy is being a bank.

WHY SO MUCH BAD STRATEGY?

Bad strategy has many roots, but I'll focus on two here: the inability to choose and template-style planning—filling in the blanks with "vision, mission, values, strategies."

The Inability to Choose

Strategy involves focus and, therefore, choice. And choice means setting aside some goals in favor of others. When this hard work is not done, weak strategy is the result. In 1992, I sat in on a strategy discussion among senior executives at Digital Equipment

Corporation (DEC). A leader of the minicomputer revolution of the 1960s and 1970s, DEC had been losing ground for several years to the newer 32-bit personal computers. There were serious doubts that the company could survive for long without dramatic changes.

To simplify matters, I will pretend that only three executives were present. "Alec" argued that DEC had always been a computer company and should continue integrating hardware and software into usable systems. "Beverly" felt that the only distinctive resource DEC had to build on was its customer relationships. Hence, she derided Alec's "Boxes" strategy and argued in favor of a "Solutions" strategy that solved customer problems. "Craig" held that the heart of the computer industry was semiconductor technology and that the company should focus its resources on designing and building better "Chips."

Choice was necessary: both the Chips and Solutions strategies represented dramatic transformations of the firm, and each would require wholly new skills and work practices. One wouldn't choose either risky alternative unless the status quo Boxes strategy was likely to fail. And one wouldn't choose to do both Chips and Solutions at the same time, because there was little common ground between them. It is not feasible to do two separate, deep transformations of a company's core at once.

With equally powerful executives arguing for each of the three conflicting strategies, the meeting was intense. DEC's chief executive, Ken Olsen, had made the mistake of asking the group to reach a consensus. It was unable to do that, because a majority preferred Solutions to Boxes, a majority preferred Boxes to Chips, and a majority also preferred Chips to Solutions. No matter which of the three paths was chosen, a majority preferred something else. This dilemma wasn't unique to the standoff at DEC. The French philosopher Nicolas de Condorcet achieved immortality by first pointing out the possibility of such a paradox arising, and economist Kenneth Arrow won a Nobel Prize for showing that "Condorcet's paradox" cannot be resolved through cleverer voting schemes.

Not surprisingly, the group compromised on a statement: "DEC is committed to providing high-quality products and services and being a leader in data processing." This fluffy, amorphous statement was, of course, not a strategy. It was a political outcome reached by individuals who, forced to reach a consensus, could not agree on which interests and concepts to forgo.

Ken Olsen was replaced, in June 1992, by Robert Palmer, who had headed the company's semiconductor engineering. Palmer made it clear that the strategy would be Chips. One point of view had finally won. But by then it was five years too late. Palmer stopped the losses for a while but could not stem the tide of ever more powerful personal computers that were overtaking the firm. In 1998, DEC was acquired by Compaq, which, in turn, was acquired by Hewlett-Packard three years later.

Template-Style Strategy

The Jack Welch quote about "reaching for what appears to be the impossible" is fairly standard motivational fare, available from literally hundreds of motivational speakers, books, calendars, memo pads, and Web sites. This fascination with positive thinking has helped inspire ideas about charismatic leadership and the power of a shared vision, reducing them to something of a formula. The general outline goes like this: the transformational leader (1) develops or has a vision, (2) inspires people to sacrifice (change) for the good of the organization, and (3) empowers people to accomplish the vision.

> "Scan through template-style planning documents and you will find pious statements of the obvious presented as if they were decisive insights."

By the early 2000s, the juxtaposition of vision-led leadership and strategy work had produced a template-style system of strategic planning. (Type "vision mission strategy" into a search engine and you'll find thousands of examples of this kind of template for sale and in use.) The template looks like this:

> *The Vision.* Fill in your vision of what the school/business/nation will be like in the future. Currently popular visions are to be the best or the leading or the best known.
>
> *The Mission.* Fill in a high-sounding, politically correct statement of the purpose of the school/business/nation. Innovation, human progress, and sustainable solutions are popular elements of a mission statement.

The Values. Fill in a statement that describes the company's values. Make sure they are noncontroversial. Key words include "integrity," "respect," and "excellence."

The Strategies. Fill in some aspirations/goals but call them strategies. For example, "to invest in a portfolio of performance businesses that create value for our shareholders and growth for our customers."

This template-style planning has been enthusiastically adopted by corporations, school boards, university presidents, and government agencies. Scan through such documents and you will find pious statements of the obvious presented as if they were decisive insights. The enormous problem all this creates is that someone who actually wishes to conceive and implement an effective strategy is surrounded by empty rhetoric and bad examples.

THE KERNEL OF GOOD STRATEGY

By now, I hope you are fully awake to the dramatic differences between good and bad strategy. Let me close by trying to give you a leg up in crafting good strategies, which have a basic underlying structure:

1. *A diagnosis:* an explanation of the nature of the challenge. A good diagnosis simplifies the often overwhelming complexity of reality by identifying certain aspects of the situation as being the critical ones.
2. *A guiding policy:* an overall approach chosen to cope with or overcome the obstacles identified in the diagnosis.
3. *Coherent actions:* steps that are coordinated with one another to support the accomplishment of the guiding policy.

I'll illustrate by describing Nvidia's journey from troubled start-up to market leader for 3-D graphics chips. Nvidia's first product, a PC add-in board for video, audio, and 3-D graphics, was a commercial failure. In 1995, rival start-up 3Dfx Interactive took the lead in serving the burgeoning demand of gamers for fast 3-D graphics chips. Furthermore, there were rumors that industry giant Intel was thinking about introducing its own 3-D graphics chip. The diagnosis: "We are losing the performance race."

Nvidia CEO Jen-Hsun Huang's key insight was that given the rapid state of advance in 3-D graphics, releasing a new chip every 6 months, instead of at the industry standard rate of every 18 months, would make a critical difference. The guiding policy, in short, was to "release a faster, better chip three times faster than the industry norm."

To accomplish this fast release cycle, the company emphasized several coherent actions: it formed three development teams, which worked on overlapping schedules; it invested in massive simulation and emulation facilities to avoid delays in the fabrication of chips and in the development of software drivers; and, over time, it regained control of driver development from the branded add-in board makers.

Over the next decade, the strategy worked brilliantly. Intel introduced its 3-D graphics chip in 1998 but did not keep up the pace, exiting the business of discrete 3-D graphics chips a year later. In 2000, creditors of 3Dfx initiated bankruptcy proceedings against the company, which was struggling to keep up with Nvidia. In 2007, *Forbes* named Nvidia the "Company of the Year."[2]

• • •

Despite the roar of voices equating strategy with ambition, leadership, vision, or planning, strategy is none of these. Rather, it is coherent action backed by an argument. And the core of the strategist's work is always the same: discover the crucial factors in a situation and design a way to coordinate and focus actions to deal with them.

ENDNOTES

[1] Nelson himself was mortally wounded at Trafalgar, becoming, in death, Britain's greatest naval hero. The battle ensured Britain's naval dominance, which remained secure for a century and a half.

[2] The effectiveness of even good strategies isn't permanently assured. ATI, now part of AMD, has become a powerful competitor in graphics processing units, and Nvidia has been challenged in the fast-growing mobile-graphics business, where cost is often more important than performance.

READING 02

The Role of the Chief Strategy Officer

Taman H. Powell
Cardiff Business School

Duncan N. Angwin
Oxford Brookes University Business School

By understanding how the duties of the chief strategy officer (CSO) can vary significantly from organization to organization, boards and CEOs can make better decisions about which type of CSO is necessary for their leadership teams.

The chief strategy officer (CSO) is a comparatively new but increasingly important role in many organizations. To explore the role of the CSO, we conducted 24 interviews with CSOs at U.K. companies that are part of the FTSE 100 Index, across a number of industrial sectors. Secondary data—company reports, strategy documents and presentations—were used to complement the interviews. All interviews were conducted either at the CSO's office or via telephone and followed the same semistructured outline and set of questions. They were transcribed verbatim and analyzed through qualitative data management software.

From the outset, it was clear that there was a variation in CSO roles, focused on two dimensions. The first dimension was the stage of the strategy process in which the CSO was involved. Our findings identified a significant demarcation between whether the CSO was focused on the formulation of the strategy or the execution of the strategy.

The second dimension of variation was how the CSO engaged in the strategy process. Some CSOs were facilitators, advising business units during the strategy formulation or assisting in the execution. Other CSOs were enactors, far more likely to execute the strategy process by themselves or with their team.

Based on variation in the roles carried out by the CSOs, we have developed a typology of four CSO archetypes.

1. INTERNAL CONSULTANT

CSOs of this type focused almost exclusively on strategy formulation by themselves or with their strategy team. The execution of the strategy—ownership and responsibility for its implementation—resided firmly with the business units. These CSOs carried out activities similar to traditional management consultants. As one of them stated, "It's very much like what an external consultant would do; the only difference is that we're internal." As a result, we have called this archetype the "Internal Consultant."

This type of CSO adopted a very rational approach to the development of strategy. One of them described the role as "getting the facts on the table, coming up with options, evaluating such options and then recommending [the best] one to the business."

Given the nature of their role, the Internal Consultant CSOs often viewed themselves, as one of them put it, "as a kind of flexible, analytical resource" that was "parachuted in to wherever there was a particular issue that needed additional analytical backing, maybe a bit of objectivity, or at least a slightly more neutral perspective."

The majority of Internal Consultant CSOs we interviewed had a background in consulting. Upon

Taman Powell and Duncan Angwin, "The Role of the Chief Strategy Officer", MIT Sloan Management Review. 54 (1), 2012, pp. 15–16.

leaving consulting, they joined the corporate world as a CSO or a member of that team, and they then carried out the role very much as if they were still external consultants. The CSO role for this archetype was seen largely as a transition into a role that leveraged their skills and had a future in managing a business with profit-and-loss responsibility. As such, these CSOs saw themselves working in the role for a number of years, then transitioning to a managerial role in the business.

2. SPECIALIST

The second archetype was the "Specialist," a CSO chosen for highly specialized skills that were not present within the organization. A classic example of a Specialist CSO is someone brought aboard to maintain a mergers-and-acquisitions capability. Another common focus for Specialists is dealing with government or regulations. This is particularly evident in highly regulated industries in which policy decisions can have a critical impact.

What separates Specialists from other CSO archetypes is their level of segregation from business units. They frequently act in a secretive manner, with only the CEO and other relevant C-level executives aware of their actions. Their activities—mergers and acquisitions, or lobbying government or regulatory bodies—are inherently sensitive and as such are kept from the organization at large.

The effectiveness of these CSOs was dependent upon both their specialized skills and their contacts outside the organization. As such, the majority of Specialists were recruited from investment banks, regulatory bodies or government. In contrast to the Internal Consultant archetype, Specialists were more likely to move to another organization in a similar role—thereby continuing to leverage their capabilities and connections.

3. COACH

The third archetype was the "Coach." The Coach was very much a facilitator, who focused on strategy formulation with the business units. Specifically, these CSOs leveraged their access to, and history with, the CEO and the board of directors to help the business units develop strategies that the board and CEO would approve.

In contrast to the Internal Consultants, the Coaches did not develop the strategy themselves. Instead, they viewed their role, as one CSO said, as working to "provide information to help people create strategy" and to "make sure people are talking to each other."

The Coaches viewed their role as advising CEOs and their teams in developing their business strategies. In turn, the business units would then take the strategies that had been facilitated by the CSOs to seek approvals, budgetary and otherwise, from the board and from the CEO.

In contrast to Internal Consultants and Specialists, who were generally recruited from outside the organization, Coaches were typically recruited from those in senior roles in a business unit. Coaches also tended to remain in their CSO role for an extended period—often working for a number of CEOs during their tenure. The extended nature of the role was critical, as this type of CSO focused on coaching the business units on (a) how to formulate a strategy and (b) how to get the strategy approved by the senior executive team. The role, therefore, required deep knowledge of the senior executive team and the strategy process—something only attainable after spending years inside the organization.

4. CHANGE AGENT

The final archetype was the "Change Agent." As with Specialists, Change Agents focused on execution. In contrast to Specialists, Change Agents acted through the business units as facilitators to ensure that strategies were enacted with fidelity. One such CSO described the role as "an enabler. Sometimes the gears don't mesh in an organization. And you're there to try and bring the people together."

Change Agents spent the majority of their time with business unit heads working on implementation. As one said, "Where most time goes is once you've done the business planning or once you've done the corporate strategy, you then end up with a series of conclusions and action points, and actually what I spend most of my time doing is then trying to implement the decisions that we arrive at toward the end of those two processes."

As with Coaches, the success of the Change Agents depends upon their knowledge and network within the organization. As such, the Change Agent also tends to be recruited from within, generally from among people in senior roles with the business units. Change Agents also tend to remain in their role for an extended period—often working for a number of CEOs during their tenure.

WHAT TYPE OF CSO IS NEEDED?

While the Specialist may be appropriate for organizations undertaking significant merger and acquisition activity or in highly regulated industries where the organizations want to influence the dialogue, the other CSO archetypes focus on different stages of the strategy process—either formulating the strategy for the business units (Internal Consultant), facilitating the strategy approval process between the business unit and senior management (Coach) or facilitating the strategy execution with the business unit (Change Agent). An organization should choose its CSO based on the stage of the strategy process most in need of resources and attention. By understanding how the duties of the CSO can vary significantly, boards and CEOs can make better decisions about which type of CSO is necessary for their leadership teams—and set proper expectations for the role that the CSO will play.

READING 03

Managing the Strategy Journey

Chris Bradley
McKinsey & Company

Sven Smit
McKinsey & Company

Lowell Bryan
McKinsey & Company

Regular strategic dialogue involving a broad group of senior executives can help companies adapt to the unexpected. Here's one company's story, and some principles for everyone.

Back in 2009, as the senior-management teams at many companies were just beginning to emerge from the bunkers to which they'd retreated during the peak of the financial crisis, we wrote an article[1] whose premise was that pervasive, ongoing uncertainty meant companies needed to get their senior-leadership teams working together in a fundamentally different way. At the time, many companies were undertaking experiments, such as shortening their financial-planning cycles or dropping the pretense that they could make reasonable assumptions about the future. But we suggested that the only way to set strategy effectively during uncertain times was to bring together, much more frequently, the members of the top team, who were uniquely positioned to surface critical issues early, debate their implications, and make timely decisions.

Since then, we have continued to evolve our thinking about how companies should undertake strategy development in the 21st century. For starters, we uncovered strong evidence that a great many companies are generating strategies that, by their own admission, are substandard. We reached that conclusion after surveying more than 2,000 executives about a set of ten strategic tests—timeless standards that shed light on whether a particular strategy is likely to beat the competition—and learning that only 35 percent of their strategies passed more than three of these.[2] This unsettling statistic raised additional questions about the effectiveness of companies' annual planning processes, which still were the most-cited triggers for strategic decision making among survey respondents (Exhibit 1).

We also have been engaged with a number of companies (in industries ranging from telecom to health care to mining to financial services) as they've begun to embrace more frequent strategic dialogue involving a focused group of senior executives. These companies, in effect, have started on a journey—a journey to evolve how they set strategy and make strategic decisions. Their journey isn't complete, and neither is ours, but we've learned more than enough to take stock and pass on some ideas that we hope will be useful to leaders in many more organizations.

In this article, we want to focus on the big things that top teams need to do. The starting point is for them to increase the time they spend on strategy together to at least match the time they spend together on operating issues. Our experience suggests this probably means meeting two to four hours, weekly or every two weeks, throughout the year. Devoting regular attention to strategy in this way makes it possible to:

- Involve the top team, and the board, in periodically revisiting corporate aspirations and making any big, directional changes in strategy required

EXHIBIT 1 The Annual Planning Process Is Frequently the Primary Trigger for Strategic Decision Making.

%

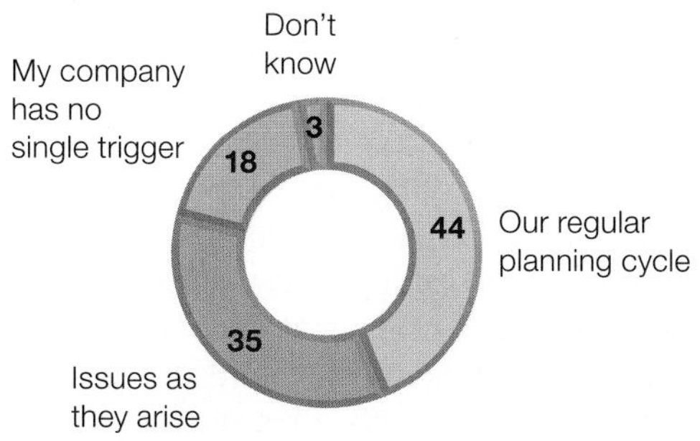

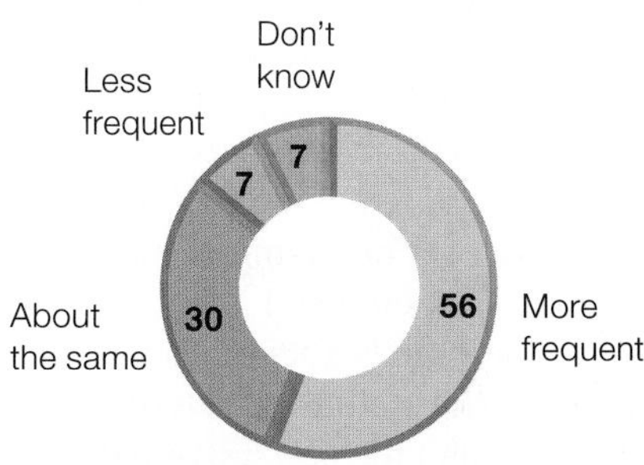

Source: Jan 2010 McKinsey survey of 2,135 executives around the world, representing the full range of industries, regions, tenures, functional specialties, and company sizes

by changes in the global forces at work on a company.

- Create a rigorous, ongoing management process for formulating the specific strategic initiatives needed to close gaps between the current trajectory of the company and its aspirations.
- Convert these initiatives into an operating reality by formally integrating the strategic-management process with your financial-planning processes (a change that usually requires also moving to more continuous, rolling forecasting and budgeting approaches).

To explain what this looks like in practice, we'll ground our discussion of these issues in the (disguised) experience of a global bank that took some severe hits during the 2008 financial crisis.

SETTING ASPIRATIONS AND DIRECTION

Like many banks, the institution had responded by writing off most of its bad assets, raising capital, shrinking its balance sheet, and slashing expenses. Sometime in 2010, in the midst of the annual long-range financial-planning processes, the CEO and the board realized that while the institution was recovering from its financial losses, it didn't know where its future growth would come from. Nor was it clear what would be reasonable growth aspirations in an era of regulatory constraints on the bank's balance sheet.

The CEO decided, in concert with his board, to halt work on their long-range plan and to launch a concentrated surge of activity to refresh the bank's strategy. To start the process, the CEO invited the heads of his three major lines of business—the Global Investment Banking Group, the Global Asset Management Group, and the Domestic Bank—to meet regularly on how they could create a strategy for growth within the constraints of the new era. Out of necessity, given the issues being discussed, these biweekly meetings were broadened over time to include the chief risk officer, the chief technology officer, the CFO, and a new hire responsible for moving the work of this new strategy council forward.

Changing the strategy of a large bank, or any large company for that matter, is a bit like turning a supertanker. The momentum of the institution is so strong that the ability to change direction quickly is limited. After all, the focus of the senior- and top-management teams of most corporations, most of the time, is on near-term operating decisions—particularly on delivering earnings in accordance with the financial plan. As a result, many, if not most, of the decisions that shape the future of organizations are made unconsciously in the flow of running the businesses or through annual planning processes that suffer from trying to cover all businesses and issues simultaneously (or through one-off projects).

In a reasonable time period, though—say, 18 months to two years—it is possible to change direction considerably. In our example bank, a key moment came when the leadership team coalesced on a shared understanding of the institution's competitive position, its "business as usual" financial trajectory, and a realistic set of future aspirations.

There was a significant gap between the bank's trajectory and goals, and an obvious set of "no regrets" moves to help close it. For example, the first major strategic decision that emerged from this council was to increase the bank's focus on balance sheet optimization and on risk-adjusted returns on equity. This would be critical in the new era of balance sheet constraints, and it led to a second major decision: to ensure that the bank's now-scarce balance sheet resources were being devoted to serving (and earning better returns from) its best, core customers.

After the top team committed itself to this direction, it quickly made difficult related moves, such as exiting some noncore businesses and reorganizing the bank along its core-customer group lines. That meant refocusing the Global Investment Banking Group by creating a far stronger focus on cross-silo customer relationship building, breaking up the Domestic Bank and Global Asset Management Group, and then reformulating them as a Domestic Retail Banking Group, a Domestic Corporate Banking Group, and a Global Private Banking and Wealth Management Group. It also led to the departure of the head of the Domestic Bank.

However, everyone also agreed that the answers to many of the specific choices the bank needed to make about where and how to compete were not obvious and that many early ideas for expanding the business were at best vague and at worst fraught with significant risk. Also unclear was the right timing and sequencing for decisions such as whether to scale up investments with a number of global technology players supporting digital-banking partnerships or whether the bank should consider an aggressive push into the midsized-corporate and small-business markets as competitors were pulling back to minimize risks. So the top team and the board defined these choices as "issues to be resolved" and decided to go on a journey to address them. In other words, the surge effort was not the end of the process of formulating the corporate strategy but rather had served only to jump-start it.

INSTALLING A RIGOROUS ONGOING STRATEGY PROCESS

Once the concentrated surge of activity was over, the senior-management team's focus shifted from changing direction to resolving these outstanding issues. Addressing ambiguous critical issues in the flow of running a large company is a challenge different from making obvious directional changes in response to fundamental environmental changes, such as responding to a shift in regulation. The differences are largely in granularity and timing. In other words, it was fine that out of the surge effort our global bank had decided to emphasize balance sheet optimization and increase its focus on core customers, but what did that really mean? Which specific customers would be prioritized? What packages of services would be offered to which customer groups, and at what target returns? How would "deprioritized" customers be handled? What specific investments were needed, and what returns could the bank expect to earn on them?

These difficult questions benefited from serious top-management attention. Their diversity and complexity also underscore how important it is for the success of the journey model to have an agreed-upon process for surfacing, framing, and prioritizing the critical issues to be debated and addressed through the top-management strategic forum. Even with extra commitment, the amount of time the senior team has for meetings is quite finite. Our experiences suggest some rules of thumb for keeping things manageable:

- Set a practical limit to the number of issues that can be pursued simultaneously at the corporate level; usually, given the time needed for review and debate at the strategy forum, no more than 15 to 25 can be managed in parallel.
- Develop a pragmatic approach for prioritizing issues. One way is to give each member of the forum a set number of slots on the agenda to bring forth whichever issues for review he or she

thinks are most important. A few slots for critical issues—such as how to improve capital budgeting, which affects many different businesses—can be reserved for the corporate-wide perspective.

- Trade off quantity in favor of quality. If something deserves to be discussed by the top-management strategy forum, the staff work undertaken to address the issue should meet a high standard, and any recommendation made should be "owned" by relevant line managers.

Since some or perhaps many of a strategic-management forum's members won't have significant experience as strategists, it's worth pausing for a moment to reflect on the skills they may need to raise the right issues and discuss them effectively. Strategy capabilities aren't the focus of this article (for a related perspective, see "Becoming more strategic: Three tips for any executive," on **mckinseyquarterly.com**). That said, after we made the unsettling discovery that a great many leaders thought their strategies were failing the ten tests mentioned earlier, we began thinking about what specific things companies must get right to build strategies sufficient to meet those tests. We concluded that moving from idea to operating reality requires seven distinct modes of activity, summarized in Exhibit 2.

At the bank, the entire top team, as well as the project teams its members lead, has needed to employ many of these skills. One thing we've seen is that the bank's ability to manage uncertainty, which cuts across at least four of the seven modes highlighted in Exhibit 2 (forecasting, searching, choosing, and evolving), is a work in progress, as is the case at many firms. As a result, there is a tendency to leap from diagnosis to commitment without doing enough work on forecasting, exploring alternatives, and constructing packages of choices—or, for that matter, thinking about how a strategy should evolve as the passage of time resolves uncertainties embedded in the assumptions underlying it. At the global bank, developing these uncertainty-management skills is part of the journey that is still under way.

CONVERTING STRATEGY INTO OPERATING REALITY

At the end of the day, strategy is about the actions you take. Therefore, one of the highest priorities of a top-management strategy forum is to ensure disciplined implementation of key strategic initiatives. A big advantage of the journey approach is that the process of debating and deciding on changes in strategic direction helps top-management teams get behind the new direction, particularly if the CEO holds the entire team collectively accountable for accomplishing it.

But more is needed. In our experience, the key is to take a disciplined approach to converting strategies into actions that can be incorporated in financial plans and operating budgets. One important capability that companies must develop to do this well is rolling forecasting and budgeting, so that needed investments can be made in a timely manner rather than waiting for the next annual planning cycle. In Exhibit 3, we show an example of the process of transforming a critical question—what are the retail bank's specific near-term opportunities in "big data"?—from idea into operating budget.

Obviously, an initiative must be fairly advanced—and granular—to justify putting the needed investments and expected returns into the rolling forecast and, eventually, into the formal annual fiscal budget and long-range plan. In our experience, it can easily take 18 months or longer to go from introducing a raw idea to putting it in the budget. When executives who have worthy ideas lack the budgets to pursue them with a sufficient full-time staff, we've found that it's valuable to fund their exploration with a small "pot" of corporate seed capital, to keep this spending separate from the operating budget (and safe from being squeezed out by earnings pressure).

Although the journey is continuous, the board and the management team itself need to take stock of progress periodically. Moreover, companies still must produce and execute against annual financial plans and budgets. For most public companies, this requirement will mean continuing to have a formal board review of strategies, financial plans, and progress being made against them, every six months or so. A board meeting in the spring might be dedicated to reviewing the progress in agreed-upon changes in strategic direction; a late-fall board meeting could be used to compare the financial plans for the coming year (and for the next several years) with the company's aspirations. These formal reviews are important checkpoints.

Having said that, a journey approach should affect the way a board works with management as

EXHIBIT 2 Moving from Ideas to Execution Requires Seven Distinct Modes of Activity.

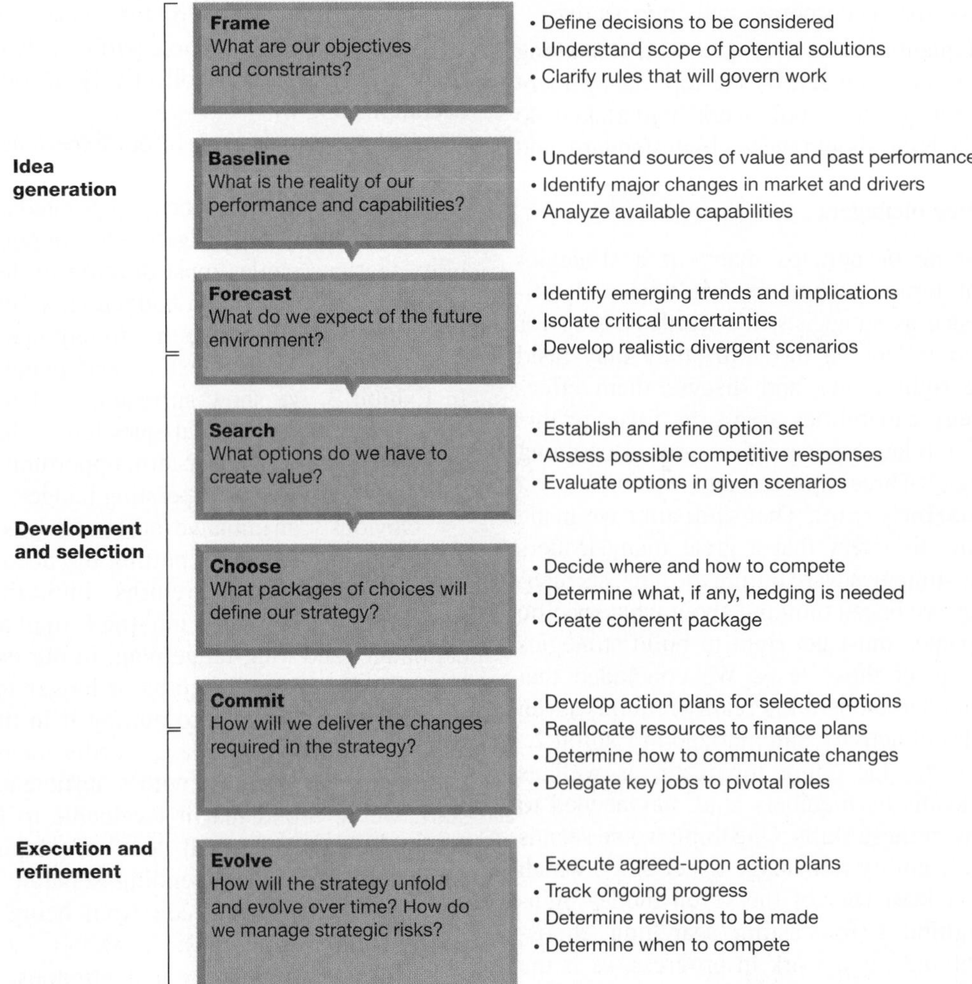

well. The board should expect that strategic issues will be raised and strategic initiatives launched whenever top management feels that they are sufficiently important. That launch may or may not coincide with the timing of formal strategic reviews with the board. The board indeed should expect that the strategy of the company will not be carved in stone but rather that meetings of the board will be used as necessary to get it involved in the debate on major issues and in the continual evolution and refreshment of the enterprise's strategic direction. Such a dialogue should improve the board's understanding of *alternatives* to chosen strategies, and that can enhance the quality of decision making and lend a valuable perspective down the road if things don't work out as planned.

The big difference between the journey model and others is that when a company isn't making sufficient progress, it doesn't pretend things are fine. Rather, these shortcomings are a call to action. If actual results begin to diverge significantly from aspirations (and related metrics of progress), that should trigger an in-depth review to explore whether a midcourse correction in strategy is needed, whether the company simply isn't executing against its strategy, or, as a last resort, whether it's time to revisit its aspirations—and make them more realistic.

As the global bank in our example entered 2012, it realized that the aspirations it had set in early 2011 still exceeded its current trajectory, particularly in the Global Investment Banking Group

EXHIBIT 3 A Rolling Process of Forecasting and Budgeting Transforms a Critical Strategic Issue into an Operational Initiative.

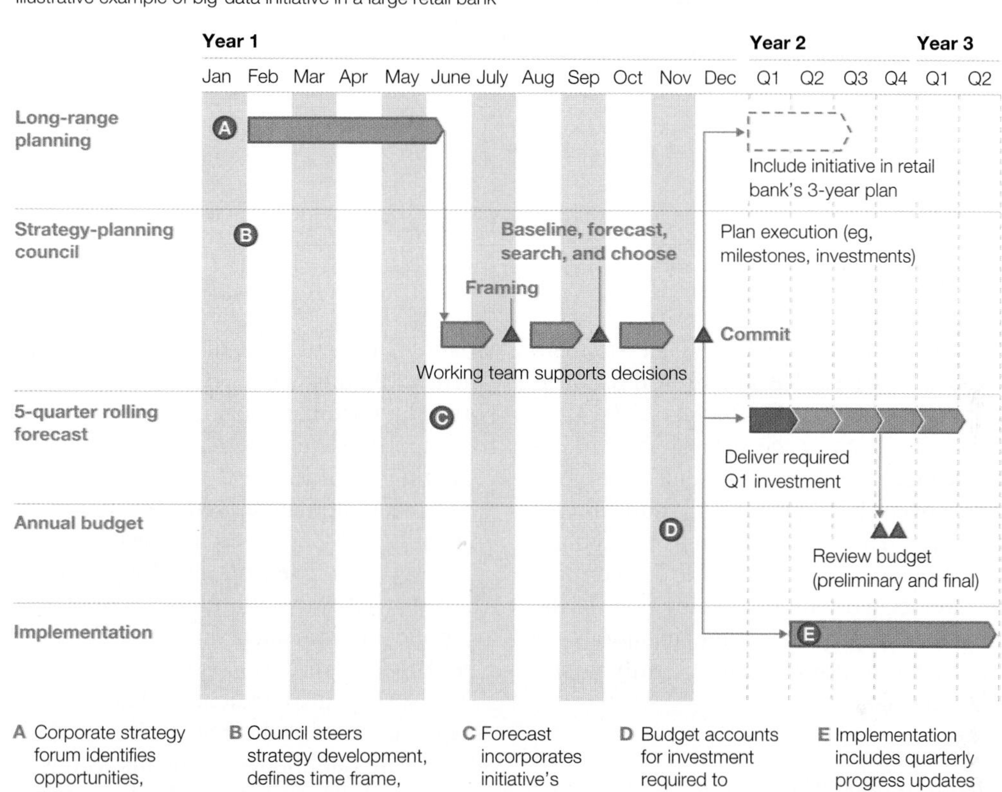

and the Domestic Retail Banking Group. As a result, the global bank has requested that not just these two groups but also the other two identify new initiatives they could undertake to help close the gap. The jury is still out on whether they will be able to do so or, instead, will need to revise their aspirations downward.

• • •

To create shareholder wealth in our turbulent 21st century, companies need to spend as much time on building and executing strategies as on operating issues. Those that do will build institutional skills and generate strategic ideas that evolve over time. Rather than fear uncertainty and unfamiliarity, these strategic leaders can embrace them, and make the passage of time an ally against competitors that hold back when the future seems murky.

ENDNOTES

[1] Lowell Bryan, "Dynamic management: Better decisions in uncertain times," mckinseyquarterly.com, December 2009.

[2] For more on the tests, which we have discussed and refined with more than 1,400 senior strategists around the world in over 70 workshops, see Chris Bradley, Martin Hirt, and Sven Smit, "Have you tested your strategy lately?," mckinseyquarterly.com, January 2011. For more on the survey results, see "Putting strategies to the test: McKinsey Global Survey results," mckinseyquarterly.com, January 2011.

READING 04

The Balanced Scorecard in China: Does It Work?

Kaisheng Zeng
Sun Yat-sen University, China

Xiaohui Luo
Sun Yat-sen University, China

The balanced scorecard (BSC) is a strategic management system that has been developed and applied in the West for 20 years. The BSC was introduced in China at the turn of the millennium and is widely used in profit and non-profit organizations, from headquarters to subsidiaries in the country. . . . This article attempts to summarize the limitations of the BSC . . . , to determine the obstacles associated with the deployment of the BSC in China, and to provide recommendations for Western firms in terms of how to successfully implement the BSC in China.

1. THE BALANCED SCORECARD IN CHINA

The balanced scorecard (BSC) was introduced in China much later than in most Western nations. Even in the West, the effectiveness of the BSC has been questioned, sparking more debate than the advocates of the BSC had likely expected. In China, the implementation of the BSC faces even more obstacles, often beyond what its users imagine. Many Western researchers (e.g., Brignall, 2002; Neely, 2005; Nørreklit, 2000) found that the BSC has unavoidable limitations as a strategic management system, and this is particularly true when it is used in emerging Asian economies, such as China.

The BSC experienced a half-hearted reception when it first appeared in China at the turn of the millennium. China was experiencing a "cooling-off period" after a long run of enthusiastic adoption of Western management theories and tools (Wu, Boateng, & Drury, 2007). Chinese managers had found that the benefits of applying Western management tools did not meet their initial high expectations, and scholars began to question the suitability of importing Western management theories without adapting them to the Chinese culture despite lacking a clear alternative. In the beginning, the adoption rate of the BSC was very low in China. According to a survey conducted by the Hong Kong China division of CPA Australia in 2002, only around 5% of respondents indicated that their firms had adopted the BSC at various levels ("Hong Kong," 2002). This survey also indicated that only 25% of the respondents knew the BSC well even though most of them were qualified accountants who were expected to be involved in strategy planning and in designing performance measurement systems.

Things have changed recently. In 2008, a survey conducted by Sheng, Xiong, and Su (2008) showed that 53% of respondents reported that their firms had implemented the BSC in varying degrees, ranging from minimum-standard (i.e., a performance measurement system containing the four perspectives of the BSC) to fully developed (i.e., a strategic management system under the BSC framework). Among all the respondents' firms, 8% had a multidimensional framework for performance measurement that combined financial and non-financial perspectives under the BSC, 15% not only used the four perspectives of the BSC but also had analyzed strategy by employing cause-and-effect chains, and 30% had fully developed the

Kaisheng Zeng and Xiaohui Luo, "The Balanced Scorecard in China: Does it Work?" *Business Horizons*. 56 (2013), pp. 611–620. Reprinted with permission of Elsevier.

BSC as a strategic management system. The survey concluded that the BSC had spread in China, and the implementation rate was similar to that in many Western nations.

The above two surveys seem to show a promising future for the BSC in China, where the number of both foreign firms and local firms is huge. However, some other reports (e.g., Lu & Du, 2007) have revealed that there is a high implementation failure rate for the BSC in China. Deciding whether or not to use the BSC seems to have become a dilemma both for Western managers, who are familiar with Western management tools but not with Chinese culture and business situations, as well as for local managers, who are familiar with local environments but not with Western management tools. On one hand, managers in China need the BSC to achieve organizational goals and improve profits, while on the other hand, they are risking their future with a high failure rate.

What has happened to the BSC in the West? What is happening to the BSC in China? It may be time to explore the reasons behind the unsuccessful implementation of the BSC in China. However, one will never have a comprehensive view on the effectiveness of the BSC without both an overall review of the BSC literature from the West and an extension of the research into China. Until recently, few articles dealing with the BSC in China were published, particularly in high-ranking Chinese journals. The number of articles published in lower-ranking Chinese journals was small, and the articles primarily introduced the BSC, such as its contents, its superior characteristics, and its theoretical backgrounds (Duh, Xiao, & Chow, 2009). Furthermore, to our knowledge, research on the effectiveness of the BSC in emerging economies is rare. Our article attempts to address the above gaps in theory and practice by summarizing key limitations of the BSC reported in the Western literature and then to extend the research into one of the largest emerging economies—China. We also offer recommendations for firms getting ready to implement the BSC and for enterprises trying to improve existing BSC systems.

2. WHAT HAPPENED TO THE BSC IN THE WEST: RESEARCH ABOUT ITS LIMITATIONS

As a new management tool, the BSC has received wide attention from both practitioners and academics in Western nations since it was developed in 1992 by Kaplan and Norton. Not long after it was introduced, the BSC came into wide usage in many organizations, including 60% of Fortune 1000 firms (Silk, 1998). At the same time, the BSC became the ongoing dominant topic related to performance measurement in academic journals, and Kaplan and Norton's (1992) publication has been one of the most cited articles (Neely, 2005). However, the reported high failure rate of the BSC along with the mixed research findings about its effectiveness have resulted in questions about the validity of some assumptions underpinning the BSC (Ittner & Larcker, 2003; Lipe & Salterio, 2000; Nørreklit, 2000). Based on the existing literature (primarily Western), we summarize the limitations associated with the BSC.

2.1. Ambiguous Validity of the Cause-and-Effect Relationship

Advocates of the BSC assume that there exists a cause-and-effect relationship between the perspectives of measures, including financial performance, customer relations, internal business processes, and learning and growth (Kaplan & Norton, 1992, 1996). For instance, better-trained employees (i.e., learning and growth) will lead to business process improvement, which will in turn lead to more satisfied customers and better financial outcomes. As the last three perspectives are non-financial measures, the cause-and-effect relationship implies that non-financial measures can be used to predict future financial performance.

However, some scholars have argued that the "linear" cause-and-effect relationship is an oversimplification of reality and that this set of relationships is in fact recursive and dynamic (Brignall, 2002). Others have even questioned the existence of the causal relationships between the perspectives of measures. Nørreklit (2000) suggested that there is no cause-and-effect relationship among the four perspectives of the BSC. For example, customer satisfaction does not necessarily improve financial performance because even though customers are satisfied, they may still choose to buy from a competitor if that competitor's products are more attractive to them. Nørreklit's (2000) opinion is partially supported by some empirical evidence indicating that financial performance is not necessarily improved after using the BSC's non-financial measures (Neely, 2005). Furthermore, as there is little or no guidance given in the BSC literature on how to set up these causal relationships, organizations often failed to establish such causal links among the four perspectives (Ittner & Larcker, 2003). Therefore, if the validity of the cause-and-effect relationship is ambiguous, if the set of causal relationships is hard to establish, and if empirical evidence suggests that non-financial measures are not necessarily the drivers of financial measures, users and researchers may question the effectiveness of the BSC.

2.2. Strategic Control Barrier

Kaplan and Norton (1996) noted that the BSC is not just a performance measurement system but also a strategic control system that is able to handle the problem of strategy implementation. Therefore, as a strategic control system, the BSC should be able to provide feedback on strategy implementation to managers and help them make adjustments in strategic plans, and it should be able to signal external changes to managers and help them respond to the changes by adjusting strategy.

However, it was argued that the BSC is a hierarchically top-down model that is not rooted in the organization or in the environment, thus making it questionable as a strategic control tool (Nørreklit, 2000; Simons, 2000). Nørreklit (2000) pointed out that since the measures in the BSC are defined by top management with little involvement of frontline workers, employees can only react rather than act on their own. As a result, a barrier exists between the strategy expressed in the plan and the strategy expressed in the actions actually undertaken. Furthermore, the BSC is problematic if the plan itself is not correct because management only pays attention to making the plan but not receiving feedback from local users. It is even more problematic that the BSC does not reflect the changes of external environments because it has no direct relationship with the market (Nørreklit, 2000). As a result, some researchers have criticized the BSC for giving inadequate feedback on strategy content and for not providing enough information about external environments, thus disabling its use for strategic control (Veen-Dirks & Wijn, 2002). Therefore, if the BSC does not provide a valid strategic control model and if it cannot solve the problem of strategy implementation, its effectiveness as a strategic management system may be questionable.

2.3. Common Measure Bias

Kaplan and Norton (1996) stated that the BSC provides a multidimensional view of strategy and that each business unit in an organization should thus develop and use both common measures and unique measures. They suggested that measures that are common across different units tend to be financial measures, such as return on assets and net income, while measures that are unique to a particular unit are more likely to be non-financial measures capturing the unit's business strategy.

However, Lipe and Salterio (2000) found that superior managers tend to simplify performance measurement by only relying on common measures when they evaluate the performance of multiple subordinate units. Consequently, unique measures are often disregarded or even ignored by superior managers in performance evaluations. As unique measures are often non-financial and common measures are often financial, the above study implied that the three non-financial perspectives of the BSC may not affect superiors' evaluations and that the financial measures may have a stronger effect on unit managers' decisions because they drive the evaluations. Follow-up studies showed similar results and indicated that common measure bias does exist in performance evaluations of multiple units due to the cognitive limitations of human beings (e.g., Dilla & Steinbart, 2005; Libby, Salterio, & Webb, 2004). Therefore, if common measure bias exists, it may affect managers' ability to properly evaluate a specific unit's performance. Also, if non-financial measures are underused, this may prevent an organization from fully benefiting from the BSC, which was designed to incorporate a broad set of non-financial measures into decision making. Finally, if unique measures reflect key aspects of a unit's strategy, inattention to them may undermine the effectiveness of the BSC.

2.4. Obese and Static Nature

According to Kaplan and Norton (1992, 1996), the BSC contains a large set of measures designed to capture business strategy and reflect all areas important to an organization. Typically, each of the four perspectives under the BSC framework includes 5–7 measures for a total of 20–28 measures in one BSC setup.

However, the number of measures in a BSC system is not consistent with a finding from psychological research suggesting that human beings have difficulty handling more than seven measurements simultaneously (George, 1956). It was reported that if an individual is asked to do too many things concurrently, no single initiative receives enough attention to ensure success, so people should focus on a small number of measurements (Malina & Selto, 2001; Simons, 2000). The large number of measures in the BSC, together with the lack of normative guidelines for performance evaluations, makes using the BSC a complex and relatively unstructured task (Dilla & Steinbart, 2005).

Opponents have also argued that the BSC is a static model because it cannot solve the time lag problem and does not reflect changes in external environments (Veen-Dirks & Wijn, 2002). Neely (2005) further suggested that the implementation of an obese and static BSC system may potentially risk performance management. Therefore, the obese and static nature of the BSC may undercut its potential usefulness. A summary of Western research about the limitations of the BSC is presented in Table 1.

3. WHAT IS HAPPENING TO THE BSC IN CHINA: MORE OBSTACLES

3.1. Four Cases in China

Although some studies have shown that the BSC has been widely used in China, other studies (e.g., Lu & Du, 2007) have indicated that there is a high failure rate of BSC implementation in the country. If these studies reveal the true situation of the BSC in China, then people may ask what is happening to the BSC in China and what the possible reasons are behind the failure to implement the BSC in the country. These questions warrant further investigation. Thus, we conducted in-depth interviews in four foreign firms in China that are using the BSC in order to find out what obstacles they face. Among these four firms, two come from the United States and another two from the United Kingdom. As for their industries, two firms operate in the service industry, one in manufacturing, and one in wholesale and retail trade.

We chose to investigate these foreign firms for three reasons. Firstly, the BSC was innovated in the United States, so the four foreign firms may be more familiar with the BSC than many local firms. Secondly, the foreign firms are subsidiaries of Anglo-American multinational companies, so it may be easier to identify what obstacles they face when implementing the BSC in China. Thirdly, the foreign firms have implemented the BSC for more than five years, a longer period than that of many local firms.

We interviewed three people in each firm: the general manager or the deputy general manager and then two departmental managers. Each interview lasted around 45–90 minutes, and we took notes during the interviews. We asked both semistructured and open-ended questions to discover possible obstacles the firms faced when implementing the BSC in China.

Our investigation yielded two main findings. First, the four limitations found by Western scholars summarized and presented in the preceding section also exist when foreign firms implement the BSC in China. Second, there are two main obstacles associated with the use of the BSC in Chinese management situations, which we will call "cultural barriers" and "matching barriers." We will discuss these two obstacles in detail in the following paragraphs.

3.2. Cultural Barriers

The BSC was developed and has been applied in the United States, and as such, it contains Anglo-American cultural features. When the BSC is transplanted into the Chinese cultural setting, it faces an obstacle in terms of cultural adaptation because local culture shapes people's behavior and management practices. In our investigation, we found that the BSC faces two main cultural barriers in China when it is implemented.

3.2.1. The BSC Facing Confucianism Confucianism is regarded as the traditional Chinese culture and emphasizes conflict avoidance, indirect expression, face saving, relationships, harmony, a long-term perspective, and so on (Westwood & Lok, 2003). The BSC is rooted in Anglo-American culture and can be characterized as direct, strict, formal, target oriented, and competition promoting. When the BSC's cultural features meet Confucian values, a number of challenges may arise in foreign firms. For instance, when the BSC causes conflict, local employees may not be happy with accepting the American style of direct objection and assertive negotiation because they have been told their entire

TABLE 1 Western Research about the Limitations of the BSC

Problems with the BSC	Description of the Problems	Symptoms to Look For
Ambiguous validity of the cause-and-effect relationship	Advocates of the BSC assume that there is a cause-and-effect relationship between the perspectives of measures (Kaplan & Norton, 1992, 1996). However, some scholars argue that there is no cause-and-effect relationship among the four perspectives of the BSC (Brignall, 2002; Nørreklit, 2000).	• Improving customer perspectives (e.g., customer satisfaction) does not necessarily improve financial outcomes because satisfied customers may still choose to buy products from other companies (Nørreklit, 2000). • Non-financial measures in the BSC are not necessarily the drivers of financial measures (Neely, 2005). • Organizations often fail to establish such causal links among the four perspectives because there is little or no guidance given in the BSC literature on how to set up these causal relationships (Ittner & Larcker, 2003).
Strategic control barrier	Advocates note that the BSC is not just a performance measurement system but also a strategic control system (Kaplan & Norton, 1996). However, some scholars argue that the BSC is a hierarchically top-down model that is not rooted in the organization or in the environment, thus making it questionable as a strategic control tool (Nørreklit, 2000; Simons, 2000).	• The measures in the BSC are defined by top management with little involvement of frontline workers; thus, employees can only react rather than act on their own (Nørreklit, 2000). • The BSC does not reflect changes in external environment because it has no direct relationship with the market (Nørreklit, 2000). • The BSC gives inadequate feedback on the content of the strategy (Veen-Dirks & Wijn, 2002).
Common measure bias	Advocates of the BSC state that each business unit should develop and use both common measures and unique measures (Kaplan & Norton,1996). However, some scholars have found that not all the measures in the BSC are treated equally during the performance evaluation process (Lipe & Salterio, 2000).	• Superior managers tend to simplify performance measurement by only relying on common measures when they evaluate the performance of multiple subordinate units (Lipe & Salterio, 2000). • Unique measures are often disregarded or even ignored by superior managers in performance evaluations (Dilla & Steinbart, 2005).
Obese and static nature	According to Kaplan and Norton (1992, 1996), the BSC contains a large set of measures. However, some scholars have suggested that the implementation of an obese and static BSC may potentially risk performance management (Neely, 2005).	• The fact that there are too many measures in a BSC system is not consistent with a psychological research finding suggesting that human beings have difficulty handling more than seven measurements simultaneously (George, 1956). • The BSC is a static model because it cannot solve the time lag problem and does not reflect changes in external environments (Veen-Dirks & Wijn, 2002).

lives to be non-assertive and indirect and to care about others' face *(mianzi)* when handling conflicts. In addition, disagreements may occur between a firm's headquarters and local subsidiaries because the Western headquarters will usually focus on targets and on using the BSC to achieve objectives, while local managers—who value maintaining relationships and harmony—place emphasis on long-term relationships *(guanxi)*. Moreover, influenced by such Confucian values as harmony, face saving, and long-term perspective, local employees tend to prefer comity. As a result, they are used to a flexible and informal management style and may be hesitant to implement a strict and formal BSC system.

3.2.2. The BSC Implementation with High Power Distance and Low Individualism In Hofstede's model (1980), power distance and individualism are widely used in identifying the cultural differences between the United States and China. Chinese culture is expected to have high power distance and low individualism, while American culture is at the opposite end. Rooted in the American culture, the BSC works only after there is active involvement, smooth vertical communication, and competition among individuals. Consequently, the BSC is not easily transferred to high power distance/low individualism situations, which often symbolize low levels of empowerment and high emotional reliance on the group. For example, when using the BSC, local managers become accustomed to the centralized decision-making process with low levels of empowerment for their subordinates because Chinese leaders have traditionally been regarded as having "paternal relationships" with their followers. Managers are expected to shoulder the responsibility of looking after their subordinates, treating them well and securing continuing employment. The subordinates respect the individuals who are in charge and accept that power is distributed unequally. Local employees seldom raise challenging questions or objections to superiors' decisions and do not directly express their ideas. Consequently, low employee empowerment leads to low employee involvement and less fluent vertical communication under the BSC framework. When the BSC encourages competition between individuals, local employees may be reluctant to become involved because they rely on the group emotionally and prefer group-based activities and rewards. Thus, many local employees are hesitant about the implementation of the BSC.

People from different cultural backgrounds have different attitudes toward the same management system (Chow, Harrison, Lindquist, & Wu, 1997). A management system found to be effective in one cultural background may not necessarily be effective and may even be dysfunctional in another cultural background. Cultural barriers influencing the effectiveness of the BSC in China will arise if the cultural features of the BSC fail to merge with Chinese culture.

3.3. Matching Barriers

Western firms that set up joint ventures with local firms in China also need to be aware of matching barriers because their local partners usually have existing management systems already in place. Therefore, the need to merge two management systems is most likely to occur when a new management system, such as the BSC, is implemented in these joint ventures. According to our research, we found that the BSC faces three main matching barriers with existing management systems in China when it is implemented.

3.3.1. Matching with Existing Planning Systems Many senior and elderly Chinese managers experienced China's transition from a centrally planned economy to today's market-oriented economy. Thus, Western management theory, such as organizational strategy and strategic planning, is relatively new to them. As a result, the planning systems in place at many local firms are not typical strategy planning systems by Western standards. Without a strong modern strategy planning system, the implementation of the BSC will be problematic because a well-designed strategic plan is a prerequisite of the BSC. Being unfamiliar with Western management tools, some local managers intend to use the BSC to help them build a strategy, but this is really a case of putting the cart before the horse because the purpose of the BSC is not to formulate a strategy but to implement one. Therefore, a matching barrier usually exists between the existing planning system and the implementation of the BSC.

3.3.2. Matching with Existing Performance Measurement Systems When it was introduced in China, the concept of management by objectives was modified and renamed as the target responsibility system. The use of the target responsibility system spread across the whole country as a modern performance measurement system in the early 1980s, a time when China was experiencing a period of enthusiasm for Western theories and practices (Wu et al., 2007). Since then, a large number of local firms have adopted the target responsibility system. Under the target responsibility system, managers usually need to achieve several objectives within their tenures, which tends to make them focus more on short-term benefits. However, conflicts will arise between this short-term-oriented performance measurement system and the long-term goals of the BSC. The implementation of the BSC is time consuming and costly, and there is usually a time lag before profit growth. Hence, it may take a long time to recognize the benefits of BSC adoption. If financial performance does not improve in the short run, managers and employees may begin to doubt the BSC's effectiveness as well as its three non-financial perspectives. In joint ventures, many of the managers come from local partners and are recruited locally; thus, their doubt may eventually lead to resistance to BSC implementation.

3.3.3. Matching with Existing Information Technology Systems As discussed in the preceding paragraph, Chinese managers and employees place great emphasis on financial performance and thus rely heavily on financial measures. As a result, the information technology (IT) systems in many local firms usually contain only financial data about the business. Although some local firms have adopted enterprise resource planning (ERP) systems, their IT systems often have data on financial and internal business perspectives but seldom include details about customer perspectives or learning/growth perspectives (Beiman, 2006). Consequently, the existing IT systems in many local firms obviously cannot meet the requirements of the BSC, which contains a diverse set of performance measures for its four perspectives. Without the support from IT systems, managers will have difficulty tracking, analyzing, and adjusting performance objectives, and thus, there is a high likelihood that they will not realize the full benefits of the BSC. The two obstacles associated with the implementation of the BSC in China are summarized in Table 2.

TABLE 2 Obstacles Associated with the Implementation of the BSC in China

Problems with the BSC	Description of the Problems	Symptoms to Look For
Cultural barriers	The BSC is rooted in Anglo-American culture, which differs very much from Eastern culture. Chinese cultural values—such as Confucianism, high power distance, and low individualism—may cause problems when using the BSC in China.	• Local employees may not be happy to accept the American style of direct objections and assertive negotiation because they emphasize conflict avoidance, indirect expression, and saving face. • Local managers, who tend to place more emphasis on long-term relationships *(guanxi)* and who are accustomed to a more flexible and informal management style, may be hesitant to implement a strict and formal BSC system. • Chinese culture has high power distance, which often symbolizes a low level of empowerment. A low level of empowerment leads to low employee involvement and less fluent vertical communication under the BSC framework. • Chinese culture has low individualism, which often symbolizes emotional reliance on the group. Thus, when the BSC encourages competition between individuals, local employees may be reluctant to participate because they prefer group-based activities and rewards.
Matching barriers	Western firms that set up joint ventures with local firms in China will face matching problems with the existing planning systems, performance measurement systems, and IT systems of their local partners.	• The strategy planning systems in many local firms often do not adhere to Western standards and thus cannot meet requirements of the BSC. • Under existing performance measurement systems, managers usually need to achieve several objectives, which tends to make them focus more on short-term benefits rather than on the BSC's long-term goals. • The IT systems in many local firms usually contain only financial data and thus cannot provide enough support for the implementation of the BSC.

4. HOW SHOULD WESTERN FIRMS PREPARE FOR AND IMPLEMENT THE BSC IN CHINA?

China ranks first among developing countries in terms of receiving foreign direct investment. The country has now attracted investment from a large number of Western firms, including many of the world's top 500 companies. When Western firms invest in China, they also bring advanced management systems with them into the country. The implementation of these systems in China, however, is met with far more challenges than what most managers imagine because the cultural and business environments differ significantly between China and the West. These differences often make the use of the BSC in China problematic. In this section, we make recommendations to Western firms on how to prepare for and implement the BSC in China.

4.1. Recommendations for Preparing for the BSC

If Western firms intend to use the BSC in their subsidiaries in China, how should they prepare for implementation? We suggest overcoming the cultural barriers first. Here are two recommendations.

4.1.1. Know More about Your Chinese Employees In the late 1970s, China implemented the one-child policy and the open-door policy. The former created a generation of only children in stark contrast to their parents' generation for whom large families were the norm. The latter allowed foreign-owned firms to expand their business into China. When Western firms expand globally, they recruit staff for their subsidiaries from the local workforce. Consequently, a majority of the employees recruited by Western firms in China are from the generation born after the implementation of the one-child policy. Influenced by the only-child family environment, China's economic boom, China's oriental culture, and Western ideas, these only-child employees are better educated, more knowledgeable, and more skilled in terms of modern scientific technology. Compared to their parents' generation, they are more studious, more accepting of new things, more creative, and burning with curiosity. However, they tend to be more self-centered, less independent, and more self-willed. Consequently, many of them have weak communication skills and are relatively lacking in team spirit and self-confidence (Ruan & Liu, 2007). Knowing more about Chinese employees is helpful for Western firms to figure out what kind of training and guidance should be provided when implementing the BSC, which we will discuss in Section 4.2.2.

4.1.2. Build a Strong Organizational Culture for the BSC The BSC is a management system involving all the people who work in an organization. Local employees bring local culture with them when they are recruited in Western firms. Thus, conflicts between employees and advanced management systems seem unavoidable. Because an organizational culture is likely to moderate the impact of local culture, developing a strong organizational culture for the BSC is a good solution to overcoming cultural barriers (Hodgetts & Luthans, 2003). The organizational culture should emphasize three dimensions: empowerment, consistency, and adaptability. The purpose of strengthening an empowerment culture is to increase employees' commitment and their sense of belonging to the organization and thus make local employees more willing to use the BSC. Reinforcing a consistent culture aims to promote common behavioral norms and the alignment of leaders and followers, hence improving coordination and integration across the organization for the preparation of the BSC. Strengthening an adaptability culture aims to help employees emphasize flexibility and adaptation and thus heighten local employees' acceptance of organizational change, such as BSC implementation. Therefore, developing a strong organizational culture for the BSC will help local employees prepare for organizational change and for future engagement in the BSC.

However, organizational cultural change is one of the hardest things to undertake because it requires employees to change their mindset and behavior to follow a new organizational culture. Whether or not a company is able to achieve this change depends on employees' recognition of, involvement with, and commitment to the change rather than on managers' wishes. If employees do not recognize the significance of the cultural change, it will take a long time for this change to occur. Costa and Kallick (2000) suggested that it could take around 3–5 years to build up new mindsets among people. Therefore, we recommend three steps to develop a strong organizational culture in terms of empowerment, consistency, and adaptability. Firstly, a recruitment process should be designed to attract and select those employees most suited to a specific organization's culture. Secondly, a friendly working environment should be created to arouse employees' interest in and recognition of the importance of organizational cultural change. Then organizational cultural training should be provided to improve employees' knowledge of the new organizational culture. Employees' adaptation to organizational cultural change may be a long and complex learning process, so persistent efforts may be required.

4.2. Recommendations When Implementing the BSC

If Western firms are ready or have already started to use the BSC in China, how can they ensure a successful BSC implementation? We suggest four ways to deploy the BSC.

4.2.1. Adapt the BSC to the Local Management Situation Western firms must be aware that simply transferring the BSC from the parent companies into their subsidiaries in China is not feasible and that modification or revision is needed to make the BSC fit into local management situations. Revising the BSC can be initiated in one of two ways. The first way is to start with a simple BSC model before implementing a more complex model, especially when the local employees have little knowledge of the BSC. A simple BSC model may include only some of the BSC perspectives, and the cause-and-effect relationships may not be necessary for implementation at this stage. Then, a fully developed BSC model could be implemented when the employees become more familiar with it. Using this step-by-step approach, Western firms may increase their chance of succeeding in the use of the BSC.

The second way to revise BSC use in China is to deploy the BSC at the department level before cascading to individuals. There are two reasons for this. One is that many Chinese managers will feel embarrassed when giving low scores during individual performance assessments because of the conflict-avoidance and face-saving nature of the Chinese culture. If they tend to give high scores to all subordinates, then the use of the BSC becomes meaningless. Another reason is that many only-child employees prefer group-based rewards when they feel a lack of confidence in the workplace and have a need for more safety by sharing risk. Thus, by deploying the BSC at the department level instead of the individual level, a compromise is reached.

4.2.2. Provide Precision Training and Guidance Many Western firms in China provide training for their employees, particularly when implementing new systems. They are usually able to recruit young employees who are well educated. Their creativity, skillfulness, and knowledge may lead many of their managers to believe that giving them full rein would be of great benefit to the company. However, these young employees may never fully adapt to the BSC system if they cannot overcome their only-child characteristics, such as weak communication skills and lack of self-confidence, which often manifest as indirectness and conflict avoidance. Therefore, precision training should be provided for the following three purposes. The first purpose is to improve employees' communication skills and encourage teamwork. The second purpose is to enhance employees' self-confidence and help them become more active at work. The third purpose is to improve employees' ability to work independently and enhance their sense of responsibility. Furthermore, together with training, detailed guidelines and guidance are also needed to improve employee competence and achieve successful BSC implementation.

4.2.3. Overcome the Matching Barriers We have three recommendations for Western firms in China to overcome the matching barriers that were discussed in Section 3.3. Firstly, a detailed and feasible strategic plan and a well-designed strategy map are prerequisites of successful BSC implementation. Secondly, any existing financially focused, short-term-oriented performance measurement systems should be modified to reflect the BSC's multidimensional and long-term purposes. Finally, a competent IT system is fundamental for successful BSC implementation. Many Chinese companies usually focus on financial data, and little information exists about non-financial perspectives. Thus, when Western firms use the BSC in China, they may need to convince their Chinese partners to build up a database that includes data about each of the four perspectives in the BSC framework.

4.2.4. Overcome the Limitations We have three recommendations for Western firms in China to overcome the limitations of the BSC, which were reviewed in Section 2. Firstly, a well-designed strategy map and a comprehensive business analysis are essential to make the cause-and-effect relationship in the BSC framework work. Secondly, top management should utilize both common and unique measures to properly evaluate performance. Thirdly, Western executives should remember to avoid putting too many measures in one BSC setup. According to psychological research, an individual is only capable of handling around seven measures simultaneously (George, 1956).

5. IMPLICATIONS FOR MANAGEMENT PRACTICE AND RESEARCH

This article summarizes the limitations of the BSC from Western literature to uncover the obstacles associated with deploying the BSC in China as well as provides some recommendations for Western firms to successfully implement the BSC in China.

This article tries to send novel and important messages to managers, signaling that the BSC faces more obstacles in cultural and business environments that differ from the West. More work needs to be done to make the BSC suitable for firms in the Chinese context. The BSC was produced in the United States and is rooted in the Anglo-American culture. Thus, managers should prepare to overcome cultural barriers when they transplant the BSC from the West to Eastern cultural contexts. At the same time, managers should prepare to conquer the matching barriers discussed in this article to achieve compatibility with existing local systems.

This article also tries to convey some valuable messages to scholars, showing that it is time to study the BSC in emerging economies, investigate how oriental wisdom and the Western-designed BSC can be merged into systematical unity, and innovate a new and locally adaptable strategic management system.

REFERENCES

Beiman, I. (2006). Using the balanced scorecard methodology to execute China strategy. *Cost Management, 20*(4), 9–19.

Brignall, S. (2002, July). The balanced scorecard: An environmental and social critique. In *Proceedings of the 3rd International Conference on Performance Measurement,* Boston.

Chow, C. W., Harrison, P., Lindquist, T., & Wu, A. (1997). Escalating commitment to unprofitable projects: Replication and cross-cultural extension. *Management Accounting Research, 8*(3), 347–361.

Costa, A. L., & Kallick, B. (2000). *Habits of mind.* Alexandria, VA: ASCD.

Dilla, W. N., & Steinbart, P. J. (2005). Relative weighting of common and unique balanced scorecard measures by knowledgeable decision makers. *Behavioral Research in Accounting, 17,* 43–53.

Duh, R., Xiao, Z. J., & Chow, C. (2009). The commentary on China's management accounting research. *Accounting Research* (China), *20,* 72–81.

George, A. M. (1956). The magic number seven, plus or minus two: Some limits in our capacity for processing information. *The Psychological Review, 63*(2), 81–97.

Hodgetts, R. M., & Luthans, F. (2003). *International management: Culture, strategy, and behavior.* Boston: McGraw-Hill/Irwin.

Hong Kong strikes a perfect balance. (2002). *Australian CPA, 72*(10), 62–64.

Ittner, C. D., & Larcker, D. F. (2003). Coming up short on non-financial performance measurement. *Harvard Business Review, 81*(11), 88–95.

Kaplan, R. S., & Norton, D. P. (1992). The balanced scorecard—Measures that drive performance. *Harvard Business Review, 70*(1), 71–79.

Kaplan, R. S., & Norton, D. P. (1996). Using the balanced scorecard as a strategic management system. *Harvard Business Review, 74*(1), 75–85.

Libby, T., Salterio, S. E., & Webb, A. (2004). The balanced scorecard: The effects of assurance and process accountability on managerial judgment. *Accounting Review, 79*(4), 1075–1094.

Lipe, M. G., & Salterio, S. E. (2000). The balanced scorecard: Judgmental effects of common and unique performance measures. *Accounting Review, 75*(3), 283–298.

Lu, J., & Du, B. (2007). The implementation of the balanced scorecard in China. *Jiangsu Commercial Forum, 24*(10), 153–154.

Malina, M. A., & Selto, F. H. (2001). Communicating and controlling strategy: An empirical study of the effectiveness of the balanced scorecard. *Journal of Management Accounting Research, 13,* 47–90.

Neely, A. D. (2005). The evolution of performance measurement research: Developments in the last decade and a research agenda for the next. *International Journal of Operations and Production Management, 25*(12), 1264–1277.

Nørreklit, H. (2000). The balance on the balanced scorecard: A critical analysis of some of its assumptions. *Management Accounting Research, 11*(1), 65–88.

Ruan, Y., & Liu, S. (2007). The characteristics of the "only-child" in China and recommendations for their education. *Chinese Modern Education, 44,* 28–31.

Sheng, C., Xiong, Y., & Su, W. (2008). Survey on the balanced scorecard: From performance evaluation to strategic management. *Journal of Shanghai Lixin University of Commerce, 22*(1), 37–45.

Silk, S. (1998). Automating the balanced scorecard. *Management Accounting, 79*(11), 38–44.

Simons, R. (2000). *Performance measurement and control systems for implementing strategy.* Upper Saddle River, NJ: Prentice Hall.

Veen-Dirks, V. P., & Wijn, M. (2002). Strategic control: Meshing critical success factors with the balanced scorecard. *Long Range Planning, 35*(4), 407–427.

Westwood, R., & Lok, P. (2003). The meaning of work in Chinese contexts: A comparative study. *International Journal of Cross Cultural Management, 3*(2), 139–164.

Wu, J., Boateng, A., & Drury, C. (2007). An analysis of the adoption, perceived benefits, and expected future emphasis of Western management accounting practices in Chinese SOEs and JVs. *The International Journal of Accounting, 42*(2), 171–185.

Competing in Network Markets: Can the Winner Take All?

David P. McIntyre
Providence College

Asda Chintakananda
Nanyang Technological University

Products as varied as software, credit cards, and even coffee makers are influenced by network effects whereby the product's value is contingent upon the number of people using it. In turn, markets for these products offer lucrative returns to managers who can leverage the dynamics in their favor. This article describes recent research focusing on the factors that influence success and failure in network markets. We offer recommendations and initiatives that increase the likelihood of success in network markets for entrepreneurs and incumbents alike.

1. STRATEGY IN NETWORK MARKETS

In mid-2008, social networks were at a crossroads. Both MySpace and Facebook had tens of millions of unique monthly visitors, yet there was significant uncertainty regarding the future of social networks. Which platform would win the battle for users and visitors? Could both maintain a viable position in the market, or was this a winner-take-all competition, with no possibility of multiple competing networks? The stakes were substantial as users, advertisers, and game developers all wanted to associate with the most popular platform: users to maximize their potential for social interaction, and advertisers and developers to maximize potential revenue streams. In addition, powerful competitors like Google and upstarts such as Twitter sought to expand their own presence in this burgeoning market.

The high stakes in this battle—and Facebook's eventual dominance of social networks—are grounded in a relatively simple social dynamic: consumers often prefer to be part of a large network of other users of the same product. For example, users of online auction sites such as eBay value a large potential audience of buyers for their goods just as credit card users desire a large number of retail settings where their cards can be used. These "network effects" have important implications for management in various industries—from social networks to coffee makers—and strongly influence various facets of the market including new product development, diffusion, and competitive success or failure for firms (Eisenmann, 2007; Eisenmann, Parker, & Van Alstyne, 2011; McIntyre & Subramaniam, 2009).

The essential features of network effects are well-established: when consumers desire interaction and compatibility with others, one company often ends up dominating the market for a given good (Farrell & Saloner, 1985; Katz & Shapiro, 1985; Schilling, 1998). This phenomenon of winner-take-all markets is driven by both direct and indirect network effects. *Direct network effects* occur when consumers value a large network of users for a given product; the larger the network, the more value it offers to consumers. For instance, Facebook's large network of users currently offers consumers a substantial cohort with which they can interact and share information. *Indirect network effects* are the benefits to consumers of the variety and availability of complements to the core product (Venkatraman & Lee, 2004). For example, in each generation of

David McIntyre and Asda Chintakananda, "Competing in Network Markets: Can the Winner Take All?" *Business Horizons*, 57, 2014, pp. 117–125. Reprinted with permission of Elsevier.

video game consoles, the console with the largest network of users will tend to have a wide variety of game titles available, as producers of these titles hope to reach the largest possible audience.

In tandem, the presence of direct and indirect network effects in a given market is thought to offer positive feedback to early leaders in such markets because firms with an early, large *installed base* of users will tend to be favored by consumers; as this user base grows, it becomes more attractive to potential consumers (Eisenmann, Parker, & Van Alstyne, 2006; Schilling, 2002). In turn, more complements will be available for the leading product. As Sony's Blu-ray technology gained traction over the competing HD-DVD format, movie studios and retailers offered a greater number of Blu-ray movie titles. When consumers find increasing value in a growing installed base and a wide variety of available complements, one product (and its sponsoring firm) may eventually "lock-in" the market for a given good. For instance, Microsoft's traditional dominance in office productivity software is thought to be partly a function of network effects, which created strong barriers to competitors entering the market (Brynjolffson & Kemerer, 1996; Liebowitz & Margolis, 1999).

However, despite the depth of research on network effects and their impact on competitive outcomes, at least two factors suggest the need for a more comprehensive understanding of these dynamics for managers in "network markets": markets where network effects may strongly influence competition. First, extant views of strategy in network markets focus largely on first-mover advantages to establish an early network of users, yet early movers also risk being locked out of the market due to an insufficient grasp of user needs (Schilling, 1998). Not all dominant firms in network markets were first movers: Facebook and Apple were relatively late movers in social networking and digital music, yet were still able to achieve dominance in their respective markets. Second, the influence of network effects appears to be both increasingly common and increasingly complex across markets. For example, while products like smart phone operating systems and video game consoles may exhibit certain features of network effects, they do not appear to engender the classic winner-take-all dynamics described in previous research, as multiple firms have been able to achieve sustainable positions in these markets. In addition, network effects are often associated with high-technology markets, yet their influence may also extend to more conventional markets such as real estate, credit cards, and health maintenance organizations (HMOs).

Given the increasing prevalence and complexity of network effects, this article offers four critical considerations for managers in network markets. First, what determines the intensity of network effects for a given product or market? Second, can network effects be strategically generated and/or manipulated in favor of one firm? Third, given that network markets tend to strongly favor large incumbents with a large base of users, how can entrepreneurs and small businesses overcome existing dynamics? Finally, how can incumbents best defend their competitive position in network markets? In addressing these questions, we hope to illustrate the complexity of competitive dynamics in network markets yet also provide insights regarding effective strategy frameworks.

2. WHAT DETERMINES THE INTENSITY OF NETWORK EFFECTS?

Some markets, such as social networking, appear to exhibit classic dynamics of network effects whereby consumers value the largest possible cohort of other users of the product. In these markets, the conventional wisdom holds in that once a given firm establishes a critical mass of adopters, the market tends to tip in favor of that firm (Chacko & Mitchell, 1998; Schilling, 2002; Shapiro & Varian, 1999). Thus, one technology (and its sponsoring firm) will usually dominate the market as a result of consumers' strong desire for interdependence, in tandem with a relatively low cost of expanding scale in many of these markets. For instance, eBay was able to achieve market dominance in online auctions due to a combination of preemption—launching the site before potential competitors—and low marginal costs of facilitating additional users.

Yet online auctions and social networking represent a relatively small subset of markets influenced by network effects because the value of the product to a consumer is dependent almost exclusively on the size of the product's installed base. Put another way, products such as Facebook and eBay would have zero value to an individual user in the absence of a network of other users; interaction is essential to the value of the product. These "pure" network markets are highly susceptible to the theoretical consequents of strong network effects, including strong first-mover advantages, tipping points, and market dominance by a single product.

While other markets may be influenced by consumers' desires for interdependence, they may not exhibit the familiar narrative of extreme first-mover advantages and lock-in by a single product (McIntyre, 2011a; Suarez, 2005). In many markets, consumers may enjoy the compatibility benefits of a large network, yet the core product can also be enjoyed by an individual user independent of any direct network interaction. Consider the video game console market, where participants enjoy multi-user games online or exchanging games with friends, but can also play in solitude. Similarly, users may find some direct or indirect network value from smart phone operating systems like iPhone or Android from the availability of applications or compatibility with other devices, yet they can also enjoy features such as games and Internet connectivity, which are not directly dependent on the number of other users of the same operating system.

These different manifestations of network effects in high-technology markets can be viewed as a function of the *network intensity* of a given market: the extent to which the value of a given product to a consumer is dependent on the size of an existing installed base of other users of the product (McIntyre & Subramaniam, 2009; Suarez, 2005). Figure 1 illustrates this notion in the context of two markets. In the first market, consumers largely value intrinsic characteristics of the product that are independent of installed base size. In the second, network intensity is much higher, as consumers derive value largely from the existence of a large installed base. What

FIGURE 1 Factors Influencing the Network Intensity of a Market

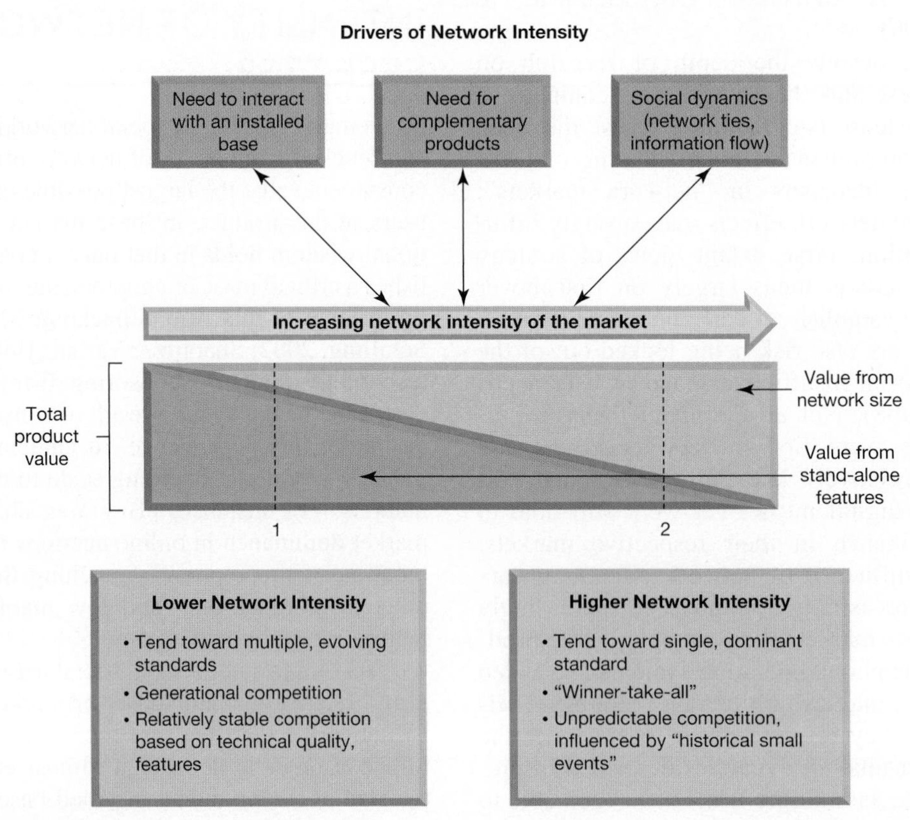

factors determine the differences between relatively competitive settings such as smart phone operating systems and winner-take-all markets such as online auctions? As illustrated in Figure 1, network intensity is driven by at least three aspects of a product: (1) the value derived by consumers from interacting with a large installed base for a product, (2) the availability of complementary products, and (3) the strength of ties among users.

First, the value of a network product is contingent on the existence of a large installed base of other users of the technology. Though a large installed base may be associated with many other benefits for the firm, like brand loyalty and fixed cost spreading, network effects specifically derive from the value of consumer interaction with the base. As noted previously, online auction websites would have little residual value to a consumer in the absence of a network of other users with whom to interact. Second, the availability and scope of complementary products will often condition the value of a technology for consumers. High-definition televisions would offer little incremental value to consumers without a wide variety of available HD programming (Gupta, Jain, & Sawhney, 1999). Finally, the frequency and depth of interaction among users may foster stronger ties among an installed base, thereby impacting the overall network intensity of a technology. Users of social networking sites, for example, may interact frequently with relatively small but strong networks of other users of the site.

3. HOW CAN NETWORK EFFECTS BE STRATEGICALLY GENERATED AND MANIPULATED?

Our current understanding of network effects is limited by the assumption that they are a market-level phenomenon based on the intrinsic nature of the market's core technology. Yet recent research suggests that while certain aspects of network effects are central to the nature of the underlying technology (e.g., online auctions), there are cases where network effects can be enhanced at the firm level by effective management (Eisenmann et al., 2011; Fuentelsaz, Garrido, & Maicas, in press). In other words, firms may be able to strategically manipulate the network intensity of a given market in their favor. Such manipulation can take at least three forms: (1) increasing customer participation through information and opinions about the product, (2) increasing opportunities for customer interaction with other customers, and (3) effectively managing complements to the core product.

Increasing customer participation through information and opinions can not only heighten the time that the customer spends with the product, but can also increase the value that the customer gains from the product. For instance, Amazon.com's online retailing business does not appear to exhibit strong network effects for consumers, as multiple channels exist to purchase the company's goods, yet by allowing customers to rate and review products and in turn rate the value of these reviews, Amazon created an informational or "meta" network effect whereby consumers may value a review that has been highly rated by many other users of the site. Amazon reviewers also benefit from being top reviewers and in turn become more loyal. Similarly, many online travel sites such as TripAdvisor allow users to rate travel destinations, as well as the utility of the reviews themselves. When a large base of users has rated a particular destination and/or its corresponding reviews highly, consumers may infer additional value or accuracy in the ratings. Increasing customer participation in order to enhance network products is not limited to online activities. In MBA seminars, for example, students may benefit from greater participation of other students within the "same network" or cohort; the more students present in class and the more these individuals contribute to group discussions, the more beneficial the collective learning experience.

Network intensity may also increase when there are more opportunities for interaction among users of the firm's products. The increasing prevalence of online gaming is one example of this phenomenon: individual users of video games could desire compatibility with a large base of other users. Cell phone service providers have also employed this approach with mobile-to-mobile service plans, via which consumers have an incentive to interact with a network of users of the same product. While cell phones by themselves exhibit relatively modest network effects (i.e., users of a particular product and service plan can freely interact with users of other products), such plans increase consumers' desire to join the same network of users of a common product and/or service plan. Increasing opportunities for interaction are not limited to digital industries. For example, universities may increase the value of alumni association membership by organizing activities where members can network and socialize more frequently. By having members interact with one another more often, universities may not only increase the value of network membership, but also offer complementary goods and services (e.g., engraved office supplies or discounted tickets to sporting events). Members could thus find greater opportunities for information exchange or social interaction within the network as well as an increasing number of complements which add value to their network membership.

Finally, indirect network effects can be fostered by the effective management of complements. Given that the availability and variety of complementary products strongly influence consumers' product adoption choices (Schilling, 2002), firms can add significant value to their core products by enabling the development of diverse complements. Firms may develop complementary products internally, allow third parties to develop complementary products for their goods, or allow for a combination of both. In the case of Visa Inc., the company offers complementary products and services through its credit cards directly (e.g., auto collision damage waiver program, travel rewards, store discounts). Green Mountain Coffee's single-cup brewing products enhance customer value by providing complementary "K-cups" from Starbucks, Dunkin Donuts, and other brands. Apple directly offers a variety of complementary products for the Macintosh computer including AirPort (wireless modem), Time Capsule (hard drive), and Thunderbolt Display (monitor); it also endorses a line of products by third party developers including Harman Kardon (wireless speakers) and LaCie (Thunderbolt drives). The availability of such complements not only enhances the current value of the core product, but also conditions consumers' expectations about the emergence and durability of the product itself (Clements & Ohashi, 2005; Gupta et al., 1999; Venkatraman & Lee, 2004). Thus, more users may be driven to the core product by the existence of complements, thereby increasing the installed base and reinforcing the value of a large network to other users.

4. HOW CAN ENTREPRENEURS OVERCOME NETWORK DYNAMICS?

Entrepreneurs who wish to enter markets where strong network effects exist may face difficulty in determining how and when to properly do so. If an existing firm has locked in the market due to strong advantages in installed base and complementary products, it will be very costly to replace such an incumbent, let alone viably enter the market (McIntyre & Chintakananda, 2013). New entrants would have to make significant investments in order to tip the market away from the dominant incumbent, and there are no guarantees that potential consumers would switch to the new entrant's offering. Google faced this problem in its early attempts to enter the social networking market through Google Buzz. As many potential users already had Facebook accounts—the social media giant boasted over 400 million active users at the time—and didn't see the need for duplicate services, Google Buzz failed to gather traction. Less than 2 years after its launch, Google announced discontinuation of Google Buzz.

How, then, can entrepreneurs and new entrants effectively enter a market where an incumbent already enjoys a large installed base? If network intensity is strong, entrepreneurs must quickly build an installed base while enhancing the network effects of their product as described previously. Such opportunities typically become possible when a new technology arrives, existing technology becomes widely accessible, or when the emergence of a new consumer sector occurs (Leiblein & Ziedonis, 2007). For example, Facebook entered the social networking market after MySpace, Hi5, and Orkut had already reached millions of dedicated users, but was able to gain traction and leap ahead of its competitors by providing users free rein in the development and addition of apps to their pages (e.g., games, newsfeeds, blogs). These apps increased Facebook users' connectivity with other users, which in turn increased the overall value of the product to consumers.

Entrepreneurs who want to enter markets with lower network intensity may actually benefit from having an existing competitor in the market that has gained some traction. The characteristics of markets with lower network intensity, in which consumers place emphasis on the quality and the branding of the product, provide opportunities for multiple competitors to coexist (Chintakananda & McIntyre, in press). Research has shown that in markets where multiple players co-exist, early entrants tend to pave the way for others by providing essential information such as level of consumer demand, production and distribution process, marketing tactics, and organizational development (Lieberman & Montgomery, 1988). This allows firms to learn from the early entrants, avoid costly mistakes, and resultingly experience a higher rate of success. These dynamics lessen the urgency for firms to invest significantly in market development to attract customers and develop a large installed base. As a matter of fact, firms are likely to compete more effectively by waiting for a more advanced technology to become available or for the cost of technology to decline so as to compete at a cost advantage.

Advantages gained through late or deferred market entry can be seen in the video game console market, where there is relatively low network intensity. For instance, Sony delayed the release of its PlayStation3 technology to allow developers to finalize game development and allow its Blu-ray DVD technology to mature, even after Microsoft had entered the market with its comparable Xbox system. Google took advantage of a similar opportunity: Yahoo entered the search engine market before Google, placing emphasis on being a portal and a one-stop shop service provider, but found little success. Recognizing this strategic error, Google decided to focus solely on providing search functionality, later adding the development of several complementary technologies.

In sum, entrepreneurs seeking to enter a market influenced by network effects should ask three critical questions prior to the entry decision. First, what is the source of network effects in this market? As noted earlier, network effects derive from the benefits of a large installed base, the existence of complements, and/or the strength of ties among users. When network effects are solely a function of installed base size, entrepreneurs should focus on providing early users value via product giveaways or enhanced functionality of a product. Users of existing products must have an incentive to switch to the entrepreneur's offering; in this case, the costs of abandoning an existing installed base must be more than offset by the benefits of either lower financial costs of an alternative product or enhanced quality or functionality of a new alternative. However, if network effects manifest in the form of smaller, stronger networks of users, greater opportunities may exist for niche players in the market. For example, Nintendo was able to overtake Sega in the 16-bit video game market by developing a smaller yet stronger network of users who in turn were more responsive to pricing and advertising efforts (Shankar & Bayus, 2003).

Second, how strong are network effects in a given market? In network-intensive markets that are dependent on information exchange or direct consumer interaction—such as online auctions—entrepreneurs should enter the market as early as possible to establish an early installed base, which will attract other users and complementors of the core product. Alternatively, new entrants may concede the core market to incumbents who have already leveraged network effects in their favor and instead focus on developing complementary technologies. Zynga, for instance, has successfully leveraged the installed base advantages of social networks by creating a complement to the core network. If network effects are weaker, entrepreneurs may benefit from delaying market entry until uncertainty regarding consumer preferences and technological features has subsided. Ultimately, the ability to accurately assess the network intensity of a new market may be the most important capability for entrepreneurs in these settings. Underestimating network intensity could lead firms to delay product releases until they are locked out of the market by earlier entrants (Schilling, 2002). Likewise, overestimating network intensity could lead to the premature release of products on the part of firms, resulting in goods of lower quality or insufficient fit for consumers. Simply put, will the size of a product's total installed base influence future adoption decisions by consumers? Will the availability of complements influence adoption decisions? If so, the high network intensity dynamics illustrated in Figure 1 are likely.

Finally, is there a dominant standard that has already locked in the market? The most solid entry barriers in network markets occur when strong network effects are coupled with the emergence of a dominant standard which has already locked in the market (e.g., Microsoft's advantage in office productivity software). These scenarios are the least attractive for entrepreneurs; new entrants simply cannot offer users the network benefits of an entrenched incumbent and may not have the vast financial resources required to develop and market a viable alternative product. In such cases, technological discontinuities or the emergence of new consumer segments may offer the best chances for entrepreneurial success. Part of Microsoft's success in office productivity software is due to the fact that it complements the Windows operating system—a dominant standard on its own—but as Windows' dominance in PCs and laptops is eroded by alternative devices like tablets and smart phones, there may be greater opportunities for new entrants to develop productivity software that is optimized for these devices.

5. HOW CAN INCUMBENTS BEST DEFEND THEIR DOMINANCE IN NETWORK MARKETS?

A significant body of literature in economics and strategic management has examined the dynamics by which a single firm can come to dominate a network market. However, such situations do not imply a perpetual barrier to potential entrants, as cases of entrenched incumbents being leapfrogged by smaller competitors are abundant. Furthermore, the benefits of network effects may eventually experience diminishing returns to network size in certain contexts. For example, in many peer-to-peer (P2P) networks, the influence of "free riders"—people who use network resources but contribute few or none of their own—begins to outweigh the benefits of additional network members at some point (Asvanund, Clay, Krishnan, & Smith, 2004). Similarly, in MBA seminars, students may benefit from greater participation from other students within the same network, but only to a certain class size; once enrollment gets too large, cohesive class discussions become more difficult, thus diminishing the collective learning experience from the same network.

Incumbents also face challenges; consumers' concerns about complementary goods and privacy issues are just two of these hurdles. Consider that while the number of Google Android mobile phone users has surpassed that of iPhone users, Google's app sales—via its dedicated store, Google Play—lag behind those of Apple. Hence, consumers may receive mixed signals about the overall value of the competing technologies, as one firm provides greater direct network value through installed base (Google), while another provides greater indirect network value through complements (Apple).

Privacy concerns can be seen in social networking sites' recent efforts to capitalize on users' private data to generate revenue, which in turn has begun to evoke feelings of distrust among some users (Angwin & Singer-Vine, 2012). Consequently, incumbents in network markets who enjoy structurally favorable positions should focus on at least three factors to enhance the likelihood of continued success: (1) increasing the quality of the core product and complementary products, (2) increasing the quality of interactions among users of the product, and (3) enhancing trust with users (i.e., protecting consumers' private data).

Product quality in network markets has been a source of significant debate among economists and management theorists. Historical narratives offer evidence of ostensibly inferior technologies dominating these markets (Cowan, 1990; David, 1985) as consumers value a cohort of compatible users over higher-quality alternative products. The persistence of the QWERTY keyboard layout is an example of an inferior technology locking in the market due to network effects and insufficient incentives for alternatives to emerge. However, competing evidence suggests that consumers will gravitate toward high-quality and user-friendly products, even when network benefits are strong (McIntyre, 2011a; Tellis, Yin, & Niraj, 2009). For instance, recent outrage over the poor quality of Apple's proprietary Maps software for iOS suggests that network effects do not simply subsume quality concerns among consumers. Thus, dominant incumbents in high network intensity markets should continuously invest in R&D efforts to improve the technical quality of their core products, even if the incentives to do so seem limited due to their leading structural position in the market (McIntyre, 2011b).

The value of incremental improvements in product quality in this context merits additional consideration of what constitutes "quality" regarding network-intensive technologies. We use quality here to describe the relative superiority of stand-alone aspects of the technology, such as speed or ease of use. In this sense, firms that have achieved dominance in high network intensity markets can reinforce their lead by increasing the quality of the core technology. For example, a social networking site may offer consumers not only a large installed base, but also a more intuitive interface and more features than new entrants. As illustrated in Figure 1, the total value of a technology to consumers in a high network intensity market can be conceptualized as the sum of its network value and its stand-alone value. Given that new entrants to these markets will, by definition, offer consumers none of the former, they must focus on the latter. Incumbents which are able to offer both a large installed base and comparable or superior quality relative to new entrants will have created a significant competitive advantage and a substantial barrier to prospective competitors' entry into the market. Yet incumbents which produce lower-quality products run a greater risk of being leapfrogged or overtaken by a new entrant, as they provide relatively less total value to consumers than an incumbent which produces optimal quality. In other words, they are lowering the costs for current users to switch to a higher-quality, smaller-network new entrant. Aside from the quality of the core product, dominant incumbents should also continuously monitor the quality of their complementary products to ensure a superior ecosystem. Continued adoption of a network also entails having excellent complementary products that enhance the utility of the core product. Apple, for instance, has been able to maintain quality complementary products for its own core goods due to rigorous screening and acceptance systems of complementary applications. This has led to enhanced perception of reliability and continued use of Apple products.

Improvements in the technical or engineering quality of a product certainly offer consumers greater value relative to competitors. However, a well-funded new entrant may be able to match or exceed these dimensions of quality via radical enhancements to the functionality of existing products. Therefore, incumbent firms should also focus on quality characteristics of the installed base itself. For example, consumers evaluating alternative online gaming systems may gauge not only the absolute size of a system's installed base, but also the perceived proficiency and sophistication of the gamers who comprise the base. Similarly, users of online dating sites such as match.com may derive value not solely from the actual number of other users of the site, but also from the perceived quality of the network in terms of appealing personal characteristics. By creating Groups, Facebook allowed its users to gather with friends among common interest rather than publicly share information and interact with all their friends on Facebook; this not only enhanced the quality of users' friends within a group, but also allowed users to interact in a more optimal network size, thereby reducing potential issues with diminishing returns to network size.

Lastly, besides the quality of the product and the characteristics of the installed base, it is increasingly vital that users trust the network provider. By adopting a networked product, users implicitly trust the provider in several ways: that the product will be viable and supported in the future; that complements will be available; and perhaps most importantly, that privacy will be protected. The interconnectivity of networks across industries has allowed users to share their personal and private information with other users, as well as the sponsoring firm, as never before. This has given firms the ability to customize their services, thereby enhancing the quality of their network and interconnectivity among users. It has also provided opportunities to generate newer sources of revenue through cross-selling and advertisements. However, firms' ability to leverage their users' personal information has caused great concern among many. Consider that Instagram recently had to revise company policy that provided it with the ability to exploit users' photos and other data sans compensation. Backlash was fierce against the perceived betrayal, with Instagram losing as much as 25% of its installed base. To uphold users' trust, incumbents must maintain an explicit and consistent policy regarding the nature of data that is collected and shared with parties outside the network. Incumbents must safeguard users' private information and obtain their permission for any other new data sharing or commercial purposes. Such transparent policies may cause firms to forsake short-term revenue opportunities, but will enhance the perceived quality of their networks in the long-term, thus further reducing the incumbent's risk of being overtaken by a new entrant to the market.

6. CONCLUSION

Markets influenced by network effects exhibit complex competitive dynamics yet offer potentially lucrative outcomes for entrepreneurs and managers who are able to harness these dynamics in their favor. This article has described the basic dynamics of network markets and four critical considerations for managers in both incumbent and new entrant firms in these markets. Given the increasing number of competitive settings influenced by network effects, a robust understanding of their antecedents and consequences is a critical capability for researchers and practitioners of management, innovation, and strategy.

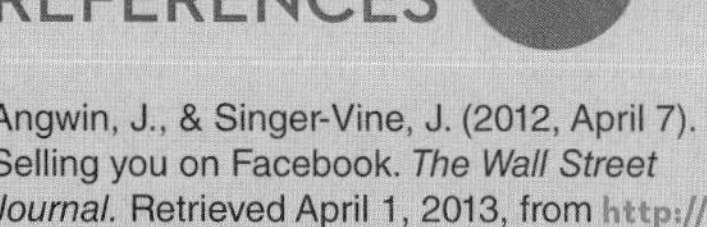

REFERENCES

Angwin, J., & Singer-Vine, J. (2012, April 7). Selling you on Facebook. *The Wall Street Journal.* Retrieved April 1, 2013, from http://online.wsj.com/article/SB10001424052702303302504577327744009046230.html

Asvanund, A., Clay, K., Krishnan, R., & Smith, M. D. (2004). An empirical analysis of network externalities in peer-to-peer music-sharing networks. *Information Systems Research, 15*(2), 155–174.

Brynjolffson, E., & Kemerer, C. (1996). Network externalities in microcomputer software: An econometric analysis of the spreadsheet market. *Management Science, 42*(12), 1627–1647.

Chacko, M., & Mitchell, W. (1998). Growth incentives to invest in a network-externality environment. *Industrial and Corporate Change, 7*(4), 731–744.

Chintakananda, A., & McIntyre, D. (in press). Market entry in the presence of network effects: A real options perspective. *Journal of Management.*

Clements, M., & Ohashi, H. (2005). Indirect network effects and the product cycle: Video games in the U.S., 1994–2002. *Journal of Industrial Economics, 53*(4), 515–542.

Cowan, R. (1990). Nuclear power reactors: A study in technological lock-in. *Journal of Economic History, 50*(3), 541–567.

David, P. (1985). Clio and the economics of QWERTY. *American Economic Review, 75*(2), 332–337.

Eisenmann, T. (2007). Internet companies' growth strategies: Determinants of investment intensity and long-term performance. *Strategic Management Journal, 27*(12), 1183–1204.

Eisenmann, T., Parker, G., & Van Alstyne, M. (2006). Strategies for two-sided markets. *Harvard Business Review, 84*(10), 92–101.

Eisenmann, T., Parker, G., & Van Alstyne, M. (2011). Platform envelopment. *Strategic Management Journal, 32*(12), 1270–1285.

Farrell, J., & Saloner, G. (1985). Standardization, compatibility, and innovation. *RAND Journal of Economics, 16*(1), 70–83.

Fuentelsaz, L., Garrido, E., & Maicas, J. P. (in press). A strategic approach to network value in network industries. *Journal of Management.*

Gupta, S., Jain, D., & Sawhney, M. (1999). Modeling the evolution of markets with indirect network externalities: An application to digital television. *Marketing Science, 18*(3), 396–416.

Katz, M. L., & Shapiro, C. (1985). Technology adoption in the presence of network externalities. *Journal of Political Economy, 94*(4), 822–841.

Leiblein, M. J., & Ziedonis, A. A. (2007). Deferral and growth options under sequential innovation. In J. J. Reuer & T. W. Tong (Eds.), *Advances in strategic management: Real options theory* (Vol. 24, pp. 225–245). Amsterdam: Elsevier.

Lieberman, M. B., & Montgomery, D. B. (1988). First-mover advantages. *Strategic Management Journal, 9*(S1), 41–58.

Liebowitz, S., & Margolis, S. (1999). *Winners, losers, and Microsoft.* Oakland, CA: The Independent Institute.

McIntyre, D. (2011a). In a network industry, does product quality matter? *Journal of Product Innovation Management, 28*(1), 99–108.

McIntyre, D. (2011b). Where there's a way, is there a will? Installed base and product quality in a high-technology setting. *Journal of High Technology Management Research, 22*(1), 59–66.

McIntyre, D., & Chintakananda, A. (2013). A real options approach to releasing "network" products. *Journal of High Technology Management Research, 24*(1), 42–52.

McIntyre, D., & Subramaniam, M. (2009). Strategy in network industries: A review and research agenda. *Journal of Management, 35*(6), 1–24.

Schilling, M. (1998). Technological lockout: An integrative model of the economic and strategic factors driving technology success and failure. *Academy of Management Review, 23*(2), 267–284.

Schilling, M. (2002). Technology success and failure in winner-take-all markets: The impact of learning orientation, timing, and network externalities. *Academy of Management Journal, 45*(2), 387–398.

Shankar, S., & Bayus, B. (2003). Network effects and competition: An empirical analysis of the home video game industry. *Strategic Management Journal, 24*(4), 375–384.

Shapiro, C., & Varian, H. (1999). *Information rules.* Boston: Harvard Business School Press.

Suarez, F. (2005). Network effects revisited: The role of strong ties in technology selection. *Academy of Management Journal, 48*(4), 710–722.

Tellis, G. J., Yin, Y., & Niraj, R. (2009). Does quality win? Network effects versus quality in high-tech markets. *Journal of Marketing Research, 46*(2), 135–149.

Venkatraman, N., & Lee, C. (2004). Preferential linkage and network evolution: A conceptual model and empirical test in the U.S. video game sector. *Academy of Management Journal, 47*(6), 876–892.

READING 06

BlackBerry Forgot to Manage the Ecosystem

Michael G. Jacobides
London Business School

BlackBerry's story underlines a new truth about the competitive landscape we live in: success or failure isn't a function of a good product or service, or a well-run, cost-effective company with a sound capital structure. It also requires an effective strategy to manage your ecosystem.

This was Blackberry's failure, leading it to be sold as a last-ditched effort to revive it. Things looked very different in 2007. The problem is that the company had become complacent about its remarkably loyal customers and didn't recognise the threat posed by rival ecosystems. Like many established firms before it, BlackBerry blew the chance to become a nodal player and leverage the energies of its complementors, in the way that Apple does with its apps.

But incumbents don't always have to lose in the game of value capture. So BlackBerry's demise isn't just another illustration of an industry leader eclipsed by upstarts. By playing their cards right, incumbents may be able to sustain their position and both create a value proposition that will appeal to the end customer, and keep their suppliers and complementors in check. Value migration has its own rules.

SHAPING THE EXPERIENCE

In the July 2013 *Harvard Business Review,* Wharton's John Paul MacDuffie and I report the results from our research on how value migrates in industry ecosystems. We consider why in sectors such as the computers of the 1980s value can migrate from the former integrated firms, giants such as IBM, to the new specialists that spring up in the industry ecosystem, such as Microsoft and Intel, and see what makes the "bottleneck," the core of the system's value, shift around in the sector.

We then look at why other sectors, such as automobiles, despite the hype, expectations of change and value chain reconfiguration, have been remarkably stable. Despite the massive outsourcing that has happened in cars, value appropriation (in terms of share of market capitalisation in the ecosystem) still rests with car manufacturers and not the ever-growing component makers.

Our research offers an explanation about what drives value to move or not.

MANAGING DIFFERENTIABILITY

We find that firms that succeed are those that proactively manage the structure of their sectors and keep a set of suppliers working for them in hierarchical, closed supplier networks. IBM made the mistake of opening up its sector through a set of standards that ultimately led to its demise, whereas today's Apple has a carefully controlled set of suppliers and complementary players to support its value proposition.

The solution is not to be vertically integrated but, rather, to control by managing differentiability, ie being the actor along the value chain who guarantees the product quality and shapes the experience—as well as managing the replaceability of other actors along the value chain. Automobile manufacturers have kept the lion's share of the sector as they managed to control the sector and shape the experience.

Bain & Company famously predicted in the 1990s that cars would soon look like computers, with giant suppliers ruling the sector. Yet this doesn't look likely to us. Rather than seeing the car industry go the way of the computer, Apple is now pushing the computer sector to increasingly resemble cars: hierarchical, tightly managed supplier networks, a keen eye for technology integration, a focus on the differentiation in the eyes of the final customer. Apple, unlike BlackBerry, hasn't just grasped the importance of a solid value proposition; it is focused on managing the ecosystem and bringing value its way.

Of course, life always looks easier when you're the kingpin of the ecosystem. What's exciting is to consider not only how successful kingpins can defend their position, but also how upstarts might upset the sector. By becoming go-to outsourcees, leveraging the need of incumbents to save on assets, and patiently moving up the food chain to become solutions providers, or by carefully managing the standards game to gain a toehold in broader markets, aspiring entrants may emulate the shift of firms like Huawei or Hon Hai from subassemblers to industrial giants.

"Unlike BlackBerry, Apple has focused on managing the ecosystem and bringing value its way."

There is no denying that strategy has become more complicated, and that it's far easier to analyse than engage in real-time problem solution. But if we start looking more carefully at what drives the movement of value in our industries we may be able to rethink our strategies before it gets to be too late to respond.

Dynamic Capabilities: Routines versus Entrepreneurial Action

David J. Teece
University of California at Berkeley

INTRODUCTION

I focus this short note on the role of individual executives in the dynamic capabilities framework. Unlike ordinary capabilities, certain dynamic capabilities may be based on the skills and knowledge of one or a few executives rather than on organizational routines.

The thesis advanced here is that, in both large and small enterprises, entrepreneurial (managerial) capitalism is required to establish and sustain superior financial performance. This entrepreneurial management involves not merely the practice and improvement of existing routines or even the creation of new ones. In dynamically competitive enterprises, there is also a critical role for the entrepreneurial manager in both transforming the enterprise and shaping the ecosystem through *sui generis* strategic acts that neither stem from routines (or algorithms) nor need give rise to new routines.

DYNAMIC CAPABILITIES

Dynamic capabilities are higher-level competences that determine the firm's ability to integrate, build, and reconfigure internal and external resources/competences to address, and possibly shape, rapidly changing business environments (Teece, 2007, 2010; Teece et al., 1990, 1997). They determine the speed at, and degree to which, the firm's particular resources can be aligned and realigned to match the requirements and opportunities of the business environment so as to generate sustained abnormal (positive) returns. The alignment of resources both inside and outside the firm includes assessing when and how the enterprise ought to form alliances with other organizations.

Dynamic capabilities have grown in importance as the expansion of trade has led to both greater specialization and more rapid competitive responses. To make the global system of vertical specialization and cospecialization work, there is an enhanced need for the business enterprise to develop and maintain asset alignment capabilities that enable collaborating firms to combine assets so as to deliver value to customers.

Dynamic capabilities can usefully be thought of as falling into three clusters of activities and adjustments: (1) identification and assessment of an opportunity *(sensing);* (2) mobilization of resources to address an opportunity and to capture value from doing so *(seizing);* and (3) continued renewal *(transforming).* These activities must be performed expertly if the firm is to sustain itself as markets and technologies change, although some firms will be stronger than others in performing some or all of these tasks.

Dynamic capabilities are "strategic" and distinct from ordinary capabilities. Firms can maintain and extend competitive advantage by layering dynamic capabilities on top of ordinary capabilities.

A firm's ordinary capabilities, if well honed, enable it to perform efficiently its current activities. However, dynamic capabilities, when combined with a good strategy (Rumelt, 2011), enable the enterprise to position itself for making the right products and targeting the right markets to address the consumer needs and the technological and competitive opportunities of the future. Dynamic capabilities help the organization (especially its top management) to develop conjectures, to validate or reject them, and to realign assets as required.

Strong dynamic capabilities are critical to success, especially when an innovating firm needs to pioneer a market, or a new product category. Dynamic capabilities, particularly those resting on entrepreneurial competences, are important to the market creating (and co-creating) processes associated with capitalist economic systems.[1]

ROUTINES, CAPABILITIES, AND IDIOSYNCRATIC ACTION

Ordinary capabilities are perhaps rooted more firmly in routines than are dynamic capabilities. A routine is a repeated action sequence, which may have its roots in algorithms and heuristics about how the enterprise is to get things done. Organizational routines, including those related to organizational transformation, transcend the individuals involved, although the routines can, for some purposes, be usefully studied as developed and embedded in the minds of multiple employees (see, e.g. Miller et al., 2012).

Capabilities change over time. Although most underlying routines tend towards stability/inertia, they can, under conditions of moderate turbulence in the environment, adapt, as suggested by the model of Pentland et al. (2012).

Capabilities are built not just on individual skills but also on the collective learning derived from how employees have worked together, as well as on special equipment or facilities to which the firm has access. The longer an organization has been around, and the larger it is, the less its capabilities depend on particular individuals. The risk of extreme dependence on founders usually dissipates after 5 to 10 years, the length of time being a function of the industry and the particulars of the business.

The literature has identified a plethora of particular routines that constitute the underpinnings and microfoundations of capabilities. For instance, Eisenhardt and Martin (2000) identify cross-functional R&D teams, new product development routines, quality control routines, technology transfer and/or knowledge transfer routines, and certain performance measurement systems as important elements of dynamic capabilities.

Winter (2003) approaches dynamic capabilities as being rooted in higher level change routines that require investment and must be maintained. He differentiates dynamic capabilities from ad hoc problem solving, but this may sometimes be a false dichotomy.

Teece (2007) identifies a comprehensive portfolio of microfoundations (building blocks) for dynamic capabilities that include change routines (e.g. product development along a known trajectory) and analytical methodologies (e.g. investment choices). Fast-moving competitive environments require continuously modifying, and, if necessary, completely revamping what the enterprise is doing so as to maintain a good fit with (and sometimes to transform) the ecosystem that the enterprise occupies.

Responding to—or instigating—change in the business environment involves diagnosing the structure of any new challenges and then choosing an overall guiding policy that builds on the firm's existing competitive advantage (see Rumelt, 2011). The dynamic capabilities that make it possible to succeed in this endeavour involve good strategizing as well as good execution. Creative managerial and entrepreneurial acts (e.g. creating new markets) are, by their nature, strategic and non-routine, even though there may be underlying principles that guide the choices.

Enterprise-level dynamic capabilities, in other words, consist of more than an aggregation of routines. Routines identify how projects are run, but not necessarily how projects are identified, prioritized, and selected. For example, strategizing and asset orchestration (identifying complementarities, buying or building missing assets and then aligning them) can only be routinized in a limited sense. Many strategic actions and transformations require actions that one may never replicate.

Although some elements of dynamic capabilities may be embedded in the organization, the capability for evaluating and prescribing changes to the configuration of assets (both within and external to the organization) rests on the shoulders of top management.[2] It is not by accident that, in the marketplace for professional services, there are turnaround CEOs and other turnaround specialists. This reflects either that some companies have failed to build change routines, or perhaps that these capacities lie outside the organization because they are perceived as being needed only occasionally. It is impossible (or prohibitively expensive) to keep full-scale transformational capacities resident inside the organization. There are almost no studies of which this author is aware directly on this topic, which makes it an obvious candidate for future research.

As noted, it is often extremely difficult, if not impossible, to routinize change beyond recognizing shared principles that should be adhered to in order to deal with it. Any routines underlying the enterprise's dynamic capabilities need to be tied to real-time knowledge creation and general enough to avoid overly focusing managerial attention on the lessons of the past (Eisenhardt and Martin, 2000). Even in less volatile settings, rules and procedures are likely to require constant revamping if superior performance is to be sustained. It is often difficult to routinize such activities partially, let alone in their entirety.

The thesis here is that top management's entrepreneurial and leadership skills around sensing, seizing, and transforming are required to sustain dynamic capabilities. Put differently, an important managerial function—perhaps the most important—is to achieve semi-continuous asset orchestration and renewal, including the redesign of routines. Periodic, if not continuous, asset orchestration (i.e. asset alignment, coalignment, realignment, and redeployment) is necessary to minimize internal conflict and to maximize complementarities inside and outside the enterprise.

The entrepreneurial management required for a business to possess dynamic capabilities is different but related to other managerial activity. Entrepreneurship is about sensing and understanding opportunities, getting things started, and finding new and better ways of putting things together. It is about creatively coordinating the assembly of disparate and usually cospecialized elements. Entrepreneurial management has little to do with standardized analysis and optimization. It is more about figuring out the next big opportunity or challenge and how to address it—rather than maintaining and refining existing procedures.

We have come to associate entrepreneurship with the individual who starts a new business that provides a new or improved product or service. However, it is important to recognize that the entrepreneurial management function embedded in dynamic capabilities is not confined to start-up activities and to individual actors. It is associated with a new hybrid: entrepreneurial managerial capitalism.

Entrepreneurial managerial capitalism involves calibrating opportunities and diagnosing threats, directing (and redirecting) resources according to a policy or plan of action, and possibly also reshaping organizational structures and systems so that they create and address technological opportunities and competitive threats. Argote and Ren (2012) show how this transformational capability resides in part on an organization's existing transactive memory systems and, presumably, other social relations within the organization, as advocated by Hodgson (2012).

THE RELEVANCE OF CORPORATE HISTORIES

The study of individual corporate histories is an avenue for research and, in particular, for understanding the origins of capabilities and for assessing evidence on whether higher-level dynamic capabilities can usefully be thought of as being rooted in routines. Apple is a case in point.

At Apple, former CEO Steve Jobs was legendary for driving his engineers to high achievement (Kahney, 2008). Jobs' presence has been seen as critical to the success of Apple. Epochs when he was present can be compared with those when he was absent (providing a degree of controlled or natural experiment). His great importance to the enterprise is consistent with Apple's declining performance after he was ousted as CEO in 1985, and with the firm's stellar performance since his return in 1997. Under his leadership, Apple was transformed from a computer company called Apple Computer to a personal computer, mobile communications, and media distribution company, now called simply Apple.

Jobs took a deep personal role in innovation at Apple. In an interview (Burrows, 2004) about product development at Apple, Jobs described it as a mixture of creativity and routines:

> . . . there is no system. That doesn't mean we don't have process. Apple is a very disciplined company, and we have great processes. But that's not what it's about. Process makes you more efficient. But innovation comes from people meeting up in the hallways or

> calling each other at 10:30 at night with a new idea, or because they realized something that shoots holes in how we've been thinking about a problem. It's ad hoc meetings of six people called by someone who thinks he has figured out the coolest new thing ever and who wants to know what other people think of his idea. And it comes from saying no to 1000 things to make sure we don't get on the wrong track or try to do too much. We're always thinking about new markets we could enter, but it's only by saying no that you can concentrate on the things that are really important.

Jobs' description succinctly illustrates the theories advanced here. He seemed to say that, while Apple's ordinary capabilities are based in processes, its product development is several parts routine but at least one part "something else." The something else is non-routine strategizing and entrepreneurial activity, some of which might appear rather ad hoc. Apple's success appears to have stemmed in part from Jobs' prioritization of possibilities based on his deep understanding of the market and an uncompromising insistence on ease of use and appealing design. This approach can be routinized to some extent (the organization comes to know what Steve likes) but Apple and its customers unquestionably benefited from the touch of a creative and brilliant conceiver of new (categories of) electronics products that appeal to consumers around the world.

As Apple's history suggests, there are, of course, risks in relying on a particular talented individual, especially if those talents don't translate into a set of replicable internal routines. Jobs himself was aware of this. In 2008, before his second medical leave, he established an internal business school in which academics were brought in to prepare cases about how key past decisions, such as the creation of the Apple Store, were reached (Lashinsky, 2011). By having executives teach these cases to the company's managers, Apple's high-level routines and top management processes are propagated among its current and future leaders.

Some individual talents, or "traits," can, over time, be embedded in corporate culture and organizational routines either formally (Apple University) or by repeated demonstration and communication. In the case of sensing capabilities, for example, the more desirable approach in many cases is to embed scanning and interpretive processes throughout the organization, while providing the necessary feedback channels to top management. This approach will not always be optimal. As shown by Turner and Fern (2012), an established routine can adapt to certain types of contextual change, but can be a source of inertia at other times of turbulence.

Any enterprise will be vulnerable if the sensing, creative, interpretive, and learning functions are left to the cognitive capacities of a few individuals. In a clear example of an endeavour to embed sensing and seizing deep into the organization, IBM has successfully routinized its selection, evaluation, and exploitation of "emerging business opportunities" in a process that has resulted in billions of dollars in additional revenue (O'Reilly et al., 2009). Similarly, Cisco has routinized its selection and integration of acquisition targets (Mayer and Kenney, 2004).

Routinized procedures such as those at IBM and Cisco can help management teams to look beyond a narrow search horizon tied to established competences (Levitt and March, 1988). Business history is replete with examples of companies that faced major problems from becoming trapped in their deeply ingrained assumptions, information filters, and problem solving strategies, including General Motors, Digital Equipment, and IBM (in the 1980s) (Henderson, 1994). Their legacy routines and assumptions over time become maladapted. The question is whether (1) they could have had change routines that would have automated their transformation, or (2) their CEOs simply failed at the tasks of diagnosing the challenges and effectuating needed transformation that couldn't reasonably have been routinized.

CONCLUSION

The importance of routines to ordinary capabilities is undisputed. For dynamic capabilities, the respective roles of routines and particular (non-routine) action by top management offer a rich and important area for research. Even though managers are often called on to strategize and to implement change, the manner in which this occurs can hardly be considered entirely routine. Indeed, the existence of an industry of restructuring and change consultants, and of so-called "transformational CEOs," challenges the notion that all dynamic capabilities can be reduced to firm-specific routines, at least in the manner that some have suggested (e.g. Eisenhardt and Martin, 2000; Feldman and Pentland, 2003; Zollo and Winter, 2002).

Another of the determinants of whether or not the decisions of individual managers and a firm's dynamic capabilities are mediated by "patterned" routines may be firm size, as suggested by the IBM example above. A smaller firm might lack the organizational and technological slack to repetitively evaluate potential opportunities.

The study of managerial dynamic capabilities is challenging because they are often tied to complex corporate histories. Although managerial dynamic capabilities can to some extent be traced by using large datasets (e.g. Adner and Helfat, 2003), they can best be analysed through in-depth qualitative research (e.g. Danneels, 2011). This empirical literature is still at an early stage and opportunities abound to dig deeper into the linkages between individual or small-group managerial actions, dynamic capabilities, and long-run firm performance. The research paradigm of dynamic capabilities is still relatively new. Accordingly, illuminating case studies—hinted at in the history of Apple since its founding—are likely to yield powerful insights.

ENDNOTES

[1] The entrepreneurial creation and co-creation of markets is often required to ensure the generation and appropriability of returns from innovation (Pitelis and Teece, 2009). The internet keeps generating a myriad of such requirements every day.

[2] However, governance structures (e.g. the composition of boards of directors) will play an important role in selecting and, to some extent, monitoring top management.

REFERENCES

Adner, R. and Helfat, C. E. (2003). "Corporate effects and dynamic managerial capabilities." *Strategic Management Journal,* 24, 1011–25.

Argote, L. and Ren, Y. (2012). "Transactive memory systems: a micro foundation of dynamic capabilities." *Journal of Management Studies,* 49, 1375–82.

Burrows, P. (2004). "The seed of Apple's innovation." *businessweek.com* (12 October). Available at http://www.businessweek.com/print/bwdaily/dnflash/oct2004/nf20041012_4018_db083.htm?chan=gl (accessed 24 March 2010).

Danneels, E. (2011). "Trying to become a different type of company: dynamic capability at Smith Corona." *Strategic Management Journal,* 32, 1–31.

Eisenhardt, K. M. and Martin, J. A. (2000). "Dynamic capabilities: what are they?" *Strategic Management Journal,* 21, 1105–21.

Feldman, M. S. and Pentland, B. T. (2003). "Reconceptualizing organizational routines as a source of flexibility and change." *Administrative Science Quarterly,* 48, 94–118.

Henderson, R. M. (1994). "Managing innovation in the information age." *Harvard Business Review,* 72, 100–6.

Hodgson, G. M. (2012). "The mirage of microfoundations." *Journal of Management Studies,* 49, 1389–95.

Kahney, L. (2008). *Inside Steve's Brain.* New York: Portfolio.

Lashinsky, A. (2011). "How Apple works: inside the world's biggest startup." *Fortune* (online date 25 August). Available at http://tech.fortune.cnn.com/2011/08/25/how-apple-works-inside-the-worlds-biggest-startup/ (accessed 24 December 2011).

Levitt, B. and March, J. G. (1988). "Organizational learning." *Annual Review of Sociology,* 14, 319–40.

Mayer, D. and Kenney, M. (2004). "Economic action does not take place in a vacuum: understanding Cisco's acquisition and development strategy." *Industry and Innovation,* 11, 299–325.

Miller, K. D., Pentland, B. T. and Choi, S. (2012). "Dynamics of performing and remembering organizational routines." *Journal of Management Studies,* 49, 1536–58.

O'Reilly, C. A., Harreld, J. B. and Tushman, M. L. (2009). "Organizational ambidexterity: IBM and emerging business opportunities." *California Management Review,* 51, 75–99.

Pentland, B. T., Feldman, M. S., Becker, M. C. and Liu, P. (2012). "Dynamics of organizational routines: a generative model." *Journal of Management Studies,* 49, 1484–508.

Pitelis, C. N. and Teece, D.J. (2009). "The (new) nature and essence of the firm." *European Management Review,* 6, 5–15.

Rumelt, R. P. (2011). *Good Strategy, Bad Strategy: The Difference and Why It Matters.* New York: Crown Business.

Teece, D. J. (2007). "Explicating dynamic capabilities: the nature and microfoundations of (sustainable) enterprise performance." *Strategic Management Journal,* 28, 1319–50.

Teece, D. J. (2010). "Technological innovation and the theory of the firm: the role of enterprise-level knowledge, complementarities, and (dynamic) capabilities." In Rosenberg, N. and Hall, B. (Eds), *Handbook of the Economics of Innovation,* Vol. 1. Amsterdam: North-Holland 1, 679–730.

Teece, D. J., Pisano, G. and Shuen, A. (1990). "Firm capabilities, resources, and the concept of strategy." Center for Research in Management. University of California, Berkeley, CCC Working Paper 90–8.

Teece, D. J., Pisano, G. and Shuen, A. (1997). "Dynamic capabilities and strategic management." *Strategic Management Journal,* 18, 509–33.

Turner, S. F. and Fern, M. J. (2012). "Examining the stability and variability of routine performances: the effects of experience and context change." *Journal of Management Studies,* 49, 1407–34.

Winter, S. G. (2003). "Understanding dynamic capabilities." *Strategic Management Journal,* 24, 991–5.

Zollo, M. and Winter, S. G. (2002). "Deliberate learning and the evolution of dynamic capabilities." *Organization Science,* 13, 339–51.

READING 08 

Meta-SWOT: Introducing a New Strategic Planning Tool

Ravi Agarwal
St Norbert College, Wisconsin

Wolfgang Grassl
St Norbert College, Wisconsin

Joy Pahl
St Norbert College, Wisconsin

INTRODUCTION

SWOT analysis is widely taught and seemingly intuitive, but it is has come under serious criticism on theoretical grounds. Critics maintain that it relies on subjective intuitions, is unsystematic, eschews quantification, and lacks predictive power. Its use as a stand-alone tool instead of a model for situational analysis as part of a more comprehensive toolset for strategy development has also been criticized (Fehringer, 2007). In a comparative evaluation of 24 techniques used for strategic analysis, SWOT does not rank highly (Fleisher and Bensoussan, 2002). Not surprisingly, there is evidence that managers make little use of it as a planning tool in business practice. A survey of more than 100 managers reveals significant distrust of the method (Finnegan, 2010). According to a study based on 212 interviews with executives of *Fortune* 1000 companies, SWOT analysis actually harms performance (Menon *et al.*, 1999). Some scholars deny that SWOT analysis serves any useful purpose at all (Hill and Westbrook, 1997; Armstrong, 1984). Another study regards the process as so flawed that it required a "product recall" (Hill and Westbrook, 1997).

Yet the basic intuition behind SWOT analysis appears to be sound. It assumes that successful strategies are based on a good fit between internal resources and external possibilities. Distinctive capabilities and competencies of organizations must "hook onto" factors in the political, economic, social, technological, and regulatory environments that require and support such competencies. There is much evidence that a strong fit between context and resources positively impacts performance (Drazin and Van de Ven, 1985; Lukas *et al.,* 2001; Venkatraman and Prescott, 1990; Zajac *et al.,* 2000; Garlichs, 2011). Reactions by strategic planning experts to the limitations of SWOT analysis have therefore been of two types: some simply ignore it as a useful tool in favor of other approaches whereas others have attempted to make it more "rigid" and increase its validity and usefulness for organizational purposes.

This paper takes the second approach and seeks to develop the basic model of SWOT into a decision-support tool. The criterion of strategic fit will be preserved but embedded into a new model of planning. What must be discarded is the rigid classification of external factors into opportunities or threats and of internal factors into strengths or weaknesses, in favor of decisions on a scale. The new approach still requires judgments, but these no longer have to be made in a categorical sense, for example by classifying a factor as either a weakness or a strength. Rather, such judgments allow for gradations and comparative evaluation. What must also be improved is the unsystematic, *ad hoc* generation

Ravi Agarwal, Wolfgang Grassl, and Joy Pahl, "Meta-SWOT: Introducing a New Strategic Planning Tool," *Journal of Business Strategy,* 33, no. 2 (2012), pp. 12–21.

of factors considered in strategy formulation. An ordered process is necessary, and it shall be driven by a seminal idea: available resources in an organization determine suitable markets more often than given conditions in the business environment allow for the creation of successful strategies to capture them. This is a key insight of the resource-based view of the firm. The new method of planning thus relies on a more structured approach, facilitates analysis with competitors, and guides decision-makers in a seamless process of data elicitation to a list of prioritized strategic objectives that are consistent with the mission of the organization. It is implemented in a tool that has been named Meta-SWOT.[1]

"According to experts, the quality standards for strategic planning techniques can be summarized in the acronym 'FAROUT.' They must be future-oriented, accurate, resource-efficient, objective, useful, and timely."

META-SWOT: THE THEORETICAL RATIONALE

Approaches to strategic planning can be classified into outside-in and inside-out models, depending on whether the resources and capabilities of an organization or its micro- and macro-environments are considered the levers from which to start. For decades, the industrial organization model that economists developed in the 1930s dominated thinking about strategy. It assumed that economic structure (or the factors that define the competitiveness of the market) determines the conduct of firms, which in turn determines the performance of an industry (or its success in generating profits and growth). Strategy formulation was outside-in, basically as a process of adaptation to opportunities in the environment. However, much research, including new thinking in economics, together with the business experience of the last several decades, has raised the question of whether internal factors must always adapt to external ones. Must decision-makers really take a specific business environment as given and devise strategies to capture perceived opportunities in order to be successful? Many relevant studies can be summarized by saying that market-share objectives harmed profits and put the survival of firms at risk (Armstrong and Collopy, 1996; Armstrong and Green, 2007). On the contrary, business history shows that some of the most successful companies—one need only think of the Hudson's Bay Company, Red Bull, or Google—have not merely adapted to a given context but have instead created markets and shaped their competitive environments. Based on this insight, the resource-based view (RBV) assumes that successful organizations are driven by their distinctive capabilities and competencies, and that a firm's resources are therefore more critical to the determination of strategic action than is its external environment. This approach takes an inside-out view of strategy. After all, the situation of an organization is better known to planners, and internal data are usually more readily available: "the RBV is an inside-out perspective on organizations that seeks to identify the characteristics of firms with superior performance" (Rouse and Daellenbach, 2002, p. 966). The guiding idea is "build on your strengths" rather than "catch a star—if you can," for by the time organizations have tooled up for the catch, the star may already have fallen. SWOT analysis only matches current strengths and weaknesses with current opportunities and threats, which may have worked decades ago but no longer fulfills the needs of a much more dynamic and volatile business climate.

The RBV understands each firm as a unique bundle of resources typically in three categories: tangible assets, intangible assets, and capabilities (Galbreath and Galvin, 2004). Tangible assets (e.g. financial and physical) and intangible assets are resources that a firm has (e.g. intellectual property, organizational assets, reputation), and capabilities are what a firm can do (e.g. its know-how). Resources and capabilities thus are different constructs (Amit and Schoemaker, 1993). Resources are tradable and non-specific to the firm whereas capabilities are firm-specific (because they reside in people) and are used to engage the resources within the firm. For our purposes, strict distinctions between resources and capabilities are not necessary (Conner, 1991; Barney, 1991). Neither do we need to distinguish "strategic" resources from others, since most resources are in fact easily imitable or tradable. It is understood that some capabilities are of a more complex nature and are created by combining less complex resources and capabilities. In the RBV, these resources and capabilities are the key determinants of competitive advantage, and strategic planning must start with them.

One challenge of course remains: how can a firm identify which of these resources and capabilities are capable of creating a sustainable competitive advantage? Barney (1991) sets forth four criteria for resolving this question. In order for a resource or capability to be strategically beneficial it must be valuable, rare, inimitable, and non-substitutable. Similarly, Prahalad and Hamel argue that in order to determine whether a capability constitutes a core competence—a basis for a firm's competitive advantage—the capability must grant the firm "potential access to a wide variety of markets" and must significantly enhance the benefits of the final product or service as perceived by customers (Prahalad and Hamel, 1990, p. 83). These two criteria together define if a resource or capability is "valuable." The other tests are that a resource or capability must be rare relative to demand for it, difficult for competitors to imitate, and (as a special case of inimitability) not be substitutable by another resource or capability that competitors might develop. Firms must also be able to capture these advantages in order to be successful.

Four criteria then define the potential of resources and capabilities for creating successful strategy. Within the RBV, they are known as the VRIO conditions (Barney, 1991):

- *V (value).* Does the resource or capability enable a firm to exploit an environmental opportunity and/or neutralize an environmental threat?
- *R (rare).* Is this resource or capability currently controlled by only a small number of competing firms?
- *I (inimitable).* Do firms without this resource or capability face a cost disadvantage in obtaining or developing it?
- *O (organization).* Are a firm's policies and procedures organized to support the exploitation of its valuable, rare, and costly-to-imitate resources and capabilities?

In this perspective, an organization must turn to its internal resources and capabilities to guide its strategy process if it hopes to successfully navigate an increasingly turbulent external environment. Scanning of the external environment then always takes place against the background of existing internal factors. Yet conditions in the business environment still determine which resources and capabilities can be leveraged to capture opportunities or alleviate threats:

> *Nothing is a strength or a weakness except vis-à-vis the competition* (Mooradian *et al.*, 2012, p. 224; italics in the original).

In other words, strategists cannot judge the relative merit or strategic value of a particular internally controlled resource or capability in isolation from their assessment of the external environment, for every internal factor either supports or does not support a potential in the environment by allowing for it to be captured. But planning must start with what an organization has and can do, not with a random search for opportunities in the business environment. The VRIO criteria then prioritize these resources and capabilities with a view to capturing the right external factors in formulating dynamic strategies (Warren, 2008, pp. 89ff.). In this sense, the proposed approach to strategic planning is really an inside-out-inside model. Successful planning, after all, is not a linear but an iterative process.

However, not all resources and capabilities that can be successfully leveraged must already exist; organizational development allows for the extension of existing factors or the creation of new ones. The RBV suggests a possible trade-off between investing in existing core competencies and investing in capabilities that could become core competencies in the future. It has been described as the "sustainability-attainability dilemma" (Miller, 2003). A resource or capability that meets the VRIO criteria will be sustainable by the firm that currently possesses the resource, but it will also be hard, if not impossible, to attain others. Therefore practitioners are left with a problem: if inimitability is the key to achieving a competitive advantage, how can their firm act to create such advantage with resources and capabilities it does not already have? The answer may lie in a firm's ability to build on its asymmetries. These are processes, skills, and assets that are unique to the firm, non-substitutable, and inimitable; competitors cannot copy these asymmetries at a cost that will allow them to earn economic rents. The one criterion that is thereby relaxed is "valuable." Firms are able to "reconceptualize" these asymmetries by

"In order for a resource or capability to be strategically beneficial it must be valuable, rare, inimitable, and non-substitutable."

"The deficiencies of SWOT analysis have prompted to improve it and others to discard it as a method for crafting strategy."

creating organizational processes and designs that can realize the untapped value in them, and in doing so are able to match them to market opportunities. This discovery is important because it adds a crucial innovative quality to the RBV. Meta-SWOT assists decision makers in discovering these asymmetries and in recognizing how they may become valuable to the organization in the future.

Resources and capabilities are then evaluated according to the VRIO framework on rarity, inimitability and organization. The "valuable" criterion is not assessed in the process until the resource in question is matched to the external environment. This is because by definition the "value" of a resource resides in its ability to exploit opportunities or neutralize threats in the external environment, and it thus operationalizes the idea of strategic fit (Barney, 1991).

Relevant factors in the business environment are then identified independently of the internal analysis. Political, economic, socio-cultural, technological, ecological, and legal (PESTEL) factors need to be considered (Carpenter and Sanders, 2007, p. 91). They are judged according to their expected impact, the probability that these trends will increase, and the perceived urgency for the organization to address them. This assessment now allows for judgments about strategic fit, i.e. about how well resources and capabilities support opportunities or alleviate threats in the environment. No classification into opportunities and threats is undertaken, in order to avoid the circularity of reasoning that is typical of SWOT analysis, which often categorizes as opportunities those environmental forces which match an internal strength. Since strategy needs to address both opportunities and threats, only the ability of given resources and capabilities to deal with either is deemed relevant.

Lastly, the idea of strategic fit is also operationalized by judging the degree to which resources and capabilities support organizational objectives. These judgments then automatically generate a list of pairs between resources or capabilities and environmental factors that are closest and of overriding importance. The most serious limitation of the model is of course that combinations between an internal and an external factor may be generated by accident but not have any real bearing on each other. The judgment of decision-makers is indispensable here, but it comes in only at the end of the structured process. Factor combinations can be dropped from the list and other factor pairs rearranged according to perceived priority. The outcome is a prioritized list of strategic priorities that depends on all the previous assessments. According to the logic of RBV, the strength of resources or capabilities, and their strategic fit with environmental factors, is prioritized over the strength of these factors alone. This appears to be a crucial advantage over SWOT analysis.

META-SWOT: THE METHOD AND TOOL

General

According to experts, the quality standards for strategic planning techniques can be summarized in the acronym "FAROUT." They must be future-oriented, accurate, resource-efficient, objective, useful, and timely (Fleisher and Bensoussan, 2002). These criteria informed the method used in developing Meta-SWOT, which is implemented in an Excel workbook consisting of a title sheet and seven interconnected worksheets. Its purpose is to guide decision-makers in a seamless process from an initial phase of brainstorming to the generation of a ranked list of strategic priorities. The tool allows for unlimited revisions of inputs, as decision-makers change their assessment in the course of a planning exercise. The method can easily be replicated on spreadsheets.

All questions are asked about the organization for which a strategy is to be developed rather than about its competitors. Assessment of internal and external factors by way of multifactor scoring is a standard procedure in strategy formulation. With the exception of the question about priority levels of organizational goals, all questions are asked on a five-point scale, which appears to allow for sufficient (or even maximum) reliability (Dawes, 2008). The order of items is not of relevance (with the exception of the final prioritized strategy recommendation). The process is presented in a flow diagram (Figure 1). The case under analysis is a small specialty foods and kitchenware retailer.

Worksheets

Worksheet resources and competition collects classification data relating to the planning project and the planning horizon, and to overall organizational objectives, which can be weighted by their degrees of priority. It is assumed that organizational objectives are given or defined in the context of a strategic planning exercise. Critical success factors must then be identified that describe which resources and capabilities are required for success in the respective industry, and their relative importance is determined on a percentage weighting scale. In order to generate a map, the list of internal factors must be reduced by first identifying two overriding dimensions on

FIGURE 1 Flow Diagram of Meta-SWOT

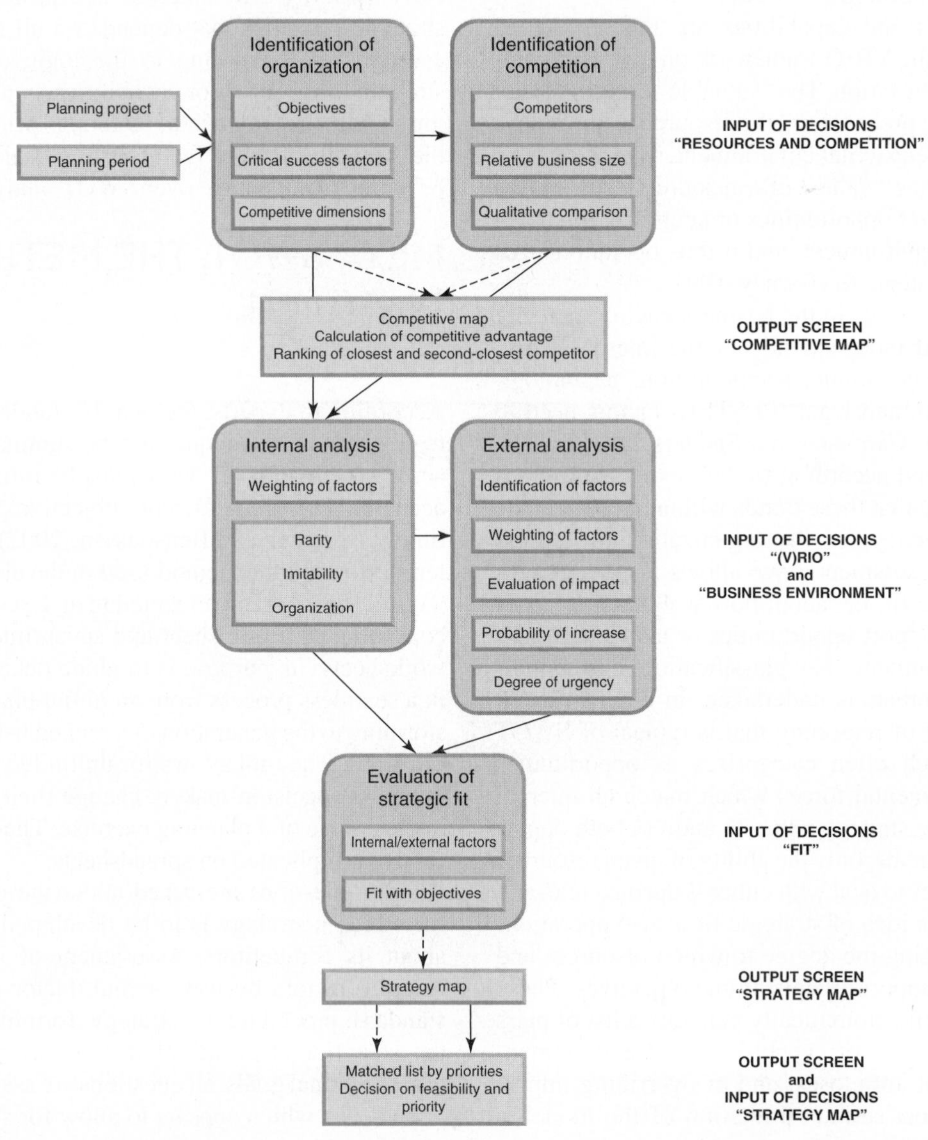

which companies in that particular industry compete and by then deciding to which of them individual resources and capabilities relate. Next, a list of competitors is generated, and the estimated sales volume of the organization in comparison with competitors (or their respective divisions) must be indicated. The perceived performance of the organization against each competitor on all resources and capabilities must be estimated on a five-point scale. Differently from SWOT analysis, internal factors are thus not generated from the mere imaginative capacity of decision-makers, but the firm is evaluated according to how well it matches what the competitive environment requires for success. Evaluation by soliciting judgments is not done for the firm in isolation but always with respect to its competitors, which again relates resources and capabilities to the competitive environment.

These decisions generate a table on a worksheet competitive map which calculates the competitive advantage of all competitors, both in absolute values and normalized to the mean of competitors, which is defined as the sum of scores achieved on the two competitive dimensions. The absolute and normalized rank order by competitive advantage is calculated, and a macro reveals the closest and second-closest competitor for the organization depending on the minimization of distance in Euclidean space. A map allows for a visualization of the competitive field as defined by the previous data input. It may be understood as a positioning map reflecting the perceptions of decision-makers (Figure 2).

The worksheet (V)RIO serves to collect data about the evaluation of resources and capabilities of the organization according to the VRIO framework (by leaving "value" to a future step). Answers about degrees of agreement are elicited to the following statements:

1. Rarity:
   - (R1) Our competitors cannot do this.
   - (R2) Our competitors do not have this.
   - (R3) Our competitors cannot acquire this.
2. Imitability:
   - (I1) Our competitors cannot copy this.
   - (I2) Our competitors cannot easily develop this.

"In a comparative evaluation of 24 techniques used for strategic analysis, SWOT does not rank highly."

FIGURE 2 Screen Shot of Competitive Map

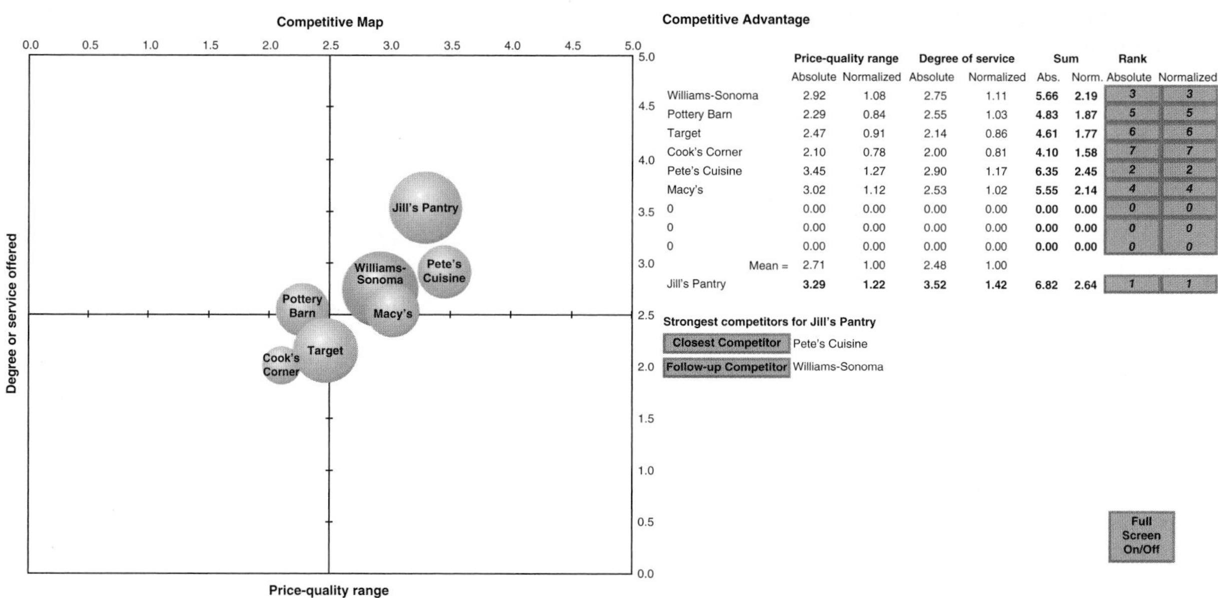

	Price-quality range		Degree of service		Sum		Rank	
	Absolute	Normalized	Absolute	Normalized	Abs.	Norm.	Absolute	Normalized
Williams-Sonoma	2.92	1.08	2.75	1.11	**5.66**	**2.19**	3	3
Pottery Barn	2.29	0.84	2.55	1.03	**4.83**	**1.87**	5	5
Target	2.47	0.91	2.14	0.86	**4.61**	**1.77**	6	6
Cook's Corner	2.10	0.78	2.00	0.81	**4.10**	**1.58**	7	7
Pete's Cuisine	3.45	1.27	2.90	1.17	**6.35**	**2.45**	2	2
Macy's	3.02	1.12	2.53	1.02	**5.55**	**2.14**	4	4
0	0.00	0.00	0.00	0.00	**0.00**	**0.00**	0	0
0	0.00	0.00	0.00	0.00	**0.00**	**0.00**	0	0
0	0.00	0.00	0.00	0.00	**0.00**	**0.00**	0	0
Mean =	2.71	1.00	2.48	1.00				
Jill's Pantry	**3.29**	**1.22**	**3.52**	**1.42**	6.82	2.64	1	1

3. Organization:

- (O1) We benefit from this factor through our reporting structure.
- (O2) We benefit from this factor through our budgeting process.
- (O3) We benefit from this factor through our compensation policy.

For some planning purposes, the three organizational items may appear of little relevance, or answers cannot be given. Choice of the "neutral" option prevents these items from influencing the aggregate average scores. Items carry equal weight, and the interval level of measurement is assumed.

The worksheet business environment elicits an identification of relevant PESTEL factors and an estimate of their relative importance. Both the statics and dynamics of the environment are assessed by deciding on the likely impact of external factors on the success of the organization (as operationalized by organizational objectives) and on the probability that these factors will increase in importance over the planning period. The degree of urgency of addressing the respective factors is assessed independently in order to avoid strong assumptions about consistency in judgments. The question about urgency introduces a time scale into the measurement exercise and facilitates the generation of prioritized strategic action steps.

The worksheet FIT asks decision-makers to decide, for each resource and capability, to which degree it relates to the important factors in the external environment. If an internal factor has no obvious bearing on an external factor, "very weakly" should be chosen. Fit is measured by the number of internal factors and how strongly they collectively match external factors. The average aggregate score represents the "value" of resources and capabilities in the VRIO model. The use of a continuous scale is expected to mitigate the problem of uncertainty in the categorization of factors into strengths or weaknesses. Lastly, the fit of resources and capabilities with organizational objectives is assessed by the degree of perceived match. It expresses the intuition that a resource may strongly correspond to an environmental factor without being very relevant for the organization.

Based on these decisions, a chart is automatically displayed on the worksheet strategy map that depicts the previous assessment and visualizes the subsequent generation of action steps. Resources and capabilities (blue bubbles) are located towards the right of the chart if they are relatively rare and inimitable and enjoy organizational fitness. They are positioned towards the upper end if they are characterized by a high degree of strategic fit; the bubble size expresses the degree of fit with objectives. The relevant factors of the business environment are plotted on the same chart, horizontal positions expressing perceived strength of impact, vertical positions expected increase, and sizes of bubbles express degrees or urgency. For both sets of data, locations in the upper-right quadrant indicate high ratings on both dimensions, and locations towards the right or the upper edge of the chart high ratings on at least one dimension of measurement. The third is the relative bubble size (Figure 3).

On the worksheet strategy development, pairs of internal and external factors are automatically generated based on three criteria: minimization of distance between the two types of factors, location maximally to the right and the upper edge, and bubble sizes. The list is subjected to judgments by decision-makers as to which combinations have a true bearing on each other such that an internal factor supports an external one. Irrelevant pairs can be dropped, and for perceived matches, three degrees of priority can be expressed. The list is then reordered to formulate the outcome of the planning exercise—a prioritized strategy.

AND SO WHAT?

The deficiencies of SWOT analysis have prompted some to improve it and others to discard it as a method for crafting strategy. Managers tend to attribute to it only a modest usefulness for actual planning exercises but still regard it as a valuable tool for structuring thought (Finnegan, 2010). Meta-SWOT therefore seeks to reinvent SWOT analysis in a substantially altered form by retaining its basic approach. The new method removes many of the shortcomings of SWOT by being more future-oriented, accurate, resource-centered, objective, useful, and timely. No longer are all factors of equal weight, since quantification at the ordinal level is possible. This allows for differentiation between factors according to their importance. The tool still relies on subjective judgment, and to some extent this will remain indispensable in strategic planning.

FIGURE 3 Worksheet Strategy Map

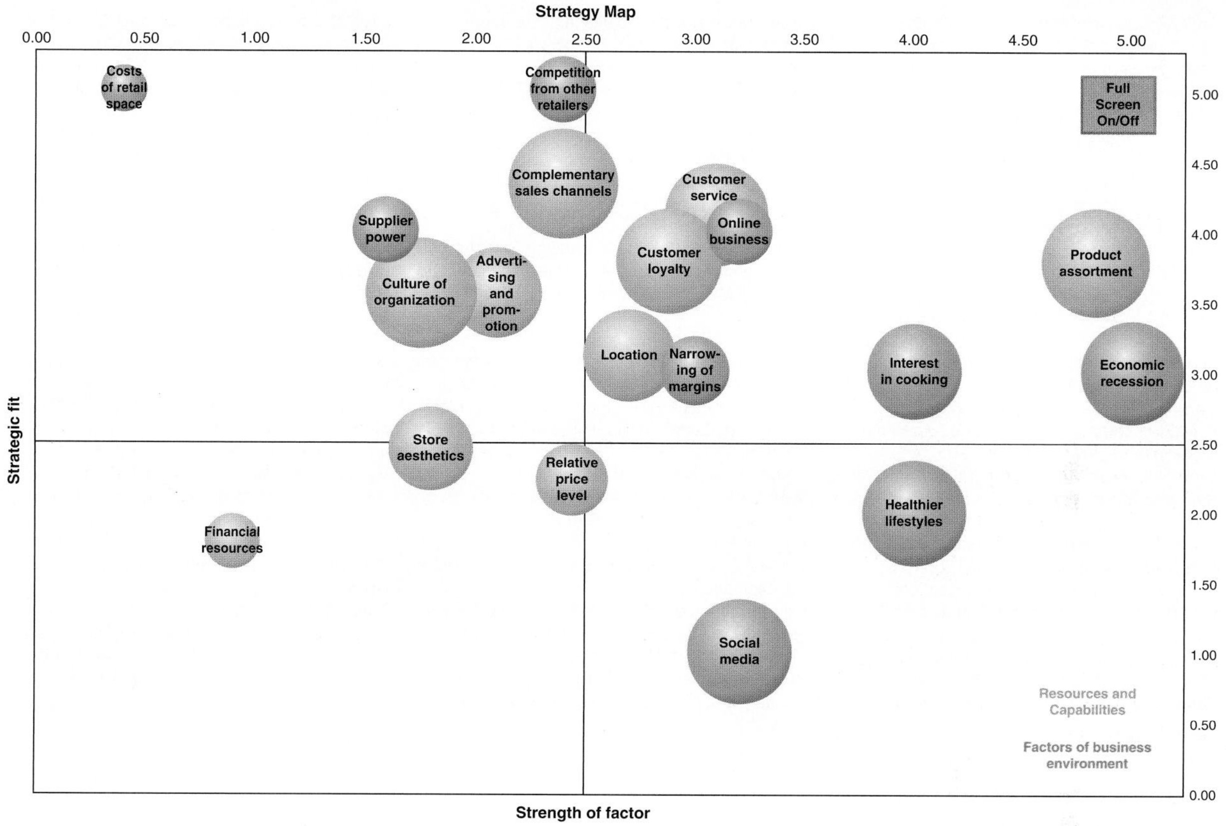

However, comparative assessment could be converted to metric measurement wherever data are available. Maybe most importantly, ideas derived from the RBV of the firm make Meta-SWOT more guided by the resources and capabilities of organizations than simply by market opportunities, without eschewing the importance of finding a good match between internal and external factors. Strategy-making is understood as a matching process driven by what an organization controls and is good at rather than by often unattainable opportunities in the business environment. Steps in a strategic action plan are prioritized by their degree of urgency or timeliness. By guiding the process of strategy formulation in a systematic and iterative fashion rather than jumping to conclusions, Meta-SWOT is a more reliable aid for decision-making than most of the alternatives proposed in the literature.

ENDNOTES

[1]The Greek preposition meta has three basic meanings that express what the new method intends to accomplish. Meta means "after" in the temporal or spatial sense, "(together) with," and in composites it signifies change (as in "metabolism" or "metaphor"). Meta-SWOT wants to change and amend SWOT analysis and in this sense replace it.

REFERENCES

Amit, R. and Schoemaker, P.J.H. (1993), "Strategic assets and organizational rent," *Strategic Management Journal,* Vol. 14 No. 1, pp. 33–46.

Armstrong, J.S. (1984), "Don't do SWOT: a note on marketing planning," available at: http://manyworlds.com/exploreco.aspx?coid=CO85041445304

Armstrong, J.S. and Collopy, F. (1996), "Competitor orientation: effects of objectives and information on managerial decisions and profitability," *Journal of Marketing Research,* Vol. 33, pp. 188–99.

Armstrong, J.S. and Green, K.C. (2007), "Competitor-oriented objectives: the myth of market share," *International Journal of Business,* Vol. 12, pp. 117–36.

Barney, J.B. (1991), "Firm resources and sustained competitive advantage," *Journal of Management,* Vol. 17, pp. 99–120.

Carpenter, M.A. and Sanders, W.G. (2007), *Strategic Management: A Dynamic Perspective,* Prentice Hall, Upper Saddle River, NJ.

Conner, K.R. (1991), "A historical comparison of resource-based view and five schools of thought within industrial organization economics," *Journal of Management,* Vol. 17, pp. 121–54.

Dawes, J. (2008), "Do data characteristics change according to the number of scale points used? An experiment using five-point, seven-point and ten-point scales," *International Journal of Market Research,* Vol. 50, pp. 61–77.

Drazin, R. and Van de Ven, A.H. (1985), "Alternative forms of fit in contingency theory," *Administrative Science Quarterly,* Vol. 30, pp. 514–39.

Fehringer, D. (2007), "Six steps to better SWOTs," *Competitive Intelligence Magazine,* Vol. 10 No. 1, pp. 54–7.

Finnegan, M.F. (2010), "Evaluating SWOT's value in creating actionable, strategic intelligence," MSc thesis, Mercyhurst College, Erie, PA.

Fleisher, C.S. and Bensoussan, B.E. (2002), *Strategic and Competitive Analysis: Methods and Techniques for Analyzing Business Competition,* Prentice Hall, Upper Saddle River, NJ.

Galbreath, J. and Galvin, P. (2004), "Which resources matter? A fine-grained test of the resource-based view of the firm," in Weaver, K.M. (Ed.), *Creating Actionable Knowledge. Academy of Management Proceedings,* pp. L1–L6.

Garlichs, M. (2011), *The Concept of Strategic Fit,* Diplomica Verlag, Hamburg.

Hill, T. and Westbrook, R. (1997), "SWOT analysis: it's time for a product recall," *Long Range Planning,* Vol. 30 No. 1, pp. 46–52.

Lukas, B.A., Tan, J.J. and Hult, J.T.M. (2001), "Strategic fit in transitional economies: the case of China's electronics industry," *Journal of Management,* Vol. 27, pp. 409–29.

Menon, A., Bharadwaj, S.G., Adidam, P.T. and Edison, S.W. (1999), "Antecedents and consequences of marketing strategy making," *Journal of Marketing,* Vol. 63 No. 2, pp. 18–40.

Miller, D. (2003), "An asymmetry-based view of advantage: towards an attainable sustainability," *Strategic Management Journal,* Vol. 24, pp. 961–76.

Mooradian, T.A., Matzler, K. and Ring, L.J. (2012), *Strategic Marketing,* Prentice Hall, Upper Saddle River, NJ.

Prahalad, C.K. and Hamel, G. (1990), "The core competence of the corporation," *Harvard Business Review,* Vol. 68 No. 3, pp. 79–91.

Rouse, M.J. and Daellenbach, U. (2002), "More thinking on research methods for the resource-based perspective," *Strategic Management Journal,* Vol. 23, pp. 963–9.

Venkatraman, N. and Prescott, J.E. (1990), "Environment-strategy coalignment: an empirical test of its performance implications," *Strategic Management Journal,* Vol. 11, pp. 1–23.

Warren, K. (2008), *Strategic Management Dynamics,* Wiley, Chichester.

Zajac, E.J., Kraatz, M.S. and Bresser, R.K. (2000), "Modeling the dynamics of strategic fit: a normative approach to strategic change," *Strategic Management Journal,* Vol. 21, pp. 429–53.

Are You Ready for the Digital Value Chain?

Rüdiger Stern
Accenture

Matthias Ziegler
Accenture

Music, books, art, maps, the ways we communicate—these and countless other things that used to be primarily physical or analog are now digital as well, and that has changed the ways we live, work, learn and play. But that is just the tip of the iceberg. Today, technology is enabling the digitization of almost everything—even manufacturing. Want your own special protective case for your mobile phone? One device manufacturer has made available digital files that will let consumers design a custom case for their phone, then have the case made on a 3D printer.

In fact, innovative examples of digitization are arising across the entire corporate value chain—not just manufacturing but also new-product development, sourcing, marketing, distribution and service (see chart, next page). Sooner or later, every company will have to deal with the impact of digitization on its business model. Innovative digital solutions can reduce costs and add value at every stage of a product's lifecycle, both within each stage of the value chain and across its entirety. Digitization enables businesses and governments to operate with greater transparency and efficiency, and it boosts consumers' access to everything from innovative products to public services.

Although the focus of media reports is often on specific examples of digitization, it is essential for businesses to see the bigger picture—the truly revolutionary possibilities available by harnessing the synergies of a fully integrated digital value chain. Companies also now need to see data management as a core competence. In the digital age, data is a strategic asset. A company's data must be able to yield the relevant information for improved or new products and services across intelligent, digital networks.

INNOVATIVE APPLICATIONS ACROSS THE DIGITAL VALUE CHAIN

How is digitization altering specific steps in the value chain, and even optimizing the makeup of the chain itself? The marketplace is seeing vibrant innovation in many specific areas; the next step will be to integrate these one-off innovations to help create an end-to-end digital value chain that creates unparalleled business opportunities.

Sourcing and Procurement: eKanban

Kanban is a scheduling system for lean and just-in-time production. For decades, Kanban has been helping companies keep inventories low by ensuring that goods and equipment arrive just before a production run begins. Today, electronic Kanban (eKanban) uses the Internet to route messages to external suppliers, providing real-time visibility into the entire supply chain. These methods can lead to a host of benefits, including lower inventory stock levels, less physical transportation, a reduction in working capital and increased liquidity.

Auto manufacturer BMW implemented an eKanban system together with Lear Corp., a supplier of car seats. Based on BMW's daily demand and supported by an enterprise resource planning

Digital Applications Can Innovate within One Part of the Overall Corporate Value Chain or Several, and May Even Lead to the Emergence of New Value Networks

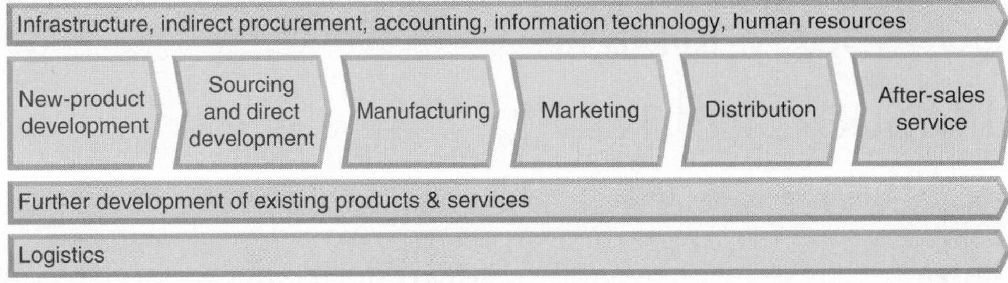

Source: Accenture Analysis.

system interface, forecast delivery schedules are sent to Lear in real time, and the supplier then has 300 minutes to produce and deliver the seats directly to the assembly line. In its first year of operation, the eKanban system produced savings of more than $82.6 million.

Manufacturing: RFID

In addition to the 3D printing innovation mentioned earlier, other digital developments are helping to make the overall supply chain more intelligent, which, in turn, makes the manufacturing process leaner and faster.

For many companies, the inability to locate a crucial component in the warehouse can jeopardize an entire assembly cycle. Today, technologies such as RFID tags are enabling organizations to transform their existing hybrid supply chain structures into more open, agile, flexible and collaborative digital models. For example, TAP Maintenance & Engineering has introduced state-of-the-art RFID technologies into its daily engine-maintenance operations. As part of the new solution, RFID ultra-high frequency labels are codified, printed and attached to the engine components undergoing maintenance. This process enables the engine-maintenance department to identify each component in all the subsequent processes, providing transparency and visibility of information that supports faster and more error-free maintenance.

Marketing: Gamification

Digital channels are enabling companies to create deeper and longer-term relationships with those who buy and use their products. Consider how 100-year-old alpine equipment company Rossignol is developing "gamification" tools as a way to move closer to its customers. Tapping into the fact that skiers and snow-boarders love to gather at the end of the day and relive their best runs, Rossignol's mobile Ski Pursuit app helps track users' daily and season-long performance. Ski Pursuit also enables skiers to share details of their statistics via Facebook and Twitter.

The companies mentioned above are important pioneers. At the same time, these function-oriented innovations are only the first step. As the industry moves forward, the more important development will be in creating truly intelligent digitized value chains.

CREATING AN INTELLIGENT VALUE CHAIN

What are the possibilities for companies when digitization does not just improve one part of the value chain but optimizes multiple aspects of it? One peek into the future is happening today at Trumpf, a German producer of intelligent machine tools and industrial laser systems. Going beyond just improving the efficiency of manufacturing, Trumpf is mining the information provided by its machines to gain deeper, actionable insights and also to network those machines together in an intelligent way to create smart factories. Connected in this way, the machines can autonomously exchange information, trigger actions and control one another.

Several advanced technologies are at the heart of the system. A cloud-based platform provides remote diagnostics. Trumpf software for production control takes the inventories and the urgency of order processing into account and allows the production status to be remotely monitored via an application. In the future, machines will be controlled using iPads, and laser lenses will be equipped with RFID chips that will signal when it's time for them to be cleaned.

IS YOUR BUSINESS READY FOR THE NEXT WAVE OF DIGITIZATION?

One important way to prepare for the coming of the digital value chain is to perform a short diagnostic, a self-assessment that can help executive decision makers plot a course toward their digital future.[1] Areas of inquiry include:

1. What impact will digitization have on your products, services, organization, processes and end-to-end value chain?
2. What opportunities do you have to leverage digital technologies such as 3D printing, eKanban or RFID in your products, services, organization and processes?
3. What steps are you taking to embed digitization into your value chain—R&D, marketing, sourcing, production and service, as well as upstream and downstream value chain processes?
4. What data will be required to optimally digitize your value chain, and what portion will come from internal vs. external sources?

All industry sectors are likely to be transformed by the increasing digitization of the value chain. Although pursuing point solutions in one part of the chain is a good start, it will also be vital to adopt an end-to-end and holistic digital mindset. That perspective can help identify the potential for intelligent products and networks across extended value chains, and help companies stay relevant to digitally empowered consumers around the world.

ENDNOTES

[1]See http://www.accenture.com/us-en/Pages/insight-why-ceo-needs-digital-vision.aspx.

Limits to Growing Customer Value: Being Squeezed between the Past and the Future

Marc Logman
Logical Management

Marketing managers often have to balance between marketing exploitation strategies (reaping value from what already is known) and marketing exploration strategies (reaping value from new sources). However, do marketing strategies once exploited or explored in a certain way or direction leave enough potential for further exploration? Based on the various cases of Apple, Alpro, Intel, Nutella, Patagonia, and Ryanair, this article shows that several risks and limits come into play when trying to answer this question. Companies may get squeezed between the past and the future while facing the pressure of temporal consistency driven by past behavior and experiencing the limits of future growth in the dominant customer value drivers. To counter this problem, companies often start integrating new value drivers in their story, leading to other risks, such as incompatibility with existing drivers. The cases discussed in this article reveal that companies may have to accept more sacrifices in order to increase returns within their growth trajectory. Value engineering will become a crucial discipline for companies to survive in many industries. This article gives a step-by-step approach on how to implement this in an organization.

1. THE RISKS AND LIMITS OF MARKETING EXPLORATION STRATEGIES

Marketing managers often have to balance between marketing exploitation strategies (reaping value from what already is known) and marketing exploration strategies (reaping value from new sources) (Kyriakopoulosa & Moorman, 2004). *Marketing exploitation strategies* are defined as strategies that primarily involve improving and refining current skills and procedures associated with existing marketing strategies. *Marketing exploration strategies* are defined as strategies that primarily involve challenging prior approaches to interfacing with the market. This means making adjacency moves beyond the core—targeting new markets/segments, changing positioning of customer value, or adjusting the marketing mix (e.g., launching new products or channels)—overall enabling the company to grow financially (Logman, 2007, 2008a; Zook, 2004).

Figure 1 summarizes the four perspectives of marketing strategy, comparing exploitation against exploration. As Figure 1 depicts, exploitation is driven by vertical thinking across the four perspectives within an existing marketing context. Exploration is driven by lateral/horizontal thinking in which an adjacency move is made in at least one of the four perspectives, creating a new context.

Focusing too much on exploitation could result in co-evolutionary lock-in, a process that increasingly ties the success of a company's strategy to that of its existing product-market environment, making it difficult to change strategic direction (Burgelman, 2002; Slotegraaf & Dickson, 2004). Sometimes

Marc Logman, "Limits to Growing Customer Value: Being Squeezed Between the Past and the Future", *Business Horizons*. 56 (2013), pp. 655–664. Reprinted with permission of Elsevier.

FIGURE 1 Marketing Strategy Components and Dynamics

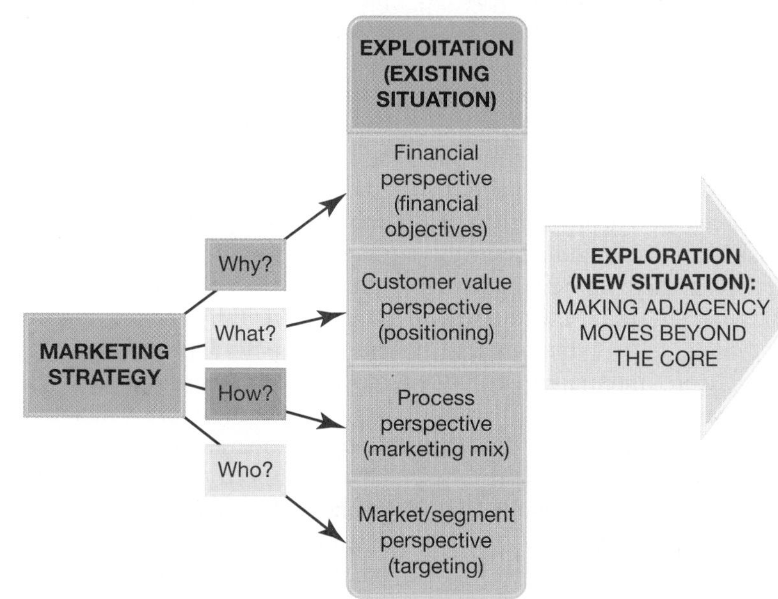

companies simply have no other choice than to leave their strict exploitative logic and move to a more explorative logic. Exploration is driven by abductive thinking in which the decision maker imagines various growth paths of what "may be" instead of sticking to what "must be" (Logman, 2011a, 2011b; Martin, 2009). For instance, although many low cost carriers (LCCs) continue enjoying rapid growth, signs indicate that the market for LCCs is becoming more limited due to increasing route density problems, primarily in Europe but seemingly also in North America. This explains why LCCs have been trying to adapt their strategies to assure future growth by shifting to primary airports, facilitating transfers, engaging in code sharing, entering alliances, and acquiring other airlines (de Wit & Zuidberg, 2012). Some pilots of LCCs such as Ryanair revealed that they are put under pressure to save fuel as much as possible, which may be at the cost of safety, although Ryanair itself denies this is the case.

Fine-tuning a business model and its associated marketing strategy over time is an important key to growth (see also Kapferer, 2012). Patagonia has recently shown how you can successfully do this. In its newest campaign, Patagonia encouraged consumers to buy less of its new apparel. However, an undercurrent of Patagonia's message is that consumers should buy high-quality apparel that will last a very long time and for which a premium price is commanded (Lowitt, 2011). From a financial perspective, the higher price may offset the potential decrease in quantity sold. Moreover, from a market/segment perspective, this strategy extends the customer basis, attracting customers who make decisions based on sustainability considerations, and attracting customers who can now sell their used Patagonia apparel for cash to buy new apparel. From a process perspective, many explorative adjacency moves can still be made, including working with retailers and consumers to recycle clothing that has been too worn to be resold and then selling the used materials back to its upstream suppliers at a lower price than comparable virgin materials. Sekerka and Stimel (2011) argue that sustainability as a value theme—as in Patagonia's case—may not be durable forever, forcing companies to change or add new customer value drivers in their story at some point in time.

In this context, a crucial question remains: Do marketing strategies once exploited or explored in a certain way or direction leave enough potential for further exploration? Based on recent cases, we will show that several risks and limits come into play when trying to answer this question. We begin with an in-depth analysis of some of Apple's strategic marketing moves. Amit and Zott (2012) revealed how Apple alters its business model as it launches new products. The timing of its launches plays a crucial role in its success. As an example, Apple launched the iPhone at a point in time when innovation was almost dead in the mobile phone industry, but after its successful launch of the iPod (the iPhone being an advancement of the iPod). Past strategic behavior forces a company to respect a certain temporal consistency of ongoing innovation, making the company highly path dependent; future strategies will be directed or even limited by past strategies (Turner, Mitchell, & Bettis, in press; Vergne & Durand, 2010). More importantly, it may leave less potential for new value paths (Garud, Kumaraswamy, & Karnøe, 2010; Gáspár, 2011). To illustrate these risks in more detail, we will rely upon two products that were recently launched by Apple: Apple Maps and the iPad mini.

2. THE RISK OF TEMPORAL INCONSISTENCY: THE CASE OF APPLE MAPS

At the Worldwide Developers Conference (WWDC) in June 2012, Apple announced that it would no longer use Google Maps, but instead would start using its own mapping system with data provided by TomTom, a Dutch manufacturer of navigation systems. This was not an obvious adjacency move beyond its core because, unlike Google, the company has no experience in geo-data. Apple's core is mainly built around its hardware (iPod, iPhone, iPad, and iTV) and its associated services/software (App Store and iTunes). Nevertheless, Apple still has a way to go to becoming an expert in cloud services, such as the Maps application. Mapping systems are built on data sets that have to be optimized and updated constantly, and from this perspective, Google has an enormous lead.

Apple's lack of experience became obvious shortly after its launch, as the maps application was criticized for misidentifying cities, incorrect icons, and even for failing to display certain locations. Tim Cook, CEO of Apple, recognized the problems and wrote a letter to apologize. This letter, addressed to Apple's customers, ended with the statement that everything Apple does is aimed at making the best products in the world. The letter exemplifies how Tim Cook mainly views Apple from a product perspective, not a customer perspective. It suggests that product innovation may become an obsessive goal and not a means to deliver customer value (Dawar, 2012). Consequently, more and more people—even some of the real Apple advocates—are starting to perceive Apple's recent moves as being too self-centered.

However, if you look at Apple's logic from another perspective, it may make more sense. The mapping functionality is becoming one of the key tools in using smartphones; and gaining more control of something that is getting a higher strategic customer value is certainly a logical explorative move, as it keeps Apple's customers from giving Google any more valuable data for their maps. Google's operating system Android, with its apps, is now the world's most commonly used smartphone platform, used by many phone manufacturers. Therefore, allowing Google to keep control of a key piece of Apple's mobile operating system iOS with its Google Maps is almost unacceptable.

Apple's temporary shortcomings can make sense, as they may be the best source for getting in-depth feedback from customers. In turn, this creates opportunities for improving the new mapping software and functionality well beyond what would have been possible with the product that Apple previously borrowed from Google. Capron and Mitchell (2012) state that the crowd-sourcing benefits that internal control makes possible will compensate for the costs of users' dissatisfaction for a couple of weeks. According to them, Apple's logic is that product innovation is not only a goal but also a means to challenge and test what customer value is really about today. This is in line with entrepreneurial marketing principles in which initial sacrifices may yield important returns afterward (Logman, 2011b; Read, Dew, Sarasvathy, Song, & Wiltbank, 2009). When Apple launches a new product, it induces immediate reactions—even from people that haven't bought the item yet—and perhaps this is the dominant factor in its marketing strategic logic, not the innovations as such.

What is important in this case (as shown in Figure 2) is the fact that immediate customer value may not always be guaranteed when a company faces the pressure for temporal consistency: in Apple's case, that of ongoing innovation. This pressure for temporal consistency is strengthened by competitive

FIGURE 2 Risks in the Apple Maps Case

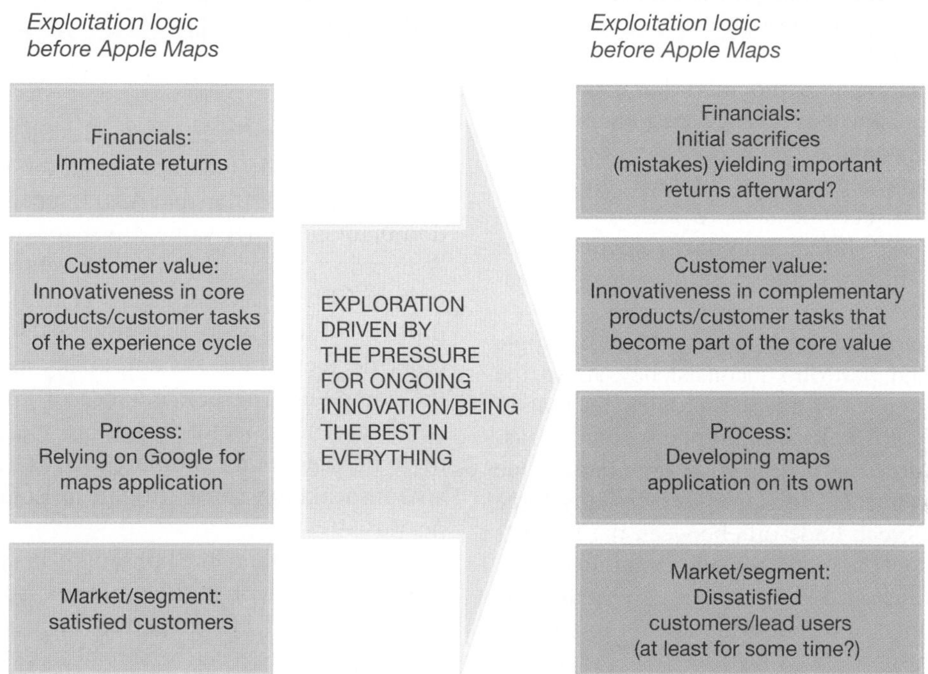

reactions. Samsung's recent marketing campaigns, for instance, point out that Apple is often lagging in the latest innovation. Second, the campaign depicts Apple fans as people that are not very smart, waiting in long lines for a technology that, according to Samsung, is not exciting anymore (Enderle, 2012).

In sum, Apple's exploitation logic before its Maps launch, where its innovations lead—almost immediately—to satisfied customers and high financial returns, is replaced after its Maps launch by a logic in which important sacrifices come into play.

Besides temporal inconsistency, companies like Apple start facing another problem: that of portfolio inconsistency. To illustrate this problem, we rely upon another product launch of Apple: the iPad mini.

3. LIMITS TO THE CUSTOMER VALUE POTENTIAL: THE CASE OF APPLE'S IPAD MINI

In October 2012, Apple announced the launch of the iPad mini. In terms of customer value, the iPad mini, with a 7.9-inch display, is $100 more expensive than Google's competitive product Nexus 7. The latter has half the memory of the iPad mini, but has a sharper, similarly sized screen, and a faster processor. Comparatively, the iPad mini is thinner, lighter, and has more apps.

As Apple pursues its marketing exploration strategy by launching new products, it is not only a question of how these relate to competitive products, but even more importantly how they fit into Apple's own product portfolio. The iPad mini may excite customers who value the Apple brand and are looking for something between the 4-inch iPhone 5 and a 9.7-inch iPad. Of course, reference frameworks may exceed product categories when price ranges start overlapping. This is a new situation for Apple, as price was never an issue for Apple buyers. However, a company may reach a situation in which products start cannibalizing each other as the complementary potential to add value becomes more limited. Adding the iPad mini to Apple's product portfolio may not only induce serious cannibalization with the larger iPad, but also with the iPhone, or even the iPod touch, as price becomes the main customer value driver in considering which Apple product to buy. This has important consequences for Apple, as the company captures the main part of its profits the moment a device is sold. Conversely, a company like Amazon accrues more profits over the lifetime of its customers with every purchase on their platform (Adner, 2012).

In sum, marketing exploration that is driven by portfolio expansion may change customers' reference frameworks and decision criteria in evaluating various product categories (see Figure 3). In Apple's case, price may become a more important driver as price ranges of different product categories start overlapping. This may induce serious cannibalization and affect Apple's overall profitability.

Besides temporal inconsistency, as in the Apple Maps case, and portfolio inconsistency, as in the Apple iPad mini case, another problem is that of reaching limits to exploration in one particular customer value driver. Relying on a dominant value driver—innovativeness in Apple's case—may force companies to break trade-offs between the benefits of that driver and the sacrifices, such as higher costs. This will be illustrated with another case in the next section, focusing on recent evolutions in the microprocessor industry.

4. TRADE-OFFS LIMITING FUTURE GROWTH: THE CASE OF THE MICROPROCESSOR INDUSTRY

If you look at marketing strategies that have characterized well-known companies in the microprocessor industry, like Intel and AMD, speed has been the dominant customer value driver for many decades. A microprocessor serves as the central processing unit, or CPU, of a computer. It generally consists of millions of transistors that process data and control other devices in the system, acting as the brain of the computer. The performance of a microprocessor is a critical factor impacting the performance of a PC and other similar devices (more extensive information can be found in Logman, 2011b, pp. 34–39).

An important breakthrough in the industry was the launch of multicore processors that offer enhanced overall system performance and efficiency, as computing tasks can be spread across two or more

FIGURE 3 Risks in the iPad Mini Case

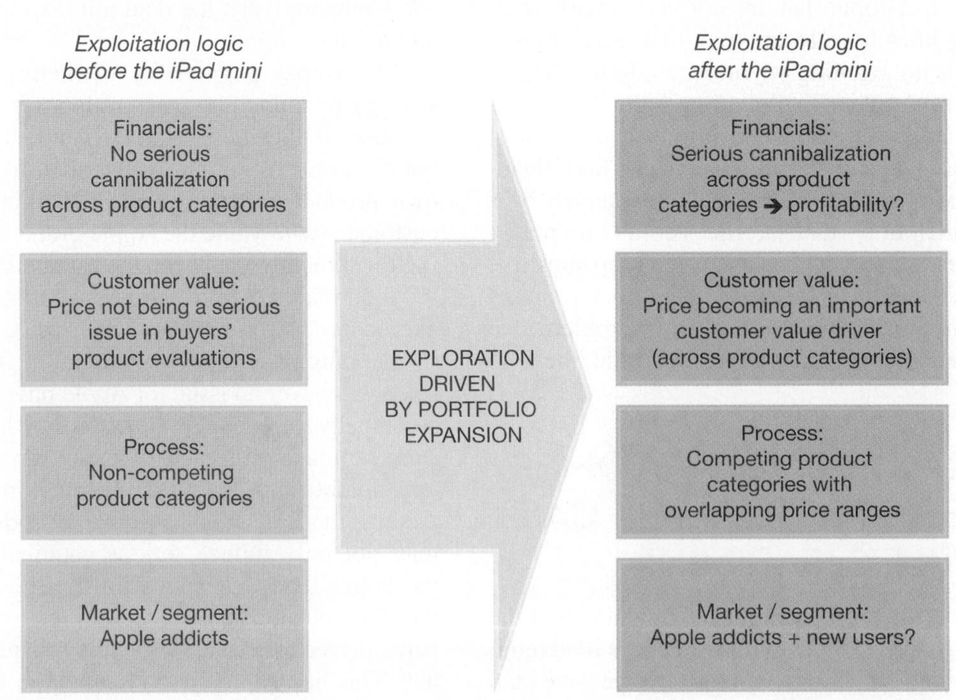

processing cores, each of which can execute a task at full speed. Moreover, performance is increased without greatly increasing the total amount of power consumed and the total amount of heat emitted (Bourzac, 2010). This breaks the trade-off between speed and energy costs (see Figure 4).

Software has to be written and rewritten to take advantage of the parallel, or multithread, processing power and specific computing environment. Automatic compiling would allow increasing speed at no additional software development cost, breaking the second trade-off of speed versus programming costs/time (see Figure 4).

In an effort to compete, all the major software and chip companies, along with many academic researchers, are working on compilers that can handle such tasks (Cass, 2010). These compilers will help in overcoming an important sacrifice: the conversion time that software developers face today. The development of automatic compilers would replace the programmer's job.

As long as these compilers are not available and programmers have to spend too much time on conversion tasks, hardware and software manufacturers—the clients in this case—may experience that the benefits, like speed, of more sophisticated multicore systems are outweighed by the sacrifices, like programming time. The case therefore shows that exploring a customer value driver, such as processing speed by players in the microprocessor industry, also demands overcoming important sacrifices. As Figure 5 depicts, breaking trade-offs that limit the growth in the customer value driver—speed—is not the only challenge semiconductor companies face in exploring market opportunities.

Besides parallel computing, the developer community is moving toward heterogeneous computing where a graphics processing unit, or GPU, is used to accelerate the application as a co-processor to the CPU. As the number of mobile devices and applications increases, the importance of systems that integrate CPU and GPU into a single silicon chip increases as well. In addition, as we move more and more from a content creation to a content consumption and data-intensive computing context, expectations may lead to a gradual shift in heterogeneous computing solutions where the GPU may become more important than the CPU. New operating systems, in particular Windows Vista, have already made the GPU more significant. Killer mass-market applications and new hardware would admittedly make the GPU more dominant in the processor architecture, as well as disruptive to the CPU in the long term. Some GPU believers argue that ultimately GPUs will replace CPUs. One important application, Microsoft Office, has begun to offer GPU acceleration for some of its graphical elements: WordArt and PowerPoint transitions. Effects like refraction and ripple (Adobe) are also accelerated by the GPU. Moreover, video and photo watching and the growing importance of visual design in sites such as Pinterest will make the GPU more dominant in everyday computing. New hardware, including the iPad, can accelerate this process, too, by emphasizing the importance of visual and graphical effects.

FIGURE 4 Breaking Trade-Offs in the Customer Value "Speed" (microprocessor industry)

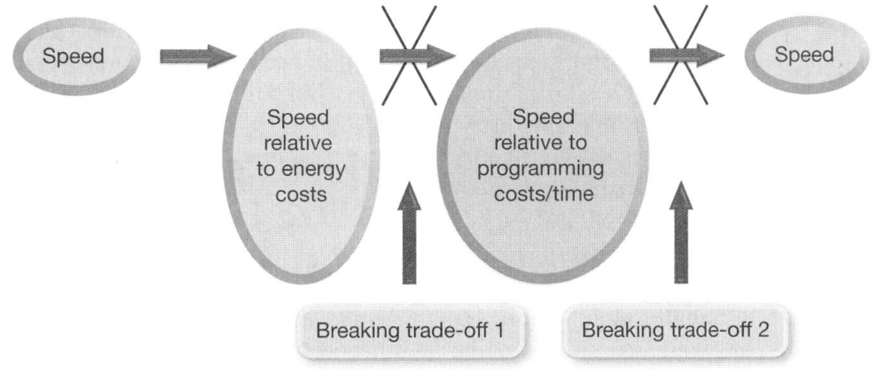

FIGURE 5 Challenges for Players in the Semiconductor Industry

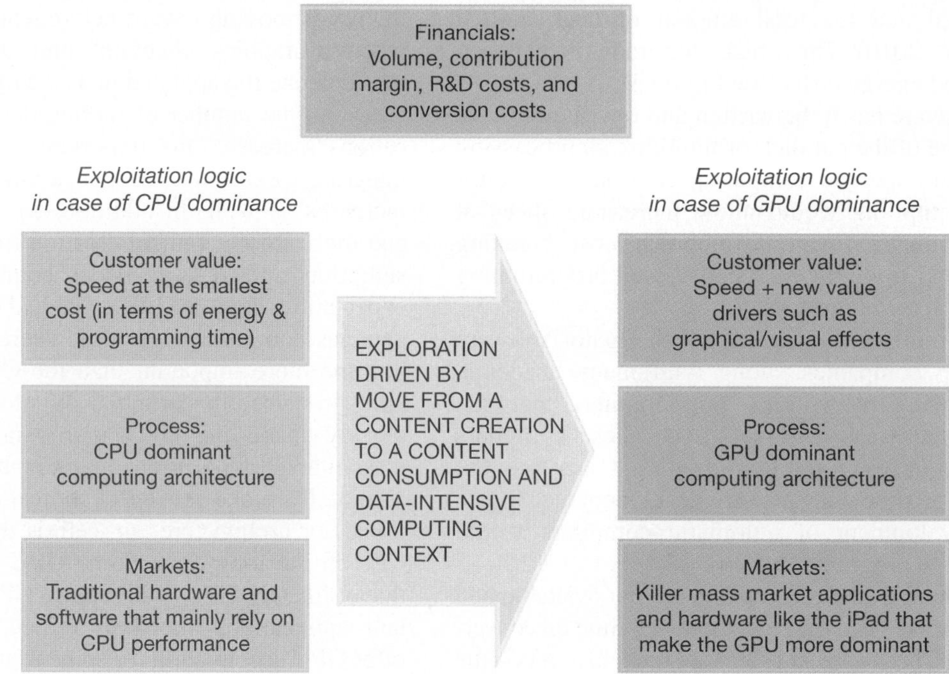

For a company similar to Intel, which relied for a long time on the successful exploitation of its core CPU business, this is certainly an exploration challenge. Conversely, this is an interesting evolution for a company such as Nvidia, which unlike Intel has its roots in GPU and visual computing.

Nevertheless, despite the GPU advantages, the programming efforts required for optimal GPU use remain very time consuming, making it less attractive for hardware and software manufacturers. Therefore, as long as mass markets cannot be reached, companies like Nvidia will have to rely mainly upon typical GPU markets, including the gaming and video screen industries.

It is not a coincidence that the significance of heterogeneous computing, and the GPU in particular, catches the interest of many chip manufacturers. AMD, ARM, Texas Instruments, and two smaller chip companies have teamed up to create a nonprofit that will try to unseat Intel's x86 dominance in computing. They have formed the Heterogeneous Systems Architecture Foundation, which, as they state, will standardize a single architecture for low-power computing as well as simplify the parallel-programming model used with multicore graphics processors and other systems on a chip. Hence, this consortium is trying to deal with two sacrifices that limit the current customer value of heterogeneous computing, those of energy costs and programming time.

The microprocessor industry case shows that new customer value drivers, such as visual effects, certainly have a lot of exploration potential. Still, trade-offs between benefits and sacrifices have to be broken in order to reach full potential.

Lastly, in exploring customer value, we will examine adding new value drivers to existing ones, which may not be straightforward. To show this, we will rely upon two examples from the food industry: Alpro and Nutella.

5. LIMITS OF ADDING NEW VALUE DRIVERS: THE CASES OF ALPRO AND NUTELLA

Alpro, acquired in 2009 by Dean Foods, is the European pioneer in the development of 100%

plant-based drinks and soya-based food products (e.g., margarine, dessert, yogurt, cream).

To complete Alpro's range of soya products, the company acquired the tofu/meat substitute producer SoFine Foods in 2006. This move was quite logical, as the company still relied upon its distinguishing soya ingredient. Additionally, in both product categories, similar segmentation criteria may be used. For instance, some people buy soya-based products out of health necessity, others buy it out of free will. However, the specific motivation may be inherently related to the product category: eating meat substitutes may be driven by vegetarian/vegan motivations whereas drinking soya milk may be driven by an allergic reaction to cow milk.

Another important growth move took place in 2012 when Alpro launched two new products: Alpro Almond milk and Alpro Hazelnut drink. This time the exploration move may be perceived as less logical, at least from a product point of view, as the company no longer relies upon the ingredient soya, which has made the company successful. With this move, Alpro strengthens its plant-based position, resulting in a change to the Alpro logo. The word "soya" has been replaced by the promise "Enjoy Plant Power!" to widen the emphasis from soya products to 100% plant-based products, and allow Alpro to offer an even wider range of sustainable, healthy food products. By the same token, the motivations to use the product are extended. For instance, with these products, the company targets a broader group of people that are curious and open to a nut taste. Not surprisingly, curiosity and discovery were the key themes Alpro used in its recent marketing campaign to intrigue and educate consumers about how they can enjoy plant power (Baker, 2012). As companies start integrating new customer value drivers in their marketing campaigns, the precise choice and order of words in their marketing campaigns become more important and even more risky. Moving from the customer value healthy to tasty may continue to be a difficult move due to the prejudice that healthy food cannot be that tasty (see Figure 6).

But other people may argue it is still a more logical move than the opposite one, moving from tasty to healthy, as Ferrero's chocolate hazelnut spread case of Nutella shows. In 2011, the company—in an effort to reach a broad target group—discovered the risks of integrating multiple themes in their marketing communication when Athena Hohenberg, a San Diego–area mother of a 4-year-old, sued the company. She was shocked to learn from friends that Nutella was in fact not a healthy, nutritious food as she interpreted, but instead was the next best thing to a candy bar. She won the suit, which has been settled for $3.05 million, of which $2.5 million will be divided among consumers. Anyone who bought Nutella within a specified period could file a claim. As a result, Nutella removed the communication phrase "An example of a tasty yet balanced breakfast" and replaced it with "Turn a balanced breakfast into a tasty one." By doing this, the brand implicitly states that you can add Nutella as a tasty food to healthy food.

The cases of Alpro and Nutella show that adding new value drivers in a company's growth path may not be straightforward, as they may be inconsistent with the dominant value drivers that have been previously emphasized. It is not a coincidence that Nutella is falling back on its core driver, taste, on which it has become path dependent. Emphasizing the taste of Nutella, the company explores new market contexts, such as foodservice, where it can highlight Nutella as a delicious ingredient in breakfast and brunch menus.

FIGURE 6 Limits to Customer Value Exploration in Alpro and Nutella's Case

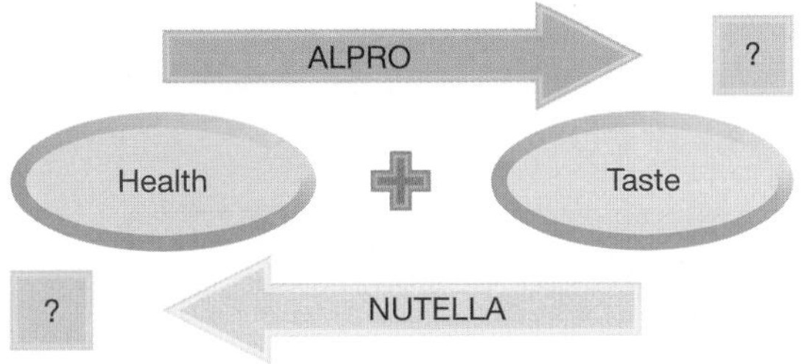

6. IMPLICATIONS

The previous discussion shows that a marketing exploration strategy may not only be limited by resources/processes or financial constraints (as has been discussed extensively in the management and marketing literature; for example, Brush, Ceru, & Blackburn, 2009), but also by customer value constraints (see Figure 7).

First, the number of possible adjacency moves around a customer value driver to new markets/segments, new product categories or channels, and new profit zones may become limited after some time—as was illustrated at the beginning of the article with the low cost carrier and Patagonia examples.

Second, a company may become too dependent on certain dominant value drivers from the past, and face time pressure to come up with new consistent moves for which the company lacks and/or lags the necessary competencies, as in Apple's iPad Maps case. This is in line with the observation made by Crittenden and Crittenden (2012) that the past has lost much of its value as a predictor of the future.

Third, from a future point of view, value creation may reach its limits as the potential for adding value becomes smaller and cannibalization within a company's product portfolio becomes almost inevitable, as in Apple's iPad mini case.

Fourth, relying on one dominant value driver may force companies to break trade-offs that limit future growth along that value dimension—as was shown in the semiconductor case. Companies may get squeezed between the past and the future when facing the pressure of temporal consistency driven by past behavior and experiencing the limits of future growth in the dominant value drivers. Making repeatable adjacency moves, as Zook (2012) proposes, may become problematic if a company sticks to one dominant value driver from which earlier growth moves were made. To counter this problem, companies often start integrating extra value drivers in their story (see arrow at the bottom of Figure 7). However, at that stage another problem may occur, as consistency with existing value drivers cannot always be guaranteed as more drivers are added (see Alpro and Nutella case).

The cases discussed in this article reveal that many companies may have to accept more sacrifices such as temporal mistakes, cannibalization, and breaking the existing exploitation logic if they want to pursue their growth exploration paths in the future.

Lastly, as the exploration moves of companies continue, marketing strategies will probably become fuzzier, as in fuzzy logic, as they will be more about integrating new value drivers to some extent—not a strict black or white situation—and learning/experimenting with what really makes sense.

FIGURE 7 Customer Value Exploration

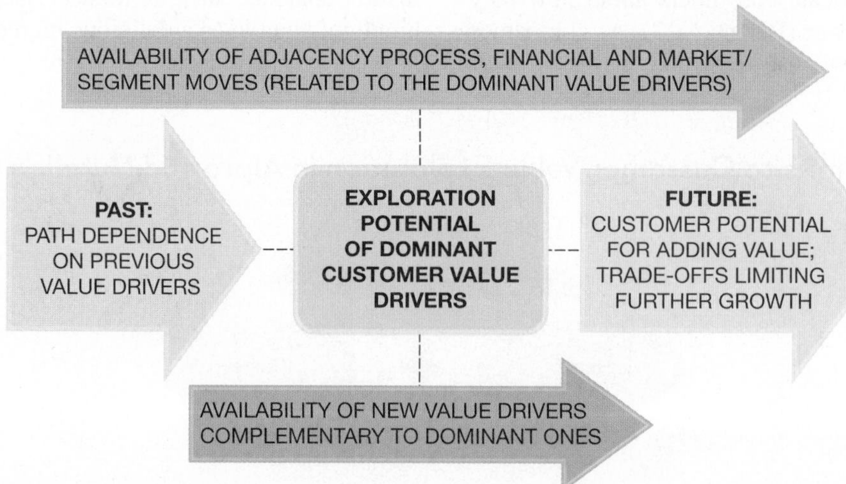

7. RECOMMENDATIONS

The risks and limits discussed in this article certainly illustrate that value engineering, in which benefits and sacrifices of customer value are analyzed in detail, will become more crucial as companies pursue their marketing exploration strategies (Logman, 2008b). This is in line with the suggestion of Rust, Moorman, and Bhalla (2010) that the marketing department must be reinvented as a customer department built around customer value—equity, as they call it.

Relying upon the four perspectives of the marketing strategy framework of this article (see Figure 1), we suggest that a value engineering (VE) team should be composed of people from various departments including marketing and sales for customer value and market/segment insights, R&D for process insights, and finance for value to the company insights.

To analyze and measure the exploration potential of customer value drivers that characterize the company or brand marketing strategy, a step-by-step approach similar to the integrative framework of Martin (2007) may be used, but applied in a more dynamic value engineering context. This approach would consist of the following steps.

7.1. Step #1: Definition and Decomposition of Dominant Value Drivers

The VE team should define the dominant customer value drivers, during the entire customer experience cycle, that characterize the current marketing strategy. Next, the value drivers should be decomposed in two categories: benefits to the customers (e.g., innovativeness) and sacrifices to the customers (e.g., higher costs). Finally, the team has to define the markets/segments, their underlying processes—such as the marketing mix and value chain—and important financials that are directly related to the dominant customer value drivers.

7.2. Step #2: Generation of Possible Exploration Moves

As a second step, the VE team has to figure out what possible exploration, or adjacency, moves can be made around each of the dominant customer value drivers. These moves may be taken from:

- A process perspective—for example, extending the product portfolio or launching new distribution channels.
- A market/segment perspective—for example, finding new market applications or new customer segments.
- A customer value perspective—for example, changing or adding new value drivers.
- A financial perspective—for example, finding new profit zones or extra cash flow.

7.3. Step #3: Analyzing Causality

As a third step, the VE team has to analyze how factors within and across the four perspectives relate before and after the exploration moves. Causality may change after pursuing certain exploration moves. We have seen some interesting examples in the cases discussed in this article (see Figures 2, 3, and 5).

7.4. Step #4: Envisioning the System Architecture

As a fourth step, the VE team has to figure out which factors condition some exploration moves. As discussed in this article, certain exploration moves may be highly dependent on previous moves due to the pressure for temporal consistency. Other moves by the company may be highly dependent on moves of complementary players, suppliers, distributors, or other stakeholders. We previously examined how exploration moves of CPU or GPU players may depend on the performance of new operating systems and software applications. As long as these other players are not moving, certain exploration options may be uninteresting for some time. Therefore, decisions of different players in the market may become interrelated.

7.5. Step #5: Making Choices

A last step is deciding on the exploration path(s) with the highest potential based on all four perspectives. In making this decision, the VE team may face various types of contradictions (Logman, 2009; Stacey, 2007, pp. 14–15):

- A *dichotomy*—a polarized opposition, requiring an either/or choice, where one exploration option is more attractive than the other.

- A *dilemma*—a polarized opposition, requiring an either/or choice between equally unattractive exploration options—taking the best from the worst.
- A *duality*—a polarized opposition that can be resolved by thinking in terms of a both/and choice, but in which the different exploration options are planned sequentially or separated in place—for instance, by pursuing one option in one market and another option in another market.
- A *paradox*—a polarized opposition, or trade-off, that can be broken by thinking in terms of a both/and choice synchronously.

A final consideration is that the VE team should take care that certain exploration paths don't induce too much path dependence, leaving enough potential for making other exploration moves in the future. In other words, it is always beneficial to keep some components in your marketing strategy that still offer enough flexibility for making changes.

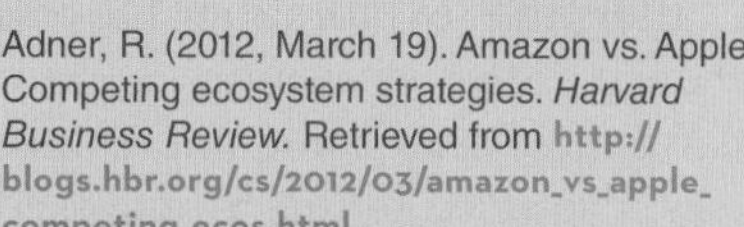

REFERENCES

Adner, R. (2012, March 19). Amazon vs. Apple: Competing ecosystem strategies. *Harvard Business Review.* Retrieved from http://blogs.hbr.org/cs/2012/03/amazon_vs_apple_competing_ecos.html

Amit, R., & Zott, C. (2012). Creating value through business model innovation. *MIT Sloan Management Review,* 53(3), 41–49.

Baker, R. (2012, March 12). Alpro ramps up marketing for NPD. *Marketing Week.* Retrieved from http://www.marketingweek.co.uk/news/alpro-ramps-up-marketing-for-npd/4000574.article

Bourzac, K. (2010, April 20). Designing for mobility. *MIT Technology Review.* Retrieved from http://www.technologyreview.com/article/418584/designing-for-mobility/

Brush, C. G., Ceru, D. J., & Blackburn, R. (2009). Pathways to entrepreneurial growth: The influence of management, marketing, and money. *Business Horizons,* 52(5), 481–491.

Burgelman, R. A. (2002). Strategy as vector and the inertia of coevolutionary lock-in. *Administrative Science Quarterly,* 47(2), 325–357.

Capron, L., & Mitchell, W. (2012, October 5). *Why Apple made the right call on Apple Maps. Harvard Business Review.* Retrieved from http://blogs.hbr.org/cs/2012/10/why_apple_made_the_right_call_on_maps.html

Cass, S. (2010, April 20). Multicore processors create software headaches. *MIT Technology Review.* Retrieved from http://www.technologyreview.com/article/418580/multicore-processors-create-%C2%ADsoftware-headaches/

Crittenden, V. L., & Crittenden, W. F. (2012). Strategic marketing in a changing world. *Business Horizons, 55*(3), 215–217.

Dawar, N. (2012, October 1). Apple, directionless? *INSEAD Blog Network.* Retrieved from http://blog.insead.edu/2012/10/apple-directionless/

de Wit, J. G., & Zuidberg, J. (2012). The growth limits of the low cost carrier model. *Journal of Air Transport Management, 21,* 17–23.

Enderle, R. (2012, November 10). *How Samsung, Microsoft, and stupidity are staining Apple's brand image.* Retrieved from http://www.digitaltrends.com/apple/how-samsung-microsoft-and-stupidity-are-staining-apples-brand-image/

Garud, R., Kumaraswamy, A., & Karnøe, P. (2010). Path dependence and creation. *Journal of Management Studies, 47*(4), 760–774.

Gáspár, T. (2011). Path dependency and path creation in a strategic perspective. *Journal of Futures Studies,* 15(4), 93–108.

Kapferer, J.-N. (2012). Abundant rarity: The key to luxury growth. *Business Horizons, 55*(5), 453–462.

Kyriakopoulosa, K., & Moorman, C. (2004). Tradeoffs in marketing exploitation and exploration strategies: The overlooked role of market orientation. *International Journal of Research in Marketing, 21*(3), 219–240.

Logman, M. (2007). Logical brand management in a dynamic context of growth and innovation. *Journal of Product and Brand Management, 16*(4), 257–268.

Logman, M. (2008a). Contextual intelligence and flexibility in today's marketing environment. *Marketing Intelligence and Planning, 25*(5), 508–520.

Logman, M. (2008b). Customer value as an ideation tool. *Value World, 31*(1), 3–13.

Logman, M. (2009). The dynamics towards multiple strategic options: A conceptual approach. *The Open Business Journal, 2,* 108–111.

Logman, M. (2011a). Realism versus simplicity in strategic marketing planning: The impact of temporality. *Marketing Intelligence and Planning, 29*(7), 662–671.

Logman, M. (2011b). *Entrepreneurial marketing: A guide for startups and potential growth companies.* Philadelphia: Garant/Coronet Books.

Lowitt, E. (2011, October 3). Patagonia's "buy less" campaign may lead to more revenue. *Harvard Business Review.* Retrieved from http://blogs.hbr.org/cs/2011/10/patagonias_buy_less_campai.html

Martin, R. (2007). How successful leaders think. *Harvard Business Review, 85*(6), 60–67.

Martin, R. L. (2009). *The design of business: Why design thinking is the next competitive advantage.* Boston: Harvard Business School Press.

Read, S., Dew, N., Sarasvathy, S. D., Song, M., & Wiltbank, R. (2009). Marketing under uncertainty: The logic of an effectual approach. *Journal of Marketing, 73*(3), 1–18.

Rust, R. T., Moorman, C., & Bhalla, G. (2010). Rethinking marketing. *Harvard Business Review, 88*(1/2), 94–101.

Sekerka, L. E., & Stimel, D. (2011). How durable is a sustainable enterprise? Ecological sustainability meets the reality of tough economic times. *Business Horizons, 54*(2), 115–124.

Slotegraaf, R. J., & Dickson, P. R. (2004). The paradox of a marketing planning capability. *Journal of the Academy of Marketing Science, 32*(4), 371–385.

Stacey, R. D. (2007). *Strategic management and organisational dynamics.* Harlow, UK: Prentice Hall.

Turner, S. F., Mitchell, W., & Bettis, R. A. (in press). Strategic momentum: How experience shapes temporal consistency of ongoing innovation. *Journal of Management.*

Vergne, J.-P., & Durand, R. (2010). The missing link between the theory and empirics of path dependence: Conceptual clarification, testability issue, and methodological implications. *Journal of Management Studies, 47*(4), 736–759.

Zook, C. (2004). *Beyond the core: Expand your market without abandoning your roots.* Boston: Harvard Business School Press.

Zook, C. (2012). *Repeatability: Build enduring businesses for a world of constant change.* Boston: Harvard Business School Press.

Organizational Ambidexterity: Balancing Strategic Innovation and Competitive Strategy in the Age of Reinvention

Idris Mootee
Idea Couture Inc.

In today's extreme competitive environment, the most successful companies are those that are ambidextrous. Managers must craft and execute a competitive strategy that works for their company's product-market context while simultaneously re-examining each of the 5Cs, with a view to how their strategic innovation will impact each of the five elements. Readers will learn how to achieve that balance in this article.

In many circles today, "reinvention" seems to be the operative word. At least it should be, as every organization needs to find ways of coping with the dynamic, unpredictable change that is impacting it at all levels. Today, organizations desperately need to reinvent themselves completely in order to win in tomorrow's market place. Reinvention means throwing away existing strategies and even best practices.

Every CEO understands the pressing need for a clear competitive strategy as well as the need for strategic innovation. In fact, a CEO must understand this need, because unless companies have a clear idea about how they are going to be distinctly different and how they should differentiate themselves from the competition, they are going to get overtaken—if not become a spent force—by the hyper-intense competition. But that's only half of the story.

The other half is the daunting challenge of striking a balance between competing effectively in today's marketplace while strategically innovating to capitalize on tomorrow's opportunities, or inventing tomorrow's business. Developing such strategic ambidexterity is critical if an organization is to maximize value creation over the long run. However, for the most part, it remains a relatively rare capability. This article suggests how C-suite executives can develop this ambidexterity.

COMPETITIVE STRATEGY

Let's begin by examining the concepts of "competitive strategy" and "strategic innovation."

Competitive strategy represents the choices that a company makes to configure itself, and deploy its resources and capabilities to compete against industry rivals or new entrants. It is important to note that this definition applies to strategy in a well-defined, product-market context.

Strategic innovation means applying strategic foresight to imagine a future, thereby creating a new market or disrupting the established market. This can take the form of new product or service categories, or processes and business models that can fundamentally change the mental models and rules of competition.

Prudent managers design and execute the competitive strategy that will enable their organizations to succeed today, while simultaneously engaging in

Idris Mootee. "Organizational Ambidexterity." *Ivey Business Journal*. 76, no. 6 (2012), pp. 1–4.

strategic innovation efforts that will lay the groundwork to compete in the future.

THE COMPETITIVE STRATEGY FRAMEWORK: THE 5 C'S

The following framework highlights five, key interrelated components of competitive strategy:

- Customers
- Competitors
- Channel configurations
- Cost structure
- Core capabilities

The successful company is one that deftly manages the inter-relationships among these components to deploy a competitive framework in which it can leverage its advantages to fulfill customer needs better than its rivals.

1. Customers

Good strategy is about focus, and one of the most crucial parts of this focus is the task of identifying which customer segments it should serve. Generally speaking, it is more effective to focus energy on serving a set of distinct customer segments well than to attempt to be all things to all people—often a recipe for peril.

Treating one's customers as one, homogenous whole can lead to sub-optimization, as people will respond in very different ways to the same offering. Customers differ on myriad dimensions, including geographic, demographic, psychographic and behavioral—all of which shape their varying needs and preferences. And of course, customers also vary in terms of their potential profitability to a company—certainly a key consideration.

In order to succeed, companies must segment the market in ways that are appropriate to their business and then select those key segments that it can serve most effectively and profitably. Once these segments are identified, the company should then target its offerings to meet these customers' needs and so improve its competitive position.

It is also important to note that this is not a stationary target. Customer segments' needs evolve, as does their profitability relative to new and emerging segments. Managers must keep a watchful eye and continue to monitor and act accordingly.

2. Competitors

A company must be acutely aware of its competitors and their offerings in order to better serve their chosen customer segments. Indeed, the competition is a key element of a company's operating context, one that must be considered when developing and honing its own differentiated offering. Given the dynamic nature of competition, companies should continually assess themselves versus their rivals, vis-à-vis the key success factors of the specific product-market theater.

A well-known challenge for many companies is the need to adapt quickly and properly to the rapid, continuous change that threatens its competitive position. However, there is a select group of savvy companies that bypass the traditional hand-to-hand combat of direct competition by offering something entirely different and new—strategic innovation at play. These companies find a strategic window and open it when there is an intriguing potential for a fit between new success factors and its own distinctive competencies.

An emerging technology may create or destroy opportunities in one market or allow companies to simply modify existing products to fit in with the needs of a new customer segment with high-growth potential.

Technological control is not, however, necessarily a critical success factor. Keniche Ohmae, a renowned strategist, argues that the most effective shortcut to a competitive leadership position is an early concentration of major resources in a single, strategically significant function in order to excel in that area, and consolidate the lead in the other functions.

3. Channel Configurations

Managers must thoroughly understand the channel dynamics of their companies in order to compete effectively. It is critically important to analyze channel choices and options as part of the strategic process.

Unfortunately, channel options are often ignored and most companies seldom confront head-on the choices of channel mix, e.g. whether to appoint an exclusive dealer network or push for intense distribution. Such a decision should not simply be determined by the characteristics of the product or service. On the contrary, these are highly strategic choices that must be made after much discussion and consideration.

Distribution strengths often play a distinctive role in reinforcing superior product performance and maintaining a strong market position in the end-user market. And, in the case of information products, the channel may be the defining elements of the product.

Passive acceptance of existing channel choices has become increasingly risky for two reasons. Companies in all industries are facing increasingly high sales costs, with little evidence of increased productivity to offset these costs. And customers continue to place a high demand on manufacturers that permit direct communication and information flow, forcing companies to reconsider the use and design of traditional channels.

4. Cost Structure

It is vital to have a deep understanding of the relative cost standing of one's company. Cost relates almost directly to scale and scope. Until recently, decisions on scale and scope were always guided by two rules of thumb: bigger is better, and, keep as many activities as possible under one roof to remain in control and maximize revenues. In the past, adherence to these beliefs led to extensive vertical integration and continuously striving for scale and mass marketing with a strong volume orientation—all of which led to a high cost burden.

5. Core Capabilities

As the elements of a company's playing field are framed and focused, managers must examine organizational capabilities closely and assess their alignment with the competitive market demands. The importance of having the right capabilities for the chosen product-market focus cannot be overstated. This is why the assessment exercise is crucial. Examples of relevant and beneficial capabilities include logistics excellence in the retail sector, and design and engineering excellence in the consumer electronics arena.

An organization's capabilities are the product of a number of inter-connected factors, including skills, culture, processes and behavior. Companies should examine the particular market dynamics closely to determine which capabilities are needed to compete and to what extent it possesses these capabilities. Some capabilities are latent and can be fully actualized by making adjustments. Others can be acquired and developed, though the question remains whether this can be done within a reasonable timeframe, given the rapid pace of change.

In sum, managers must ensure that their organizations possess and deploy the capabilities that are most relevant to their chosen product-market focus in order to compete.

FOUR ARCHETYPES OF STRATEGIC INNOVATION

In addition to making incremental innovation a part of the competitive strategy for today's product-market context, managers need to keep a watchful eye on the future and act accordingly. Opportunities are plentiful for the future, but the questions remain: What are they and how to capitalize on them? Cost control and cash management are important for the short-term but they will not position a company to be a leader in the future. That's why companies need a mindset that says: "We're not only competing for today—We're going to create a new future."

One needs to be realistic about the operating environment as well as the resources and capability available. The trick is to take care of both, but in a way that moves the company towards a desirable future state. This could involve a re-examination to determine which consumer needs have shifted and which industry boundaries have become blurred, in order to capitalize on white-space opportunities that emerge.

The following sections introduce four potent archetypes of strategic innovation that a company can deploy:

- Attacking the mass market by designing a new value configuration;
- Opening a new market by maximizing economies of scope through horizontal integration, value bundles and friendly customer experience;
- Opening a new market by maximizing economies of scale through vertical and virtual integration;
- Pursuing the unserved, under-served or non-consumers by servicing to that segment.

1. Attack the Mass Market by Designing a New Value Configuration

Many companies find themselves in an arms race with competitors, one that is based on a well-worn set of performance criteria. Often, a scenario of frequent one-upmanship typically plays out, resulting in incremental improvements along these criteria, following a predictable path. However, some companies courageously and deliberately step out of the tried and true and boldly attack the market with a new value configuration. They change the rules of the game by introducing new performance criteria that influence consumer behavior.

Let's take the case of the console video game industry. For many years, rivals Sony, Microsoft and Nintendo engaged in a seemingly never-ending series of successive battles involving faster chips and better graphics, as these were the established performance criteria. Then, in 2006, Nintendo stepped into the pantheon of great innovations with the introduction of its revolutionary and wildly successful Wii console. The Wii was designed not to compete on speed and graphics. Rather it introduced totally different performance criteria such as playability and accessibility to more family members, and just plain old-fashioned fun. In effect, Nintendo deliberately chose a new mode of competition, and invested in designing and developing an offering that would outpace the competition along the newly defined performance criteria. The rest is history.

2. Open a New Market by Maximizing Economies of Scope by Exploiting Opportunities through Horizontal Integration, Value Bundles and Customer Experience Design

The business world is littered with examples of companies that have tried—without effect—to diversify through horizontal integration and sell new and unrelated products under their brand. Many of these companies clumsily bolt on the new offerings, ignoring the better-off test, that is, determining if and how the new venture benefits from its association with the company (e.g. brand relevance and power, ability to leverage existing infrastructure, etc.). On the other end of the spectrum, there are great companies that develop interfaces prized by their customers, and which they use as monetizable platforms that enable horizontal integration and lead to successful outcomes.

A shining example of the latter is Apple Inc. Among Apple's truly brilliant moves was the creation of the seminal iTunes store. As everyone knows, it served initially as a store for music files only—a companion for its iPod product. This interface gained solid traction with millions of users and provided Apple an invaluable platform for integrating video, and famously, apps, which opened an entirely new, tremendously successful market for the company. Consumers were primed and ready for the new offerings. This also opened up a host of opportunities, including bundling. All of this was predicated on the development and ownership of a key consumer interface—Itunes.

3. Open a New Market by Maximizing Economies of Scale by Exploiting Opportunities through Virtual Vertical Integration

Historically, a company would need a tremendous amount of capital in order to reach scale and vertically integrate its operations. And as companies reached scale, they made decisions about which customer segments to serve, and conversely, on which segments to not serve (or under-serve). This presented an intriguing opportunity for companies to deliver on customers' unmet needs in creative ways.

Today, the size of capital commitments required to achieve vertical integration has fallen dramatically, due to the emergence of virtual integration. That is, companies can choose to lease expensive value-chain elements such as a manufacturing capability in order to step in and deliver an offering that fulfills needs that are under-fulfilled by the industry giants. Firms can in effect find a niche, open a new market and enjoy economies of scale in a cost-effective, asset-light fashion that affords the flexibility to scale up and down, depending on performance.

4. Pursue the Unserved, Under-served or Non-traditional Consumers with Tailored Offerings and New Business Model Design

Competitors often leave white-space opportunities in the market that can serve as promising growth areas. This is certainly the case with customer segments, many of which remain unserved or under-served, or that do not contain traditional consumers, e.g. recent immigrants. Rather than going with the crowd and overlooking these segments, a forward-thinking company could take a close look at them and determine whether there is a way to create an offering that would drive value by serving them in a creative way.

Western Union is an example of a company that capitalized on this type of white-space opportunity. Many recent immigrants have a need and desire to send money to relatives in their home countries, but these needs were not adequately served by many major banks, which may not have chosen to focus on this customer segment. In effect, Western Union has become an invaluable service for the customers in this segment and has created a market that drives value.

Given the realities of today's extreme competitive environment, the most successful companies are those that are ambidextrous. Managers must craft and execute a competitive strategy that works for their company's product-market context today while simultaneously re-examining each of the 5Cs, with a view to how their strategic innovation will impact each of the five elements.

Strategy is all about focus, but unfortunate side effects are inertia and the emergence of blind spots. Companies can strategically innovate in their core and future businesses and play two games at the same time, if they are successful in discovering a new strategic position. Striking the right balance between competing today and investing for tomorrow is a key ingredient for creating long-term, sustainable competitive advantage. Organizations with rigid, top-down hierarchical management structures have high levels of control, low connectivity and are less agile. Organizations that are flat and decentralized are more agile and able to react to external changes. We need to consider a new organizational design that can both manage stability and handle change. The ability to continuously adjust and adapt strategic and tactical moves as a function of strategic ambitions and new consumer behavior will inspire new business models and innovative ways to create value for a company. This is the ultimate sustainable competitive advantage.

Pioneering and First Mover Advantages: The Importance of Business Models

Constantinos Markides
London Business School

Lourdes Sosa
London Business School

Pioneering has both advantages and disadvantages. Which effect will predominate will depend to a large extent on: (i) the business model that the pioneer utilizes to exploit the first-mover advantages (FMAs) associated with early entry: (ii) the business models that late entrants adopt to attack the pioneers; and (iii) the business model that the pioneer uses to respond to these attacks. Studies that do not explicitly control for the business models being used by firms will provide biased estimates of the importance (or sustainability) of first-mover advantages.

INTRODUCTION

Nobody in the literature denies that pioneering has both advantages and disadvantages (e.g. Lieberman and Montgomery, 1988; Schnaars, 1994). Therefore, the bulk of academic research has focused on identifying the factors that influence the relative magnitude of these effects and so determine the conditions under which pioneering is a profitable strategy. A rather long list of factors has now been developed, broadly divided into three categories (Gomez et al., 2011): (i) factors such as firm-level resources and capabilities that allow a pioneer to exploit first-mover advantages, or FMAs (e.g. Fuentelsaz et al., 2002; Robinson and Chiang, 2002; Teece et al., 1997); (ii) factors such as switching costs and preemption of scarce assets—known collectively as isolating mechanisms—that constrain latecomers from catching up with the pioneers (e.g. Day and Freeman, 1990; Golder and Tellis, 1993; Mueller, 1997); and (iii) factors such as environmental uncertainty, market transparency and the stage of the industry life cycle that determine the initial FMAs enjoyed by the pioneer as well as their sustainability (e.g. Gans and Stern, 2010; Geroski, 1995; Suarez and Lanzolla, 2007; Teece, 1986).

Perhaps surprisingly, the literature does not explicitly consider either the strategy (or business model) that the pioneer uses to exploit FMAs or the strategy/business model that later entrants use to attack the pioneer as important determinants of the profitability of pioneering. A business model has been defined as "the content, structure and governance of transactions designed so as to create value through the exploitation of opportunities" (Amit and Zott, 2001: 511). Several authors interpret a business model as an activity system made up of a number of interdependent activities such as the firm's value-chain activities, its choice of customers and its choice of products and services (e.g. Afuah, 2003; Casadesus-Masanell and Ricart, 2010; Hedman and Kalling, 2003; Markides, 2008; Teece, 2010; Zott and Amit, 2010; Zott et al., 2011). The right choice of interdependent activities determines the performance of the system.

Our thesis is that the business models that pioneers or late entrants adopt could have a big impact on the usefulness and sustainability of first-mover advantages. Yet, the existing literature on FMAs has largely ignored the business model concept. Granted, the literature does consider the firm's resources or capabilities as important determinants of FMAs.

Constantinos Markides and Lourdes Sosa, "Pioneering and First Mover Advantages: The Importance of Business Models", *Long Range Planning*, 46, 2013, pp. 325–334. Reprinted with permission of Elsevier.

For example, Lieberman and Montgomery (1998, p. 1113) argue that: "Ultimately, the sustainability of a first-mover advantage depends upon the initial resources captured by the pioneer, plus the resources and capabilities subsequently developed, relative to the quality of resources and capabilities held by later entrants. . . . " But resources and capabilities are not the same thing as the business models that different firms use to fight in a market. Resources and capabilities are inputs into a firm's business model but the same resources can be used to develop totally different business models. Thus, one does not equal the other.

Even casual observation of anecdotal evidence ought to alert us to the importance of this variable and how different it is from resources and capabilities. For example, in the well-known story of Xerox versus Canon, late entrants such as IBM and Kodak failed to undermine Xerox's significant FMAs in the copier market while another late entrant (Canon) did so quite effectively. All of the late entrants faced the same variables listed above (i.e. Xerox's resources, the isolating mechanisms protecting Xerox's FMAs and the environmental factors facing the industry), yet one late entrant was successful in undermining Xerox's FMAs while two others were not. What could explain the difference? Several researchers pointed to the different business models that the various players brought into the fight (e.g. Markides, 1997; Porter, 1985). As we argue in this paper, our inability to explicitly account for the different business models employed by the various firms in an industry is a serious shortcoming of the existing literature on FMAs. It casts doubt on the accuracy of the results that the existing literature has provided on the relationship between FMAs and performance.

BUSINESS MODELS CAN EXPLAIN THE SUCCESS OF PIONEERS

It is often assumed that first-movers in a new market enjoy FMAs and utilize these advantages to dominate the market. Nothing could be further from the truth. The fact of the matter is that the early pioneers of a new market are almost *never* the ones that dominate a market (Markides and Geroski, 2005).

Consider, for example, the car industry. Long before Henry Ford introduced the Model T in 1908, the industry was populated by hundreds of firms. Indeed, more than one thousand firms populated the industry at one time or another. 14 firms entered into the fledgling US market between 1885 and 1898; 19 entered in 1899, 37 in 1900, 27 in 1901 and then an average of about 48 new firms entered per year from 1902 until 1910 (Utterback, 1996). Thereafter, the surge subsided: from 1911 until 1921, an average of 11 new automobile producers started up per year but that seems to have been it—very few firms entered the industry after the early 1920s. These features of the early evolution of the car industry are by no means unique to that industry. You see the same pattern unfolding in industry after industry (Utterback, 1996). For example, in the TV industry thirty firms were producing TV sets in 1947, forty more entered the following year and another 71 entered between 1949 and 1953.

The interesting question is: what happened to all these early entrants? And the answer is that most of them die, never to be heard of again. For example, from a peak of about 275 car manufacturers in 1907, a mere 7 were left by the late 1950s. And from a peak of 89 TV manufacturers operating in 1951, numbers sagged to less than 40 before the end of the 1950s.

Who, then, ends up dominating the mass market that grows as soon as the dominant design emerges? According to Markides and Geroski (2005), it is those companies that were "lucky" enough to either possess the dominant design at the time of its establishment or jump into the market right when the dominant design was to emerge. But jumping in at the right time is not enough to conquer the market. Not only do the eventual winners time their entry into the market to perfection but they also undertake a series of actions that grows the market from a niche into a mass market. Put simply, they adopt a business model that allows them to grow the mass market and dominate it in the process.

According to Markides and Geroski (2005), the main elements of the winning business model are the following:

1. Target the *average* consumer (rather than the *early adopters*) by emphasizing different product attributes to those that the pioneers focus on. In particular, instead of emphasizing the functionality of the product, emphasize low prices that help grow the market;

2. Support low prices by driving down costs. To do so, the winning firms build market share quickly so as to enjoy economies of scale and learning benefits. This can be achieved by creating bandwagon effects;
3. Reduce customer risk through branding and communication. The winning firms help build as big a consensus as possible across consumers to broaden the initial installed base and widen the ultimate market;
4. Build the distribution that can serve the mass market;
5. Create alliances with key suppliers and producers of complementary goods, so as to control key inputs and the provision of complementary goods;
6. Protect the market by exploiting first mover advantages

There may be more actions that the winning firms can take to consolidate the early market. But the important point to note is that winning the market is not a matter of luck or good intentions. It is the by-product of an innovative business model.

BUSINESS MODELS CAN EXPLAIN THE SUCCESS OF LATE ENTRANTS

Innovative business models are not only important to early entrants who enter at the beginning of an industry's evolution. They are also important for latecomers who attack the established players long after the industry has grown into a mass market.

What is it that we know about business models and market entry by late entrants? One of the most robust findings from academic studies on new market entry is that most new entrants fail (e.g. Geroski, 1995). For example, several studies of market entry in the US, Canada and the UK have reported that about 5–10% of new entrants disappear within a year of entry, about 20–30% disappear within two years and some 50% disappear within five years of entry (e.g. Geroski, 1991, p. 27). These results are consistent with a study by Dunne et al. (1989) that found that 64% of their sample of new US firms had exited within 5 years of entry while a full 79% had ceased trading 10 years after commencing operations. The failure rate of new entrants is so high that economists have come up with the "revolving door" analogy to describe the entry process: new entrants are like people going through a revolving door, exiting the room as soon as they enter it (e.g. Audretsch, 1995).

Of course, we would expect most entrants to fail early on in a new industry's evolution, especially in its "era of ferment" (Utterback, 1996). However, the reported high failure rates are observed at all stages of an industry's evolution, not just in its era of ferment. This suggests that FMAs can persist for long periods, giving incumbents a competitive advantage over later entrants.

Another robust finding on new market entry is that most entrants imitate the incumbents when they enter. Imitative entry has been estimated to be 90% of all entry with the remaining 10% being taken over by entrants that utilize innovative strategies (e.g. Geroski, 1991, p. 230). Yet another finding is that it takes 10–12 years for the profitability (ROI) of the entrant to be equal to that of the mature business (Biggadike, 1979), a fact that has serious implications on how patient any new entrant ought to be before giving up.

Given these facts on market entry, the high failure rate of new entrants should not be a surprise. When they enter a new market, entrants are in effect attacking the established players there (i.e. the pioneers or early-movers). By virtue of being in the market before the late entrants, these pioneers (i.e. established firms) enjoy first-mover advantages (FMAs) such as economies of scale, knowledge of the market, control of scarce assets and consumer inertia. In addition, the market under attack is their home, which implies that incumbents will fight to the death before giving it up. This suggests that unless the entrants have some serious advantages over the established firms (such as superior and patented technology) or unless they utilize an innovative strategy to attack, the established firms will most likely win out. Since we know that 90% of all entrants use imitative entry to attack (Geroski, 1991), it should not come as a surprise to know that most of them fail, and they do so fairly regularly and fairly quickly.

Yet, without disputing the statistics, we all know of examples of companies that entered new markets (at various stages of their evolution) with great success. In several instances, not only did they survive but often managed to emerge as one of the leaders in the industry! IKEA did it in the furniture retail business, Canon in copiers, Bright Horizons in the child care and early education market, MinuteClinic in the general health care industry, Starbucks in coffee, Amazon in bookselling, K-Mart in retailing, Southwest, easyJet and Ryanair in the airline industry, Enterprise in the car-rental market, Netflix and Lovefilm in the DVD rental market, Honda in motorcycles and Home Depot in the home improvement market. The list could go on!

So, why do some late entrants succeed when most fail? The literature has identified several reasons for the late entrants' success (e.g. Schnaars, 1994; Tellis and Golder, 1996 and 2001; Zhang and Markman, 1998). One of them is the business model that late entrants adopt to attack the pioneers (e.g. Markides, 1997; Porter, 1985; Shankar et al., 1998). Specifically, the probability of success in attacking established competitors through market entry is increased if the entrant adopts an innovative strategy, one that avoids imitation and instead disrupts the established players. As proposed by Porter: "The cardinal rule in offensive strategy is not to attack head-on with an imitative strategy, regardless of the challenger's resources or staying power" (Porter, 1985, p. 514). Adopting such strategy does not guarantee success but it improves the odds of success for the late entrants.

Consider, for example, Enterprise Rent-a-Car, the biggest car rental company in North America. Rather than target travellers as its customers (like Hertz and Avis did), Enterprise focused on the replacement market (i.e. customers who had an accident). Rather than operate out of airports, it located its offices in downtown areas. Rather than use travel agents to push its services to the end consumers, it uses insurance companies and body shop mechanics. Rather than wait for the customer to pick up the rental, it brings the customer to the car. In short, Enterprise built a business model that is fundamentally different from the ones utilized by its biggest competitors. This allowed it to start out in 1957 as a new start-up firm in the industry and grow into the biggest competitor in less than 50 years.

The generalization that emerges from case studies like Enterprise is that late entrants can overcome the FMAs enjoyed by incumbents and succeed in attacking them by utilizing an innovative business model—one that undermines the very FMAs on which incumbents rely. If, for example, Unilever enjoys control of the supermarket shelf by virtue of being an early mover, a late entrant can undermine this FMA by adopting a business model that uses online distribution as one of its key components. Similarly, if British Airways enjoys control of airport gates by virtue of being an early mover, a late entrant can neutralize this FMA by adopting a business model that utilizes alternative airports for its operations.

The importance of an innovative business model in overcoming early movers' FMAs is also evident in the writings of both Michael Porter and Clay Christensen. For example, in describing how to successfully attack a market leader, Porter (1985) proposed that a challenger must utilize an innovative business model that meets three basic conditions:

- it must possess a sustainable competitive advantage over the leader, in either cost or differentiation;
- it must have proximity in the leader's other inherent advantages; and
- it must have a way of impeding leader retaliation.

We see the same emphasis on innovative business models in Christensen's (1997) work on disruptive innovation. Specifically, as argued by Christensen (1997) and Bower and Christensen (1995), *disruptors* (i.e. late entrants) use all three of Porter's conditions in staging their attacks against the established players (i.e. first-movers). By being *good enough* in whatever value proposition the established player is offering, they achieve proximity to the established firms' inherent advantages; by being *superior* in another dimension of the value proposition, they achieve competitive advantage; and by using a business model that is not only different from the business model of the established firm but also *conflicts* with it, they impede leader retaliation.

A potential criticism of the proposition that late entrants (such as Enterprise, Amazon and Southwest) succeed in entering established markets by utilizing innovative business models that undermine the early-movers' FMAs is that these companies are not really late entrants but pioneers of new markets themselves. For example, Amazon in e-retailing and Southwest in low-cost, no-frills air transportation can both be viewed as disruptors that have started whole new markets. They can, therefore, be viewed as first-movers themselves rather than as late entrants.

Whether disruptors create "new" markets or simply enlarge existing ones is of course a subjective issue and there is no right way to answer it. However, the pertinent question that needs to be answered (even if we accept that these disruptors created "new" markets) is the following: "did the pioneers of the established markets (such as the main airline companies) suffer (i.e. lost the benefits of their FMAs) as a result of the creation of these new markets (such as low-cost, no-frills flying)?" The answer is obviously "yes." Therefore, the creation of these new markets that came about by the introduction of a new business model has eroded the advantages of early FMAs. And that is exactly our proposition—new business models have the potential to erode the sustainability of FMAs irrespective of whether the markets they create are new or not.

Another potential criticism is whether the use of an innovative business model is equally important at every stage of an industry's evolution. For example, it has been suggested that FMAs tend to erode over time so that after some time, they cease to be important drivers of competitive advantage (Abernathy and Utterback, 1978). Several authors (e.g. Agarwal et al., 2002 and Suarez and Lanzolla, 2007) have pinpointed the "onset of maturity phase" as the critical point in the evolution of an industry after which FMAs lose their potency. The implication of this is that latecomers can succeed in entering a market without using an innovative business model if this market has already reached maturity. Could it be, for example, that Honda (a late entrant) succeeded in entering the US auto market not because it utilized an innovative business model to undermine the established firms' FMAs but because it entered once the market had matured and the drivers of competitive advantage had shifted away from the FMAs?

Again, it is true that there are many reasons why a firm may succeed and an innovative business model is only one of them. However, the available empirical evidence suggests that utilizing an innovative business model is an important driver of success both early in an industry's evolution (e.g. Markides and Geroski, 2005) as well as late in its evolution (after the onset of the maturity phase). For example, Markides and Geroski (2005) showed that *early* in an industry's evolution, the firms that succeed in scaling up a new market (and by definition end up capturing most of the value) are not the early pioneers but those firms that follow "fast-second," utilizing an innovative business model. Similarly, Christensen's (1997) work on disruptive innovation has demonstrated that disruptors succeed in entering *mature* industries primarily on the back of a business model that "breaks the rules of the game" in the industry. Thus, an innovative business model is important for success no matter what the stage in an industry's evolution. This is not to deny that an innovative business model may be *more* important for success earlier rather than later in the evolution of an industry. But this should not take away from the fact that an innovative business model is an important determinant of success whatever the stage in the industry's evolution. As Porter (1985) argued, attacking the pioneers on the back of an innovative business model increases the probability of success whatever the stage of the industry's evolution.

The same argument could be made with respect to order of entry effects—specifically, should a late entrant who enters soon after the pioneers utilize a different business model from a late entrant who enters a long time afterwards? We are not aware of any empirical studies that explored this question directly but based on the principle that the probability of success is higher for entrants who attack established firms on the back of an innovative business model, we can provide a tentative answer to this question. Specifically, we would expect that the late entrants who enter *early* should adopt a business model that differentiates them from the pioneers. Similarly, the late entrants who enter *late* should adopt a business model that differentiates them not only relative to the pioneers but also relative to the early latecomers. Thus, the later an entrant enters a market, the more difficult its task of identifying an innovative business model that would differentiate it relative to all the other market participants.

A final criticism of our thesis is whether late entrants who utilize innovative business models can be assessed as "successful" because of the market share they capture or because of their profitability. As argued by Szymanski et al. (1995) and Tellis and Golder (1996), how we measure performance makes a difference. There aren't any studies that have specifically examined this question but anecdotal evidence suggests that the generalization that innovative business models increase the success rate of late entrants is not affected by how we measure the success of these late entrants.

BUSINESS MODELS CAN EXPLAIN THE SUCCESS OF INCUMBENTS IN RESPONDING TO INNOVATIVE LATE ENTRANTS

Innovative business models are not only important in explaining the success of late entrants. They are also important in explaining how successful the established firms (i.e. pioneers) are in responding to innovative late entrants (e.g. Porter, 1985, chapter 14). We can see this by looking at the literature on disruptive innovation (Christensen, 1997).

As we already argued, the late entrants that succeed in attacking pioneers are those that exploit an innovative business model. However, not all late entrants that use innovative business models succeed in their attacks. For example, both Seiko (in watches) and Bic (in razors) attacked the pioneers in their markets (SMH and Gillette respectively) using innovative business models. Yet, despite their early success, both failed to make significant inroads. What determined the late entrants' success or failure was not only the innovativeness of their business models but also how the established firms (i.e. pioneers) responded to their attacks.

Specifically, we know that two specific business models employed by pioneers worked very well in limiting the success of their attackers (Markides, 2012). The first was to find ways to reduce the price of their established product while at the same time raising its existing value proposition (such as performance) to higher levels. Doing so allowed them to achieve low cost *and* differentiation at the same time and made life more difficult for the late entrants. The best way to see how this worked out is to compare an industry that failed to do so against one that did it successfully.

Fast moving consumer goods companies (FMCG) like Unilever and Procter & Gamble have lost enormous market share over the last twenty years to low cost disruptors producing private label products. Research by Glemet and Mira (1993) has shown that some products (such as wine, cheese, syrup, rice and pasta) are more susceptible to the private label threat than others (such as deep-frozen food, coffee, yogurt and chocolate). The difference is all down to innovation: products in which the incumbents had stopped investing lost share to private labels while products in which the incumbents continued to invest stood their ground. Specifically, private label products tend to do well when: (a) the incumbents charge "excessive" price premiums not justified by quality; (b) the incumbents have stopped innovating in these products (as measured by percent of new products introduced in the last 5 years); and (c) the incumbents have cut advertising investment in these products (Glemet and Mira, 1993). All this suggests that if the pioneers (i.e. incumbents) stop innovating in their products, the late entrants (i.e. disruptors) will inevitably catch up.

Compare how the FMCG players responded to the low-cost disruption in their markets with how Gillette responded to a similar threat. After seeing a quarter of the market being won over by Bic (in less than ten years), Gillette set about to change people's perceptions on what to expect from their razor. Through a series of innovative product introductions (such as the Sensor, the Mach 3 and the Fusion), Gillette redefined what "performance" meant in this market. They also innovated in the disposable space—for example, in 1994 they introduced the Custom Plus line that was a disposable with a lubricating strip. In late 2002, they announced the introduction of a new line of disposable razors with proprietary technology (rumoured to be a disposable version of a triple-blade razor, its premier product in refillables). By successfully raising the bar in this market, Gillette managed to convince consumers that they should expect more from their razors and that Bic was not really "good enough" for them. In the process, they succeeded in maintaining their leadership position in refillables while capturing a 45% market share in disposables.

Achieving low cost and differentiation at the same time is the first way that pioneers can use to respond to their attackers. A second way is to shift the basis of competition altogether, away from what the late entrants are trying to catch up with (i.e. performance) to another product benefit. For example, SMH was able to shift customer attention away from performance to style and design, an area the late entrant (Seiko) was not even considering. Nintendo also succeeded in doing this in its response to Sony's and Microsoft's entry in the home games console market. But achieving such a feat requires the support of a fundamentally different business model—one that is not only different from what the established player is using in its main market but also from the business model of the disruptor. An example may help clarify this point.

The coffee industry was revolutionized in the early 1990s with the introduction of Nestlé's Nespresso system (the pioneer). The system consisted of stylish coffee machines designed to make espresso using thimble-sized capsules filled with highest-quality coffees. It allowed for the quick preparation of single-serve, high quality espressos and cappuccinos at home. The new system gave rise to the premium, single-portion coffee market which quickly grew to dominate the overall coffee market, at the expense of more traditional R&G coffee. The rapid growth of this market attracted entry from numerous other coffee players (the late entrants). For example, Kraft introduced Tassimo in 2004; Lavazza introduced Espresso Point in 1994; Procter and Gamble introduced Home Café in 2004; Sara Lee's Dutch subsidiary, Douwe Egberts, introduced the Senseo system in 2001; and Melitta introduced the Melitta One:One system in 2003. Of all these late entrants, the only one that achieved success over the pioneer was Sara Lee DE's Senseo system.

The big difference between Sara Lee DE and all the others was the business model that they used to enter the single-serve coffee market. Whereas all other players adopted a business model that was similar to the one that Nespresso pioneered, Sara Lee DE adopted a totally different one. For example, rather than target wealthy households (as Nespresso did), Senseo went after the mass market. Rather than focus on espresso-drinking countries like Switzerland, Italy and France (as Nespresso did), Senseo focused on roast and ground (R&G) coffee-drinking countries like Germany and the Netherlands. Rather than offer machines that prepared espresso and cappuccino coffee (as Nespresso did), Senseo offered single-serve American coffee. Rather than position its product as a luxury item and distribute it through exclusive department stores (as Nespresso did), Senseo was positioned as a mass-market product, sold through mass-market department stores. In short, Senseo entered the market on the back of a business model that was radically different from the business model that Nespresso introduced (and all other players imitated) in this market. The end result was that Senseo was the only one to make any inroads in the new market that Nespresso created.

These examples highlight a simple point: how pioneers (i.e. incumbents) respond to an attacker could have a big effect on how successful the late entrants are in overcoming the early pioneers' first mover advantages. Specifically, if the pioneer succeeds in developing an innovative business model to counter-attack the late entrants' own innovative business models, the probability that it will protect its FMAs will be higher.

IGNORING BUSINESS MODELS CAN BIAS THE RESULTS

Our discussion so far suggests that FMAs are important but more important is *how* firms exploit them. Pioneering as a strategy has both advantages and disadvantages. Which effect will predominate depends on (i) the business model that pioneers use to consolidate a young market; (ii) the business model that late entrants utilize to attack the early pioneers; and (iii) the business model that pioneers use to defend their market against the latecomers. Yet, the business model variable is absent from every study on FMAs. What are the implications of such an omission?

Any econometric equation that aims to explain the performance of a firm as a function of a set of independent variables must control for any variable that influences *both* the dependent and independent variables. In this specific case, the firm's business model influences both the dependent variable (firm performance) and the independent variable (first-mover advantages). This implies that any examination of the correlation between performance and FMAs must explicitly control for the business models of both the pioneer and the late entrants. Failure to do so will produce a biased estimate of the correlation between performance and FMAs. Yet, past studies on this topic have done exactly this.

This may explain the conflicting *empirical* results found in the literature on the existence of FMAs. As already shown by VanderWerf and Mahon (1997), the likelihood of finding first-mover advantages is greatly affected by the methodology used. They specifically examined 4 questioned research practices (i.e. sample selection; specification of the dependent variable; specification of the independent variable; and statistical method used) and found that the likelihood of finding a positive relationship between performance and pioneering was only 8 percent when none of the four questionable research practices were used (versus 99 percent when all four methods were used). Our thesis in this paper is that failure to explicitly control for business models could be another questionable research practice that prevents us from identifying the true relationship between performance and pioneering.

In saying this we hope to shift the literature towards a contingency approach to FMAs—namely, that performance is not a consequence of FMAs per se but of the degree of *fit* between FMAs and a firm's business model. It is the *implementation* (i.e. exploitation or defending) of FMAs that will determine success, not the mere presence or size of these FMAs. Although researchers tend to shy away from incorporating the business model variable in their work on the basis that we do not have a clear definition of what a business model is, nothing could be further from the truth. As argued by Markides (2008, pp. 2–6), several useful definitions of business models exist and can be constructively used in our research. It is only by explicitly incorporating this concept in our work that research on FMAs can take a leap forward.

REFERENCES

Abernathy, W.J., Utterback, J., 1978 June–July. Patterns of Industrial Innovation. Technology Review, 40–47.

Afuah, A., 2003. Business Models: a Strategic Management Approach. McGraw-Hill/Irwin, Boston.

Agarwal, R., Sarkar, M.B., Echambadi, R., 2002. The conditioning effect of time on firm survival: an industry life cycle approach. Academy of Management Journal 45 (5), 971–994.

Amit, R., Zott, C., 2001. Value creation in e-business. Strategic Management Journal 22 (6–7), 493–520.

Audretsch, D.B., 1995. Innovation and Industry Evolution. MIT Press, Cambridge, MA.

Biggadike, R., 1979 May–June. The risky business of diversification. Harvard Business Review, 103–111.

Bower, J., Christensen, C., 1995 January–February. Disruptive technologies: catching the wave. Harvard Business Review, 43–53.

Casadesus-Masanell, R., Ricart, J.E., 2010. From strategy to business models and onto tactics. Long Range Planning 43 (2–3), 195–215.

Christensen, C., 1997. The Innovator's Dilemma: When New Technologies Cause Great Firms to Fail. Harvard Business School Press, Boston, MA.

Day, G.S., Freeman, J.S., 1990. Burnout or fadeout: the risks of early entry into high technology markets. In: Lawless, M.W., Gomez-Mejia, L.R. (Eds.), Strategic Management in High Technology Firms. JAI Press Inc, Greenwich, CT, pp. 43–65.

Dunne, T., Roberts, M., Samuelson, L., 1989 November. The growth and failure of US manufacturing plants. Quarterly Journal of Economics 104 (4), 671–698.

Fuentelsaz, L., Gomez, J., Polo, Y., 2002. Followers' entry timing: evidence from the Spanish banking sector after deregulation. Strategic Management Journal 23, 245–264.

Gans, J., Stern, S., 2010. Is there a market for ideas? Industrial and Corporate Change 19 (3), 805–837.

Geroski, P.A., 1991. Market Dynamics and Entry. Basil Blackwell Ltd, Oxford.

Geroski, P.A., 1995. What do we know about entry? International Journal of Industrial Organization 13, 421–440.

Glemet, F., Mira, R., 1993. The brand leader's dilemma. McKinsey Quarterly (2), 3–15.

Golder, P., Tellis, G., 1993 May. Pioneer advantage: marketing logic or marketing legend? Journal of Marketing Research 30, 158–170.

Gomez, J., Lanzolla, G., Maicas, J.P., 2011. The Role of Industry Dynamics in the Sustainability of First Movers' Advantages. City Business School. Unpublished Manuscript.

Hedman, J., Kalling, T., 2003. The business model concept: theoretical underpinnings and empirical illustrations. European Journal of Information Systems 12 (1), 49–59.

Lieberman, M., Montgomery, D., 1988. First mover advantages. Strategic Management Journal 9 (Special issue, Summer), 41–58.

Lieberman, M., Montgomery, D., 1998. First-mover (dis)advantages: retrospective and link with the resource-based view. Strategic Management Journal 19, 1111–1125.

Markides, C., 1997. Strategic innovation. Sloan Management Review 38 (3 (Spring)), 9–23.

Markides, C., 2008. Game Changing Strategies: How to Create Market Space in Established Industries by Breaking the Rules. Jossey-Bass, San Francisco.

Markides, C., 2012. How disruptive will innovations from emerging markets be? Sloan Management Review 54 (1, Fall), 22–25.

Markides, C., Geroski, P., 2005. Fast Second: How Smart Companies Bypass Radical Innovation to Enter and Dominate New Markets. Jossey-Bass, San Francisco.

Mueller, D., 1997. First-mover advantages and path dependence. International Journal of Industrial Organization 15, 827–850.

Porter, M.E., 1985. Competitive Advantage. Free Press, New York.

Robinson, W., Chiang, J., 2002. Product development strategies for established market pioneers, early followers and late entrants. Strategic Management Journal 23, 855–866.

Schnaars, S., 1994. Managing Imitation Strategies. The Free Press, New York.

Shankar, V., Carpenter, G., Krishnamurthi, L., 1998. Late mover advantage: how innovative late entrants outsell pioneers. Journal of Marketing Research 35, 54–70.

Suarez, F., Lanzolla, G., 2007. The role of environmental dynamics in building a first mover advantage theory. Academy of Management Review 32 (2), 377–392.

Szymanski, D.M., Try, L.C., Bharadwaj, S.G., 1995. Order of entry and business performance: an empirical synthesis and reexamination. Journal of Marketing 59, 17–33.

Teece, D., 1986. Profiting from technological innovation: implications for integration, collaboration, licensing and public policy. Research Policy 15, 285–305.

Teece, D.J., 2010. Business models, business strategy and innovation. Long Range Planning 43 (2–3), 172–194.

Teece, D., Pisano, G., Shuen, A., 1997. Dynamic capabilities and strategic management. Strategic Management Journal 18, 509–533.

Tellis, G., Golder, P., 1996 Winter. First to market, first to fail? Real causes of enduring market leadership. Sloan Management Review, 65–75.

Tellis, G., Golder, P., 2001. Will and Vision: How Latecomers Grow to Dominate Markets. McGraw Hill, New York.

Utterback, J., 1996. Mastering the Dynamics of Innovation. HBS Press, Boston.

VanderWerf, P., Mahon, J., 1997 November. Meta-analysis of the impact of research methods on findings of first-mover advantage. Management Science 43 (11), 1510–1519.

Zhang, S., Markman, A., 1998 November. Overcoming the early entrant advantage: the role of alignable and nonalignable differences. Journal of Marketing Research 35, 413–426.

Zott, C., Amit, R., 2010. Business model design: an activity system perspective. Long Range Planning 43 (2–3), 216–226.

Zott, C., Amit, R., Massa, L., 2011. The business model: recent developments and future research. Journal of Management 37 (4), 1019–1042.

READING 13

Adding Value through Offshoring

Joan Enric Ricart
IESE, University of Navarra, Spain

Pablo Agnese
Pompeu Fabra University, Spain

For decades, offshoring involved little more than moving call centers to countries with lower labor costs. But things have changed. Today's new generation of offshoring increasingly features value-added services, such as highly complex software projects or specific R&D functions. These changes are forcing companies to rethink their internationalization strategies in order to incorporate more of these kinds of value-added offshoring processes.

In this article, the authors discuss the risks and opportunities that managers must consider when offshoring, and they propose six steps aimed at creating value rather than simply reducing costs.

The U.S. sitcom *Outsourced* is based on an all-too-real premise: An American manager named Todd suddenly finds his departmental functions being outsourced to a call center in Mumbai.

"Todd, we decided to restructure Order Fulfillment."

"Restructure how?"

"Offshore the whole department."

(Laughs.) "Good one."

"I'm not kidding. Check out this spreadsheet. Any American job that's done on the phone or online is going overseas. The savings are incredible."

"You can't outsource Order Fulfillment. Our catalog is patriotic knick-knack. If a factory worker from Wisconsin calls the 800 number to buy this and gets a person from another country, he will flip out. You expect me to walk in there and tell everyone, 'I'm sorry, your job has been outsourced?'"

"I'll do it."

"So I'm fired, too?"

"No, not at all. We need you in India. Someone has to train the new guy."

"What does this new guy get paid?"

"Half a million . . . rupees. That's $11,000 a year to do your job. As in, eight for the price of one."

In real life, as in fiction, the arguments made by numerous companies to offshore services in the 90s usually followed this same script. Those years saw offshoring as little more than simply moving call centers to countries with lower labor costs.

But things have changed. Today's new generation of offshoring increasingly features value-added services, such as highly complex software projects or specific R&D functions. Gone are the days of simple cost reduction, which favored the routine use of call centers and overseas software developers for minor projects.

Two of Spain's biggest banking groups, BBVA and Santander, exemplify the new and improved offshoring trend.

Less than a decade ago, BBVA was running its entire back office out of Madrid. Five years later, it had relocated these operations, first to the southern Spanish city of Malaga, before outsourcing two-thirds of its operations to low-cost destinations such as Buenos Aires, Mexico City, and Lima. BBVA is currently doing the same with its remaining administrative activities in the other geographic areas where it operates.

Santander has taken a much more radical approach. Since 2000, the banking group has progressively transferred software development, computer centers, and business operations to three subsidiaries. These, in turn, were given the freedom

Joan Enric Ricart and Pablo Agnese. "Adding Value through Offshoring." *IESE Insight,* no. 10 (2011), pp. 60–66.

to concentrate, outsource, or transfer part of those activities as they saw fit, but always under the supervision of the banks. At the same time, Santander has developed a single, shared technology platform and common processes, among which offshoring is just one facet of an overall operating strategy.

This article is based on studies conducted by the Offshoring Research Network, which is associated with IESE's Center for Globalization and Strategy. For companies interested in moving operations overseas, our research shows that offshoring has become a critical component of a business strategy aimed at creating value.

For those who have not yet made the leap, an understanding of the current state of offshoring is essential. First, we explain the factors that have contributed to transforming this business practice. Then, we weigh up the benefits and risks, before sharing some of the tools that will help you to define a successful international offshoring strategy suited to your organization.

THE IT IMPETUS

How did offshoring get to be so popular? Undoubtedly, the development of information technology, fuelled by the Internet, gave rise to a certain set of functions that could be relocated more easily, and influenced which business relationships could be maintained through offshore destinations.

Information and communications technology (ICT), such as Voice Over IP and telepresence, became not only much cheaper, but also, with the advent of more collaborative applications and cloud computing phenomena, more comprehensive. This enabled companies to carry out high value-added activities far from home with the maximum degree of reliability and efficiency. With digitization, distance ceased to be a problem and, in many ways, disappeared.

The Telemedicine Clinic is a good case in point. What began life in 2003 as a means to centralize diagnostic services performed by hospitals in Sweden has since expanded to become a full radiology solutions provider to where public hospitals across the European Union are able to subcontract their diagnostic services. A specialist based in Barcelona, for example, can have immediate access to X-rays taken in Sweden, and on-call specialists in Sydney make sure that quality readings are provided day or night.

Eventually, offshoring evolved beyond providing technical support services, to actually being a source of new professional expertise in the form of research and development. Such was the path taken by General Electric, IBM, and Cisco. This went hand in hand with the proliferation of professional services firms and management consultancies, which specialized in offshoring and facilitated these tendencies even further.

FROM COST SAVINGS TO HEAD-HUNTING

In 2009, the Offshoring Research Network surveyed senior executives representing more than 2,000 companies and 4,300 offshore projects in four continents. While these executives continued to cite "labor cost savings" as the top advantage of offshoring, the survey also turned up significant numbers of executives who valued, for instance, the benefits of access to qualified personnel or greater organizational flexibility (see Exhibit 1).

EXHIBIT 1 More than Cost Savings

Companies increasingly value offshoring from the viewpoint of access to talent and improved flexibility.

	Finance & Insurance	High Tech	Manufacturing	Professional Services	Consumer Goods	Software
Labor costs	92	84	78	82	78	86
Other costs	74	68	70	66	74	56
Access to talent	67	65	61	55	53	63
Growth strategy	56	69	69	64	74	62
Organizational flexibility	70	53	77	70	85	64

Source: "Taking Offshoring to the Next Level." The 2009 Offshoring Research Network Corporate Client Survey Report.

There are two main reasons behind this. First, many have come to the realization that "labor cost savings" cannot serve as the only source of competitive advantage, as there will always be someone who can do it cheaper.

Also, what's happening is that, thanks to better education, the supply of skilled labor in offshore destinations has improved significantly over the years. This means that these workers are able to take on and carry out new business tasks requiring high levels of knowledge.

Our research corroborates the development of talent and knowledge as a critical element in offshoring strategies—a development that reinforces the association of offshoring with value creation processes. As our analysis shows, improving the quality of skilled workers worldwide will encourage product development offshoring, as opposed to just offshoring lower value activities.

This shift has been partly driven by emerging countries making a firm commitment to invest in education and infrastructure. Several studies, including the one by the Offshoring Research Network, reveal explosive growth in the number of engineering and computer science graduates, especially in the two major offshoring destinations of India and China. No wonder the U.S. administration is concerned, as reflected by President Obama's pledge in 2010 for the United States to "produce eight million more college graduates by 2020, because America has to have the highest share of graduates compared to every other nation."

This growth in the availability of skilled labor has led to the emergence of clusters specialized in offshoring activities, like investment banks in Mumbai or call centers in Bangalore. The phenomenon is not restricted to the Asian giants. There are now IT-associated clusters in Latin America, too, from Guadalajara, Mexico, to Recife, Brazil, and Córdoba, Argentina.

Having clusters concentrated together in one area makes it easier for companies and universities to exchange ideas and people, with universities tending to become the main recruitment centers. Clusters can also generate pools of talent with specific capabilities, making these offshore destinations even more attractive.

But the picture is not entirely perfect. Some of these regions have suffered significant inflation as well as high turnover of labor.

BENEFITS NOT WITHOUT RISKS

The positive effects of offshoring on the productivity of companies and—by extension—the economy, are well-documented (see the box "An Argument Blown Out of Proportion").

One study of 450 U.S. industries found that, between 1992 and 2000, offshoring succeeded in boosting productivity by as much as 10 percent. Another study, of 35,000 British production plants over a three-year period, estimated that increasing offshoring activities by 10 percent saw a corresponding 0.37 percent rise in total-factor productivity. Meanwhile, a study of 83 Japanese industries found that, between 1980 and 2005, a 1 percent rise in offshoring resulted in an improvement in total-factor productivity of between 0.5 percent and 2 percent.

Other studies, however, underscore the risks of offshoring, such as the problems associated with limiting the number of offshore destinations. A 2009 McKinsey survey found that 70 percent of offshore centers, whether company-owned or outsourced, were concentrated in just three countries: India, China, and the Philippines.

The risks of such concentration include unstable currencies and wages, intense competition for employees and regulatory limits—none of which compensate for the lower labor cost advantage. Certainly, the emergence of clusters in other parts of the world will undoubtedly help to mitigate such risks through a wider geographic distribution of activities.

The Offshoring Research Network study highlights the primary risks perceived by senior management, and how their perceptions changed from 2007 to 2009 (see Exhibit 2). Of particular note are the changes in how managers rank data security and the quality of the services provided. This should come as little surprise, since the financial crisis that erupted during this period made these issues of paramount importance for company survival.

DESTINATIONS Á LA CARTE

Most services offshoring used to go primarily to India (Hyderabad, Bangalore, Delhi, and Mumbai), Eastern Europe (Prague and Budapest) and Russia (mainly Moscow). In recent years, however, some of these cities have become less attractive in terms

AN ARGUMENT BLOWN OUT OF PROPORTION

The Impact of Offshoring on Employment in Countries of Origin Is Neither as Significant nor as Lasting as Some Would Portray

The argument that offshoring leads to serious job losses has found sympathizers in the media and certain political spheres. There is no shortage of voices advocating a return to tighter regulation and protectionism. But many of these fears are unfounded, and taking the measures some call for would bring results diametrically opposed to the desired ones.

HIGHER PRODUCTIVITY, MORE DEMAND

The greater efficiency and productivity obtained through offshoring exerts downward pressure on domestic prices, which, over time, raises demand for goods and services, and thus, for labor. How? By being more productive, companies can offer lower prices, which stimulates demand for their products and services, thereby boosting domestic job demand. This line of reasoning is supported by Mary Amiti and Shang-Jin Wei, who, in a 2006 study of U.S. industries, noted sufficient consequent growth in demand to offset any negative effects. More recent research by Pablo Agnese on the offshoring experiences of Japan found very probable gains in employment and productivity for local firms.

IMPACT ON EMPLOYMENT LESS THAN BELIEVED

The impact of offshoring on labor markets in the economies of origin is neither significant nor lasting. With few exceptions, the research agrees that any negative consequences are nil or negligible. Despite the recent crisis, Forrester stands by its estimates that, by 2015, the United States will have exported about 3.3 million service jobs—far from the alarming 40 million predicted in other reports.

RELEASED RESOURCES BRING LONG-TERM GAINS

Alarmist figures pale further against employment projections of the U.S. Bureau of Labor Statistics, which foresees the creation of 160 million jobs for the same year, 2015. While some workers may be affected in the short term, as jobs they used to perform go overseas, the new resources that are freed as a result of offshoring open up new opportunities for employees and employers alike. In the long run, labor markets in the economies of origin find themselves performing new activities or entering whole new sectors.

EXHIBIT 2 Risks to Consider

Managers perceive service quality and data security as the primary risks associated with offshoring.

	Finance & Insurance	High Tech	Manufacturing	Professional Services	Consumer Goods	Software	Average 2007/2008	Average 2009
Service quality	70	56	54	53	35	46	51	65
Data security	72	47	43	36	33	31	43	59
Loss of control	45	44	44	42	34	33	43	44
High turnover	42	42	47	33	17	42	41	39
Cultural differences	37	50	47	32	28	26	32	40

Source: "Taking Offshoring to the Next Level." The 2009 Offshoring Research Network Corporate Client Survey Report.

of labor costs and infrastructure, as they have been inundated with demand. New offshoring destinations have emerged, with unique selling points of their own.

Dubai and the United Arab Emirates, for example, have focused on internationality, state-of-the-art infrastructure, a stable and qualified workforce, low taxes, and five-star attractions. Cape Town, South Africa, stresses its highly qualified workforce, strong insurance and professional services sectors, alongside its well-developed telecommunications network. Morocco specializes in customer service and back-office functions for many French and Spanish companies, since many of its workers speak both languages. Vietnam boasts a large number of math graduates who also speak English, French, German, or Russian.

Given the expanding choice of destinations, managers who consider offshoring will need to compile lists of locations and weigh their suitability based on the following criteria: costs, availability of skilled labor, local or regional market potential, quality of infrastructure, the country's risk profile, and the political and business environment.

FINDING THE RIGHT STRATEGY

Are managers fully aware of what they face in implementing offshoring strategies? Until now, services offshoring has followed the traditional strategy applied to industrial processes—that is, identifying any repetitive and nonstrategic processes that can be relocated to geographic areas with lower labor costs.

Experience shows that this approach is not enough. To make offshoring decisions, one must have a clear strategy of activity assignment for different locations. This requires a systemic view of the changes in the business model.

In line with IESE Prof. Pankaj Ghemawat's globalization theories, we consider three types of strategies that yield different business models: aggregation, adaptation, and arbitrage. They usually come two at a time; rarely all three at once.

Aggregation means exploiting economies of scale through the use of regional business units offering a standardized product or service. Here, the purpose of offshoring is to centralize the activities in a specific geographic region to gain efficiencies through economies of scale.

Adaptation, on the other hand, seeks to compete through personalized dealings with customers at the local level. Unless the locations share many traits, it is very hard to think of offshoring processes designed according to the framework of this type of global strategy.

Arbitrage involves exploiting the differences that may arise between countries where the different business units are located. Most offshoring processes are associated with this last strategy. The goal is to take advantage of other economies with lower wages and, as recent research indicates, the possibility of competing for talent at a global level.

What happens when your existing strategy is incompatible with offshoring—that is, when your business model is not flexible enough to integrate it? This is a question that should make managers reconsider the pros and cons of the drive toward offshoring at all costs.

CHOOSE YOUR STRATEGY WISELY

Implementing all three of the previously mentioned strategies often results in friction or imbalances between them, or between the business models involved. Sometimes offshoring strategies will force changes in the current orientation that can be very hard to assume, especially if the process involves changes to the long-term business model.

The experience of the companies studied shows that it isn't necessary to "go all out" when embarking on a strategy of global scale. Instead, it's enough to focus on one or two strategies, at most. It should be remembered that the optimal strategy depends not only on conditions in the market or sector, but also on the company's position relative to its competitors.

Managers also need to consider whether a strategy based on activity offshoring is the most appropriate when it comes time to take action. Other options might be more suitable to the company's situation and market conditions. Productive resources—labor services, know-how, raw materials—allotted to arbitrage, for example, could be used for other purposes, such as tasks related to adaptation or aggregation strategies.

Thus, the final decision of whether or not to go for offshoring must take into account the company's comparative advantages.

AN ADVANCED OFFSHORING MODEL

The case of Santander illustrates some of the salient aspects of offshoring processes.

The banking group has concentrated most of its software development activities in its subsidiary, Isban. With this centralization in a single unit, and all banks sharing the same technology platform, the group reaps enormous benefits from aggregation.

Meanwhile, Santander leaves control of the management of these processes to those banks that have a manager for operations and technology. This enables total adaptation to the idiosyncrasies of each context.

Furthermore, by operating this way in all the countries where the group is present, Santander can move its software factories to locations that provide the maximum benefits of arbitrage.

Ultimately, with this model, Santander obtains benefits from each of the key aspects of its international strategy. It gains flexibility and resilience, making the group better able to react to adverse conditions, as well as better able to challenge its main competitors.

Admittedly, this three-pronged strategy is rare and seems to work only in companies with large infrastructure and vast experience. Even then, implementation is not easy and requires three critical elements.

First, there needs to be a common transaction platform flexible enough to serve the needs of each bank, while at the same time being uniform enough to achieve the benefits of aggregation.

Second, there needs to be a complex system of governance that balances efficiency improvements, acceptable risks, and the quality of services.

Third, there needs to be an unequivocal desire to serve the client banks.

Yet if the functioning and coordination of these tasks is correct, the results are extremely positive, as has been the case for Santander.

SIX STEPS TO FOLLOW

Formulating an appropriate strategy is tricky, and following generic advice can lead to disaster. Instead, we offer you a sequence of specific steps that can help to guide managers.

1. **Think big picture, not item by item.** Offshoring that's not linked to the overall strategy can be a one-way ticket to failure. In the search for the best capabilities at the best price, a company must adapt both its global strategy and its organization.
2. **Decide what you want to outsource and how.** Defining a global strategy requires deciding which activities or processes are suitable for offshoring, how—through subsidiaries or outsourcing—and where. Study the complexity or simplicity of your processes and services, and the interdependencies between them, to identity the most outsourceable. You should also take into consideration issues such as whether these processes require some sort of presence or physical proximity, or specific company expertise. You will need to review this analysis from time to time, since studies show that these situations are changeable.
3. **Examine destinations carefully.** You should take into account variables such as labor costs, availability of talent, market potential, quality of infrastructure, acceptable risks, and the environment of each destination.
4. **Adapt your organization to the new reality.** According to our studies, in most companies, adapting business processes to the new reality entails a long learning curve. Therefore, it pays to make the transition with the help of a specialized company.
5. **Develop local talent.** Another organizational difficulty is learning how to attract, manage and develop talent in the destination countries. Again, this task is easier if you hire the services of an experienced, specialized provider in the chosen country, as BBVA did. If you opt for full outsourcing, it is important that you create some way of incorporating their know-how; otherwise, you run the risk of these operations being held hostage by the local talent.
6. **Govern your offshored business.** Finally, the company needs to develop management mechanisms to oversee activities in different parts of the world, often with different suppliers. The development of sound governance capabilities is vital.

Activity offshoring is evolving rapidly toward ever-higher levels of complexity. The sequence from labor costs to skilled personnel to value creation illustrates the continuous evolution and adaptation of firms to the technological revolution. But companies shouldn't underestimate the risks. Prudence may be the most useful tool in your approach to offshoring—even more so in times of crisis.

READING 14

Reverse Innovation: A Global Growth Strategy That Could Pre-empt Disruption at Home

Vijay Govindarajan
Tuck School of Business at Dartmouth

Chris Trimble
Tuck School of Business at Dartmouth

As western companies increasingly target emerging markets to help drive growth, they will likely find that the traditional strategy of global localization will prove inadequate. An alternative is the new concept of reverse innovation. Historically, multinationals innovated in rich countries and sold these products in poor countries. Reverse innovation is doing the opposite.

For decades, multinationals adopted a strategy of global localization, or "glocalization"—that is, trying to modify the products developed for rich countries to suit local conditions. The problem with this strategy is that it effectively restricts the multinational to playing at the top of the market pyramid in emerging economies, with products that only the most affluent could possibly afford. What companies like GE have since come to recognize is that in order to be able to take full advantage of the growth opportunities presented in countries like India and China they also need to be able to offer products at much lower price points. The only way they can do that is to innovate specifically for those markets in a back-to-zero fashion.

But reverse innovation implies more than just zero-based innovation for emerging markets. Reverse innovation also highlights the potential for very low price-point innovations originating in the developing world to generate new market demand back in the richer economies. A good example is the portable ultrasound machine. This was developed originally by GE in the early 2000s to meet the particular needs of the Chinese market, and the PC-based technology advances involved have since helped propel the growth of a $250M business opportunity for GE globally, through finding many new applications in the US and other advanced economies (see box, "Reverse Innovation at General Electric").

Historically, developed world multinationals, especially winners, struggle in emerging markets. This is because the optimal organization that led to success in a developed economy does not support reverse innovation. Companies that practice the more conventional global localization strategy need to solve several major challenges in order to innovate successfully given local conditions. New organizational models are required. Multinationals like GE, PepsiCo, P&G, and Deere are creating full business capabilities—including product development, manufacturing, and marketing—in emerging markets.

However, for many executives perched in rich countries, it's tempting to disregard the reverse innovation challenge. "Why should innovation for emerging markets ever be necessary? Why can't we just export the products and services that we already have?" Unfortunately, the implicit assumption that emerging countries will follow the same pattern of development as rich nations simply doesn't match the facts. India, for example, has the potent advantage of being able to tackle old problems with new technology. Also, the needs of consumers must be addressed under local conditions—different

Reprinted from "Reverse Innovation: A Global Growth Strategy That Could Pre-empt Disruption at Home," by Vijay Govindarajan and Chris Trimble, *Strategy and Leadership,* Vol. 40, No. 5, pp. 5–11.

REVERSE INNOVATION AT GENERAL ELECTRIC

At the turn of the millennium, GE Healthcare had established strong positions in the rich markets of the world, but the results from developing countries like China were disappointing. Relying on a strategy of localizing the products that it had developed for rich countries was constraining the company from fully participating in the growth of the Chinese economy. This changed when GE finally came to recognize that customer priorities were essentially different in rich and poor country markets. In wealthy countries, customers valued performance and functionality, while in poorer countries the priorities were price, followed by portability and ease of use, because the basic demographics and infrastructure are very different.

The state-of-the-art, feature-rich, high technology ultrasound equipment that GE Healthcare sold to large hospitals in the developed world at price points of $100,000 and above was suitable only to serve a very small proportion of the Chinese population in the larger city locations. Most of China's population still relied on low-tech hospitals in relatively remote areas, and there was no way that even a scaled-down, feature-reduced version of the company's existing ultrasound offering would be able to meet the need. A radical solution was called for, one developed specifically for the particular requirements of the local market. To meet this need, GE engineers found a way to develop a compact, portable, "good enough" ultrasound device, based on combining a regular laptop computer with some sophisticated software. Within five years the company had managed to produce a version that could sell for as low as $15,000 (a "50 percent solution at a 15 percent price").

This new low-price, portable technology, developed by GE specifically to meet the distinct requirements of emerging markets, has since found exciting new applications in more developed economies in situations where features are less important than price, portability and ease-of-use, such as at accident sites or in emergency rooms and operating theaters.

Adapted from Immelt, J.R., Govindarajan, V., and Trimble, C., "How GE is disrupting itself," *Harvard Business Review*, October, 2009, pp. 56–65.

infrastructures, geographies, cultures, languages and governments.

Because of the vast differences of the developing economies, business leaders who have grown up in, worked in, and are steeped in the traditions of rich countries face a tremendous challenge. For them, reverse innovation begins not with inventing, but with forgetting. The lesson for these executives trying to grow in emerging markets: let go of what you've learned, what you expect and what has brought you your greatest successes. You must let go of the dominant logic that has served you well in rich countries. If you want to use today's science and technology to address unmet needs in the developing world, then you must start with humility and curiosity. In fact, it's best to assume that you've just landed on Mars.

So where should you look out for the most promising opportunities to reverse innovate? From this "new planet" vantage point, you can observe five enormous needs gaps that separate emerging markets from rich countries and think of them as among the most promising starting points. None of the needs gaps are likely to be closed simply by adapting innovations already developed for rich countries.

HOW REVERSE INNOVATION BEGINS: STUDYING THE FIVE GAPS

The five gaps are the performance gap, the infrastructure gap, the sustainability gap, the regulatory gap and the preferences gap.

1. The Performance Gap

With little money in their pockets, buyers in the developing world cannot demand the sky-high levels of performance that we are accustomed to in rich countries. Indeed, in many cases, they cannot afford even what those in the rich world would consider to be low-end products. However, that doesn't mean these potential customers don't need innovation.

Consider a typical "good-better-best" product lineup. The good product offers 80 percent performance at an 80 percent price, the better product offers 90 percent performance at a 90 percent price, and the best product gives 100 percent performance at a 100 percent price.

The easy thing to do, when trying to address needs in emerging economies, is to customize the good product a bit, perhaps by watering it down to a fair product that offers 70 percent performance at a 70 percent price. Typically, however, such an offering captures only a small slice of the market. Instead, developing nations are most eager for breakthrough new technologies that deliver decent performance at an ultralow cost—that is, a 50 percent solution for as little as a 15 percent price. It is impossible to design to that radical ratio if you begin with the existing offering. The only way to get to an entirely new price-performance curve is by starting from scratch.

For example, Nokia managed to capture an enormous market share of 60 percent in India by creating an ultra-low-cost handset that some users have bought for as little as the equivalent in rupees of $5—discounted from a published price of $20 to $30, which is still a mere fraction of the retail price of high-end rich-world phones. How did Nokia do it? By re-imagining the cell phone. The company slashed costs by producing only a few basic models at a time when its global competitors offered dozens or more. Nokia made some customization, such as adding Hindi-language text messaging, but it did so with software, not hardware—a far less costly approach. It also added functionalities to the handset, such as powerful flashlights that rural customers with irregular electricity valued. Nokia clearly understood the differences in needs—the performance gap, in particular. It created an offering that met real needs at a realistic price.[1]

2. The Infrastructure Gap

The rich world has extensive infrastructure in place; the poor world does not. One naturally thinks of the rich world's well-developed infrastructure as a powerful asset. New products can be developed in the rich world under the assumption that a solid and reliable infrastructure is in place. However, a lack of infrastructure can actually be an advantage in the innovation game. Difficult constraints, such as unreliable electric power, inspire creative workarounds that sometimes lead in unexpected directions. There are also major differences between rich and poor countries in infrastructure markets themselves. In fact, reverse innovation opportunities are particularly robust in this area. For starters, as developing countries build out their infrastructures for the first time, demand for construction services is very strong. Developing countries are robust construction markets; rich countries are tepid replacement markets.

Furthermore, when rich countries adopt innovative infrastructure technologies, they must make the new systems compatible with those that already exist. Rich countries are thus constrained by choices they made decades ago. Developing countries, unencumbered by legacy systems, have the flexibility to leapfrog to breakthrough technologies. As a result, we have a seemingly odd state of affairs. Infrastructure is often painfully absent in the developing world, but where it exists, it is frequently cutting-edge.

There are already several examples of third-world nations with first world infrastructure. Indeed, when traveling one sometimes wonders which are the developed and which are the developing countries. Take a flight from New York's JFK Airport to Beijing, compare the airports, and you'll see a striking difference. Or make a cell phone call in rural Vermont and then in rural Morocco. (One reason Nokia captured its high market share in India was that it built advanced wireless infrastructure in rural areas of the country.) The developing world's rapid investment in wireless telecommunications has affected more than phone calls. Poor countries have leapfrogged brick-and-mortar banking to mobile banking for the masses, and they are also the early adopters of telemedicine technologies.

3. The Sustainability Gap

As the world economy grows, the clashes between economic activity and environmental concerns will only become more severe. Nevertheless, the intensity will not rise uniformly around the globe. In some cases, intensity is highest in the developing world. Take the case of China's extreme air-pollution problems. As a point of comparison, on an air quality scale of 1 to 500 (where 1 is cleanest and 500 dirtiest), Beijing often hits the 500 mark; a score of 100 would be unacceptable in the United States. Small wonder that China is charged up about electric cars.

"Reverse innovation also highlights the potential for very low price-point innovations originating in the developing world to generate new market demand back in the richer economies."

"A lack of infrastructure can actually be an advantage in the innovation game. Difficult constraints, such as unreliable electric power, inspire creative workarounds that sometimes lead in unexpected directions."

The electric-car concept is a century old, but it has remained impractical for want of a cost-effective battery. Local companies are rising to the challenge. A little-known Shenzhen-based firm called BYD has announced a plug-in electric car with a lithium-ion ferrous-phosphate battery—a non-catchy name for what investors hope will be a catchy battery. One indication of the company's promise: Warren Buffet took a 10 percent ($230 million) stake in the company.

If the 5.8 billion of the world's poor consume and produce goods in ways that are environmentally unsound, the results will be catastrophic for poor countries—and for the planet. The only way poor countries can sustain economic growth is through "green" solutions. As a result, emerging markets are likely to leapfrog to several next-generation environmentally friendly technologies.

4. The Regulatory Gap

Regulation is a double-edged sword. New regulation almost always arises in the wake of misfortune or "bad" behavior in some market that, in retrospect, is judged to have been too free. The rich world, because of its older economies and its cultural and legal traditions, has advanced regulatory systems that, when applied effectively, keep markets fair and consumers and workplaces safe. But regulatory systems can also be needless barriers to innovation when they become labyrinthine, technologically obsolete, or captured by vested interests that seek to sustain the status quo. Under such conditions, innovation in the developing world may enjoy the advantages of lower friction and faster progress. In making this observation, we do not mean to suggest that low levels of regulation in an emerging market are either a good thing or a bad thing; it simply is what it is, and it may sometimes provide an advantageous medium for certain innovations.

For example, Diagnostics For All is a Boston-area start-up that has developed paper-based diagnostic tests the size of a postage stamp. When chemicals embedded in the paper react with blood, urine, saliva, or sweat, the paper changes colors. It is a quick, simple, and inexpensive alternative to diagnostic machines that cost tens of thousands of dollars and produce results requiring expert interpretation. Despite the attractiveness of such a product in rich-world markets, Diagnostics For All chose to commercialize its technology first in the developing world, where the company could circumvent the slow and painstaking US Food and Drug Administration approval process and sidestep resistance to change (and even hostile lobbying efforts) from established players who rely on high reimbursements tied to expensive equipment.

5. The Preferences Gap

One of the more enjoyable aspects of traveling the globe is discovering, from country to country, a rich diversity of tastes, habits and rituals. Often this diversity is revealed in seemingly mundane consumer products, such as snack foods. Many of the nutritional staples that anchor diets in developing countries are rarely consumed in the rich world. In India, for example, PepsiCo is developing new snack foods based not on corn (ubiquitous in the rich world), but on lentils—hardly a food most Americans grow up eating.

As these five substantial gaps suggest, developing-world customers have problems that have not already been solved in the rich world (see Exhibit 1).

Furthermore, poor countries have the relative luxury of addressing their challenges with modern technologies that simply weren't available when rich countries addressed similar needs decades ago. Therefore, capturing opportunities in the poor world means starting from scratch. Reverse innovation is what we call clean-slate innovation.

EXHIBIT 1 Why Reverse Innovation Must Be Clean Slate Innovation

The five needs gaps between emerging economies and the rich world are so substantial that emerging-economy needs can only rarely be addressed simply by making adaptations to rich-world products.

Gap	Description	Implication	Example
Performance	Because of their low incomes, customers in poor countries are prepared to make significant sacrifices in performance—at the right price	Design to deliver a 50 percent solution at a 15 percent price	Nokia cell phones
Infrastructure	Rich-world infrastructures are fully built; emerging-economy infrastructures are under construction	First, customers in poor countries need solutions that do not depend on reliable infrastructure Second, infrastructure builders in poor countries can immediately adopt cutting-edge solutions	Portable, battery-powered electrocardiogram machines for use where electric power is unreliable Indian telecoms leapfrogging to wireless technology in the absence of landline phones
Sustainability	Poor countries face many of the most daunting sustainability challenges on the planet	Poor countries are more eager than rich ones for next-generation environmental solutions	Electric cars in China
Regulatory	Regulatory systems in emerging economies are less developed and present fewer delays when a company is bringing innovative solutions to market	New products may pass through regulatory hurdles in poor countries first	Diagnostics For All
Preferences	Each country has distinct tastes and preferences	Innovation efforts must take these differences into account	The prevalence of lentil-based foods in India

Note: © 2012 Vijay Govindarajan and Chris Trimble, *Reverse Innovation: Create Far From Home, Win Everywhere* (Harvard Business Review Press, 2012).

REVERSE INNOVATION AS COMPETITIVE THREAT

So far, our message has been simple:

- There are huge opportunities in the developing world.
- Developing nations are different—not just a little, but *very* different.
- Innovators win, exporters lose.

That's a good start, but it is not the full message, because it overlooks the full consequences of inaction. To fail at reverse innovation is not just to lose out on an opportunity abroad. The stakes can be much more meaningful than that. A loss abroad can lead to an even bigger loss at home.

Why? Because, although reverse innovations are adopted first in the developing world, that isn't the end of the story. The global economy is richly interconnected. Reverse innovations can have global impact. Ultimately, they have the potential to migrate from poor countries to rich ones. This migration is, at first glance, counterintuitive. After all, the dramatic needs gaps are what create the opportunity for innovations in emerging markets in the first place. Given those gaps, how could such innovations possibly be eagerly adopted in rich countries?

We believe there are two distinct mechanisms. Reverse innovations become attractive to the rich world through either a "marginalized market" sooner or a mainstream market later.

ENTERING MARGINALIZED MARKETS

In the rich world, marginalized markets are underserved or ignored not because they don't need innovation, but because they're too small to justify a costly innovation investment. But what if, for every marginalized potential customer in the rich world, there are fifty similar customers in the developing world? When an otherwise marginal market is multiplied by fifty, it suddenly looks much more interesting.

For example, the very low end of the automotive market in the rich world has long been marginalized. Companies like Ford and Audi have targeted their innovation efforts at rich or middle-class customers. Poor buyers get whatever is left over after the features they can't afford have been stripped out. This may seem like a sensible approach, but it really only makes sense to an executive with rich-world blinders on. The low end of the market is a gold mine, not a ghost town, if your vantage point is Delhi instead of Detroit.

On March 23, 2009, the automotive division of legendary Indian business conglomerate Tata launched the Nano. At just over $2,000, Nano is by far the world's most affordable car. Tata practiced "frugal engineering": it challenged every standard industry assumption to achieve its ultra-low-cost position by using clever designs, new materials and supplier partnerships. The launch suddenly and dramatically changed the size and composition of the automotive market in India. By some estimates, the Nano will make car ownership possible for 65 percent more Indians of the middle class, all of them eager for a safer alternative to motorbikes.

It is a huge opportunity. Nonetheless, it was overlooked not just by one or two rich-world automakers, but by all of them. These automakers have not just lost an opportunity; they have put themselves at risk close to home. Tata Motors plans to scale up the Nano platform and launch it in Europe and the United States, and it now seems just a matter of time before Tata becomes a significant new competitor at the low end of the market, challenging traditional industry giants like Honda and Ford.

The banking industry has similarly ignored the low end of the market. Muhammad Yunus capitalized on the opportunity by founding Bangladesh's Grameen Bank, unleashing the microfinance revolution (and, in 2006, taking home the Nobel Peace Prize). To enable the poor to start small businesses, Grameen makes tiny loans, ones that are too small to be profitable for large banks. At every turn, Yunus challenged the conventional wisdom of large commercial banks. Banks lend to the rich; Grameen lends to the poor. Banks lend to men; Grameen lends to women. Banks operate in urban areas; Grameen operates in rural areas. Banks ask for collateral; Grameen extends trust. Banks have legal contracts; Grameen relies on peer pressure. If one member of a borrowing group defaults, no more loans will be made to the entire group. Since its inception in 1983, Grameen has lent over $9 billion, with a 98 percent recovery rate.

From its beginnings in Bangladesh, the microcredit banking model has spread to over one hundred countries. Today, it has even gained a foothold in a marginalized banking market in the United States—poor neighborhoods in New York City.

DISRUPTING MAINSTREAM MARKETS

When a reverse innovation is embraced by the mainstream, it becomes a powerful force—one that holds tremendous opportunities for those with their eyes open and terrifying risks for incumbents with their eyes shut. When this happens, established players stand to lose something even more precious than opportunities forgone. They stand to lose long-held market positions. We can see this already happening in the case of GE's portable PC-based ultrasound innovation designed for emerging markets. In the years since its introduction almost a decade ago, GE has continued to improve image quality to the point where newer "premium" versions have already moved beyond the confines of applications in "marginalized" markets in developed countries, like accident sites and emergency rooms, to offer a range of mainstream cardiology, radiology, and obstetric functionalities for long the preserve of more expensive, centrally-installed, equipment.

"Reverse innovations can have global impact. Ultimately, they have the potential to migrate from poor countries to rich ones."

Reverse innovations don't always flow uphill into mainstream markets, but conditions are ripe whenever there is a trend that slowly closes the needs gap. Because of the gap, the poor-world

EXHIBIT 2

Destination	Time Frame	Driving Force	Consequence of Inaction	Example
Marginalized market	Immediate	Niche markets in the rich world with needs similar to the mass market in poor countries	Lost opportunity	Microfinance in poor neighborhoods in New York City
Mainstream market	Delayed	A trend that closes the needs gap	Erosion, possibly severe, of existing market position in the rich world	Portable ultrasound devices that improve in performance to the point that they can compete with traditional devices

Note: © 2012 Vijay Govindarajan and Chris Trimble, *Reverse Innovation: Create Far From Home, Win Everywhere* (Harvard Business Review Press, 2012).

innovation will likely be unattractive in mainstream rich world markets on the day that it is introduced, but over time and with further development, it may, as in the case of GE's portable ultrasound machine, become attractive to more and more customers and eventually disrupt established rivals (see Exhibit 2).

ENDNOTES

[1] Juan Alcacer *et al.*, "Emerging Nokia?" Case 710-429 (Boston: Harvard Business School Publishing, 2011).

READING 15

How Emerging Giants Can Take on the World

John Jullens
Booz & Company

The trick is to learn to innovate and manage quality while remaining nimble.

Many of today's emerging giants face an existential threat they didn't see coming: The headlong growth that put them on the map isn't enough to sustain them when their industries mature or their geographic markets experience the kind of cooldown that's occurring right now in China and India.

Companies in developing countries are often so focused on chasing growth that they fail to invest in improving their capabilities in areas such as innovation, operations, and brand management. So even if they have enormous reach and revenues in the billions, they're unprepared when growth slows and competition from increasingly savvy developed-world multinationals intensifies. They lack the tools—and the structure—to remain profitable in a slower economic environment by becoming efficient and gaining competitive advantage in new markets. Some, including the once high-flying Chinese automakers BYD and Chery, have landed hard.

It's critical that the next generation of emerging-market corporations heed this lesson and develop enterprise capabilities from the very beginning—even as they battle for early advantage by seizing nascent business opportunities. Great Wall, which has seemingly emerged from nowhere to become one of China's most successful automakers, and the appliance maker Haier, which in 30 years transformed itself from a local manufacturer of poor-quality refrigerators into a world-class competitor, have achieved this ambidexterity. Unless emerging-market companies can become capabilities-driven, they're doomed to follow BYD and Chery—and may eventually fall victim to a shakeout in their industries.

PLAYING CATCH-UP

Companies in emerging markets embody a contradiction: They are both first movers and latecomers. They're among the first to have made cars, appliances, or computers in their home countries, but they're way behind multinationals that have been honing their capabilities, technologies, and brands for decades.

As first movers, they have typically pursued rapid top-line growth at all costs, acquired technologies by all means legal and sometimes illegal, and simply copied the products and processes of developed-market companies. They have mastered the local business landscape and learned to cater to customers who are just joining the consumer economy. Their speed and agility have served them well—indeed, some scholars have argued that opportunism, tenacity, ingenuity, and connections with local power brokers are the only capabilities emerging giants need.

But in their eagerness to get ahead, many of these companies have neglected to lay the foundation for profitability in any environment other than a rapidly expanding market. They often don't know how to compete on quality, for example, or on the strength of design ideas, or on innovative branding.

HOW ONE CHINESE CAR COMPANY CAME UP SHORT

Founded in 1995 by Wang Chuanfu, BYD was originally a low-cost manufacturer of rechargeable lithium ion batteries for cell phones. Wang had considerable expertise in batteries but virtually none in automotive technology. That didn't stop him from buying a state-owned automobile maker in 2002 and envisioning a central role for battery technologies in the rise of electric vehicles.

Although the company borrowed ideas from Japanese manufacturing (and reverse-engineered popular Japanese car designs), it shunned Japan's reliance on intensive automation and employed thousands of workers to produce not only cars but most of the needed parts, from braking systems to CD players. To boost sales, it rapidly expanded dealerships in China, set aggressive sales targets, and pushed inventory to dealers in pursuit of those targets.

In 2008 Warren Buffett bought 10% of the company, dramatically enhancing its brand value and increasing BYD's sales in the United States. In 2009 its F3 model was the best-selling sedan in China, with more than 250,000 cars sold. The company's sales hit a peak of about 500,000 units in 2010.

But soon after, BYD began to falter. Consumer demand for electric vehicles was weak, and China Central Television questioned the company's quality standards. Indeed, BYD ranks below the industry average in a number of J.D. Power studies, including initial quality and dependability.

BYD did a few things right, from adopting a bold vision to establishing a position as a technology leader. But that vision wasn't rooted in reality: Widespread consumer adoption of battery-powered passenger vehicles is still far in the future (if it occurs at all). And the company's emphasis on technology made a good start in establishing a strong competitive position, but a vehicle maker must be known as reliable, too. BYD's stumbles resulted from a failure to develop sophisticated capabilities such as new-product development, demand forecasting, capacity planning, inventory management, and customer insight. The company may have to accept being a niche player, selling electric passenger cars and buses.

As they expand, they lose managerial control and begin suffering operational problems—poor product quality, poor inventory management, low employee satisfaction levels—that become worse over time.

It's easy to see how emerging-market corporations get themselves into this position of weakness. Copying established companies' products and processes can seem like a great strategy when markets are young and growing by double digits. Moreover, many of these emerging giants are still run by their founders—industry veterans with powerful connections to key government officials—who tend to make decisions on the basis of their own experiences. They fail to realize that their organizations have outgrown their management structures or are overextended, with too many employees, too many facilities, and too many commitments to volume levels. They don't notice until too late that a changing business climate poses challenges the company isn't prepared to face.

> "Companies in emerging markets embody a contradiction: They are both first movers and latecomers."

Over the past decade China's leaders have been pushing its economy toward greater reliance on domestic consumption as a driver of growth. That uneasy transition is partly responsible for lower revenue increases at many Chinese companies. Maintaining profitability in this environment requires companies to become more productive and to shift their marketing efforts from enticing wide-eyed new consumers to winning over competitors' customers.

Meanwhile, developed-world multinationals have learned a thing or two about emerging markets, and some have become formidable players there.

So emerging giants must now compete against one another and against foreign multinationals on efficiency, marketing, branding, service, quality, innovation, and, in many cases, managing acquisitions. In other words, they need enterprise capabilities that create value, are difficult to copy, and can be translated into profits.

BYD lacked a wide range of those. After dominating in the global battery market, it chased a grandiose vision of becoming the world leader in electric vehicles. The company expanded rapidly and tried to diversify in order to preempt competitors. But it never mastered the notoriously complex process of automobile product development; it overestimated how quickly its markets would grow; and it fell short on product quality.

As better-made vehicles from competing manufacturers eroded its market share, BYD's unit sales fell by 15% in 2011 and stayed flat in 2012. Only now is the company beginning to appreciate the importance of the capabilities it lacked, including product development, quality management, and network management. Although BYD has had some recent success in selling electric buses to the city of Los Angeles and the Amsterdam airport, its passenger car business continues to struggle. (See the sidebar "How One Chinese Car Company Came Up Short.")

Chery, too, lacked a number of capabilities, most noticeably for managing multiple brands and models. Its strategy for China was to develop car models for practically every taste and income level. In 2009, when its lineup already included nine passenger vehicles, one commercial vehicle, and one minivan, the automaker added 15 new and redesigned models. By 2012 it was producing more than 30 models, and it couldn't generate enough sales per model to cover its investments in product development, plant capacity, and tooling.

Instead of slowing down and adopting a more balanced approach to growth, Chery aggressively expanded its dealer network. But the sales volume couldn't support all those dealerships. Many dealers got fed up and quit. After reaching a sales peak of about 600,000 units in 2010, Chery's sales numbers dropped steeply. Its chairman, Yin Tongyue, has acknowledged that Chery needs to improve its portfolio and sales management. The company has reduced the number of brands and models and cut personnel by more than a quarter. Nevertheless, sales have continued to decline. In the first half of 2013 they were down by 18%.

THE RIGHT CAPABILITIES AT THE RIGHT TIME

It takes a long time to acquire capabilities—even longer in China and other developing countries, where companies face a lack of competent suppliers, distribution networks, and qualified candidates to fill managerial positions. In deciding when and how to do so, the best approach is to develop capabilities in four stages:

1. Seize the Moment

Business opportunities—such as industry privatization or the emergence of a new customer segment with money to spend—are fleeting, so it's critical that companies move quickly and be tenacious. In this early stage they typically don't have the time or inclination to invest in anything more than rudimentary capabilities in payroll, finance, factory operations, and employee management.

2. Build Strength

Once the company is up and running, its strategic focus should shift to getting the business model right and becoming profitable. It's at this stage that many companies neglect to develop the basic capabilities they'll need when the industry matures, such as innovative product design and engineering and quality management—not just in manufacturing but in other activities. Every company needs specific competencies that are aligned with its strategy.

A good way to attain them is to learn—through licensing or contract manufacturing, for example—from companies that already have advanced capabilities. Galanz, a Chinese company that started as a duck feather dealer, became a respected maker of microwave ovens and other appliances after working as a contract manufacturer for Toshiba and other global players.

3. Scale and Consolidate

Next companies must focus on scaling up to become leading players in the domestic market and on consolidating their positions, often by acquiring competitors. But they must not overstretch management

GREAT WALL: FIRST STRONGER, THEN BIGGER

Great Wall began in 1984 as a vehicle-repair collective and grew by focusing on the manufacture of pickup trucks and SUVs for the Chinese market. Its approach all along has been "Be stronger and then be bigger," in the words of its low-key chairman, Wei Jianjun.

As part of its effort to improve R&D, the company invested in a world-class testing facility that includes a 250-meter crash-test track. Although it is largely vertically integrated, Great Wall outsources noncore parts to outside suppliers. To maintain high quality standards, it has formed alliances with global suppliers such as Bosch, Borg-Warner, Delphi, and ZF for core parts. It cooperates with these suppliers to develop technologies, an approach that has enhanced its R&D strength.

Great Wall also expanded its dealer network carefully, assessing the local market before opening new dealerships and then refraining from overstocking them. The company trains dealers to improve their service capabilities, resulting in greater satisfaction and loyalty among dealers as well as customers.

Not until 2008 did the company start making sedans. When it moved into the sedan market, it built on its existing platform and released just a few models. Instead of trying furiously to grow the top line, it concentrated its resources on developing and improving those models in a market segment where it could compete successfully. Great Wall's early sedans were unpopular, but it was able to pivot quickly to make improvements.

Having established itself in sedans, the company intends to manufacture SUVs that can rival vehicles produced by joint ventures in China. It recently announced its intention of becoming the first Chinese automaker to enter the highly competitive U.S. market by 2015. But Great Wall's president, Wang Fengying, says the company values product and operational quality above export scale.

resources or become an ill-functioning collection of poorly integrated business units: They should keep product lines and markets relatively narrow and fill capability gaps through greater investment in, for example, R&D, acquisitions, and partnerships.

The Chinese automotive supplier Wanxiang took this approach, building capabilities step-by-step. The company initially focused exclusively on improving quality performance and lowering its costs for just one product line: universal joints. It was able to win lucrative contracts with world-class multinationals such as Bosch and Delphi, and gradually it developed from a domestic tier-three supplier into a global tier-one supplier by expanding into other parts. In the process Wanxiang acquired, merged with, or established 30 companies around the world.

4. Move Up and Out

At this stage companies are typically expanding into higher-value customer segments and international markets. This kind of breakout growth requires that they have a portfolio of strong brands to compete across multiple price points, innovation capabilities and advanced technology to develop premium products, sophisticated marketing and sales capabilities, and a means of integrating them all into a complete system that confers a distinct competitive advantage.

Back in the 1990s, China International Marine Containers (CIMC), recognizing that China would soon play an important role in world trade, expanded its presence in the country's coastal regions. During the scale-and-consolidate stage it focused exclusively on low-tech dry-goods containers and then used an IPO to grow and acquire its local competitors, becoming the largest dry-goods container manufacturer in China. Ultimately, it expanded into refrigerated containers through acquisitions and a licensing agreement with a German competitor, Graaff, and invested heavily in its own technology. Only after its global market share exceeded 50% did CIMC start to move into new areas of growth—and always with an eye to making use of its capabilities in low-cost manufacturing.

Great Wall, too, followed the right pattern in acquiring capabilities. From the very beginning it has focused on becoming proficient at automaking rather than trying to achieve rapid top-line growth. During its start-up stage it found opportunity as a niche player, making pickup trucks and low-end SUVs, and began building its know-how in product development, safety technology, sheet-metal stamping, and total quality management. During its growth stage it improved its R&D, honed product quality, and adopted foreign standards for safety as well as emissions. During its scaling-up stage it prioritized its original products but moved judiciously into making sedans.

Great Wall's cautious expansion of its product line didn't limit its growth: Sales rose sharply from just over 100,000 vehicles in 2008 to well over 500,000 in 2012. During the first six months of 2013 Great Wall's sales grew by 43%. The company has recently pulled ahead of BYD and Chery in both sales and profits. In 2012 its gross margin stood at a healthy 27%, in comparison with about 12% for BYD. (See the sidebar "Great Wall: First Stronger, Then Bigger.")

"Haier changed its pyramidal, hierarchical, and siloed structure into a project-based network."

A NEW STRUCTURE FOR STAYING NIMBLE?

Emerging-market companies that have moved into the fourth phase of development have typically outgrown the top-down management style of their early days. They must organize themselves to simultaneously coordinate their global operations and remain agile.

The matrix structure used by virtually all established multinationals is too rigid, but a good alternative is not yet clear. Managers at a few emerging-market corporations that have reached this stage are experimenting with new structures—for example, breaking up into nimble, globally dispersed, semiautonomous units held together by governance organizations that provide services and disseminate best practices. The units may be empowered to enter and exit partnerships quickly in order to pursue opportunities.

Haier is one such corporation. In the early years its business model was based on its executives' belief that the company must differentiate itself by improving product quality and building a valued brand. Haier entered into a joint venture with Germany's Liebherr to strengthen its manufacturing skills, make higher-quality products, and become a leading local Chinese manufacturer of refrigerators. After years of growth and development that included acquisitions and a strategic push to become more customer-oriented, Haier changed its pyramidal, hierarchical, and siloed structure into a project-based network.

This radical new structure is aimed at reducing bureaucratic distance from customers. The company has been broken up into more than 2,000 semiautonomous teams of 10 to 30 employees with their own P&Ls. One team might focus on a given air conditioner model, another on a refrigerator. Below the teams are two tiers of units that oversee functions such as marketing, supply chain management, sales, product development, and manufacturing of all Haier products. The units in those tiers provide services to the semiautonomous teams; indeed, formal service contracts govern their interactions.

Is this the emerging giant of the future? It's difficult to say. But Haier has become the world's leading manufacturer of household appliances. It has succeeded not only in defending its home market against stronger, better-endowed foreign competitors, but also in opening up new markets for itself in the United States and Europe. Other companies will no doubt join Haier in experimenting with organizational structures aimed at allowing them to grow while retaining speed and agility.

Although emerging-market companies can learn much from the capabilities of established multinationals, this article isn't intended to advocate that they imitate the conventional management and planning styles of those organizations. Most developed-world multinationals are too slow and inflexible to seize dynamic opportunities in developing countries, and they lack local companies' ties with government and knowledge of markets and customers. Emerging-market companies thus have an advantage on their home turf and in countries with similar business environments. Their problem for the long term is sustaining that advantage as they grow larger and significantly more complex and as their markets mature.

READING 16

Why Conglomerates Thrive (Outside the U.S.)

J. Ramachandran
Indian Institute of Management, Bangalore

K. S. Manikandan
Indian Institute of Management, Tiruchirappalli

Anirvan Pant
Indian Institute of Management, Calcutta

Conglomerates may be regarded as dinosaurs in the developed world, but in emerging markets, diversified business groups continue to thrive. Despite the recent global economic slowdown, their sales rose rapidly during the past decade: by over 23% a year in China and India, and by 11% in South Korea. Business groups accounted for 45, 40, and 20 of the 50 biggest companies (excluding state-owned enterprises) in India, South Korea, and China, respectively, according to a recent McKinsey study.

They may be called different things in different countries—*qiye jituan* in China, *business houses* in India, *grupos económicos* in Latin America, *chaebol* in South Korea, and *holdings* in Turkey. But no matter where they are, business groups are becoming increasingly diversified. On average, they set up a new company every 18 months, more than half the time in a sector unrelated to their existing operations. Most of them are profitable. In India, they deliver above-average performance: Companies belonging to the largest Indian business groups generated higher returns on assets from 1997 to 2011 than the rest of the companies listed on the Bombay Stock Exchange, according to a study we conducted, and more than 60% of those groups generated better returns than a comparable portfolio of standalone companies did.

The success of the business group—a network of independent companies, held together by a core owner—in most emerging markets is remarkable for several reasons. First, it defies history. Conglomerates were all the rage in the United States and Europe for decades, but hardly two dozen of them survive there today. By the early 1980s, they had been laid low by their poor performance, which led to the idea that focused enterprises were better at creating shareholder value than diversified companies were. Most conglomerates shrank into smaller, more specialized entities.

The multidivisional company is the dominant structure for managing multiple business lines in the West today. But it, too, faces challenges. Pioneered by DuPont and General Motors in the 1920s, the divisional structure was supposed to improve the parent's ability to deal with diversification. But the problems associated with the structure—extra layers of senior executives, opaque accounting, the inability of headquarters to cope with different businesses, and so on—have often made the whole less valuable than the sum of its parts. If that isn't happening with business groups, they must be more effective in some way—and it's important for executives to understand how.

Second, the unbridled expansion of business groups challenges the conventional wisdom that they have succeeded in developing countries mostly because they've been able to compensate for institutional voids there and, in the process, catalyzed their own growth. Since the early 1990s, however, economic reforms in those nations have led to the creation of new institutions modeled along Anglo-American lines: Legal infrastructures and corporate governance requirements have been strengthened, and sophisticated market intermediaries have emerged. Although institutional voids have contracted, and markets have become relatively more efficient, business groups haven't imploded, suggesting that making up for institutional inadequacies may not be their only raison d'être.

Of course, countries take generations to develop efficient markets and institutions, so it may be too early to conclude that. However, business groups are neither a temporary phenomenon nor found only in developing countries; many, such as the Tata Group in India (which dates back to 1868), Jardine Matheson in Hong Kong (1832), Doosan in South Korea (1896), and Mitsubishi in Japan (1870), were born over a century ago.

Third, business groups in developing countries have grown mainly through diversification, even though U.S. investors believe that diversification destroys value. On Wall Street the typical conglomerate discount ranges from 6% to 12%. That makes the structural choices today rather stark: If a CEO can convince Wall Street that a new business relates to the current one, it can be accommodated in the form of a division. Otherwise, the CEO will be compelled to divest or let go of the opportunity, regardless of its promise, in order to retain the benefits of a focused enterprise. Not surprisingly, in recent times conglomerates such as Fortune Brands, ITT, McGraw-Hill, and Tyco have all broken up into more focused entities.

Business groups represent an alternative to this "divisionalize or divest" approach. We've done five years of research on them in India, and we've found that, because of the way they are structured, they can manage a portfolio of enterprises better than multidivisional companies can. Another major factor in their effectiveness, we've observed, is that their leaders have stopped relying on family members and associates to oversee companies and created a formal management layer, called the group center, which is organized around the office of the group chairperson. That mechanism is helping smart business groups spot more opportunities and capitalize on them while retaining their identity and values.

"U.S. investors think diversification destroys value. On Wall Street the conglomerate discount ranges from 6% to 12%."

HOW BUSINESS GROUPS ARE DIFFERENT

Business groups are distinct from multidivisional organizations in two ways. One, unlike corporate divisions, the companies (or affiliates) of a business group are legally independent entities. The Tata Group, for instance, comprises around 100 listed and unlisted entities (some of which have more than one division). Each affiliate has a separate board of directors, is answerable to its own shareholders, raises capital from investors on its own, independently develops and executes strategies, and creates its own incentives for managers. To borrow a term that Anand Mahindra, the chairperson of India's Mahindra Group, likes to use, a business group is a "federation" of companies.

Two, in business groups, there's a high level of involvement between ownership and management. In some groups, the core owners, who may hold large equity interests in affiliate companies, directly participate in overseeing them—as CEOs, functional heads, or board members. An investment committee, composed of representatives of the core owner and the top management of the key affiliates, usually reviews and approves all major investment decisions of the group and its affiliates.

These features help business groups better navigate the challenges of operating diverse businesses in three critical areas:

Decision Making

In multidivisional organizations, the top management teams of divisions are empowered to make decisions—in theory. In practice, corporate headquarters casts a long shadow over divisional management. And that destroys value. Michael Goold, Andrew

IDEA IN BRIEF

The Challenge

Companies in developed markets haven't been able to come up with a structure that allows them to seize different kinds of business opportunities. Because investors believe that focus is critical, companies are usually forced to set up separate divisions or divest businesses that aren't related to the core business.

The Argument

CEOs and entrepreneurs would do well to look at the way business groups in emerging markets, such as China, India, and South Korea, are structured. Not only are they flourishing, but they're becoming more diversified over time.

The Takeaways

Instead of organizing businesses as divisions, groups in emerging markets set them up as separate, independently listed companies, and create a formal management layer called the group center to oversee them all. The group's core owners work with the group center to spot new opportunities and to capitalize on them while retaining the group's identity and values.

Campbell, and Marcus Alexander of the Ashridge Strategic Management Centre summed the reason up when they asked: "Why should the parent's managers, in 10% of their time, be able to improve on the decisions being made by competent managers who are giving 100% of their efforts to the business?"

By contrast, the structure of a business group—especially the presence of separate boards of directors with distinct fiduciary responsibilities—affords the affiliates' top management greater autonomy. The legal separation of each business also ensures that it's affected less by the parent's dominant logic than the divisions in a company would be.

Incentive Design

While multidivisional organizations can base their incentives on the performance of each business, the

Two Ways to Structure Diversified Enterprises

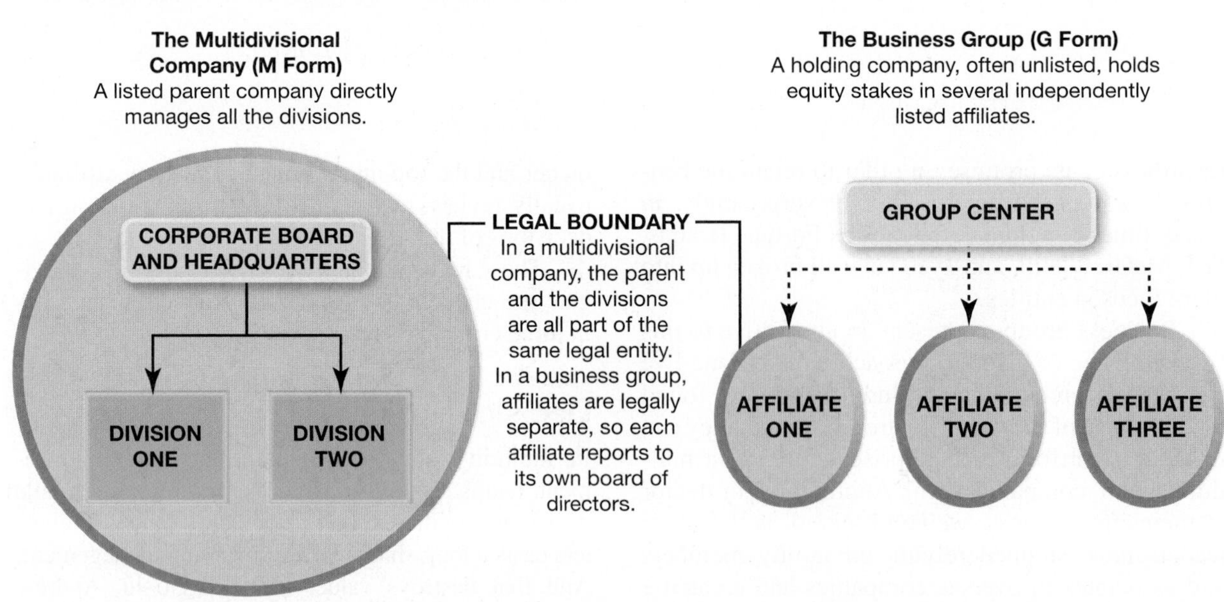

HOW TATA'S GROUP CENTER DROVE CROSS-BUSINESS INNOVATION

Although household water purifiers were widely available in India for many years, they were unaffordable to the poor, who didn't have access to clean drinking water.

Then in 2009, Tata Swach, a low-cost water purifier, was launched. The result of years of work among three Tata companies—TCS, Tata Chemicals, and the Titan Company—this purifier is based on natural ingredients and nanotechnology.

Tata Swach's origins lie in research first carried out by TCS, a software services company. The company developed an early prototype but declared it unviable and not a fit with its software business, and shelved the project. In 2006, R. Gopalakrishnan, a senior member of Tata's group executive office, stumbled across the prototype at TCS and became intrigued by it. He revived the project, suggesting that Tata Chemicals, with its expertise in chemical-processing technologies, take the lead. The chemical company and the software service provider started working together on it; later the group's watchmaker, the Titan Company, which had developed precision engineering capabilities, joined in. Today Tata Swach provides potable water that meets the stringent standards of the U.S. Environmental Protection Agency at a cost of less than one paisa a person a day. But without the interventions of the group center, that collaboration among the three businesses would not have been possible, and Tata Swach would never have come to market.

task is not without challenges. After all, a single corporate entity can tolerate only so much variation in incentives. Moreover, it's impossible to create a separate market-based measure of performance for each division.

Because each affiliate in a business group is legally independent, it has greater latitude to tailor its performance measurement systems to its distinctive needs. Its stock price also provides an accurate market-based measure of performance. The combination of greater autonomy in making decisions and more-appropriate rewards increases managers' psychological ownership of the affiliates, inspiring greater entrepreneurship.

Resource Allocation

In a multidivisional structure, business divisions allocate capital more efficiently than external capital markets could, because their executives have better information. At the same time, divisions have only limited control over free cash flows; surplus cash usually flows to headquarters, which makes the call on redistributing it. This centralized system is susceptible to supply-and-demand mismatches, bureaucratic delays, and favoritism. In business groups, however, each affiliate retains the capital it raises and the cash it generates, largely mitigating those problems. Further, the affiliate can raise capital directly from the financial markets, which usually ensures better valuations.

In addition, membership in a business group provides access to the highly diverse resources of sister companies, and that allows affiliates to tap greater growth opportunities. Our statistical analysis of a large sample of Indian companies from 1994 to 2010 suggests that affiliates of the biggest business groups had greater access to business opportunities than standalone companies did. And the affiliates of more diversified groups had access to even more opportunities than those belonging to less diversified groups.

A group's core owners often play a critical role in exploiting these opportunities. Because their associations with affiliates are long-term (whereas the average CEO tenure in the United States is now just six or seven years), they have a rich understanding of all the affiliates' capabilities, knowledge, and assets. And their shareholdings give them the influence to coordinate those resources in novel combinations. For these reasons, business groups often spot—and seize—opportunities that multidivisional organizations can't. (See the sidebar "How Tata's Group Center Drove Cross-Business Innovation.")

Given these capabilities, it's not surprising that the portfolio of most groups consists of many unrelated businesses. The Tata Group, for instance, comprises affiliates operating in a wide range of sectors including automotive, chemicals, communications, consumer products, energy, engineering services, financial services, hospitality, information technology, and steel. Similarly, the Aditya Birla Group comprises 56 companies running businesses as diverse as cement, textiles, telecommunications, financial services, and retailing.

THE ROLE OF THE GROUP CENTER

Business groups may be positioned to pursue opportunities in unrelated industries, but the coordination of strategies across affiliates is still difficult. The affiliates' legal independence, industry specialization, and autonomous resource allocation processes can set off centrifugal forces that reduce a group to little more than a portfolio of stocks. What's more, the heads of groups don't have the same hierarchical authority over affiliates that the CEOs of multidivisional firms do: Though the leaders of the affiliates do answer to the core owners, they don't report to them; they report to their own boards of directors. In fact, group heads sometimes have to deal with affiliates that want to chart out destinies independent of the parent group.

Yet, as we have said, the unique value creation potential of business groups lies in coordinating the activities of affiliates. In India in particular, that task was traditionally handled by an inner circle of trusted managers and relied heavily on the group head's personal charisma, as well as on complex holding structures, interlocking directorates, and informal mechanisms, such as family loyalties. However, the effectiveness and legitimacy of the informal coordination methods were constrained after the Indian economy opened up to local and foreign competition, and global corporate governance standards became the norm.

Several Indian groups imploded, but the progressive ones chose to increase their capacity to manage new businesses. As the policy environment became less restrictive, the owners shifted their role from helping their affiliates gain access to the corridors of government to helping them formulate strategic goals, build organizational capabilities, find resources, and achieve their growth aspirations. Over time, the process led to the development of the group center—a formal management layer at group headquarters.

In 1998, for instance, the Tata Group announced the creation of a group executive office that would strengthen its relationship with its affiliates and review strategy issues. Soon after, several groups, such as the Aditya Birla Group, the Murugappa Group, and the Mahindra Group, announced the formation of group centers that would explore synergies between businesses and forge strategic plans. The job of coordination in the business group has shifted to the group center, which acts as a centripetal counter to the forces of fragmentation.

HOW THE GROUP CENTER ADDS VALUE

To add value, group centers guide activities along two dimensions: strategy and identity.

Strategy Work

The group center helps affiliate companies develop and reshape their strategic frames. From its vantage

Business Group Affiliates Outperform Other Enterprises

From 1997 to 2011, companies belonging to the 50 biggest Indian business groups had higher returns on assets than the rest of the corporations listed on the Bombay Stock Exchange.

DATA CMIE PROWESS

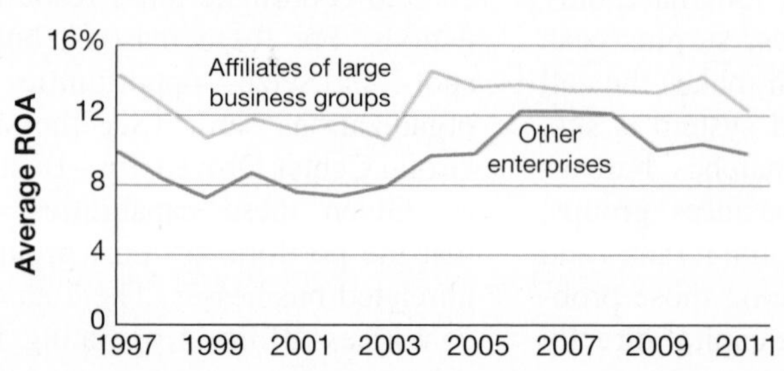

HOW TO ASSESS YOUR GROUP CENTER

1. Identify Your Center's Strengths and Weaknesses

Group centers, which oversee all the affiliates in business groups, often have different focuses. To find out what kind of center you have, rate your organization on the traits listed at right, on a scale from 1 to 6, and then calculate the average score for each column.

SCORING SCALE
1 = Strongly disagree
6 = Strongly agree

2. Determine Which Category Your Center Belongs To

Plot your two scores on the *x* and *y* axes and see which quadrant your center lands in. *Absentee landlords* don't appear to add much value; groups with this type of center could be under pressure. *Clan leaders* and *venture capitalists* may not be leveraging their full potential. If your center falls into one of these categories, consider broadening the scope to include both strategy and identity activities. The most effective centers are *evangelical architects;* they help deliver the best performance and ensure a group's long-term survival.

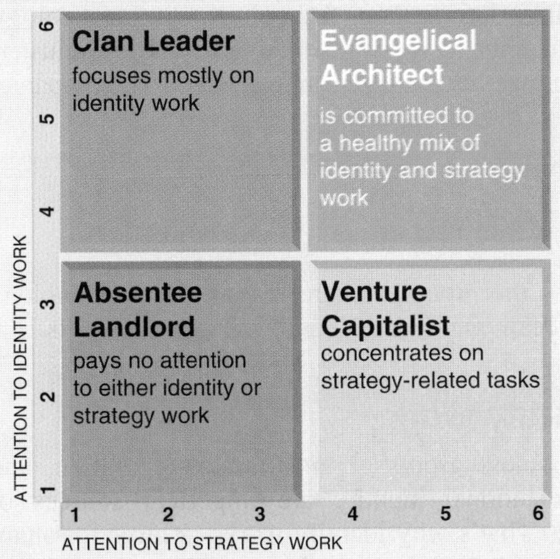

Attention to Identity Work		Attention to Strategy Work	
1. Employees of our affiliate companies value membership in the group.	____	1. Senior managers in our affiliate companies habitually consider the consequences their strategic initiatives will have for the group.	____
2. Employees of our affiliates always carry business cards with the group logo.	____	2. We've designated a number of senior group executives to identify new long-term opportunities for the group.	____
3. A set of guiding principles for employees of all affiliates has been developed and articulated.	____	3. In the past three years, we've identified at least one new long-term opportunity that wasn't being pursued by any affiliate.	____
4. Senior managers in our affiliates refer to group principles whenever they confront ethical or strategic choices.	____	4. Our group center has specialized management expertise that it makes available to affiliates.	____
5. Our group systematically recruits managerial talent that can be shared by affiliates, in addition to the recruitment that the affiliates conduct.	____	5. We've instituted structural mechanisms to provide mentoring to senior managers at our affiliates.	____
6. We conduct group-level competitions for process excellence, product innovation, and business creativity.	____	6. In the past year, we've made up for the financial shortfall of at least one affiliate by pursuing a new strategic initiative.	____
7. Customers pay a premium in the marketplace for our group brand.	____	7. We've created groupwide platforms to disseminate best business practices and processes to affiliates.	____
8. Our group's reputation carries significant weight in the talent market.	____	8. Directors of all our affiliates interact on a regular basis in formal and informal settings.	____
9. We make substantial, recurring investments in developing, communicating, and protecting our group identity.	____	9. We have created mechanisms for developing new strategic initiatives that involve partnerships among our affiliates.	____
10. Group representatives work with affiliates' executives to manage any significant engagement with external stakeholders, such as the government, the media, or business partners.	____	10. In the past year we've launched at least one new product or service that synthesized the resources and capabilities of multiple affiliates.	____
Identity work average score	____	**Strategy work average score**	____

point, the group center can challenge the assumptions that affiliates hold and spur them to set their sights higher. Typically, the center drives a three-part agenda:

Sensing Distant Opportunities Most multidivisional companies find it tough to manage opportunities across varying time horizons; they often require different kinds of resources, mindsets, skills, planning and budgeting systems, and performance measurement processes. Unlike multidivisional companies, though, business groups can create different systems for different horizons. When a group center identifies a promising nascent business, it can incubate that business in an affiliate, in a specialized entity, or by setting up a new company, where it won't distract other affiliates from focusing on their existing businesses.

In the 1990s, Anand Mahindra asked a number of people at his headquarters to scout for opportunities beyond his group's tractor and utility-vehicle businesses. Among the pitches he received was one for a time-share-based hospitality business. Back then, time shares in India were associated with shady operators and had a bad name. Mahindra sensed an opportunity to leverage his group's impeccable reputation and invested some $5 million in the business. By 2012, Mahindra Holidays & Resorts had become the market leader, with a stock market valuation of over $500 million when it first went public. It has built a base of more than 150,000 members today, delivered high levels of service—and wiped away the sector's unsavory image in the country.

Pursuing Stretch Opportunities Often the group center induces affiliates to look beyond their current environment and resources and develop more-audacious strategies. Because its executives work closely with decision makers across the group—sometimes as directors on boards, sometimes as mentors to the affiliates' CEOs—they generally gain valuable expertise and experience in nonroutine events, such as M&A. By sharing those capabilities with affiliates, the group center can assist them in achieving ambitious goals.

In 2007, the Aditya Birla Group's flagship, Hindalco, India's largest integrated aluminum producer, bid for Atlanta-based Novelis, the world's leading producer of rolled aluminum. Although it was not performing well, Novelis was four times the size of Hindalco, and many believed that the Indian company was overreaching. The bid had unqualified support, however, from the group center, which thought that the acquisition would give Hindalco global scale, a portfolio of premium products, and technological expertise. Hindalco eventually bought Novelis for $6 billion and turned it around. Executives at the group center played a crucial role in the cross-border acquisition and in teasing superior performance out of it. They deployed key personnel to integrate the American and Indian operations and help rework Hindalco's strategic plans to take advantage of Novelis's distinctive capabilities.

To ensure that affiliates are constantly thinking about stretch goals, the group center must engage with the affiliates' teams on an ongoing basis. For instance, every major Tata company has a business review committee—made up of that affiliate's top leaders and key members of the group center—that works with it to redraw its horizons.

Shepherding Cross-Business Opportunities Some opportunities call for creative collaboration among affiliates. The group center can identify potential synergies that typically wouldn't be apparent to individual affiliates and set up initiatives that foster the exchange of capabilities and ideas. The Tata Group Innovation Forum, for example, sponsors five innovation clusters in the areas of engineering, information technology, nanotechnology, plastics and composites, and water. These clusters bring together managers and experts from companies across the group to share research and technology road maps and identify joint innovation projects.

"Executives in the group center played a key role in Hindalco's $6 billion acquisition of Novelis and its integration and turnaround."

Identity Work

A business group's brand, motto, reputation, and organizational identity are important sources of value. That's why identity work—a lever for shaping the beliefs, perceptions, and motivations of customers, business partners, employees, and talent—is usually an integral part of the group center's activities.

Because the affiliates are autonomous and have different aspirations, the center's first challenge is to manage the presence of multiple identities. The creation of a robust and meaningful überidentity that can help executives "think like one group" is crucial to cohesion. The überidentity will lend stability and continuity to the group as the environment changes and provide the boundaries within which affiliates can articulate their individual identities. The Murugappa Group, for instance, has built a corporate brand around the core values of moderation and helping the community. The group believes that the brand has kept it in good stead even as it diversified away from its traditional businesses of manufacturing abrasives and bicycles to making fertilizers and pesticides and, more recently, providing financial services.

A second challenge is that the group's intangible resources, particularly the parent brand, can be devalued by affiliates' actions. Such problems can be prevented only if the intangibles have a guardian.

The group center's identity work has three objectives:

Refresh Identity The center must periodically rejuvenate the group identity and brand. Five years ago the Godrej Group embarked on a complete makeover of its corporate brand after research determined that consumers associated it with the image of a frumpy old woman. After studying the group's heritage and key business lines, consultants helped articulate a unifying aspirational proposition—"Brighter Living"—and revamped the Godrej logo to incorporate vibrant colors and contemporary motifs. This repositioning also led to a new brand architecture, which distinguished between businesses that were master branded (such as Godrej Properties), platform branded (Godrej Interio furniture), and endorsed (Real Good Chicken). The Godrej name dominated the master brands but was used as a prefix to the platform brands and was not part of the endorsed brands. The platform and endorsed brands are allowed to embody values other than Brighter Living. That new architecture, the group center felt, was essential to transform the Godrej brand into a strategic asset.

Safeguard Values The center should reaffirm the group's identity in day-to-day workings and manage that identity's alignment with key strategic decisions. But the center's paramount role is to act as the custodian of values, as Anand Mahindra said in an HBR interview several years ago.

In the late 1990s, the Tata group executive office received a proposal from an affiliate that wished to produce movies. Senior executives were concerned that movie production, then tainted by the financial ties some producers had to organized crime, was incompatible with the group's purpose of "improving the quality of life of local communities." Ultimately, the group executive office decided to turn down the proposal.

Systems that ensure proper communication of the group's identity and values are critical. The Tata Group has codified the values that it stands for in the Tata Code of Conduct, which it expects its affiliates to abide by. R. Gopalakrishnan, a key member of the group executive office, refers to it as the group's bible; it provides guidance on the dilemmas and questions that crop up in the course of business every day.

> "The Tata Code of Conduct provides guidance on the dilemmas that crop up in business every day."

A particularly potent way of embedding values across affiliates is to develop a cadre of key executives who can be transferred among them. At the Tata Group, a program known as TAS (formerly Tata Administrative Services) has been nurturing talent since 1956. TAS trains managers centrally, assigns them to affiliates in keeping with the latter's needs, and helps them move up and across companies as their careers progress. Similarly, the Mahindra Group has a cadre of managers, many of them graduates of India's leading business schools, that it rotates through the various companies in the group.

Multiply Goodwill Systematically channeling resources for socially responsible activities through a group center increases their impact. A centralized agency that guides and coordinates social initiatives can generate enormous economies of scope.

Take the Aditya Birla Centre for Community Initiatives and Rural Development. Headed by Rajashree Birla, the matriarch of the Birla family, it focuses on education, health care, sustainable living, and rural infrastructure development. The center is setting up a vocational training facility in the state of Kerala, which will begin operating in early 2014. The 23rd facility run by the Aditya Birla Centre, it will provide skills development in careers such as tailoring, carpentry, construction, and plumbing to around 10,000 people every year.

LEVERAGING THE GROUP CENTER

Business groups in developing nations may be flourishing now, but they could face greater challenges as the institutional environments in which they operate become more like those in the United States. Outperforming standalone companies in more-efficient markets will be tougher, as will retaining a group identity in a global marketplace. To keep groups competitive, group centers will need to focus intensely on both strategy and identity.

But not all group centers are ready to handle that task. We believe that centers fall into four basic categories (see the exhibit "How to Assess Your Group Center," page R-100). Some pay no attention to either identity or strategy work; they belong in the *absentee landlord* category. In our experience, the long-term survival of groups with this kind of center is endangered unless a charismatic owner and his or her top management can miraculously compensate for the center's lack of initiative. A center that is a *clan leader,* on the other hand, pays attention to identity work but neglects strategy work. It sustains the identity that binds the affiliates together and protects the group's reputation but shows little concern for coordinating the pursuit of growth opportunities. Lacking a common strategic vision and unable to get affiliates to work together on new projects, this kind of center frequently fails to demonstrate the value of belonging to the group. That often raises questions about the legitimacy of the owner's control.

A *venture capitalist* group center conscientiously shapes the group's strategy, identifying opportunities and assisting affiliates with resource and leadership challenges. This type of center doesn't cultivate and communicate a common identity, however, so it doesn't energize affiliates with a collective purpose or support them with a group brand. The fourth category of center is the *evangelical architect*—which is committed to both identity and strategy work. Such centers undertake initiatives that enhance the groups' performance as well as their longevity.

As the business environment and leadership priorities change, group centers must evolve, moving from one category to another before they achieve the right balance. For example, between 1938 and 1991, chairman J.R.D. Tata held the Tata Group together by sheer dint of personality. When Ratan Tata took over as chairman, in 1991, Tata Sons, the holding company, was a passive shareholder that exercised little influence over the affiliate companies.

After rejuvenating the group's flagship companies, Tata Steel and Tata Motors, Ratan Tata spent the next few years strengthening the group's identity. His initiatives—the Tata Code of Conduct, the Brand Equity and Brand Promotion Agreement, the Tata Business Excellence Model, and the makeover of Tata Administrative Services—embedded a core set of values in everyday work throughout the affiliates. This task was coordinated by the newly formed group executive office.

Later, Ratan Tata and the group executive office complemented the identity work by building new capabilities for strategy execution: They developed expertise in cross-border acquisitions, formed a business review committee in every major affiliate, created the Tata Group Innovation Forum, and launched other initiatives. Thus, the group executive office became an evangelical architect.

CEOs in North America and Europe who are managing business portfolios should take a close look at how their counterparts in India, China, and other emerging markets are tackling this challenge. There's already at least one sign that the latter's approach is spreading. In 2011 the Agnelli family, major shareholders in Fiat SpA, implemented a new plan for accelerating growth: It would break Fiat into two legally independent entities, a car company and an industrial unit consisting of its agricultural equipment, construction machinery, and Iveco truck operations. Fiat is in the process of transforming itself from a multidivisional company into a business group. In order to generate long-term value, the Agnellis will probably have to create a group center—just as business groups in emerging markets have done.

In a sense, the business group liberates strategy from structure. Though structure is supposed to follow strategy, the former's limitations seem to have decided strategy until now. Too often the need to pass up opportunities in order to satisfy shareholders' expectations has inhibited companies' growth. A business group, particularly one led by a dynamic group center, enables the pursuit of shareholder value at the affiliate level as well as strategic value at the group level. That makes the business group a winning organizational structure even if it isn't popular in North America—yet.

READING 17

Diversification: Best Practices of the Leading Companies

Graham Kenny
Strategic Factors

1. A BAD REPUTATION

Everyone knows how huge General Electric, or GE, is but may not realize how highly diversified it is as well, with operation in many areas. These include jet engines and replacement parts; rail system products and maintenance services; power plant products and services; gas, steam and aero turbines; advanced turbine machinery; major appliances such as refrigerators, freezers, ranges, cook tops, dishwashers; lighting products; electrical control equipment; plastics; commercial finance; magnetic resonance and CT scanners; US network television services—and this is merely a sample.

With customers in over 160 countries and more than 300,000 employees worldwide, GE is also one of the world's most esteemed companies, being regularly named among *Fortune* magazine's "Most Admired Companies" and ranked highly in Barron's annual survey of the world's most respected companies. GE is rated well on corporate governance, too. In terms of financial strength, the company has been given the highest AAA rating by Innovest and regularly outperforms most other large companies on the most fundamental measure of all: return on shareholders' funds, also known as return on equity.

Yet GE's highly diversified business model is shunned by many CEOs, senior executive teams and boards. The reason? The message has gone out that diversification is bad and focus is good. (No one seems to pause and ask: If focus is so good, why do the most focused firms of all, small businesses, fail at such alarming rates?)

This article takes a fresh look at diversification to find out why so many managers and boards are fearful of it. And, by showing how to make diversification a success, we encourage companies to get over the barrier that prevents them from benefiting from a range of potential business opportunities. (See Box 1, "The Diversification Project.")

2. SLOPPY ANALYSIS

Sloppy analysis is one major contributor to diversification's bad reputation. It's all too easy to write off the failure of a diversified business as "too diversified." Here is a case in point. By 2006, Burns Philp had become Australia's 95th largest company by market capitalization. In December of that year it was delisted, having been taken over by the Rank Group. But it was an earlier period that ultimately led to the company's near collapse and salvage acquisition.

In many of its moves, Burns Philp failed to understand the industries it was getting into. In one case this involved the US spices market and the intensity of the competition it would face, especially from a major player, McCormick & Co. In the US spices market McCormick held a 30 percent share and fought Burns Philp's entry into the market by escalating payments to retailers to get the best positions on supermarket shelves. Burns Philp's management misread the situation and the consequent bidding war that would take place. McCormick was prepared to "fight to the death," to quote Burns Philp's CEO at the time.

The press and pundits leapt on Burns Philp's case. "Too diversified!" they bellowed. Indeed, this is the argument in many analyses of failures of this

Graham Kenny, "Diversification: Best Practices of the Leading Companies." *Journal of Business Strategy.* 33, no.1 (2012), pp. 12–20.

BOX 1. THE DIVERSIFICATION PROJECT

The purpose of my research was to understand the features of successful diversifiers; what causes diversified firms to fail; what successful diversifiers and successful focused firms have in common (Kenny, 2009).

The initial identification of the pool of successful diversifiers came from a study by Marakon Associates. They identified 88 successful diversified companies from around the world with market values over $500m (Kaye and Yuwono, 2003). Along with other firms from other sources I chose four of the top 22 of these to study in depth. These were GE (US), Wesfarmers (Australia), Bidvest (South Africa) and ITC (India). Being geographically spread was one of the criteria. Other diversifiers studied in depth were Burns Philp (an Australian diversified failure) and the Australian department store chain David Jones (failed in its attempt to diversify). Two focused successes also came under the microscope—McDonald's and Westfield.

The major selection criterion employed to be classed as a success, for both diversified and focused firms, was the achievement of an ROE of at least 14 percent for the ten previous consecutive years. This benchmark was derived from *Standard & Poor's Quality Rankings* and placed the companies in at least the A minus category of firm performance (Standard & Poor's, 2005).

type. But it is simplistic. Rather than "diversification" being the culprit, we have identified at least eight drivers of Burns Philp's failure:

1. lack of effective management at the division level, cited by the CEO at the time;
2. expansion overseas, with the cultural and regulatory differences and complexities this implies, e.g. Italy, US, Germany;
3. expansion via acquisition, with all the consequent integration requirements;
4. overpayment for acquisitions, with the resulting expense burden;
5. failure to exercise effective due diligence in acquisitions, e.g. checking for hidden liabilities;
6. lack of understanding of the industries it was getting into, e.g. the US spices market;
7. rash expansion, resulting in head office staff being stretched and unable to react to crises effectively; and
8. lack of management discipline, i.e. inability to put in place essential measures, systems and processes.

None of these are inherent in diversified companies. A focused firm on an expansion route could just as easily stumble over the same obstacles.

3. ONION ANALOGY

A second driver of diversification's bad reputation is the way we look at it. This gives rise to what we call the onion analogy. Onion is good for you, but too much can actually kill you. So there must be some optimal level.

The onion analogy is based on the corporate perspective on diversification. This involves viewing the various activities and businesses of a diversified firm, such as GE, from the head office, looking down. It leads CEOs to consider whether the head office adds value by providing needed services and capabilities to the various businesses. And this is fine. But this same perspective also induces CEOs and boards to overemphasize the relatedness among their businesses, even if they are unrelated. Followers of the onion analogy, including some academics, posit that moderately diversified companies outperform focused companies on the one hand and highly diversified companies on the other. This produces an inverted U-shaped curve with performance on the "Y" axis—too little diversification, no good; too much diversification, also no good (Palich *et al.,* 2000).

The concern about becoming too diversified is that there can be an ever-increasing strain on top management to manage an increasingly unconnected (and therefore less familiar) portfolio of businesses. Were senior management to be responsible for developing the competitive strategies and detailed operational plans across business units as diverse as home improvement, energy, industrial and safety products, insurance, and chemicals and fertilizers, to take one diversified situation, they would certainly experience "strain." But successful diversifiers do not do this. CEOs and senior management at companies such as General Electric, Wesfarmers, Bidvest and ITC act as support staff to their divisions. As Warren Buffett, CEO of Berkshire Hathaway, understands, the "heavy lifting," the development of business-unit strategies and operational plans, is delegated to division management. So the "strain" on head office is kept to a manageable level by being continually parcelled out.

But let us look at the optimum-level hypothesis a different way through a business-unit perspective rather than a corporate one. This requires us to restate the optimum-level case thus: firms whose business units are highly related to each other, such as in a focused company, are outperformed by those whose business units are moderately unrelated to each other. The latter also outperform firms whose business units are highly unrelated to each other. Since business units are the drivers of corporate performance, this argument says that business units perform better when being somewhat unrelated to other business units rather than highly related or highly unrelated. From a business-unit perspective there seems no sense to this argument.

We look next at the particular practices that successful diversifiers follow to achieve success.

4. SELECTING CAPABLE DIVISION MANAGERS

Michael Porter made the point many years ago that "competition occurs at the business-unit level. Diversified companies do not compete; only their businesses do" (Porter, 1987). Successful diversifiers never forget this axiom. Divisions are the cutting edges of diversified firms and their leaders make all the difference. Business-unit managers have to be capable. Without high-performing individuals in place, diversification will struggle because the managerial load will get shifted back to the company's corporate center. If this leads to the head office developing the strategies and operational plans for the company's diverse businesses, then the writing is on the wall for the company as a whole.

The previous CEO of GE, Jack Welch, lauded by many as the US's most effective CEO in recent decades, had this to say regarding his role and the importance of effective division managers: "[My job] is to put the best people on the biggest opportunities . . . and [make] the best allocation of dollars," not to decide how to "produce a good [television] program . . . [or] build an engine" (Slater, 1999a). The latter is the role of the divisions.

Wesfarmers, like GE, is highly diversified and very successful. It has 200,000 employees, making it Australia's biggest private sector employer. It is a top-ten company with a market capitalization of about $38 billion, with businesses in retailing (Coles, Kmart, Target), home and office supplies (Bunnings, Officeworks), insurance, resources (coal mines), chemicals, energy and fertilizers (includes plastics), industrial safety, and more.

Michael Chaney, who until a few years ago was the CEO of Wesfarmers, is unequivocal about the importance of having effective business-unit managers to make a diversified company work. As individual divisions are run autonomously at Wesfarmers, business-unit managers need, of course, to know their industry and be able to focus on key financials, such as return on capital employed. But additionally, he says, these "above-the-waterline characteristics" need to be supplemented by "below-the-waterline characteristics," including emotional intelligence, i.e. interpersonal sensitivity; broad-scanning interests; and reflection on how big issues might affect a business. Commercial nous, Chaney says, is another component, as are integrity and the ability to communicate. This latter skill is essential if a business-unit manager is going to motivate others. Chaney has also pointed out the need for Wesfarmers managers to have conceptual thinking skills so that they do not become tunnel-vision managers, but instead can think outside of the box.

5. SECURING COMPETITIVE ADVANTAGE

Jack Welch sought to secure competitive advantage for GE via its business units by establishing a system in which division managers acted like small business owners. That way, he felt, they would know their customers and their needs, respond to them promptly and produce a real competitive edge. "We [have] to find a way to combine the power, resources, and reach of a big company with the hunger, the agility, the spirit, and the fire of a small one," he said (Slater, 1999b).

To achieve this, GE stripped away layers of management that clogged the organization and laid bare the divisions and business units, directly exposing them to competitive pressures. Talking about transforming GE into a successful diversifier, Welch has said: "We found ourselves in the early 1980s with corporate and business staffs that were viewed—and viewed themselves—as monitors, checkers, kibitzers, and approvers. We changed that view and that mission to the point where staff now sees itself as facilitator, adviser, and partner of operations, with a growing sense of satisfaction and cooperation on both sides. Territoriality has given way to a growing sense of unity and common purpose" (Slater, 1999b).

Wesfarmers has a similar story. A former outsider, who was subject to a takeover by Wesfarmers, comments on how autonomy operates within the company to secure competitive advantage: "Wesfarmers' philosophy of autonomy and financial rigor has been clearly apparent since the takeover. This is in contrast to previous experience with high degrees of operational scrutiny and financial hurdles which were sometimes unclear, or known to just a few. The approval process underpinning capital investments, divestments or acquisitions has been supportive of the ROC [return on capital] ethic" (Chaney, 2004).

6. ESTABLISHING A SUPPORTIVE CORPORATE CENTER

A division within a diversifier succeeds if the business unit itself delivers competitive advantage and it is given appropriate support by the corporate center. A key characteristic of the center in successful diversifiers is that it provides clear guidelines and it can handle diversity, i.e. it refrains from meddling with the way the various divisions achieve their competitiveness. A hands-off yet supportive policy is not easy to achieve, as interfering can become the norm.

There are three main reasons why meddling occurs. One is the lack of competent managers at business-unit levels. The second is the lack of clear lines of authority and responsibility between head office and divisions. I addressed both of these previously. The third is that head office has not clearly defined its role. This includes:

- keeping external stakeholders adequately informed;
- developing innovative financial approaches;
- ensuring that the company is seen as a reputable, responsible corporate citizen;
- ensuring the company is equipped to respond to unforeseen crises; and
- ensuring that the corporate culture is communicated throughout the company.

This list comes from Wesfarmers, with 130 staff located at its corporate center. Numbered in the center's total is the CEO, the Chief Financial Officer (CFO), group accounting, corporate human resources, head office corporate affairs, business development, group legal, group risk management, corporate tax and corporate treasury. Group accounting is the largest of these, but business development contains 20 analysts.

Wesfarmers headquarters is always careful not to tell its divisions how to run their businesses. Its aim is to "add value" by assisting, not interfering unless results require drastic action. The latter rarely occurs. This hands-off yet supportive approach has the effect of producing a highly competent group of division managers.

7. INSTALLING APPROPRIATE PERFORMANCE MEASURES

We have seen that having skilled managers in place is a precursor to employing diversification successfully. But good managers can go bad in poor systems. Recognizing this, successful diversifiers ensure that their performance measures are sound and that they encourage the right behavior.

Bidvest has its headquarters in South Africa but runs significant operations in the UK, Central and Eastern Europe, Singapore, Hong Kong and greater China, New Zealand, and Australia. With 107,000 employees, its foundation business is food service, which means providing supplies to hotels, restaurants, clubs and canteens. Bidvest is also in freight handling, contract cleaning and security, financial services, office and industrial products, and motor vehicle sales. The company is renowned for its ability to correct underperforming acquisitions. Every business that has been acquired by Bidvest has

"The message has gone out that diversification is bad and focus is good."

proved more profitable after takeover than before. How do they do it?

Bidvest's model, like GE's and Wesfarmers', encourages managers to run their businesses as independent, decentralized units, but at the same time they are subjected to what Bidvest calls "the discipline of constant measurement." This balance between entrepreneurial freedom and accountability through measurement rigor appears to be the real alchemy of Bidvest's success as a diversifier.

Bidvest uses profit and return on funds employed (ROFE) as the key performance measures for its divisions. It defines ROFE as trading income divided by net operating assets, and it fills the equivalent role of GE's ROTC (return on total capital) and Wesfarmers' ROCE (return on capital employed). Yet unlike GE and Wesfarmers, Bidvest doesn't enforce a standard percentage for ROFE across all business units. For some, it could be quite high, for others relatively low. An individual target depends on prior history. Improving profit and ROFE is what's important at Bidvest.

GE, Wesfarmers and Bidvest each see return-on-capital performance measures, such as ROCE, as discouraging division managers from pursuing growth for growth's sake or to satisfy ego. Return-on-capital performance measures are far removed from revenue-building, market share or customer base as the ultimate measures of success or the justification for business expansion. Performance measures such as ROCE also hold managers back from taking a devil-may-care attitude to expenditure. In addition, such measures are congruent with the ultimate performance measure employed by successful diversifiers for the corporation as a whole: return on equity.

8. SETTING EFFECTIVE INCENTIVES

ITC, one of India's foremost companies, has a market capitalization of over $22 billion and a turnover of $6 billion. It employs over 26,000 people at more than 80 locations across India.

Rated among the World's Best Big Companies and Asia's "Fabulous 50" by *Forbes* magazine, ITC has also been named among "India's most respected companies" by *Business World* and among "India's most valuable companies" by *Business Today.* ITC also ranks among Asia's 50 best performing companies, compiled by *Business Week.*

ITC's diversified presence extends to cigarettes, hotels, paperboards and specialty papers, packaging, agri-business, branded packaged foods, information technology, lifestyle retailing, and gifts and stationery. While it is a market leader in its traditional businesses, it is rapidly gaining market share even in its nascent businesses of branded packaged foods, branded apparel, personal care and stationery. ITC's diversification is aimed to create multiple drivers of growth.

The compensation policy of ITC includes a significant variable pay component comprising performance-linked bonus payments and an Employee Stock Option Scheme structured towards aligning individual performance with the company's strategic goals.

Like ITC, Bidvest is enthusiastic about using "incentivization" to attract and retain motivated people and, when applied to its decentralized management system, encourages managers "to seek returns in open competition with their peers." It also produces an "owner-manager mind-set" that, they say, "drives us forward." Division managers send financial reports to Bidvest's CEO monthly and are rewarded via a base salary, an annual short-term incentive and a long-term incentive. The base salary is set at the market rate or lower, while the short-term incentive is based on a percentage of division profit and on achieving a benchmark for return on funds employed (ROFE). Only after a division manager reaches the division's threshold ROFE does the percentage profit calculation kick in.

GE rewards its division managers via fixed salaries and bonuses. Depending on the staff member's organization level, the bonus can come in the form of cash or shares or a combination of both. The practice of providing incentives beyond a fixed salary is widespread in GE.

"The concern about becoming too diversified is that there can be an ever-increasing strain on top management to manage an increasingly unconnected (and therefore less familiar) portfolio of businesses."

In the case of successful diversifiers, their CEOs and division managers are subject to systems that are heavily weighted towards their achieving a high return on investment for the entity they manage—and ultimately for the company as a whole and its shareholders. Through these systems, CEO, division and business-unit performance is aligned with an increase in the value of the company, a prime indicator of which is return on equity for the company as a whole.

9. ALIGNING THE CORPORATE CULTURE

Divisions in diversified companies will by definition be very different in their operations, the industries they work in, their customer bases and the like. Successful diversifiers are very tolerant of these differences. But they use culture to unify the organization.

GE has one culture across all of its varied divisions. Describing itself as "imagination at work," GE's culture is a major driver of how the company operates, its policies and procedures, and what it will and won't take on. It has been distilled to four values that read as actions: imagine, solve, build, and lead. Each of these is defined in detail. Here's part of how it describes "imagine": "Imagine is a sense of possibility that allows for a freedom beyond mere invention. Imagine dares to be something greater. At GE, Imagine is an invitation to dream and do things that you did not know you could do."

ITC enshrines its culture in a number of ways. One is its mission statement: "To enhance the wealth-generating capability of the enterprise in a globalizing environment, delivering superior and sustainable stakeholder value." It then backs this up with six "core values": trusteeship; customer focus; respect for people; excellence; innovation; and nation orientation. These are aimed "at developing a customer-focused, high-performance organization which creates value for all its stakeholders."

Wesfarmers summarizes its culture as four ingredients: shareholder focus; growth philosophy; structure; and climate. As with GE, these are defined in detail. For instance, in the case of "growth philosophy," it says: "It is impossible to predict the future with any reliability so we grow our business by taking incremental steps, learning as we grow."

While there are individual corporate differences, five fundamental and distinctive themes run through the cultures of successful diversifiers:

1. *Growth.* Business growth is important to all of them.
2. *Autonomy.* Division managers need to run their businesses as if they were their own—like a McDonald's franchise.
3. *Return on investment.* They're not in the business of growing for growth's sake, nor just for profit; they need to produce an economic return that can be justified *objectively.*
4. *Stakeholder focus.* They recognize clearly whom they depend on for success, i.e. customers, suppliers, employees, etc.
5. *Integrity.* First-class corporate governance and proper dealings are important to all of them.

10. PAYING THE RIGHT PRICE

One of the routes to business growth that successful diversifiers employ is acquisition. It would seem axiomatic that you should not pay too much when acquiring a business. But what is "too much"?

A problem arises regarding the computed value of an acquisition because accountants cannot agree on how to value a firm—not the value of *a* particular firm, but how to value a firm. There are at least six methods for conducting an evaluation so the negotiations for the purchase of a company can start with a very broad range. We see this played out every day with public companies in the press. But it happens on many more occasions with private companies. It is critical to know how to play the valuation game—as successful diversifiers do.

Successful diversifiers also try to avoid the danger of getting caught up in a deal's own momentum, the weight of effort that goes into the transaction process. This is geared to overcoming problems and achieving a positive outcome. But "deal fever" leads to the feeling among the acquiring team that it's "too-late-to-pull-out." Hence, deals get done under the weight of their own momentum even if they are not, in the final analysis, good ones.

CEO hubris, i.e. insolence or excessive self-confidence, can derail a deal. Boards and CEOs need to be cautious here. Hubris often explains the large size of premiums paid for some acquisitions. Mathew Hayward and Donald Hambrick reviewed a range of acquisitions over $100 million and researched 106 transactions. In their *Administrative Science Quarterly* article, they conclude that CEO

> "Michael Chaney, who until a few years ago was the CEO of Wesfarmers, is unequivocal about the importance of having effective business-unit managers to make a diversified company work."

hubris is highly associated with premiums paid for acquisitions (Hayward and Hambrick, 1997). They also find that the greater the CEO hubris and acquisition premiums, the greater the shareholder losses.

Executive teams can guard against getting caught up in a deal's own momentum and CEO hubris by remaining objective and focusing on the numbers.

11. INTEGRATING ACQUISITIONS

Successful diversifiers are great integrators. Diversification won't work well unless acquisitions are integrated successfully. Bringing the acquired firm "into the fold" effectively means not alienating its employees. To put this more positively, a smooth integration process has employees in the acquired business feeling accepted. It also includes getting the systems of the two organizations working well together—computer systems, measurement systems and a range of human resources systems. Some studies blame poor integration for up to 70 percent of all failed acquisitions.

To avoid an integration mess, effective up-front planning and extensive follow-through is needed. Brian Joffe, the CEO of Bidvest, maintains that a key to a successful acquisition is communication in the initial stages, post acquisition. Areas covered by his company are future direction; corporate objectives; performance measures and everything that can help people make sense of how they are going to be working under the new arrangement. If all this is clear, Joffe says, a company will achieve a successful result nine times out of ten. When Bidvest buys a business, it gets the key people together, explains its philosophies, describes its objectives, details its performance measures, and then empowers staff to get on with the job.

Wesfarmers has developed its own "integration framework," a "how to" for handling the acquisition process. The company follows it in every merger, even though it requires the allocation of a considerable amount of resources. For example, in the case of its acquisition of the company Howard Smith, Wesfarmers assigned a senior manager and around 60 staff to the job of successfully integrating the new purchase. It took about six months and progress was measured against a timeline that showed the tangible benefits for Wesfarmers.

12. DIVERSIFICATION AND BUSINESS GROWTH

In approaching the issue of diversification, managers need to keep an open mind. In evaluating alternatives in growing a business, such as being a focused firm or a diversified one, senior executive teams and boards need to avoid getting caught up in the prevailing orthodoxy, share market hype or press hysteria. These are often uninformed by fact and fuelled by prejudice, special interests and rumor.

To beat the current downturn and to come out of it stronger than the competition, managers have to be prepared to entertain fresh ideas and different opportunities. Rather than seeing diversification as the leper of management, something organizations do not want to touch, it should be on their agenda for growth. If not, CEOs and boards may be incurring a serious opportunity cost. They should *not* be frightened to stray from what they see as "core business."

> "A division within a diversifier succeeds if the business unit itself delivers competitive advantage and it is given appropriate support by the corporate centre.

REFERENCES

Chaney, M. (2004), "The Wesfarmers' culture," presentation at Wesfarmers Best Practice Conference, 2004.

Hayward, M.L.A. and Hambrick, D.C. (1997), "Explaining the premiums paid for large acquisitions," *Administrative Science Quarterly,* Vol. 42 No. 1, pp. 103–27.

Kaye, C. and Yuwono, J. (2003), *Conglomerate Discount or Premium? How Some Diversified Companies Create Exceptional Value,* Marakon Associates, Chicago, IL, London and New York, NY, August.

Kenny, G. (2009), *Diversification Strategy,* Kogan Page, London.

Palich, L.E., Cardinal, L.B. and Miller, C.C. (2000), "Curvilinearity in the diversification-performance linkage: an examination of over three decades of research," *Strategic Management Journal,* Vol. 21 No. 2, pp. 155–74.

Porter, M. (1987), "From competitive advantage to corporate strategy," *Harvard Business Review,* May–June, pp. 43–59.

Slater, R. (1999a), *The GE Way Fieldbook: Jack Welch's Battle Plan for Corporate Revolution,* McGraw-Hill, New York, NY.

Slater, R. (1999b), *Jack Welch and the GE Way,* McGraw-Hill, New York, NY.

Standard & Poor's (2005), *Standard & Poor's Quality Rankings: Portfolio Performance, Risk and Fundamental Analysis,* October.

READING 18

Pragmatic Business Ethics

David De Cremer
China Europe International Business School (CEIBS)

Henri-Claude de Bettignies
INSEAD

Our workplaces include many difficult moral choices. On a daily basis we are confronted with a wide range of ethical dilemmas. Do our decisions and actions confront us with conflicts of interest? Should we pay the bribe? How safe should be our product? Will those actions damage our reputation or not?

These are important questions to ask, but at the same time it is clear that it is not easy to provide an answer to many of the most regularly asked questions.

Due to the pressure to succeed in business and make profits, we face the challenge of having to make choices that can lead us in opposite ways. As a result, conflicts of interest easily arise. Ethics becomes something that is not easy to define—let alone comply with. As a result, good people can end up doing bad things.

A vast amount of research supports the notion that people move from the good to the evil side when put in situations to do so. The famous simulated jail experiment by social psychologist Philip Zimbardo demonstrated that when students played the role of a prison guard, normative and institutional norms pressured them to behave aggressively and abusively towards students playing the role of prisoners. The roles of prisoners and guards activated certain expectations and behaviours that encouraged students to cross the fine line between good and evil.

Business is no exception to this. In this arena, people are also driven by implicit expectations and norms that can lead them into ethical misconduct. Even if people do not get killed, lives can be ruined in different ways when businesses cross the ethical limits and commit fraud, use deceptive commercials and engage in corruption. The fact that it's all a part of business induces us to tolerate some level of moral disconnection.

Research shows that in people's minds business is associated with notions of competition and greed. And the mere fact that this association is alive and kicking exerts implicit influences on how we act. Indeed, there is some degree of general acceptance that in business people will act in line with these implicit assumptions of greed and competition. Even more so, this implicit connection has become so accepted that it is equally acceptable to say that if you can't stand the heat of the business kitchen then stay out of it. In other words, business is not an easy game, violations of ethics can happen, but they are part and parcel of the game.

In business, ethics are treated highly pragmatically. This is exemplified by two popular business observations:

- It's okay to push the limits but not cross the boundaries of the law
- Ethics is about grey zones, so, it's hard to take responsibility.

What do these sayings imply and why are they easily accepted in their use?

PUSHING THE LIMITS BUT NOT CROSSING THE BOUNDARIES

Business ambition often lies in the extent to which one is willing to push the limits. If you are truly motivated to achieve the best outcome possible, you need to be willing to make every effort imaginable. At the same time, we, of course, add that this all has to happen within the limits of what is legally permitted. As a result of this kind of thinking, business has created a tick-box mentality. Specifically, to determine ethical limits we no longer rely on our own moral values. Instead, we check the existing laws and rules to see what is *not* legally acceptable. In fact, we have actually evolved in such ways that we do *not* always check which actions and decisions are legally acceptable. No, we only focus on what is not legally acceptable. The advantage of this approach is that if the law does not mention that it is not acceptable then by definition it should be acceptable.

This attitude of pushing the limits effectively clouds our own moral limits and, as a result, increases the chances that we eventually will cross the boundaries. What at first seems like a small deviation—not severe enough to be seen as ethical misconduct—may after a while turn into a full-blown instance of corruption or fraud.

In managerial accounting, for example, these kinds of slippery slopes can easily emerge, when debts of one year are passed on to the next year, with the hope that profits will be high enough next year to straighten out the accounts. However, if the profits are not as forecasted one runs the risk of beginning to slide down a precipitous and slippery slope one cannot escape from. In a similar vein, companies may be motivated to delay payments or to book risky orders ahead of time to ensure that managers can get their performance bonuses. Or, misleading information may be used in ways that while no lies are actually told, some information is simply not mentioned.

After a while, a whole new reality is created based on missing information. This effectively deceives the business' stakeholders. As business owners may determine that this kind of unethical behaviour is not necessarily illegal, grey-shaded areas are quickly created and unethical behaviour escalates. As a result, it is no surprise that pushing the limits becomes synonymous with good business. At the same time, however, it becomes clear that pushing the limits as a business model becomes fertile ground for confusion and uncertainty about what is morally acceptable and what is not.

GREY BY DEFAULT

Despite the fact that everyone in business is aware that the "pushing the limit" approach creates grey zones, allowing for more opportunities to deceive, the system continues. Even more, this system is unquestioned and becomes the default setting. Business is comfortably grey. Research in the behavioural sciences shows that as long as people can rationalise behaviours they can feel comfortable with them. Put differently, as long as we can justify our actions, we will not feel that we are pushing the limits in unacceptable ways, let alone crossing the boundaries. Specifically, these studies show that people have no problem lying about their performances and actions, as long as they have enough information available that they can use to justify their choices. If business transactions take place in situations where it is easy to imagine that different results could be achieved, people are more inclined to deceive and lie about their actions. Certain lies are justified as they do not feel unethical. The fact that the circumstances allow for an initial lie not to be perceived as a lie means that people can maintain their positive image as an honest business man or woman.

Justifying small and initial unethical actions is a survival strategy, used especially under threatening situations to one's reputation and business identity. Research shows that the survival strategy to justify unethical actions is particularly activated when people suffer from loss of sleep, feeling depleted (physically and emotionally) and when potential losses of one's wealth are salient. Sound familiar? Business provides ample opportunities for excessive

"This attitude of pushing the limits effectively clouds our own moral limits and, as a result, increases the chances that we eventually will cross the boundaries."

workloads, feelings of depletion, lack of sleep and financial challenges. The presence of these circumstances elicits the kind of justification processes necessary to push the limits of what is allowed, eventually ending in boundaries being crossed.

A PARADOX

It is important to realise, however, that by the implicit (and sometimes even explicit) use of these self-justification processes we actually deceive ourselves. We make ourselves believe that we do not cross the boundaries, simply by pushing them a little bit—a clear act of ethical fading. We become blind to the fact that we are actually crossing the boundaries. And after some time, we encounter a variety of conflicts of interest that are no longer easily solved. A paradox thus seems at work. We argue that business situations are often intrinsically grey zones but, by means of our own behaviour, we actually create these grey zones or at least promote and foster their existence.

Awareness is a necessary first step. Human nature means that whenever we behave badly we easily forget about moral principles and agreed upon codes of conduct. So, if we ever become aware of how our actions contributed to the grey zones our self-preservation and self-serving strategies come into play again. It will not bother us too much when finalising the desired deal if it takes place in the grey zone.

WHAT TO DO?

An endless long-term continuation of this process will lead to failures in our market and business systems. The financial crisis in 2008 was a perfect example of this. So, what to do? The most common response is to create more control systems, rewarding the behaviour we would like to see and punishing the behaviour that we wish to avoid. Although this may give some positive short-term results, the inherent nature of a control system will not help in the long-term. As one executive told us, the use of rules and controls is a guide in the absence of judgments. And it is exactly these judgments that are needed. We would like to see a situation emerge where business people are able to judge whether we have crossed moral boundaries or not. In other words, that we become aware of our moral compass and allow it to influence our decisions.

A more direct way of pointing out the potential failure of control systems is by saying that the more controls we want, the less we may understand the reason behind the control. By using control systems to regulate our moral decisions and actions, we as humans detach ourselves from any sense of responsibility—after all, it is the system that is now responsible for the moral culture of our business. The result of this is that we all start suffering from moral amnesia. Under those circumstances, the action or decision that is most favourable to one's own interest will then become the most justifiable option.

For the survival of our business systems it is imperative that managers are made aware of the psychology behind decisions taken in the context of moral dilemmas. We need to understand that we are not perfect rational beings and that we make mistakes—and sometimes these are moral mistakes. The first thing to grasp is this imperfect image of us as humans and start working with it in developing the responsible leaders we need.

Awareness is a first step to changing behaviour but we also need to develop corporate cultures which foster the strengthening of people's moral compasses, while inducing an open and trustworthy leadership that allows discussions of the grey zones we all encounter in business and how they come about. It is thanks to awareness—along with vision and imagination—that responsible leaders will be able to take actions conducive to a culture that respects people and contributes to the common good. The poor image of business and the lack of trust in its leaders can be changed if they learn how to navigate in the grey zone (that they have often created) through their own awareness of and reliance upon a strong moral compass. A long journey is ahead of us.

"Research shows that the survival strategy to justify unethical actions is particularly activated when people suffer from loss of sleep."

Leaders as Stewards

Gary Hamel
London Business School

What matters are bedrock values.

If you are a leader, you are a *steward*—of careers, capabilities, resources, the environment, and *values*. Unfortunately, some managers behave like *mercenaries*—by mortgaging the future to inflate short-term earnings, putting career ahead of company, exploiting vulnerable employees, preying on customer ignorance, or manipulating the political system to reduce competition. Managers now need to embrace the *responsibilities of stewardship*.

Stewardship implies five things: 1) *Fealty*—a propensity to view the talents and treasure at your command as a trust rather than as the means for personal gain; 2) *Charity*—a willingness to put the interests of others ahead of your own; 3) *Prudence*—a commitment to safeguard the future as you take advantage of the present; 4) *Accountability*—a sense of responsibility for the systemic consequences of your actions; and 5) *Equity*—a desire to ensure that rewards are distributed in a way that corresponds to *contribution* rather than *power.*

These virtues seem to be scarce in leaders today. But if today's leaders seem especially amoral, it's because a globally matrixed economy magnifies the effects of executive malfeasance. In a networked world, lax security standards can imperil the confidential information of a hundred million consumers or more. A failure to exercise due diligence over a vendor can result in a worldwide food contamination scare. And a decision that puts quality at risk can provoke a global recall.

Since the decisions of global actors are *uniquely consequential,* their ethical standards must be *uniquely exemplary.* It's a good thing when influential leaders are held to high standards, as the Web amplifies the impact of ethical choices. *Word-of-mouse* quickly turns a local misdemeanor into a global cause celebre. Companies are castigated for turning a blind eye to the subpar employment practices of their suppliers. There are no dark corners on the Web—miscreants will be ousted. We expect the same high standards of *equity* and *fair play* to apply *everywhere,* and are offended when they don't. And that displeasure can quickly congeal into a global chorus of indignation.

The intermeshing of big business and big government is another force bringing values to the fore. As citizens and consumers, we know that when lobbyists and legislators sit down to a lavish meal, our interest won't be on the menu. Democracy and the economy do better when power isn't concentrated; but since it often is, we must ensure that those occupying positions of trust are, in fact, trustworthy.

We need a values revolution in business. In one Gallup study, only 15 percent of respondents rate the ethical standards of executives as *high* or *very high.* This distrust poses a threat to capitalism. Companies don't have *inalienable rights* granted to them by a Creator—their rights are *socially constructed,* and can be reconstructed any time.

The values revolution has started. Between 2005 and 2010, U.S. assets invested in *socially responsible* funds grew by *34 percent* while *total assets* grew by 3 percent. Today, of the $25 trillion under management in the U.S., *one dollar in eight is invested in*

Gary Hamel, "Leaders as Stewards," *Leadership Excellence,* Vol. 29, No. 8, 2012, p. 5. Reprinted with permission of Gary Hamel.

socially oriented funds. A decade ago, no car magazine would have noted a vehicle's CO2 emissions; now most do. A decade ago, *Fair Trade* wasn't a marketing pitch; now it is. A decade ago, few paid attention to executive pay; now millions do.

Are you going to be a values leader or a values laggard? It's easy to excoriate fraudster CEOs and greedy bankers, but what about *you?* You can't expect *others* to be good stewards if you're not. Though some executives cast a bigger moral shadow than others, we must all shoulder responsibility for protecting capitalism from ethical vandals.

From Adam Smith to Ayn Rand, the defenders of capitalism have argued that the common good is maximized when every individual is free to pursue his or her own self-interest. I believe this to be true, with one caveat: Like nuclear fission, ***self-interest works only as long as there's a containment vessel—a set of ethical principles that ensures enlightened self-interest doesn't melt down into unbridled selfishness.*** Sadly, the groundwater of business is now heavily contaminated with the runoff from *morally blinkered egomania.*

TAKE THIS SELF-TEST

In recent years, many leaders have blithely dodged their stewardship responsibilities. That's why *executives* languish near the bottom of the trust table. So, ask yourself, ***am I really a steward?*** Take this ***five question self-test:*** 1. *Fealty?* Like the executor of an estate, do I see myself as a fiduciary? 2. *Charity?* Like a self-sacrificing parent, am I willing to put the needs of others first? 3. *Prudence?* Like a committed conservationist, do I feel responsible for protecting and improving the legacy I have inherited? 4. *Accountability?* Like the captain of a vessel, do I understand I am responsible for my wake—for the distant ripples created by my decisions? 5. *Equity?* Like a conscientious mediator, am I truly committed to finding *the most equitable outcome for all?*

If you're struggling to think through what this means in practice, when you take a job, assume that these five things are true: *1. Your widowed mother has invested her life's savings in your company. She's the only shareholder and that investment is her only asset. Obviously, you'll do all you can to ensure she has a secure retirement. The idea of sacrificing the long-term for a quick payout will never occur to you. 2. Your boss is an older sibling. You respect him, but you don't hesitate to offer frank advice when you think it's warranted—and you'll never suck up. 3. Your employees are childhood chums. You give them the benefit of the doubt and do all you can to smooth their path; however, when needed, you remind them that friendship is a reciprocal responsibility. 4. Your children are your primary customers. You want to please and delight them, not deceive and exploit them. 5. You're independently wealthy. You work because you want to—so you never sacrifice your integrity for a promotion or a glowing performance review. You would quit before you compromise.*

Nourish the seeds of stewardship in your leadership and, by example, in the lives of others. What *matters now* is what has always mattered—*bedrock values.*

READING 20

Attract Top Talent

Gary Hamel
London Business School

Become a passion multiplier.

The inventors of *modern management,* born in the 19th century, would be surprised to learn that their inventions *(workflow optimization, variance analysis, capital budgeting, functional specialization, divisionalization,* and *project management)* are still cornerstones of 21st century management. Organizations still try to strap rancorous, free-thinking people into *the straitjacket of institutionalized conformity.* Now, we're on the verge of a *management revolution.*

Three discontinuities will end management as we know it: 1) dramatic changes—ultra low-cost competitors, commoditization of knowledge, more customer power, new social demands—emphasize *innovation over optimization* and *change over continuity;* 2) web-based collaboration tools and networks—an alternative to formal hierarchy; 3) the new expectations that *Generation Facebook* will bring to work (they see the Web as the *ubiquitous operating system* of their lives, the means by which they learn, play, share, and connect).

12 POST-BUREAUCRACY REALITIES

Gen F expects the *social environment* of their work to reflect the *social context* of the Web. They'll use 12 realities to determine if your company is *with it.*

1. ***All ideas compete on an equal footing.*** On the Web, every idea has the chance to gain a following. No one has the power to kill a subversive idea or squelch an embarrassing debate. Ideas gain traction based on their *perceived merits,* not on the political power of their proponents. By dis-associating *share of voice* and *share of power,* the Web undermines the ability of the elites to *control the conversation* or *set the agenda.*
2. ***Contribution counts for more than credentials.*** When you post a video to YouTube, no one asks you if you went to film school. When you write a blog, no one cares if you have a journalism degree. Position, title, and academic degrees—the usual status differentiators—don't carry much weight online. On the Web, what counts is not your résumé, but what you can contribute.
3. ***Hierarchies are built bottom-up.*** In any Web forum, some individuals command more respect and attention, and thus have more influence. However, they aren't appointed by some higher authority. Their clout reflects the freely given approbation of their peers. On the Web, *authority* trickles *up,* not *down.*
4. ***Leaders serve rather than preside.*** On the Web, every leader is a servant leader; no one has the power to command or sanction. Credible arguments, demonstrated expertise, and selfless behavior are the only levers for getting things done. Forget this online, and your followers will soon ***desert you.***
5. ***Tasks are chosen, not assigned.*** The Web is an opt-in economy. Whether contributing to a blog,

Gary Hamel, "Attract Top Talent," *Leadership Excellence,* Vol. 30, No. 1, 2013, p. 4. Reprinted with permission of Gary Hamel.

working on an open source project, or sharing advice in a forum, people choose to work on the things that interest them. Everyone is an independent contractor and everyone scratches their own itch.

6. ***Groups are self-defining and self-organizing.*** On the Web, *you choose your compatriots.* In an online community, you can link up with some individuals and ignore the rest, share deeply with some folks and not at all with others. No one can assign you a boring task, or force you to work with dimwits.
7. ***Resources get attracted, not allocated.*** In organizations, resources get allocated top-down, in a politicized, budget wrangle. On the Web, human effort flows toward ideas and projects that are attractive (and fun) and away from those that aren't. Individuals decide, moment by moment, how to spend their time and attention.
8. ***Power comes from sharing, not hoarding.*** The Web is also a gift economy. To gain influence and status, you have to give away your expertise and content, quickly; if you don't, someone else will beat you to the punch and garner the credit. Online, there are many incentives to share and few to hoard.
9. ***Mediocrity gets exposed.*** In organizations, employees don't get to rate much of anything. As a result, we often find a *conspiracy of the mediocre:* "I won't question your decisions or effectiveness, if you don't question mine." On the Web, if you're inadequate *you'll be found out,* as disgruntled customers have a *global soap box.* Few companies seem eager to give employees an internal platform for challenging decisions and polices.
10. ***Dissidents can join forces.*** In a hierarchy, it takes great courage to *speak up,* and it's hard to know whether anyone else has a similarly rebellious mind. Individuals who feel isolated and vulnerable are unlikely to protest. The Web makes it easy to find and connect with individuals who share your dissenting point of view. Agitators who might have been marginalized in a top-down organization can rapidly mobilize like-minded confederates in the Web's densely-connected *thoughtocracy.*
11. ***Users can veto most policy decisions.*** Online users are opinionated and vociferous, and they'll quickly attack a decision or policy change that seems contrary to the community's interests. Only by giving users a say in key decisions can you keep them loyal. Since *users* own the online community, policies have to be socially constructed.
12. ***Intrinsic rewards matter most.*** The Web is a testament to the power of *intrinsic rewards.* Think of all the articles contributed to Wikipedia, all the open source software created, all the advice freely given, all the photos submitted to Flickr. Add up the hours of *volunteer time* and it's obvious that *people will give generously of themselves when they can contribute to something they care about.*

To attract creative young workers, you need to reinvent your management practices to align with these expectations. We're enamored with the Web because it's a *passion multiplier.* ***Online:*** *No one can kill a good idea. Everyone can pitch in. Anyone can lead. No one can dictate. You get to choose your cause. You can easily build on top of what others have done. You don't have to put up with bullies and tyrants. Agitators don't get marginalized. Excellence wins over mediocrity. Passion-killing policies get reversed. Great contributions get recognized and celebrated.*

How many of these things can be said of your firm? Only by exemplifying all the passion-boosting attributes of the Web can you create organizations that *magnify* human passions.

Building Superior Capabilities for Strategic Sourcing

Steffen Fuchs
McKinsey & Company

Gillian Pais
McKinsey & Company

Jeff Shulman
McKinsey & Company

Purchased materials and services often make up 60 to 80 percent of a product's cost. Companies that don't invest in the purchasing team's capabilities are throwing away value.

Jack Welch once notoriously said that "engineers who can't add, operators who can't run their equipment, and accountants who can't foot numbers become purchasing professionals." Hyperbole aside, General Electric's legendary boss was reflecting a common perception: the purchasing function is little more than a necessary evil in business. No surprise, then, that many companies underinvest in the purchasing team's capabilities and leave sourcing out of strategic decision-making processes in favor of functions, such as manufacturing and sales, that drive revenue.

Over time, of course, a negative compounding effect sets in: up-and-coming talent flows to the higher-status functions, often exacerbating the capabilities mismatch when difficult sourcing negotiations come up. If a supplier's heavily supported sales team squares off against an underdeveloped purchasing team, the result, like that of a football match between Fiji and Brazil, is fairly predictable.

Yet purchased materials and services make up 60 to 80 percent of a product's total cost in many industries. As a result, companies that do not invest appropriately in the purchasing team's capabilities and culture are throwing away more value than they realize. Organizations that employ leading-edge purchasing practices achieve almost double the margins of companies with below-average purchasing departments (20.2 percent versus 10.9 percent, respectively).[1] Among the dimensions that affect purchasing's success, capabilities and culture were correlated 1.5 to 2.2 times more strongly with a company's financial performance than the others we studied (exhibit).

We have developed an approach that emphasizes speed and scale to build and institutionalize capabilities, so that performance improves rapidly and continues to get better over the long term. When applied to purchasing, the approach helps to raise the function's profile and to give high-performing procurement professionals more leadership-development opportunities and exposure to senior management. In our experience, companies that employ this program in purchasing are able to attract and retain better purchasing talent and capture the financial impact more quickly and sustainably. This article will discuss how the approach has improved the performance of purchasing organizations and helped several of them realize their goals.

IDENTIFYING AND BUILDING CAPABILITIES

To turn the purchasing function into a high-functioning strategic asset, an organization must

This article was originally published in *McKinsey Quarterly*, www.mckinseyquarterly.com.

EXHIBIT Capabilities and Culture Are Key to Purchasing Success

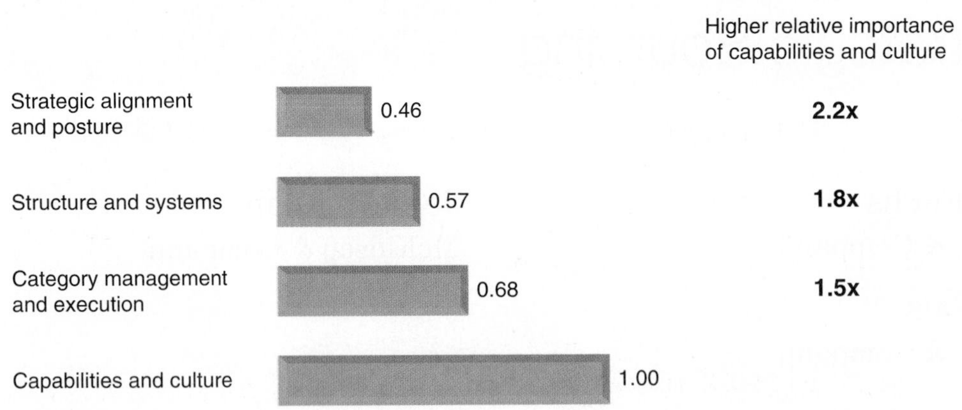

[1]Normalized; analysis based on a multiple regression using partial-least-squares optimization to solve multicollinearity.

first identify the specific capabilities that will create the most value. They vary by company but may include technical skills such as the ability to reverse-engineer a supplier's cost structure accurately or to conduct a thorough supply-market analysis that produces insights leading to a competitive advantage. Leadership capabilities—such as the ability to navigate complex cross-functional interests, to manage the trade-offs required to meet competing needs, and to identify alternatives with perspicacity and tact—may also be important.

A company can figure out which capabilities have the greatest potential to contribute to performance by conducting a bottom-up assessment of its technical and leadership capabilities and comparing them with relevant benchmarks. For one leading chemical company, this type of assessment revealed a need to improve advanced "should-cost" analytics (that is, clean-sheet modeling) and cross-functional leadership. The company created a tailored capability-building program to build these specific skills. One year later, it was routinely convening cross-functional sourcing teams and using clean-sheet-based negotiations to capture savings that ranged from 10 to 20 percent for many categories.

Beyond building individual employees' skills, an organization must embed them in its processes, systems, and tools. For example, after completing an initial phase of capability building for individuals, a leading basic-materials company took the next step. This effort included the implementation of an improved organizational structure to place a greater focus on value-generating priorities: transactional activities, such as purchase-order processing, were organizationally separated from strategic activities, such as category management. Data-collection tools and clear processes were instituted to support a more strategic kind of category management. The company also worked to ensure that the right individuals were placed in the right roles. Finally, performance-management systems were put in place to measure and provide incentives for total-cost-of-ownership savings and continuous improvement.

USE REAL WORK AND ADULT-LEARNING PRINCIPLES

According to our research, the traditional method of providing corporate training, through infrequent classroom sessions, is one of the least effective ways to build capabilities. Adults retain new ones more successfully if learning occurs through shorter, more frequent interventions in which the content is delivered "just in time." That is, when training is tied to real work and the specific activities an individual must complete, trainees get immediate practice in incremental new skills that directly affect their day-to-day responsibilities. Over time, these new skills build on each other and develop into a complete set of improved capabilities.

One of the most effective ways to act on these adult-learning principles and scale new capabilities quickly is the "train the trainer" approach. In this technique, a small number of highly skilled and motivated change agents go through a structured "field and forum" program covering technical and leadership capabilities. While these change agents are in this program, they are expected to transfer their newly acquired capabilities to others by acting as mentors for a cohort of key purchasing employees going through an actual category-sourcing process. These purchasing staffers, with some further training, then go on to become coaches and mentors themselves. Through this approach, a combination of coaching and on-the-job training creates an organizational-talent engine that scales up new capabilities rapidly.

The global chemical company mentioned above followed this approach for its purchasing-transformation program. The company's purchasing leaders identified a core set of trainers, who were 100 percent dedicated to driving change in the organization. Every week, these trainers received seven hours of technical and leadership training, and in tandem each of them co-led a cross-functional category-sourcing team. Over the course of 16 weeks, the trainers led their teams through the full sourcing process while also receiving regular coaching, training, and mentoring from their leaders. At the end of the period, the trainers unanimously declared that this experience had been the most transformative time in their careers, both professionally and personally, and that it helped improve their own skills and mind-sets, as well as the attitudes and capabilities of their colleagues. The trainers went on to train others independently and to become highly respected leaders in the organization. Many were recognized by C-level executives for their achievements.

SCALE UP AND INSTITUTIONALIZE

After the first phase of individual and institutional capability building, a company must focus on scaling, across the entire organization, the new way of doing business, so that it is sustainable over the long term. For example, at the basic-materials company mentioned above, this scale-up was accomplished by first setting an austere goal of 7 percent cost reductions across the entire third-party spending base and creating a clear action plan to reach that level in two years. This plan involved a sequence of category-sourcing efforts, with assigned team members and a center of excellence of core trainers and leaders to provide category teams with the necessary capabilities and expertise. A robust mechanism reported results to the whole organization to build excitement and credibility for the cost reductions. Two years later, the organization is well on its way to achieving what many thought a nearly impossible goal.

The final important piece in the capability-building effort relates to culture: creating an environment in which purchasing professionals are proud of the value they add to the organization and have the confidence to take a leadership role in finding and delivering new sources of value. Such cultural change is the bedrock of a sustainable transformation in a purchasing organization. Companies can push this change by creating highly visible senior role models who act out the new culture. These companies do so in several ways: instituting joint purchasing councils with responsibility for ensuring cross-functional collaboration and making use of the right forums to publicize successes throughout the organization and build excitement. Continuing to measure the attitudes and mind-sets of the staff carefully (using employee questionnaires and focus groups, for example) and then making targeted interventions to address challenges are important as well.

For example, at one leading global chemical company, a "victim" mind-set predominated in the purchasing function. Professionals within the group felt directionless and disheartened by an environment in which key sourcing decisions were often made without their involvement. To change this attitude, the company made sure senior leadership was involved in redesigning the purchasing organization, developing and institutionalizing a formal sourcing process, and implementing new databases and tools. Executives participated in weekly stakeholder meetings and periodic gatherings to address concerns as they arose. The company also made a significant effort to communicate the project's successes to the whole organization. Eighteen months after launch, the purchasing transformation was on track to exceed some radical savings goals in many categories. The transformation was recognized as one of the most significant efforts the company had ever undertaken, not only because of the bottom-line impact, but also because the project fundamentally changed the way the organization operated.

• • •

Companies that have invested in developing best-in-class purchasing capabilities have nearly double the margins of those that have not. By identifying the capabilities that will drive value, building them in real work situations using adult-learning principles, and institutionalizing them, a company can create sustainable performance improvements that enhance the bottom line.

ENDNOTES

[1] These figures are derived from McKinsey's proprietary Global Purchasing Excellence surveys and research on more than 500 companies around the world.

READING 22

How Collaboration Technologies Are Improving Process, Workforce and Business Performance

Mary Hamilton
Accenture

Allan E. Alter
Accenture

Alex Kass
Accenture

Companies need their critical workforces to perform smarter, faster and more productively. Achieving that goal requires embedding collaborative technologies deep into processes and incentivizing collaborative behaviors—ultimately transforming the way organizations turn knowledge into action. Collaboration platforms should do more than help employees talk about their work; they should create new ways for employees to do their work.

Although collaborative technology solutions have been around for many years they are kind of like Olympic competitors with a slew of silver medals but no golds: high achievers that have yet to achieve their highest aspirations.

Certainly there is no lack of collaboration technologies in the marketplace. Vendors are offering businesses a growing range of these tools, including Facebook-like social platforms such as Chatter, Yammer and Jive, as well as employee crowdsourcing tools such as AnswerHub and Spigit, to the list of collaboration technologies.

And executives are sold on the need for enterprise social technologies to improve collaboration, especially in supporting the work of today's enormous global organizations. A 2013 Avanade survey found that 77 percent of decision makers are using such technologies, and 82 percent of businesses that use collaboration tools want to use even more in the future.

Successful and innovative collaboration solutions are already in place at many companies. Consider consumer products giant Unilever's "Creating Brands for Life" social media marketing strategy, which aims to turn customers into advocates for the company's brands. Making campaigns like this work requires plenty of coordination between central marketing staff, local teams and external creative talent. That coordination is provided through Unilever's digital platform for social marketing, which enables teams to create their own internal sites where marketers and their partners converse and access marketing materials.

Yet many executives sense they should be getting more value from these tools. According to a 2011 Forrester Research report, 64 percent of executives surveyed said their companies were realizing only a subset of potential benefits from collaboration technologies.

Why have these solutions advanced only to silver-medal status instead of the gold? One sticking point is that they need to do more than just make it easier for employees to share knowledge and communicate; collaboration technologies must help shape how work is performed and enable teamwork that leads to better results, greater innovation and higher productivity. After all, collaboration literally means "working together"—co-laboring, not just co-talking. As one executive said in the course of our research, "Collaboration tools cannot just be about better knowledge sharing; they need to improve the speed and effectiveness of people's efforts."

How can executives use collaboration tools to truly transform workplace performance? Three strategies can help companies achieve the large gains in productivity, decision making and innovation they seek from these technologies.

1. Embed Collaboration Technologies within Business Processes

New collaboration technologies do more than just digitize old ways of doing things; they make new ways of doing things possible. This is accomplished in part by embedding the technologies into the way work is performed so that using them becomes a natural and accepted part of the job. It's also important to set objectives in specific terms related to an industry and to job roles, and to measure results. For example, for an insurance company, the goal of "increasing knowledge sharing" is noble but vague. A better goal would be, "improving underwriters' speed and effectiveness in pricing insurance policies."

Through the use of collaboration technologies that improve the manner in which work is done, companies have achieved impressive results. For example, by sharing experiences and ideas via an online platform, employees in CEMEX's alternative fuels program reduced CO_2 emissions by 1.8 million metric tons per year, saving the company more than $140 million while earning $80 million in sales of CO_2 credits. By more readily sharing documents and quickly locating experts to answer questions, sales teams at GE Aviation were able to complete in minutes work that had previously taken more than one week.

Collaboration technologies can also provide guidance about how particular processes can be optimally performed to improve quality and increase productivity. For example, "social workflow platforms" provide a collaborative environment that can guide groups through an optimized and standardized workplan, with roles, tasks and templates laid out in advance. Team members can then use the platform to hand off work, conduct discussions, share updates, review checklists and obtain approvals. The platform's tagging, searching and messaging features make it easier to ask for help, locate documents that can be reused and share best practices.

Executives can then use workstream analytics to study how effectively processes are being performed and where they can be improved, and also how well teams are collaborating.

2. Shape the Collaborative Behaviors That Drive Results

Simply making collaboration technologies available is not enough. Equally important is engaging in the change management activities that shape, encourage and incentivize desired collaborative behaviors.

Early approaches to incentivizing participation in knowledge sharing often focused on quantity of postings, not quality. Looking for a better way to encourage the use of collaboration tools, EMC Corp., a leading hardware and cloud-based computing company, decided to turn collaborative participation into a game with winners and awards. The company's Jive-powered enterprise social network had grown to 240,000 users within four years, but customers, employees and partners were not using the network as much as expected. EMC implemented a gamification approach to support its Recognition, Awards and Motivation program. Employees win points for completing tasks, answering questions or doing other work on the social network. Employees who complete "missions"—a sequence of relevant achievements—receive awards and corporate recognition for their expertise. The result: a 21 percent increase in total activity, helping to shape behaviors that actually support timely business outcomes.

3. Unleash the Full Power of Enterprise Talent

Effective collaboration technologies support not only how people work today but how they will need to work in the future. Increasingly, companies are embracing new operating models in which multiple organizations—the company, its vendors, its outsourcers, its partners and others—work together toward a unified goal. Such an operating model will be successful only if people from the different organizations collaborate effectively.

A related trend has to do with how talent is sourced and deployed. Just as companies' operating models are increasingly built on combinations of organizations, so workforces are becoming combinations of internal, external and contingent employees.

Consider how crowdsourcing and the social web are already enabling firms to hand off some tasks to workers outside the enterprise. Salesforce.com uses LiveOps' "cloud contact center" to deliver global customer support services, which involves tapping contractors who work from home and set their own hours. The platform tracks performance and rewards high performers with recognition, more work and better pay. One advantage of this approach: It allows organizations to scale their customer contact needs quickly to respond to sudden spikes in demand.

In the future, these same concepts and technologies are likely to be applied to more kinds of knowledge work. Take, for example, an automotive engineer in Germany who needs help creating engineering drawings. That engineer could use enterprise collaboration technologies to route a request for help to the company's most relevant intranet sites. A retired engineer in Michigan or a young engineer in Europe could offer to assist, and receive not just pay but a reputation-enhancing public review for completing the job well. Mechanisms like these could help companies quickly and seamlessly plug their skills gaps.

CONCLUSION: EXPECTING MORE

Executives are right to expect more from the new wave of collaborative technologies. Adding social networking and crowdsourcing to collaborative tools provides new potential to improve organizational agility, increase productivity, aid decision making and spark idea generation. Rather than accept just modest improvements from these technologies, executives should aim high and pursue the greater gains that can come by embedding collaboration into specific processes, incentivizing collaborative behaviors and thinking more strategically about these important technologies.

READING 23

The ROI of Employee Recognition

Jill Jusko
Industry Week

Done right, reward and recognition programs deliver more than soft benefits—they drive company performance.

If your company's reward and recognition program does not boost corporate performance as much as you would like, it may be your own fault. Try focusing on the behaviors you want, suggests consulting group Bersin by Deloitte.

"Nearly 80% of organizations unfortunately focus on ad-hoc or tenure-based recognition programs that fail to reinforce consistent messages or make a strategic impact," says Bersin's Stacia Sherman Garr, principal analyst, performance management. "Used correctly, employee recognition is an important talent management tool."

Seco Tools, for example, incorporates several reward programs as part of a comprehensive package of human resources initiatives. Driving performance is a significant component of those programs, says Dan Sikora.

"We are an EBIT-driven company," says Sikora, director of operations and human resources for the Troy, Mich.-based provider of metal-cutting solutions for the manufacturing industry.

Examples of Seco Tools' programs include small rewards given in recognition of performance that goes "above and beyond" daily job duties, with the recipients nominated by managers. "It is used sparingly for exceptional performance," Sikora says.

Another program, LIFE (Little Improvements from Everyone) promotes innovation, not simply in product development but across the organization. Work groups or individuals submit LIFE ideas via a structured process. The performance-driven keys to the program are this: The improvement idea must be tied to money savings or revenue generation, and the idea must be *implemented,* not merely generated, to be rewarded. Those whose ideas are implemented participate in a quarterly drawing, with the winner of the drawing receiving a gift card and recognition at the quarterly all-employee meeting. The quarterly award winners and their spouses also join senior executives for an annual dinner.

"We recognize when they are at work, they are away from home. We're showing we appreciate their contribution," Sikora says.

A third program delivers career development opportunities to participants while promoting company performance. Individuals chosen for the talent program are presented with a project to pursue during an approximately eight-month period. Importantly, the projects are not theoretical; they are actual problems faced by the company and ones which senior executives are having difficulty resolving.

The results have been excellent with regard to improving company performance. "Every proposal has turned into an implementation, and the program engages and motivates," Sikora says.

For participants in the program, the reward is the opportunity for career growth—a factor Sikora says is of growing importance to new recruits.

While participants in the talent program are not guaranteed a job promotion or pay raise, Sikora says what they do gain is greater opportunity to

Reprinted from *Industry Week,* Vol. 262, Issue 2, February 2013, pp. 40–41.

> "If you truly believe that engagement drives motivation, then people are more productive."
>
> —Dan Sikora

interact with senior executives, a work challenge outside of their everyday duties that expands their skills, and greater recognition from the company as promotion-worthy candidates when job opportunities arise.

"It is a rocket-booster to career development," Sikora explains.

The company tracks the ROI of its HR programs in multiple ways, including with such typical metrics as employee turnover and new-hire stay rates. For programs like LIFE, Seco Tools tracks the costs avoided or reduced for each implementation.

"Another financial one I keep a close eye on is productivity. Reason being, if you truly believe that engagement drives motivation, then people are more productive," Sikora says, while acknowledging that external factors also influence this metric. Nevertheless, "I believe it has enough of an influence that I track it and use it as an indicator of success."

For companies trying to improve or implement their own reward and recognition programs, Bersin & Associates offers these suggestions:

- Set the tone for recognition with senior leaders and clear goals.
- Develop clear recognition criteria.
- Use technology; it boosts performance. Bersin by Deloitte suggests IT aids performance because it makes recognition more accessible to employees, can adapt to changing business needs and enables more frequent recognition.
- Make recognition a multifront offensive.
- Provide recognition that employees value.

"It is all about execution," adds Seco Tools' Sikora. Managers must support the programs and not simply see it as something to "check off" as done. Citing the LIFE program, he notes that every person who generates an idea receives a response. "It dies unless you have the discipline to provide feedback."

READING 24

The Critical Few: Components of a Truly Effective Culture

Jon Katzenbach
Booz & Company

James Thomas
Booz & Company

Rutger von Post
Booz & Company

Forget the monolithic change management programs and focus on the elements of your culture that drive performance.

Sometimes corporate culture manifests itself in a make-your-own-taco party in the office kitchenette. Sometimes you can see it when an outdated phone bank is converted into an on-site ice cream shop. And sometimes it's on display when senior leaders pick up paintbrushes to turn formerly bland office walls into electric blue work spaces. These are examples of the "Culture Blitz" at work at Southwest Airlines Company, where a 40-year culture is still going strong and is further invigorated by traveling teams who volunteer every year to visit hundreds of employees to show their appreciation. And it's infectious.

Mary Widen is a Southwest Culture Blitz member who will never forget the first time she "hokeyed" an airplane. (Although the hokey is in fact a line dance, at Southwest it's also the name of the small carpet sweeper used to clean the plane between flights.) It's traditionally the responsibility of the flight attendants to clean the plane, but once in a while Culture Blitz members take over this task and give the flight attendants time off and bags of snacks. "The flight attendants were in shock—you would have thought I had given them a bag of jewelry. They were yelling 'thank you' at me long after I had walked away. It was their unexpected good moment of the week, and they were so grateful. And that refuels you. And those good feelings last long after the hokeying is complete. People keep in touch after, and that makes Southwest feel like a real family," says Widen.

These are the types of experiences that a strong culture creates. To sustain such a culture, Southwest and other enterprises understand that key behaviors have to be actively managed and made visible. Companies with the most effective culture seek out and continually reinforce what Charles Duhigg, author of *The Power of Habit: Why We Do What We Do in Life and Business* (Random House, 2012), calls "keystone habits." A keystone habit, Duhigg has noted, is "a pattern that has the power to start a chain reaction, changing other habits as it moves through an organization." Companies that recognize and encourage such habits stand to build cultures with influence that goes beyond employee engagement and directly boosts performance.

Too few leaders recognize the outsized influence of these key behaviors, however. Their efforts to improve performance remain ill focused and diffuse. They find it hard to resist the temptation to pile one directive on top of another; even when those efforts are aligned to the same ultimate goals, they often undermine one another. Further, when those efforts are focused on significant changes to the culture, they are almost always too comprehensive, programmatic, esoteric, and urgent. Leaders fail to appreciate how deeply culture can be ingrained in people's beliefs and habits—and, therefore, how very difficult it will be to change behavior in a way that will last.

We have found, through numerous cultural interventions with a wide range of organizations, from HP and Bell Canada to major enterprises in India, Australia, and the Middle East, that companies that eschew all-encompassing culture change initiatives and instead focus on three specific elements—critical behaviors, existing cultural traits, and critical informal leaders—have the most success. We call these "the critical few."

The first elements, critical behaviors, are those ways of doing things in your current operations that can easily spread from one employee to another; they have the potential to generate a real business impact, particularly when they become habitual and widespread. Moreover, you would recognize them right away if respected leaders at various levels throughout the organization started putting them into practice.

The second piece, existing cultural traits, refers to three or four emotional elements of the current culture that are distinctively clear, wisely profound, emotionally powerful, and widely recognized; these traits together are a manifestation of the organization's collective sense of identity. They play a prominent role in supporting the most important behaviors.

And the critical informal leaders are those few authentic individuals who motivate others by what they do and how they do it. They are recognized by their colleagues as credible, trustworthy, and effective—and they know how to influence behavior.

In our experience, a sharp focus on the critical few reduces complexity and begets more positive, informal, and lasting cultural impact on performance—and it does so much faster than top-down messaging and formal programmatic attempts. This approach takes into account the emotional dimension of human behavior. Most people instinctively resist change, particularly when it is thrust upon them in large doses, because it feels different and complex, and makes them uncomfortable. Top-down messaging alone—no matter how compelling and inspiring—seldom produces a lasting effect on how we feel about what we do.

Individuals are simultaneously emotional and rational, so how we *feel* about something often gets in the way of how we *think* about it. This is particularly the case when human beings are confronted with complexity. When it comes to changing something important about what we do and how we do it, we crave simplicity so we can navigate the fear of the new and unknown—and it really helps when we can look to peers and colleagues for insight, support, and encouragement, if not positive personal experience. When people we trust and admire clearly model and encourage a few key behaviors, those behaviors spread much more quickly, and they stick.

If you don't have your culture firmly established, a taco party or a hokey won't get you there. But if you get these three critical elements in sync, your culture's positive impact will be felt on the bottom line much sooner than you might expect.

IDENTIFY THE CRITICAL BEHAVIORS

Pinpointing a few critical behaviors is priority number one. Once the behaviors that embody the cultural priorities that a company seeks are identified, clarified, and supported widely, you can focus on harnessing them to strengthen and modify the existing culture. But even while we focus first on the critical behaviors, you will see just how interwoven the elements of the critical few are.

As you set out to find and prioritize those critical behaviors that are going to make the biggest difference in performance, it might be tempting to address the ones that are holding you back, meaning those you most want to change or eliminate. You'll be tempted to take on the biggest pain point, the behavioral elephant in the room—be it a lack of innovation, people not giving honest feedback to colleagues, or employees resisting collaboration with people outside their own teams.

Instead, take stock of the positive aspects of your current culture and consider which elements could be harnessed to drive the behaviors you seek most. At the same time, ask yourself:

"Top-down messaging alone—no matter how compelling and inspiring—seldom produces a lasting effect on how we feel about what we do."

- How visible would these behaviors be if a senior executive or an authentic informal leader started exhibiting them? (Would others throughout the organization see and recognize the change?)
- Will these behaviors be contagious enough to be spread through social networks and peer relationships? (Will key people begin to envy and emulate them?)
- What potential do the behaviors have to create real, measurable business impact? (Can you find ways to measure and track the impact early on?)

At the start of Southwest's entrepreneurial journey, cofounder Herb Kelleher and his top team were determined to sustain a culture based on a few very simple, coherent behaviors that aligned with their low-cost route strategy: (1) cultivate collaborative and fun interactions across the company; (2) make every traveler feel good and enjoy personal interactions with Southwest people; (3) follow through on every traveler concern, and tell it like it is when the unexpected occurs; and (4) do it all on the cheap.

Kelleher's simple strategy and operating model for Southwest Airlines was tightly connected with what soon became a remarkably instinctive culture. It has energized caring behaviors among employees, delighted target customers, and rewarded early shareholders. Kelleher believed (and his successors still maintain) that how you treat your employees determines how they treat customers—and happy customers are what will sustain attractive shareholder returns over time. Southwest flipped the hierarchy that most organizations follow—i.e., shareholders first, customers second, and employees last. Although the culture continues to evolve over time, it remains closely aligned with this simple formula.

Shaping a corporate culture is much easier to do when an enterprise is starting out small, as when Kelleher laid the cultural groundwork at Southwest. But no matter the organization's size or level of maturity, shaping culture takes insight, persistence, and courage from leaders at multiple levels, especially when they are expecting culture to drive growth. It helps if leaders' cultural intent is both simple and behaviorally clear, as Kelleher's has been: Hire people who are naturally friendly and fun, make sure they learn how to connect in positive ways with customers, and discipline them to be relentlessly frugal. In retrospect, these have been the critical few behaviors that have produced the lowest fares and among the most satisfied and loyal customers in the U.S. airline industry for nearly 40 years.

HONOR THE EXISTING CULTURE

Your organization may have many admirable cultural traits, but you need to focus on those three or four traits that are distinctively clear, wisely profound, emotionally powerful, and widely recognized. If you go mining for more, not only will you hit rapidly diminishing returns, but you will also make even the strongest traits seem somehow tenuous, and the entire process will lose credibility.

It is a leader's responsibility to determine the existing cultural traits that the organization will preserve and build upon. At one industrial manufacturer, the CEO enlisted a senior culture team to help him catalyze key existing traits similar to those many aspire to: speed, sensible risk, accountability, and customer-centricity. In another example, for a leading energy company in the U.S., unveiling significant traits—which the company termed "performance imperatives"—was a process of broader management team discussion and discovery. The performance imperatives were resourceful execution, enterprise-wide perspective, active accountability, and people development.

Almost every organization has a few key cultural traits that are distinctively positive. Whether these elements are displayed on posters in the corridors or etched on desk ornaments—or not visibly celebrated at all—they are an integral part of the company's true cultural situation. Properly recognized and drawn upon, they provide the workforce a sense of pride and purpose.

But even after the priority traits have been declared, senior leaders can't expect them to immediately inspire the right behaviors, in the right way, at the right time. When employees hear about the traits, they need to be able to recognize and personalize them. The traits need to feel specific to the real world people work in every day. Getting to this point is a process.

Begin by prioritizing your existing cultural traits on the basis of relevance, importance, and urgency. In addition, it is essential to shape, validate, and refine them using the insights and reflections of informal leaders in key populations. These individuals are often

FOUR SIGNS THAT YOUR CRITICAL FEW BEHAVIORS ARE WORKING

To sustain a true competitive edge, your culture should accelerate business performance. This is the ultimate goal of the critical few. Four indicators can reveal that your culture is boosting the business.

1. *Your culture taps into the waiting reserves of energy within lots of people.* If you have a culture focused on a certain set of performance outcomes, and employees buy into it, people start reinforcing one another informally. Simply put, they increasingly help one another feel good about what they need to do. As a result, you gain a greater level of emotional commitment to the work that matters most.
2. *Your culture guides down-the-line decision making.* If you have a strong culture, you don't need to have prescribed policies for every permutation of a situation. Employees can rely on cultural influences to help determine what they should do—they will act with speed, and they'll take initiative. You simply do not need all those formal sign-offs when you have the right kind of cultural support. When nobody is there to give the approval, the culture guides the individual in how to act.
3. *Your culture builds enduring execution capability.* Over time, critical behaviors are repeated; as they turn into habits, people become faster and better at executing. You see evidence of greater customer loyalty, higher levels of the kinds of employee engagement that matter most for performance, higher degrees of emotional commitment to what the organization is focused on, a more rigorous pursuit of continuous improvement, and greater resilience in downturns.
4. *Behaviors in normal times emulate positive behaviors during crisis situations.* We often hear executives praise the collaborative, selfless, and energetic behaviors of their people during a crisis—and lament the fact that they don't see more of those kinds of interactions normally. This difference is in large part explainable by the activation of cultural forces that occurs during a crisis. When you are focused on activating those forces all the time, you get that "special" level of performance all the time.

found on or close to the front line, and they have a strong and genuine connection with other employees. Use this combined leadership wisdom to decide what you want to accomplish most urgently, and carefully consider what makes sense at this stage of your company's life cycle. Addressing these issues will help you home in on the cultural traits that are most important for your organization to pay attention to *now.*

FOCUS ON THE CRITICAL INFORMAL LEADERS

You've picked the behaviors you need to change or energize. You understand which facets of your existing culture can help spread the new behaviors you are seeking. Now, focus your efforts on a critical few groups and specific people within the organization who can help bring this transformation about and make it last.

Since culture is the self-sustaining pattern of behaving, thinking, believing, and feeling in a given population, you are simply not going to change very much about it very rapidly. You will be similarly frustrated if you try to start with the people who most ardently object to what you're trying to achieve. Instead, be laser-focused and pick the corners of your organization where there is both a need and a willingness to grapple with culture and where a spreading of your critical few behaviors could translate into real business impact. You are looking for a manager and team who "get it," "need it," and "want it."

Next, within that team, enlist some "special forces" you can work with—people who are recognized by their colleagues as credible, informal leaders and who exemplify one or more of your critical few behaviors. These are people who have already cracked the code—they know how to effectively translate your critical few behaviors into specific actions within the company's current culture and operating model. In many cases, these individuals are instinctive motivators (we call them "pride builders"). In other cases, they are the hubs of useful informal networks and natural connectors across parts of the formal organization. The insights and special skills they possess enable them to get things done in ways that most in the regular forces can't.

> "Enlist some 'special forces'—credible leaders who know how to translate your critical few behaviors into specific actions within the company's current culture."

And here comes another big difference between the critical few approach and traditional change management: You're not going to use these people as ambassadors or change agents to carry your message, or to train others in planned programs, or to report on implementation milestones. Rather, you're going to learn from them—what they do differently that appeals to their co-workers on an emotional level, what works, what doesn't—and then work with them to codesign a specific set of tools that will encourage others to follow their lead.

These individuals have an emotional energy that you will see once you've tapped into it. Spend time talking with them and learning what energizes and motivates them. Pride builders and connectors are constructive. They don't focus on the downside; they naturally seek collaborative ways to enable improvement.

Our work with an industrial manufacturing company recovering from severe financial distress from the recession provides a good example. As we noted earlier, the CEO had set four top cultural priorities: speed, sensible risk, accountability, and customer-centricity. He recruited a senior culture team and tasked its members with learning more about how these priorities were already being manifested in different parts of the company. To that end, they identified and spent time with small groups of people—informal leaders who were among the most respected by their colleagues. To identify these individuals, they drew on official sources like HR records and annual reviews, but they relied more heavily on their own experience and judgment—as well as on the judgment and experience of insightful colleagues around the complex organization. They were seeking authentic informal leaders (the best of whom are well known in most organizations, although seldom well utilized) who exemplified through their behaviors the cultural traits the CEO had set as priorities. Senior team members continually cross-checked their initial judgments with others who had worked with and knew the candidates personally. They also collected stories and anecdotes that demonstrated behaviors that the informal leaders themselves were sometimes not even conscious of doing because they had become habits. Indeed, these behaviors often proved critical in moving the company's strategic priorities forward.

The senior culture team eventually identified and assembled informal leaders across North America whose behavior the company wanted to see more of, and enlisted their help in spreading their cultural and behavioral insights across the organization. These informal leaders were provided with a "safe space" to talk frankly about the issues they saw and how they were being addressed. The senior culture team often brought other C-level leaders as well as the CEO into those gatherings. Senior leaders were advised beforehand that when in these gatherings, they were not to behave as "the boss." Their role was to listen and learn, and when they did that well, it broke the conversation wide open.

The CEO and other senior leaders were able to get a ground-level authentic view of the day-to-day challenges that stood in the way of achieving their cultural and behavioral priorities. Their senior presence, in turn, energized the frontline individuals who had previously seen some of their leaders, and certainly their CEO, only on TV. As the initial groups of informal leaders gained confidence and visibility, the company was able to take advantage of their ideas and their energy throughout the organization—and they replicated the process by identifying more informal leaders and convening more information discussions in different critical populations in North America. The senior culture team also took advantage of electronic networking opportunities where peers and colleagues could share experiences and stories of "behavior successes" with one another online. The result: a viral movement that accelerated and became an emotional complement to programmatic efforts that enabled a swift and lasting financial recovery.

It is no secret that we take a great many of our behavioral cues from the people around us; "how we do things around here" means more than impersonal directives from on high. This social proof of what we do can be compelling and long lasting.

SECOND THOSE EMOTIONS

As you work to put the critical few into practice in your own organization, remember to focus on integrating emotional support. It is particularly important to avoid the trap of relying too heavily on conventional approaches to culture change and change management: programmatic consistency, process rigor, engagement tracking, and so on. Neither should you get too caught up in focusing on rational arguments and shared values, relying on hierarchical channels, and motivating through "stretch targets."

These approaches are seductive simply because they work well in addressing noncultural challenges. But when applied directly to culture, they overlook the kind of emotional commitment on which lasting cultural impact is based.

Resist these traps and focus on the critical few behaviors—with all their innate emotional power—that can have the greatest impact on your business (see "Four Signs That Your Critical Few Behaviors Are Working," page R-133). Find the individuals in your organization who are already influencing and living them—their enthusiasm and leadership among their peers will be easy to spot—and preserve those elements of your culture that drive the business forward.

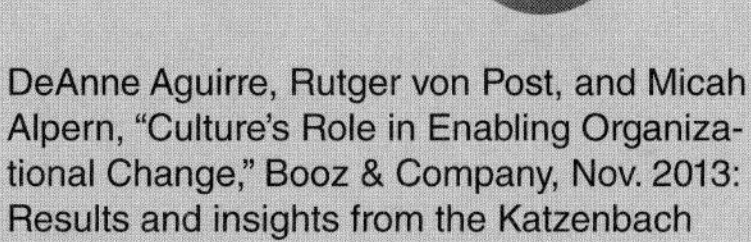

DeAnne Aguirre, Rutger von Post, and Micah Alpern, "Culture's Role in Enabling Organizational Change," Booz & Company, Nov. 2013: Results and insights from the Katzenbach Center's 2013 Culture and Change Management Survey.

George C. Halvorson, "The Culture to Cultivate," *Harvard Business Review*, July 2013: The CEO of Kaiser Permanente writes that instilling a foundational culture of continuous improvement is the only way to unify an organization as large and diverse as his.

Jon R. Katzenbach and Adam Michaels, "Life in the Matrix," *s+b*, Autumn 2013: Essential analysis of the major cultural shift required as companies evolve away from traditional hierarchies.

Chuck Lucier, "Herb Kelleher: The Thought Leader Interview," *s+b*, Summer 2004: The cofounder of Southwest Airlines discusses his company's people-centered culture.

The Katzenbach Center at Booz & Company website, booz.com/global/home/what-we-think/katzenbach_center: Ongoing source of research and insight on culture change theories and methods.

For more thought leadership on this topic, see the *s+b* website at: strategy-business.com/organizations_and_people.

READING 25

How Strategists Lead

Cynthia A. Montgomery
Harvard Business School

Seven years ago, I changed the focus of my strategy teaching at the Harvard Business School. After instructing MBAs for most of the previous quarter-century, I began teaching the accomplished executives and entrepreneurs who participate in Harvard's flagship programs for business owners and leaders.

Shifting the center of my teaching to executive education changed the way I teach and write about strategy. I've been struck by how often executives, even experienced ones, get tripped up: they become so interested in the potential of new ventures, for example, that they underestimate harsh competitive realities or overlook how interrelated strategy and execution are. I've also learned, in conversations between class sessions (as well as in my work as a board director and corporate adviser) about the limits of analysis, the importance of being ready to reinvent a business, and the ongoing responsibility of leading strategy.

All of this learning speaks to the role of the strategist—as a meaning maker for companies, as a voice of reason, and as an operator. The richness of these roles, and their deep interconnections, underscore the fact that strategy is much more than a detached analytical exercise. Analysis has merit, to be sure, but it will never make strategy the vibrant core that animates everything a company is and does.

THE STRATEGIST AS MEANING MAKER

I've taken to asking executives to list three words that come to mind when they hear the word *strategy.* Collectively, they have produced 109 words, frequently giving top billing to *plan, direction,* and *competitive advantage.* In more than 2,000 responses, only 2 had anything to do with people: one said *leadership,* another *visionary.* No one has ever mentioned *strategist.*

Downplaying the link between a leader and a strategy, or failing to recognize it at all, is a dangerous oversight that I tried to start remedying in a *Harvard Business Review* article four years ago and in my new book, *The Strategist,* whose thinking this article extends.[1] After all, defining what an organization will be, and why and to whom that will matter, is at the heart of a leader's role. Those who hope to sustain a strategic perspective must be ready to confront this basic challenge. It is perhaps easiest to see in single-business companies serving well-defined markets and building business models suited to particular competitive contexts. I know from experience, though, that the challenge is equally relevant at the top of diversified multinationals.

What is it, after all, that makes the whole of a company greater than the sum of its parts—and how do its systems and processes add value to the businesses within the fold? Nobel laureate Ronald Coase posed the problem this way: "The question which arises is whether it is possible to study the forces which determine the size of the firm. Why does the entrepreneur not organize one less transaction or one more?"[2] These are largely the same questions: are the extra layers what justifies the existence of this complex firm? If so, why can't the market take care of such transactions on its own? If there's more to a company's story, what is it, *really?*

This article was originally published in *McKinsey Quarterly,* www.mckinseyquarterly.com.

In the last three decades, as strategy has moved to become a science, we have allowed these fundamental questions to slip away. We need to bring them back. It is the leader—the strategist as meaning maker—who must make the vital choices that determine a company's very identity, who says, "*This* is our purpose, not *that*. *This* is who we will be. *This* is why our customers and clients will prefer a world with us rather than without us." Others, inside and outside a company, will contribute in meaningful ways, but in the end it is the leader who bears responsibility for the choices that are made and indeed for the fact that choices are made at all.

THE STRATEGIST AS VOICE OF REASON

Bold, visionary leaders who have the confidence to take their companies in exciting new directions are widely admired—and confidence is a key part of strategy and leadership. But confidence can balloon into overconfidence, which seems to come naturally to many successful entrepreneurs and senior managers who see themselves as action-oriented problem solvers.[3]

I see overconfidence in senior executives in class when I ask them to weigh the pros and cons of entering the furniture-manufacturing business. Over the years, a number of highly regarded, well-run companies—including Beatrice Foods, Burlington Industries, Champion, Consolidated Foods, General Housewares, Gulf + Western, Intermark, Ludlow, Masco, Mead, and Scott Paper—have tried to find fortune in the business, which traditionally has been characterized by high transportation costs, low productivity, eroding prices, slow growth, and low returns. It's also been highly fragmented. In the mid-1980s, for example, more than 2,500 manufacturers competed, with 80 percent of sales coming from the biggest 400 of them. Substitutes abound, and there is a lot of competition for the customer's dollar. Competitors quickly knock off innovations and new designs, and the industry is riddled with inefficiencies, extreme product variety, and long lead times that frustrate customers. Consumer research shows that many adults can't name a single furniture brand. The industry does little advertising.

By at least a two-to-one margin, the senior executives in my classes typically are energized, not intimidated, by these challenges. Most argue, in effect, that where there's challenge there's opportunity. If it were an easy business, they say, someone else would already have seized the opportunity; this is a chance to bring money, sophistication, and discipline to a fragmented, unsophisticated, and chaotic industry. As the list above shows, my students are far from alone: with great expectations and high hopes of success, a number of well-managed companies over the years have jumped in with the intention of reshaping the industry through the infusion of professional management.

All those companies, though, have since left the business—providing an important reminder that the competitive forces at work in your industry determine some (and perhaps much) of your company's performance. These competitive forces are beyond the control of most individual companies and their managers. They're what you inherit, a reality you have to deal with. It's not that a company can never change them, but in most cases that's very difficult to do. The strategist must understand such forces, how they affect the playing field where competition takes place, and the likelihood that his or her plan has what it takes to flourish in those circumstances. Crucial, of course, is having a difference *that matters in the industry.* In furniture—an industry ruled more by fashion than function—it's extremely challenging to uncover an advantage strong enough to counter the gravitational pull of the industry's unattractive competitive forces. IKEA did it, but not by disregarding industry forces; rather, the company created a new niche for itself and brought a new economic model to the furniture industry.

A leader must serve as a voice of reason when a bold strategy to reshape an industry's forces actually reflects indifference to them. Time and again, I've seen division heads, group heads, and even chief executives dutifully acknowledge competitive forces, make a few high-level comments, and then quickly move on to lay out their plans—without ever squarely confronting the implications of the forces they've just noted. Strategic planning has become more of a "check the box" exercise than a brutally frank and open confrontation of the facts.

THE STRATEGIST AS OPERATOR

A great strategy, in short, is not a dream or a lofty idea, but rather the bridge between the economics of a market, the ideas at the core of a business, and action. To be sound, that bridge must rest on a foundation of clarity and realism, and it also needs a real operating sensibility. Every year, early in the term, someone in class always wants to engage the group in a discussion about what's more important: strategy or execution. In my view, this is a false dichotomy and a wrongheaded debate that the students themselves have to resolve, and I let them have a go at it.

I always bring that discussion up again at the end of the course, when we talk about Domenico De Sole's tenure at Italian fashion eminence Gucci Group.[4] De Sole, a tax attorney, was tapped for the company's top job in 1995, following years of plummeting sales and mounting losses in the aftermath of unbridled licensing that had plastered Gucci's name and distinctive red-and-green logo on everything from sneakers to packs of playing cards to whiskey—in fact, on 22,000 different products—making Gucci a "cheapened and overexposed brand."

De Sole started by summoning every Gucci manager worldwide to a meeting in Florence. Instead of telling managers what he thought Gucci should be, De Sole asked them to look closely at the business and tell him what was selling and what wasn't. He wanted to tackle the question "not by philosophy, but by data"—bringing strategy in line with experience rather than relying on intuition. The data were eye opening. Some of Gucci's greatest recent successes had come from its few trendier, seasonal fashion items, and the traditional customer—the woman who cherished style, not fashion, and who wanted a classic item she would buy once and keep for a lifetime—had not come back to Gucci.

De Sole and his team, especially lead designer Tom Ford, weighed the evidence and concluded that they would follow the data and position the company in the upper middle of the designer market: luxury aimed at the masses. To complement its leather goods, Ford designed original, trendy—and, above all, exciting—ready-to-wear clothing each year, not as the company's mainstay, but as its draw. The increased focus on fashion would help the world forget all those counterfeit bags and the Gucci toilet paper. It would propel the company toward a new brand identity, generating the kind of excitement that would bring new customers into Gucci stores, where they would also buy high-margin handbags and accessories. To support the new fashion and brand strategies, De Sole and his team doubled advertising spending, modernized stores, and upgraded customer support. Unseen but no less important to the strategy's success was Gucci's supply chain. De Sole personally drove the back roads of Tuscany to pick the best 25 suppliers, and the company provided them with financial and technical support while simultaneously boosting the efficiency of its logistics. Costs fell and flexibility rose.

In effect, everything De Sole and Ford did—in design, product lineup, pricing, marketing, distribution, manufacturing, and logistics, not to mention organizational culture and management—was tightly coordinated, internally consistent, and interlocking. This was a system of resources and activities that worked together and reinforced each other, all aimed at producing products that were fashion forward, high quality, and good value.

It is easy to see the beauty of such a system of value creation once it's constructed, but constructing it isn't often an easy or a beautiful process. The decisions embedded in such systems are often gutsy choices. For every moving part in the Gucci universe, De Sole faced a strictly binary decision: either it advanced the cause of fashion-forwardness, high quality, and good value—or it did not and was rebuilt. Strategists call such choices identity-conferring commitments. They are central to what an organization is or wants to be and reflect what it stands for.

When I ask executives at the end of this class, "Where does strategy end and execution begin?" there isn't a clear answer—and that's as it should be. What could be more desirable than a well-conceived strategy that flows without a ripple into execution? Yet I know from working with thousands of organizations just how rare it is to find a carefully honed system that really delivers. You and every leader of a company must ask yourself whether you have one—and if you don't, take the responsibility to build it. The only way a company will deliver on its promises, in short, is if its strategists can think like operators.

A NEVER-ENDING TASK

Achieving and maintaining strategic momentum is a challenge that confronts an organization and its leader every day of their entwined existence. It's a challenge that involves multiple choices over time—and, on occasion, one or two big choices. Very rare is the leader who will not, at some point in his or her career, have to overhaul a company's strategy in perhaps dramatic ways. Sometimes, facing that inevitability brings moments of epiphany: "eureka" flashes of insight that ignite dazzling new ways of thinking about an enterprise, its purpose, its potential. I have witnessed some of these moments as managers reconceptualized what their organizations do and are capable of doing. These episodes are inspiring—and can become catalytic.

At other times, facing an overhaul can be wrenching, particularly if a company has a set of complex businesses that need to be taken apart or a purpose that has run its course. More than one CEO—men and women coming to grips with what their organizations are and what they want them to become—has described this challenge as an intense personal struggle, often the toughest thing they've done.

Yet those same people often say that the experience was one of the most rewarding of their whole lives. It can be profoundly liberating as a kind of corporate rebirth or creation. One CEO described his own experience: "I love our business, our people, the challenges, the fact that other people get deep benefits from what we sell," he said. "Even so, in the coming years I can see that we will need to go in a new direction, and that will mean selling off parts of the business. The market has gotten too competitive, and we don't make the margins we used to." He winced as he admitted this. Then he lowered his voice and added something surprising. "At a fundamental level, though, it's changes like this that keep us fresh and keep me going. While it can be painful when it happens, in the long run I wouldn't want to lead a company that didn't reinvent itself."

ENDNOTES

[1] For more, see Cynthia Montgomery, *The Strategist: Be the Leader Your Business Needs,* New York, NY: HarperCollins, 2012; and "Putting leadership back into strategy," *Harvard Business Review,* January 2008, Volume 86, Number 1, pp. 54–60.

[2] R. H. Coase, "The nature of the firm," *Economica,* 1937, Volume 4, Number 16, pp. 386–405.

[3] For more on managerial overconfidence, see John T. Horn, Dan Lovallo, and S. Patrick Viguerie, "Beating the odds in market entry," mckinseyquarterly.com, November 2005; as well as Dan Lovallo and Olivier Sibony, "The case for behavioral strategy," mckinseyquarterly.com, March 2010, and "Distortions and deceptions in strategic decisions," mckinseyquarterly.com, February 2006.

[4] For more detail on the Gucci case, see Mary Kwak and David Yoffie, "Gucci Group N.V. (A)," Harvard Business Publishing, Boston, May 10, 2001.

PHOTO CREDITS

Image research by David Tietz/Editorial Image, LLC.

CHAPTER 1

Opener: © Greg Hargreaves/Getty Images; p. 6: © McGraw-Hill Education/John Flournoy, photographer; p. 11: © Eric Carr/Alamy.

CHAPTER 2

Opener: © Fanatic Studio/Getty Images; p. 26: © George Frey/Getty Images; p. 29: © McGraw-Hill Education/Andrew Resek, photographer; p. 39 (top): © Jason Reed/Reuters/Corbis; p. 39 (bottom): © Jay Mallin/Bloomberg via Getty Images.

CHAPTER 3

Opener: © Bull's Eye/Imagezoo/Getty Images.

CHAPTER 4

Opener: © Matt Zumbo/Getty Images; p. 101: © Sean Pavone/Alamy.

CHAPTER 5

Opener: © Digital Vision/Getty Images; p. 123: © McGraw-Hill Education/John Flournoy, photographer; p. 133: © Huntstock/Getty Images; p. 135: © Martin Klimek/Newscom; p. 137: © David Paul Morris/Getty Images.

CHAPTER 6

Opener: © Bull's Eye/Imagezoo/Getty Images; p. 150: © PRNewsFoto/Gilt GroupeAP Images; p. 153: © David Paul Morris/Getty Images; p. 158: © Jb Reed/Bloomberg via Getty Images; p. 163: © Aerial Archives/Alamy.

CHAPTER 7

Opener: © Ian McKinnell/Getty Images; p. 188: © Ken James/Bloomberg via Getty Images; p. 194: © John Greim/LightRocket via Getty Images; p. 204: © Kevin Lee/Bloomberg via Getty Images.

CHAPTER 8

Opener: © Alex Belomlinsky/Getty Images; p. 224: © McGraw-Hill Education/Eclipse Studios; p. 247: © Daniel Acker/Bloomberg via Getty Images.

CHAPTER 9

Opener: © Fanatic Studio/Getty Images; p. 259: © Helen Sessions/Alamy; p. 266: © PRNewsFoto/Novo Nordisk/AP Images; p. 271: © Jb Reed/Bloomberg via Getty Images; p. 273: © Vivien Killilea/Getty Images.

CHAPTER 10

Opener: © Ingram Publishing; p. 300: © Lou-Foto/Alamy; p. 303: © Kumar Sriskandan/Alamy.

CHAPTER 11

Opener: © Bull's Eye/Imagezoo/Getty Images; p. 326: © Imaginechina/AP Images; p. 333: © Corey Lowenstein/Raleigh News & Observer/Getty Images; p. 335: © BananaStock/Jupiterimages.

CHAPTER 12

Opener: © Fanatic Studio/Getty Images; p. 345: © George Frey/Getty Images; p. 358: © Nacho Doce/Reuters/Corbis.

COMPANY INDEX

D

E

F

G

H

I

J

K

L

S

T

U

NAME INDEX

A

B

C

D

E

F

G

SUBJECT INDEX

C

D

E

F

G

H

I

N

O

P

V

W